VIRTUOSO GOLDSMITHS

AND THE TRIUMPH OF MANNERISM

1540-1620

J. F. Hayward

SOTHEBY PARKE BERNET

Produced by
Sotheby Parke Bernet Publications Limited
34/35 New Bond Street, London W1A 2AA

Edition for the United States of America available from
Biblio Distribution Center for
Sotheby Parke Bernet Publications
81 Adams Drive, Totowa, New Jersey 07512
and from the co-publishers
Rizzoli International Publications Inc.
712 Fifth Avenue, New York 10012

ISBN 0 85667 005 7
Library of Congress Catalog Card Number: 76-14042

Text setting by TBF (Printers) Limited
Printed in Holland by Koninklijke Drukkerij G. J. Thieme bv
Bound in Great Britain by W. & J. Mackay Limited

Contents

List of Colour Plates

Acknowledgements

IT is imposible to record the names of all the institutions, Museum colleagues, collectors, dealers and friends in many countries who have assisted me with information, advice and with facilities for study in the course of the many years during which this book has been in preparation. They include:

AUSTRIA
Oesterreichisches Museum für angewandte Kunst: Dr. G. Egger
Graphische Sammlung, Albertina: Dr. W. Koschatzky
Kunsthistorisches Museum, Vienna: Dr. M. Leithe-Jasper, Dr. E. Neumann, Dr. B. Thomas

BELGIUM
Culturdienst, Province of Antwerp: Dr. P. Baudoin
Museum Vleeshuis, Antwerp: Dr. F. Smekens
Musées Nationaux, Bruxelles: M. J. Squilbeck

CANADA
Royal Ontario Museum, Toronto: H. Hickl-Szabo

FRANCE
Musée du Louvre: M. S. Grandjean, M. B. Jestaz

GERMAN DEMOCRATIC REPUBLIC
Grünes Gewölbe, Dresden: Dr. V. Arnold, Dr. J. Menzhausen
Historisches Museum, Dresden: Dr. J. Schöbel
Schlossmuseum, Weimar: Dr. W. Scheidig

GERMAN FEDERAL REPUBLIC
Stadtarchiv Augsburg: Dr. H. Deininger
Städtische Kunstsammlungen, Augsburg: Dr. H. Müller
Kunstgewerbemuseum, Charlottenburg Schloss, Berlin: Dr. Dreier
Museum für Kunst und Gewerbe, Hamburg: Dr. L. Möller, Dr. H. Jedding
Badisches Landesmuseum, Karlsruhe: Dr. J. Fritz, Dr. E. Petrasch
Residenzmuseum, Munich: Dr. H. Brunner, Dr. H. Thoma
Bayerisches Nationalmuseum, Munich: Dr. U. Krempel, Dr. K. Maurice, Dr. T. Müller, Dr. R.

Rückert, Dr. H. Weihrauch
Dr. H. Seling of Munich
Dr. R. Fritz of Münster
Germanisches Nationalmuseum, Nürnberg: Dr. E. W. Braun, Dr. K.. Pechstein, Dr. A. Schönberger, Dr. E. Steingräber
Staatsarchiv Nürnberg: Dr. Schnelbögl
Württembergisches Landesmuseum, Stuttgart: Dr. W. Fleischhauer, Dr. M. Landenberger
Veste Coburg: Dr. H. Kohlhaussen

HOLLAND
Rijksmuseum, Amsterdam: Dr. J. Verbeek, Mvr. D. de Wit- Klinkhamer

ITALY
Museo degli Argenti, Florence: Dr. K. Piacenti-Aschengren
Museo Naz. di Capodimonte, Naples: Dr. L. Penta, Dr. R. Causa
Marchese Giunta di Roccagiovane of Rome

SWEDEN
Kungl. Livrustkammaren, Stockholm: Dr. G. Ekstrand
Nationalmuseum, Stockholm: Dr. C. Hernmarck

SWITZERLAND
Historisches Museum, Basel: Dr. H. Reinhardt
Historisches Museum, Bern: Dr. R. C. Wyss
Schweizerisches Nationalmuseum, Zürich: Dr. A. Gruber, Dr. H. Schneider

U.K.
British Museum: Mr. H. Tait
Courtauld Institute of Art: Sir Anthony Blunt
Victoria and Albert Museum: Mr. C. Blair, Mr. R. Lightbown, Mr. C. Oman, Mr. P. Ward-Jackson
Worshipful Company of Goldsmiths, London: Miss

S. Hare, Mr. G. Hughes
Ashmolean Museum, Oxford: Mr. G. Taylor
Wallace Collection, London: Mr. A. V. Norman,
Mr. F. Watson
Mr. A. Grimwade of Christie's, Mr. P. Pouncey of
Sotheby's
Mr. R. Vander and Mr. M. Wellby, London

U.S.A.

Walters Art Gallery, Baltimore: Mr. R. Randall Jr.
Metropolitan Museum of Art, New York: Dr. Y.
Hackenbroch, Miss J. MacNab
Museum of Art, Toledo: Mr. O. Wittman

U.S.S.R.

Hermitage Museum, Leningrad: Dr. L. Tarassuk

Without the generous co-operation of the above
and of many others who will, I hope, accept my
apologies for my failure to name them, the problems of identifying the work of the sixteenth-century goldsmiths would have been beset with even
more difficulties.

Acknowledgements are due to Her Majesty
Queen Elizabeth II and to the many museums,
private collectors and dealers who have granted
permission for pieces in their possession to be illustrated. A generous grant towards the cost of publication has been made by the Pasold Foundation and
financial support has been received from the Worshipful Company of Goldsmiths. The staff of
Sotheby Parke Bernet Publications has shown
immense patience in dealing with a repeatedly
amended text.

Special thanks are due to Dr. I. Grabowska of the
National Museum, Cracow, and to Dr. I. Weber of
the Staatliche Münzsammlung, Munich, for their
critical reading of the text in the earlier stages of its
preparation, to Dr. C. Hernmarck for generously
sharing with me his comprehensive knowledge of
the subject; and to my wife for her constant encour-
agement and advice without which the book would
never have been completed.

Introduction

DURING the hundred years between 1530 and 1630 style in the goldsmiths' workshops was determined by three successive interpretations of classical art; first the purity and harmony of proportion of the Renaissance, then the sophistication and invention of Mannerism and finally the monumentality and vigour of Baroque.

The sixteenth century was a period of dramatic shifts of emphasis in the field of goldsmiths' design. While the Renaissance remained the dominant influence, the interpretation of classical art was far from consistent. The century begins with Italy as the centre from which knowledge of and the taste for antiquity was diffused throughout Western Europe. At first the remnants of Roman civilisation uncovered in Italy were credited with a degree of excellence and an authority that was beyond question. Venetian engravers reproduced details of pilasters, reliefs and architectural friezes exactly as they found them in the ruins. They were followed a generation later by Roman engravers who engraved sets of designs showing antique bronze and marble vases and ewers, in which archaeological accuracy, though claimed, was no longer achieved. Alongside the legacy of classical art, the Orient exercised powerful influence, particularly on goldsmiths' designs. The mauresque, introduced to Europe via Venice, was first exploited by an Italian engraver, but was almost immediately adopted by the French master, du Cerceau, and thereafter by the Fleming, Balthasar Sylvius of Antwerp. His book of mauresques, first published in 1554, was the most influential of its time; it was issued and re-issued in various languages throughout the sixteenth century and into the early seventeenth century.

During the second quarter of the sixteenth century teams of Italian artists went north of the Alps to seek employment at northern courts, the most important group being that which introduced and developed Italian Mannerism at the palace of Fontainebleau. What they achieved there was seized upon and further exploited by French and Flemish engravers to a degree of exaggeration that would not have been acceptable south of the Alps, where classical precept was still present in the form of Roman remains. The northern goldsmiths abandoned harmonious Renaissance proportions and ideals in favour of a more sophisticated approach before they had fully understood them. From the Low Countries Mannerism spread over the German-speaking territories, taking the place of the hybrid Renaissance and indigenous Teutonic style evolved by the *Kleinmeister* of southern Germany. From the mid-century onwards the main trend is a shift northwards of both ideas and of the artists who propagated them. It is true that many northern masters went to Italy to study but most returned to practice their skill in their own country.

To such an extent does the north dominate the art of the goldsmith during the second half of the century — in spite of the achievements of Benvenuto Cellini, Manno di Sbarri and Antonio Gentile — that there is a risk of underestimating the contribution of the Latin south. The fact that so little survives to illustrate the quality of Italian Renaissance goldsmiths' work weights the balance further in favour of the north.

Though the grotesque was born in the ruins of ancient Rome, the Flemish engravers interpreted this decorative style in a manner far removed from the moderation of their

Italian precursors. The central importance of Flemish design in the triumph of northern Mannerism is illustrated by the fact that the greatest of the German goldsmiths, Wenzel Jamnitzer, derived his characteristic manner from a Flemish source, that the leading goldsmith at the court of the Tuscan Grand Duke was a Dutchman from Delft, and that the finest armours made for the courts of the Habsburg Emperor and for the Kings of France and Sweden were decorated with embossing and damascening by the Antwerp goldsmith, Eliseus Libbaerts. Whereas in the south the classical cameo and excavated sculpture constituted a standard of excellence that could only be rivalled but never excelled, in the north the Flemish and German goldsmiths drew upon a far wider range of subject matter. Prompted by their patrons, who called for ever new inventions, they ran the whole gamut of ornament, adding motif to motif in their determination to leave no space unfilled. The casts from nature practised by the Paduan bronze sculptors were exploited by Wenzel Jamnitzer and his followers to create a whole realm of naturalistic ornament undreamt of in the early Renaissance.

Northern Mannerism took on a new form that amounted to anti-classicism and it was once again a Flemish-born master, Erasmus Hornick of Antwerp, who contributed most to this new direction. He outstripped his German contemporaries, Hirschvogel and Dietterlin, in evolving distorted, even monstrous forms. In this descent to the *bas fonds* to discover decorative ideas the northern masters had no competition from the south, and the shift of emphasis from south to north was from classical restraint to a masochistic delight in deformity.

By the end of the century the production of designs for goldsmiths was largely in the hands of Flemish or Dutch engravers, some of them families with several members, among them the two Collaerts, father and son, de Bruyn, the two de Brys, father and son, and the de Passe family. During the sixteenth century the goldsmith was often also an engraver, just as the engravers were called upon to excute the engraved ornament on the more important pieces. The most original German designer of the end of the century, Christoph Jamnitzer, was at the same time one of the most gifted goldsmiths of his generation.

In the last quarter of the sixteenth century a new dimension was given to northern goldsmiths' work by the fashion for miniature works of sculpture in precious metal, which were put on display at the great banquets, at which the buffet loaded with tier upon tier of silver vessels had long been the main decoration. The goldsmiths met the new challenge with consummate skill and the many masterpieces of sculpture that they produced in their difficult techniques of embossing, casting and assembling are fully equal to the better-known small bronze sculptures of the time. Mannerism was so dominant in the decorative vocabulary of the goldsmiths that it was not till well into the seventeenth century that the Baroque revived their faith in Rome and the classical tradition.

This book is mainly concerned with the second half of the century when Mannerism was the dominant influence. Its origin lies in a series of studies of goldsmiths' work of the second half of the sixteenth century, which were published in the *Connoisseur* and the *Burlington Magazine* in England and in *Antichita Viva* in Italy, with particular reference to the *oeuvre* of a hitherto almost unknown Flemish goldsmith and designer, Erasmus Hornick. As the range and quantity of Hornick's output of designs was revealed it became evident that, in order to appreciate his significance as an exponent of Mannerism, that refined yet ambiguous version of Renaissance style, it was necessary to survey the impact of that style on European goldsmiths' work as a whole. Almost every aspect of Mannerist design is represented in the large number of drawings by Hornick that survive; it is for this reason that he plays a central role in this book, and not because it is claimed that he was a major contributor to its development. In fact, like many of his contemporaries, he derived most of his ideas from earlier designs and from contemporary sources. Mannerism was a fashion with many variations rather than a consistent and independent style and it cannot be understood in isolation from the Renaissance against which it reacted. Two chapters of this book are, therefore, devoted to a short study of Renaissance goldsmiths' work, while in subsequent chapters the original and fantastic forms devised by the Mannerist goldsmiths are examined in greater detail. Frequent reference is made to the international character of Mannerist art and it might thus seem proper to deal with Europe as a whole; I have, however, chosen to discuss the development of taste and style in the goldsmith's art of each country separately. My reason is that, although the Mannerist rejection of the Renaissance made itself felt in most European countries during the sixteenth century, its manifestations were not uniform and differed according to the social conditions and aesthetic tradition of each nation.

This book is primarily concerned with secular plate; firstly because of the greater variety of form and ornament found on pieces made for the table or cupboard (in its archaic sense of a board to display cups) and secondly because of the scarcity of original drawings for church plate of this period, which was, moreover, of uniform pattern in both Roman Catholic and Lutheran regions. Only when a significant style or period cannot otherwise be adequately presented are vessels made for the altar illustrated. This applies most cogently to Spanish goldsmiths' work, the best of which in this period is ecclesiastical.

During the sixteenth century, gold and silver were far more precious than they are today; a very small silver coin would cover a man's need for a week and the gap in wealth between the owner of a princely treasury and the common man was inconceivably wide. Study of the inventories of sixteenth-century treasuries of royalty or noblemen have shown how wide a range of vessels was made of precious metal. Most were concerned with the service of wine or beer, but other items include salts, bowls, trenchers, dishes, spice-plates and spice-boxes, pepper-pots, sauce-boats, chafing-dishes, table-fountains, candlesticks and prickets, as well as a variety of kitchen plate. Surviving pieces are not so various; the majority are wine-cups, ewers, beakers and tankards, all vessels connected with drinking. In the chapters that follow, discussion is confined to those pieces that express something of the spirit of Mannerism. Other vessels, such as dishes, plates, spoons and the simpler forms of beaker, are omitted, not because examples do not survive, but because they are not relevant. Many types of sixteenth-century goldsmiths' work, which for functional or other reasons did not inspire the imagination of the goldsmith, are passed over.

During the sixteenth century greater demands were made by the client upon the goldsmith than just the competent exercise of the techniques of his craft. The more complex the form, the more recondite the classical allusions in its decoration and the more abstruse the philosphical programme upon which its ornament was based, the more worthy was a vessel of admiration. Designs were usually based upon some familiar object, such as ewer, basin, vase or cup, but during the second half of the century the useful form was treated as a theme upon which elegant or fanciful variations could be played. The artists who by their pattern-books determined the forms of gold and silver vessels drew increasingly upon their own fantasy in re-interpreting classical models to accord with modern taste. In arriving at an approved design the customer had more influence than would now be thought usual. The artist did not claim that his own inspiration must be allowed free rein and in subsequent chapters evidence will be presented to show the close relationship which often existed between goldsmith and client. In the more important commissions the form that was eventually evolved made few concessions to function and was intended to be appreciated as an essay in virtuosity. Even the virtuoso goldsmith was, however, sometimes compelled to accept more modest orders to keep his workshop busy. A large workshop would receive commissions of all kinds from ruling princes, noblemen, rich merchants and the bourgeoisie, there was no question of confining production to articles with pretensions to aesthetic significance. Though they are not included among the illustrations in this book, silver vessels of quite modest design and quality exist, which bear the maker's marks of well-known and highly respected masters.

The standard piece of plate in the sixteenth century, judging by surviving examples, was the standing cup. With its tall stem and tall cover reaching up to a decorative finial this was primarily a ceremonial object intended for display rather than use. The survival of so many underlines the importance attached in the period to silver as a sign of social status and financial security. In spite of the contemporary interest in virtuosity in design and execution, most sixteenth-century vessels were subject to certain established conventions. From the abandonment of the Gothic style until the latter part of the century the design and decoration of the cover of a cup repeated on a smaller scale that of the foot and stem. The finial on the cover was either a figure in the round or a vase of flowers in cut and bent sheet silver. The coat-of-arms of the owner was introduced at some point; on a standing cup it was engraved on a shield held by the finial figure, on a tazza, bowl or basin on a boss set in the centre and on a tankard or flagon on the cover. Construction methods were also uniform in most countries; from the central point of the base of both cup and cover a silver tube rose vertically over which the various elements that composed the stem were slipped and held in place by locating pins. Into the top of this tube was screwed the bowl in the case of the cup and the finial in the case of the cover. The ornament on the foot, bowl and base of cover was usually embossed, while the other elements were cast. In most countries the foot and stem of the tazza were constructed in the same way with a central vertical tube, but some German goldsmiths cast the foot and stem in one.

Few sixteenth-century silver vessels remain in the condition in which they left their maker's workshop. Changing taste has led to alterations either of function or decoration. Damage in use which necessitated repairs also may have fundamentally changed the appearance of a piece; the part most frequently damaged was the cover, which was most likely to be accidentally dropped and the finial either damaged or broken off. It is, therefore, exceptional to find the original finial still intact. Tankards were usually finished with a flat top, in the centre of which was set an engraved or enamelled disc bearing the arms of the owner. This again rarely survives as, when the piece passed into the possession of another person, the coat-of-arms was removed and replaced, not by another coat-of-arms, but by a figure or baluster finial. The alteration can usually readily be seen, as the figure in the centre of the cover does not accord with the tall thumb-piece set behind it. Another alteration often found is the removal of the coat-of-arms that filled the central boss or print of a sixteenth-century basin and its replacement by a plaquette or a plain disc of silver. Other pieces may even have been adapted to serve a purpose other than that for which they were originally intended; this may have happened soon after their making or at a comparatively recent date. Thus the so-called Töbing Cup in the Lüneburg Ratsschatz was, according to an old inventory note[1], in 1566 put together from various earlier elements. In this case the combination was intentional, but cups composed of numerous elements held together by a central stem have often been wrongly assembled after being unscrewed for cleaning. Ignorant servants entrusted with this work have also mixed up elements from different cups when reassembling them and, once these have passed out of the family of the original owners, they can never be put right again. Evidence of later repairs or alterations is often found on otherwise authentic objects, but such pieces are, as far as possible, not illustrated in this book.

Inasmuch as this is a study of the history of a fashionable style, it is concerned with those countries or cities that created fashion and not with those in which it was merely followed. This means that the countries of Scandinavia and much of Central Europe are omitted and certain others, such as Portugal, are dealt with very briefly. The English style, though not a contributor to the mainstream of European development, is sufficiently individual to warrant detailed study.

The amount of information available concerning the art of the goldsmith in the various countries of Europe, however, is far from consistent, and this is reflected in the length of the chapters. So much is known about the work of German sixteenth-century goldsmiths and so much silver of the period remains that it is not practicable to discuss each centre of production at equal length. In dealing with the German cultural region, which extended beyond the boundaries of modern Germany and Austria to Bohemia, Poland and Hungary in the east, to Switzerland in the south and to Denmark and the Baltic countries in the north, I have concentrated on the main centres, Augsburg and Nürnberg, referring only briefly to the more outstanding masters who worked in Hamburg, Munich, Dresden and elsewhere. The recent survey by Dr. Kohlhaussen of early Nürnberg silver[2] describes and illustrates a large proportion of the surviving German silver made between 1340 and 1540. In view of this I have not dealt fully with German silver of the first half of the sixteenth century. Though concerned only with Nürnberg silver, Kohlhaussen's book illustrates many unmarked pieces, which are not now generally accepted as Nürnberg, and does, therefore, cover a somewhat wider field than he intended. In this connection it should be remembered that many young goldsmiths went to Nürnberg as journeymen and, having learnt the prevalent techniques and style there, moved elsewhere but continued to work in the Nürnberg fashion. Only in the case of the German cultural region is it possible to discuss the style of individual goldsmiths; elsewhere the trend of fashion is dealt with by reference to vessel types rather than makers.

In an article written on Nürnberg goldsmiths' work in 1949[3] Professor E. W. Braun stressed the need for a comprehensive study of German goldsmiths' work which would cover the large volume of supporting material extant such as drawings (*Visierungen*), engravings and woodcuts, the considerable number of models of wax, stone, terracotta and wood and, finally, the plaquettes. In his monumental study, Kohlhaussen included such material insofar as it was relevant to Nürnberg prior to 1540. In this book I, also, have – though inevitably on a less ambitious scale – referred to and illustrated contemporary goldsmiths' models, drawings and printed designs. The number of such designs that has survived is surprisingly large and I have selected only a few from an immense corpus. Working drawings, which were used, worn out and eventually thrown away, are rare, but examples can be seen pinned up above the bench at which the goldsmiths work in the painting from the *Studiolo* of the Grand Duke Francesco I de' Medici (pl. 1). Original designs drawn by graphic artists as sources of ideas for goldsmiths and their clients are more numerous, having been preserved in the print-rooms and private collections of European princely and noble houses.

The determination of the origin of hall-marked silver usually presents no difficulties, but in the sixteenth century many of the finest pieces, in particular those made by court craftsmen, were not submitted for assay and marking. Some can be recognised on stylistic grounds, but others can only tentatively be attributed to a country of origin. The goldsmiths have generally tended to be conservative, and a design which gave satisfaction might well continue in use for as long as a century after its first invention. In the same way there was a considerable time lag between the development of a new style by graphic artists and its adoption by the goldsmiths. In the absence of a hall-mark, therefore, the terminal dates of a piece of silver may well be as far as fifty years apart. It has been usual in recent years for books on silver to reproduce the marks as well as the objects on which they are struck. Although this practice is undoubtedly of value to the student and collector it has not been followed in the present work, mainly because of the large number of illustrations drawn from almost every quarter of the western world. The question of marks is, in any case, of lesser importance here; firstly because so many of the pieces are unmarked or struck with unidentified marks, and secondly because the subject of this book is less concerned with the detailed study of the work of individual makers than with stylistic evolution as a whole. In the sixteenth century the maker's mark was usually a symbol of some sort and, unless the original mark plates in which mark and name of the goldsmith are recorded have survived, it is rarely possible to link one with the other. In those cases where the marks of an illustrated piece are reproduced in one of the standard books on silver, the corresponding reference is given. Objects made of gold were not normally hall-marked during the sixteenth century, so the problem of identification of marks does not arise in their case.

The goldsmiths of the sixteenth century showed outstanding mastery of sculpture in precious metal and, because, or perhaps as a result of this, sculpture played a more important role in goldsmiths' work of the time than in subsequent periods. The larger examples have been melted but a great many smaller ones in the form of human figures or animals have survived, mostly of German origin. A number of these are illustrated and the technique of their production is discussed at length.

A chapter of this book is devoted to subjects that are not as a rule treated in books on gold and silver, namely the role of the goldsmith in the production of armour and swords and also of articles of base metal; the latter a particularly complex one as it covers so wide a field. Apart from making articles of base metal which were more usually of silver, the goldsmith chased and gilded small bronzes, produced clock- and watch-cases, mathematical instruments, and cast bronze and embossed copper ornaments for a range of objects such as furniture, horse-harness, firearms and armour. Very little research has been carried out on this subject, with the exception of clock-cases, and no more than a general survey is attempted here.

1 W. Scheffler: *Die Goldschmiede Niedersachsens,* Vol. II, p.907 '*1566 aus verschiedenen alten Teilen zusammengesetz*'.
2 H. Kohlhaussen, *Nürnberger Goldschmiedekunst des Mittelalters und der Dürerzeit,* Berlin, 1968.
3 'Uber einige Nürnberger Goldschmiedezeichnungen aus der ersten Hälfte des 16ten Jahrhunderts' *94 Jahresbericht,* Germanisches Nationalmuseum, Nürnberg, 1949, p.9.

Part One

TEXT

CHAPTER ONE

The Study of Silver

THE basic problem to be faced in discussing sixteenth century silver is the identification of source; first the country of origin and then, where possible, the maker. On the silver vessel itself the most valuable evidence is the town mark, the maker's mark and, if present, the date letter. Where all three are present, the problem of identification is not difficult to solve. Though the practice varied from country to country and from city to city, most of the surviving silver vessels of the sixteenth century bear at least one stamped mark, most frequently the mark of the goldsmith who submitted the piece for assay. The town mark often accompanies the maker's mark but date letters are far less common though they are usually found on English, French, Flemish and Dutch silver. The presence of a maker's mark normally implies that the piece was made in the workshop of that particular maker. A goldsmith's workshop was likely to consist of two apprentices and two or more journeymen, so the master who presented the piece for assay might not have touched it himself, but could have left it entirely to his assistants. Furthermore, if a goldsmith received a large order for a service of vessels, he might put some of the work out to other masters. The guilds were constantly urging the more successful makers to pass on orders to their poorer brethren. If, however, the goldsmith who had received the initial order also supplied the metal to his colleagues, then he might himself have to take responsibility for its purity and in that case it would be his mark and not that of the actual maker which would be struck upon the piece. It follows that a maker's mark cannot be regarded as conclusive proof that the piece was produced by the maker in question, though in most cases this would be so. Again, if a piece of exceptional importance was required, the goldsmith might engage the services of a specialist chaser or engraver, who would execute all the decoration; the name of the latter would not as a rule appear at all, though a few pieces are known on which the signature of the chaser accompanies the mark of the goldsmith. Prominent masters were prepared to work on vessels that would subsequently be struck with the mark of a less distinguished craftsman. It is thought, for instance, that Hans Jamnitzer, son of the famous Wenzel, and himself one of the most skilled of the Nürnberg chasers, provided the embossed reliefs for a casket submitted for assay by, and bearing the mark of, Hans Straub.[1] In the same way, the great silver altarpiece commissioned from the Hamburg goldsmith, Jacob Mores, for the chapel of the Danish royal palace of Frederiksborg near Copenhagen, was marked by Mores, though he had only supplied the design and the execution had been entrusted to other masters.

When a piece of silver was assayed it was necessary to take a small scraping, usually from the underside of the vessel, for testing. If it was made up of several separate parts, then a scraping was taken from each. On English silver the removal of silver for assay can rarely be detected, whereas in the case of the German, Central European, Dutch and Scandinavian silver it took the form of a zig-zag groove (*Tremulierstich*) that went sufficiently deep to be readily recognisable. If this is present, one can expect to find a town and a maker's mark as well. If it is not accompanied by these other marks, it is likely that the assay has taken place at a later date, unless, of course, the piece has been altered and that part which bore the town and maker's marks has been removed. It is not unknown for a piece of silver to be re-assayed on importation in another country; in this case it may have two town marks, two maker's marks (the second one being that of the goldsmith who imported it and submitted it for re-assay) and two or more assay scrapes.

A feature of Mannerist fashion which will frequently be noticed in the course of this book is the preference for feet and bases of small size. Subsequent owners sometimes found these small feet impracticable and had a larger foot rim added. The goldsmith might well have his addition marked and, if the cup itself were unmarked, the whole might well be attributed to the maker of the foot ring alone. This has actually happened in the case of the cup illustrated in pl.553, the foot ring of which bears the mark of a goldsmith in the small Swiss town of Sitten. In view of the exceptionally high quality of this cup such an attribution seems unlikely. Just as one must guard against the danger of accepting the maker's mark as final proof of origin, so also is it wrong to assume that all unmarked pieces of high quality must have been made in one of the European artistic centres. Much Hungarian silver is unmarked, but we know on the evidence of a few marked pieces (pls. 581-2) that, when an important commission was received, the Hungarian goldsmiths were capable of work of exceptional merit.

Many of the finest examples of European goldsmith's work are unmarked. They were for the most part made for one of the ruling princes whose commissions were exempt from the guild regulations relating to assay and hall-marking. Though it is usually possible to make broad distinctions and to separate, for instance, southern European from northern European goldsmiths' work, it is often difficult in the absence of a town or maker's mark to be sure of the origin of a given piece. The international character of the style favoured in the European courts and, to a lesser extent, by other customers of the goldsmiths can be attributed to two main causes: first the determination of the ruling princes not to lag behind in following the march of fashion and, secondly, the constant exchange of craftsmen between one country and one city and another. Not only was fashion itself international, though Italy was the ultimate source of most innovation, but so also were the artists who created it. Goldsmiths and hardstone cutters moved from court to court seeking employment. The many disasters that made human life so brief and uncertain in the sixteenth century, such as warfare, the sudden death of the prince, plague or lack of money or clients, were always interrupting their work and compelling them to move on to another place of employment. The goldsmith was accustomed to such moves; he had probably been sent from his home village to another city to be apprenticed; his period as a journeyman took him outside his own country, possibly even half across Europe. Finally, if business was poor he would seek the right to work in another town where prospects were better. The tools of his craft were few and could be moved without much trouble.

Even at the court of Cosimo I de' Medici, rightly regarded as one of the most influential breeding grounds of the Italian Mannerist fashion, many of the goldsmiths were of German or Flemish origin. Thus Cellini, in a memorandum[2] submitted to the *Soprasindichi* in 1570, states 'French, German and Flemish craftsmen, who had worked in my service in France, came to find me here in sufficient numbers'. So also in Rome the goldsmiths' shops gave employment to many Germans and Flemings; in 1544 Cellini's rival for papal commissions, Tobia da Camerino, had two German goldsmiths in his employ, one of whom received a third of the profits of the business. The foreigners penetrated not only to the greater cities of Italy but also to the provinces. In 1578 Casolino, the court goldsmith to the Farnese Dukes of Parma and Piacenza, engaged a German, Agostino Smit (sic), to assist him in his Parma workshop and, seven years later, in 1585, another foreign-born goldsmith called Gottardo was engaged to work with Smit. Genoa, being a seaport, was also strongly subject to foreign influence and gave employment to many foreign goldsmiths. Among these was the Portuguese, Antonio de Castro, master of the ewer and basin illustrated in pls. 342 and 345, and the Flemish goldsmith who signed and dated a fine embossed dish now in a Paris private collection: *Gio. Aelbosca Belga F. Ge^a 1626*.[3] It follows that great caution must be used in identifying a style as national.

Certain features can be recognised as typical of a given locality, and England on the outskirts of Europe developed vessel types that were not known on the mainland. The goldsmiths employed together in the service of a prince evolved a distinct court style, but this was not by any means a national style as it was composed of elements drawn from various sources. The most individual was that developed by the goldsmiths employed by the Emperor Rudolph II in his court workshop in Prague.

A major feature of this period is the large-scale production of magnificent vessels of semi-precious hardstone and, in particular, of rock-crystal. The interest in intaglio cut rock-crystals probably grew out of the practice of collecting classical cameos and intaglios in the early Renaissance. Lorenzo de' Medici had an important collection of both hardstone cups and ancient cameos in Florence, including the famous antique carnelian of Apollo and Marsyas, which was mounted in gold by Lorenzo Ghiberti[4]. Rock-crystal vessels had been produced in medieval Europe, mostly in Venice, but possibly somewhere within the territories of the Dukes of Burgundy as well. The medieval rock-crystal vessels were only shaped and cut with facets and it was not until the Renaissance that rock-crystals were intaglio cut with figure subjects. The art first flourished in Rome but later spread to the main European capital cities. It appealed to the princely collector of the sixteenth century as much on account of the extreme difficulty encountered by the craftsman in working the material as of the exquisite effect of the finished article. Such vessels were mainly intended to decorate the buffet but sometimes had more practical uses; the French royal inventory of 1560 includes, for instance, a chalcedony *pot de chambre*.[5] In this book I have not studied these hardstone vessels at length as they have been treated in great detail by Heikamp in his study of the treasury of Lorenzo il Magnifico, by Kris in his *Steinschneidekunst in der italienischen Renaissance* and most recently by Alcouffe in his investigations of the former French royal collections.

Some of the most attractive and ingenious achievements of the goldsmith were, however, the enamelled gold mounts they made for these hardstone vessels and for this reason a considerable number are illustrated. Being made of gold, the mounts are not marked and are, with rare exceptions, by anonymous masters. Moreover, many of the finest hardstone vessels of the sixteenth century and, in particular, the most richly mounted, have been stripped of their gold and jewelled mounts at a later date and survive only as torsos. The reason for this brutal despoliation was sometimes simply lack of appreciation of works of art that were regarded as old-fashioned, but more often it was the need to recover the precious metal in order to use it for some other purpose. The hardstone itself had no intrinsic value and has, therefore, survived in an unmounted state, or, not infrequently, has been re-mounted in less expensive material such as gilt-bronze or even brass. Vessels mounted in this way can be seen in the former royal collections in the Louvre, Paris, and in the Schatzkammer of the Munich Residenz. The finest hardstone vessels were mounted in gold but many rock-crystals had silver-gilt mounts, indicating that this material was less highly prized than the coloured stones. Even in the case of the latter, gold was sparingly employed; silver-gilt was often used wherever the difference would not be apparent. A much higher proportion of vessels made of non- or semi-precious materials, but mounted in precious metal, has survived than of those entirely of gold or silver. This fact must be taken into consideration when studying sixteenth-century goldsmiths' work; otherwise a mistaken impression might be gained of the proportion of decorative to functional vessels produced by the sixteenth-century goldsmiths.

Innumerable representations of Mannerist silver can be found in sixteenth- and seventeenth-century paintings. Artists liked to introduce handsome plate into their pictures; for its decorative effect or for its usefulness in filling up awkward spaces. A buffet laden with white and gilt plate would help to fill a background, while a few large vases were equally useful in the foreground. Displays of plate were usual in paintings that represented religious, mythological or historical subjects involving banquets. Rottenhammer portrayed the 'Marriage at Cana' taking place in a palace worthy of a prince and packed with magnificent silver and gilt vessels. Any painting that showed an opulent interior called for at least a few pieces of plate. In such pictures the plate depicted might be more or less generalised without attention to precise detail, but there were at least two classes of paintings in which the vessels were accurately shown. These were still life paintings and representations of collector's cabinets, both specialities of Flemish and Dutch masters. The paintings were mostly executed during the seventeenth century, but the vessels depicted were often of earlier date. Such was the accuracy of still life paintings by masters such as Willem Kalf (1619-1693) that it has been possible to identify surviving vessels shown in them (see p.300).

The pattern of survival of sixteenth-century silver is quite irregular. Germany, England and the Low Countries are well represented whereas Italian and French silver of this period is extremely rare. Spain and Portugal retain vast quantities of ecclesiastical plate but very little that was intended for domestic use. In the case of the German-speaking area not only has much domestic plate survived, but also many goldsmiths' models in wood, bronze, lead and pewter. These, for obvious reasons, correspond to the extant pieces made of precious metal and are of more use in explaining the process of manufacture than the stylistic development, which is, however, adequately covered. The makers of pewter usually followed fashions in precious metal and, where no examples of the latter have survived, it is sometimes possible to obtain an idea of current fashion in the goldsmiths' shops by examining contemporary pewter. This applies with particular force to France, where little silver but much pewter survives. French ceramic wares of the sixteenth century were also closely related to contemporary silver designs, particularly in the case of green pottery made at La Chapelle des Pots; the models made there include ewers and pilgrim flasks which were directly inspired by the corresponding silver vessels. The influence of contemporary silver design can also be recognised in Saint Porchaire pottery and the wares of Bernard Palissy and his followers (see p.184).

As drinking habits varied in northern and southern Europe, so also the vessels used differed. The tankard which was a standard piece of plate in England, Germany, the Netherlands and Scandinavia was unknown in Italy, Spain and France. The tall beaker was also a mainly northern type; in the Middle Ages it had sat directly on the table but towards the middle of the sixteenth century it was given the added dignity of foot and stem and sometimes cover as well. The set of six or twelve low beakers which could be placed one on top of the other and surmounted by a cover (*Satz-* or *Setz-becher*) was a German speciality. The use of brown speckled stoneware jugs with silver mounts as beer jugs seem to have been confined to England; in Germany and Holland only the white Siegburg ware was considered worthy of mounting in this way.

Drawings of vessels of precious metal, mostly vases and ewers, dating from the sixteenth century, survive in large numbers and collections of them are to be found in the Print Rooms of the larger cities of Europe and the United States of America. Most are Italian or copied from Italian originals. Some are well known, such as those in the Uffizi in Florence or the Cabinet des Dessins of the Louvre. I have published many of those in the Victoria and Albert Museum, the Fitzwilliam Museum, Cambridge, the Bayerische Staatsbibliothek, Munich, and some of those in the Oesterreichisches Museum für angewandte Kunst, Vienna[6]. The Holbein drawings in Basel and the Nürnberg drawings in the library of Erlangen University are adequately published, but few of those in the library of Christchurch, Oxford, are known and the great collection of Etienne Delaune drawings of jewellery in the Ashmolean Museum has yet to be published. The majority of the drawings in Vienna, both in the Albertina and the Museum für angewandte Kunst await investigation. This research is less rewarding than might at first sight appear as the number of original designs is limited and there are innumerable copies, especially those after Giulio Romano. Two of the richest collections are those of the Bibliothèque Nationale in Paris and the Berlin Kunstbibliothek. The resources of the former await publication, whereas the French drawings in the Berlin library have been published by Berckenhagen.[7] An important collection of Italian Renaissance drawings of goldsmiths' work is preserved in the folio volume no. 196 in the Royal Library at Windsor. The volume was put together by the Roman seventeenth-century collector, Cassiano del

Pozzo, from whom it passed to the Albani family and thence via Consul Smith to the royal collection. It is particularly rich in drawings by Perino del Vaga (or Luzio Romano) and Giulio Romano, the latter including a design for a chafing-dish bearing the Farnese arms.[8] Other designs that can be connected with actual commissions are a basin with Gonzaga arms[9] by Alfonso Ruspagiari of Reggio Emilia (1521 - 1576) and a ewer with the Borghese eagle and dragon on the handle.[10] These have been summarily catalogued by Sir Anthony Blunt,[11] but would merit further research. Finally there are the three hundred odd drawings in the Basel Kupferstichkabinett, usually known as the *Baseler Risse*. These are original drawings by goldsmiths working in Nürnberg, Augsburg and Basel, which were assembled by Basilius Amerbach of Basel during the latter part of the sixteenth century. They cover the late Gothic, the transitional and the Renaissance styles and constitute the most valuable source of information on South German design in the first half of the century. They cover ecclesiastical and secular plate and include some dagger-sheath designs as well. Some are of mediocre quality and do not approach the originality of Holbein, but they well represent the average production of the time. Few of them have been published.

These drawings of goldsmiths' work served various purposes; the most useful from our present point of view are those executed by the goldsmith himself. Most valuable of all are the actual sketch-books of working goldsmiths. Unfortunately these are excessively rare; only two are known to me, though it is probable that others lie unrecognised in the libraries of Europe. The only sketch-book that has been adequately studied is that of Wenzel Jamnitzer in the Berlin Kunstbibliothek, which is discussed in detail on p.203. It is no longer complete and many of the drawings are so faint as to be barely recognisable. The second sketch-book is also in a poor state of preservation. It is now in the Pierpont Morgan Library, New York and consists of fifteen sheets with drawings on both sides of each sheet. An inscription in a later hand on the first page states that it was produced by Rafaele da Montefeltro to contribute to the eternal glory of Benvenuto Cellini, the sculptor of Florence who died in 1570, but the authenticity of this inscription is questionable. The designs it contains are mostly for jewellery or hand-mirror frames, the latter apparently derived from a series of prints by Etienne Delaune. An inscription in Italian on the last sheet suggests that the author was, in fact, Italian, but the style of the drawings as a whole corresponds to international Mannerism of the second half of the sixteenth century. Apart from the mirror frames, there are two designs for vases decorated with strapwork, while the remaining drawings represent jewellery. The circumstance that the drawings appear to be the work of an Italian, who was familiar with French designs of the mid-sixteenth century, does point to some goldsmith who followed in Cellini's footsteps and went to work in France.

Next to the goldsmith's own drawings come those commissioned by goldsmiths or their patrons from graphic masters, which related to a specific object and were not subsequently reproduced for general use. Based on them were the working drawings, probably showing only a part of the object to be made. These were followed by the craftsman as he worked on a vessel and have rarely survived, since they were roughly treated when the piece was in the making and were scrapped when it was finished. These may have been drawn out by the master goldsmith, but it is more probable that they were copied by an assistant from a rough sketch supplied by his master. The most complete collection of drawings showing all the stages of design relates to a series of armour made for the Kings of France; it is attributed to Etienne Delaune and his workshop.[12] It includes the artist's original rough sketches, his finished drawings, detailed drawings by his assistants based on the finished drawings and, finally, rough drawings made to the actual scale of the work. As this book is primarily concerned with the pieces that the goldsmiths made, the question of the original authorship of the designs they used is of secondary importance. Furthermore, it is often difficult to determine whether a drawing is the work of the master himself or of one of his workshop assistants. In this study I have devoted some attention to the problem of distinguishing between the former and the latter, but have in most cases been content to attribute drawings to the workshop of the master who was originally responsible for the style. Even a copy of a drawing is of interest, provided, of course, that it is contemporary. I have, however, endeavoured to establish the manner adopted by particular graphic artists in their designs for goldsmiths and also to estimate the influence they exercised on silver of the time, insofar as any survives. The names of many of the lesser graphic masters who supplied goldsmiths' designs have inevitably been lost and their *oeuvre* has subsequently been grouped together under the name of more prominent artists to whose style their work shows the closest resemblance. It has, for instance, been suggested that some of the vase designs formerly attributed to Perino del Vaga should be given to his assistant, Luzio Romano (see p.135). Such re-attributions, though noticed in this book, do not call for critical examination. It will suffice here to point out that the members of a workshop followed the manner of their master with remarkable fidelity. It must also be remembered that some of the surviving drawings were prepared as studies for representations of vases or other vessels in paintings and were not intended to serve the goldsmith at all. This applies in particular to vase drawings by or after Polidoro da Caravaggio; most of his designs are so fantastic that they could hardly have been translated into metal at all.

Almost as important as the extant drawings of goldsmiths' work are the printed pattern sheets or books of engraved ornament. These were sold to any goldsmith able or willing to purchase them and they had a wide distribution, often far beyond their place of origin. They remained in use for many decades and so tended to prolong the life of a particular style among provincial goldsmiths after it had ceased to be fashionable in the larger centres of the craft. The earlier prints offered ornament alone without indicating the particular article or type of article for which it was intended. The later engravers showed how the ornament might be adapted to the object and it is with this type of print that I am concerned. In the course of the sixteenth century a very large number of pattern-books intended to guide the goldsmith were published and the craftsman was so well served that he can rarely have needed to fall back on the resources of his own imagination in order to find a scheme of ornament suitable for his work. Those masters who devised ornament for goldsmiths were not, however, necessarily the most gifted in their field and it follows that only a marginal aspect of the history of ornament is studied in this book.[13] The less skilled goldsmiths were probably content to use pattern-books, but others drew also upon the great quantity of prints which, though not intended specifically for the goldsmith, showed subjects, mostly from classical mythology or the Bible, that could readily be adapted by him. The most important of these, used equally by the enamellers of Limoges and by the goldsmiths, was the *Historiarum memorabilium ex Genesi*, published in Lyon in 1558 with woodcuts by Bernard Salomon. Adapted to the round form of a tazza bowl they are frequently found in Nürnberg and Augsburg work of the latter part of the sixteenth century. Of comparable popularity were the many prints of contemporary life in Jost Amman's *Kunstbüchlein* published posthumously in 1599 in Frankfurt am Main. Not only did goldsmiths copy their subjects from prints, so also did engravers of prints copy from earlier masters: Flemish and French engravers from those of Agostino Veneziano; Paul Flindt from his near contemporary, Jost Amman. It follows that a design embossed on a northern piece of silver may be copied from a local source which has in turn been taken from an Italian original.

A detailed study of the *oeuvre* of Anton Eisenhoit of Warburg, one of the most gifted German Mannerist goldsmiths, has shown how completely dependent he was on contemporary printed sources for his designs.[14] Though many goldsmiths were able to adapt their source material and combine details from various sources, few were able to produce completely original designs. The emphasis that is now placed on originality is a comparatively recent development. Plagiarism was not regarded as in any way unworthy of a craftsman; he took whatever came to hand and either copied it exactly or adapted it to suit his purpose.

Much information concerning the purpose of various vessels produced in the sixteenth century can be gained from a codex containing one hundred drawings in the Fitzwilliam Museum, Cambridge. This book is not dated but it resembles so closely another published in 1597 by Ottavio da Strada, Court Antiquary of the Emperor Rudolph II, that it can be dated about the same period.[15] Like the drawings in the da Strada book, they are derived from originals by Giulio Romano and his workshop which were first produced at least fifty years before. The title-page of the book describes the contents as *Dissegni per far vasello di argento et oro per servitio della credenza e tavola per un gran principe fatte tutte al modo antico et come hoggi si usano in Roma per la Tavola del Papa et Cardinali et altri gran signori'.* (Designs for making gold and silver vessels for use on the sideboard and the dining-table of a great prince, all in the antique manner and like those today used in Rome for the service of the Pope, the Cardinals and other great princes). The claim that the vessels were such as were then used in Rome may not have been completely misleading, in spite of the age of the designs, inasmuch as old-fashioned plate could still have been in use on the tables of the Pope and Cardinals in Rome. On the other hand, the book certainly does not represent the type of vessel that was fashionable at the close of the sixteenth century. The title-page lists the contents of the book under thirteen different heads. There are three types of salt-cellar, large ones for the *credenza* (sideboard) (pl. 73), medium-sized for the long table when the prince gave a banquet and small ones when the prince dined alone. Two pepper-pots are shown and next a large covered tazza with two handles and a figure on top of the cover, intended to be set on the sideboard. There follow two types of tazza, both for drinking wine, and then goblets for drinking water. The two low vases, described in the list as intended for drinking water, were probably sauce-boats, while two hanging bowls, also described as for water, were probably intended for washing the hands after a meal. There follow low and tall candlesticks (pl. 70) for either the sideboard or the high table of the prince, and finally ewers (pls. 71-2) and basins for washing the hands. It is curious that this list includes no tureens nor wine-coolers, both of which were in use in the sixteenth century, but these gaps can be filled by referring to the da Strada book of designs which includes examples of each.

Of the various vessels illustrated in the Fitzwilliam Codex the only types which have survived in any number from this period are tazzas and the ewers with companion basins (pls. 341-50). The survival of the latter is the more surprising as the introduction of the fork in the early seventeenth century made the ewer and basin, which were used to rinse the fingers of the diners between courses, superfluous. These pieces were, however, the largest and most decorative and they can be seen standing in rows on the sideboard in many contemporary paintings of scenes such as the 'Feast of Nebuchadnezzar' or the 'Marriage at Cana'. Even though their original purpose no longer existed, they remained the most suitable pieces for display and were retained for this reason. The basin was provided with a central boss which fitted a recess in the base of the ewer so that it would sit firmly in the middle, but contemporary paintings usually show the basin set vertically with the ewer standing upright in front of it.

One of the most valuable features of the Fitzwilliam Codex is the information it gives concerning Italian drinking vessels. Whereas the majority of surviving northern European vessels of silver or gold are drinking vessels with baluster stems and trumpet-shaped feet, only one Italian cup of this type is recorded. The only sources of information concerning the types of drinking vessels used in Renaissance Italy are paintings and drawings. The Fitzwilliam Codex shows twenty-four drawings of three types of drinking vessel, namely low tazzas on short feet, taller ones on leafy baluster stems (pl. 74) and goblets (pl. 75). Most are of fairly simple design, which may explain why none seem to have survived to the present day. The tazzas have wide shallow bowls, a form which is far from convenient for drinking, and becomes less so as the drinker imbibes, since they require a steady hand in use. Those with wide bowl and low foot were presumably held with both hands. The solitary survivor — of gilt-copper, not precious metal — is in the Museo dell' Opera del Duomo, Florence. This tazza dates from about 1530/40; the bowl has a border embossed with bold acanthus foliage forming Renaissance masks.

The reference in the list of contents of the Fitzwilliam Codex to vessels *'per la Credenza'* is interesting because these were presumably intended for decoration and not for practical purposes. Amongst those meant for the *credenza* are the large tazzas with covers; this seems sensible as a cover is bound to be a nuisance to the drinker, but practically all the important northern European drinking cups either have, or had originally, a cover. It must have been a problem to know where to place the cover when drinking, unless the northern examples also were intended only for ceremonial use. It seems hard to credit that the demand for cups intended only for show should have been so large. The complex design and elaborate decoration of many sixteenth-century vessels suggests that utility was not greatly considered when they were being designed and made, and here we have confirmation of this from a contemporary manuscript source. This lack of concern for function applies also to the designs of Giulio Romano, one of the most prolific masters of this period. His drawings display the greatest fantasy, and yet some of his apparently most impracticable suggestions bear annotations that they were made for one or other member of the family of the Gonzaga Dukes of Mantua. In some cases one suspects that the imagination of the artist ran away with him as did that of Jacopo Ligozzi in his series of designs for glass vessels preserved in the Uffizi, Florence.[16] Though it may have been possible to execute them in so readily ductile a material as glass, they must have been of extreme fragility.

Among the contemporary sources of information the most plentiful are the inventories made after the owner's death. Most of the important inventories have now been published, among them those of the Habsburg Holy Roman Emperors,[17] of the Kings of France,[18] Philip II of Spain,[19] Henry VIII of England and his Tudor successors,[20] the Dukes of Bavaria,[21] the Grand Duke of Tuscany,[22] etc. These inventories often give some indication of the country of origin of a piece, but where the piece in question does not survive, such information is of little use. Many of the cups in the inventory of the Tudor royal plate are described as 'Almain' (German); this presumably means that the vessel in question was of German make, but one item (no. 333) is described as an 'Almain cup guilt embossed with faces and garnisshed red, blewe and grene with H and K knyt together upon the Cover.'[23] The presence of the initials of Henry and one of the three Catherines, to whom he was married, suggests that the cup was made in England, in which case one would be at a loss to explain the meaning of the term 'Almain'. It is, however, possible that the initials were added later to a cup of German origin. No. 387 in the same inventory is a 'Venetian cup', no. 190 is described as 'of Flaundours making', no. 226 is 'one Spanish cup'.[24] The various references to a 'Double Almain cup' must mean the typical German double cups of which one formed the cover of the other (pl. 482). Inventory clerks rarely concerned themselves with the marks struck on the vessels they were describing, but no. 523 in the Tudor inventory records three bowls 'of Flaunders touche'.[25] It is surprising that a clerk should have been able to recognise foreign assay marks in this way.

The 1587 inventory of the Guardaroba of the Medici Grand Dukes frequently refers to vessels as being '*alla todescha*' (in the German fashion), another term that is now meaningless. Again the inventory of the property left by Duchess Jacobäa of Bavaria, widow of Wilhelm IV, which is dated 21 February 1581, lists 'two silver handbasins, one fitting on the other, made in the French manner' and further on in the same inventory is a French gold-mounted crystal ball containing a figure of Orpheus.[26]

Correspondence between goldsmiths and their clients sometimes gives hints which, however, can all too rarely be followed up. A letter in the Munich archive, dated 13 December 1564, from Antonio Meiting of Augsburg, informing Duke Albrecht that he was sending him a water-jug of rock-crystal with gold mounts in the Spanish fashion and decorated with stars,[27] which he had just completed, leaves us wondering what mounts in the Spanish fashion looked like. As the Spanish goldsmiths of the second half of the sixteenth century were famed for their jewellery wrought in relief and enamelled, it is probable that in this case the term 'Spanish' referred to the enamelled ornament. Of much more use than the written inventories, few of which give sufficient detail to make the recognition of objects possible, should they perchance survive, are the pictorial inventories (*Bildinventaren*), which unfortunately, are far less common. Four German pictorial inventories survive, which between them illustrate a large number of sixteenth-century vessels. The earliest is that prepared for Cardinal Albrecht of Brandenburg shortly before 1530 (see p.97), the next consists of a series of miniatures in the manner of and, perhaps, by Hans Mühlich, which are now divided between the library of the Bayerisches Nationalmuseum and the Staatliche Graphische Sammlung, Munich.[28] They show enamelled gold vessels and jewels of great splendour, dating from the third quarter of the sixteenth century (pls. 161, 228). The third illustrates no fewer than 427 pieces of domestic plate and was drawn up after the marriage of Prince Wenzel Eusebius Lobkowitz in 1652.[29] While the first inventory consists mainly of ecclesiastical plate, much of it medieval, the Lobkowitz inventory is more helpful though again a fair proportion is Baroque in style and does not concern us here. Nearly all the articles illustrated appear to be of German origin and cover a period of about a century prior to the date of the inventory. There are many standing cups, six flagons, twelve tankards, nests of beakers, plates and dishes, and a large parcel-gilt wine-cooler weighing about three hundred ounces, with a cast from Peter Flötner's plaquette of 'David and Bathsheba' within a strapwork cartouche applied to the side. There are also warming-pans, perfume-burners, braziers, dish-warmers, salts with obelisk-form covers, a cheese-grater, scallop shells, (presumably for butter), cruet-stands, porringers, candlesticks, etc. Eight standing dishes with scale borders are dated 1590 and one of the five ostrich-egg cups is dated 1597. There is only one coconut cup in the inventory. Among the earlier vessels depicted are five that can be associated with the workshop of Ludwig Krug in Nürnberg. Of all this vast quantity of plate, devised for every conceivable use, only one cup is believed to have survived and the present location even of this is unknown. The last of the pictorial inventories dating from our period is that of the silver of the St. Michael Hofkirche, Munich,[30] which was prepared by an obscure artist named Müller in 1610. Most of the silver consists of altar plate but a few pieces, mostly baptismal ewers with basins, do not differ from contemporary secular plate. The plate was presented to the church by Duke Wilhelm V of Bavaria about the time that the inventory was prepared. The ewers conform to the egg shape, usual during the second half of the century, while the altar cruets, of which there were large numbers, are miniature versions of the full-size ewer. The most impressive objects shown are not of German origin; they are two silver-gilt caskets set with panels of jasper and lapis lazuli which were presented to the two sons of Duke Wilhelm by Pope Clement VIII when they left Rome after a visit to the Pope in 1593. The caskets contained relics but correspond in design to the magnificent Italian casket acquired by Duke Albrecht before 1563.[31]

Other pictorial inventories probably survive unrecognised or at any rate unpublished in the libraries of noble families; a number of detached sheets from such inventories appear on the market from time to time and are sometimes mistakenly identified as sketches for, instead of drawings after, an existing article. One such is illustrated in pl. 176. Their quality is usually unremarkable. That of the Dukes of Bavaria, attributed to Hans Mülich, is the only one that can claim any artistic distinction. Many more unillustrated inventories survive but these are of slight value unless the articles they list are available for study. Three of these inventories do, however, concern existing objects. The first is the Disposition of Duke Albrecht V of Bavaria by which he established seventeen of his most precious pieces as inalienable treasures of the Wittelsbach line. To this list his successor added ten further objects (see p.32). The second inventory is that of the gold and silver vessels left by Archbishop Wolf Dietrich von Raitenau of Salzburg.[32] A large part of this treasure has survived with the former Medici Collection in the Palazzo Pitti, Florence, though it did not actually come to Italy until the early nineteenth century. The third unillustrated inventory is that of the ducal line of Hesse-Cassel; this has been published together with illustrations of those pieces mentioned in it that still survive.[33] For Spanish silver another valuable source is available: namely the drawings submitted by candidates for admission as masters of their craft. A large number of masterpiece drawings by goldsmiths and jewellers of Barcelona survive and many of them have been published. Those of Valencia do not seem to have survived the Spanish Civil War of the 1930's but a small selection had been published previously. No masterpiece drawings by goldsmiths from other cities or countries are known to exist.

A vast amount of material has survived in the city archives of Europe, most of it unexplored. The records of the Goldsmiths' Company of London[34] have been published, though only in brief extracts but we are well served for the south German cities. The records of the goldsmiths' guilds of both Munich and Augsburg have been studied and in the case of Nürnberg there are two volumes of the decrees (*Verlässe*) of the Nürnberg City Council[35] covering the period from 1474 to 1618. These are mostly concerned with parochial matters, but give a graphic picture of the life of a Nürnberg goldsmith, showing how powerful was the City Council and how easily a master-goldsmith might find himself in the town gaol (*Loch*). The researches of A. Bertolotti[36] in Italian archives have brought to light the names of large numbers of goldsmiths who were working in the larger Italian cities in the sixteenth century. Unfortunately few, if any, of these can be associated with extant works and are seldom of relevance here.

Of the literary sources the most important is Benvenuto Cellini's autobiography (*Vita*) to which frequent reference will be made in the following pages. It is followed closely by his two *Trattati* on the art of the goldsmith and the sculptor respectively. His arrogant and boastful manner led earlier commentators to question the value of his testimony, but subsequent investigation has shown that, where they can be checked, his statements are true. His extravagant account of life in sixteenth-century Italy has attracted much research and the various editions of his *Vita* provide detailed information about him and his contemporaries; the most complete English version is that by Robert Cust,[37] in which biographical information about all the people mentioned is given. Unfortunately, the destruction of all his larger works except for the salt of François I makes it impossible to give an adequate account of his achievement. Cellini's two treatises on his art provide us with explicit accounts of methods of manufacture in the sixteenth century, as well as detailed information about the production of some of his most famous creations. They also compare his own methods with those used by contemporaries in other countries, particularly in France.

Giorgio Vasari's *Lives*[38] provide a few scraps of information about the activities of those Italian artists who at some time in their lives engaged in goldsmithing, but his value as a source for Italian goldsmiths' work as a whole is slight. The same must be said of Joachim von Sandrart's *Academie der Bau, Bild und Mahlerey-Künste* of 1675, which is in any case mostly concerned with the seventeenth century. For the lives of the Nürnberg masters the biographies of the Nürnberg historian, Johann Neudörfer,[39] are informative and and, as he was a contemporary, reliable. The best source of information about relations between goldsmiths and their customers and the process of commissioning and completing an order is the correspondence between the Augsburg diplomat and the art dealer, Philip Hainhofer, and his chief customer, Duke Philip of Pomerania.[40] Although the published material only covers the few years between 1610 and 1618, the extent of the duke's purchases and the detail in which they are discussed throw much light on an important aspect of the creation of goldsmiths' work. Of equal importance is the account-book of the Florentine court goldsmith, Giacomo Biliverti, covering the period for 1573-1587, which, together with a list of all the bills presented by Biliverti to the Grand Duke of Tuscany in respect of work carried out by him, has been published in full by W. Fock.[41] Most of the items relate to jewellers' work, but a remarkably wide range of vessels and other objects of gold and silver is included.

Contemporary sources are not invariably reliable. There is in the Berlin Kunstbibliothek a collection of twenty-four sheets of mid-sixteenth century drawings of vases, mostly of typical Mannerist design, each of which is accompanied by an annotation in a contemporary hand describing its purpose.[42] The annotations go further, however, and claim that the vessels represented are classical antiquities and were dug up in or near Rome or Naples. Verisimilitude is added to the statements by the addition in some cases of the name of the sixteenth-century collector in whose possession the piece was supposed to be. While the collectors did exist and the objects may in some cases have been in their possession, there can be no doubt that the claims made for the antiquity of the vessels represented are false. They are almost without exception typical Mannerist fantasies drawn by artists who knew little or nothing of authentic classical vases. Presumably the drawings had been prepared in Italy for sale to some northern collector of antiquities and drawings thereof, who would not be able to recognise the fact that they were all contemporary fakes. If, however, we ignore the annotations, the drawings are of interest as providing evidence of Mannerist taste and its alleged classical sources.

1   ill. Pechstein I, cat. no. 88

2   Cellini III, p.574, *lettera ai Signori Soprasindichi 'E mi venne trovare qui parecchi lavoranti Franzesi, Todeschi, Fiamminghi sufficientissimi, li quali mi avevano serviti in Francia'*

3   The subject is Columbus receiving gifts from native Indians.

4   Kris I, p.24-5.

5   Fontainebleau I, no. 272.

6   J. F. Hayward, 'The Mannerist Goldsmiths (Italian Sources) and some Drawings and Designs', *Connoisseur*, 149, 1962, p.157-165.
    ibid. 'France and the School of Fontainebleau. Part I', *Connoisseur*, 152, 1963, p.240-245.
    ibid. 'France and the School of Fontainebleau, Part II', *Connoisseur*, 153, 1963, p.11-15.
    ibid. 'Antwerp. Part I', *Connoisseur*, 156, 1964, p.92-6.
    ibid. 'Antwerp. Part II', *Connoisseur*, 156, 1964, p.165-70.
    ibid. 'Antwerp. Part III', *Connoisseur*, 156, 1964, p.251-54.
    ibid. 'Antwerp. Part IV': Italian influence in the designs of Erasmus Hornick', *Connoisseur*, 158, 1965, p.144-49.
    ibid. 'England, Part I: The Holbein designs', *Connoisseur*, 159, p.80-84.
    ibid. 'England, Part II', *Connoisseur*, 162, 1966, p.90-5.
    ibid. 'Germany, Part I'. Nürnberg', *Connoisseur*, 164, 1967, p.78-84.
    ibid. 'Germany, Part II. Wenzel Jamnitzer of Nürnberg', *Connoisseur*, 164, 1967, p.148-54.
    ibid. 'Germany, Part III, Erasmus Hornick and the Goldsmiths of Augsburg', *Connoisseur*, 164, 1967, p.216-22.
    ibid. 'Germany, Part IV, The Followers of Wenzel Jamnitzer', *Connoisseur*, 167, 1967, p.162-7.
    ibid. 'Germany, Part V, The later Mannerist Masters', *Connoisseur*, 168, 1968, p.15-19.
    ibid. 'Germany, Part VI, Christoph Jamnitzer and his contemporaries', *Connoisseur*, 168, 1968, p. 161-166.
    ibid. 'Northern Germany, Part VII', *Connoisseur*, 169, 1970, p.22-30.
    ibid. 'Disegni di Orafi del Rinascimento Tedesco', *Antichita Viva*, Florence, 1967, p.35-42.
    ibid. 'Fontainebleau nell'interpretatione degli orafi di Norimberga', *Antichita Viva*, Florence, 1968, p. 17-25.
    ibid. The Goldsmiths' Designs of the Bayerische Staatsbibliothek reattributed to Erasmus Hotnick', *Burlington Magazine*, April 1968, p.201-7.
    ibid. 'Ottavio Strada and the Goldsmiths' Designs of Giulio Romano', *Burlington Magazine*, Jan., 1970, p.10-14.
    ibid. 'Some spurious Antique Vase Designs of the Sixteenth Century', *Burlington Magazine*, June, 1972, p.378-86.
    ibid. 'The drawings and engraved ornament of Erasmus Hornick', *Burlington Magazine*, 110, 1968, p.383-89.

7   E. Berckenhagen, *Die Französischen Zeichnungen der Kunstbibliothek Berlin*, Berlin, 1970.

8   Schilling and Blunt, no. 208.

9   ibid. no. 416.

10 ibid. no. 316.

11 In the Supplement to Italian and French drawings as a second part to the *German Drawings at Windsor Castle* catalogued by E. Schilling, London. 1971.

12 B. Thomas, 'Die Münchner Harnischvorzeichnungen', *Jahrbuch*, Band 55, 1959, p.31-74; Band 56, 1960, p.7-62; Band 58, 1962, p.101-168; Band 61, 1965, p.41-90.

13 For the best analysis of the development of engraved ornament, see Berliner, *Ornamentale Vorlage-Blätter*, Leipzig, 1926.

14   A. M. Kesting, *Anton Eisenhoit, Ein Westphälischer Kupferstecher und Goldschmied*, Münster, 1964.

15   J. F. Hayward, 'Ottavio da Strada and the Goldsmiths' designs of Giulio Romano', *Burlington Magazine*, Vol. CXII, 1970, p.10ff.

16   L. Berti, *Il Principe dello Studiolo*, Firenze, 1967, figs. 142-3.

17   For the Habsburg Inventories, see Lhotsky, *Festschrift des Kunsthistorischen Museums*, 'Die Geschichte der Sammlung', Zweiter Teil, Erste Hälfte, p.209, 307, 315 etc. The most valuable of the inventories of the Emperor Rudolf, dating from 1607-11 and probably prepared by the miniaturist, Daniel Froschl, has not as yet been published, but see E. Neumann, 'Das Inventar der Rudolphinischen Kunstkammer von 1607-11', *Queen Christina of Sweden, Documents and Studies*, Stockholm, 1966, p.262. The inventory of the collection of the Archduke Ferdinand of Tirol in the Castle of Ambras is published in the *Jahrbuch*, Band Vii, 1888, Regest, pp. ccxxvi-cccxi.

18   Fontainebleau I, Vol. III, p.334, Vol. IV, p.445, 518.

19   Ch. Davilier, *L'Orfèvrerie en Espagne*, passim.

20   Collins, *Jewels and Plate of Queen Elizabeth I*, London, 1955, passim.

21   Brunner, p.7.

22   Extracts are printed by Supino, p.65ff. See also K. Piacenti, *Museo degli Argenti*, p.26-36 and Berti, pps. 52-4.

23   Collins, p.346.

24   Collins, pps. 355, 317, 325.

25   Collins, p.378, see also C. C. Oman, *English Domestic Silver*, London, 1959, pps. 50-1.

26   Ed. Rückert, *Münchner Jahrbuch der Bildenden Kunst*, 1965, p.122-132. The Medici inventory of 1587 uses the terms *'alla francese'* and *'alla tedesca'* frequently; the latter term is applied to a set of eight tazzas which from the description would now be recognised as German or of German type *'otto tazze overo bichiere d'argento dorati alla tedesca con piede alto, una testa nel mezo, atorno un cerchio di arabesco alla tedesca'* eight tazzas or beakers of silver-gilt in the German fashion on tall feet, with a head in the centre (of the bowl) surrounded by a circles of arabesques also in the German fashion.

27   Stockbauer, p.89 *'ein Wasserkrugl von Kristall, mit Gold auf die spanische Art, und mit Sternen verziert'.*

28   J. H. von Hefner Alteneck, *Deutsche Goldschmiedewerke des 16ten Jahrhunderts*, Frankfurt am Main, 1890.

29   E. W. Braun, *Die Silberkammer eines Reichsfürsten*, Leipzig, 1923.

30   Gmelin, *Alte Handzeichnungen nach den verlorenen Kirchenschatz der St. Michaels Hofkirche*, München, 1888.

31   Brunner, cat. no. 47.

32   F. Martin, *Die Salzburger Silberkammer*, Salzburger Museumsblätter, Oct. 1929, p.3.

33   A. von Drach, *Aeltere Silberarbeiten in den königlichen Sammlungen zu Cassel*, Marburg, 1888.

34   W. S. Prideaux, *Memorials of the Goldsmiths' Company*, n.d. London.

35   T. Hampe, *Die Nürnberger Ratsverlässe, Quellenschriften für Kunstgeschichte*, Vols. XI, XII, Wien, 1904.

36   *Artisti belgi et holandesi a Roma*, Firenze, 1880; *Artisti lombardi a Roma*, Milano, 1881; *Artisti urbinati in Roma*, Urbino, 1881; *Artisti modenesi, parmensi e della Lusigiana*, Modena, 1882; *Artisti subalpini in Roma*, Mantova, 1884; *Artisti francesi in Roma*, Mantova, 1886; *Arti minori alla corte di Mantova*, Milano, 1889; *Artisti veneti in Roma*, Venezia, 1884.

37   R. H. Cust, *The Life of Benvenuto Cellini*, London 2nd ed. 1935. This is particularly useful as it quotes the relevant references to Bertolotti (see note 36) and to other 19th-century sources. The most modern Italian edition is that of E. Camesasca, Milan, 1954.

38   *Le Vite di piu eccellenti Pittori.....*, ed. Milanesi, Firenze, 1868-1885.

39   J. Neudörfer, *Nachrichten von Künstlern und Werkleuten*, Nürnberg, 1547.

40   O. Doering, 'Des Augsburger Patriziers Philipp Hainhofer Beziehungen zum Philipp II von Pommern-Stettin, *Quellenschriften für Kunstgeschichte*, N.S. Vol. VI, passim.

41   Fock, p.155-176. Among the bills are several for clock or watchcases or parts thereof, silver figures after models by Gian Bologna, vases *'alla Francese'*, mounts for rock-crystal vessels and sword hilts.

42   J. F. Hayward, 'Some Spurious Antique Vase Designs of the Sixteenth Century', *Burlington Magazine*, June, 1972, p.378ff.

CHAPTER TWO

Patrons, Goldsmiths and Guilds

GOLDSMITHING is and always has been a luxury trade, which could only thrive in prosperous communities that provided a large and wealthy clientèle. In the sixteenth century goldsmiths were mostly to be found in the larger cities which were also the seat of a bishop or the place of residence of a ruling prince. The goldsmith who was employed by a court could rely on orders not only for the use of the prince and his noblemen, but also for articles of precious metal to be given as presents to other princes and their ambassadors. The last were sometimes on a vast scale and the practice of exchanging New Year's gifts between the sovereign and members of his court, as was the custom in Tudor England,[1] gave rise to new orders in plenty. Occasions such as a dynastic wedding, a coronation, a *Reichstag* of the Holy Roman Empire or a Council of the Church all offered great opportunities to the goldsmith to obtain new orders. When the Constable of Castile, Don Juan Fernandez de Velasco, and his fellow envoys from the court of Spain and the Spanish Netherlands left England in 1604 they were gratified by James I with no less than 290 ounces of gold vessels and over 28,900 ounces of gilt plate, amounting to a significant proportion of the whole Tudor treasure that had been inherited by James I just one year before.[2] Among the pieces then lost to the English royal treasury was the fourteenth-century Royal Gold Cup, one of the most historic vessels of the Crown. Other European princes were equally ruthless in disposing of the finest pieces in their treasuries once they became unfashionable. In 1570 King Charles IX of France sent as a present to Archduke Ferdinand of Tirol some of the most outstanding treasures in his possession: the Cellini Salt (pl. 313), the Saint Michael Cup (pl. 289), an onyx ewer (pl. 372) and the so-called Burgundian Court Beaker.[3] Such pieces were replaced by others of more recent fashion, thus giving more work for the goldsmiths. James I actually intended to replace the vessels that went to Spain with exact copies and had drawings made of them for this purpose, but his plan was never executed.[4] Embassies were always expensive, even when the occasion was relatively unimportant. When in July, 1585, the Prince of Sulmona came to Florence bringing with him the Order of the Golden Fleece conferred upon Francesco I, Grand Duke of Tuscany, by Philip II of Spain, he was rewarded by the Duke with a ewer and basin of solid gold valued at three thousand scudi, while the Duchess Bianca gave him, presumably as a present for his wife, a quantity of linen valued at three hundred scudi.[5]

The number and variety of commissions given to goldsmiths knew no limit; the inventories of the treasuries of monarchs ranging from the Holy Roman Emperor in Prague to that of Queen Elizabeth in London record the vast quantities of plate made of precious metal then in the possession of the European sovereigns. While a certain proportion of the wealth of a sixteenth-century ruler was kept in the form of coin, a great deal was converted by the court goldsmith into vessels of gold or silver. These pieces were placed in the treasury until such time as they were required for presentation. If, however, affairs of state made this necessary, they were melted down without hesitation. Many examples of such destruction could be quoted, but the most famous is certainly the inclusion of the Cellini gold salt in a list of vessels ordered to be melted in 1566 by the French King Charles IX. The salt was saved from the melting pot, only to be given away a few years later.[6] Even a dedicated collector of works of art such as the Basel humanist, Basilius Amerbach, included the vessels of precious metal in his possession among the specie and did not enter them in the inventory of his art collection.[7]

Although the sixteenth-century ruler maintained at his court the services of one or more goldsmiths, or, in the case of the Emperor Rudolph at Prague, a large workshop of masters who were exclusively employed by him, it was nevertheless necessary to pass on many commissions elsewhere — in Italy to Milan and in the German-speaking territories to Augsburg and Nürnberg. The objects commissioned were often of unparalleled costliness. The most extravagant of these no longer survive. Vessels were carved from semi-precious hardstones and mounted with enamelled gold and jewels with a profusion that has not been equalled since except, perhaps, for the work of the Saxon court jeweller, Dinglinger, for August the Strong, King of Poland and Elector of Saxony. The raw material, rock-crystal, agate, jasper, etc. was obtained in the Bohemian mountains and in Saxony, the gemstones that adorned them from India and from the Spanish South American Empire. The goldsmiths of cities such as Nürnberg or Augsburg, which were not the place of residence of a prince, relied mainly on orders from the City Council, the merchants and from visiting noblemen. The movements of wealthy personages were watched and the goldsmiths were ready with valuable stock to show them when they arrived. An entry in the Nürnberg records[8] for January 20, 1616, shows that the Bürgermeister of the city announced that on the following Thursday a visit from the Archduke Maximilian, *Hoch und Deutschmeister* of the *Deutsches Ritter Orden* was expected, and further that he intended to purchase a number of important jewels for presentation to the wife of the Emperor (Matthias) on the occasion of her coronation as Queen of Bohemia. It was decided that the Chamberlain of the Order should be asked when the Archduke was arriving, and that the goldsmiths, the official in charge of the Assay and also Petzolt and (Christopher) Jamnitzer should be informed so that, if they had any drinking-cups or jewels, they could get them ready.

The sixteenth-century goldsmith enjoyed one considerable advantage over his medieval predecessor: the vastly increased supply of precious metal available to be worked, which followed on the discovery of the New World and the exploitation of the South American gold and silver mines. The precious metal was first imported to Spain, but was soon distributed over Europe, partly in order to pay for the armies stationed outside the frontiers of Spain. One indication of the change in the supply situation can be seen in the large number of vessels made of silver which would, a century earlier, have been made of bronze or brass. At the same time every goldsmith must have known, as he worked on his latest creation, that the preciousness of its material condemned it to destruction as soon as it became unfashionable or its owner needed ready money. While the painter or the sculptor was producing works of art which would continue to please future generations into a far distant future, the goldsmith could not look forward to more than a life of some thirty years or so at best for his creations, however splendid and costly they might be. Only objects made for the church were likely to have a longer life and even they were subject to the hazards of theft or wartime looting. This impermanence of his so-carefully created masterpieces was made doubly clear to the goldsmith because the precious metal he worked and the precious stones he set often came to him in the form, not of bullion or of unmounted stones, but of old-fashioned or damaged pieces, which he had first to break up before re-creating them in a new form. The goldsmith who was used to destroying the most splendid works of his predecessors cannot have failed to realise that a similar fate would almost certainly await his own productions.

The idea of preserving articles of precious metal as a permanent collection of heirlooms (*erb und haus clainoder*) seems to have originated with the Wittelsbach Duke Albrecht V of Bavaria who in 1565 enumerated seventeen objects which were to become hereditary treasures of his family in perpetuity.[9] They were to be kept in his Munich castle, the *Neuveste*. Shortly afterwards ten further pieces were added and his

Plate I
French casket covered with mother-of-pearl scales, and gilt mounts. Paris, 1533, probably by a court goldsmith.

Plate II
Italian rock-crystal ewer with enamelled and gilt mounts. Probably Florentine, mid 16th century.

successor, Duke Wilhelm V, increased the number still further. Of the original twenty-seven pieces only nine have survived to the present day in the Munich Residenz on the site of the old Neuveste. Duke Albrecht V shared the taste of his day in his liking for vessels carved from rock-crystal. A group of thirty-three rock-crystals commissioned by him in Milan did not arrive in Munich until after his death in 1579. These were added to the hereditary treasure of the Wittelsbachs by his grandson, the Elector Maximilian. Duke Albrecht also founded a *Kunstkammer* as a separate entity from the treasury. This contained a greater variety of articles than the latter; the 1598 inventory of the *Kunstkammer* enumerates no less than 3,407 items.[10] Similar collections, mostly begun during the second half of the sixteenth century, are still to be seen in Vienna, Dresden, Kassel, Paris, Madrid, Florence and Copenhagen. The contents of these collections were not regarded as functional objects, which they often were not, but as works of art that gave honour to their owners. In subsequent centuries, when they had ceased to be in fashion and their aesthetic importance was unappreciated, they were, unless protected by some legal provision such as that which established the Bavarian treasury in perpetuity, treated as just so much precious metal suitable for conversion to other purposes.

Whereas in southern Europe the major commissions for goldsmiths' work came from ruling princes, the Church and wealthy noblemen, in the north the goldsmith drew his customers from a wider range of society. The *Willkomm* (welcome) cup or beaker was an indispensable item in the treasury of every German noble family or guild. Some of these cups dated back to the Middle Ages, but other families of less ancient lineage had more modern pieces. The inventory of the property of the Fugger banking family at Schloss Kirchheim included 'a mounted ostrich egg with a silver cover in a black case together with the book used for welcoming.'[11] In addition to the nobility and the guilds, the *Stadträte* (City Councils) were important customers. It was the practice to present visiting princes or their ambassadors with a handsome cup of gold or silver-gilt when they came to stay in one of the cities and this practice was repeated, though on a less lavish scale, by other institutions. Probably the most lavish gifts were those made by the City of Nürnberg to the Emperor when he entered the city for the first time. In 1541 Charles V was presented with a silver-gilt cup embossed with figures of the seven planets and enriched with enamel, which had been purchased in the previous year from Melchior Baier for 460 florins. It contained two thousand new-minted Nürnberg gold gulden.[12] On July 3, 1612, on his return journey after his coronation in Frankfurt am Main, the Emperor Matthias received a silver-gilt cup (pl. 115) set with twenty-five precious stones containing one thousand newly minted gold gulden, each struck with the heads of the Emperor Matthias and his Empress.[13] Judging by the drawing, the cup must have seemed old-fashioned in design in 1612, but it probably served as little more than an elegant and expensive container for the gold coins.

While there were at any one time certain standard designs for presentation cups, usually derived from the pattern-books then current, great importance was placed upon originality, particularly in the case of the *Willkomm* cups. In the case of families these might take a form that reflected the military career of the owner, as for example the seventeeth-century cup of the Counts von Giech of Thurnau constructed like a mortar. In the same way vessels made for the guilds reflected the activity of the guild for which they were destined. No great exercise of the imagination was required to produce a cup in the form of an ox or a sheep for the Butchers' Guild, a shoe for the Shoemakers' Guild (pl. 524) but the contemporary admiration of virtuosity led in the second half of the century to the creation of some extravagantly designed vessels (pl. 559). Some of the finest surviving cups were originally ordered by great merchant families. The Holzschuher family of Nürnberg were particularly active patrons. Two cups made for this family are in the Germanisches Nationalmuseum, Nürnberg; the earlier is a coconut-cup from the design of Peter Flötner with reliefs carved by him (pl. 271), the later one is by Elias Lencker, the first of a famous family of Nürnberg and (later) Augsburg goldsmiths. A third Holzschuher cup, also by Elias Lencker is in the Hamburg Museum (pl. 489). Among other Nürnberg patrician families both the Tuchers and the Imhofs are represented by cups of great splendour (pl. 484, 485).

Nearly all the treasuries of the German City Councils and Guilds have disappeared. Those few that survived the terrors of the Thirty Years War were melted to pay the vast fines imposed upon the German states during the Napoleonic Wars. Some of those that were given away as presents or sold still exist and are recognisable by the inscription recording the presentation or by the engraved or cast arms or device of the city or guild in question. These presentation cups are imposing pieces, though more importance was often attached to weight of precious metal than to quality of finish. The cup of the Butchers' Guild of Augsburg, now in the Bayerisches Nationalmuseum (pl. 458) constitutes an exception, as it is of the finest quality though of moderate size. Constructed like a beaker on baluster stem, it is surmounted by a cover with a figure finial. The embossing in low relief of three figures of Virtues set within *Rollwerk* cartouches is of outstanding merit. The only treasury of which enough survives to give an adequate idea of the former riches of the City Councils is that of Lüneburg; twenty-seven pieces are in the Berlin Kunstgewerbemuseum, one still in Lüneburg and one other (pl. 526) in private possession. Lüneburg was by no means exceptional. In 1610 the City Council of Lübeck owned two hundred and fifty-five silver vessels, but in 1636, during the Thirty Years War, treasure to a value of 5000 thaler had to be sold and the remainder was melted at the time of the Napoleonic occupation.

The fact that the goldsmith dealt with precious metal, which could also be used for coinage, brought with it other possibilities; he could become a money-changer, and following from this, a banker. Provided he did not make the mistake of lending too much to unreliable and insolvent princes, the goldsmith was likely to become one of the wealthiest and most influential citizens of his community. He required a regular supply of precious metal for his work and though much was always obtained by melting down plate that was worn or out of date, increasing wealth meant a constant demand for further supplies. He made sure of this by interesting himself in silver-mining; there is much evidence of such participation in the economic life of the country by the more important masters.[14]

At no time has the goldsmith enjoyed so high a status in society as during the second half of the sixteenth century. In his autobiography Cellini makes it clear that he and other goldsmiths were used to consulting in person with Princes and Popes about their commissions:[15] at a later date, the interpretation of the royal wish would have been left to the discretion of the court chamberlain or some lesser official. It was not unusual for the Prince to visit the workshop in order to discuss projects and to examine the progress on commissions that had already been started. King Francis I, the two successive Medici Grand Dukes, Cosimo I and Francesco I, Popes Clement VII and Paul III and the Emperor Rudolph II were among those whose enthusiasm for the goldsmiths' art brought them into frequent contact with the masters they employed in their court workshops. Francesco's interest even extended to designs for goldsmiths' work. Writing to his friend Borghini on October 1, 1572, Vasari lists his projects for the Grand Duke: a palace at Capraia di Pisa, a chapel at Colle Mingoli, fountains at Castello and furthermore 'every evening the Prince (Francesco) has wished me to be present until three o'clock in the morning to draw vases as long as I live'.[16] The Elector August I of Saxony also showed a personal interest in the craft of goldsmith, for he had constructed for his own use a splendid draw-bench which is now in the Musée de Cluny, Paris. This machine is elaborately inlaid with the arms of the Elector and his spouse, Anna of Denmark, and with figure subjects. The iron parts are etched with mauresques against a blackened ground in the same manner as the arms and armour of the period. The bench, which was probably made in Dresden, is dated 1565.

The most notorious proof of the favour that might be accorded to leading goldsmiths relates to Cellini. His brother was wounded and subsequently died following a scuffle in Rome with the guard of the Bargello, in the course of which one of the latter was also killed.[17] Benvenuto swore vengeance against the man who had wounded his brother and did in fact assassinate him in the street. When the affair was reported to Pope

Clement VII, not only did he take no action against Cellini but continued to employ him and allowed him to retain his post of Master of the Dies (*Maestro delle Stampe*) to the Papal Mint. This incident occurred in 1530; four years later, during the first year of the papacy of Paul III, Cellini was insulted by his main rival for papal commissions, Pompeo de Capitaneis, and thereupon assassinated him.[18] Once again he escaped arrest as a result of a safe conduct procured by one of the Cardinals who employed him, either Cardinal Cornaro or Ippolito de'Medici. When an influential friend of the murdered goldsmith protested to the Pope that Cellini should not be allowed to go free, Paul III, according to Cellini, replied 'Know that men like Benvenuto, unique in their profession, ought not to be bound by the law; but much more so in his case, for I know how much reason he has'.[19] It is unlikely that Cellini's report of the Pope's reply is exactly correct, but there is no doubt that Paul III provided him with a safe conduct which protected him from arrest.[20] Pompeo had been one of the officers of the Papal Mint, but Cellini nevertheless thought it appropriate to ask Paul III that he should be restored to the office of Master of the Dies, the position which he had held under Clement VII, but had lost as a result of his failure to complete the chalice ordered by Clement (see p.149).

Cellini recounts with great satisfaction the high praise that his works received from the French king. He considered that his creations rivalled those of classical antiquity and he never fails to quote remarks in which the former are favourably compared with the latter. He describes (see p.173) how, when he first met Francis I and handed over a ewer and basin originally made for the Cardinal of Ferrara, the King expressed the opinion that such superb works had not been seen since antiquity. When again in 1545 Cellini finally produced his completed gold salt, Francis expressed himself in much the same way, and perhaps with more justification:[21] 'God be praised that here in our own day there be yet man born who can turn out so much more beautiful things than the Ancients'. On another occasion, when Cellini showed Michelangelo a medal that he had chased for a Sienese customer, in praising it the great man compared it favourably with an antique piece. In fact, apart from medals, coins, cameos and intaglios, practically nothing was known at this time of classical goldsmiths' work.

The European monarchs vied with each other in attracting to their courts the most skilled goldsmiths from Florence, Milan, Antwerp, Nürnberg, Augsburg, Utrecht, and other leading centres. The importance attached to the possession of highly competent court craftsmen can be judged by the trouble to which Francis I went in order to get Benvenuto Cellini released from a papal prison and brought from Rome to Paris. Even more remarkable is the story of the Strassburg-born master, Valentin Drausch, who is described as a *Goldarbeiter und Steinschneider* (goldsmith and hardstone sculptor).[22] This man had been working for Duke Wilhelm V of Bavaria, when in 1582, after the Augsburg *Reichstag* in that year, he was sent with some jewels to the Elector of Saxony, but he disappeared and sought refuge in Bohemia, taking with him a quantity of jewellery belonging to the Bavarian Duke. He was eventually located in Bohemia and thrown into prison at the request of Duke Wilhelm, but, soon after, it was revealed that he had been given a court appointment as jeweller to the Emperor Rudolph II. Drausch offered various excuses for making off with the jewels, claiming that he was owed money by the Duke and that he had been instructed to sell others belonging to the Elector. It was only after three years that Duke Wilhelm managed to get Drausch sent back from Prague to Munich, where he was nevertheless reinstated and continued to receive payments until 1593.

Though the ruling princes of the sixteenth century often took great personal interest in the activities of their goldsmiths, the general task of controlling the court artists was usually entrusted to one of them who enjoyed a higher status. Among these were Jacopo da Strada at the court of Rudolph II, Bernardo Buontalenti at that of the Grand Duke Francesco I of Tuscany and Friedrich Sustris at that of Duke Wilhelm V of Bavaria. The responsibilities of Sustris at the Munich court were precisely defined in a decree of 1587;[23] this laid down that he should make all the plans, designs and distribution of work and order and arrange everything; that all painters, sculptors and handworkers should obey him and everyone should work according to his instructions. By the appointment of a single person with overall control it was possible to achieve a more consistent policy in the production of representational and decorative art. From the goldsmith's point of view the advantages of being appointed to work for one of the courts were numerous. He was exempted from the tiresome regulations of the local guild, he achieved a higher status and, in theory at least, he was in receipt of a regular salary which assured him a reasonable living. In fact, the archives are full of letters from disappointed court artists begging for payment of moneys due to them in order to save them and their families from starvation. In the case of foreigners there was often no alternative to seeking employment at a court, as the guilds would not admit them. The most successful of all these court goldsmiths was the Florentine Giacomo Biliverti (Jacques Bylivelt, see p.152), who was entrusted not only with the negotiations with the Vatican but was sent by Grand Duke Ferdinand of Tuscany in 1597 on an embassy to Queen Elizabeth in England, conveying messages from his master and also presenting her with a casket of precious materials containing medicaments.

The goldsmith often had difficulties in obtaining payment for his work. When an article was sold directly to a customer from stock, it was up to the goldsmith to allow credit or not as his circumstances permitted, but in the case of specially commissioned objects, it was usual, once the piece was finished, to submit it to other members of the guild to obtain an estimate of its value. It is evident that fellow goldsmiths would not wish to harm a member of the guild by undervaluing his work, but should they chance to decide that the charge made was too high, the goldsmith would have little hope of securing payment in full from his customer. Such estimates (*Taxierung*) would not be required in the case of smaller commissions but were commonly called for when the object was of great value. Thus we know that Hans Schwanenburg, *Kammergoldschmied* to Duke Wilhelm V of Bavaria was ordered to estimate the value of materials, jewels and labour of the figure of St George in enamelled gold and hardstone which had been made by members of the Munich court workshop.[24] The task of estimating the value of work carried out by such a personality as Cellini must have been a most unwelcome one, in view of the drastic measures he took to revenge offences against him either real or imagined.

In sixteenth-century Europe the degree of control exercised by the guilds over their members varied greatly from country to country and from town to town. In the main centres of the craft, such as Augsburg, Nürnberg, Paris, London, Antwerp, control was strict but in Italy the opposite seems to have been the case. It is significant that the *Arte* (Guild) is very rarely mentioned by Cellini in his *Vita* in spite of the fact that he was constantly moving from one city to another. Had he lived north of the Alps he would have required the approval of both town and guild authorities before he could have taken up work elsewhere. In Italy, moreover, the goldsmiths worked in both precious and base metals. As a result a number of Italian masters combined goldsmithing with other activities in the field of sculpture and the decorative arts.[25] In northern Europe, on the other hand, goldsmiths were with rare exceptions only allowed to work in precious metal and precious or semi-precious stones. Such obligations were not always strictly observed and in practice the goldsmith seems to have been capable of turning his hand to whatever skilled task he might be called upon to perform.[26]

An important function of the guilds was to determine the tests which must be undergone by every aspirant for admission as master goldsmith. In Nürnberg the applicant for admission had to make a columbine-cup (*Akeley Pokal*), a gold ring set with a precious stone and a steel seal-die. The successful master was, therefore, equipped to be a goldsmith, jeweller or seal-die cutter. When submitting his masterpiece he had to swear that he had received no outside help, though in 1535 this regulation was relaxed to the extent that he no longer had to produce his own design. The columbine-cup was first introduced as the masterpiece in 1531. Eventually in 1572 when new regulations governing the submission of masterpieces in Nürnberg were issued, a pattern cup designed by Wenzel Jamnitzer was acquired by the guild. This was shown to aspirants on three separate occasions when they were producing their masterpiece; its form had to be followed but variations in the ornament were permitted. They were then allowed a period of approximately three months to produce their own version of the design. The example of Nürnberg was followed by the guilds of several other German cities.[27] In Augsburg the guild experienced difficulty in ensuring that the masterpiece was the unaided work of the aspirant. One would expect that their requirement that the master-piece must be made in the workshop of one of the two wardens (*Geschaumeister*) of the guild and locked away at night would have sufficed, but in 1572 a new regulation was made that any journeyman who had received help should submit another piece, while those who had helped him should be imprisoned for four or six days. The masterpiece usually took about eight weeks to make and involved great expense for the journeyman, who not only had to devote his time to it, but also had to find the precious metal.

The masterpiece was also required of applicants for freedom of the London Gold-smiths' Guild, but the regulation was not enforced with much effect during the sixteenth century — if we may judge by the terms of the preamble to the *Order for the Master-piece* made by the Goldsmiths' Company in 1607. This stated that 'very few workmen are able to furnish and perfect a piece of plate singularly...without the help of many and several hands, which inconvenience is grown by reason that many of the idler sort betake themselves to the sole practice and exercise of one slight and easy part . . . some to be only hammermen . . . work nothing but bell saltes, or only bells, or only casting bottles'.

The most responsible function of the goldsmiths' guilds was the maintenance of the requisite standard of purity in the metal used by their members. This duty was carried out by requiring the guild members to submit for assay every article they made before it was finished; if it was found to correspond to the fixed standard of purity it was struck with the town mark and, where appropriate, with the year mark or warden's mark and returned to the goldsmith for finishing. Frequent searches were made through the gold-smiths' workshops to make sure that no vessel was sold without being assayed and hall-marked. This task involved the warden in a great deal of extra work and made the office an undesirable one; some goldsmiths preferred to pay a substantial fine rather than spend so much time away from their workshops. The records of the London Gold-smiths' Company show that the prevention of sale of substandard plate by their own members and by goldsmiths working in the provinces was the most important and time-consuming activity of the Court of Wardens.

The operation of submitting a vessel of precious metal to the guild for assay and hall-marking involved the payment of a fee, which was usually calculated by reference to the weight of the vessel in question. Goldsmiths often tried and sometimes succeeded in avoiding payment of this fee; such pieces bear no assay or town-mark, but only the maker's mark. One circumstance that could lead to the evasion of assay and hall-marking was when the customer ordered a piece of silver directly from the goldsmith and provided him with the metal required to make it. In this case the vessel was never offered for public sale and might not, therefore, be noticed by the Wardens, unless they searched the workshop as well as the objects offered for sale. It was by no means unusual for the customer to hand over 'worn plate' and a considerable number of sixteenth-century pieces bear only a maker's mark. 'Worn' or old-fashioned plate which was handed over in this way for melting and re-working would usually already bear assay marks, so that further assay seemed superfluous and was, therefore, dispensed with. Submission for hall-marking could, however, only be evaded when the customer himself had complete confidence in the honesty of the goldsmith to whom he had given his commission. The obligation to submit articles of precious metal for assay was some-times extended to plate imported from another town or country and even to older unmarked pieces that had been reworked to a more fashionable or more practicable form. Such pieces lead to difficult problems of identification, as they may bear two sets of marks: those of the original maker and those of the importer. Alternatively they may bear only the marks of the importer and of the town in which he worked.

The Wardens of the guild also had the responsibility of ensuring that silver was not worked by masters belonging to other crafts or by foreign immigrants who had not gained admission to the guild, even if they had been admitted as masters of their craft elsewhere. Both tasks involved much work and made the office of Warden as onerous as it was honourable. Such craftsmen as the gunmakers and clockmakers often mounted their more luxurious pieces in precious metal and were tempted to make the mounts themselves instead of handing over the work to a goldsmith. Journeymen sometimes accepted commissions before they had submitted their masterpiece and goldsmiths from other countries or towns sought to establish themselves in the precincts of monasteries where medieval liberties to work free of guild control could be claimed. The guilds were frequently involved in what would now be called demarcation disputes. The pattern-carvers who made the wood models for casting were tempted to extend their activities and to work the precious metal as well. On the other hand the goldsmiths were doubtless tempted to extend in the opposite direction and to carve their own models, so taking work away from another craft. Certain marginal activities also led to problems. Gilding of silver was clearly a matter for the goldsmith, but gilding of base metal raised a problem of competence. Some concessions were made: the gunmakers and sword furnishers were allowed to use gold and silver to decorate their productions with damascening. In the German cities certain crafts were recognised as being independent (*Freikünstler*) and might be practiced freely as long as those who did so did not infringe upon the spheres of the established guilds. The goldsmiths who most frequently found themselves in trouble with the guilds were those employed directly by one of the ruling princes. Some had been taken into employment by the prince on account of their exceptional skill before they had submitted their masterpiece and been admitted to the guild. If this were so, they risked losing their right to have their work assayed, a circumstance that would ruin them should they lose the patronage of the prince. Particularly offensive to the guild was the fact that the vessels they made for the court were exempt from hall-marking. The goldsmiths' guild had to accept this exemption, but they did so most unwillingly. An entry in the minute book of the Court of the London Goldsmiths' Company in 1537 records the making of a silver-gilt crown for the posset-pot of King Henry VIII and mentions the fact that it was not touched (i.e. marked).[28] The guilds were well aware of the potential threat to their livelihood implicit in the existence of these court craftsmen who ignored their rules and regulations and they lost no opportunity of making life difficult for them. When a court craftsman was forced by the death of his patron or the conclusion of the work upon which he had been engaged to seek admission to the guild, the chances were that his application, even when supported by the recommendation from the prince, would be rejected. Even the Holy Roman Emperor himself did not find it easy to impose his will upon the guilds when it came to inducing them to admit as master a journeyman goldsmith who had been working as a court craftsman and had thereby offended against their regulations. Among the histories that can be followed in the archives of the city of Augsburg are those of Hans Schebel[29] and Jörg Sigman, both masters of the highest skill. Their experiences throw a fascinating light upon the problems of the sixteenth-century member of a city guild. One of the prerequisites was that every member must be of legitimate birth. In September 1552 Hans Schebel, of Hall in the Inntal, requested permission of the Augsburg goldsmiths' guild to submit a masterpiece and undertook to produce evidence concerning his legitimacy. In fact he produced a letter of legitimation from Pope Clement and also a decree from the Emperor which freed him of the stigma of illegitimate birth. His application was, however, rejected by the Augsburg guild on the grounds that his admission would bring dishonour to the craft. When Schebel threatened imperial wrath, the guild suggested he should settle somewhere else where illegitimacy was no bar. He then offered a letter of recommendation from Duke Albrecht V of Bavaria, for whom he had made a fine drinking-cup, but this again was rejected and his master, the goldsmith Weinetz, was instructed to discharge him. It was only after the Emperor had issued a further instruction that he was allowed to complete and submit his masterpiece. Even then he was debarred from taking on apprentices and journeymen employed by him could not count the time spent with him, when reckoning their period of service before becoming a master goldsmith. In January 1560 Schebel had to leave Augsburg because he had killed his brother-in-law in a quarrel about a legacy, but in August of the same year he was allowed to return again at the request of the Emperor and the usual penalty for his crime was held in abeyance — murder was more excusable than illegitimacy.

Jörg Sigman was a goldsmith who specialised in embossing armour;[30] such was the importance of the commissions for fine armours made of, or decorated with, panels of embossed and gilded copper in Augsburg that the regulations governing the use of non-precious metal by goldsmiths seem to have been less rigorously applied there. Even so, Sigman, who was not a citizen of Augsburg by birth, had his share of difficulties with the goldsmiths' guild. He had been brought to work there by the leading Augsburg armourer, Desiderius Colman, on the embossed and damascened armour made by the latter for Prince Philip of Spain. Sigman actually obtained citizenship of Augsburg through his marriage in 1550 with the daughter of an Augsburg merchant (*Krämer*). At this time he was working as a journeyman goldsmith (*Geselle*) for Desiderius Colman. According to the regulations of the Augsburg goldsmiths' guild a journeyman must have served for at least four years with not less than three master goldsmiths of the city before he could himself be admitted master. As Sigman had been employed by an armourer, the period he had spent on embossing and damascening the suit of Prince Philip, which was in excess of two years, would not count towards the four years of service as a goldsmith in Augsburg and he took the remarkable step of appealing directly to the Prince, who happened at the time to be attending a *Reichstag* in the city. In his petition he asked the Prince to use his influence to persuade the guild to offset the two years he had already spent and any additional time he might yet have to spend on the armour against the four year period of service as a goldsmith. Prince Philip acceded to the request and, although a first application to the City Council was rejected, persisted until the Council felt unable to resist further the wishes of so important a personality.

Goldsmiths whose application to submit a masterpiece was refused by the guild might either continue as journeymen in the employ of other goldsmiths, or they might try to induce another goldsmith who had been admitted master to submit their work as his own and so get it assayed and marked. This was a clear infringement of the guild regulations and such pieces are no longer identifiable, since they bear the mark of a goldsmith who did not in fact make them.

Among the goldsmiths who were employed by the Wittelsbach court at Munich in defiance of the Augsburg guild regulations were Georg Bernhard and the Hungarian, Georg Zeggin. Bernhard had worked for Duke Albrecht V of Bavaria before submitting his masterpiece and it was only as the result of a special appeal to the guild from the Duke himself that he received permission to work and have his productions assayed in 1572.[31] Subsequently he married the daughter of a member of the Merchants' Guild which saved him from persecution by the Goldsmiths, though strictly he was only allowed to sell but not make jewellery. He continued to deal in goldsmiths' work and jewellery, but in 1584 received a large and important order from Duke Wilhelm, the execution of which he evidently wished to direct. He made an arrangement, therefore, with Georg Sigman for the latter to take on the work, though it seems, in fact, to have been given to Sigman's journeyman, Matthias Wallbaum, who later became famous as the maker of elaborate caskets (see p.229). Sigman had already been in trouble with the Augsburg goldsmiths' guild and was probably under suspicion. At all events, Bernhard was accused of secretly employing a goldsmith-journeyman in contravention of the regulations and eventually all three concerned were fined. The most seriously affected was Matthias Wallbaum, as, when he applied for permission to submit his masterpiece and to marry the daughter of an Augsburg goldsmith, his application was rejected on the grounds that the years he had worked as a journeyman with Sigman could not be reckoned as part of his service and he had to serve two years longer. It appears from the records of the Augsburg guild that Jörg Sigman and another goldsmith named Christoph

Behaim had both passed on their commissions to Wallbaum, who had executed them and received payment for them. He had satisfied the two goldsmiths by making them a monthly payment.

Once admitted to the guild the master-goldsmith enjoyed the advantages of a kind of friendly society, but he had to accept considerable restrictions upon his freedom of action. The permission of the City Council was required before a goldsmith might leave his place of residence to work elsewhere, even for a limited time. The records of the City Council of Nürnberg contain many references to applications for permission to go to work for a patron in another town. Sometimes the patron made the application to the Council; in 1587 the Nürnberg goldsmith, Mattheus Karl, was invited to Dresden for one year by the Elector Christian I, because, as the request stated, 'he was very famous as a skilled goldsmith and portraitist'.[32] In 1602 he was invited again by Christian, Prince of Anhalt-Bernburg, to go to work for three years in Amberg. Even so distinguished and influential a master as Wenzel Jamnitzer had to obtain permission to go to Prague to work for the Holy Roman Emperor. It was not only German goldsmiths who had such difficulties; the Spanish goldsmith, Pery Juan Pockh, who was absent from his home town of Barcelona for thirty-seven years, from 1551 until 1587, in the service of the Habsburg court, found himself in an awkward position when he eventually returned. According to the Barcelona guild regulations a goldsmith who went abroad must return at the end of a year and a day to seek permission to stay for a further period and must also pay a fine. He offered to pay the amount due for the whole thirty-seven years but, as this was a larger sum than he could find, had to ask the guild to allow him credit for a time.[33]

The guild also restricted the number of journeymen and apprentices that a single master goldsmith might employ. This meant that no individual, no matter how gifted an artist he might be, could dominate the craft in his city. Nor could he, by accepting a larger number of commissions, become very much richer than his rivals in the city. A successful goldsmith had, as a rule, no choice other than to pass on orders that he could not fulfil with his existing staff to another goldsmith. A guild might sometimes authorise a master to take on an additional journeyman or apprentice in order to complete an important commission, but this was rarely done and then only for a limited time. Wenzel Jamnitzer himself had to refuse important orders because he lacked the staff to execute them. In 1552 three of the leading Nürnberg goldsmiths, Wenzel Jamnitzer, Bonaventura Hegner and Jakob Hoffman, were criticised because they had passed on orders for dishes by the half-dozen to journeymen instead of giving them to their brother master goldsmiths, as the guild requested them to do.[34] An order of 1572 laid down that in future no Nürnberg goldsmith might employ more than four journeymen and two apprentices in his workshop. He was, however, allowed to engage another journeyman for modelling and making patterns, provided that the latter did not sit in the same shop as the others but was accommodated in a separate room. The number of journeymen that a German goldsmith might employ at any one time varied from city to city and from time to time. In Augsburg he might not have more than three journeymen nor more than two apprentices. In Lübeck only two journeymen were allowed; in Strassburg on the other hand, there was no limitation on their number. Other regulations fixed the number of years a journeyman must have worked in the craft before he was allowed to submit his masterpiece. Here again regulations varied from town to town, becoming more strict as time passed; the reason for this was that the number of trained journeymen increased more quickly than the volume of work available. Rather than allow the master goldsmiths to suffer through the over-crowding of the craft, the period of service required from a journeyman was lengthened. In the mid-sixteenth century a journeyman who had been born in Augsburg had to have served four years before he was eligible to submit his masterpiece. If he were not a native of Augsburg the period of service was lengthened in 1555 to six years, which must have been spent with three different masters. In 1593 the total period in the craft as apprentice and journeyman was increased by the Augsburg guild to twelve years, at the same time the period of service of a journeyman not born in the city was extended to eight years. Such long periods of service were not exceptional and in Strassburg a total period of ten years was eventually imposed.

The journeyman spent some years, usually not less than three, on his travels known as 'wander years'. Here again a problem arose as the goldsmiths' guilds were not always willing to allow these years of travel to count against the period of service as a journeyman, particularly in the case of those born in other cities, as it was not easy to check the length of their period of travel. Journeymen on their travels sometimes covered great distances: a petition addressed to the Lübeck City Council by Michael Vester of Husum states that he had devoted himself to the craft since childhood, that he had been apprenticed in Nürnberg, where, when he had finished his time, his master had wished him to stay on. Subsequently he went to Rome where he had set up his own independent shop; after this he had been to Naples, Genoa and Florence. He stated that he had practised his craft throughout nearly the whole of Germany.[35] Vester was doubtless exceptionally well-travelled but the possibility of working in widely distant parts of Europe must have contributed to the development of the international style that was so characteristic of sixteenth-century goldsmiths' work. The guilds were always very aware of the risk of competition by foreigners, a term which in the sixteenth century meant not only those born abroad but even those born in another city. Suspicion of foreigners was particularly marked in England, where the goldsmiths had to face competition from Hugenot refugees from France and Flemish Protestants from the southern Netherlands. The London Goldsmiths' Company took a firm line and in 1575 and again in 1605 forbad its members to accept as apprentices those who were not children of English-born parents.

Among the many restrictions placed upon the journeyman one of the harshest was the prohibition against marrying before he had submitted his masterpiece and been made free of his craft. If he disobeyed this rule he was subject to penalties that might even force him to abandon his craft and would certainly delay his admission as master. On the death of a goldsmith his widow was allowed to carry on his business and to continue to use his name and mark so long as she was assisted by a qualified journeyman. As a result of this particular regulation the leading journeyman in the workshop often married his late master's widow and took over his business. If he did so, the fees he had to pay the guild on admission as master were substantially reduced, and, of even greater importance, he was able to start his career with an established business. This regulation had the peculiar social consequence that a goldsmith, as of course other craftsmen, was likely to be married twice: first as a youngish man to the widow of his former master and then again in later life, when he in turn became a widower, to a younger woman. Thus the pattern was established of a young man taking an older woman as his first wife and then, later in life, of an older man taking a young girl as his second wife.

The journeyman was subject to the temptation of accepting work from members of other guilds in order to supplement his income. This was frowned on by the guild, though it evidently happened frequently. He was, however, allowed to engrave and publish a pattern book of designs. Matthias Zündt, the gifted journeyman of Wenzel Jamnitzer, produced one (see p.207) and a book of designs by Bernard Zan of Nürnberg, published in 1580 (pl.181) is entitled *12 Stick zum verzaichnen stechen verfertigt Bernhard Zan Goldschmid Gesel inn Niernberg* (Twelve pieces to draw or engrave by Bernhard Zan, journeyman goldsmith in Nürnberg).

The goldsmith had to seek permission from the guild concerning what would now appear to be quite trivial matters. This is illustrated by the petition addressed by Abraham Lotter the Elder in 1572 to the City Council of Augsburg.[36] This master had since 1562 been the recipient of important commissions from the Bavarian court and in 1572 he requested permission to maintain a workshop with barred windows. This would seem to be an indispensable precaution for a goldsmith, but Lotter had to explain in his petition that he had hitherto been mostly employed on commissions for the court and also for the Emperor himself; these were for jewels, necklaces and similar articles. He pointed out that such work had to be kept highly secret and continued with the observation that he had been responsible for a number of *Inventiones* of a type that had never before been made in Augsburg and had thus improved his standard of living.

One way of evading the control of the guild was to set up as a dealer or *Krämer*. These dealers had their own guild but their regulations were less strict as they were free to trade in all kinds of wares. Among the Augsburg *Krämer* during the reign of Rudolph II was the clockmaker, Georg Roll.[37] Strictly speaking, a *Krämer* was not allowed to manufacture anything himself, but might only purchase from accredited members of the guilds. A highly skilled clockmaker, Roll not only employed other clockmakers but worked on the production of complex celestial globes for the Emperor himself; he was enabled to ignore guild regulations by pleading the Emperor's orders. In a letter he wrote to Rudolph II, Roll tells us something of the range of activity of a *Krämer* for he states that, at the *Reichstag* held in Augsburg in 1582, he offered for sale not only clocks but also silver vessels. He had also held a lottery on the same occasion in which he had included silver. In 1585 he travelled to Prague in connection with the sale of two celestial globes to the Emperor Rudolph and his brother, the Archduke Ernst, and once again took a selection of silver with him for sale. Such journeys might involve considerable risks; in 1608 three Augsburg goldsmiths, Andreas Nathan, Bernhard Manlich and Georg Beuerle, set out to travel to Moscow with a quantity of silver ware on the occasion of the marriage of the Tsar Dmitri Ivanovitch. When they eventually arrived they were arrested and flung into prison and had to be content to be allowed to return home after lengthy imprisonment and the confiscation of all their property.[38]

As a rule the master goldsmith kept a retail shop from which he sold his wares but this was not invariably so. Some masters, such as the eminent Nürnberg goldsmith, Elias Lencker, did not sell their own productions at all but passed them on to another member of their guild or to a dealer for sale. Important orders came from these dealers, some of whom were sufficiently wealthy to commission services of plate which they would offer for sale at the annual fairs held in various towns, the most important being those at Frankfurt am Main and Leipzig. An example of this is the purchase by the Archbishop of Salzburg of a set of twelve tazzas that were taken by the Augsburg goldsmith and *Krämer*, Bartolomäus Vesenmayer, to the Regensburg *Reichstag* in 1594 (see p.233). Whenever a marriage or other festivity in one of the ruling families was announced, the *Krämer* would set off with a selection of their wares in the hope of obtaining orders. One such occasion cost the younger Wenzel Jamnitzer his life in a foreign country (see p.215).

Since most goldsmiths kept open shops from which they offered their wares for sale, they resented the competition of the *Krämer* and made frequent efforts to restrict their activities, though in fact they owed much to them as, through their contacts with the European courts, they gave the goldsmiths commissions which might otherwise have been lost. In Augsburg the dealers were not supposed to sell new silver but to confine themselves to second-hand pieces, while in Nürnberg they were not allowed to sell silver made outside the city. In fact the goldsmiths' guilds had little success in controlling the *Krämer* who ignored such regulations, usually with impunity.

Closely associated with the goldsmiths, and performing an essential function for them were the pattern-carvers (see p.60). In spite of their importance to the goldsmiths' craft, every effort was made by the guilds to prevent them from becoming goldsmiths themselves. Christoph Weiditz, who was, perhaps, the carver of the figure stem of the Merckelsche *Tafelaufsatz* (pl.416), was refused permission to submit his masterpiece in 1530 on the grounds that he had not fulfilled all the necessary conditions. Although he obtained a recommendation from the Emperor, it was not until 1538 that he was formally allowed to follow his art and to engage journeymen. Even so, he was not admitted to the guild, but only tolerated, and the journeymen who had been employed by him had difficulty in getting their time recognised as counting towards the period of preparation for mastership. Some journeymen who had offended against the guild regulations were forbidden to produce completed work, but were allowed to produce models. An example is that of the Augsburg journeyman, Christoph Brunnenmayr, who had married before presenting his masterpiece. On April 29, 1593 he was informed that he was permitted 'to model and to cast for goldsmiths, in glue and other materials as they may wish and to make in wax or lead anything that they cannot furnish with patterns. Further to make all kinds of portraits and similar articles in wax and wax colours. Then also to engrave and to etch silver and to instruct apprentices and other journeymen in those arts for an appropriate fee. Also to gild and to prepare work for goldsmiths'.[39] At the same time he was absolutely forbidden to make anything himself for goldsmiths or to employ other journeymen either openly or secretly on any work. Finally, Brunnenmayr had to take an oath to the Bürgermeister and make no further claims.

Once established as a master and member of the city guild, the goldsmith still had to cope with the commercial problems of his craft. The most important commissions came from princes whose individual tastes had to be satisfied. If the customer were to die before taking delivery of his order, the goldsmith was left with a costly article that might be very difficult to sell elsewhere. Study of the illustrations to this book will demonstrate the impractical nature of much of the silver made for the great patrons. The contemporary attitude can be explained by the following quotations: Cellini relates how while he was working in Rome he was commissioned by the Bishop of Salamanca to make 'one of those great water-vessels called *acquareccie,* which are used as ornaments to place on sideboards'.[40] In another passage he gives the height of one such vase as nearly three feet (87 cm.). In 1550 the Milanese medallist and rock-crystal carver, Jacopo da Trezzo, wrote from Spain to Duke Cosimo de' Medici to enquire whether the vessel he had commissioned was 'a cup to drink from or only to look well' (*un vaso per bever o per sol bel vedere*).[41]

Pieces of such elaboration as those chosen to illustrate this book cannot have constituted more than a small proportion of the output of a typical sixteenth-century goldsmith and many of them would have been beyond his competence. The average master would have been mainly occupied with the production of useful plate, dishes, plates and beakers, of which he would have held a stock. The more important pieces would have been specially commissioned by the customer, who would have paid for the precious metal in advance or would have supplied it in the form of worn plate. Not even the wealthiest goldsmith would have been able to stock the hardstone vessels mounted in enamelled and jewelled gold that were the highest expression of his art. These were mostly produced by goldsmiths working for one of the princely courts outside the control of the guilds, but they also found their way into the possession of rich merchant families. The rock-crystal tazza bearing the arms of two merchant families families, Krafter of Augsburg and Ott of Ulm (pl. 338), was presumably given as a wedding present on the occasion of the union of members of these two families.[42]

The inventory of the contents of Benvenuto Cellini's workshop, prepared in 1538 when he was taken to prison in the Castel Sant' Angelo, shows how little was kept in stock even by so prominent a master.[43] Apart from unmounted stones, a large number of rings, gold scudi and gold medals, the only finished articles of precious metal in his possession were an enamelled gold *Agnus Dei,* a dagger with gold mounted lapis handle, three gold chains and the following articles of silver: a basin with a figure within it,[44] two cups composed of eight members, four candlesticks of six pieces each, a tazza and a number of fragments of silver weighing together eleven and a half pounds. The inventory made after his death in 1570 is much longer and shows that he owned a villa outside Florence as well as his town house. He had, however, very little in the way of precious metal, presumably because he was in later life mainly active as a sculptor.

Further light on the problems of the goldsmith in holding stock is thrown by a letter written in 1610 by Phillip Hainhofer to Duke Philipp of Pommern about a commission the latter had authorised. Hainhofer states that he has advanced 60 thaler for the silver required as few of these people (the Augsburg goldsmiths) have much stock or cash, with the exception of Lencker who is a man of substance: most of them consume all their money by drinking.[45] The ruling princes who were the customers were themselves often short of ready money and for this reason entrusted their orders for jewels and vessels of precious metal to bankers such as the Fuggers, who were better able to allow them credit than the goldsmith himself. Nevertheless the state archives of the former European kingdoms contain many appeals from artists endeavouring to obtain payment for articles delivered years and sometimes decades earlier.

The designer has never played a more important part in the goldsmiths' art than in the sixteenth century. When, as in the early eighteenth century, fashion favoured pure form without added embellishment, the goldsmith could work on his own without the need to call in the help of a designer, In the sixteenth century not only was originality of form expected but a vessel was judged by the variety, the fantasy and the extravagance of its ornament. In order to satisfy his clients the goldsmith often had to seek assistance outside his own workshop. It is not, therefore, surprising that a larger volume of drawings of goldsmiths' work survives from the sixteenth century than from any other period of comparable duration. Assistance was also likely to be needed in order to plan the character and arrangement of the scenes from mythology, biblical or Roman history that adorned the more important pieces. The many scenes on the Lercaro ewer and basin (pls. 342, 345) or on the set of twelve tazzas made for Cardinal Aldobrandini (pls. 363, 364, 365) were not copied from engravings or illustrations in books extant at the time, but were specially designed in consultation with humanists who had the requisite knowledge of classical antiquity. In the same way the masters who carved figure subjects on rock-crystal vessels obtained their designs from graphic artists. Giovanni Bernardi was, for instance, supplied with drawings by Perino del Vaga, one of the leading Roman Mannerists (see p.135). Artists of the calibre of Benvenuto Cellini were capable of working out their own schemes; his account of the ideas that lie behind the gold salt he made for King François I (see p.148) shows how much thought went into the design and production of an important piece of plate. Seldom, if ever, have the artistic ideals of a period been so clearly reflected in the decorative arts as in the second half of the sixteenth century. The preoccupation of artists with the literary content of their productions brought them into close contact with humanists and philosophers; in modelling their vessels they were giving expression to ideas as well as creating forms.

An exchange of correspondence between Wenzel Jamnitzer and his patron, Archduke Ferdinand of Tirol,[46] in the late 1550's and early 1560's gives an interesting picture of the lengthy procedure that attended the manufacture of an important piece of plate, in this case a table-fountain, and also of the leisurely course of the exchange of ideas between artist and client. The fountain was first mentioned in August 1556 when Jamnitzer wrote to the Archduke explaining that, owing to the importance of the work he was already committed to do for the Emperor Maximilian in Vienna (presumably on a table-fountain commissioned by the latter), he was unable at the moment to proceed with the Archduke's order. He suggested that as a preliminary step he should instruct an artist to produce a series of designs for the fountain.[47] For this purpose he recommended his assistant, Jacopo da Strada, whom he described as a diligent workman, an Italian by birth and a fellow citizen of Nürnberg who was skilled in painting and in other crafts.[48] In view of the difficulties involved in the production of the fountain, which was to represent 'Adam and Eve in Paradise', Jamnitzer suggested that da Strada should visit the Archduke in person, show him his scale model and discuss the project in detail. Da Strada then wrote himself to the Archduke, explaining that it was impossible to represent so complex an object by drawings alone and suggesting that he should make a model as did architects when preparing to build a palace. He suggested certain other features that should be incorporated in the design: silver fishes in the water and semi-precious hardstones such as agate, carnelian and sardonyx. Finally he offered to go to Prague, or wherever the Archduke might happen to be, to discuss the fountain, but only on condition that he should be entrusted with the whole work, presumably to the exclusion of Wenzel Jamnitzer. In January 1557 da Strada set off for Prague, taking with him a number of the figures of small animals and insects cast directly from nature that were a speciality of the Jamnitzer workshop. These were to be included with a quantity of castings of animals and birds as well as certain *Stufen* (specimens of silver ore) that were already in the Archduke's possession.

Eventually da Strada gave up his part in the table-fountain, perhaps because his insistence on exclusive control was not conceded. Nevertheless the piece made some progress and in the summer of 1558 the Archduke asked Jamnitzer to go to Prague for a consultation. In March of the following year Jamnitzer wrote about the current difficulties in the production of miniature figures of animals for the 'Garden of Eden'. He was unable to find carvers who could make them on a sufficiently small scale and thought it would be better to model them and then cast them in silver. He countered the Archduke's suggestion that he should send two carvers to Prague to work under his supervision by saying that he could not persuade them to leave their homes and families. In April 1559 Jamnitzer was at last able to announce that he had discovered a carver and goldsmith who would go to Prague, though the man could not be spared long enough from his workshop to finish all the work. This goldsmith was Matthias Zündt, whose engraved designs for goldsmiths' work are discussed on p.207. According to Jamnitzer, Zündt could model the animals in wax, cast and chase them and also colour them. This reference to colouring does not in this case mean true enamelling, but more probably the application of the type of lacquer known as *Kaltemail,* which was much used for insects and leaves cast from nature. Eventually Jamnitzer completed the model of the base of the fountain, which he sent to the Archduke with the suggestion that it should be veneered with ivory, boxwood, ebony and sandalwood and enriched with silver reliefs or figures. Finally, in May 1559, Matthias Zündt was sent off to Prague and at the same time Jamnitzer wrote to point out that Zündt would be able to produce all the minute animals that were required. The reference to Zündt's skill in producing such minute animals and insects is of interest as in his 1551 book of engraved designs he does incorporate some figures of insects meant to be cast from nature. In spite of Zündt's visit the fountain was still under discussion in January 1561; there was not enough silver available and the base was unsatisfactory. The last mention of it dates from April 1561, and it must be assumed that the production was finally abandoned, perhaps because of lack of precious metal. Ferdinand of Tirol retained his interest in minute animals cast from nature in silver and in 1565 ordered two dozen small animals and also a supply of grasses.

In his dealings with Wenzel Jamnitzer and the Archduke, da Strada showed an unusual independence of spirit, but he was a goldsmith of exceptional talents which he exploited to the full. His career was so varied that it is worth recounting in some detail. He was born in Mantua and was presumably trained as a goldsmith there. His name is probably an Italianised version of the Flemish Van der Straet, but he regarded himself as Italian and usually wrote in that language. After completing his training in Italy he succeeded in the early 1540's in entering the service of the Fugger banking family, and spent two years purchasing classical coins and marbles for them in Italy. In 1546 he applied for permission to reside in Nürnberg; in his application he described himself as a painter (*Maler*). Such was his reputation that his request was granted within twenty-four hours.[49] Shortly after receiving his residence permit he asked that he might, although still a journeyman, be allowed to execute in his own home certain goldsmith's work that had been commissioned from him by Giovanni, Marchese di Marignano, an Italian nobleman who, after fighting in the service of the Duke of Milan, had entered that of the Emperor Charles V. This request, together with permission to engage a Nürnberg master goldsmith or a journeyman to assist him, was granted for a period of one year only.[50] Such exceptional concessions can only have been granted through the influence of Wenzel Jamnitzer with whom he had presumably entered into some form of association. The classical learning he had acquired in Italy was doubtless of great importance when such articles as the Archduke's fountain had to be designed. Da Strada had another advantage in that he was an expert on the design of water-pumps and was, therefore, fully competent to deal with the technical problems of making a complicated table-fountain, which, like that of the Emperor Maximilian II, would surely have incorporated various kinds of waterworks. Although the fountain was never completed, da Strada received from the Emperor the considerable reward of 100 thaler as well as 54 gulden for an *Ehrenkleid* (suit of clothes).[51]

In 1549 da Strada was granted citizenship of Nürnberg and thus obtained the right to settle permanently in what was then the centre of the goldsmiths' craft in German-speaking Europe. He must, nevertheless, from an early date have recognised that the knowledge of classical antiquities he had acquired in Italy, together with his familiarity with the Italian language and the country, offered him a more brilliant future than the safer but bourgeois life of a successful Nürnberg goldsmith. Within three years of the grant of citizenship he was, in July 1552, already applying for and being granted permission to leave the city for three years in order to prepare the publication of a treatise on his own collection of classical coins in Lyons, a work that was published in 1553.[52]

Jacopo da Strada had the good fortune to be one of the few individuals in northern Europe who were experts on classical antiquities just at the moment when a number of rich and powerful princes were seeking to acquire them. It was presumably his appreciation of this advantage that enabled him to treat the leading Nürnberg goldsmith, Wenzel Jamnitzer, in so cavalier a manner. In 1556 he set off again on a buying mission for the Fuggers and in 1558 he was granted permission to live in Vienna for three years. How he was occupied there is not recorded, but there can be little doubt that it was his knowledge of antiquities and the possibilities of acquiring them, rather than his skill as a goldsmith, that made him welcome at the Habsburg court. His ability to recognise the false from the true must have been particularly valuable at a time when so many Italian artists were engaged in the production of fake antiques.

In 1559 or 1560 da Strada was a member of the commission appointed to advise on the redesigning of the uncompleted tomb of the Emperor Maximilian I and, with effect from 1 April, 1564, he was granted an annual salary of 100 gulden as a court servant.[53] In the following year he was lent by the Emperor to Duke Albrecht V as architectural adviser in order to design a special building to house the ducal collection of antiquities and also to purchase more objects to fill it. In 1567 he again set off for Italy where he made vast purchases on the Duke's behalf.

Da Strada's qualifications as an art expert did not go unquestioned. On 7 September, 1569, Cardinal Otto von Augsburg wrote to the Duke of Bavaria on the subject of the purchase of antiquities from Rome and Venice as follows[54] 'It is said that the Duke has sent a certain Jacob Strada to Venice, and that he has purchased antiquities for 7000 Kroner which are of no special merit and far too expensive. Da Strada had previously bought similar articles for the Fuggers and was not well thought of. It is further said that the Duke proposed to send this same da Strada to Rome, many await this and have increased the price of antiquities accordingly. If the Duke wished to have something complete, then he should inform (the Cardinal) and take honourable people into his service like Mgr. Gorimberti, etc. and he would hope to get something rare at a low price.'

In 1567, in spite of his activities on behalf of the Duke of Bavaria, da Strada was appointed Imperial Court Antiquary (*Hofantiquar*), a position he had already held unofficially since 1564, and which carried an incomparably higher status than that of a Nürnberg goldsmith. He remained in Vienna until his retirement in 1579.

A man of immense diligence, his activities included the publication of a lexicon of eleven different languages, upon which he had worked for seventeen years. He also produced a series of seven volumes of transcripts of antique inscriptions and was held in such high esteem at the imperial court that the Emperor Maximilian II wrote in 1579 to the Duke of Bavaria asking his support in financing their publication. The most striking evidence, however, of da Strada's status at court is provided by the portrait that Titian painted of him in 1568 (pl. 4). This shows him wearing a fur-trimmed robe with a golden chain of four loops and a pendant gold medal round his neck and holding in his hand an antique marble statue. A cartouche, which is, however, believed to have been added by his son, describes him as *Civis Romanus Caes. Antiquarius et Com. Belic.* (Imperial Antiquary and Military Counsellor).

1 For New Year's and other gifts of silver to Queen Elizabeth I, see Collins, p.542-599.

2 Collins, p.136.

3 M. Leithe Jasper, 'Der Bergkristallpokal Herzog Philipps des Guten von Burgund' *Jahrbuch*, Band 66, 1970, p.227.

4 Collins, p.137.

5 Berti, p.39.

6 Plon, p.392.

7 P. Ganz, Oeffentliche Sammlungen, Basel, *Berichte LIX*, 1907, p.1-68.

8 Hampe, no. 2742.

9 The 1565 inventory is printed in full by J. Stockbauer, p.87ff.

10 See Brunner, p.19.

11 Georg Lill, *Hans Fugger und die Kunst*, Leipzig, 1908, p.155.

12 For the gift to Charles V see A. Kircher, *Deutsche Kaiser in Nürnberg*, Veröffentlichungen d. Ges. f.Familienforschung in Franken, 7. Nürnberg, 1955, p.63, for that to Matthias, see Kris III, p.22n. At the Regensburg Reichstag in 1532, Charles V had received a more modest gift from the city: a pretty cup and cover embossed with portraits of the Electors (*eine hübsche scheuern mit einer deck und ausgetriben Churfürsten pildungen*). See Pechstein, 'Merckelsche Tafelaufsatz', *Nürnberger Mitteilungen*, Band 61, 1974, p.91-2.

13 Kris III, p.22.

14 For further information see the catalogue of the exhibition *Spätgotik am Oberrhein*, Badisches Landesmuseum, Karlsruhe, 1970, p.224.

15 That Cellini was not boasting in this case is proved by a letter written by Cosimo I to Cellini in 1549 about some small vases, quoted Supino, p.48 '*Con la vostra lettera habbiamo ricevuto li schizzi de' vasetti che ci havete mandati, et vi avisseremo quali souo quelli che piu ci piacono et se vorremo che se metta alcuno in opera.*'

16 Berti, p.229 '*ogni sera il Principe a voluto che io sia in camera per disegni di vasi fino a 3 ore, tanto che pure io son vivo*'.

17 *Vita*, I, caps. 47-8.

18 *Vita*, I, cap. 70.

19 ibid. cap 74, '*Sappiate che gli uomini come Benvenuto, unici nella loro professione, non hanno da essere ubbrigati alla legge; or maggiormente lui, che so quanto ragione e gli ha*'.

20 Fabriczy, 'Documenti inediti su Benvenuto Cellini' *Arch. Storico dell' Arte,*Anno VII, Fasc. V, 1894, p.372ff.

21 *Tratto dell' Oreficeria*, cap XII, *A questi il re disse "Ringraziato sia Iddio che alli di nostri e nato anche degli uomini, i quali le opere loro piacciono molto più chè quelle degli antichi"*.

22 For a full account of this incident, see Stockbauer, p.135ff.

23 H. Brunner, *Die St. Georgs-Statuette in München*, Stuttgart, 1968, p.19; the terms of the decree stated that Sustris '*Intentionen, disegna and austailung machen unnd alle ding bevelchen und angeben . . . Ime alle Maler, Scolptori unnd Handwercksleut gehorsamb sein . . . Jeder sein Arbeit nach seinem bevelch, angeben und haissen*'.

24 ibid. p.18.

25 See Vasari's account of the great variety of work undertaken by Francesco di Girolamo dal Prato, *Le Vite* VII, p.43.

26 In Augsburg, for instance, goldsmiths were permitted to clean up and finish bronzes. The bronzes cast from models by Hubert Gerhard which had been commissioned for a large fountain in the Fugger family Schloss Kirchheim were finished by six Augsburg goldsmiths, including such well-known masters as Hans Hübner, Adam Rebhuhn and David Altenstetter, H. Weihrauch, *Bildwerke in Bronze*, Bayerisches Nationalmuseum, München, 1956, cat. no. 171.

27 The Augsburg regulations were similar: namely, a gold ring, a seal and a drinking-cup made to a fixed design. See Weiss, p.49.

28 Prideaux, Vol. I, p.49.

29 Weiss, p.121.

30 A. Buff, 'Urkundliche Nachrichten über den Augsburger Goldschmied, Jörg Sigman', *Zeitschrift des hist. Vereins für Schwaben und Neuburg*, 1892, p.149ff.

31 Krempel, p.140.

32 Hampe, no. 918 (4.8.1587).

33 Davilier, p.208. Pockh's letter to the Barcelona *Gremio* is dated 19.X.1587.

34 Hampe, no. 3395, '*Scheurn halbtutzetweise zu machen geben*'.

35 Hach, p.19-20.

36 See Krempel, p.138.

37 M. Bobinger, *Kunstuhrmacher in Alt Augsburg*, Augsburg, 1969, p.36-7.

38 H. Neubauer, 'Ein Augsburger Bericht über die Moskauer Wirren.' *Studien zur Geschichte OstEuropas, III Teil.* Wiener Archiv für Geschichte des Slaventums und OstEuropa, Graz, 1966, p.136.

39   'für die Goldschmiede zu formen und zu giessen, in Laym und Zeug wie es begeren und wa sie mit Patronen nit versechen, Inen dasselbe von Wax oder Pley zuzurichten. Item in Wax and Waxfarben allerlei Contrafeit und dergleichen sachen zu machen. Dann auch zu reissen und radieren und dessen die Goldschmieds-Jungen oder Gesellen um gebührliche Belohnung zu unterweisen. Degleichen den Goldschmieden zu guelden und aufzubreitten'.

40   Vita, I. 22, 'un vaso grande da acqua, chiamato un' acquereccia, ch'e per l'uso delle credenze che in su(n) esse si tengono per l'ornamento'.

41   Supino, p.54.

42   See Sotheby's catalogue, Thirty Renaissance Jewels from the Lopez-Willshaw Collection, 13.X.70, lot 14.

43   Plon, p.380.

44   This basin was being made for Cellini's chief patron and protector, Cardinal Hippolito d'Este.

45   Doering, p.66; for Hainhofer's protracted negotiations with Lencker, see Doering, passim.

46   D. Schönherr, 'Wenzel Jamnitzer's Arbeiten für Erzherzog Ferdinand,, Mitteilungen des Instituts für Oest. Geschichtsforschungen, Vienna, Vol. IX, 1888, p.289ff.

47   The exact wording is 'Mittlerweil einen kunstlichen maler ein Visierung oder etliche über mehrbmeltes Werk reissen und stellen lassen'.

48   'er habe als bald mit einen fleissigen des Malens und anderer dergleichen Künsten wohlverständigen Gesellen mit Namen Jacob Strote einen italiener und auch Nürnberger Bürger gehandelt, dass er sich zu solchen Vorhaben gebrauchen lassen wollen'.

49   Hampe, nos. 2994-5 (1-2.xi.1546).

50   Hampe, no. 3012 (12.3.1547).

51   Jahrbuch VII, Regest. no. 4943 (8.2.1557).

52   Hampe, no. 3390 (26.7.1552).

53   Jahrbuch VII, Regest,. no. 5046.

54   Stockbauer, p.13.

55   Jahrbuch VII, Regest. no. 5091.

Plate III
Classical Roman sardonyx vase from the collection of Lorenzo the Magnificent with parcel-gilt mounts
probably by one of the court goldsmiths. Mid 16th century.

Plate IV
Florentine lapis lazuli vase designed by Bernardo Buontalenti and supplied with enamelled gold mounts
by Giacomo Biliverti. Dated 1583.

CHAPTER THREE

The Craft of the Goldsmith

WHEN considering the working methods of the sixteenth-century goldsmith it is necessary to set aside romantic conceptions of the nobility of handwork. The goldsmith had an eminently practical approach to his craft and took as much interest in methods of increasing efficiency and reducing costs of production as any modern factory manager. The introduction of labour-saving devices does not accord with the idealised picture of the master-craftsman which has been inherited from nineteenth-century writers, but, in fact, processes such as casting stems, borders and finials in series, turning columns on a lathe and producing friezes or cornice ornaments by means of a stamp were all in use by the second half of the century. Among Wenzel Jamnitzer's innovations was a process for reproducing ornament by mechanical means, a form of repeating stamp. The use of a stamp to produce strips of continuous ornament was not new, but Jamnitzer seems to have used a revolving stamp, thus avoiding ugly breaks where the strips were joined.[1] His revolving stamp was used to produce the friezes and figured borders that appear on so many of his works and on others made under his influence (pls. 428, 429). The idea of turning silver columns on a lathe is believed to have been devised by the Cordoba goldsmith, Juan Ruiz, who thus solved the problem of producing economically the large number of columns and colonettes required in the construction of Spanish ecclesiastical plate and, in particular, the custodias. A letter written in 1574 by a certain Baron von Sprinzenstein to Grand Duke Francesco de' Medici concerning a project for a Mint suggested even more advanced industrial processes, for he states that the building could be used not only for stamping coins but for a thousand other most beautiful objects, such as friezes and plaques for writing desks, medals of every kind and silver flasks with the finest relief ornament.[2] There is, however, no evidence to show that whole vessels were manufactured by stamping at so early a date.

In the sixteenth century two main methods were employed in the production of silver vessels: raising and casting. The former involved the highly skilled process of the gradual hammering up of a flat plate of silver with various tools until the intended form of the vessel was achieved. The ornament was then embossed in the body of the vessel, though it might also be cast and applied. If the object was cast, a model or models were necessary from which the casts were made (see p.59). The parts of the completed vessel, that is handle, foot and spout, were attached either by screws or by being soldered. The ornament of cast vessels might either be cast in one with the body or attached separately. When the parts of a vessel had to be attached, solder with a lower melting point than the vessel itself had to be used. The excessive use of low-grade solder sometimes gave rise to disputes between the guilds and their members, some of whom were not above increasing their profit margins by using more solder than was strictly necessary and so adding to the weight and hence the price of their wares. Besides cast or embossed ornament a piece might be further decorated with engraving or etching, both techniques being applied to either cast or wrought objects. If the vessel had a cover, this was usually finished with a finial, which might take the form of a figure, a group of figures, a baluster, a coat-of-arms or, in the case of German goldsmiths' work, a vase of flowers in cut and bent silver sheet (pl. 490). The German goldsmiths made another use of sheet silver, this was to form the scrolled ornaments which were placed at each end of the baluster stem of a standing cup and, sometimes, on the cover as well. While the cup was usually gilt, the scrollwork was left white, providing an attractive colour contrast. A high proportion of sixteenth-century silver is gilt, often re-gilt but sometimes original, in which case the colour is lighter — of a rather lemon hue. It is unlikely that plate intended for constant use would be gilt and the conclusion to be drawn is that most of the extant vessels of this period were meant for show. The custom of gilding plate seems to have existed generally in western Europe, the chief exception being the northern Netherlands where the practice was less widespread, especially in the seventeenth century.

There were local preferences in the type of decoration used; engraved ornament was more usual in northern Europe than in Italy or Spain, where borders were more likely to be worked in relief. Nowhere was engraved decoration more exploited than in England and the northern Netherlands; tankards, flagons and beakers were engraved all over whereas elsewhere they would be embossed. Etched borders on silver seem to have been confined to the Teutonic cultural area. Though the technique had already been practised by the armour decorators (*Ätzmaler*) during the fifteenth century, it does not seem to have been taken up by goldsmiths until it was exploited by Wenzel Jamnitzer. It was used by him on the bowl of the Merckel table centre (pl. 420); thereafter it became a standard feature of the German drinking vessel until ornament in higher relief came in with the baroque. Etched ornament was usually confined to borders, either the foot rim or the upper border of the bowl of a drinking-vessel or tazza, but sometimes, as on the large standing cup by Linhardt Bauer of Strassburg (pl. 542), it played a more important rôle. The thematic range of etched ornament was limited by its very nature; it usually comprised some simple repetitive design, such as true arabesques (*mauresques*) in which no living image was introduced, some abstract classical pattern or a highly conventionalised acanthus leaf. Its very low relief provided an ideal foil for the higher relief achieved with embossed decoration.

A great many of the finer vessels and nearly all the hardstone cups and the jewels of the sixteenth century were decorated with enamel, either *champlevé*, that is, set in recesses cut in the metal and finished flush with the surface, or *en rond bosse*, that is, laid over surfaces modelled in relief. Both techniques had been practised in the Middle Ages, the latter having been exploited with particular skill by the Burgundian goldsmiths of the second half of the fourteenth century. The second technique was mainly used in the sixteenth century for the figures modelled in the round that surmounted the covers or embellished the stems of standing cups. Enamelling was a specialised craft, and though the leading goldsmiths might have employed an enameller, others would put out enamelling to a specialist who worked for the trade as a whole. While vessels of gold were decorated with *champlevé* enamel in translucent or opaque colours, silver, especially in Germany, was more frequently enamelled with the cold process known as *Kaltemail*. This was only a form of lacquer; it was not fired and, though it doubtless stood up to use for a time, it was far less durable than fired enamel. It is rarely found in good condition now, having been damaged or destroyed by subsequent cleaning. The sixteenth-century goldsmith not only showed little concern for the practical problems of using the vessels he made, he also tended to ignore the difficulty of keeping them clean. Both Wenzel Jamnitzer and Matthias Zündt made use of a finial for cup or ewer-cover in the form of a vase of flowers of cut and painted silver sheet (pl. 136). In the design illustrated, not only is the finial constructed in this way, but bunches of fruit with delicate foliage grow out from the junction of stem and body as well. Such details would have been extremely difficult to clean by the primitive methods then in use.

In the sixteenth century the distinction between the goldsmith and the jeweller was less clear than it became in subsequent centuries. In addition to making hollow-ware (cups, tankards, bowls, plates and dishes) and flat-ware (spoons and forks) they also manufactured jewellery which was then worn in great profusion. While ladies wore head ornaments, necklaces, girdles, brooches, rings and pendants as well as countless jewels sewn at intervals on their dresses, noblemen rivalled them with hat-ornaments, rings, sword- and dagger-hilts and sword-belt mounts, all of gold or gilt and often enriched with enamel as well. Since jewels were neither signed nor marked, it is rarely possible to ascribe a surviving example to an individual master, but evidence for the production of jewellery by leading goldsmiths can be found in the accounts of German and Italian courts and also in the sketch-book of Wenzel Jamnitzer in the Berlin Kunstbibliothek (see p.104). This includes designs for watches, settings for jewelled pendants and one for a jewel of the Order of the Golden Fleece.

While the larger workshops covered a wide field of production, there was a trend towards specialisation in the smaller ones. This was particularly marked in the main centres of German goldsmithing, but much the same development took place in Antwerp, Paris and London (see, for instance, the strictures of the London Goldsmiths' Company about specialisation on p.39). If we take a typical piece of Augsburg silver such as the tazza illustrated in pls. 441, 443 as an example, we will find that it was probably produced in three different workshops: the casting pattern for the stem came from the pattern carver; the foot and the bowl were then raised and the stem cast in the goldsmith's shop, probably by two different specialist craftsmen; the bowl was then sent off to another workshop to be embossed and chased with some figure subject; then finally the whole tazza was fitted together, screws attached to the base of the bowl and the foot and the stem bored and female threads cut for assembly. The partly finished piece was then submitted to the guild for assay and, when it had passed, it was finally gilded and polished. The many different patterns of silver mounts used to adorn the caskets, tabernacles and house-altars supplied by the two Augsburg masters, Boas Ulrich and Matthias Wallbaum, are so similar that one suspects that they all came from a single workshop specialising in their production, although the completed articles bear the marks of the two different masters.

Other types of specialisation developed in individual towns. Lapis lazuli was worked in Florence, coral was carved in Palermo and Genoa, while shell cameos were cut in Paris and, later, in Naples and the nearby town of Torre del Greco. The exact source of the mother-of-pearl scales that were used in large numbers for mounting in silver vessels in Bavaria, Saxony and also in England is not known, but many of them probably came ready-made from the Eastern Mediterranean and were then mounted with precious metal in Europe. There is a marked difference in quality in these mother-of-pearl vessels, depending on their source. Coral was used for handles for knives, forks and spoons and to provide finials for cups. The most ingenious use of the material is on the figure of Daphne by Wenzel Jamnitzer in the Musée de Cluny, Paris.[3] In this case the nymph is depicted at the moment when she is in the process of being changed into a tree and her hair and hands are turning into branches of coral. The ebony required for constructing the gold- or silver-mounted caskets made in Florence, Augsburg and Nürnberg was obtained in Portugal, whither it was brought in Portuguese ships trading with the Far East. Such was the importance and costliness of ebony that in Augsburg it was struck with the pine-cone town mark to guarantee its authenticity.

Division of labour was already an established practice in the sixteenth century. One proof of this is the fact that the figure finials of the covers of cups made by different masters come from the same mould and must, therefore, have been purchased ready-made from a goldsmith who specialised in their production. The most impressive account of this division is given in a letter written by Hainhofer to Duke Philipp of Pommern in December 1610.[4] He lists the twelve craftsmen who were then working on a silver sewing-basket (Nähkorb) that was being made for the Duke, the delivery of which was taking a long time: 'the woman Schwarz, who is plaiting the silver wire, Lencker doing a relief for the cover and four figures of eagles, Maulbrunn decorating the relief with gilt borders and precious stones; the woman Lotter making silver flowers, Gottfried Münderer casting insects and grasses from nature, Rigelstain painting the flowers [presumably with cold enamel], Achilles Langenbucher enamelling insects on the inside. Schwegler putting musk in a small box [pomander?], Valti Michael enamelling the arms and fruit on the handle; Philip Froscher making the lock, Daniel Griesbeck carving the hard-stones, Miller making the straps'. Finally when all these had completed their work, a case with silk lining had to be made. It is difficult to imagine just what these elaborate sewing-baskets were like. Another one was ordered by Duke Wilhelm of Bavaria from his court goldsmith, Georg Bernhard of Augsburg; it was intertwined with wreaths of flowers in bloom and took several months to make — rather less than that made for Duke Philipp.

Goldsmiths also engaged in activities that fell outside the craft such as banking, dealing in antiques, genuine or spurious, or as merchants by buying and selling the works of other masters. Another outlet was the publication of collections of their designs as pattern-books of engraved ornament for the use of contemporaries working in the same or other crafts. The more ingenious were inventors, such as Jacopo da Strada who invented water-pumps and wheels, Erasmus Hornick who devised military equipment or Wenzel Jamnitzer who produced a book on the science of perspective. When carving or modelling was required they were often capable of the most exacting work and it has been suggested that even the coconuts mounted in standing cups were carved by the goldsmith himself.[5]

When a goldsmith received a commission for an important piece of plate, his usual procedure was first to make a drawing and, when this had been submitted to and approved by the customer, a model. In the *Vita* Cellini relates how he was commissioned by Pope Clement VII to make a chalice 'After I had served the Pope for a time making him various small articles, he instructed me to prepare a drawing for a magnificent chalice, which I did and at the same time made a model. This was of wood and wax.'[6] He also had models made of a vessel he proposed to his chief patron, Cardinal Hippolito d'Este. The register of the Cardinal's expenses for the year 1540 include the payment of thirty *baioques* to a wood-turner 'For a wood model of a cup given to Master Benvenuto, the goldsmith in respect of a silver cup he has to make for the most Reverend Cardinal.'[7]

There can have been no uniform custom governing the distribution of commissions. Sometimes the intending customer would go first to his favourite goldsmith and the latter would approach the designer; in other cases the customer obtained the design himself and then gave it to the goldsmith or even left the choice of goldsmith to the designer. It is probable that in northern Europe only an exceptionally gifted goldsmith was able to produce his own original designs. Most vessels were made according to established types and if something different were required, a pattern-book would provide the necessary ideas.

The Italian goldsmiths did not rely on printed pattern-books to such an extent as their northern contemporaries; they seem either to have produced their own designs or to have obtained drawings from a graphic artist. The number and variety of extant Italian sixteenth-century drawings for goldsmiths is very large; many are, moreover, the work, not of obscure artists, but of some of the leading masters of their time. This circumstance goes far to explain the varied character of such drawings, and also the frequent lack of concern of the artist for so practical a question as the eventual function of the piece he was designing. Vasari,[8] on the other hand, implies that the goldsmith usually produced his own designs, stating 'at that time it was the custom, and no man was considered to be a good goldsmith unless he was a good designer and a good master of relief work as well'. Whether a graphic artist was called in to supply the design depended no doubt on the status of the goldsmith. Thus, when as a young man first establishing himself in Rome, Cellini obtained a commission to make a large vase (*acquereccia*) for the Bishop of Salamanca through Raphael's assistant, Luca Penni, the design was provided by Penni. Subsequently Cellini became more independent, as is shown by the following story he tells in the *Vita*.[9] It appears that when in 1528 he went to Mantua, Duke Federigo Gonzaga commissioned him to make a reliquary and instructed Giulio Romano to supply a design for it. According to Cellini's not necessarily accurate

THE CRAFT OF THE GOLDSMITH

account, Giulio tactfully replied, 'My Lord, Benvenuto is a man who does not need other people's sketches, as your Excellency will be very well able to judge when you see his model'.

When Cellini was working in Paris from 1540 to 1545 in the service of François I, he supplied all his designs himself, or so he subsequently informed Duke Cosimo I: 'that great king Francis paid for thirty good assistants chosen by me, and with their help I could busy myself with all the important works I have mentioned, all of which were made from my drawings'.[10] An incident which threw a less flattering light on his skill as a designer occurred on one occasion when he had been summoned to see the Pope and granted a commission for a model of a new gold coin. On this occasion Cellini's *bête noir*, Baccio Bandinelli, happened to be standing by and could not resist the opportunity to observe slightingly 'When it comes to such fine things one must provide goldsmiths with drawings for them to follow'. Cellini replied with characteristic force that he did not require Bandinelli's drawings to assist his art, but on the contrary hoped in due course through his drawings to give Bandinelli cause for concern.[11]

The contract between a Genoese nobleman and his goldsmith for the production of the ewer and companion basin illustrated in pls. 342 and 345 gives us a picture of the arrangements which were made in Italy when an important commission was awarded (see p.161). This contract was signed on 11 May, 1565, between the *Magnifico* Francesco Lercaro and *Maestro* Antonio de Castro of Genoa, who undertook to make the two vessels within fourteen months to a model supplied by his client. The precious metal, 'sixteen pounds in weight,' was supplied by Lercaro and the goldsmith was to receive on completion of his task two hundred *scudi d'oro* for his work. In the event of a dispute as to the terms of the agreement or the quality of the piece, another goldsmith, Lazzaro Scorza, was named as arbitrator.

The Weimar archives contain an enlightening exchange of correspondence relating to the Augsburg goldsmith, Hans Schebel, and his patron, Duke Wilhelm of Sachsen-Weimar.[12] In 1571 the duke decided to have a fine silver-gilt cup made and, as a preliminary step, obtained from an unknown source the design illustrated in pl. 164. This was then shown to certain Augsburg goldsmiths who were invited to estimate the cost of making it. According to contemporary practice they submitted their offers in terms of thaler per mark of silver, and the figure at which they arrived was the high one of 20 thaler per mark weight. A note on the bottom of the drawing gives the estimated weight as 22 marks so the total cost would have been in the neighbourhood of 450 thaler. The reason for the high cost of this cup was doubtless its complex design, characteristic of Mannerist taste. The duke's agent, Matthis Haug, wrote to his master explaining that it was not possible to make the cup in the way intended. It would have to be wrought and not cast. In a letter written to the Duke he states 'but if I may be allowed to counsel your Grace, then I would accept this [i.e. an alternative] design which does not cost so much, and it could be made on a smaller scale, and, if most of the work were to be cast, then your Grace could certainly buy it for 18 Gulden [per mark weight]. If, however, the cup has to be made from the drawing which your Grace prefers and must, therefore, be wrought, then 20 thaler per mark will not be sufficient to pay for it. Therefore, I would beg your Grace to let me know whether you wish to have the wrought or the cast cup.'

The alternative design sent by Matthis Haug from Augsburg is illustrated in pl. 165. It does not seem to be so very much less ornate than the first cup and the considerable difference in cost − 12 thaler as against 20 thaler per mark − seems surprising, the more so as the alternative was to be enamelled without extra charge. The explanation must lie in the vastly higher cost of embossing as opposed to casting. The first cup was evidently to be made to an original design: most of the ornament on both the bowl and the cover would have to be embossed, chased and finished by hand, and new casting models would have to be supplied by the pattern-carver (*Formschneider*) for the stem. The only details that would have involved no extra work were the two lion masks with rings in their mouths, the two female masks on opposite sides of the bowl, the brackets in the form of half-figures on the foot and the cherubs' and horses' heads on the cover. All these features would have been cast and patterns could have been purchased or perhaps hired from a pattern-carver in Augsburg or Nürnberg.

The bowl of a cup was usually the most carefully decorated part; when this was cylindrical or conical, it might be embossed in the flat, then brought to the appropriate shape and soldered up the vertical seam. In this case the bowl would be composed of two separate members, the inner bowl which was undecorated, and the outer member, which was a decorated sleeve placed over the former. The inner bowl was attached to the stem by a vertical screw and was finished with a moulding at the top to keep the outer sleeve in position. There were other ways of making a decorated bowl. It could also be constructed of two or three panels, embossed in the flat and then soldered together, or again it might be raised from flat plate and embossed and chased in its final shape of a tapering cylinder. The first-mentioned method could not have been used in the case of the design in pl. 164 as the serpentine profile is too complex. This would have to be raised from flat plate, embossed from the inside and chased from the outside. The design for a cast bowl shown in pl. 165 was probably not new; in this case the patterns would already have been in existence and little preliminary work would have been required when the cup was made. The bowl of a cast cup was constructed of two or three segments which were cast, soldered along the seams and then carefully chased over to conceal the soldered joints. The manuscript notes on the side of the drawing in fig. 165, which are in Haug's handwriting, explain that the cover and the bowl with the scenes of Adam and Eve in the Garden of Eden would be cast; so also would the stem and most of the foot, though Haug does not mention this in his notes. The only wrought work would, therefore, have been the lip of both cover and bowl, perhaps part of the shallow cup-like member from which the bowl rises, and the lowest member of the foot.

Duke Wilhelm did not, in fact, accept the less expensive cast design but decided to discuss the matter in person with his agent, Haug, at the Leipzig fair in 1571. A letter written by Haug in May, 1572, indicates that his brother, who was at the time in Augsburg, had finally given instructions as to the design that was to be executed. He informed the duke that it would be delivered in some three to four weeks. He sent on to say that a cup weighing 17 marks could be obtained in Augsburg from stock and that this would cost 17 gulden (slightly under 12 thaler) per mark, and even cheaper therefore, than the cast cup decorated with the Garden of Eden. The correspondence between the duke and his agent Haug also refers to two designs for chalices which were sent to the duke in July 1571. One of these is still preserved in the Weimar archive (pl. 163). In this case three Augsburg goldsmiths were invited to submit estimates for making it, namely the Hans Schebel mentioned above, Philipp Zwitzel and Wolf Schyrer.[13] It appears from the correspondence that Schebel was commissioned to produce the chalice at a price of 16 thaler per mark, but he died before completing it. In this case the high price may have been due to the lavish enamelled ornament on both bowl and foot.

While the two less accomplished drawings in pls. 163 and 165 can, on the strength of the correspondence, be attributed to Augsburg and very probably to Hans Schebel himself, the third design is of unknown origin. It is the work of a far more competent and imaginative designer and may have been executed by an artist who specialised in such drawings. There is, unfortunately, no evidence to show where the duke obtained it: the many annotations provide no clue as they are all in the hand of Matthis Haug, who was himself a goldsmith. While the Adam and Eve Cup conforms to a well-known type of which several examples survive, that decorated with masks (pl. 164) is more sophisticated in taste and it is not difficult to understand that the duke, following contemporary Mannerist fashion, found it more desirable.

Another account of the negotiations which preceded the commissioning of an important piece of goldsmiths' work dates from the early seventeenth century. It comes from that extremely useful source, the correspondence between Duke Philipp II of Pommern-Stettin and his agent, Hainhofer.[14] The duke had some silver plaques embossed after the Golzius engravings of the Passion of Christ. He wished to complete the series and asked Hainhofer for his advice. The latter in turn consulted Rottenhammer who recommended Bayr, de Vos or, best of all, Christoph Lencker. Hainhofer then suggested that the duke should send a plaque or a plaster cast from one of them for use as a model. He explained that the series could be divided between the three masters and each be given one or more engravings to follow. The duke sent two of the plaques to Augsburg and Hainhofer gave them, together with one of the engravings, to Lencker, with whom he now began to discuss the question of price. It is interesting to note that Lencker criticised the reliefs: while he did not consider them to be bad, he found that the master did not understand perspective and that he should have embossed the buildings in the upper background in lower relief. Lencker himself preferred a less clear delineation of the background.

If the commission was sufficiently important, a preliminary rough model was made to show the customer the effect of the projected piece. Once this first model had been seen and approved, others had to be constructed. For every piece of cast work or cast ornament on a silver vessel the following processes were necessary. First a positive model was produced, usually carved in wood. From this a negative was made, probably of plaster and glue. From this a new positive was made, this time of wax, which was sufficiently soft to be pressed into the recesses of the negative. When flat panels of ornament were to be cast, it was important to make sure that the wax positive was of fairly even thickness, otherwise the metal would not cool evenly and the panel might be distorted. In removing this wax positive, the negative might be damaged, hence the importance of having the original wood positive from which new negatives could always be made. The wax was then encased in plaster or some form of clay, the exit holes for the wax, entrance holes for the molten metal and air vents were bored, the wax was melted out and molten silver poured in. When the metal had cooled the mould was broken away and the casting removed. The external surface of the metal was then chased with gravers and punches as necessary in order to sharpen the relief and bring out the detail.

This elaborate process was only necessary when it was intended to make more than one cast from the model. If it was to be used once only, the first two steps could be omitted and the cast made directly from the wax. Cellini describes the process of making models in his *Trattato*,[15] as follows: 'You may then proceed to fashion in wax whatever graces you may wish to place at lip or handle, improving on the model or design with which you started. These finished you may make them in all sorts of different ways, so many that it would be wearisome to recount. The easiest of these was that which I usually employed, and particularly in the vase I made for King Francis I'. He then goes on to describe his process, which was the usual lost wax (*cire perdue*) method mentioned above.

A simpler process, used in the case of less important pieces, was for the silver to be cast in sand into which the model had previously been pressed, making a negative impression. In this process objects to be made in the round were cast in two halves and soldered up the seam. This was done in order to produce a hollow casting, thus reducing the weight of precious metal and so economising on cost. If it was necessary to make a large number of casts from one model, patterns were made of lead. In the *Trattato* Cellini refers to their production: 'When the moulds (from the wax models) are made with due observance to the undercutting, lead castings are made from them, and these as well cleaned and worked up as the master may be minded; then they are cast in silver. This is a particularly good way, because when the master has his lead model and has finished it to suit his purposes, it can serve ever so many more times than a single casting'.[16] According to Cellini the best kind of casting sand was found in the bed of the Seine in Paris. He states that he used to take the sand for casting from the river near the Sainte Chapelle. It had the advantage of being very soft and did not need to be dried. 'When you have made it the shape you want, you can pour into it while it is still moist your gold, silver, bronze or any other metal. This is a very rare thing and I have never heard of it occurring anywhere else in the world'.[17]

Though the larger workshops would have produced their own models, they were also made by specialist pattern-carvers. The original model was carved in some soft wood such as lime or pear. A few examples have survived; there is in the Metropolitan Museum, New York, a complete model for a tazza carved in three parts, bowl, stem and base (pls. 733, 735) and the Germanisches Nationalmuseum, Nürnberg, has a model for the cover of a bowl as well as a group of models for pendant jewels, all dating from the middle or second half of the sixteenth century.[18] The most remarkable of these rare survivals is a set of four models carved in pearwood for the panels of a table-clock (pl. 730). A harder material, such as boxwood, might also be used, or even honestone, in which Peter Flötner carved the models for his plaquettes. Models for reliefs might also be chiselled or embossed in copper. It is clear that the real merit for producing the superb ornament on sixteenth-century goldsmiths' work belongs properly to the master who carved the model. Little is known of these carvers — *Bildschnitzer* or *Formschneider* — for the most part they are anonymous, though among them may be reckoned such outstanding masters as Peter. Flötner, Hans Kels, Hans Schwarz and Victor Kayser. One of the most skilled of these carvers was François Briot of Montbéliard (Mömpelgard), then belonging to the territories of the Duke of Württemberg. His models seem to have been used only by the makers of decorative pewter vessels (*Edelzinn*) (see p.328). There were, of course, exceptions and some goldsmiths were capable of the finest sculpture as well. Others employed a journeyman specifically for the purpose of making patterns: the Augsburg regulations refer to the employment of a journeyman '*zum possieren und patronenmachen*'. On the whole, however, just as the German Renaissance bronzes were once credited to the founders such as Pancraz Labenwolf, who had cast them, but are now recognised as the achievement of *Bildschnitzer*, such as Hans Peisser,[19] so also must the fine cast work be regarded as the work of a *Bildschnitzer* whose model was employed by the goldsmith. The credit for embossed ornament remains, of course, with the goldsmith. Whether he had a drawing, a wax or lead relief to copy, the process of hammering the silver sheet from the underside and chasing or chiselling it from the upper side required the exercise of the highest skill.

During the sixteenth and early seventeenth centuries, when almost the whole surface area of vessels of precious metal was covered with ornament, cast, embossed, engraved or etched, the possession of a good collection of patterns from which moulds for cast ornament in relief could be made was one of the most important elements in the equipment of a goldsmith's workshop.[20] In an age when there was no protection by patent law for the inventor, one would expect them to have been closely guarded. That this was usually the case is indicated by an entry in the records of the Nürnberg City Council on 19th December, 1549, according to which the Nürnberg goldsmith, Peter Kuster, was required to state truthfully how he had come into possession of Wenzel Jamnitzer's models and his stake (*Kunsteisen*) and that in the event of his refusal he should be committed to prison.[21]

A fortunate chance has preserved in the Historisches Museum, Basel, a large number of lead or pewter patterns used by the Jamnitzer workshop in the second half of the sixteenth century.[22] These formed part of the *Kunstkammer* of the Basel humanist, Basilius Amerbach, who is believed to have purchased them, or some of them, before 1580 from a Basel goldsmith, Johann Hoffmann (master 1543, died 1572), or from his estate. Amerbach also had a large number of patterns going back to the end of the previous century. It is believed that these also came from Hoffmann, who had acquired them as part of the contents of the house of another Basel goldsmith, Balthasar Angelrot (died 1544). As Amerbach was an enthusiastic collector of all kinds of antiquities as well as being a much-travelled man, he may have purchased part of the collection directly from a Nürnberg goldsmith.[23] The collection is particularly rich in the various sets of Flötner plaquettes, including the Muses, Vices, Virtues, etc. There are also reliefs modelled after prints by the Nürnberg *Kleinmeister* and after Holbein's *Bauerntanz* (Peasants' Dance). These last were used to decorate a silver wine-can of the Basel *Weinleute-Zunft* (Vintners' Guild) dating from 1613, nearly three-quarters of a century after Holbein's death, in the Historisches Museum, Basel.[24] It seems strange that so large a number of patterns should have been allowed to pass out of the Jamnitzer workshop at so early a date, for their possession would have enabled a rival goldsmith to have produced a convincing imitation of a Jamnitzer piece. As a rule the models and lead patterns were passed on in the workshop; the will of the famous Leipzig goldsmith, Hans Reinhart the Elder, dated 1579, two years before his death in 1581, specifies that *'alles Werkzeug mit Blein und Modellen'* should be divided between his two sons. There can, however, be no doubt that models from the Jamnitzer workshop were available to goldsmiths elsewhere; there is no other way of accounting for the existence of vessels made by goldsmiths in other German cities decorated with borders and friezes cast from Jamnitzer models. It might be thought that such models would soon become out of date and lose their value, but this was not so in the aesthetic climate of the time. Mannerist taste was not offended by the adding, even the superimposing of one ornament upon another. Thus a decorative device worked out in 1560 could still be used on a vessel made a quarter of a century later. It was probably this interest in piling up ornament that accounts for the sale of pattern-books, such as that of Hans Brosamer, in a second edition long after the style depicted was out of date.

A striking feature of the Jamnitzer patterns in the Amerbach *Kunstkabinett* is the perfection of their finish, which surpasses that of the finest silver vessels. They were cast in plaster or clay or a composition of clay and casting sand, in which a more perfect result could be obtained than with casting sand alone.[25] Plaster alone would provide a perfect impression but great difficulty was experienced in keeping the plaster moulds dry: if the plaster absorbed too much moisture the steam produced when the molten metal was introduced into the mould would damage the cast. While many of the lead plaques in the Amerbach collection were intended to serve as patterns, it is probable that others were made purely as records of decoration used in the workshop. Among the latter are those taken from panels of etched ornament (pls. 429-435).

Goldsmiths' patterns came in other materials besides the wood, stone and pewter mentioned above. Those of bronze or brass were produced by another craft in Germany, the *Patronengiesser* (pattern-casters). The *Patronen* they made provided only a rough approximation of the relief that was required and were as a rule only used when a large number of reliefs to a standard design were to be made. The process was for a thin silver sheet to be pressed or hammered on to the bronze pattern thus giving the main outlines of the design, the details being added by hand chasing afterwards. The *Patronen* were in relief, but a second type was cut intaglio. The goldsmith pressed thin sheets of silver into these intaglio patterns thus producing ready-made reliefs. The plaquette collection of the Berlin Kunstgewerbe Museum includes a bronze plaquette cast intaglio with the subject of Christ in the *Noli me tangere* scene.[26] When a particular model, such as a frieze or border ornament, was in constant demand, a lead pattern would soon become worn and indistinct, so the design was embossed in copper or cast in bronze instead. These must be distinguished from the *Patronen* because they were used as casting patterns and not for hammering on to. Very few of these bronze patterns have survived, probably because of the high value of the metal.

During the last quarter of the sixteenth and the first quarter of the seventeenth century, it was usual for the central area of a tazza bowl to be decorated with a relief subject drawn from Scripture or mythology. These reliefs were embossed and chased by hand by specialist craftsmen who worked for a number of goldsmiths. It follows that the mark struck on the foot or bowl of a tazza is not necessarily that of the artist who executed the relief which is its most important feature. The more gifted goldsmiths were capable of producing their designs directly by adapting prints; in a few exceptional cases the goldsmith may even have produced the original design himself. Others seem to have required the intermediate state of a plaquette to help them translate the light and shade of an engraving into the varying relief of the scene to be embossed on the tazza bowl. Lead plaquettes were, therefore, made from original reliefs in other materials and sold to the goldsmiths to be copied. When, during the seventeenth century, tazzas ceased to be fashionable and were not yet recognised as works of art, many were destroyed but the central panel with its finely-chased scene was sometimes cut out and preserved. This accounts for the existence of a number of detached silver plaquettes that were originally part of tazzas.

The interest of collectors in plaquettes, particularly those of bronze, dates from the sixteenth century. Those made as patterns for goldsmiths were of lead, but the demand from collectors led to the production of bronze casts from the lead versions. The lead ones, being made of so soft a metal, were often much worn and as a consequence the bronze casts made from them were of inferior quality. Casts were also made from some of the silver plaquettes cut out of tazzas; and, being taken from originals of harder metal, were of better quality. Thus the extant plaquettes may be original patterns in boxwood or stone, embossed silver reliefs, casts from them in silver or lead or aftercasts in bronze from these silver or lead casts. Lead plaquettes after models by Nürnberg pattern-carvers were sold by merchants at trade fairs and their wide distribution in northern Europe accounts for the repetition of the same design on silver vessels made by gold-smiths in towns geographically remote from one another. The moral taint which today is attached to plagiarism did not exist in the sixteenth century and a goldsmith would not hesitate to take a mould from a detail modelled by another master if it would serve his purpose. Nevertheless it was accepted at the time that embossed work ranked more highly than casting.

Tazza bowls provided the goldsmith with a particularly suitable surface upon which to display his skill in embossing and chasing. The process of decorating a tazza bowl, a dish or the cylindrical body of a cup or tankard in relief called for a skill quite different from that needed to provide a model for casting. It was, therefore, entrusted to a different specialist craftsman. In the case of a tankard the goldsmith could usually follow his printed source exactly, but when decorating a tazza bowl the artist might have to adapt a rectangular print to a circular shape. After this had been done, the design was drawn or traced on the back of the piece to be decorated. The outlines were then pricked with a fine punch; the traces of the pricks can sometimes be seen on the backs of finished pieces. The rough design was then put in from the back, using tools of various sizes and shapes made either of metal or of boxwood (snarling irons). While this was done the sheet or vessel was placed on a bed of pitch, which provided a sufficiently elastic support.[27] This finished, the dish was turned over and the detail put in from the front, using finer tools. Finally the background was given a matt finish with minute punches. In the course of this process of embossing or chasing, metal was not removed from the silver vessel but worked from one position to another to create the relief and the detail of the design. When the goldsmith was decorating the bowl of a tazza he worked the piece in the form it would eventually take, with the exception that the rim of the tazza was sometimes added after the centre had been chased. In the case of a tankard, the emboss-ing might be applied to the already assembled body. On the other hand, it might be carried out when the body was in the form of a flat sheet with curved top and bottom. After the chasing had been completed, the sheet was rolled into a drum, soldered up the seam and the tankard assembled.

Cellini gives a clear account of his technique for embossing a relief on a medallion: 'After having made a model in wax and decided what design he wishes to follow the artist takes a sheet of gold which is thin at the sides and a little thicker in the middle. This done, he begins very gradually to work on it from the back and to emboss it a little following the model. In this way it is not necessary to use a bronze pattern, for in the time required to cast the bronze pattern, one will have got well ahead with the work.....I made a medal for a certain Sienese gentleman, Girolamo Marretti, in the way described above. The subject of the relief was Hercules holding open the lion's mouth; I wrought both Hercules and the lion in almost full relief, so that they were only attached to the ground by little tabs. I achieved this without using a bronze pattern, working slowly first from the back and then from the front.'[28]

That embossed work was more costly and more highly regarded than cast work is shown by the transactions relating to the cup ordered by the Duke of Sachsen-Weimar (see p.57) and by the following incident concerning a Lübeck goldsmith. In an undated petition that can be placed towards the end of the sixteenth century, a journeyman-goldsmith, Berend Krumtunge, requested Arend Bonnus, the Bürgermeister of Lübeck to allocate him one of the goldsmiths' booths in the city.[29] He stated that, in return, should there be among the Bürgermeister's plate a piece of insufficient quality of ornament, he would be pleased to decorate it with fine ornament and entirely with embossed work, nothing being cast from patterns, in whatever manner would please him and further that he would not charge a single penny for the work. Nevertheless, even with cast work the goldsmith was able to express something of his own taste and skill. The fine sand in which silver was cast, described by Cellini as *arena di tufo*, left a minute granular surface and as a rule the whole piece was worked over (chased up) by the goldsmith after being freed from the casting mould. In this process he could alter the detail of the ornament and add character to the expression of a figure or a mask.

The highest demands were placed on the skill of the goldsmith when he made figure sculpture in the round. This might either be cast by the *cire perdue* process or wrought from sheet. Such sculpture was by no means an innovation of the Renaissance: figures of saints and angels had been much used in the decoration of medieval monstrances or chalices and the most obvious form for a reliquary that contained a fragment of some Saint was either a full length or a bust figure wrought in silver. The collection of relics assembled by Archbishop Albrecht of Brandenburg, the pictorial inventory of which was completed in 1525, included a large number of such reliquary figures and busts wrought in silver. So little medieval secular silver survives that it is impossible to speak with any certainty of its character, but two late fifteenth-century salts at Oxford University, the Huntsman Salt at All Souls and the Monkey Salt at New College, both have figure stems. The inventory of the plate of King Henry VIII of England also makes it clear that many of the more handsome vessels were adorned with sculpture in precious metal.

In his treatise on sculpture Cellini describes the production of such figures; he relates that the Roman goldsmith, Caradosso, one of the very few rivals whom he admired, followed a complex process, first preparing a model in wax from which he cast a bronze figure. He then cut out a gold sheet of approximately the right size and shape, which he placed over the model and finally worked the gold into the shape of his model with the help of long wooden hammers.[30] Cellini, on the other hand, omitted the stage of making a bronze model and, after completing his wax, set to work immediately on shaping his gold sheet, bending it and hammering it from both sides. The wax model was, therefore, used only for guidance in working the metal. In this way Cellini was able to produce his finished figure much more quickly than Caradosso.

Cellini's ambition was to become a sculptor rather than a goldsmith and the first commission he received from François I after his arrival in Paris was for a series of life-size statues to be wrought in silver. These were to represent gods and goddesses and were to decorate the gallery of the King's new palace at Fontainebleau. Cellini[31] gives a detailed account of their manufacture; first he made a full-size clay model, then he proceeded straight to the task of embossing the various sheets that were to compose his figure. Arms, legs and body were hammered out in separate pieces and then the head was wrought in one piece like a vase. Finally each element was soldered to the next and the figure completed. Even the smaller figures of the Cellini Salt are constructed in the same way from gold sheet; presumably in this case the saving in precious metal of embossing rather than casting had some bearing on the method used. No larger scale silver statues made in this way are known to survive from the sixteenth century, but in the gardens of the Mirabell Palace of the Archbishops of Salzburg there is an almost life-size copper figure of Pegasus built up from sheets joined together.

One of Cellini's tasks when working for François I in Paris was to produce a figure of colossal size; in discussing it he comments on the capacity of the French goldsmiths 'I have described above the beauty of all the things made in the great city of Paris, and I have never seen anywhere in the world such perfect hammer-work as in that city, but with all their technique not even the best masters were able to give that statue (a life-size silver figure) either grace, beauty or style. The reason is that they did not know how to solder, so that when they came to join the legs, arms and head to the body, they had to attach them with silver wire.'[32] He goes on to say that 'Whilst in Paris I used to work on the largest kind of silver work that the craft admits of, and, moreover, the most difficult (i.e. life-size sculpture). I had in my employ many workmen and inasmuch as they learnt very gladly from me, so I was not above learning from them.'[33]

The extent to which goldsmiths were themselves able to produce the models they required in order to cast or work up from sheet figure sculpture in silver is a subject that is still open to discussion. There was, moreover, a distinction between the practice in Italy and in Germany. Whereas the Italian goldsmith would produce a model in the manner described by Cellini, his German contemporary would be more likely to carve his model or to have it carved in boxwood or pearwood. This called for a special skill which did not lie within the range of the average goldsmith. It is evidently impossible to arrive at a final ruling, as some goldsmiths might acquire skills that were outside the competence of others. The part played by the goldsmith might in some cases be the relatively minor one of executing something that had been designed and modelled by another master. The best known example relates to the leading Nürnberg goldsmith, Melchior Baier, who, when he produced the silver reliefs for the altar commissioned by King Sigismund I of Poland for his sepulchral chapel in the cathedral of Wawel, hammered his silver sheet over bronze plaquettes (*Patronen*) that had in turn been cast from wood models carved by Peter Flötner.[34] In the same way, it has in recent years been realised that the attribution of German Renaissance sculptures to the bronze founders, such as Benedikt Würzelbauer or Pankraz Labenwolf, is to confuse the technical artisan with the artist.

The ability of even the great Wenzel Jamnitzer to produce the models for figures he subsequently cast in the round has been questioned. The evidence on this particular point is somewhat contradictory. That he did not necessarily produce the figure sculpture which accompanied or embellished his own works can be proved by reference to the four gilt-bronze figures that originally formed the base of the great table-fountain he made for the Emperor Maximilian II and that are the only remaining parts of it (see p.130). These have been attributed by both Feulner[35] and by Meller[36] to the Dutch master, Gregor van der Schardt; they certainly show an Italianate elegance that is foreign to Jamnitzer's manner. Weihrauch[37] has thrown doubt on the attribution to Jamnitzer of the magnificent boxwood model (pl. 731) for the 'Mother Earth' stem of the Merckelsche *Tafelaufsatz*, this in spite of the fact that the original drawing (pl. 132) for the fountain is generally accepted as an autograph work of Jamnitzer. As an alternative the name of Christoph Weiditz has been suggested. Weihrauch even questions whether Wenzel Jamnitzer ever used the sculptor's tools, referring in this connection to a commission given to Jamnitzer by the Archduke Ferdinand of Tirol for four figures of the Evangelists. In a letter referring to this commission Jamnitzer states that he has spoken with the sculptor who would model them, with the master who would cast them in bronze, and with the man who would finish and gild them, and that the final price would be 30 florins.[38] In this case there is no doubt that Jamnitzer's role was that of agent. On the other hand the portrait of Wenzel Jamnitzer by the *Wanderkünstler*, Nicholas de Neufchatel, in the Musée d'Art et d'Histoire at Geneva (pl. 5)[39] executed about 1560-65, shows him surrounded by the typical productions of his art among which is a silver figure of Neptune holding a trident and, next to it, a pencil sketch of the same figure. This does not really settle the matter as it merely indicates that Jamnitzer provided the original drawing and presumably cast the figure in silver. It does not establish who was responsible for the casting pattern, which alone called for the skill of a sculptor. The silver vase set in a niche in the background to the right of the sitter is also of interest; not only is it embossed or cast with the crowded arrangement of strapwork enclosing terms and masks which is found so frequently on surviving Nürnberg silver of this date, but the flowers it contains are also cast in silver in allusion to Jamnitzer's famed skill in this particular respect. On the whole the credit should probably be given to Jamnitzer for his models; Sandrart in his brief biography of the master specifically describes him as *'ein guter Bosierer in Wachs von allerley Figuren, Bildern und Zieraten'* (a good modeller in wax of all kinds of figures, pictures and ornaments).

Wenzel Jamnitzer's grandson Christoph also had himself painted holding a model for a figure sculpture. The painting is the work of Lorenz Strauch and is dated 1597; the master goldsmith is shown holding a modelling tool in his right hand and a wax model of a Bacchus in his left (pl. 6). The fact that the model is evidently of wax implies that Christoph wished to emphasize the point that he could produce his own models. This is also suggested by his sketches in the sketch-book which he took over from his grandfather.[40] These show drawings of an Atlas figure which he subsequently executed as the stem of a globe-cup in the Royal Palace, Stockholm. While the Atlas derives from a bronze by Sansovino, Christoph did not fail to contribute something of his own to these models he copied from Italian sources. Apart from being a sculptor, Christoph Jamnitzer was also a draughtsman of considerable skill; this is indicated by his drawings preserved in the Berlin Kunstbibliothek and by two particularly attractive sheets of drawings of putti in the Germanisches Nationalmuseum, Nürnberg[41]

That Wenzel Jamnitzer was considered by later generations to have been a gifted sculptor is shown by the following extract from an undated, probably eighteenth century, advertisement for sale of a silver-mounted coconut-cup by Jamnitzer which was dated 1593 and was, so it was stated, worthy of being presented to 'Emperors, Kings, Electors and Princes'. After describing the cup in great detail it concludes with the statement 'The master of this valuable cup was Wenzel Jamnitzer, a Nürnberg goldsmith who also carved stone, ivory and coconuts with such artistry that neither before nor since has anyone equalled him either in goldsmiths' work or in carving'.[42] Wenzel Jamnitzer died in 1585, eight years before the date on the cup, but as this accompanied a coat-of-arms painted on a separate glass medallion, it could well have been added by a later owner.

Jamnitzer was on terms of close friendship with the sculptor, Andreas Albrecht, for in 1552 he obtained permission for Albrecht to spend two years in Lyon without loss of his rights as a citizen of Nürnberg on the grounds that he considered him to be so good an artist. Two years later he intervened again on Andreas' behalf to have the permit extended for an additional year.[43] Whether he also employed him is not known, but it seems likely. Among Jamnitzer's rivals in Nürnberg was Flötner's patron, Jacob Hofmann. The fact that he employed Flötner would seem to suggest that he was not able to produce his own models, but when he was admitted as a citizen of Nürnberg, he was actually described not as goldsmith but as sculptor (*Bildschnitzer*).

In spite of the considerable demand there must have been for figure sculpture in precious metal in the second half of the sixteenth century, either to form the stem or finial of a cup, or to adorn the sides of a shrine or casket it was not easy to find competent sculptors in Augsburg. That this was so is shown by an interesting exchange of correspondence between Duke Albrecht V of Bavaria and his agent in Augsburg, Marx Fugger, in 1576. The work for which the sculptor was required was to make a figure for the top of a reliquary to be presented to Philip II of Spain (see p.226). The choice eventually fell on a foreign goldsmith, Andreas Attemstett, and the first reference to him is in a letter[44] from Fugger to the Duke in which he states 'Now I think that your Grace should have the model made of lead, bronze or silver by Hadrian von Friedberg, and from this model the golden figure can be cast subsequently: as your Grace should know there is no goldsmith in the city here who can bring out the muscles and similar features in a statue as well as Hadrian'. Subsequently, on 3 February, 1576, Fugger writes again that Hadrian is working on the model and it will be something fine, for in producing a model in the antique manner there is no man in all Germany who can be compared with him.[45] Finally, on 8 February, Fugger sent Hadrian's model, which had been made in wax. He explained that the figure would be wrought except for the hands and feet which would be cast but these would remain hollow.

The Hadrian in question is believed to be the Dutch goldsmith, Andreas Attemstett[46]

(1528-1592) who was born in Groningen and from 1562 was employed by the Bavarian court. Apart from the evidence provided by Fugger's letters a further testimonial to Attemstett's exceptional skill can be found in a decree issued by the Emperor Rudolph II in 1582 requiring the city of Augsburg to admit him as a citizen and permit him to follow his craft despite the guild regulations to the contrary. In his petition to the Emperor in the year 1582 Attemstett gives some information about his work in the following terms, stating that 'I have learnt the goldsmith's craft both in embossed work and in modelling figures in the round both of gold and silver in Italy and other Provinces to such an extent and without exaggeration been so far gifted by Almighty God that I hope that no-one in Augsburg can equal me let alone do better.'[47] So confident of his skill was Attemstett that he repeated this claim on his tombstone: *Plastes, auri et argenti caelator, in orbe et urbe nulle secundus.*

It is often assumed that goldsmiths of the past maintained a consistently high standard of workmanship, and suspicion has as a result been thrown unjustly upon the authenticity of pieces which, though of second quality, are in fact genuine. Quality varied according to price then just as it does now; the main function of the guilds was after all to maintain purity of metal not quality. Even leading goldsmiths produced results that failed to satisfy their customers: thus a large table service delivered by the noted Nürnberg goldsmith, Melchior Baier, in 1532 to Cardinal Bernhard von Cles, Bishop of Trient, was criticised by its recipient on the grounds of the poverty of its workmanship in a letter he wrote to the Nürnberg humanist, Dr. Scheuerl, who had negotiated the commission.[48] The most likely complaint, to judge from surviving pieces, would relate to the engraved ornament; this might be of inferior quality because the goldsmith had carried it out himself instead of hiring a specialist engraver. The most likely risk that would be run by the purchaser would be to pay the cost of sterling standard silver for pieces in which an excessive amount of low grade solder had been used. More serious, but less frequent, was the practice of dishonest goldsmiths of making a cup of copper, then silvering it before its final gilding. In this case, a purchaser who lightly scraped the surface in order to ascertain whether it was of silver, would find the silver under the gilding and assume that he was acquiring a vessel entirely of precious metal.

As has been already mentioned, the craft of the goldsmith included mastery of the technique of seal die-cutting. There are repeated references to commissions to goldsmiths in Italy, Germany and elsewhere for the production of seal or medal dies. The art of cutting intaglio designs in hardstone was not far removed from that of cutting steel dies in which medals might be struck; Vasari makes this clear in his statement that the dies could be cut with wheels 'just as intaglio work is done in crystals, jaspers, chalcedonies and other oriental stones'. Though some goldsmiths were doubtless capable of working in hardstone, as a rule this was a separate art and the masters of whom one hears, such as Valerio Belli of Vicenza (known as *il Vicentino*), Matteo del Nassaro, Giovanni de Bernardi da Castel-bolognese, while they cut coin dies, did not usually carry out ordinary goldsmiths' work.

When working a transparent material such as rock-crystal the artist could see without difficulty how his work was progressing but his task was more difficult when he was engaged upon an opaque material such as metal or stone. Vasari[49] tells us that 'oriental stones are carved with wheels by means of emery, which cuts its way through any sort of hardness of any stone whatever'. He goes on to explain that the gem-cutter must repeatedly test the effect of the intaglio he is cutting by means of wax impressions, so that he can go on removing material 'where he thinks it necessary, until the final touches are given to the work.'

While the hardstone collection of Lorenzo de'Medici was provided with simple mounts that did little more than protect the edges of the vessels they enclosed, in the course of the sixteenth century the mounts became increasingly important. In the case of the Holbein cup (pls. 645-7) the mounts are already so rich as to overpower the rock-crystal vessel. As the art of engraving rock-crystal with figure subjects was developed, mainly in Milan, the gold mounts were of more restrained design in order to give full effect to the rock-crystal cutting. The hardstone vessels of the first half and on into the third quarter of the sixteenth century were cut from a single piece, but towards the end of the century, in an attempt to achieve more original and fantastic effects, they were constructed of several pieces joined together by collars of enamelled gold. In the case of articles so precious as carved hardstones it was essential to prepare one or more models for submission to the customer. As in the case of the goldsmiths' work, these might be of wood or wax or both, that is, a wood base upon which ornamental details were applied in wax. Fock quotes an account submitted by the sculptor, Orazio Mochi, in respect of four wax models to serve as designs for consideration for a hardstone vase.[50]

1   Doppelmayr, *Historische Nachricht von den Nürnbergischen...Künstlern*, Nürnberg, 1730, *'Er war der erste in Nürnberg, der mit einer besonderen Pressen Gold und Silber so schön druckte, als wann sie getrieben wären'*. The same author attributes the invention to another Nürnberg master as well, namely, Hans Lobsinger (1510-1570), who was also expert in casting figures from nature. After recounting his various skills Doppelmayr states *'dann aber noch andere verfertigte, mit dem Beyhülfe man alle Metallen so sauber in Figuren zu drucken vermogte, als wann sie getrieben wären'*. None of these stamped figures seem to have survived. As a rule casting was the preferred method when numbers of the same type of ornament or figure were required. Stamped plaques with the symbols of the Evangelists are found on late medieval crosses but this method seems to have been abandoned by the sixteenth century.

2   Berti, p.295, *'da più V. A. Ser. ma si potrà servire di detta edifitio non solamente per stampare tenari, ma ancora mille altre cosse bellissime come fresi e piastri per scrittoi, medaglie di ogni sorte, fiasgetti dargento con bellissimo relievo'*.

3   ill. Rosenberg II, pl. 41. Another version of this figure bearing the mark of Barthel Jamnitzer is in the Grünes Gewölbe, Dresden, ill. Rosenberg I, pl. 58.

4   Doering, 5-15 Dec. 1610, p.69-70. No sewing basket of comparable proportions and elaboration survives, but there is a simple one, now incomplete, in the Munich Schatzkammer, cat. no. 615. The basket is constructed of plaited silver wire, the cover is a plaquette embossed by or in the manner of Hans Jamnitzer.

5   Written communication by Dr. R. Fritz of Münster.

6   Vita I, 56 *'Seguitando appresso di servire il papa or di un piccolo lavoro or di un altro, m'impose che io gli facessi un disegno di un calice richissimo; il quale io feci il ditto disegno e modello. Era questo modello di legno e cera.'*

7   Plon, p.168 *'Per un modello de legno de una coppa datto a Mo Benvenuto, aurefice, per tirare una coppa de argento che lui ha da fare per il Rmo. Cardle.'*

8   Vasari, Vol. VI, p.135 *'Perciocche in que' tempi usavano; e non era tenuto buono orefice chi non era buon disegnatore, e che non lavorasse bene di rilievo'*.

9   Vita, I, 40, *'Io fui messo in opera da un certo maestro Nicolo milanese, il quale era orefice del duca di detto Mantova. Messo che io fui in opera, di poi dua giorni appresso io me ne andai a visitare misser Iulio Romano pittore eccelentissimo, gia ditto, molto mio amico, il quale misser Iulio mi fece carezze inestimabile, ed ebbe molto per male che io non ero andato a scavalcare a casa sua; il quale viveva da signore e faceva una opera pel duca fuor della porta di Mantova, luogo detto al Te.....Subito el ditto misser Iulio con molte onorate parole parlò di me al duca; il quale mi commesse che io gli facesse un modello per tenere la reliquia del Sangue di Christo che gli hanno, qual dicono essere stata portata quivi da Longino; di poi si volse al ditto misser Iulio, dicendogli che mi facessi un disegno per detto reliquiere. A questo, misser Iulio disse "Signore, Benvenuto è un uomo che non ha bisogno delli disegni d'altrui, e questo vostra eccellenzia benissimo lo giudichera quando la vedrà il suo modello".'*

10   *'Quel gran re Francesco mi teneva pagati piu di trenta lavoranti buoni a mia scelta, e con quelli io potevo impiegare me con tutte le dette importante opere, le quali tutte si facevano con i miei disegni'*.

11   *'A questi orafi, di queste cose belle bisogna lor fare è disegni. Al quale io subito mi volsi e dissi che io non avevo bisogno di sua disegni per l'arte mia; ma che io speravo bene con qualche tempo che con i mia disegni io darei noia all'arte sua'*.

12   This correspondence was first referred to by R. Bergau in *Wenzel Jamnitzer's Entwürfe*, Berlin, 1881. More recent investigations by Dr. Scheidig of the Staatliche Kunstsammlungen, Weimar, have shown that Bergau's account was incorrect in many details, and the corrected version is given here.

13 Philip Zwitzel belonged to a well-known Augsburg goldsmith family, he died in 1603. Wolf Schyrer or Scheurer was born in 1529 and died in Augsburg in 1605.

14 Doering p.50.

15 *Trattato dell' Oreficeria* XXII, 'Comincerai con la cera a farvi quelle galanterie che si 'ntervengono alla bocca et al manico, migliorando dal modello o disegno che arai fatto in prima. E finito bene con la cera detta tutti li sopradetti ornamenti, questi si forano in diversi modi; e quai modi non ci parra fatica a dirli tutti. Il piu facile che io ho sempre usato, e maggiormente in quel gran vaso che io dico aver fatto al re Francesco'.

16 *Trattato dell' Oreficeria* XXIV. 'E formate che le sieno in quel modo che sia possibile rispetto à sottosquadri . . . queste si gettano di piombo, e da poi si rinettano et assottigliansi in quel modo che torna bene al maestro; di poi si formano e gettansi d'argento in nelle medesimi staffe. E questo modo è bonissimo, perchè quando il maestro l' ha di piombo, e' la puo assottigliare nel modo sopra detto a suo proposito: e le dette forme di piombo possono servire da poi tutte le volte che uno se ne voglia servire'.

17 *Trattato dell' Oreficeria*, XIII, 'e mi sovviene una di queste arene rarissima, la qual si e nel fiume della Senna di Parigli...questa è sottilissima da per se, et ha una proprieta diversa dall'altra, che adoperandola in nel modo che si fa alle altre terre con le staffe, e non accade rasciugarla come alle altre terre si fa quando l'uomo ha formato quel che è vuole; ma subito formato che tu hai l'opera tua cosi umidiccia...vi si può gettar drento oro, argento et ottone, e tutti quei metalli che ti vengono in proposito. Questa e cosa rarissima, che mai l'ho sentito dire che tal cosa sia in altra parte del mondo'.

18 One of these models is illustrated in *Deutsche Kunst und Kultur*, Nürnberg, 1952, pl. 136.

19 See K. Pechstein, 'Der Bildschnitzer Hans Peisser', *Anzeiger des Germ. Nationalmuseums*, Nürnberg; 1973, p.84 and 1974, p.38ff.

20 When a goldsmith moved from one town to another he took his collection of models and drawings with him, as did Jacopo da Strada when he left Mantua. I. Weber, *Anzeiger des Germ. Nat. Museums*, 1966, 'Die Tiefenbronner Monstranz', p.76, n. 190 quotes a law suit between two goldsmiths in the year 1489-50 in which one accused the other of having improperly disposed of designs as well as clothing and tools, which had been left in pawn with him.

21 Frankenburger, p.6, no. 22.

22 They are described in the *Kunstkammer* inventory as 'blyin und silberne bildlin, vögelin, fischlin, thierlin, engelin, und ander vil Stück wie die Goldschmid bruchen'.

23 *Jahresbericht, Oeffentliche Sammlungen Basel*, Vol. LIX, 1907, p.25 Basilius Amerbach prepared two inventories, of which the first was dated 1565 and the second 1586, he died in 1591 within a few years of completing his second inventory. The first inventory shows that he owned five drawers full of goldsmiths' equipment, consisting of over 100 tools, 773 models made of wax, wood, clay and lead, stamps and dies for seals and coins and impressions thereof and 709 engravings. Some or all of these models and tools were acquired from a Basel goldsmith, Urs Schweiger and his brother Hans. Both were born in Augsburg and part of the collection of tools, models etc. had belonged to their father, Jörg Schweiger, a goldsmith of Augsburg.

    By 1586 Amerbach had acquired two more drawers full of goldsmiths' models, one containing plaquettes after models by Peter Flötner, the other the collection of models from the Jamnitzer workshop, which, it appears, had belonged to the Basel goldsmith, Jacob Hoffmann (died 1572). The inventory lists the contents of the cabinets as follows: the first cabinet, mainly tools; the second, models made of wood, plaster, wax and paper; the third, mainly wax impressions from seals; the fourth, models of plaster and terra-cotta; the fifth, models of lead and copper, including foliage, jewels, feet for cups and dagger-sheaths; the sixth the Flötner plaquettes, copper (bronze) plaquettes and roundels. In addition to the pieces he collected Amerbach inherited 31 vessels and spoons from the philosopher Erasmus, as well as a number of gold rings and of antique gold and silver coins. The whole collection was acquired by the city of Basel in 1662.

24 ill. F. A. Dreier, 'Hans Jakob Sprüngli aus Zürich', *Zeitschrift für Schweizerische Archäologie*, Band 21, 1961, pl. 6.

25 Early sources give varying accounts of the methods used by goldsmiths to produce fine castings. W. Salmon in his *Polygraphice*, London, 1677, states that fine casting sand mixed with bole (yellow clay) was used to provide the material of the mould, but that the impression was made in a lining of fine tripoli powder which was spread over the mould.

    Chambers Dictionary of 1786 states that goldsmiths commonly used powdered bone of cuttle-fish as a material in which to make fine castings that would require the minimum of finishing.

    Dossie in his *Handmaid to the Arts* (2nd edition, London, 1764) discusses the problem of the most suitable material, stating that if plaster is used difficulty is likely to be encountered in drying it out, especially if of great thickness. 'Figures, Beasts etc., may be cast of lead or any other metal in the moulds of plaster; only the expense of the plaster and the tediousness of its becoming sufficiently dry, when in a very large mass, to bear the heat of melted metal, render the use of clay, compounded with some other proper materials preferable where large subjects are in question. The clay in this case should be washed over till it be perfectly free from gravel or stones, and then mixed with a third

Plate V
Rock-crystal vase by the Saracchi family of Milan, the body intaglio-cut with the arms of the Dukes of
Bavaria, the mounts of enamelled and jewelled gold. About 1578.

Plate VI
Milanese rock-crystal dragon ewer, attributed to the Saracchi workshop. Late 16th century.

or more of fine sand to prevent its cracking....Whether plaster or clay be used for the casting of the metal, it is extremely important to have the mould perfectly dry, otherwise the mixture being rarified will make an explosion that will blow the metal out of the mould'.

In another pasage Dossie describes the method of making casts of very small articles in the manner practised by Wenzel Jamnitzer. 'There is a method of taking casts in metals from small animals and the parts of vegetables...the proper kinds of animals are lizards, snakes, frogs, birds or insects, the cast of which being properly coloured will be exact representations of the originals.

A casting chest is prepared of clay, the insect or flower to be cast is suspended in it by a string. Due quantity of plaster of Paris and calcined talc in equal quantities with a quantity of alumen plumosum (talc) is then mixed with water to the right consistency. The chest is then filled with the composition but at some time a straight stick as well as a number of pieces of thick wire must be inserted so as to touch the object to be cast. These are drawn out when the composition is set to provide pouring channels and also air vents. The mould is then heated until it is red-hot. The insect or leaf is thus completely calcined to ashes — which may then be blown out through the pouring channels and air vents. When cold the mould must be blown and shaken, alternatively it may be filled with quicksilver, as dust will rise to the top and pour out with it. The mould is then heated and the molten metal poured in. The mould is cooled and soaked in water so that the cast may be removed'.

26 There are also three sixteenth-century intaglio bronze plaquettes in the Museo Nazionale, Capodimonte, Naples.

27 Vasari, vol. VII. p.43, describes how the goldsmith, Girolamo da Prato, produced embossed representations of parts of the body for votive offerings. He placed a layer of wax, tallow or pitch between the silver sheet and his bench and hammered his work into this.

28 *Trattato dell' Oreficeria*, cap. XII, p.699, '*Avendo fatto il modello di cera, e resolutosi a quel che l'uomo voglia fare, e' si piglia la piastra d' oro in nel modo sopradetto, cioè che la sia sottile dagli lati, et un poco grossetta in mezzo. Fatto questo, si comincia pian piano con i ceselletti grossi a darle da rovescio, e fassi gonfiare un poco di bozze secondo che mostra il tuo modelletto; et a questo modo e' non occorre adoperare il bronzo, perchè innanzi che tu abbia gittato la tua medaglia di bronzo, tu arai condotta la tua opera molto bene innanzi...in questo modo sopra detto io feci un medaglia a un certo Girolamo Marretta Senese, nella qual medaglia si era uno Ercole che sbarrava la bocca a lione; e l'Ercole et il lione gli avevo fatti di tutto rilievo, che a pena e' si tenevano al campo con certe piccole attacature. E tutto questo era fatto nel sopradetto modo, senze bronzo, dando pian piano or da rovescio or da ritto tanto*'.

29 Hach, p.38. '*da etwa unter dessen Silberzeug ein Geschirr oder sonsten wäre, da etwa nicht gutte Kunst und Form daran wäre, daselbige dermassen fein zurichten und ganz und gar anders mit getriebener Arbeit und nicht von Patronen gegossen verarbeiten, dass E. E. Hochw. und Herrlichk. Lust daran haben soll, und begehr darumb nicht einzigen Pfenningk*'. This is a curious offer, for it would be exceedingly difficult to add further embossed ornament to an already finished object without distorting its shape.

30 *Trattato dell' Oreficeria*, cap. XII, *Lavorare di Minuteria*. '*Caradosso usava di fare un modelletto di cera appunto come ei voleva che la sua opera stessi; di poi pigiliava il suo bel modelletto; e ripieno tutti e sottosquadri, formava il detto modello, e lo gittava in bronzo, di ragionevol grossezza. Dipoi tirave una piastra d'oro alquanto grossetta in mezzo, non tanto pero che con facilita ei non l'avesse potuta piegare a suo modo, e la detta piastra era alquanto un poco piu grande due coste di coltello che il detto modello; di poi pigliava la detta piastra ben ricotta, et avendola tirata con poco colmetta, questa metteva sopra il detto model di bronzo, et con certi ceselletti, prima di legno da scopa, o di legno di corniolo, che son migliori, pian piano cominaiva a dargli la forma di quella figura, o, figure, che lui voleva fare*'.

31 *Trattato dell' Oreficeria*, cap. XXV.

32 *Trattato dell' Oreficeria*, cap. XXV, '*come per adietro io ho detto, per le tante faccende che si fanno in quel gran Parigi, io non viddi mai lavorare in altra parte del mondo con piu sicura practica di tirare di martello, che si fa in questa citta, e con tutta questa loro bella practica, mettendosi tutti quei migliori maestri a fare la detta statua, mai la condussero che l'avessi grazia, o bellezza o arte; il perche non la seppono mai saldare di modo che nel commettere le gambe, le braccia e la testa al corpo furno necessitati a legarla con fili di argento*'.

33 ibid. '*Io lavorai in Parigi opere di argento le maggiori che mai di tale arte si possa fare, e le piu difficile; e perche io mi servivo di molti lavoranti, e si bene come loro volentieri imparavano da me, ancora a me giovava imparare qualche cosa da loro*'.

34 Kohlhaussen, p.437.

35 A. Feulner, *Die deutsche Plastik des 16ten Jahrhunderts*, 1925, pls. 5, 6.

36 S. Meller, *Die deutschen Bronzestatuetten der Renaissance*, Munich, 1926, pl. 49.

37 H. Weihrauch, *Italienische Bronzen als Vorbilder deutscher Goldschmiedekunst'*, *Festschrift Theodor Müller*, Munich, 1965, p.263ff.

38 '*mit dem Bildhauer der sie bossiert, mit dem, der sie von Messing giesst, und mit dem, der sie*

verschneidet und der sie vergoldet'.

39   A contemporary replica of this portrait in the Historisches Museum Basel shows the same vase but partly gilt instead of white. While the figure of Neptune is white, the replica shows it gilt.

40   K. Pechstein, 'Eine unbekannte Entwurfsskizze für eine Goldschmiedeplastik von Christoph Jamnitzer', *Zeitschrift für Kunstgeschichte, Jahrgang 1968, p.314.*

41   Nos. Hz. 3899, 4069.

42   Frankenburger, p.41 *'Der Meister dieses kostbaren Pokals war Wenzel Jamnitzer, ein Nürnberger Goldarbeiter, der aber auch zugleich Steine, Elfenbein, Coccus Nüsse so künstlich geschnitten, dass vor und nach ihm keiner war, der es ihm weder in der Goldarbeit noch im Schneiden gleich gethan hätte'.*

43   ibid. ps. 8, 12, nos. 29, 41.

44   Stockbauer, p.96 *'Nun gedenkt mich aber dass E.F.G. das aus Blei, Kupfer oder Silber dem Hadrian von Friedberg machen lassen, von welchem man das goldne konnte abgiessen: den E.F.G. sollen wissen dass kein Goldschmied in der Stadt hier ist, der die Musculos und Art in einem Bilde besser kann herausbringen, als der Hadrian'.*

45   ibid. p.97, *'etwas Schönes werden, denn in Stellung eines Bossiments secundum venam antiquitatis ist keiner in Teutschland, der es ihm gleich mache'.*

46   This identification is due to Dr. Ulla Krempel. He is first mentioned in Munich in 1561, lived from 1563 to 1582 at Friedberg near Munich and from 1582 until his death in Augsburg. Hadrian is a possible variation of Andreas. See also Werner, *Augsburger Goldschmiede*, Augsburg, 1913.

47   Quoted from Krempel, p.140 *'das Goldschmied Hanndwerkh von getribener Arbait und Runnden Pilderen, aus Silber und Gold (ohne rheum zemelden) in Italia und andren Provintien dermassen erlehrnet uund von got dem Allmechtigen begabt, das mir solche Arbait verhoffentlichen, khainer in Augsburg gleich, vil weniger bevorthuen soll'.*

48   Kohlhaussen, p.440.

49   Vasari, I. p.164ff *'e quelle pietre orientali che noi dicemmo di sopra, s'intagliano di cavo con le ruote per forza di smeriglio, che con la ruota consuma ogni durezza di qualunque pietra si sia. E l'artifice va sempre improntando con cera quel cavo che e lavora; ed in questo modo va levando dove piu giudica di bisogno e dando fine all' opera... E di questa professione abbiamo visto opere mirabili e divinissimi, antiche e moderne'.*

50   Fock, p.112, where other references to models for hardstone vessels are cited.

CHAPTER FOUR

The Renaissance

THE Renaissance was a period of tranquillity between the taut emotionalism of late Gothic and the sophisticated ingenuity of Mannerism. In decorative art its expressions display logical arrangement, perfection of proportion, harmonious design and graceful profile. It was, however, no more than a brief moment in the history of the applied arts, and its principles were already being abandoned in Italy when they were first understood north of the Alps. In northern Europe Gothic survived until the second quarter of the sixteenth century, while by the 1540's Mannerist ornament was already creeping into goldsmiths' designs. This meant that in the north the Renaissance determined fashion in the goldsmiths' shops for barely twenty-five years. The rapid eclipse of so gracious a style is not easy to explain. It may be that during the Renaissance the emphasis on beauty of form and proportion exerted too great a restraint on the artists' independence and that they turned with relief to Mannerism, which placed more value on intellectual content (*concetto*) than on purity of form.

The moment at which the classical revival of the Renaissance reached the goldsmiths' shops of Europe varied from country to country. Italy was over a generation ahead of northern Europe in this respect and it was not until actual vessels, drawings of them, or printed pattern books by Italian masters, illustrating the style (or what was thought to be the style) of the ancient Roman goldsmiths penetrated north of the Alps that traditional Gothic forms were abandoned there. Once the Italian designs were available, they were eagerly followed by northern goldsmiths and the new style passed rapidly from one region and one city to another. While the original designs were Italian, they were soon copied by graphic artists working outside Italy. The latter, experimenting in a style that was unfamiliar, followed their sources closely, creating a uniformity that is a marked feature of Renaissance design. The pattern sheets of Italians such as Agostino Veneziano and Leonardo da Udine were followed in France by Jacques Androuet du Cerceau and the monogrammist ACD, in Germany by Albrecht Dürer the Younger, Albrecht Altdorfer, Heinrich Aldegrever, Daniel, Hieronymus and Lambert Hopfer and Hans Brosamer, in Switzerland and, subsequently, in England by Hans Holbein. Their designs show striking similarity, not only because they derive from a common Italian source, but also because they copied from each other.

The most important source of information available to the Italian graphic masters, and through them to the goldsmiths, in reviving classical ornament was the painted decoration of villas and palaces found under the ruins of ancient Rome. The best preserved and most influential of these was the Domus Aurea of the Emperor Nero, the ruins of which had been used to form part of the foundations of the baths of the Emperor Titus.[1] Its walls and ceilings, decorated with compartments enclosing figures and surrounded by floral scrolls, were buried well below the ground level of the fifteenth century and were, therefore, incorrectly assumed to have formed part of a grotto. It was this misunderstanding that led to the use of the term *grottesche* for Renaissance decorative schemes based on the fresco and stucco ornament of classical Rome. Some of the typical features of Mannerist art can already be recognised in the decoration of the Domus Aurea, such as the delight in metamorphosis, expressed in the mingling of animal and vegetable forms. Even the bound satyrs, which were later so beloved of the Flemish Mannerist designers, are represented; they presumably derived from the bound prisoners of Roman triumphs. The main distinction between antique and Renaissance grotesques is that the former were more linear, the latter more plastic in treatment. The most famous Renaissance decorative scheme based on the grotesques of the Domus Aurea is that of the Loggie of the Vatican, which was carried out by Raphael and his assistants between 1516 and 1519, It was, however, preceded by paintings by Signorelli, Perugino and Pintoricchio in which grotesques were used as decorative features framing a scene, and also by a series of engraved sheets of ornament by Italian engravers. There was a marked contrast between the grotesques of the Loggie and those devised by the masters of engraved ornament. Whereas the former are playful and highly imaginative, the latter are crowded and composed of ponderous elements copied from the sculptured reliefs of classical Rome. It was this heavier style that was to influence the goldsmiths.

The significance of the grotesque is that it was the earliest Renaissance ornament used by the goldsmiths; moreover the masters who designed and engraved these grotesques were familiar with classical vessel forms and included them in their decorative schemes. A number of Italian masters who were active in the last decade of the fifteenth and the first of the sixteenth century produced them: Nicoletto da Modena, Fra Antonio da Monza, Giovanni Antonio da Brescia, Giovanni Pietro da Birago and Zoan Andrea of Mantua.[2] Their earliest prints of ornament were pilaster panels composed of a vertical central feature, usually a tall vase or candelabrum, around which acanthus foliage, figures, trophies of arms and classical vases or ewers were placed symmetrically (pl. 7). The most elaborate vase forms are found in a set of engravings of pilaster ornament, formerly attributed to Zoan Ándrea but now thought to be the work of Giovanni Pietro da Birago.[3] Zoan Andrea, who was a contemporary of Andrea Mantegna at Mantua, was also familiar with classical vessel forms. Among his engravings is a design for a fountain of classical form with a typical Renaissance vase stem with putto supporters and pendent swags of foliage surmounted by a figure of Neptune.[4] The earliest engraving of vessels after Roman originals seems to be the plate by Giovanni da Brescia (pl. 8). This shows two pieces, a vase with a mask embossed on the body and a bowl supported by a tripod. It is sufficiently detailed to have served as a design for a practising goldsmith.

Nicoletto of Modena is known to have studied the Domus Aurea for he inscribed his name there when he visited it in 1507 as did Giovanni d'Udine, another early designer of grottesche. His work is of significance in a wider context, for his engravings were known to artists north of the Alps at an early date; the relief decoration of the Fugger chapel in the Annakirche, Augsburg, which was completed in 1518, is based on one of his prints.[5]

Following the example of the wall paintings of the Domus Aurea, Nicoletto da Modena developed an arrangement of compartments flanked by figures that was to become a standard device in the sixteenth century. This consisted of a centrally placed square or circular compartment, usually containing a scene from classical mythology set within a larger compartment, the intervening spaces being filled by standing or reclining figures. In one of Nicoletto da Modena's designs the central panels are enclosed by a narrow intersecting band which starts at the top as the extension of two dragon's tails and, after winding round two groups of five panels, terminates at the bottom in a dolphin.[6] From this modest beginning was to evolve, after a somewhat tentative development at the hands of Agostino Veneziano, the system of strapwork ornament that played so dominant a role in the decorative art of the mid and later 16th century. This strapwork appears in more robust form in the curious rolled over leather-like terminals of the figures decorating the base of Bandinelli's group of 'Hercules and Cacus' in front of the Palazzo Vecchio, Florence. This is dated 1533 and was therefore executed about the same time as the decoration of the Galerie François I at Fontainebleau, in which

Rosso and Primaticcio revolutionised the grotesque and transformed it into a system of ornament that was to dominate European decorative art for the remainder of the century and even longer. Mannerist ornament was thus the invention of two masters whose training had followed the usual course of the Italian Renaissance. The system of Fontainebleau with medallions enclosing scenes from classical history or mythology or landscapes, set within elaborate strapwork cartouches interspersed with figures and animals derives directly from the Roman grotesque. But the Fontainebleau masters such as the etcher, Antonio Fantuzzi, and the engraver, René Boyvin, found in northern Europe a more willing market for their prints than had the Italian engravers of the early Renaissance. It is, perhaps, for this reason that Mannerist ornament was more widely and ingeniously exploited in northern than in southern Europe.

Though Italian Renaissance masters drew their inspiration from classical sources, they did not merely copy them. This is shown by their introduction of other themes and, in particular, of the mauresque. This was a design composed of flat stylised vegetable forms, which was derived from a Near Eastern source. Nicoletto da Modena introduces less stylised arabesque-like forms into his grotesques at an early date, but the first printed pattern book of mauresques to appear in Europe is signed by the master 'F'. He is identified by Berliner as Domenico da Sera[7] and the book is believed to have appeared in the 1520's.

The popularity of the true Moslem arabesque, then usually described as a mauresque, is one of the more surprising incidents of the Renaissance. This form of ornament had been known in Spain during the Middle Ages, but was now introduced through Venice and soon became an important element in the goldsmiths' vocabulary of ornament. It was formerly held that Saracenic workmen, who had established themselves in Venice during the twelfth or thirteenth century, were responsible for its introduction to Italy, but more recently it has been suggested that Moslem craftsmen would not have been allowed to practice their craft in a Christian city during the Middle Ages.[8] It is at all events certain that large basins and ewers damascened with gold and silver were produced for Italian customers by Saracenic masters in the late fifteenth or early sixteenth centuries and these were soon copied by Italians in Venice and, perhaps, elsewhere. The engraved ornament of these last vessels is usually a mixture of Renaissance and Near-Eastern elements.

The pattern-book of the master 'F' (Domenico da Sera?) was soon followed by Francesco Pellegrino's '*La fleur de la science de broderie, façon arabisque et ytalique*' published in Paris in 1530. The title seems to indicate that this type of decoration was first associated with embroidery. The author of this substantial book of sixty sheets of designs was a Florentine artist who had been brought to work at Fontainebleau as an assistant to Rosso Fiorentino. Pellegrino's designs were soon followed by another similar publication in France by Jacques Androuet du Cerceau. This appeared in Paris about 1540 and was plagiarised in England by Thomas Geminus. Thereafter books of mauresques were published in the Low Countries by Balthasar Sylvius and in Zürich by Peter Flötner. Early Renaissance taste seems to have accepted so peculiar a combination as ornament of oriental derivation applied to vessels of impeccable classical form. One of the earliest examples of this combination is the salt-cellar, of either Italian or perhaps French origin illustrated in pl. 243. The design is of pure classical taste with a frieze of dancing maidens, yet the upper border is engraved with mauresques.

During the sixteenth century there was a switch of emphasis of production from ecclesiastical to secular plate. The reason for this was the greater wealth of the merchant class who now joined the aristocracy and church as major sources of commissions. The first consequence of the adoption of the Renaissance style by the goldsmiths was the abandonment of tall Gothic forms in favour of rather squat designs in which the horizontal was more strongly stressed than the vertical. This trend is evident in all countries of western Europe, but is more particularly noticeable in secular plate, though the standing cup and cover continued to be a dominating object on the table. In the case of ecclesiastical plate, where tradition was stronger, there was little change. While the detail of ornament was now classical instead of Gothic, the shapes and profiles of monstrances, chalices and reliquaries remained much the same. It was in northern Europe, especially in Germany, that both the ornament and the flowing perpendicular movement of late Gothic lasted longest.

The foot of a Renaissance vessel is of adequate proportions to support the bowl, the handle occupies a functional position and, most important of all, the piece is constructed in a series of horizontal members, each of which is clearly separated from that above and below by a moulding or frieze (pl. 290). The late medieval secular standing cup was supported on a trumpet-shaped foot; in place of the knop, a leaf-cresting descended from the base of the bowl enclosing the upper part of the stem. The central point of the baluster stem of a Renaissance cup is marked by a disc-shaped knop, derived from the knop of the medieval chalice, which in turn was based on the Romanesque drinking-cup. During the second half of the sixteenth century the disc knop was replaced by one of vase form, which became a consistent feature of northern drinking vessels.

Two conflicting movements can be traced in the goldsmiths' art of the Renaissance; while the determining factor was clearly the revival of classical antiquity, an interest in naturalism was also expressed and can be recognised in the many drinking-cups formed like apples, pears or exotic fruits. This trend was more marked in northern Europe, in particular in the designs of Albrecht Dürer and in surviving vessels made under his influence or in some cases after his designs. One of the chief aims of the Renaissance goldsmith was to equal the achievements of his classical Roman predecessors and the highest praise he could receive was the recognition of his work as worthy of comparison with that of ancient Rome. This attitude is illustrated by a passage in Cellini's *Vita*. He relates as one of his greatest triumphs the incident when he showed to Michelangelo a gold relief of Hercules overcoming the Nemean lion which he had wrought himself.[9] After studying it for a while the great master said 'If this work were made to a larger scale in marble or bronze and to so beautiful a design, it would astonish the world; I find it to be so beautiful made in this size that I do not believe the goldsmiths of antiquity would ever have done it so well'.

When sixteenth-century vessels, that were thought by their creators to derive from classical Roman originals, are examined, it is striking how little they resemble what we now recognise as classical antiquities. With the exception of coins, the source material available to the early Renaissance designer was not made of precious metal at all, but of marble or bronze. Virtually no classical goldsmith's work was to be seen until the discovery of Pompeii and Herculaneum two centuries later; in their endeavour to reconstruct the style of the ancient Romans the Renaissance designers had to combine ideas draw from such disparate sources as architecture, sculpture, decorative painting, cameos and intaglios. Such was the uncertainty about the nature of the vessels used in classical antiquity that an artist of the Fontainebleau school in depicting a banquet has set on the table as a sauce-boat a vessel which is derived from a Roman lamp.[10]

A natural consequence of the Renaissance was an increased interest in artefacts surviving from classical Rome. From the point of view of the goldsmith the most useful were cameos, intaglios and gold coins, all of which could be incorporated in new pieces, thus giving them an aura of antiquity. While the first two existed in some quantity, the gold coins were difficult to obtain and it was often necessary to make do with contemporary copies which were then passed off as genuine antiquities. Most surviving vessels decorated with antique cameos or coins, such as the clock-salt in pl. 251 or the coin-cups in pls. 283, 284, 256 and 278 are set with sixteenth-century reproductions. The best documented example is the gold bowl in the Grünes Gewölbe, Dresden,[11] which is set with twenty-two casts from Roman coins. This was presented in 1508 by Augustin Kesenbrot of Olmütz, Chancellor of King Ladislaus II of Hungary, to an association of humanists known as the Danubian Society. A number of other bowls decorated with classical Greek or Roman coins survive. As a rule they rely on the coins for their ornament but are otherwise plain. The gold bowl illustrated in pl. XII is somewhat of an exception in that it stands on foot and stem like a tazza and has enamelled gold enrichment as well. The presence of the latter detracts from the classical Roman character that was the usual aim of the Renaissance goldsmith; it also suggests a date towards the middle of the sixteenth century, somewhat later than other recorded examples. The practice of decorating drinking vessels with coins set in the bowl or drum continued during the second half of the century, but the coins were usually contemporary. The cup of Christof Reinfart of Worms of 1571, is set with fifty-three coins, of which only thirteen are antique (pl. XIX).

Most of the surviving Italian, Spanish and French silver in early Renaissance style was made for the service of the altar, and, in order to obtain an adequate picture of the appearance and development of secular plate, we have to rely mainly on pictorial sources. At first sight the large number of paintings of the Adoration of the Kings, in which richly decorated vessels containing the offerings of gold, frankincense and myrrh are shown, would seem to provide the best source of information. One of the most comprehensive displays of Italian silver is to be seen in Filippino Lippi's fresco of St. Philip exorcising the Devil in the Strozzi Chapel in the church of Santa Maria Novella, Florence. These representations, though doubtless based on contemporary types, are not altogether reliable, as the artist's imagination so often played some part in their delineation. The most satisfactory source is, therefore, to be found in the drawings that were prepared for the goldsmith. Even these must be treated with discretion, for the graphic artist wielding his pencil is likely to devise adventurous forms which the goldsmith may not be able to translate into terms of precious metal. Between the artist's design and the executed silver vessel there was once a working drawing, in which the flights of the artist's imagination had been brought down to earth, but such working drawings have hardly ever survived and, apparently, not at all in the case of Italian and French goldsmiths' work of the Renaissance.

The earliest surviving secular vessels that show Renaissance detail formed part of the collection of silver-mounted hardstone cups of the Florentine Lorenzo de'Medici. They were wrought by the Florentine goldsmith, Giusto da Firenze, in the third quarter of the fifteenth century.[12] Giusto's mounts still show a mixture of Gothic and Classical elements, but other cups in the same collection are already mounted in a pure Renaissance style. These were either not mounted until the early sixteenth century or, possibly, later mounts were substituted for the Gothic ones. They show a purity of style that is rarely seen either in contemporary designs or in surviving Italian goldsmiths' work. This restraint may have been because more importance was given to the hardstone vessel than to the mount and the goldsmith was prevented from displaying his ability to the full. The vases in the Medici collection were, or were thought to be, of antique origin and for this reason an effort was made to mount them in the fashion of classical antiquity. That this was not necessarily successful is shown by the sardonyx vase illustrated in pl. III. The mounts in this case bear no resemblance to their supposed prototype. On the other hand, the Italian goldsmiths of the Renaissance sometimes achieved a most convincing copy of a classical frieze as on the salt-cellar illustrated in pl. 243.

The importance accorded to the collection of Lorenzo il Magnifico at the time can be judged from a letter written to Isabella d'Este, the wife of Francesco Gonzaga of Mantua.[13] She had heard that some of the vases from the Medici collection were to be sold and wrote to her agent, Francesco Malatesta, asking him to consult Leonardo da Vinci about their value. He replied on May 3, 1502, 'I have shown them to Leonardo Vinci, the painter, as Your Highness desired. He praises them all, but especially the crystal vase which is all of one piece and very fine, and has a silver gilt foot and cover and Leonardo says that he never saw a finer thing. The agate one also pleases him, because it is a rare thing and of large size, and is all in one piece, excepting the foot and cover, which are silver-gilt; but it is cracked. That of amethyst or as Leonardo calls it, of jasper, is transparent and of variegated colours, and has a masssive gold foot, studded with so many pearls and rubies that they are valued at 150 ducats. This greatly pleased Leonardo, as being something quite new and exquisite in colour. All four have Lorenzo Medici's name engraved in Roman letters on the body of the vase, and are valued at very high prices: the crystal vase at 350 ducats: the jasper vase at 240 ducats: the agate vase at 200 ducats: and the jasper vase on a plain stand at 150 ducats'. Malatesta also sent coloured drawings of four of the vases but the prices proved too high for Isabella d'Este and she made no acquisitions from the collection.

The Renaissance style in the goldsmiths' shops of western Europe was surprisingly uniform during the first three decades of the sixteenth century. Once the style was familiar, the goldsmith could indulge his imagination, but in the early days he kept close to the pattern-book. Vessels such as tazzas, which were common to most European countries, were so similar that they can barely be distinguished if the goldsmith has not struck his mark, even when produced in towns geographically remote from each other. This uniformity was not exclusive to the goldsmiths' shops; it is typical of the applied arts of the Renaissance as a whole and presents a marked contrast to the many local variations found in late Gothic art. While fashion in design was uniform, there were variations in the types of vessel used in different countries. Thus the tankard was confined to the beer-drinking regions and was unknown in France and the Mediterranean countries. The beaker was also a northern form and does not seem to have penetrated to Italy or Spain. In the same way the tall standing cup that was so popular in northern Europe and, in particular, in the German speaking regions, seems, to judge by the surviving examples, to have been unknown in Italy and Spain. This type of cup, which was also produced in the Netherlands, in England, Switzerland and, perhaps, in France as well, was regarded in the last country as specifically German. This is indicated by the inscription '*Couppe à la mode dallemagne*' on the du Cerceau drawing of such a cup illustrated in pl. 24. The large vases, either with or without cover, which Cellini describes as '*acquareccie*' of which a drawing is illustrated in pl. 9, seem to have been confined to Spain and Italy and not to have been made north of the Alps. On the other hand the ewer and basin were fairly international and varied little from country to country.

With very few exceptions the work of the medieval goldsmith is anonymous; there is usually no maker's mark, nor is the designer's name known. During the Renaissance no such obscurity surrounds the goldsmith. The most prominent masters of the age produced designs for them: Raphael, Michelangelo, Rosso, Dürer, Holbein to mention but a few. Benvenuto Cellini, the most famous goldsmith of all time, was a goldsmith of the Renaissance before he became one of the leading protagonists of Mannerism. He also produced lengthy and instructive treatises on his art, as did subsequently the German masters, Wenzel Jamnitzer and Hans Lencker, and the Spanish master, Juan de Arfe. The Renaissance artist *par excellence* was a person of universal genius; the Renaissance goldsmith also possessed a wide range of competence. Many other examples will be referred to in the course of this book, but Ludwig Krug of Nürnberg can be taken as a typical master goldsmith of his time. He followed the same craft as his father, worked flat plate, modelled and cast silver statuettes. He is recorded as a sculptor in stone from 1514, as a bronze sculptor from 1515, as a draughtsman and engraver from 1516 and finally as a designer of woodcuts and a medal die-cutter between 1525 and 1527. He is believed to have been a painter as well, though no paintings from his hand have as yet been identified.

1   For a detailed study of the Domus Aurea see Nicole Dacos. *La Découverte de la Domus Aurea et la fonction des grotesques à la Renaissance.* London, 1969.

2   For a discussion of these masters see Berliner, Textband, p.138-145 and *Early Italian Engravings,* National Gallery of Art, Washington, 1973.

3   ill. Berliner, Vol. I, pls. 83-86, but see also *Early Italian Engravings,* Washington 1973, for more recent attributions.

4 ill. *Early Italian Engravings* pl. 100.

5 Berliner, Textband, p.14-15. Vol. I, pls. 29-30.

6 ibid. Vol. I, pl. 30.

7 Berliner, Vol. I, pls. 83-90.

8 H. Huth, 'Sarazenen in Venedig', *Festschrift für Heinz Ladendorf,* Köln, 1970. p.57ff.

9 *Trattato dell' Oreficeria,* cap. XII, p.699. '*se questa opera fussi grande, o di marmo o di bronzo, condotta con questo bel disegno, la farebbe stupire il mondo, si che di questa grandezza io la veggo tanto bella, che io non credo mai che quegli orefici antichi facessero tanto bene'.*

10 For an illustration of this engraving by the monogrammist L.D. see Fontainebleau II, Cat. no. 385.

11 ill. Sponsel. Vol. II, pl. I. Kohlhaussen, Cat. No. 416.

12 ill. Heikamp and Grote, pls. 23, 24, 46-50.

13 A. Luzio, *Archivio Storico dell' Arte,* Rome, 1888, Vol. I, p.181. The full text of the letter, which is dated 12.V.1502, runs:

Ill ma Madonna mia

Per Alberto Chavalaro mando a la S.V. li disegni de li vasi et quella me ha scripto per la sua de 2 del presente, disegnati per iusta misura et choloriti de li proprii cholori ma non con el proprio lustro perchè questo è impossibile a li dipintori a saperlo fare. Et perchè la S.V. possa ellegere quello chè piu li piacerà, m'e parso mandar li disegni de tutto quatro li vasi. Li ho facti vedere a Leonardo Vinci depintore, si come la S.V. me scrive: esso li lauda molto tutti, ma specialmente quello di cristallo, perche è tutto de uno pezo integro e molto netto dal piede e coperchio in fiora che è di argento sopra indorato, et dice el prefato Leonardo che mai vide el mazor pezo. Quello di agata anchora li piace, perchè è cosa rara et è gran pezo, et è un pezo solo, exceptel piede e coperchio che è pur de argento indorato, ma è rotto si come la S. V. pora vedere per le virgule signate in el corpo di esso vaso. Quello di diaspris simplice è uno pezo netto et integro, et ha el piede come ho ditto de sopra de argento sopradorato. Quello de amatista, overo diaspris, si come Leonardo lo bateza, che è di varie misture di cholorite et e transparente, ha el piede de oro masizo et ha tante perle et rubini intorno che sono indichate di prezio de 150 duc. Questo molto piace a Leonardo, per esser chosa nova et per la diversità de cholori mirabile. Tutti hanno intagliato nel corpo del vaso littere maiuschule chè dimostrano el nome de Laurenzo Medice.

CHAPTER FIVE

The Renaissance Goldsmiths

Italy

THE chief Italian centres of the craft were Rome, Florence, Milan and Venice, but there were probably few cities that could not claim a skilled goldsmith. The fact that Cellini spent his working life in Rome and Florence, apart from the not infrequent occasions when he was compelled by warfare, plague or the consequences of his own unruly life to move and seek employment elsewhere, implies that the best commissions were to be had in those cities. The demand for fine goldsmith's work was greater in Italy than in the kingdoms north of the Alps owing to the existence of a large number of small but rich Italian principalities, each with their independent or semi-independent ruler. These either retained their own court goldsmith or competed with each other to secure the services of the most competent masters. The Popes and Cardinals also provided a constant source of important commissions and their wealth attracted to Rome the more ambitious goldsmiths not only from Italy but from the Netherlands, Germany and Spain. The significance of Rome as a source of commissions was, however, completely eliminated in 1527 when the city was captured and looted by an Imperial army, composed mainly of German and Spanish troops. The Sack of Rome was the more drastic as the Imperial commander, the Constable Charles de Bourbon, who might have restrained his men, fell in the initial assault on the city. Clement VII abandoned the city and the occupation lasted six months, during which time those who possessed any fortune were compelled to ransom their lives by surrendering their wealth. When eventually the Imperial army withdrew they left a city from which a large proportion of the inhabitants, including all the artists, had fled, and there can have been few commissions for goldsmiths, the more so as all the precious metal in the city had been removed by the troops who did not hesitate to use torture to discover the whereabouts of hidden treasure. The only artist who seems to have saved much from the Sack was Benvenuto Cellini who escaped to Florence with the money he had earned as a soldier fighting in the defence of the Castel Sant' Angelo. The Sack marked the end of the Renaissance in the city; by the time artistic life was resumed there, another manner was in fashion.

The effect of the Sack can be measured by the fact that five years later in 1532 the Rome goldsmiths' guild, the *Confraternita di San Eligio*, numbered only thirty master goldsmiths and eighteen workmen. Pope Clement VII was a lavish patron of the goldsmiths and in 1532 presented no fewer than fifty vases, caskets, etc., of rock-crystal and other precious materials to the Florentine church of San Lorenzo for use as reliquaries, many of which are still preserved in the treasury of the Capella dei Principi attached to San Lorenzo or in the Plazzo Pitti. These, however, mostly came from the Medici treasury in Florence and were not of Roman manufacture.

The earliest representations of goldsmiths' work in engraved ornament are merely decorative adjuncts, inserted to fill a space in a pilaster panel (pl. 7). The engraver did not aim at archaeological accuracy, though some of the vessels shown are of recognisably antique form. Starting out from such modest beginnings the designers soon evolved vessels of more complex form, such as that in the drawing illustrated in pl. 9, which is attributed to a Paduan master. The early Renaissance style represented by this drawing can no longer be studied in secular plate, but is still to be found, though in less elaborate form, in ecclesiastical plate such as the reliquary of Saint Eutitius[1] in the Spoleto Gallery, or in the simple gilt-copper cross-foot (pl. 715).

The next generation of Italian masters of engraved ornament claimed that their prints reproduced the exact forms of excavated vases and ewers. Between 1530 and 1544 three sets of engravings were published by the Venetian, Agostino dei Musi, also known as Agostino Veneziano, by Leonardo da Udine, and by Enea Vico respectively. The first of these produced a set of twelve sheets signed A.V. and dated either 1530 or 1531. Each sheet is inscribed '*Sic Roma Antiqui Sculptures ex Aere et Marmore faciebant*'. The second set by Leonardo da Udine consisted of ten sheets '*ex romanis antiquitatibus*' dated between 1542 and 1544, while Enea Vico's set, the precise extent of which is not known, is inscribed '*Romae ab antiquo repertum*'. It is uncertain to what extent the Renaissance designers had original excavated vases available to copy, but, judging by the representations of antique vessels provided in the three aforementioned sets of engravings, it seems likely that they were in more or less fragmentary condition and that a great deal of imagination was used in conjecturally restoring the missing parts. While the bodies of the vases were copied fairly faithfully from the classical originals (pl. 11), the handles and spouts with their relief ornament, which were evidently missing, were replaced with quite fantastic conceits (pl. 14). As might be expected, Agostino dei Musi's reconstructions of 1530-31 (pls. 11 and 12) are the most restrained, while Enea Vico's of 1543 display more sophisticated vessel forms and mannered detail (pl. 13). It is possible that the sources used by these sixteenth-century engravers were not actual vases but representations of them on reliefs from antique sepulchral monuments.[2] These last might be more adventurous in conception than vessels that were made for practical use, but even so there can be no doubt that the Italian masters of ornament took great liberties with their sources in spite of their claims to the opposite.

Among the gold or silver-gilt vessels that are frequently represented in Italian Renaissance painting one of the most usual is a large vase without a cover and with two handles. Cellini's second employer in Rome, Lucagnolo di Jesi, made one of these for Pope Clement VII (1523-1534) of which he says[3] 'Lucagnolo's was a huge silver piece, used at the table of Pope Clement, into which he flung away bits of bone and the rind of various fruits while eating: an object of display rather than of necessity. The vase was adorned with two fine handles, together with many masks, both large and small and masses of foliage, in as exquisite a style of elegance as could be imagined, on seeing which, I said it was the most beautiful vase I ever set eyes upon'. Cellini was working for Lucagnolo between 1523 and 1524 and the vase to which he referred probably resembled the type illustrated in pl. 9. Drawings of this early period are rare, but the style of the early decades of the century is represented by this and by another drawing, formerly attributed to Baldassare Peruzzi, for a circular dish or bowl supported by three putti on a baluster stem and triangular base (pl. 10). While it would be difficult to find a parallel to this piece in extant Italian silver, it does recall the design of altar candlesticks of the period, such as the bronze Paschal candlestick in the Santo at Padua,[4] an object of elaborate but logical and dignified form that was completed by Andrea Riccio of Padua in 1516. An authentic but rather damaged drawing by Peruzzi in the British Museum[5] represents a large dish or basin decorated with scenes from the Old Testament story of Joseph and with the destruction of Pharaoh's army on the central boss. An interesting feature of the design is the way in which the various scenes round the border are separated from each other by groups of columns; this solution of the problem of showing different subjects on a continuous frieze was also used by the goldsmith who wrought the dish (pl. 266). Peruzzi's drawing dates from the second decade of the century and reflects the style of Raphael. In comparison with designs such as those in pls. 9 or 10, which were also supposedly based on classical antiquity, Agostino Veneziano's engraving of a Roman vase reconstructed from the evidence of excavations in Rome (pl. 11) seems extremely sober.

Few drawings by Raphael for goldsmiths have been identified: among the Windsor Castle drawings is a single sheet from his hand with on the verso a rapidly sketched design for the border of a tazza;[6] the theme being just such nymphs and tritons as were later employed by Salviati. The goldsmith Cesarino of Perugia made two bronze salvers to the order of Agostino Chigi in 1510 from Raphael's designs and Raphael also designed the bronze perfume-burner of François I (see p.85). While the drawings almost invariably show pieces of complex design, extant examples of Italian Renaissance silver are usually of unpretentious character, such as a plain unmarked tazza in the Untermyer Collection.[7]

Valerio Belli

The first of the Italian Renaissance masters who is sufficiently well represented by extant examples of his work for us to arrive at any comprehensive idea of his manner is Valerio Belli of Vicenza. He was born in 1460 and went to Rome to work for Leo X (1513-1522) and remained there in the employ of Clement VII (1523-1534). Active as a medal die-cutter, rock-crystal carver and to a lesser extent as a goldsmith, his work is recognised by the rock-crystal panels which he signed, but it is very probable that he was responsible for some at least of the mounts of precious metal in which they were set. Contemporary documents refer to him as *Aurifex* (goldsmith) as well as *Excellentissimo gemmarum scultore* (highly gifted gem carver).

During his long stay in Rome, which lasted until 1530, he was much influenced by contemporary artists there, in particular by Raphael and Michelangelo; according to Vasari he collected drawings by these two masters. He also collected antiquities excavated from ancient Rome and purchased plaster casts of both ancient and modern works. His rock-crystal intaglios gained a high reputation; moulds were taken from them, from which casts in bronze and lead were made and sold to collectors and to goldsmiths as models.

Belli's most famous work is the rock-crystal casket in the Museo degli Argenti, Florence,[8] usually known as the *Cassetta del Belli* (pl. 244). This was commissioned by Pope Clement VII as a present to François I on the occasion of the marriage of his son, the future Henri II to Catherine de' Medici. It bears the date of its completion in 1532, but several earlier pieces of ecclesiastical plate by Belli have been identified in recent years. The earliest is a reliquary of the Holy Cross[9] in the Treasury of San Marco, Venice, which can be dated about 1508; this is followed by the basin in the Munich Residenz which bears the arms of Pope Leo X and must therefore have been completed before 1521 (pl. 245). Of particular splendour is the altar set of cross and two candlesticks in the Victoria and Albert Museum, which appears to date from about the same period as the basin. This altar set was formerly identified with one that was being made by Belli for Pope Clement VII in 1533 and was first paid for by Paul III in 1546 after the death of its maker. This identification is, however, not altogether convincing as the style of ornament seems archaic for the 1530's. All these objects dating from the 1510-20 decade are of silver or silver-gilt, enriched with translucent polychrome enamels and mounted with rock crystal plaques. The plaques are not signed but are so similar to Belli's signed works that their attribution can be accepted without question. They stand out among other Italian goldsmiths' work of the Renaissance on account of their architectural construction and the restrained nature of their decoration, which expresses so justly the Renaissance ideal. Their effect is greatly enhanced by the translucent enamelled ornament; on the reliquary this is confined to formal scrollwork, but subsequently flowers were introduced, though still of conventional design. It seems likely that Valerio Belli was the maker or, at any rate, the designer of these mounts, whereas those on the casket commissioned by Clement VII may be by another hand. Valerio Belli went to Venice in the late 1520's but he seems to have had earlier contacts with the city, for the reliquary of 1508 was made for a member of the Morosini family, while the altar set in London came from the Grimanis, both influential Venetian patrician families.

The exquisite sense of proportion and classical design of the Italian Renaissance seen in the works of Valerio Belli is also shown by the miniature gold casket in the form of a sarcophagus, illustrated in pl. 246. It is difficult to determine what purpose this attractive piece was originally intended to serve, unless as a valuable receptacle for some even more precious jewel. The absence of any religious symbol in its decoration makes it unlikely that it was intended to contain a relic. The frieze which surrounds the casket is composed of scrolling foliage inhabited by minute figures of birds, while the terminals are of varying design. Cellini also took an antique source for a casket when he first went to Rome and entered the employment of Giovanni de Georgis, known as Firenzuola; his first commission was to make a salt cellar of sarcophagus form for an unnamed cardinal. This was to be 'a little casket, copied from the porphyry sarcophagus before the door of the Rotunda (i.e. the Pantheon). Beside what I copied, I enriched it with so many elegant masks of my own invention....It was about half a cubit in size, and was so constructed to serve for a salt cellar at table'.[10] The salt does not survive but it was presumably a larger version of the Italian gold casket described above, though the latter is probably somewhat earlier in date. The Pantheon sarcophagus was of classical origin and the success with which Cellini completed this task encouraged him to study other classical remains in Rome. Caskets of various sizes and materials have survived in some number from the Italian Renaissance; the finest of them is that of silver-gilt in the Munich *Schatzkammer*. This is decorated with the most restrained Renaissance ornament alternating with small diamonds, rubies and emeralds in collets enamelled white, blue and black. The four corners are embellished with engraved mauresques and set with diamonds; as the casket is included in the Disposition of Albrecht V of 1565, it must have been regarded as one of the treasures of the Wittelsbach Dukes of Bavaria.[11] Of about the same date, but constructed of more various materials, is the silver-gilt and rock-crystal casket in pl. 247. In this case the mauresques, instead of being confined inconspicuously to the corners, form the main feature of the decoration. The original purpose of this casket is uncertain. Larger caskets of similar construction are believed to have contained layettes and to have been presented to noble ladies after the birth of their first-born son. The smaller ones were intended, like the mid-sixteenth-century casket containing the relics of Saint Felix, formerly in the Vienna Schatzkammer,[12] to serve as reliquaries. This casket is of enamelled gold set with rock-crystal plaques, engraved with figures copied from the predella of the painting of the Entombment by Raphael in the Vatican. Here the decoration of enamelled mauresques is on the underside of the base.

Another workshop that followed a manner very similar to that of Valerio Belli is represented by a magnificent service of altar plate in the Museo dell' Opera, presented to the Cathedral of Siena by Pope Alexander VII (1655-57), and by a ewer formerly in the Hermitage, Leningrad, (pl. II). The fact that the service was given in the seventeenth century led one writer to assume that it was of seventeenth-century manufacture, but it can hardly be later than the mid-sixteenth. It consists of chalice, paten, pax, incense-boat and cover with spoon, incense burner, holy water bucket and sprinkler, tazza, a pair of cruets and a pair of tall altar candlesticks.[13] The service is of rock-crystal with mounts of silver-gilt enriched with polychrome translucent enamel. The rock-crystal elements are carved with spiral gadroons similar to the bowl of the ewer illustrated in pl. II and probably come from the same workshop. The bowl of the tazza in the service is supported on a stem composed of three twisted snakes, similar to the two snakes that form the handle of the ewer. While the colour scheme of the enamels of the altar service is clearly related to the earlier Valerio Belli group, the ornament now consists entirely, or, in the case of the ewer, mainly, of large naturalistic flowers rendered in translucent enamels with the greatest subtlety. Such features as the intertwined snake stem of the tazza, the mauresque border and the snake handle of the ewer can scarcely be much earlier than the middle of the century. The presence of this altar service in Siena suggests a Tuscan, probably Florentine, origin, an idea supported by the existence of a further piece, apparently from the same workshop, in the Medici Treasury. This is a rock-crystal bowl on low foot with the foot and cover of silver-gilt profusely enamelled with naturalistic flowers. The bowl is cut with gadroons in a similar manner to the ewer illustrated in pl. II. The splendid preservation of this vessel and the beauty of the rock-crystal cutting combine to make it one of the most pleasing surviving examples of Italian Renaissance goldsmith's work. It represents the full flowering of this style just before it gave way to the more sophisticated manner of the third quarter of the century. Snake handles and spouts of shell form supported by mermaids are found not only on the ewer (pl. II) and on the tazza in the altar service in Siena, but also on two vessels from the former French royal collection that are now in the Prado with the Trésor du Grand Dauphin. All four have rock-crystal bodies cut with spiral gadroons. A similar rock-crystal body can be seen on the French ewer from the royal collection (pls. 370-1). Furthermore, the maures-ques on the ewer (pl. II), while of silver-gilt instead of gold, do recall the type of enamelled mauresques associated with French mid-sixteenth century goldsmiths' work. There is, at present, insufficient evidence to draw definite conclusions from these facts. The rock-crystal bodies were, in any case, probably Italian, and the *basse-taille* enamelled flowers, though later in date and more naturalistic in treatment, are closely related to the enamelled decoration on the Valerio Belli altar set in the Victoria and Albert Museum and the Leo X basin in the Munich Schatzkammer.[14]

France

The identification and dating of French silver is rendered somewhat easier than Italian by reason of the French system of marking, which included the striking of a date letter as well as both town and maker's mark. Unfortunately the system was less effective than that followed in England as the form of the letters used in the date-letter cycles did not vary greatly and it is difficult to be certain to which cycle a particular letter should be assigned. The Gothic style persisted in France into the early sixteenth century; this is illustrated by the nef of Anne of Brittany in the treasury of Rheims Cathedral, which is believed to have been presented to her on the occasion of her entry into Tours in 1501. It would presumably have been new or at any rate of recent manufacture at the time, but its design shows no trace of Renaissance influence. On his accession to the throne of France, François I, a typical Renaissance prince, lost no time in inviting to France and appointing to his court foreign masters whose art might bring fame and honour to him. Among the few records relating to the various vessels he acquired at the beginning of his reign is Marcantonio Raimondi's engraving of the perfume-burner that Raphael designed for him shortly before his death in 1520. In this vessel three figures support the burner which is shaped like a wine-cooler and is supplied with a cover pierced with fleurs-de-lys, while the sides are decorated with salamanders in relief.[15] So large a vessel did not long survive the moment when it ceased to be fashionable, but it lasted long enough to provide the model for the funeral monument to contain the heart of his successor, Henri II, designed by Germain Pilon. The re-use of a design some fifty years after its first conception and at a time when fashion had turned against the High Renaissance, is a tribute to the timelessness of Raphael's invention. Among the foreign-ers brought to Paris was the goldsmith, medal die-cutter and hardstone carver, Matteo dal Nassaro, who came from Verona and who seems to have been established in Paris in the first year of the new king's reign.[16] He set up a grinding mill for cutting stone on a barge anchored in the Seine and it is possible that hardstone vessels, such as the agate cup (pl. 254) and the onyx ewer (pl. 372), may have been roughed out in this mill. Their form is so harmonious and graceful that one is inclined to look for Italian influence in their production. The main impact of Italian taste, however, came later with the estab-lishment of the colony of Italian artists in the palace of Fontainebleau and the summon-ing of Benvenuto Cellini in 1540 to work for the French court.

A general impression of the state of the goldsmiths' art in France, or at any rate in Paris, can be gathered from the numerous references to the subject made by Cellini both in his *Vita* and the two *Trattati* on goldsmithing and sculpture. In the five years Cellini spent in Paris between 1540 and 1545 he had ample opportunity to judge the skill of his French rivals. He thought very highly of Paris and described it as the 'most wonderful city in the world' where 'they practise every branch of every art'. In another passage[17] Cellini tells us how he entrusted a youth with the task of making a pair of vases weighing twenty pounds apiece. After melting and casting the silver the youth set to work on them, cleaning off the edges and then hammering them into shape 'He turned out both vases with great care and admirable technique without any correction or other work. As more work of this kind is done in Paris than in ten other cities of the world, the craftsmen there from constant practice acquire such marvellous technical skill. I should never have believed it had I not seen it for myself. Then, at first, I thought it was the quality of the silver that gave them an advantage, because they work here with a finer quality of silver than anywhere else; but my workman said no, and that silver of baser alloy would serve his purpose equally well. I tried him and found that it was so'.

Among the very few pieces of silver that can be attributed to French goldsmiths of the first half of the sixteenth century are two nefs in the Victoria and Albert Museum (pl. 252) and the British Museum (pl. 253) respectively. The identification of the date letter cycle of the first is so uncertain that it has been attributed to 1482, to 1505 and to 1528. In fact the Renaissance character of the base seem to preclude the earliest date which has been given to it by one writer.[18] Even the intermediate date of 1505 seems early if it is compared with the nef of Anne of Brittany in the treasury of Rheims Cathedral.[19] A production of more distinctly Renaissance character is the most attractive little ship in pl. 253. This piece is not marked so the attribution to a French source is based on nothing more than the presence of a French motto on the knop. The fact that the motto is also that of the city of Bar le Duc has given rise to the suggestion that it may have been made in that town, probably about 1530-1540.[20] Also unmarked is the silver-gilt casket in the British Museum (Waddesdon Bequest), the angles of which are set with caryatid figures, while on the cover are figures of Neptune and Amphitrite, their bodies of Baroque pearl.[20] This casket is further ornamented with diamonds and coarse emeralds and leads on to another group of French silver objects that have recently been recognised as proceeding from one workshop that was probably associated with the French court.

The Paris Court Workshop

This group can be associated with the court because at least two of the pieces are believed to have been presented by French sovereigns. They are closely similar in style and appear to date from the decade between 1530 and 1540, slightly later than the Burghley nef in the Victoria and Albert Museum. The group consists of a casket in Mantua Cathedral, another of larger size in a London private collection (pl. I and pl. 248) a ciborium (pl. 250) and a pair of candlesticks among the plate of the Chapel of Saint Esprit[22] in the Louvre and, finally the clock-salt from the Tudor Royal Treasury, now at Goldsmiths' Hall, London (pl. 251). Of all these pieces only the two caskets are marked, with the Paris hall-marks for 1532-3 and 1533-4 respectively and with an unidentified maker's mark, the initial B. With the exception of the two caskets, which are covered with mother of pearl scales, each piece is constructed in part of rock-crystal, but without the carved ornament that distinguishes Milanese rock-crystal vessels of the period. The mounts are of gilt-silver with acanthus leaf enrichment, set with numerous pearls and precious stones in cusped collets. The sides of the caskets, the base of the salt and the knop of the reliquary are set with large projecting cameo busts carved in shell in a manner that was fashionable in early Renaissance decorative art throughout western Europe. The same medallion heads or busts were a common architectural ornament of the first half of the century. The pieces from this workshop share other common features such as large numbers of pendant pearls, free-standing brackets and claw-

Plate VII
Smoky quartz cup attributed to Ottavio Miseroni in the Imperial Court workshop, gold mounts. Prague, early 17th century.

Plate VIII
Rock-crystal vase with gilt mounts, attributed to the Imperial Court workshop. Prague, early 17th century.

and-ball feet. Their design as a whole is somewhat naive in its combination of Gothic and Renaissance features, this being most markedly so in the case of the clock-salt (pl. 251). Whereas one might have expected to find in objects made for the French court in the 1530's a pure classical manner, these have an almost provincial air with their crowded ornament. The appearance of the candlesticks from the altar of the Chapel of the Saint Esprit is not improved by the fact that they have been made up with the help of rock-crystal stems taken from earlier pieces which did not, in fact, match. The candle-sticks seem quite old-fashioned in comparison even with the huge pair of sticks, six feet in height which were presented by the officials and merchants of the city of Paris to Eleanor of Austria in March, 1530, on the occasion of her solemn entry into the city after her marriage to François I.[23] These last conform to the Italian style of the early Renais-sance.

The ciborium and the pair of candlesticks were evidently presented by King Henri II to his newly-founded Order of the Saint Esprit and were presumably taken from the royal treasury. They may have been part of the plate of a royal chapel, but it is conceiv-able that they had originally a secular use, in which case the figure on top of the ciborium (pl. 250) would have been added to make it suitable for ecclesiastical purposes. It does not appear to be part of the original design of the vessel. The candlesticks have also been altered. Originally supplied with sockets into which candles could be inserted, they have been fitted with prickets and larger drip-pans to serve as altar candlesticks when they became part of the plate of the Order.

From the English point of view the most interesting of the group is undoubtedly the clock-salt (pl. 251) from the treasury of King Henry VIII, which was very probably presented to the English king by François I of France. This remarkable object is evidently either no. 913 or 914 of the 1574 inventory of the jewels and plate of Queen Elizebeth I. As a result of subsequent alterations, which have deprived the piece of the original receptacle for the salt and also of its cover, it is not now possible to identify it with certainty. The inventory description of no. 914[24] is the more complete and corre-sponds fairly closely with what remains of the original salt:

> Item oone Sault of Siluer and guilt with a Couer standing vpon vj rounde balles of Jasper with vj white Agathe heddes standing in Collettes of siluer within the same a rounde Christall and therin a Clocke with a Chime and other Jointes of latten and Irone appertaigning to the same. The Sault garnisshid with course stone and cartaigne hanging pearles. The couer garnisshid with smale counterfet Emeraudes having a man sitting vpon an Egle vpon the toppe of the couer lacking diuers stones poiz together cviij oz.

While the salt now has a restored cover which probably but not certainly follows its original form ,the ciborium in the Louvre (pl. 250) remains apart from the finial figure in original condition with its cover and complete garnish of stones and pearls, mostly of inferior quality. As a whole the pieces in this group are of great splendour, though it is, perhaps, surprising that the stones are of such poor quality. A colourful effect is achieved as a result of the combination in these pieces of rock-crystal, enamel, silver-gilt and precious or counterfeit stones and pearls.

The only other clock-salt of which an illustration survives is that shown in a painting from the pictorial inventory of the treasures of Duke Albrecht V of Bavaria (1550-1579) by the court artist, Hans Mühlich (pl. 161). This inventory, now broken up, is shared between the Bayerisches Nationalmuseum and the Graphische Sammlung, Munich. Curiously enough this salt was a far more costly piece than that of Henry VIII; it was constructed of enamelled gold and set with far better stones than the indifferent ones of the latter. The French royal treasury at Fontainebleau also included at least one clock-salt, which is described in the *Inventaire des Joyaux de la Couronne de France* drawn up on 20 Feb. 1560, as follows:

> *No. 143 Ung cristal ou il y a ung orloge, le dessus servant de salliere ayant une petite figure au dessus emaillé de blanc.*

Jacques Androuet du Cerceau

The most influential French designer of the mid-sixteenth century was Jacques Androuet du Cerceau, best known as an architect and author of a series of books on architecture. His curious name derives from the circle device that served as his shop sign. None of his buildings is known to survive, but a large number of drawings and etched designs of ornament for furniture, silver, etc. are attributed to him. The dates of his life are not definitely established; he is thought to have been born in Paris between 1510 and 1515.[25] Assuming that the traditional dating of his birth is correct, his designs for goldsmiths can be divided into three groups: first, those in more or less pure Renaissance manner but showing some northern influence; secondly, those derived from Italian Renaissance and early Mannerist sources, and, thirdly, those in which the influence of the French school of Fontainebleau is dominant. This last group presumably belongs to the latter part of his life and is discussed in a subsequent chapter (see p.76). The designs in it were of considerable importance in disseminating the Italian Mannerist style in France and in the Low Countries.

Du Cerceau is known to have worked in Paris, in Orleans, in Montargis and, towards the end of his life, in Paris again. His early style in goldsmith's work is represented by a series of etchings, mostly of ecclesiastical plate, and by three collections of drawings in the Cabinet d'Estampes of the Bibliothèque Nationale, Paris, in the Kunstbibliothek, Berlin[26] and in private possession respectively. It is not certain that all three are autograph, but they are all based on his work. The Paris codex consists of thirty-four drawings, including eleven described as 'Coupes à la mode d'Allemange' (pl. 24). The codex in Berlin is interesting, not only for its contents, but because the first sheet bears the English royal arms, presumably of Henry VIII. It consists of forty-nine sheets, one with the coat-of-arms and forty-eight drawings of vases, ewers, etc. The third codex contains eighteen sheets, including some of church furniture, two cups in the German fashion (but not so described) and one fountain. The binding in which these last drawings are contained appears to be Flemish, suggesting that the author may have been a Flemish follower of du Cerceau.[27] This codex (pls. 19-23) shows some Gothic influence in the strongly vertical construction and the foot of one of the vessels has the complex-shaped profile typical of late Gothic church pieces.

Du Cerceau's secular designs make much use of gadrooning (pls. 15, 20, 22), applied masks, medallion heads (pl. 18), acanthus foliage and garlands suspended from ribbons or masks (pls. 16, 18). Peculiar to du Cerceau are the delicately drawn and symmetrically arranged fronds of foliage which fill the spaces between mouldings and borders. This detail is repeated in many of the du Cerceau drawings and can be seen on those of a standing cup (pl. 24), a flask (pl. 21) and a ewer, though in the last the leafy fronds develop into dolphins, a typically French solution, (pl. 23). None of these drawings include the mauresques that are otherwise so usual in mid-sixteenth-century designs, and one can, therefore, date them at the latest to the early 1540's. They are not dissimilar to those in Hans Brosamer's *New Kunstbüchlein von mancherley schönen Trinckgeschirren* (A new design book of some fine drinking vessels), but as neither du Cerceau's designs nor those of Brosamer are dated, it is impossible to establish which appeared first. One may have copied from the other, but it is also possible that both were interpreting in their own manner the fashionable style of the period. Du Cerceau's earlier designs were very conservative in comparison with the style introduced to France by the goldsmiths working under Benvenuto Cellini.

Du Cerceau's manner can be recognised in the St. Michael Cup in the Kunsthistorisches Museum, Vienna, (pl. 289), formerly regarded as one of the cardinal pieces of French Renaissance gold plate, but now held to be more probably of Antwerp make (see p.107). It was presented along with the Cellini Salt, (pl. 313) and the onyx ewer (pl. 372) by King Charles IX to the Archduke Ferdinand of Tirol, when the latter acted as his proxy on his marriage with Elizabeth of Austria. The fact that it was presented by a French king has in the past been accepted as sufficient proof of its French origin but a study of contemporary inventories shows that royal treasuries included vessels from different countries.

In his second group of goldsmiths' designs, which probably date from about the middle of the century, du Cerceau drew heavily on Italian sources and, in particular, on the engravings of Enea Vico and Agostino dei Musi as well as on the very popular ones after Polidoro Caldara. Out of a group of fifty-five etched designs by du Cerceau in the Prints and Drawings Department of the Victoria and Albert Museum eight are copied from Vico, five from Agostino des Musi and six from Polidoro.[28] In these designs (pl. 25) du Cerceau shows little awareness of what was going on in Fontainebleau and adds nothing of consequence to the Italian prints he copied. Drawn as they are from so many sources, du Cerceau's etched designs are of varied character and give at first an impression of a breadth of invention that he did not in fact possess. They include a ewer in the manner of Giulio Romano with the body in the form of a seated faun between whose legs is an old man's head, another, tall and slender with conical body widening towards the lip, and a third with cartouches of strapwork with rolled over ends in the Fontainebleau manner applied to the body. Du Cerceau seems to have copied these designs without discrimination and many are of poor form. His best work of this period is to be found in a set of nine tazzas on tall stems; these may well derive from his own invention, for they are certainly French in style. The bowls are decorated with mauresques, interlacing strapwork, pendant ribbons or swags of fruit such as may be seen on the St. Michael gold cup (pl. 289). Though du Cerceau must have exercised a great influence on French design, there are few surviving pieces in which his manner can be recognised. Among them is one of the finest vessels surviving from the treasures of the French crown. This is the magnificent standing cup of agate mounted in enamelled gold, set with cameos of Roman Emperors and enriched with jewels in the Galerie d'Apollon at the Louvre (pl. 254). The presence of the royal crown surmounting the cameo of a Roman Emperor at the top of the cover implies that the cup was made for a King of France, who can only have been François I. Although the cup is unmarked, its resemblance to du Cerceau's manner, combined with its history, establish its French origin. The attractive briar-rose trails executed in translucent enamel have not been noticed on contemporary French jewels, but can be found later in the jewellery designs of Etienne Delaune.

A near contemporary of du Cerceau is known only from the monogram of the initials ACP or CAP, with which he signed his etched designs. He produced a series of eighty etchings of drinking goblets, beakers, tazzas and vases (pls. 26 and 27) each signed with monogram and datable shortly before the mid-sixteenth century. They were formerly attributed to Polidoro da Caravaggio[29] (see p.134), but lack the originality and ebullient Mannerism of the Italian master.

Shell Cameos

A feature of French goldsmiths' work, especially during the first half of the century, is the frequent use of carved shell cameos as applied ornament.[30] Similar shell cameos are, however, found on German vessels and some of the latter have been attributed to the Nürnberg goldsmith, Ludwig Krug, as, for instance the standing cup (pl. 270). These cameos are used on the most extensive scale on the shell-altar from the treasury of Cardinal Albrecht von Brandenburg of about 1525, now in the Bayerisches Nationalmuseum,[31] and on a cup attributed to Ludwig Krug, formerly at Schloss Raudnitz in Bohemia, but now lost. The frame of the shell altar was certainly German and the cameos, if French, must have been imported. Some of the cups embellished with these cameos are of distinctly international character, and their identification rests on the nationality of the cameos. If, however, as seems likely, there was trade in these cameos, they lose their value as evidence of the origin of the pieces to which they are applied. The silver gilt cup enriched with cameos in the British Museum (pl. 255) is here included as conjecturally French, but the cup in Budapest (pl. 270) is German and the shell reliefs on it are copied from prints by Albrecht Dürer, though these would have been available also to French shell carvers. It will be noticed that the cameos on the clock-salt and the associated objects from the same Paris workshop are carved in high relief, while those on the shell altar and the two cups mentioned above are much flatter. There also exists a small group of flasks carved in shell and mounted in silver. One of these is illustrated in pl. 369; it is certainly of French origin. That such carved shells were exported from France is proved by the presence in the Kunsthistorisches Museum, Vienna, of a similar one with mount struck with the Vienna mark.[32] Of about the same date as the two shell-mounted cups in London and Budapest is the hardstone serpentine cup with silver-gilt mounts in Budapest (pl. 256), in which the place of shells is taken by thirty-six sixteenth-century casts from antique Roman coins. In spite of the French inscription the origin of even this cup is uncertain. The inscription might have been executed in Germany for a foreign customer or could be a later addition. In general character the cup resembles south German work more than French, though our knowledge of the latter is still insufficient to support definite conclusions.

The Iberian Peninsula

Spain

Up to the middle of the sixteenth century the goldsmiths of Spain were subject to medieval regulations but in 1552, by order of Charles V, they were officially recognised as *artifices*, that is, artist craftsmen whose work was not merely manual but also required an understanding of the sciences and the arts. Their new status is well reflected in Juan d'Arfe's treatise on sculpture and architecture, *De Varia Commensuracion para la Esculptura Architectura,* published in Seville in 1585-7 (see p.192). Though the Spanish goldsmiths were organised in guilds and were obliged to strike their marks on the pieces they made, to which the town mark was added after assay, in practice the marking regulations were not consistently enforced. Much silver is unmarked and, as a result of the strong conservatism of Spanish taste, combined with the absence of any date letter system, it is difficult without further evidence to determine at all precisely the exact date of a piece.

While a greater quantity of sixteenth-century ecclesiastical silver has survived in Spain and Portugal than in any other country, secular plate of the same period is very sparsely represented, though there is more in Portugal than in Spain. Whereas in northern European countries the great majority of surviving pieces of secular plate, other than spoons, are drinking vessels, few of these are preserved in Spain or Portugal. On the other hand, a number of ewers with their companion basins have survived, usually because they have been taken over for use at the altar. One writer on Spanish silver[33] has endeavoured to account for this disparity in the rate of survival of ecclesiastical and secular plate by suggesting that the sumptuary laws were more effectively enforced in Spain than elsewhere. The extreme piety of the Catholic population of Spain may, however, have led to much secular plate being bequeathed to the Church — as was so much jewellery. Whereas the jewels could be used to adorn statues of the Virgin, the plate was melted down and converted into the huge custodias which are a typical feature of Spanish ecclesiastical silver. It is also possible that the production of altar plate may have been greatly in excess of that intended for the domestic household. In a country such as Spain where the influence of the Church was so strong this cannot be excluded.

Though few pieces of Spanish Renaissance secular plate survive, two valuable sources of information are to be found in the series of drawings submitted by candidates for admission as masters of the goldsmith's craft to the guilds of Barcelona and Valencia respectively. Others may survive in other Spanish cities but have not as yet been investigated and published. These drawings extend back in date to the beginning of the sixteenth century but the majority of those that have been published in modern times show jewellery rather than vessels. Those of Renaissance date are distinctly international in style and, had one not known their provenance, it would have been hard to determine. Those from Valencia include a number of salts profusely decorated with the standard Renaissance elements of ornament. These Spanish drawings do not show the variety found in contemporary German or Italian designs, but the latter were the work of experienced masters while the former are only sketches by young men at the beginning of their artistic career.

An exceptional feature of Spanish silver is the absence of any single dominating centre. Whereas, in Germany, Nürnberg and Augsburg, in France, Paris and in England, London produced the vast majority of gold and silver as well as determining fashion elsewhere, in Spain there is little to choose between the work of goldsmiths in Burgos, Barcelona, Valencia, Seville, Toledo and other large provincial cities. Nor can one discover strongly-marked local styles in the sixteenth century. During the greater part of the century style in the goldsmiths' shops was derived from foreign sources. In the early decades, when some of the most sumptuous pieces were created, German and Netherlandish late Gothic fashion was dominant, transmitted by immigrant masters and, in particular, by the family of de Arfe, who originated from the town of Harff near Cologne in the Rhineland. Several generations of this family created between them the most important surviving examples of Spanish ecclesiastical plate. Spanish church plate includes the usual European types; reliquaries, chalices and patens, monstrances, altar crosses, incense boats, altar candlesticks and so on, but extends to two others that were not used elsewhere, namely a combined chalice and monstrance and, most important of all, the custodia, the large tabernacle in which the monstrance was placed. The earliest of the series of great custodias made by members of the de Arfe family to survive is that of the Cathedral of Cordoba, made by Enrique de Arfe and completed at the end of 1518. This custodia is constructed like a Gothic tower and spire; apart from the series of embossed reliefs set in the base, its style looks back to the preceding century. Subsequently de Arfe adopted the new fashion imported from Italy and helped to create that remarkably successful combination of ogival and Renaissance elements which is characteristic of Spanish church plate of the first quarter of the sixteenth century. The most famous of the custodias made by Enrique de Arfe is that of the Cathedral of Toledo, which took the nine years from 1515 to 1524 to produce. Goldsmiths had been invited to make tenders for this custodia and it is a measure of the importance of immigrant masters that de Arfe's main rivals for the commission were both foreigners from the Netherlands: Diego Copin de Holanda and the painter, Juan de Borgona. Presumably the large quantity of precious metal that was being imported into Spain from South America gave rise to important commissions, which in turn attracted foreign goldsmiths to the country. In the Toledo custodia de Arfe introduced much Renaissance detail, both in the finials and in the figure sculpture (pl. 262), but the form as a whole can best be described as late Gothic. During the second quarter of the century Gothic detail gradually gave way to that of the Italian Renaissance; at first this change in style of decoration did not, however, influence the actual form and construction of church plate. The Renaissance style that was introduced was not the pure and restrained Florentine, but followed the highly ornamental manner of Lombardy. This style, generally known in Spain as *plateresque* (meaning simply that it was derived from goldsmith's work) is best represented in Italian architecture by the facade of the Certosa of Pavia. It involved a variety of elements, including classical busts looking out of medallions, strange monsters with long undulating bodies and winged cherubs' heads. This style was not necessarily introduced directly to Spain from Italy, it may have taken a longer journey via the Rhineland. The epitaph of Jakob von Croy, Domherr of Cologne and Prince Bishop of Cambrai, in the treasury of Cologne Cathedral, executed soon after 1518, already anticipates the Spanish plateresque style.

To the early Renaissance vocabulary of ornament the Spanish goldsmiths subsequently added swags of fruit and of drapery, trophies of arms and grotesque masks, either cast or embossed. All this detail can be seen on the vast custodia of the cathedral of Santiago da Compostella (pl. 263). This was constructed between 1539 and 1544 by Antonio de Arfe, son of Enrique and belonging to the next generation of the family. Instead of following the Gothic spire form of his father's custodia, he adopted an edifice of classical style, composed of four receding openwork stories rising in tiers from a base embossed with scenes from the life of St. James. Though the detail of the ornament is classical, the general effect and proportion still recalls the Gothic custodia. The composition is highly architectural with large numbers of balusters, colonettes and pilasters divided by mouldings into several stages and enriched with openwork brackets. Even richer than the Santiago da Compostella custodia in its elaboration of profusely packed Renaissance ornament is that of the cathedral of Saragossa, which was begun in 1537 by a goldsmith named Pedro Lamaison, evidently of French origin. As, however, the models were supplied by the Valencian sculptor, Damian Forment, who had recently carved the alabaster retable of the Capilla Mayor, the general effect is entirely Spanish (pls. 260, 261).

It is a curious feature of Spanish silver that, while much of the secular plate such as the Seville tazza in pl. 264 was comparatively plain, church plate of the second and third quarters of the century was decorated with quite worldly and sometimes openly erotic subjects in addition to the usual Scriptural themes. The amorous adventures of nymphs and satyrs were not, however, confined to the vocabulary of ornament of the goldsmith, similar scenes can be found on the carved decoration of choir stalls. Those few secular pieces that are richly decorated show the same ornament as the church plate, without of course, the religious imagery. The main features are dragons and human figures amongst scrolling foliage, as on the spice dish (pl. 259), and medallion heads, usually shown in profile and sometimes projecting in high relief. Dishes were often finished with elaborate cast and pierced borders. One of the most imposing secular pieces in Renaissance style is the great silver-gilt casket (pl. 258) said to have been presented to the Capilla Real of the cathedral of Granada by King Ferdinand and Queen Isabella, though it may be questioned whether it is so early in date. This is one of the transitional pieces in which can be recognised not only elements of Gothic and Renaissance but also more exotic influences, probably derived from Moorish art. A Gothic quatrefoil pierced border can also be seen on the base of the great silver brazier (pl. 257). This vessel owes its survival to the fact that it must have been brought or sent to Vienna in the time of the Emperor Charles V and remained undisturbed in the imperial treasury.

Portugal

The most interesting productions of the Portuguese goldsmiths of the first half of the sixteenth century are undoubtedly the ewers and their companion basins in the Manueline style.[34] This was a hybrid development from three different sources, namely elements of exotic cultures encountered in the course of Portuguese explorations, half-understood Renaissance art, and survivals of Gothic. This peculiar combination produced an effect not far distant from that of the Mannerist goldsmiths' work studied in the second part of this book. In Manueline silver one finds the closely-packed all-over decoration, fantastic profiles and wealth of sculptural detail of the later style. The most persistent Gothic feature is the thistle foliage wrought in strong relief; the exotic element is to be recognised not so much in individual details of ornament as in the generally alien appearance of the vessels as a whole (pl. 268). The style had a fairly long life in Portugal, longer than did the Renaissance in northern Europe, but in the absence of date letters or even marks of any sort, it is difficult to establish the exact extent of its period of fashion. The earliest precisely datable Portuguese dish in a pure Renaissance style is illustrated in pl. 266. It is decorated with two concentric friezes of figures, those in the outer frieze being separated by baluster columns standing on plinths in the Italian manner. Another Portuguese dish (pl. 265) of about the same date displays the same feature of a profile female head embossed in the centre, but both probably replace a family coat-of-arms, which was removed when the dishes came into other hands. Some reminiscence of the Gothic can be recognised in the thistle ornament and in the rather spiky treatment of pomegranate leaves. The persistence of Gothic fashion is best illustrated by the dish in pl. 267. At first sight a purely Gothic piece, the costume of the warriors depicted in the border frieze indicates a period not earlier than the mid-sixteenth century.[35]

The German Cultural Region

During the early decades of the sixteenth century the German goldsmiths had already achieved a reputation that extended beyond the linguistic frontiers. Their work was reaching places as far apart as the Kremlin in Russia, the Santo in Padua and even remote churches in the Abruzzi. With the combined efforts of Albrecht Dürer as a designer of silver vessels and of Ludwig Krug as their maker, a standard was reached in Nürnberg that rivalled the production of any other European capital. Whereas during the latter half of the sixteenth century the goldsmiths of Augsburg equalled those of Nürnberg, in the earlier period it was to Nürnberg that the commissions of the Habsburg Emperors, the Electors of Saxony, the kings of Poland and the wealthy aristocracy went. In 1514 there were one hundred and twenty-nine goldsmiths working in Nürnberg, each of whom had two journeymen and one apprentice; in the course of the century the number declined: to sixty-seven by 1564 and fifty-eight by 1573. In fact, this decline in number of masters at work does not seem to have been accompanied by a noticeable reduction in volume of production, for a great many pieces of Nürnberg silver made in the late sixteenth century survive.

Although neither Nürnberg nor Augsburg was the seat of residence of a reigning prince, the masters working there received orders from the whole area of German culture. Moreover, they were from time to time summoned to work at one or other of the courts of the Holy Roman Empire. Such moves to a different place of work did not imply that the master concerned adopted a different style. It follows that vessels of precious metal of the type associated with Nürnberg or Augsburg may have been made in a court workshop far distant from the goldsmith's city of origin. The south German style was also spread by goldsmiths who went to work in Nürnberg or Augsburg as journeymen and learnt a manner which they subsequently practised elsewhere. The high reputation enjoyed by the goldsmiths of the larger German cities is illustrated by a matter reported in the archives of the town of Pforzheim (Baden) near Karlsruhe. In 1564 the goldsmiths there refused to have their larger pieces marked on the grounds that the presence of a Pforzheim town mark would make them unsaleable, as only pieces bearing the marks of Strassburg, Nürnberg or Frankfurt were acceptable to their customers.[35]

Both Nürnberg and Augsburg vessels are identifiable by the presence of a town mark; in Nürnberg the maker was required to stamp his own mark as well in and after 1541. The Augsburg town mark, a pine-cone, was first introduced in 1529 and it also had to be accompanied by the maker's mark. The marking of silver was, as a whole, less thorough in the German cities than in France, England or the Low Countries. Even during the second half of the century, when silver was usually struck with both maker's and town mark, there was in Germany no date letter to give the exact year of manufacture. Slight differences in the form of the Augsburg pine-cone are of assistance in dating individual pieces but do not give a precise year of manufacture. Besides the silver vessels a certain number were made of pure gold; these were not marked and their identification is extremely difficult and rarely possible at all, though a small group of enamelled gold vessels made by Hans Karl, a Nürnberg goldsmith who went to Salzburg to work for the Archbishops of Salzburg has been recognised (see p.268). It is probable that many gold vessels made in one or other of the south German cities exist but have not yet been recognised. It is, therefore, often necessary to have recourse to style criticism in order to date German sixteenth-century silver. This is made more difficult by the fact that while some masters continued over long periods to produce vessels of conservative design, the more gifted worked in an original manner.

Jörg Seld

The earliest recorded example of classical detail in northern goldsmiths' work is the Walpurga portable altar which was completed by the Augsburg goldsmith, Jörg Seld, in 1492.[36] This is an extremely early date and the introduction of such Renaissance elements as the pairs of putti in the lunettes of the altar should probably be attributed to the Italianate taste of the prelate who commissioned the piece rather than to the sophistication of the goldsmith, even though he was, at the age of about forty, at the height of his powers when he made it. The fact that Jörg Seld made this altar does not mean that in his subsequent work he abandoned Gothic forms, nor is it an isolated example of his working in the Renaissance manner. It has been suggested that some of the series of drawings of goldsmiths' work in the Historisches Museum, Basel, which are in either late Gothic or early Renaissance style, may be attributable to him. The Walpurga altar should not be regarded as the beginning of a continuous development; Gothic forms long persisted, particularly in ecclesiastical plate. The earliest piece of Nürnberg silver in the Renaissance style is a small house-altar.[37] This was commissioned by Bishop Thurzo and presented by him in 1511 to the cathedral of Breslau. Once again its Italianate chacter can be explained by the fact that the patron had travelled in Italy and was acquainted with Italian fashion.

Albrecht Dürer

The gap of nearly two decades between the appearance of Renaissance forms in Augsburg and Nürnberg respectively is probably due to the chance of survival, for Albrecht Dürer had certainly introduced the Renaissance to his city before the end of the fifteenth century. Looking through Dürer's graphic *oeuvre,* his earliest representation of goldsmiths' work showing classical detail seems to be in the 'Vision of the Seven Candlesticks' in the woodcut series of the *Apocalypse* of 1498. In this print Renaissance baluster forms appear alongside the tangled vine foliage so beloved of the German goldsmiths of the late fifteenth century. As a result of his initial training in a goldsmith's workshop, Dürer showed a sensitive appreciation of the possibilities of the new style in relation to precious metalwork. On the other hand, like Jörg Seld he had grown to maturity at a time when late Gothic was the only acceptable manner and his conversion to the Renaissance was never absolute. An important source of evidence for his silver designs is his sketch-book in the Dresden Landesbibliothek, which contains drawings in the purest Renaissance taste and others in which no hint of the Renaissance can be recognised.[38] The exact dating of these drawings is uncertain; the sheet with six designs for Gothic standing cups has been dated to 1507 or soon after while others, which show tazzas on low baluster stems decorated with restrained acanthus foliage, have on stylistic grounds been placed about 1519. There can however be little doubt that Dürer was sufficiently conversant with Renaissance ornament to have produced the latter designs at least ten years earlier. A drawing of a column surmounted by a goat, which is dated 1510, in the British Museum, already shows much Renaissance detail.[39] On the other hand, the persistence of Gothic designs well into the sixteenth century is illustrated by the carefully finished drawing of a double cup (pl. 30) in the Albertina, Vienna. Though dated 1526 the design is far more Gothic than Renaissance in spirit; this is particularly evident in the wild, almost living, foliage that adorns it. During the second and third decades of the sixteenth century there was an individual trend towards naturalism in German goldsmiths' work. This is noticeable not only in Dürer's designs for goldsmiths but also in surviving vessels. The most characteristic expression is the rendering of the bowls of cups in the form of fruit, such as apples or pears, the smooth forms of which are contrasted with the tangled foliage around them. Typical examples of this taste are Ludwig Krug's chrysoprase cup in Budapest (pl. 269), the apple-cup in the Germanisches Nationalmuseum,[40] the pear-cup, generally known as the *Maximilian Pokal* in the Kunsthistorisches Museum, Vienna,[41] and another pear-shaped cup made by H. Schröder of Lübeck.[42] This taste for naturalistic detail was later revived by Wenzel Jamnitzer and persisted throughout the century (see p.209). The transition from Gothic to Renaissance was not a difficult one for the German goldsmiths, since the spirally twisted lobate forms typical of the earlier style could so readily be turned into Renaissance gadroons; this is well illustrated by the Dürer drawing for a double cup (pl. 30).

Dürer's drawings of standing cups in the late Gothic manner sometimes show the covers with a flat-ended finial that could serve as a foot, so forming in effect a double cup. This construction, which was extremely popular in Germany (pl. 31) does not seem to have penetrated south of the Alps. The many double cups in the Tudor royal inventory are specifically described as 'Almain'. Dürer's silver designs, like those of Hans Holbein the Younger, were not reproduced at the time and had, therefore, less direct influence than those of lesser masters whose work was engraved and printed.

Albrecht Altdorfer

After Dürer the Regensburg master, Albrecht Altdorfer, was the next to concern himself with designs for the goldsmith. His style shows strong Italian influence and his set of twenty-two etchings of cups and beakers on steel represent the early Renaissance manner at its best, combining dignity of form with austerity of profile (pl. 31). His designs are similar to some of Dürer's in the Dresden sketch-book but have been variously dated to the period 1520-25 and about 1530. The earlier date seems to be the more likely, but a covered beaker in the treasury of the Deutsches Ritter Orden in Vienna,[43] which is copied directly from an Altdorfer design, dates from as late as 1534.

Among Dürer's contemporaries was the Augsburg engraver, Daniel Hopfer, who is credited with being the first to extend to silver vessels the technique of etching, which had long been applied to the decoration of armour. He was followed by his two sons, Hieronymus and Lambert; the former of whom produced a number of silver designs, some copied from Altdorfer, including an etching showing a covered beaker, a double cup and a pricket candlestick, all in the purest Renaissance style.[44] Subsequently H. S. Beham, one of the Nürnberg *Kleinmeister,* (so called not because of limited talent but of the minute scale of their prints) produced four designs for covered cups dated 1530, while Peter Flötner designed in Renaissance style two salts, an inkwell and a ewer. These prints date between 1535 and 1541. Consistent features of these designs are protruding bosses or lobes; they had been taken over from German late Gothic silver, but instead of being used with Gothic profusion were applied with due regard to Renaissance standards of proportion. The double construction (pl. 30) is to be seen in many of the designs referred to above, and the *Doppel Pokal* or *Doppel Scheuer* became one of the standard forms of the German sixteenth-century goldsmith. On later examples the two cups were of the same height which resulted in an unbalanced and top-heavy effect. The double cup should be distinguished from another type with flat finial on the cover which was not meant to serve as a foot but was set with a medal or a plaque of the owner's coat-of-arms.

The Hallesche Heiltumsbuch

A major source of evidence about German goldsmiths' work of the early Renaissance is the *Hallesche Heiltumsbuch,* a pictorial inventory of the collection of relics and reliquaries assembled by Cardinal Albrecht von Brandenburg and given by him in 1530 to the *Neue Stift* of Halle.[45] Of the three hundred and twenty-nine objects shown the great majority are Romanesque or Gothic, but some sixty-seven are in Renaissance style. As the inventory is thought to have been completed before 1527, it provides convincing evidence of the general adoption of the new style by that date. The Cardinal is believed to have been an important patron of Ludwig Krug of Nürnberg: one of the pieces illustrated is signed by him and several others are apparently his work, but the presence of as many as sixty-seven pieces implies that other goldsmiths besides Krug must have worked in the Renaissance manner.

Insofar as the present study is concerned, the Halle inventory is of limited importance as only nine of the pieces depicted seem originally to have been intended for secular use. The vessels, whether produced for secular or ecclesiastical use, show the usual Italianate elements, such as bowls and feet decorated with gadrooned or fluted ornament and baluster stems surrounded by acanthus-leaf mouldings. Among the more interesting is the pair of nautilus-shell cups composed in the form of tritons.[46] In each case the shell forms the lower part of the body of the triton, to which scaly fins and tails of silver, apparently parcel-gilt, are attached. The cover of each is modelled in the round, one as a warrior in classical armour wearing a fantastic helmet and with a shield in one hand and a scimitar in the other, the other as a woman, nude except for a transparent shift, wearing a large barette on her head and holding a globe. These cups, which are amongst the earliest mounted Renaissance nautilus-shells recorded, are at the same time the most original in design.

Two other secular pieces closely anticipate English vessels made some twenty to thirty years later; one is a silver-gilt covered tazza on a tall stem[47] which recalls the enamelled gold and rock-crystal bowl made for Henry VIII (pl. 647). Its secular origin is indicated by the finial in the form of Hercules shooting the Stymphalian bird. The rock-crystal cover is shown in the drawing as set with roundels of saints, but these were presumably originally occupied by secular subjects. The second is a small two-handled cup and cover[48] of similar but somewhat more elegant form than the English cup of 1555 in pl. 304.

A striking feature of the objects depicted in the inventory is the great wealth of sculpture, including many figures of important dimensions modelled fully in the round. Little or nothing remains of all this early Renaissance sculpture in precious metal, but the drawings of this inventory provide evidence of its range and quality, and incidentally show the foundations on which the goldsmiths of the succeeding generation had to build.

Ludwig Krug

Ludwig Krug ranks second only to Dürer as the founder of the Renaissance style in German goldsmithing. The son of a Nürnberg goldsmith, he followed closely the lead of his more famous contemporary. His earliest recognised works date from the 1515-20 period. They include the apple-shaped cup already mentioned, a number of standing cups set with shell cameos, amongst them that illustrated in pl. 270, and a reliquary and a ciborium, which figure in the *Hallesche Heiltumsbuch,* though both are now destroyed.[49] He died in 1532 so his work does not show any advanced evolution of style; it mostly shows the same combination of Gothic and Renaissance motifs that can be seen in early Dürer designs. Ludwig Krug was a sculptor of great skill; the stems of some of his cups are decorated with free-standing figures, while the finials are composed of Gothic foliage inhabited by monsters and humans, as in the magnificent chrysoprase cup and cover in Budapest (pl. 269). His figure sculpture has however abandoned the Gothic treatment in which the nudes appear helpless and unprotected; instead they show the proud confidence of Renaissance man.

The shell cameos which decorated the missing cup by Krug at Schloss Raudnitz were based on Dürer drawings, and it has been convincingly suggested[50] that the goldsmith executed them himself. According to Neudörfer, Krug was famed for his shell carvings. His most ambitious piece decorated with shell cameos is the St. Ursula Reliquary[51] (now destroyed) from the *Hallesche Heiltumsschatz*. This vessel was constructed in the form of a ship and was mounted with three rows of cameos, two around the upper part and the third around the foot. It was surmounted by a figure of the saint modelled in the round. The standing cup in the British Museum (pl. 255) should, perhaps, be considered as a Krug piece; it is included by Rosenberg amongst Krug's Nürnberg works.

Another Nürnberg goldsmith, Martin Krafft, is represented by two vessels of Renaissance design made for Cardinal Albrecht and illustrated in the Inventory of the *Hallesche Heiltumsschatz*.[52] These are a pax and a monstrance. In their design Krafft shows an understanding of Renaissance style that was exceptional in Germany at this date and rivals Krug as an interpreter of the new ideas. It is noticeable that he omits the confusing foliage and small figures which were a legacy of the late Gothic but which interfered with the architectural style of the Renaissance.

Hans Brosamer

The German Renaissance style is best illustrated in the forty sheets of the *New Kunstbüchlein von mancherley schönen Trinckgeschirren*, published by the Fulda goldsmith, Hans Brosamer, in or about 1540.[53] The date seems late when one considers the style of the vessels represented (pls. 32-5) but, as with other pattern-books, the designs had been produced over a number of years and show fashions that had been followed for at least a decade prior to the year of publication. Another series of three woodcuts dated 1533, of which the only examples are preserved in the Basel Kupferstichkabinett, formerly attributed to an anonymous Swiss master, have since been given to Brosamer, and these show that the manner of the 1540 publication was introduced earlier.[54] One of the Basel designs shows Roman medals set in the body of a cup, a practice that was particularly favoured during the second quarter of the century. Rather less convincing is Braun's attribution to Brosamer of the drawing of a covered cup with tree stem in the Germanisches National Museum; this sophisticated design with its classical medallions set in the bowl is closer in style to the manner of Peter Flötner.[55]

The influence of Albrecht Altdorfer is very marked in some of the Brosamer woodcuts. Typical features are fat and gay putti (pl. 32), leafy friezes often enclosing medallion heads in the manner of the Nürnberg *Kleinmeister*, and, of course, the favourite German form of the first half of the century, the lobate cup (*Buckelpokal*) in which base, cover and bowl are embossed with prominent lobes or gadroons. One of the designs (pl. 33) is exceptional in that the lobes are replaced by spirally wrought bosses. Brosamer also makes frequent use of a feature favoured by the Nürnberg goldsmiths: fat and heavy straps terminating in volutes which are attached either to stem or base (pl. 35). Brosamer did not always adhere to the Renaissance canon of proportion, as in the flask (pl. 35) with its huge figures supporting a medallion of the Judgement of Paris, or in the standing cup with outsize masks decorating the lower part of the bowl (pl. 34). In this, as in his other designs, the vessel is distinguished by a lively and effective profile. The 1540 set includes a design for a coconut-cup, showing that Brosamer was aware of the attractions of such exotic objects. Some of his designs are so near to the contemporary Nürnberg style that it seems likely that he had close connections there, perhaps having served as an apprentice or journeyman. That he was familiar with the city is proved by his inclusion of a view of the Nürnberg *Burg* in his woodcut of the Judgement of Paris. No piece of silver made by Brosamer is known and he was probably never a working goldsmith; there are, however, many cups in existence, mostly of south German origin that reflect his manner. Among the vessels that recall his designs is the large silver-gilt flask or pilgrim bottle in the Grünes Gewölbe, Dresden (pl. 274). This piece is not marked, but the four-sided foot on high base moulding and the rather rough quality of the embossing suggests a central European, perhaps Hungarian origin. This particular form was not confined to northern Europe; the collection of masterpiece designs submitted to the guild of goldsmiths of Valencia in Spain illustrates a similar flask by a goldsmith named Sancho.[56]

Peter Flötner

The most significant influence on design in the goldsmiths' shops of Nürnberg, and indeed the whole German-speaking area, was exercised by Peter Flötner, who came to the city as a master of his craft from Ansbach in 1522 and was admitted citizen in the following year. He is believed to have gone subsequently to study the remains of classical antiquity in Italy, returning to Nürnberg in 1530, where he established close contact with the goldsmiths. According to the Nürnberg historian, Neudörfer,[57] his main pleasure was to carve models for the goldsmiths to follow. These models were first carved in boxwood or honestone (*Kehlheimer Stein*). His most famous achievement in this genre was the production of the wood models for the twelve reliefs of the 'Life of the Virgin Mary' for the altar of the Sigismund chapel in the cathedral on the Wawel at Cracow.[58] From these models bronze patterns were cast in Nürnberg by Pankraz Labenwolf and the patterns (*Patronen*) were passed on to the goldsmith, Melchior Baier, to serve as a foundation upon which to emboss the silver plaques that were to adorn the altar.[59] In this case it will be seen that the function of the goldsmith was a relatively minor one of hammering silver sheet on to a bronze pattern.

No fewer than one hundred and thirty separate plaquettes in various materials have been attributed to Flötner; many of these were in turn used as patterns for casting relief panels which were applied to vessels of precious metal. Lead patterns were also taken from moulds after Flötner's plaquettes; these were produced in large numbers and were sold to goldsmiths over a wide area in western and central Europe, thus spreading his influence. The most frequently encountered plaquettes after Flötner's models are those representing the Virtues, Vices, Muses and Ancient German Kings. Many of the original carved honestone models for them still survive. Among the magnificent vessels created in Nürnberg under his influence is the tankard illustrated in pl. 277. Here the art of working silver in low relief can be seen at its best, both in the frieze with its three scenes from the story of the Prodigal Son and the smaller friezes above and below of foliage inhabited by birds and animals and putti respectively. The carved models of the Holzschuher Cup (pls. 271-3) are also attributed to Flötner. An outstanding example of his skill as a pattern carver is the soapstone model of a cover or base of a cup in the Busch-Reisinger Museum, Harvard University. This is carved with a frieze of putti proceeding in triumph accompanied by sea-monsters against a background of water. The carving, described as being 'as high in quality as virtually any sculpture produced at this time in Germany', derives from a drawing by Flötner in the Herzog Anton Ulrich Museum, Braunschweig.[60] Few of Flötner's designs were published but a number of his drawings have survived.[61] These are of varying quality, and follow early Renaissance fashion. Some are so close to those of Hans Holbein that they have been attributed to him. The drawings do not give an adequate idea of the quality of Flötner's carvings. Though not the first to introduce the subject to the German goldsmiths, he was one of the first to recognise the decorative possibilities of the mauresque. His pattern-book of mauresques was not published in Zürich until 1549, three years after his death. Flötner's influence on the decorative arts. especially goldsmiths' work, persisted until well into the second half of the sixteenth century, as long as the patterns cast from his models remained in use.[62] It is unlikely that he ever worked precious metal himself. This would not have been permitted by the Nürnberg goldsmiths' guild of which he was not a member.

Melchior Baier

This Nürnberg master, who must be distinguished from the later Augsburg goldsmith of the same name was admitted master in the year 1525 and according to Neudörfer produced major works in precious metal.[59] Some of the most important silver vessels in German Renaissance style are believed to have been made by him after models by Peter Flötner. Baier's identified works were made in the decade from 1530-40; they include the Cracow altar made for King Sigismund I of Poland, the Holzschuher coconut-cup and two enamelled gold cups.

The Holzschuher cup (pls. 271-3) seems at first sight to introduce a significant break with tradition, though whether this should be credited to the goldsmith Baier or to Flötner, who made the models, is uncertain. The examples of this cup and of the Cracow altar demonstrate that the part played by the goldsmith in the creation of what appear to be some of the greatest achievements of the craft was sometimes limited to the more or less mechanical execution of models and ideas provided by another artist who was not a goldsmith at all. The Holzschuher cup offers a vastly different solution of the problem of drinking-vessel design from the familiar German Renaissance lobed cup (*Buckelpo-kal*) as shown in pl. 285. It has, however, close analogies with some of Albrecht Dürer's designs dating from the beginning of the sixteenth century, such as that of a table-fountain in the Ashmolean Museum, Oxford.[63] There are also late Gothic precedents for the tree-trunk stem, but the voluptuous treatment of the nude figures around the base (pls. 272-3) points to Renaissance humanist influence. The masterly modelling of these figures and their rhythmic grouping shows that their creator was a sculptor of consider-able stature.

Besides executing Flötner's major designs,[64] Baier was a distinguished master in his own right; this is indicated by the fact that he was commissioned to work in such pre-cious materials as enamelled gold. He is thought to be the maker of the Pfinzing Cup in the Germanisches Nationalmuseum[65] and also of the agate cup of Markgraf Georg von Brandenburg-Kulmbach. The former cup, which dates from about 1534-6 is of pure Renaissance design but the latter which was made in 1536 marks a significant step in the development of Mannerist taste (pl. 275). The manifestation of the triumph of human ingenuity over nature appealed strongly to the Renaissance patron; in the case of the Markgraf von Brandenburg-Kulmbach's cup the appeal was twofold in that, through the expenditure of immense human effort, the form of a fragile shell has been wrested from a different and extremely hard material, agate. So sophisticated an approach cannot be regarded as typical of the 1530's. The cup was commissioned by a ruling prince, probably after the design of Peter Flötner, and was intended to satisfy the demands of a rarified taste formed by contact with international fashion.

In 1540 the City Council of Nürnberg purchased from Baier a silver-gilt beaker and cover decorated with embossed and enamelled representations of the seven Planets. This cup must have been of exceptional splendour for in the following year it was presented to the Emperor Charles V. This incident shows that Baier was at the time recognised as the leading Nürnberg master. Very few of his works are marked and attributions are based on style-criticism, together with evidence of Flötner's influence.

During the first half of the sixteenth century, cups decorated with classical coins were much in fashion; during the Mannerist period interest in these flagged and it was not until the second half of the seventeenth century that it revived. Two of these coin cups are attributed to Baier, both set with casts from original coins and medals. One in the Museo Civico at Padua is dated 1534, the other in a Swiss private collection is neither marked nor dated. (pl. 278). In an endeavour to accomodate the maximum number of coins in the surface of the bowl a rather ungraceful profile has been adopted.

The Nürnberg Master

Among the many unascribed examples of south German goldsmiths' work of the six-teenth century is a group of cups, all of the highest quality, which are decorated with figure subjects embossed in high relief. The group includes a covered cup in the Treasury of the Deutsches Ritter Orden, Vienna, a double cup in the Kunsthistorisches Museum, Vienna (pl. 281-2),[66] another which, however, lacks both foot, stem and cover in the British Museum[67] and a fourth piece in the Württembergisches Landesmuseum, Stuttgart (pl. 288, 288a). Of these the first is dated 1536, while the third bears the Nürnberg town mark, thus giving some indication of both provenance and period. The cup in the possession of the Deutsches Ritter Orden is decorated on foot, bowl and cover with four friezes, while that in the British Museum is decorated with two such friezes, the upper embossed with the siege of a fortified city with Saracens in the foreground and the lower with Old Testament subjects. The embossing is carried out with the greatest skill: mounted soldiers are depicted facing inwards with the horses' rumps projecting outwards from the surface of the cup. Around the base are medallion heads in high relief. The double cup in the Kunsthistorisches Museum has embossed scenes of the Passion of Christ on the stem while the bowls are embossed with medallions of eight of the Apostles and of the eight Worthies (pl. 281-2). That in Stuttgart is embossed with crowded battle scenes, perhaps representing the storming of Rome in 1527, while the centre of the cover is set with a medallion of Salome holding the head of St. John the Baptist on a dish. Inside the lid is an embossed plaquette showing the Emperor Charles V in armour mounted on an armoured horse, trampling his enemies under foot. Among the latter can be recognised the head of Clement VII with a shield of the Medici arms, the crescent of the Turks and another shield bearing a cross. The use of a cup or basin to commemorate a historical event, so frequent in the latter half of the century, was thus well established during the Renaissance. Beauty of form or elegance of outline cannot be claimed for these vessels. Their maker betrays no knowledge of the tall and more graceful forms that were being developed by his contemporaries under the influence of Mannerist art. On the other hand his skill in embossing the scenes with innumerable small figures crowded into a very limited space is outstanding. His embossed figure of Charles V inside the Stuttgart cup (pl. 288a) shows him to have been a skilled designer of medals as well. None of these vessels bears a maker's mark.

Concz Welcz

The preceding pages have been concerned exclusively with Nürnberg masters, but superlative pieces were made by goldsmiths working in towns as far remote from each other as Strassburg in the west and Cracow or Joachimsthal in the east of Europe. Only too frequently the absence of town or maker's mark prevents us from establishing the origin of such provincial pieces, but the superb drawing in the Albertina, Vienna, of a standing cup (pl. 36) is signed and dated *Concz Welcz 1532* by the Joachimsthal goldsmith of that name.[68] Like so many of the finer quality provincial pieces, this cup also shows strong Nürnberg influence, which may, perhaps, be due to its master having been apprenticed there, but this is a matter of speculation. In allusion to the chief activity of the inhabitants of Joachimsthal, the foot is covered with buildings such as would be found at the top of a silver mine. Subsequently silver *Handsteine* (pieces of silver ore in natural state carved with figures of miners and mounted on a silver foot and stem) became usual features of the *Kunstkammer;* there are many examples in the former *Kunstkammer* at Vienna and Dresden.[69] They served no purpose other than as curiosities, unless as in Concz Welcz' design the piece of ore was set in the foot, leaving the upper part free to serve as a drinking-cup.

Strassburg

During the sixteenth century Strassburg belonged to the Teutonic cultural area and the goldsmiths of the city showed no trace of French influence in their work. The city was one of the main centres of the goldsmiths' craft in western Europe and much fine silver bearing the Strassburg mark survives. Its goldsmiths came under the influence of Nürnberg; many of them were either apprenticed there or went there to work as journeymen. There were enough commissions to attract Nürnberg masters to leave their own city and settle in Strassburg. In 1506 Erasmus Krug of Nürnberg, an elder brother of the more famous Ludwig Krug (see p.98) married the daughter of a Strassburg citizen and so gained the right to live there. None of his works survive — unless perhaps the three cups described below are by him — but his son, Diebolt Krug, who was admitted master in 1545, is represented by several mounted rock-crystal vessels (pls. IX, 549).

The very fact that he was entrusted with the task of mounting such precious material as rock-crystal shows that he must have enjoyed a high reputation. In 1538 the Strassburg engraver, Heinrich Vogtherr, produced his pattern-book entitled *Fremds und Wunderbars Kunstbuchlin* which, though not aimed directly at the goldsmith, included much material that might be used as a source of ornament.

Among the few early examples of Strassburg silver are three silver-gilt covered cups of very similar design, dating from the third decade of the sixteenth century, each decorated with four rows of Renaissance casts from classical Roman coins.[70] Two were made for Count Wilhelm von Honstein, Bishop of Strassburg (pl. 283, 6), while the third (pl. 284), the only one to bear the Strassburg mark, is in the Residenz Museum, Munich, to which it came from the Wittelsbach treasure. The first two cups have been attributed by Kohlhaussen to the Krug workshop in Nürnberg,[71] but in view of the close similarity of all three and the presence of the Strassburg mark on one, it seems unreasonable to reject the Strassburg origin of the Honstein pair. It is true that they show many features found on vessels attributed with good reason to Ludwig Krug, such as the decoration of the foot with a scalloped border from which acanthus foliage emerges, but similar ornament can also be seen on cups of English make.

As further evidence of the close similarity of cups made in Nürnberg and Strassburg during the first half of the sixteenth century, the Bullinger Cup in the Zürich Museum can be cited (pl. 285). But for the marks this would certainly have been accepted as a Nürnberg piece.

Switzerland

In the fifteenth century the centre of the goldsmiths' craft in Switzerland was the town of Basel; during the sixteenth century Zürich gradually came to the forefront until, by the latter half of the century, it had gained first place. The Renaissance style made an early appearance in Basel and in the Upper Rhine area; partly through the influence of the Basel master, Urs Graf, who like so many graphic artists of his time, had also received his initial training in a goldsmith's shop. A comprehensive picture of the Basel goldsmiths' work of the late Gothic and Renaissance is given by the collection of over three hundred designs which, like the goldsmiths' models (see p.68, n.23) formed part of the Amerbach *Kunstkabinett*. The drawings include both rough sketches executed in charcoal or pen and wash and others more carefully finished with the help of rule and compass. Some of the drawings are attributed to the Augsburg born goldsmith, Jörg Schweiger, who settled in Basel in 1507, and it is probable that the late Gothic designs amongst them were brought by him from his native city. As, however, a number of the drawings relate to extant articles made by Basel masters other than Jörg Schweiger, there can be no doubt that some of them must have been produced in Basel.[72] These drawings show no specifically Swiss features; they cover the whole range of Renaissance northern goldsmiths' work and can be paralleled in surviving German examples, such as those from the Lüneburger *Ratsschatz*. They represent the transitional style from late Gothic to the Renaissance as well as the fully evolved Renaissance and illustrate with what ease the pointed lobes (*Fischblasen*) of late Gothic could be turned into the gadroons (*Buckeln*) of the following style. The great majority are of conservative design but they include cups with mauresque patterns and the latest, probably dating from about the middle of the century, is a nautilus cup. As they were collected by Amerbach, it is impossible to be certain how many or which are of Basel origin; so great is their difference in quality and so long their time span — nearly a century — that they must derive from various sources. While most are of conventional design there are a few designs for standing cups of more imposing character, comparable even with that designed by Holbein for Queen Jane Seymour. The drawings include some that were executed for they bear the armorials of their intended owners, but the unpretentious style of the majority of them points to a working goldsmith rather than an artist-designer. Many recall the goldsmiths' designs of Albrecht Dürer and there seems to have been a close relationship between Nürnberg and the Basel goldsmiths. Not only do some of the Basel designs show the influence of Nürnberg masters of the generation between Albrecht Dürer and Peter Flötner, but surviving examples of Basel silver of the same period correspond to Nürnberg types. The covered beaker of Erasmus[73] in the Basel Historisches Museum is an example. The continuence of Nürnberg influence into the second half of the century is indicated by such vessels as the Basel drinking-bowl of 1571,[74] also in the Historisches Museum, the handle of which is cast from a known model by Wenzel Jamnitzer. A lead cast of this handle is included among the Jamnitzer models in the same museum.

The Renaissance style had a long life in Basel: the superb beakers on low feet such as that formerly used for communion in the Peterskirche in Basel, which was made by the Basel goldsmith, Theodor Merian, about or only slightly before the middle of the century show a purity of style that could not have been bettered by Holbein himself.[75]

The most fully documented of the earlier Zürich goldsmiths is Jakob Stampfer (1505-1579) who, like so many of the more famous goldsmiths of the time, was also a coin and medal die-cutter.[76] He came of a family of goldsmiths, though his father, Hans Ulrich Stampfer, combined the craft with the office of *Zeugmeister* (master of the city arsenal). Jakob was apprenticed to his father and then probably went to work in Nürnberg as a journeyman; this assumption is based on the close resemblance of his early work to that of the Nürnberg master, Ludwig Krug. On the completion of his 'wander years' in 1533 he became a master-goldsmith in Zürich. His first known important commission came in 1539 from the well-known Basel collector and antiquarian, Bonifacius Amerbach. It seems strange that a prominent Basel citizen should have chosen a Zürich goldsmith, but this may have been because of the special nature of the commission — a globe cup. This cup, which is preserved in the Historisches Museum, Basel, is a double cup, with one hemisphere engraved on each half. It is apparently the earliest of the type surviving. Subsequently such cups became a speciality of another Zürich master, Abraham Gessner. The Stampfer cup is surmounted by an armillary sphere supported in a cradle; the sphere can be lifted out of the cradle, which when reversed serves as the foot of the upper hemisphere. Stampfer's other major surviving work is a standing cup commissioned by fourteen clerics as a gift for the cathedral chapter of Constance (pl. 287). The stem and the plaquettes after Flötner that decorate the bowl derive from Nürnberg, but the scrolling design on the foot seems to be an original theme of Stampfer.

The Low Countries

During the greater part of the sixteenth century the chief centre of the goldsmiths' art in the Netherlands was the city of Antwerp. Its geographical situation as a seaport, midway between northern and southern Europe, was the prime cause of the dominating position it enjoyed amongst the cities of the Low Countries. Extensive trade connections brought its merchants into regular contact with the Italian seaboard cities and with the Hanse towns of the north. It became the meeting point of influence from both north and south and its artists developed an individual version of the nascent Mannerist style, which consisted of a synthesis of elements derived from Italy, France and, to a lesser extent, Germany. The style developed in Antwerp was soon followed in the other Netherlandish cities. Antwerp was as famous for its jewellery as for its goldsmiths, but, owing to the lack of makers' or town marks on jewellery, it is impossible to distinguish the work of the Antwerp jewellers from that made in other European centres.

Many Antwerp masters emigrated to seek their fortune elsewhere; amongst those who achieved fame abroad were Hans of Antwerp, the friend of Holbein who was employed by the court of Henry VIII of England, Jan Vermeyen the Elder, court painter to Margaret of Austria, Regent of the Netherlands, his son of the same name, who was Court Goldsmith to the Emperor Rudolph II and presumed maker of his

Plate IX
Rock-crystal vase with gilt mounts, the faceted vase from Freiburg im Breisgau, the mounts by Diebolt
Krug of Strassburg. Third quarter of 16th century.

Plate X
Standing cup in the form of a trochus-shell, with gilt mounts. Probably Antwerp, about 1560.

enamelled and jewelled crown (the Habsburg *Hauskrone*); Bartholomäus Spranger, the same Emperor's Court Painter, Erasmus Hornick and Joris Hoefnagel, both of whom went to work for Rudolph in Prague.

The fame of Antwerp extended far beyond her immediate vicinity. When in 1570 the City Fathers of Genoa required four figures of Evangelists to be cast in silver from wax models supplied by a Genoese sculptor, it was to Antwerp that they turned. These figures still adorn the shrine of the Corpus Domini in the Cathedral of San Lorenzo, Genoa.[77]

Although Antwerp enjoyed so important a role during the first half of the century, few pieces of early date have survived. The extent and variety of goldsmiths' work of this period can best be recognised in the precious vessels depicted in the many Antwerp Mannerist paintings of the Adoration of the Magi. The most important extant Flemish example of goldsmiths' work of the early Renaissance is not of silver but of gilt-bronze. This is the epitaph of Jacob de Croy in the treasury of Cologne Cathedral.[78] Jacob de Croy was Prince Bishop of Cambrai and Domherr of Cologne, and the epitaph must have been completed after his death in 1516. It consists of an elaborate tabernacle with much pinnacle work enclosing a relief of the Adoration of the Magi. It is of particular interest inasmuch as it seems to anticipate the plateresque style developed in Spain by the d'Arfe family. The epitaph was cast in 1518 by Hieronymus Veldauer of Louvain, but the name of the master who originally modelled it is not known.

The two most important Antwerp cups made in the Renaissance manner are those illustrated in pls. 289 and 290. They date from shortly before the middle of the sixteenth century and are so similar in design that one is tempted to attribute them to the same workshop, although one is of gold and the other of silver-gilt. The second was presented, along with a number of other vessels, to a Rome convent by Cardinal Paolo Emilio Sfondrati (1550-1618) for use as a reliquary. The first cup, pl. 289, the St. Michael gold cup presented by the French king to Archduke Ferdinand of Tirol and now in the Kunsthistorisches Museum, Vienna, is unmarked and has hitherto been accepted as being of French origin, not only because of its history, but also because its design shows much similarity to some of the du Cerceau school drawings (see p.90). One drawing of a standing cup has a finial very similar to that of the St. Michael Cup; again the spherical member with circular recesses, perhaps intended as settings for cameos or rock-crystal plaques on the drawing, appears on the finial of the cup set with jewels in large projecting collets. Another drawing in the same set (pl. 24) shows a stem and foot of analogous design to that of the St. Michael Cup. On the other hand, as has already been noticed by Kris,[79] certain Netherlandish elements can be found in the design of the frieze around the bowl. The St. Michael Cup was already some twenty to thirty years old when it was presented to the Austrian Archduke, while that given by Cardinal Sfondrati was even older when the gift took place. The explanation of this curious lack of concern with fashionable design is that more importance was attached to the value of the cup as precious metal than to its design. The possibility cannot be excluded that the St. Michael Cup was made in France by an immigrant Antwerp goldsmith, in the same way that another master from that city, Hans von Antwerp, worked for the English crown (see p.109) but this can only be a matter of speculation.

These two cups represent the taste of a king and a cardinal respectively, but less important pieces of the same period show distinction of design and quality. A standing cup in the Bayerisches Nationalmuseum, Munich,[80] with the Antwerp town mark, is so close to contemporary Nürnberg style that one is tempted to attribute it to a master who went as journeyman to that city. Similar vessels can, however, be found among the engraved designs of the Frenchman Androuet du Cerceau, or the German Hans Brosamer, pointing again to the uniformity of Renaissance fashion. Of equal excellence, both in design and execution, is the Brussels mounted coconut cup dated 1540 (pl. 291). It shows that such superb quality was not confined to the Antwerp masters.

Secular silver of the northern Netherlands dating from the first half of the sixteenth century is of such rarity, that it is not possible to give a comprehensive account of it. The most spectacular surviving piece is the silver-mounted drinking horn of the Arquebusiers Guild of Amsterdam;[81] this bears the Amsterdam date letter for 1547, but shows many Gothic features, including the profiling of the foot, the modelling of the heraldic beasts on each side of the stem and the pierced branches in the mounts that secure the horn to the stem. In this case the persistence of Gothic design can, perhaps, be attributed to the ceremonial nature of the vessel itself, for a slightly earlier silver-mounted glass beaker[82] by a Franeker master named Feike, which must have been made during the second quarter of the sixteenth century and probably shortly before 1542 (the date of an inscription upon it), shows conventional Renaissance ornament. Both foot and cover are embossed with acanthus and vine foliage enclosing roundels chased with profile heads.

England

In comparison with other European countries, with the possible exception of Germany, England is still extremely rich in sixteenth-century plate. Even in England, however, nearly all the more magnificent pieces have been lost and a considerable proportion of those surviving are modest articles, such as the many stoneware jugs with silver mounts, popularly known as tiger-ware. The great collections, in particular that of the Crown, were destroyed or dispersed during the Civil Wars and those few institutions that have retained their plate, such as some of the colleges of Oxford and Cambridge Universities, the town corporations and the London craft guilds, were not likely to acquire pieces of the greatest splendour. The most serious loss is that of all the Tudor royal plate with the exception of three pieces, the fourteenth-century royal gold cup in the British Museum, the sixteenth-century clock-salt belonging to the Goldsmiths' Company, (pl. 251) both of which are of French origin, and the Holbein cup described below (pl. 647). In judging the influence of fashion and taste on English silver, one must therefore, take into account the fact that those pieces most likely to reflect fashionable ideas have been lost. The situation regarding English goldsmiths' work is thus the precise opposite of that in Italy and France, where in the treasuries of the former reigning houses a small number of magnificent pieces have been preserved while the more average ones have disappeared.

The goldsmiths' craft was going through a period of full employment in early sixteenth-century England. An Italian traveller,[83] Andreas Franciscus, who visited England in 1497 described the working of silver as 'very expert here (London) and perhaps the finest I have ever seen'. Another Italian, writing at about the same time, made a similar observation 'The most remarkable thing in London is the wonderful quantity of wrought silver...In one street named Cheppside leading to Saint Paul's there are fifty-two goldsmiths' shops, so rich and full of silver vessels, great and small, that in all the shops in Milan, Rome, Venice and Florence put together I do not think there would be found so many of the magnificence that are to be seen in London'. While provincial travellers were easily impressed by quantities of silver or gilt plate offered for sale, these particular observers cannot have been so naive, knowing, as they did, some of the great cities of Italy. When they visited London, the goldsmiths whose work they saw would have been following the international late Gothic style. This same style long persisted in the applied arts in England, but a powerful influence in favour of more modern fashion emanated from the court of Henry VIII. England was not by any means behind other northern European countries in the adoption of Renaissance design. Convincing proof of this lies in the so-called Howard Grace Cup, an ivory cup with silver-gilt mounts with London hall-mark for 1523 (pl. 294). While the design of the finial of this cup is still Gothic, all other ornament is of Renaissance style. Though this cup is an isolated example, this does not mean that it was unique, but simply that most other surviving examples of the period are of ecclesiastical origin, in the design of which Gothic tradition was particularly persistent.

Henry VIII, whose ambition to cut a figure on the Continent once led him to contemplate the possibility of competing for election as Holy Roman Emperor, was anxious to attract foreign artists and craftsmen to England. He was evidently successful, for several of his court goldsmiths have names that indicate a foreign origin. The most distinguished foreign artist who was attracted to England during the early years of Henry VIII's reign was the Florentine, Pietro Torrigiano, who worked on the tombs of Lady Margaret Beaufort, Elizabeth of York and Henry VII. When Torrigiano returned to Florence he tried to persuade Cellini to accompany him to England as his assistant, and it was only by chance that the great goldsmith failed to spend some of his early years in England. According to Cellini,[84] Torrigiano said to him 'I have come to Florence to recruit as many young men as I can, for I have to execute a great work for my king, and I want to have some of my fellow-Florentines to assist me; and, as your style of work and also your designs are more in character for a sculptor than a goldsmith and I have to produce large bronzes, I will make you able and rich at the same time'. Subsequently Torrigiano recounted how he had broken Michelangelo's nose, but the unpleasant impression created by this incident caused Cellini to decide against going to join him in England.

There is very little evidence of direct Italian influence in English goldsmithing and the introduction of Renaissance design is due to the presence of a number of French, Flemish and German masters who had emigrated from their own countries to escape religious persecution after the Reformation and to the presence at the court of Henry VIII of the Augsburg-born artist and designer, Hans Holbein, who first came to England for a period of two years from 1526 to 1528, but returned in 1532 and remained until his death in 1543.

Most of the evidence relating to the presence of alien goldsmiths in London dates from the latter half of the sixteenth century, but in 1533 a guild of foreign artificers known as the 'Brotherhood of the Conception of our Blessed Lady' was founded. This was, of course, still a Catholic foundation and it drew its members from craftsmen working in the City of London, Southwark and Westminster. The first group of French refugees from religious persecution arrived in 1531 and by 1550 the number of Dutch Protestant immigrants was large enough for them to found their own church in the monastery of Austin Friars. The re-establishment of the Catholic faith in England on the accession of Queen Mary in 1553 seriously threatened the future of these immigrants, who were now regarded as undesirable heretics. In 1554 all foreign craftsmen were required to leave the country within the space of twenty-four days and in 1558 steps were taken to force out those who, by taking out Letters of Denization, had escaped classification as foreigners. A Bill was passed through Parliament in that year cancelling all such Letters of Denization but the opportune death of the Queen led to the abandonment of this project.

Hans Holbein the Younger

Hans Holbein's first visit in 1526 is of no great significance in the present context. He was employed by Sir Thomas More and his family but did not succeed in obtaining the appointment to the court of Henry VIII which had probably prompted his visit. It was not until 1535 that he actually obtained the court appointment. He first received regular payments from the court in 1534, thereafter he remained a court servant until his death, producing many portraits of members of the Tudor court as well as designs for decorations, jewellery and goldsmith's work. It is, perhaps, significant that on his return journey to England in 1532 he spent four weeks in the city of Antwerp, then the centre of Netherlandish culture and in particular of the goldsmith's art. Holbein was a personal friend of the *emigré* Flemish goldsmith, Hans of Antwerp, who had been working in England for many years, certainly since 1511, the date he gave himself for his arrival in England. Holbein painted his portrait in 1532 and possibly on other occasions as well.[85] The names of both Holbein and Hans of Antwerp appear together in a commission dating from the autumn of 1533 for the construction of a silver cradle for the Princess Elizabeth, later Queen Elizabeth I, who was born on 7 September 1533. Another mentions Holbein and a second royal goldsmith, Cornelius Heyss, who was also of foreign extraction, in connection with the same cradle.[86] The name of Hans of Antwerp in the anglicised form of John of Antwerp appears frequently in Cromwell's Book of Payments. He was still active in 1547, the last year of Henry VIII's life, but he does not seem to have been employed by Edward VI. The latest reference discovered which relates to him dates from 1 July 1550, when the burial of a son was registered in the parish church of St. Nicholas Acon in the City of London. Holbein's association with Hans of Antwerp must have dated back to his first stay in London, for the portrait he painted of the goldsmith was executed immediately after his return in 1532 and it is unlikely that he would have received a commission so soon from an unknown person. That the friendship continued until Holbein's death is proved by the artist's will to which Hans was a witness, and which contained a provision for the repayment to Hans of money owed to him.

The earliest of Holbein's drawings of goldsmiths' work — a covered cup of a type now known as font-shaped (pl. 37) — was also intended for his Flemish friend. Whether it was commissioned by Hans of Antwerp or was intended as a present to him is not known; nor do we know whether the cup was to have been made by the goldsmith for his own use, though the presence of his name suggests this. Goldsmiths were often quite wealthy men in the sixteenth century and when Hans was assessed for tax in 1541 in the parish of St. Nicholas Acon, the figure arrived at was thirty pounds and thirty shillings, the same amount as that of Nicholas Lysarde, the King's Sergeant Painter.[87] It is not, therefore, improbable that the goldsmith might have been able to afford so handsome a piece of plate. Considering Holbein's achievement as a whole, his main contribution to English goldsmithing was his adaptation of Renaissance ornament to established vessel forms. Most of his designs represent known types of vessel; in the case of this font-shaped cup he was certainly no innovator. There is in the Victoria and Albert Museum a standing cup (pl. 295), now without cover, of very similar type which bears the London hall-mark for 1529-30, some two to three years earlier than the presumed date of the drawing.

The font-shaped cup had a long history in England.[88] Several examples are recorded dating from the first quarter of the century. Among the London-made examples is that of 1551, formerly belonging to the church of Deane in Hampshire (pl. 299). These cups are sometimes known as 'grace cups' on account of the words of the grace that are engraved around the rim of many, though not all, examples. That they were not ecclesiastical is proved by the clearly secular ornament applied to them; that in pl. 299 has, for instance, the helmeted head of a warrior engraved inside the bowl. A later font cup in the Moscow Kremlin[89] also has a helmeted head in the middle of the bowl, but the outer rim is engraved with arabesques instead of the words of the grace. It bears the London hall-mark for 1557. Even later provincial examples exist, that made by Peter Peterson of Norwich dates from about 1570.

The font cup was also made in another size with larger bowl and accompanied by a cover. Only three English examples are known to survive, two, together with one cover which apparently belonged to another piece from the same set, are in the British Museum, the third is in the collection of the Worshipful Company of Goldsmiths, London. This larger version (pl. 297) corresponds to what would, in the case of continental silver, be described as a tazza. Each of the three has an attractive feature that does not appear to be recorded on other silver of the period, namely the embossing of the bottom of the bowl in a honeycomb pattern (pl. 298). There is a Holbein drawing of a vessel of similar shape (pl. 38); like his other designs, it is more elegant and sophisticated than the surviving English pieces. While the latter belong to a transitional stage between Gothic and Renaissance, the comparable Holbein designs show complete mastery of Renaissance ornament.

Among the designs produced by Hans Holbein during his second period in England are two for salt-cellars, then vessels of great importance upon the table. One (pl. 39) is a forerunner of the pillar-salts so characteristic of English goldsmiths' work of the second half of the century (see pl. 670). A frieze of somewhat similar design to that on the Hans of Antwerp cup runs round the foot. An English salt of comparable form belongs to the Goldsmiths' Company in London (pl. 292). A second drawing of a salt (pl. 40) also dating from the earlier part of Holbein's English residence cannot be paralleled by any surviving piece. Both designs compare very favourably with those of the German, Hans Brosamer of Fulda, who was Holbein's chief rival in the exploitation of Renaissance forms for the benefit of the goldsmith (see pls. 32-5).

The superb silver-mounted rock-crystal ewer in pl 293 has, on the grounds of its similarity to one of the earlier drawings in Holbein's English sketch-book been identified as a piece made for the English court.[90] In fact, the drawing shows a ewer with rather corpulent body while the extant vessel is of distinctly thin and elegant proportions. This discrepancy between design and execution can be explained by the fact that the form of the vessel must have been determined by the shape of its rock-crystal body. In other respects the ewer conforms closely to Holbein's design; the gadrooned foot, the S-shaped handle and the long spout with dragon's head terminal can all be found on the drawing. The resemblance to a Holbein design does not constitute final proof that the vessel was mounted in England, but the 1574 inventory of the Tudor treasure lists a good many ewers, then known as lairs, of which several might be taken to correspond with that here discussed. Thus no. 1124 is described:[91]

Item oone Laire of Christall with a rounde foote the foote lippe and handle of siluer guilt the saide handle being an Antique Sarpent with lions heddes.

It is hardly possible to provide a definite chronology of the Holbein drawings of goldsmith's work for the English court since they cover the short period of eleven years between 1532 and 1543. One might think that the less complex designs are the earlier ones, but such considerations as the importance of the commission must have played an important part in the choice of design. Among the former is that of the great gold cup set with alternate rows of rubies and diamonds (pl. 45). There is no indication on this drawing that it was a royal commission, but in view of its costly nature it is probably a preliminary design for the cup numbered 45 in the 1574 inventory of the royal plate of Queen Elizabeth I.[92] At this time there were only ten covered cups made entirely of gold in the royal treasury, and none of the others bears the least resemblance to this drawing. The inventory description of the bowl runs as follows:

45. Item oone proper Bolle of golde the bryme of the foote parte enamelid blacke the bolle having in the middest a faire squaird Diamounde with a pointe set in a collet of golde. The Couer wrought with braunches of trees knit together and therein are set six rowes of Diamoundes being in noumber fourescore and sixtene Diamoundes having within the Couer a woman pictured the heade and Shoulders graven in a Camew and thre Lozanged Diamoundes set in Collettes of golde parte of the knoppe of the couer set with nyne Diamoundes in Collettes of golde and a Roose of Diamoundes vpon the knoppe poiz togethers. xlvj oz.

It was probably this cup that was shown to a German visitor, Lupold von Wedel, when he visited the Tower of London on 14 November 1584, and which was, in 1606, presented to Christian IV, King of Denmark. Von Wedel described it as a 'vessel set with nothing but large diamonds, on the lid were two hundred, the others could not be counted' while a reference to it at the time of its presentation to the King of Denmark called it 'a Cup of 5000 li'.[93] While the six rows of diamonds on the cover and the 'braunches of trees knit together' can be recognised in the drawing, there is no sign of the black enamel border on the foot and the knop of the cover seems to have been set with more than nine diamonds. Furthermore, the drawing shows diamonds alternating with rubies whereas the finished bowl was set with diamonds only. However, such discrepancies might easily exist between a design and the vessel as completed by the goldsmith. No drawings of the interior with the cameo in the cover and a fair square diamond with a point in the middle of the bowl exist to show how these parts appeared. In this case, Holbein was evidently called upon to design a vehicle for the display of a large number of diamonds, probably over a hundred, and there was little opportunity to display his imaginative powers. While the design of this bowl is unenterprising, the next datable Holbein drawing — the great table-fountain given to Henry VIII as a New Year's Gift by Queen Anne Boleyn in 1534 — seems to belong to another epoch altogether. Two alternative drawings for this piece survive, one showing the basin and fountain together (pl. 44), the other (pl. 43) the fountain only. There are considerable differences between the two designs but the version finally produced was probably based on the drawing illustrated in pl. 43. The 1574 inventory describes the fountain as follows:

> 998. Item oone Basone of siluer guilt the border railed with golde and set with stone and pearle in collettes of golde standing in the same a Fountain and thre women parte of them being Copper water runnyng owte at ther brestes with two borders of golde in the Fountaine lacking oone Roose of garnettes in the nethermost border with a plate of golde in the toppe of the Couer with the Quenis Armes and Quene Annes therein poiz together. cccxxxij oz.

Another description[94] given in the New Year's Gift Roll for 1534 is slightly more informative:

> By the Quene grace, a goodly gilte bason hauing a raille or bourder of golde in the middest of the bryme, garnisshed wt rubies and perles, wherein standith a fountein alos hauying a raille of golde aboute it garnisshed wt diamauntes, out wherof issueth water at the teetes of iij nayked women standing aboutes the foote of the same founteyn.

Hans of Antwerp

If the alternative design (pl. 44) had been executed and, moreover, survived, then English goldsmiths' work of the sixteenth century would have been represented by a piece worthy of comparison with the Cellini Salt. It is tempting to speculate whether Holbein's friend, Hans of Antwerp, had a hand in the production of the fountain which was actually made, for there are prominent Antwerp features in its design. If so, no record survives, for his name does not appear in the royal accounts between 1533 and April 1539 and then only in respect of a payment for carrying despatches to Germany.[95] He did, however, receive a number of commissions from Thomas Cromwell, Lord Privy Seal, and his name appears in the latter's Book of Payments from 1536 to 1539.[96] The first payment was for New Year's Gifts supplied to Cromwell in January 1537 and during the following two years frequent payments to him are recorded, mostly of minor significance. Amongst the more important orders was one for the gold cup offered by Cromwell to Henry VIII as a New Year's Gift in 1539. For this John of Antwerp received fifty-two ounces of gold and £12 in November 1538 and a further £7.7.0 in January, 1539. Another important commission related to a gold laver and trencher weighing fifty-one ounces and costing four shillings per ounce, for which he received 100 marks on 29 November, 1539.

It is not surprising to find that it was Thomas Cromwell who signed a letter of recommendation to the Wardens of the Goldsmiths' Company on 9 April, 1537 requesting the admission of John of Antwerp to the Freedom of the Company.[97] The letter states that John seeks the liberty of the city of London, but thinks it would be better to be first admitted a member of the Company. It also mentions that he has lived in London for twenty-six years, is married to an Englishwoman, has many children and proposes to stay in the country for the rest of his life. It seems surprising that a foreigner such as John of Antwerp should have been able to practise as a goldsmith in London for so long without ever becoming a Freeman of the Company that controlled the trade. Presumably he had eluded control by working for the court or those associated with it. In any case, with the support of the Lord Privy Seal he obtained the Freedom for which he had asked and was admitted to the Company on 27 September, 1537.[98]

John of Antwerp had, in fact, had trouble with the Company on more than one occasion. On 25 October, 1529, together with three other Dutchmen, he was ordered to bring in sureties to deliver all gold and silver brought to him to work, or else to keep neither shop nor workhouse.[99] The purpose of this order was presumably to ensure that he did not re-fashion old plate and return it to the owners without first submitting it to Gold-smiths' Hall for assay and the hall-mark. This practice, which was prevalent at various times, especially after the Restoration of the Stuart monarchy in 1660, is responsible for most of the unmarked English antique plate that now exists. In November 1530 another goldsmith brought a complaint against him about an apprentice,[100] but the most serious incident was on 6 November, 1536, when he was sent to the Compter (prison) for putting Andrew Pomert, a stranger and probably a fellow Fleming, to work without a testimo-nial.[101] It may well have been this last embarrassing affair that induced him to regu-larise his position by becoming free of the Company. After 1539, when he was still working for Cromwell and made the journey to Germany with dispatches, we hear no more of him for a while. Cromwell was executed in 1540 so he lost his best customer. However, in August 1545 he was sent with two others to prospect for mines in Ireland and finally in 1547, the year of Henry's death, he and Peter Richardson received the large quantity of eighty ounces of gold, worth £188, though for what purpose is not specified. Most of the references to him mention the use of gold and jewels and we can, therefore, assume that he was a jeweller as much as a worker of wrought plate. He may well have had a part in the production of such splendid vessels as the diamond-studded bowl or the enamelled gold and jewelled rock-crystal cup shown in pls. 645-8. The most carefully finished of the Holbein designs is that for the gold and jewelled cup presented by Henry VIII to Jane Seymour, probably in 1536. The first sketch for this cup is in the British Museum, while the final version is in the Ashmolean Museum (pl. 41). The cup appears in the 1574 inventory of the royal plate as item 47:

> One faire standing Cup of golde garnisshed about the Couer with eleuen table Diamoundes and two pointed Diamoundes about the Cup Seventene table Diamoundes and thre pearles pendaunt vpon the Cup with this worde bounde to obeye and serue and H and J knitted together in the toppe of the Couer and the Quene's Armes and Quene Janes Armes holdone by two boyes vnder a Crowne Imperiall.

A miniature and greatly simplified version of this cup is in the Victoria and Albert Museum (pl. 296). As it bears a maker's mark that has not been attributed, one cannot be certain of its origin, but it is here included as possibly the work of an English goldsmith under the influence of Holbein. This cup and the Seymour Cup are the earliest examples of the use of mauresque ornament on English silver. First introduced in Paris in 1530 by the Italian master, Francesco Pellegrino, it was not until 1548 that mauresques made their appearance in an English pattern-book. This was Thomas Geminus' *Morysse and Damashid renewed and encreased – Very profitable for Goldsmythes and Embroder-ers;* it was not an original work but a pirated edition of a pattern-book by the French master, Jacques Androuet du Cerceau. Presumably Holbein saw the Pellegrino pattern-book on his second journey to England in 1532. The *Rollwerk* (straps with rolled over ends) forms that were also exploited at Fontainebleau can be seen in the heraldic car-touche supported by two putti which surmounts the cover of the Seymour Cup (pl. 41) and, even more emphatically rendered, in the centre of Holbein's design for a chimney-piece for one of the royal palaces.[102] Their earliest exactly dateable appearance in Holbein's English designs is in the woodcut of Erasmus standing within an aedicule of the year 1535. This particular design includes other Mannerist features, amongst them baskets of fruit supported on the heads of male terms.[103]

In the seventeenth century the English antiquary, the Earl of Arundel, acquired an album of Holbein drawings and gave them to the Bohemian artist, Wenceslaus Hollar, who was in his employ, to copy. The Holbein originals are lost, but prints from Hollar's engravings survive; among the designs thus preserved is one for a gold mounted glass or rock-crystal beaker (pl. 42). This is of particular interest since it was made for the King himself. Though there are many gold-mounted rock-crystal cups listed in the Tudor royal inventory, it has not been possible to recognise this particular piece, so one cannot know whether it was ever made. A secular cup of similar but much simpler design, which was presented in the sixteenth century to the parish church of Cirencester,[104] is thought to have been made originally for Queen Anne Boleyn. It bears the London hall-mark for 1535. The standing mazer bowl of the Barber-Surgeons' Company (pl. 300), presented to the Company by Henry VIII in 1540, is another vessel that appears to derive from a Holbein design, though perhaps in somewhat simplified form. While goldsmiths' designs of the early sixteenth century were logical in composition, towards the middle of the century a fascination with curious or grotesque forms becomes apparent. Something of the perverse trend of Mannerist art can already be recognised in Hollar's engraving after a lost original by Holbein (pl. 46).

Amongst the last designs prepared by Holbein for the court of Henry VIII were two alternative suggestions for a time-measuring instrument[105] that was to be presented to the King by Sir Anthony Denny, his Chamberlain and personal friend, on New Year's Day, 1545. Sir Anthony had received considerable grants of land from the estates of secularised monasteries and had, therefore, every reason to make a handsome present to his royal master. The two designs represent a sand-glass and a table-clock or, perhaps, clepsydra (water-clock) respectively; of these the former seems to have been executed, but the instrument has not survived. The drawing (pl. 47) is preserved in the British Museum, the latter is known only from a contemporary copy (pl. 48) following a Holbein original.[106] Clock-cases were not usually made of silver in the sixteenth century, though there were exceptions such as the royal clock-salt (pl. 251); it is possible that Sir Anthony Denny's clock was not of silver either. It cannot be identified in the 1574 *Inventory of the Jewels and Plate of Queen Elizabeth*, but this does not prove that it was not made of precious metal, as the Jewel House Inventory was constantly being depleted by presents made to members of the court and also by the removal of articles by court officials as perquisites of office on the decease of the sovereign. The various inventories of the possessions of Henry VIII enumerate a few clocks with silver cases. Thus among 39 'Clockes at Westmr in the chardge of James Bufforth' in 1547[107] was 'A flatte square striking clocke with a case of silver and gilte having the kinges armes on thone syde and Sainte George on the Dragonne on thother Syde'.

In the introduction to his study of the Tudor Jewel House inventories, A. J. Collins suggested that the Holbein design (pl. 47) must represent one of the clock-salts of which a number existed in the Tudor treasury. The solitary example of these clock-salts that is known to survive is of French origin and of fundamentally different construction from these two Holbein drawings (see pl. 161). There would, in fact, have been no room for a salt receptacle in the Holbein design since the round boxlike member between the glass and the sundial was intended to contain the compass. Not only is there a sketch of the compass at this level, but the manuscript note on the other side confirms that it was intended to occupy this position. It is, of course, conceivable that the salt might have been placed in the base below the hour-glass. This would not correspond to the usual placing of the receptacle on the sixteenth-century drum-salt, nor to the arrangement of the extant clock-salt. The second drawing (pl. 48), which was not actually used, owes more to Italian sources. The base with its sphinxlike supporters and central roundel within a cartouche of drapery strongly recalls some of the designs associated with the school of Salviati (pl. 83).

The magnificent unmarked sand-glass in the Boston Museum (pls. 301-2) is the only surviving Henry VIII time-piece other than a watch that can be attributed to an English goldsmith. The attribution is based on its general resemblance to Holbein's designs rather than any constructional feature, and the possiblity that its design was derived from Hans Brosamer or one of his followers cannot be entirely excluded.

While fashion at court was determined by Holbein, goldsmiths outside the court circle seem to have had access to the pattern-book of Brosamer. This is usually dated to about 1540 but it does in fact represent the style fashionable in the second quarter of the century and, as has been indicated above, some of its designs must have been available at an earlier date. Examples of English silver that reflect more or less closely the Brosamer book include the Boleyn Cup of 1535 at Cirencester parish church[104] a wine cup of 1540 and another of 1545 (pl. 303); the last two are now used as Communion cups in the churches of Gatcombe, Isle of Wight, and St. Margaret Patterns in the City of London respectively. The bold gadrooned ornament on both bowl and foot of these two cups is typical of Brosamer's ornament.

When working to a familiar model the English goldsmith was perfectly competent to produce vessels of excellent proportion and profile; when, however, he was required to depart from the usual type, he needed the guidance of a design or pattern. The little cup from Corpus Christi College, Cambridge (pl. 304) illustrates the difficulties encountered by a goldsmith who lacked a sense of style. This cup was presented to the college, together with another of the same design but later date, by Matthew Parker, Archbishop of Canterbury, who must have been oblivious to its unhappy proportions.

1 ill. Rossi, fig. 35.

2 See S. Anjou, 'Two Renaissance drawings for engravings', *Röhskka Konstlsöjd Årstryck*, 1957, p.70 n.6.

3 *Vita* I, cap. 20 'Quella di Lucagnolo detto si era un vaso assai grande, il quale serviva in tavola di papa Clemente dove buttava drento, in mentre che era a mensa, ossincina di carne e bucce di diverse frutte; fatto piu presto a pompa che a necessita. Era questo vaso ornato con due bei manichini, con molte maschere piccole e grande, con molti bellissimi fogliami di tanta bella grazia e disegno quanto immaginar si possa: al quale io dissi quello essere il piu bel vaso che mai io veduto avessi'.

4 ill. Planiscig, *Andrea Riccio*, Vienna, 1927, p.244-5.

5 ill. Pouncey and Gere, *Italian Drawings, Raphael and his Circle*, London, 1962, cat. no. 241.

6 ill. Popham and Wilde, *Italian Drawings at Windsor Castle*, London, 1949, cat. no. 793. Another sketch for the Cesarino salvers is in the Ashmolean Museum, Oxford, while a more finished drawing is in the Dresden Kupferstichkabinett. See O.Fischel, *Raphael*, Berlin, 1962, pls. 232-3.

7 ill. Y. Hackenbroch, *Catalogue of the Untermyer Collection*, Revised edition, New York, 1969, no. 201.

8 Kris I, p.51.

9 Erich Steingräber, 'Das Kreuzreliquiar des Marcantonio Morosini', *Arte Veneta*, Vol. xv, 1961, p.53ff.

10 Cellini I, I cap. 14. 'Questo fu un cassonnetto ritratto da quello di porfido che e dinanzi alla porta della Rotonda. Oltra quello che io ritrassi, di mio arrichi con tante belle mascherette . . . Questo era di grandezza di un mezzo braccia in circa; ed era accomodato che serviva per una saliera da tenere in tavola'. Berti, p.54 quotes a reference in the Medici inventory to a similar salt: 'Una saliera d'argento dorato a sepultura con quatro piedi di zampe di lione, arabescato tutto il coperchio con una figura che e un fiume, con arme di palle'. The sarcophagus is probably that made for the Roman tribune, Agrippa.

11 Brunner, cat. no. 47, ill. pl. 21.

12 Sotheby's, London, 13.x.1970, lot no. 2, illustrated in colour. For the nineteenth-century copy made by the Vienna Hofjuwelier, Weininger, see Fillitz and Neumann, 1968 edition, cat. no. 61, and J. F. Hayward, 'Salomon Weininger, master faker', *Connoisseur*, 187, p.170-9.

13 The paten from this service is illustrated by Rossi, pl. LXXV. The whole service is in the Museo dell' Opera del Duomo at Siena except for the incense-burner which is in the Opera del Duomo at Orvieto.

14 For the suggestion that the Siena service is of French origin see D. Alcouffe, 'Le collezioni francesi di gemme del XVI secolo' *Arte Illustrata*, 1975, p.266.

15 Bartsch XIV, no. 489, p.364, ill. p. Jessen, *Meister des Ornamentstiches*, Berlin, 1923, Vol. I pl. 34.

16 Kris I, p.45ff. According to Vasari, Nassaro had been patronised by the French king before he went to France. Once there he was patronised by the whole court as well as the king, thus faring better than his friend and co-national, Cellini. We do not know to what extent he was a goldsmith: he produced an altar frontal with figures of gold enriched with precious stones for François I, but may have entrusted the goldsmith's work to his assistants. He was eventually appointed to the Royal Mint.

17 Cellini II, cap. XXII 'egli tiro e dua vasi benissimo senza radere e senza altro, con bellisima diligenzia et una virtuosa pratica, la qual pratica si faceva in Parigi, perchè in quella citta si lavora piu che in dieci altre città del mondo, e dove si fa assai faccende. Quella pratica assicura tanto quelli che lavorano, che di essa pratica nasce cose maravigliose, come io veddi, le quali io non avrei mai credute. E se bene noi demmo il vanto alla proprieta dello argento che in altra parte del mondo; a questo mi ripose il mio lavorante che

d'ogni bassa lega di argento gli bastava la vista di fare il medesimo. E cosi ne facemmo la prova e trovammo essere vero'.

18   Oman III, p.15, pls. viii-xi.

19   J. Taralon, *Treasures of the Churches of France*, 1966, p.267, pls. 90-93.

20   Read and Tonnochy, I, cat. no. 220.

21   The group was first published by Dr. I. Toesca, *Apollo*, Vol. XL. Oct. 1969, p.292.

22   ill. Rossi, pls. xxxv and xxxviii.

23   ill. A. Michel, *Histoire de l'art*, Paris, Vol. V, 1912, p.415.

24   Collins, p.450.

25   Geymuller in his study of the du Cerceau family gives the years between 1510 and 1515 for the period of Androuet du Cerceau's birth; A. Blunt, *Art and Architecture in France*, London, 1953, p.94 suggests 'about 1520' and in n. 22, p.106, states that 'the later date of birth fits in far better with the known facts. The whole question of his work...is still to be cleared up'. Whether the earlier drawings are by du Cerceau or by a slightly older master does not affect their significance as examples of French design for goldsmiths of the first half of the sixteenth century.

26   Geymuller, p.125-7. This codex came to Berlin from the Destailleur collection in Paris. It is curious that this book with the English royal arms should have been preserved abroad. It probably left England at the time of the Civil War and the dispersal of the English royal collection.

27   Four drawings of salts with covers in the British Museum Print Room, formerly attributed to Etienne Delaune, but evidently of earlier date belong to the same series as these eighteen sheets.

28   The Italian sources and du Cerceau derivations in the Victoria and Albert Museum Prints and Drawing Dept. are as follows:

Enea Vico	Du Cerceau
B421	E 488-1911
B422	E 478-1911
B423	E 476-1911
B424	E 512-1911
B426	E 477-1911
B427	E 4302-1910
B429	E 45-1911
B433	E 4306-1910
Agostino Venexiano	Du Cerceau
29470	E 4310-1910
B 452	E 4314-1910
B 543	E 487-1911
B 548	E 507-1911
B 549	E 479-1911
Polidoro da Caravaggio	Du Cerceau
20576.4	E 504-1911
27736.1	E 505-1911
27736.2	E 496-1911
27736.5	E 511-1911
27736.6	E 508-1911
27736.7	E 489-1911

29   Jessen, p.69.

30   R. Berliner, 'Französische Muschelschnitte', *Münchner Jahrbuch*, 1924, p.26.

31   Halm and Berliner, cat. no. 339, fig. 2.

32   A third powder flask of carved shell with silver-gilt mounts is in the Berlin Kunstgewerbemuseum, no. 79-1100, and a fourth with later mounts in the British Museum, Read and Tonnochy I, no. 230.

33   J. Hernandez Perera, *Orfebreria de Canarias*, Madrid, 1955, p.100.

34   For similar ewers and companion basins, some with more advanced Renaissance ornament, see Dos Santos, pls. 88 and 91.

35   Rosenberg II, Vol. III, p.281.

36   For a detailed discussion of Jörg Seld and an illustration of the Walpurga Altar, see I. Weber, 'Die Tiefenbronner Monstranz und ihr kunstlerischen Umkreis', *Anzeiger des Germ. Nat. Museums*, 1966, p.48ff.

37   ill. Kohlhaussen, pl. 585, cat. no. 424.

38   ill. Kohlhaussen, pl. 519, 523. For the most authoritative study of Dürer's influence on goldsmiths' designs, see G. Schiedlausky 'Dürer als Entwerfer für Goldschmiedekunst' *Ausstellungs – Katalog Albrecht Dürer, 1471-1971*, Munich, 1971, p.364ff.

39   ill. Kohlhaussen, pl. 517.

40   ibid pls. 528, 9.

41   ibid pl. 534, 5.

42   W. Paatz, 'Bildschnitzer und Goldschmiede in Lübeck', *Pantheon*, 1929, p.260.

43 ill. Kohlhaussen, pl. 707.

44 ill. Guilmard, *Les Maîtres Ornemanistes*, 1891, Vol. II, pl. 121.

45 Halm and Berliner, passim.

46 ibid. pls. 124, 125.

47 ibid. pl. 93. This vessel is attributed to Ludwig Krug.

48 ibid. pl. 38a.

49 ibid. pls. 178, 175.

50 Rosenberg I, Vol. 3, p.55.

51 Halm and Berliner, pl. 176.

52 L. Grote, 'Arbeiten des Nürnberger Goldschmiedes Martin Krafft für das Hallesche Heiltum', *Anzeiger des Germ. Nat. Museums*, 1967, p.30ff.

53 F. W. H. Hollstein, *German Engravings*, Amsterdam, 1957, Vol. IV, p.p.25 N, 540-583; this authority dates the first edition of Brosamer as 1540.

54 See E. W. Braun, 'Uber einige Nürnberger Goldschmiedezeichnungen aus der ersten Hälfte des 16ten Jahrhunderts', *94 Jahresbericht, German. Nationalmuseum*, Nürnberg, 1949, p.9.

55 Kohlhaussen, pl. 649.

56 A. Igual Ubeda, *El Gremio de Plateros*, Valencia, 1956, pl. LX. A flask with foot of somewhat similar design is illustrated in the Lobkowitz pictorial inventory, see Braun, pl. XII, 23.

57 Neudörfer, p.115 *'seine Lust aber in täglicher Arbeit war in weissen Stein zu schneiden, das waren aber nicht anderes den Historien den Goldschmieden zum Treiben und Giessen'.*

58 Kohlhaussen, cat. no. 458, pls. 650-1.

59 Neudörfer, p.125 *'Diser Bayr is mit treiben, reissen, und grossen Wercken, von Silber zu machen beruhmt, er machte dem König von Pohlen eine ganz silberne Altar-taffel, die wug CCXII Marck, zu solche Taffel macht Peter Flötner die Patron, und Figuren aus Holz, aber Pangraz Labenwolff goss dieselben holzen Patronen von Messing, über diese Messingtaffeln wurden die silbernen Blatten eingesencket und getrieben'.*

60 C. L. Kuhn, 'An Unknown Relief by Peter Flötner', *Art Quarterly*, 1954, p.108-115.

61 Bock, no. 358.

62 For a study of continuing use of Flötner plaquettes, see I. Weber, 'Bemerkungen zum Plakettenwerk von Peter Flötner', *Pantheon*, Vol. xxviii, 1970, p.521.

63 Kohlhaussen, pl. 400, p.260.

64 Neudörfer, on the other hand, states that another Nürnberg goldsmith, Jacob Hoffman, purchased most of Flötner's work *'Den mehren Theil seiner Kunst und Arbeit hat Jacob Hoffman, goldschmid, von ihm erkauft'.* See also Rosenberg I, no. 3851, p.71

65 Kohlhaussen, pls. 669-70.

66 E. Neumann, *Katalog der Sammlung für Plastik und Kunstgewerbe*, Vienna, 1966, Renaissance, fig. 50.

67 *The Waddesdon Bequest*, British Museum, London, 1927, cat. no. 96.

68 See E. W. Braun, 'Concz Welcz, der Goldschmied zu St. Joachimsthal', *Kunst und Kunsthandwerk, Vienna, 1917, p.422ff.*

69 Four examples from the Vienna collection are illustrated by Schlosser, fig. 29.

70 Kohlhaussen, cat. nos. 417, 418, 419.

71 Kohlhaussen, p.515.

72 Thirteen of the Basel goldsmiths' designs were exhibited and five illustrated in the catalogue of the exhibition of *Spätgotik am Oberrhein*, Badisches Landesmuseum, Karlsruhe, 1970. These date from before or about 1500. For a study of these designs see I. Weber, 'Die Tiefenbronner Monstranz und ihr künstlerischen Umkreis'. *Anzeiger des Germ. Nat. Museums*, 1966, p.7-87.

73 ill. *Historische Schätze Basels, Basler Kunstbücher*, 3, pl. 132.

74 ill. ibid pl. 138.

75 ill. *Historisches Museum, Basel Jahresberichte*, 1956, p.23.

76 See E. Hahn, 'Jakob Stampfer, Goldschmied, Medailleur und Stempelschneider' *Mitteilungen der antiquarischen Gesellschaft*, Zürich, 1915, Band LXXIX.

77 ill. Morazzoni, pl. 28.

78 ill. E. F. Bange, *Die deutsche Bronzestatuetten des 16ten Jahrhunderts*, Berlin, 1949, p.72: see also the exhibition catalogue, *Herbst des Mittelalters*, Kunsthalle, Köln, 1970, no. 152.

79 Kris III, cat. no. 33, p.21-3.

80 This cup was published by Kohlhaussen, cat. no. 487, as Nürnberg work. It does, in fact, bear a clear Antwerp mark which appears to be that for 1574-5, but it clearly dates from the 1540's at the latest. Presumably it was re-assayed in 1574-5: there seems to be no doubt about the identification of the date letter. The question whether it was actually made in Antwerp is therefore open.

81 ill. *Catalogus van Goud en Zilverwerken*, Rijksmuseum, Amsterdam, 1952, pl. 22.

82 Frederiks, vol. IV, no. 50, pl. 61.

83 Quoted by T. F. Reddaway, 'Elizabethan London, Goldsmiths' Row in Cheapside, 1558-1645', *Guildhall Miscellany*, Vol. II no. 5, 1963.

84 *Vita* I, 12, *Io son venuto a Firenze per levare più giovani che io posso; ché avendo a fare una grande opera al mio re, voglio per aiuto dè mia fiorentini; e perché il tuo modo di lavorare e i tua disegni son più da scultore che da orefice, avendo da fare grande opera di bronzo, in un medesimo tempo io ti farò valente e ricco'.*

85 P. Gantz, *The Paintings of Hans Holbein*, London 1950, cat. nos. 62, 63 and 64, reproduces three portraits but points out that the identification is uncertain. The sitter is a merchant of the London Steelyard, but in no case is any accessory introduced that would prove the sitter to have been a goldsmith.

86 *Calendar of State Papers*, 26 H.8, 1534, no. 1668. Payment to Cornelys Hayes for a silver cradle at the cost of £16 and, in respect of various alterations and additions £2-1-10. 'Hance', presumably Hans Holbein, received '20sh. for painting Adam and Eve upon it'.

87 L. Cust, 'John of Antwerp and Hans Holbein', *Burlington Magazine*, Vol. VIII p.356.

88 For a comprehensive list of Font cups, see N. M. Penzer 'Tudor Font-shaped Cups', *Apollo*, Vol. 66 p.174, Vol. 67 p.44 and p.82.

89 ill. Oman II, pls. 42-3.

90 See von Falke, 'Die Holbeinkanne im Kunstgewerbemuseum', *Amtliche Berichte der Kön. Kunstsammlungen*, Berlin, 1908-9, Vol. XXX, p.126.

91 Collins p.495.

92 ibid. p.278.

93 ibid. p.278.

94 ibid. p.468, no. 998.

95 In his study of the Jewel House and the Royal Collection (*Archaeological Journal*, Vol. CXVII, 1960, p.131-156) General Sitwell states that Morgan Wolfe, who was Henry VIII's principal goldsmith and held the Household appointment, would have had a monopoly in the supply of plate for the Royal Household. Wolfe is certainly likely to have been concerned with the more important orders for the Crown, but in fact many different goldsmiths are named in Henry VIII's account. Thus in March 1543 Cornelius Hayes, King's Goldsmith, was paid the large sum of £1,611-2 in respect of gilt plate given by the King on New Year's Day.

96 *Letters and Papers of Henry VIII*, Vol. XIV, Cromwell's Accounts.

97 Minute Books of the Worshipful Company of Goldsmiths, Vol. F. p.61.

98 ibid. Vol. F, p.79.

99 ibid. Vol. D, p.291.

100 ibid. Vol. D, p.336.

101 ibid. Vol. F, p.42.

102 ill. H. A. Schmidt, *Hans Holbein der Jüngere*, Basel, 1945, Vol. III, pl. 141.

103 ill. ibid. fig. 98.

104 ill. Collins, pl. III, p.196.

105 P. Ganz, *Die Handzeichnungen Hans Holbeins*, Basel, 1937, cat. no. p.52.

106 This drawing is fully discussed by Campbell Dodgson, 'Holbein's designs for Sir Anthony Denny's Clock,' *Burlington Magazine*, Vol. LVIII, p.226.

107 British Museum, Harley 1419B, fol. 192 obv. and rev.

CHAPTER SIX

Mannerism

WHILE the new interpretation given by Mannerist artists to the familiar themes of Renaissance painting and sculpture is a subject that has long attracted the attention of the art historian, the parallel and consequent changes that took place in the sphere of decorative art have not been studied so intensively. Not only do the sixteenth-century manifestations of Mannerist taste show great variations and even contradictions, so also do modern interpretations of those manifestations. From being recognised as an independent style that dominated all the arts for three-quarters of a century and almost crowded the Renaissance out of the sixteenth century, Mannerism has now been reduced in significance to little more than the last phase of Renaissance art.[1] This is not the place for yet another detailed investigation of a subject that has attracted so much discussion from art historians over the last half-century, but some indication of the significance of Mannerism in the art of the goldsmith is essential.

Vessels made of precious metal in the Mannerist taste are more plentiful than those in pure Renaissance style. The reason is that, outside Italy, the Renaissance occupied so brief a period in the history of decorative art. Mannerism as a decorative style was being developed by Italian masters in Florence and in Fontainebleau during the 1530's and 1540's and the new fashion then created reached northern artists shortly after they had mastered the classical Renaissance style. The transition from the High Renaissance style of the first half of the sixteenth century to the more sophisticated forms of Italian Mannerism did not present serious problems. Many of the features of Mannerist ornament can be recognised in earlier goldsmiths' designs: the *horror vacui*, the assembling of animal, vegetable and human forms to produce monstrous or fantastic creatures and the delight in complex profiles. The main feature that distinguishes Renaissance from Mannerist design is the absence in the latter of rational architectonic construction.

The same conservatism that caused the goldsmiths to delay so long in accepting the Renaissance also manifested itself in the early seventeenth century, when in the representational arts Mannerism gave way to Baroque. It was not only in the north but also in Italy that the first quarter of the seventeenth century can be described as a period of Mannerism in the goldsmith's art. The great ewers and basins wrought by Genoese masters in the second and even third decade of the seventeenth century (pls. 356-62) still conform to Mannerist taste as do those made by the van Vianen family in Utrecht or by the Imperial Court Workshop in Prague.

A decisive role in the creation of Mannerism in European decorative art was played by the group of Italian artists who were brought by François I to decorate his new palace of Fontainebleau in the 1530's (pl. 95). The composition of the series of frescoes in the Galerie François I and of the stucco frames enclosing them, which were created by the Florentine Rosso and the Bolognese master, Primaticcio, anticipates nearly every feature that can be recognised in Mannerist art of succeeding decades. The lion's share of the credit should probably go to Rosso, for the gallery was almost finished when he died in 1541.

The goldsmiths' art seems to have exercised a peculiar fascination upon the Fontaine-bleau masters for, among the interlacing straps terminating in volutes, which form the framework of their designs, tall attenuated vases are introduced wherever possible as decorative features on top of cornices and volutes, within niches and in the foreground of figure subjects. Though the birth of Mannerism is rightly associated with Fontaine-bleau, it was only by chance that the fashion developed on French soil. The reason for its rapid spread over the rest of Europe was the establishment at Fontainebleau of a school of graphic artists, who reproduced the main features of the decorative schemes of the frescoes while varying them by introducing some original ideas of their own. Their prints found a ready market in the north, especially in the Low Countries. Amongst the masters who contributed to the spread of the Fontainebleau style were René Boyvin, who engraved the prints illustrating the story of Jason[2] (pl. 96) after the designs of Leonard Thiry, a Flemish painter who was one of Primaticcio's assistants at Fontainebleau, and Antonio Fantuzzi, who was active there between 1537 and 1550. This artist etched numerous subjects after Rosso which he set within elaborate car-touches with figures and strapwork copied from those in the Galerie François I. The Fontainebleau style was further spread as a result of the remarkably accurate reproduc-tions of the frescoes produced in the tapestry weaving workshops that were also estab-lished there. The most valuable documentation of the Galerie François I is, in fact, to be found in the set of tapestries in the Kunsthistorisches Museum, Vienna, rather than in the much decayed paintings by Rosso and Primaticcio that remain in the Galerie itself.

A major element in the decorative scheme of Fontainebleau was a cartouche com-posed of straps with scrolled-over ends projecting in strong relief. It is not known whether Rosso himself first invented the scheme but this is likely, since, at the time he introduced it at Fontainebleau, most of his Italian contemporaries were satisfied with the *grottesche* and the candelabrum ornament of the early Renaissance. What had pre-viously only been hinted at was exploited by Rosso and Primaticcio with quite unparal-leled mastery and confidence. The introduction of these bold strapwork compositions (pls. 95 and 96) marked a distinct advance against the simple geometrical frames of the previous generation. In the manner developed by the Fontainebleau masters the straps played a dominating role, rendered in such a way as to give an impression of weight and thickness. Their ends were turned over in volutes in a manner that has given rise to the description *cuirs* (leathers). Subsequently the style moved to the Netherlands where the strapwork became more profuse and its convolutions less controlled, while the human figures, instead of perching comfortably on their scrolls, were trapped within them and held prisoner. In the north the style moved further and further away from the original Fontainebleau scheme until it reached its climax in the fantastic imaginings of Cornelis Bos (pl. 194). In Italy the Fontainebleau manner had a longer life and the Sala Regia of the Vatican, completed in 1573, is still modelled on the Galerie François I. The fashion for strapwork developed to such a degree that the cartouche eventually became more important than the subject it contained, which was almost submerged within the convolutions that enclosed it. This development can also be noticed in the design of Mannerist picture-frames, which were composed of heavy strapwork, sometimes enclosing smaller pictorial subjects.

While the masters of ornament delighted in figures writhing within imprisoning strap-work, the goldsmiths, doubtless more concerned to please their customers than to fol-low contemporary fashion to its logical end, adopted a more benign form of ornament in which, as in the Fontainebleau manner, the figures dominated the straps instead of trying to escape from them. The surrealist fantasy that the Netherlandish masters intro-duced is absent from the designs of their German contemporaries, while in the vessels of the period that survive we find an even milder version. A typical example of the less extreme manner can be seen in the pen and wash drawing of a pilgrim flask by Erasmus Hornick (pl. 157). In this attractive design the strapwork constitutes no more than a framework within and around which the figures are disposed in elegant and comfortable poses. The great advantage of this particular composition was its adaptability; while the jeweller could use it on a miniature scale to decorate a prayer-book or the back of a locket, the goldsmith found it equally useful for the body of a tankard or, on a larger scale, for the frame of a mirror. One such is the frame by Wenzel Jamnitzer,[3] which is believed to date from the 1560's (pl. 437). Another mirror frame of similar design is inset inside the lid of the reading-desk made by Elias Lencker, who was a follower of Wenzel Jamnitzer (pl. 450). This desk is believed to have been intended for Claudia de' Medici. Some of the most attractive mirror-frames of the period are to be seen in one or other of the series of paintings showing ladies at their toilet, which were so popular with painters of the school of Fontainebleau. In these the mirror is usually provided with a gilt frame and is supported on either a double stem in the form of a nude man and woman or, in the case of a portrait, believed to represent Diane de Poitiers, in the Basel Oeffentliche Kunstsammlung,[4] of a single stem composed of a man and woman in an erotic embrace. A symbol of *Vanitas,* the mirror exercised a particular fascination upon the Mannerist goldsmith and two of the most extreme versions of Mannerist taste surviving are, in fact, mirror frames, illustrated in pls. 527 and 737.

In discussing a subject so wide ranging as the art of the goldsmith in western Europe it is inevitable that many divergent trends and fashions will be encountered. It would be naive to expect to find a single style among the creations of so many masters working in different countries over the course of a century. It will, nevertheless, become clear that at least some suggestion of Mannerism is to be found in the typical examples of the goldsmiths' craft of the period, irrespective of the country of origin. In considering goldsmiths' work of this, as of other periods, we encounter one serious hindrance which is a consequence of subsequent historical events. The great innovators of the Mannerist period were Italian and French, and the style developed by the German, Flemish and English goldsmiths was, with few exceptions, derivative. Unfortunately, while German, Netherlandish and English silver of the sixteenth century is comparatively plentiful, all but a handful of the Italian and French pieces have been destroyed. This destruction makes it very difficult to estimate the importance of the latter compared with the productions of the former.

The almost universal destruction of what could now claim consideration as the finest goldsmiths' work of all time for the sake of recovering the precious metal content seems at first inexplicable. Our forefathers seem to have been completely blind to the aesthetic merits of the treasures they consigned so ruthlessly to the melting-pot. Much had to be sacrificed through sheer economic necessity, but there is another factor to be considered. Much of this magnificent plate was intended for display on the many-tiered sideboards that can be seen in contemporary paintings of interiors. Later generations have usually had little sympathy towards the more ostentatious aspects of the taste of their ancestors and it is just these pieces that were most liable to destruction. Obsession with fashion is a constant characteristic of man throughout the ages and keeping up with its movements was as important to a person of quality in the sixteenth as it is in the twentieth century. In this connection one may quote the report sent to Duke Wilhelm V by his agent, Hans Fugger on 18 November 1574. Fugger had been instructed to find some suitable presents for St. Nicholas' Day but said that he had seen a chess set in the shop of the Augsburg goldsmith, Ulrich Eberl, which was somewhat old-fashioned (*altfränkisch*), he could, however, get nothing better.[5]

During the period of some seventy years covered by the following chapters, designs in the goldsmiths' shops were governed by successive and increasingly esoteric phases of Mannerist fashion. When applied to the decorative arts Mannerism found its natural expression in the use of rare and costly materials: precious stones, semi-precious hardstones, precious metals, exotic woods and rare shells. In looking at the creations of the goldsmiths' art of this period one must rid oneself of the modern prejudice against artefacts that are evidently incapable of performing any useful function. Mannerist goldsmiths' work had a dual function, but neither had anything to do with utility. The purpose of these lavishly ornamented pieces was to demonstrate, first, the wealth and taste of the prince who had commissioned them, and secondly the technical skill of the master who had created them.

Not all goldsmiths were affected by, or, perhaps, even conscious of, the trend of fashionable taste, and vessels of more or less traditional design were produced throughout the second half of the sixteenth century. The nature of goldsmiths' work is such that we cannot expect to find more than the outward forms of Mannerism reflected in it. In Mannerist art emphasis was placed upon the irrational and the anomalous, but this was a direction that the goldsmith could not easily follow. The highly complex facade of Mannerism with its unexpected twists and turns and contrasts was by no means beyond the comprehension of a goldsmith of the calibre of Wenzel Jamnitzer, but even the greatest master was to some extent restricted by the basic forms of the vessels he wrought from expressing the full range of Mannerist ideas. The most sophisticated piece still had to be capable of standing upright on its foot or base. Nevertheless the goldsmith, working in the easily malleable and fusible precious metals, was less restricted by technical considerations from wilful indulgence in the bizarre forms and eclectic ornament inherent in Mannerism than were craftsmen working in other materials. Like other artisans in the field of decorative art the goldsmith took pride in overcoming the seemingly insuperable problems set by the designer. Freed from the limitations of function, in so far as the material and the vessel form would permit, the goldsmith's creation could become an expression of an idea, in short a work of art. From this it follows that the most characteristic examples of Mannerist goldsmiths' work were created for the collector and were intended to adorn the *Kunst und Wunderkammer*[6] rather than the dining-table.

The pre-occupation of the goldsmith with technical skill tended to blind him to beauty of form and harmony of profile. Furthermore, the obsession with profusion of ornament prevented him from achieving unity of design. The impression is sometimes given that the goldsmith has merely added one scheme of ornament on top of another without regard to the coherence of effect of the whole. In working out their programmes of ornament the Mannerist goldsmiths overlooked the problems arising from the association in close proximity of decorative styles that sprang up in different periods and circumstances. The naturalistic arabesque that had been a characteristic feature of Renaissance border ornament was replaced towards the middle of the century by the more strictly Near-Eastern and purely abstract mauresque. This exotic ornament was regularly used by the goldsmiths of the second half of the century in combination with both formal classical and naturalistic detail on one and the same piece. It is typical of this period that ingenuity was more highly regarded than unity of design. Not only was the original programme of a piece composed of eclectic elements; sometimes an object that was already richly embellished was given added decoration within a few years of its completion. Typical examples are the frame of the Dresden mirror (pl. 527), the Jamnitzer jewel-casket in the Munich Schatzkammer (pl. 427), which has been enriched with precious stones in gold collets, both inside and outside, and the Reliquary of St. George in the same treasury, the base of which was altered and enriched in 1612 and again in 1623. The climate of aesthetic opinion of this period favoured this obsession with ornament. The Mannerist patron expected to take up the piece in his hand, to examine it closely and to admire the minute detail of its craftsmanship.

In spite of the admiration accorded to originality of invention, certain conventions were introduced by the Mannerist artists, such as the ideal female nude. First devised by the Fontainebleau masters, this ideal was adopted and to some extent exaggerated by the court painters of the Emperor Rudolph II at Prague: Hans von Aachen, Bartholomäus Spranger, Joseph Heinz and Jost van Winghe. This ideal combines a long and elegant body with almost disproportionately small head, breasts and feet. The faces often display a cold, aloof and yet sensual expression. Emphasis is placed on the sexual organs; though not necessarily depicted, their position was indicated by some symbolic feature such as a ring, girdle or knot.

While continuing to employ in their compositions the familiar elements of classical ornament revived in the Renaissance, those goldsmiths who were influenced by Mannerism rejected the system of proportion and some of the conventions that had hitherto

Plate XI
Ivory beaker mounted in enamelled gold. Probably French, dated 1558.

Plate XII
Enamelled gold tazza set with antique gold coins. Probably Central European, mid 16th century.

governed the use of these elements. There was no fundamental break in the development from Renaissance to Mannerism, but classical ornament was sometimes used in so perverse a manner as to suggest a spirit of revolution. There was no lack of continuity except in some of the more extreme manifestations, and Mannerism, while rejecting what seemed to be outworn disciplines in favour of a more original if artificial elegance, did not completely interrupt the gradual evolution of style which extends from the early Renaissance to the Baroque and Neo-classicism. Some of the wilder manifestations have given rise to the suggestion that Mannerism was in general anti-classical, but the Mannerist goldsmiths continued to employ classical ornament, sometimes adding naturalistic and even exotic detail. The *enfants terribles* of the style perpetrated quite surrealistic combinations of unrelated themes, in which animal, vegetable, architectural and abstract elements were combined in fantastic conceits, but such extremes were exceptional amongst the work of the goldsmiths. One common fault of the Mannerist craftsman was his unwillingness to leave any space undecorated: obsessed by this *horror vacui* he delighted in abundant and vociferous ornament, often without paying much attention to questions of scale. While the *Maniera* was as a whole courtly and sophisticated, one sometimes suspects the goldsmith of an almost childish delight in setting familiar ornamental themes in improbable, almost anomalous juxtaposition.

The most elegant of all representations of a vessel in Mannerist taste known to me appears in Parmigianino's *Madonna del Collo lungo* in the Dresden Gemälde Galerie. In this painting, executed about 1535, an angel to the right of the Virgin Mary holds up a vase with an elongated ovoid body and a tall slender foot, foretelling the course of sophisticated taste during the following decades. While most of the goldsmiths of the time preferred to cover the surface of their vessels with profuse ornament, Parmigianino's vase is undecorated and its effect is achieved by the originality of its form. The type introduced by Parmigianino was subsequently taken up in France and long-necked vases and ewers are constant features of the paintings of the Fontainebleau school.

The term *stil rustique* has been applied by Kris[7] to one of the many divergent directions taken by Mannerist art. This trend is found in both France and Germany at about the same time, but each seems to have been a spontaneous development rather than the result of interaction. The French version is now confined to the ceramic productions of Bernard Palissy and it is not possible to establish whether the style had any effect in the goldsmiths' workshops. In the north it is best represented in the productions of the workshop of Wenzel Jamnitzer. The *stil rustique* was characterized by naturalism, a naturalism of striking realism because it was based upon casts taken directly from nature. The subjects ranged from fruits and grasses to insects and the smaller reptiles. The last must have been dead before the casts were taken, but the versions in silver have nevertheless a most lively appearance, which can only have been achieved as a result of the most careful preparation of the figures before the plaster mould was poured on them. This exploitation of naturalistic ornament did not accord with the general trend of Mannerist art which preferred to represent abstract rather than natural forms, but the climate of contemporary taste was particularly favourable to such demonstrations of human ingenuity. They constituted just the sort of conceit that appealed to the collector of the time. Casts from nature had already been known to the Paduan bronze sculptors such as Andrea Riccio, but the Nürnberg goldsmiths were able to achieve much more delicate results in precious metal than their Italian predecessors working in bronze or their French contemporaries working in ceramic.

The philosophical principle lying behind the *stil rustique* was that of the earthly source of all things. Just as in the case of a Mannerist building the ground storey was given the rough surface of the natural rock, so also the base of a silver vessel was intended to suggest the living material from which the precious metal was won. The most effective expression of this idea is to be found in the *Handsteine* (a word for which there is no precise English equivalent); these were small pieces of silver ore mounted on silver gilt stems or bases and carved with numerous figures and scenes illustrating mining or other industrial processes associated with the production and refining of silver. In some cases the order was reversed and the silver ore was placed on top of a worked silver base. The design by Concz Welcz (pl. 36) shows a mining scene on the base while the upper part of the cup is elaborately wrought.

Another aspect of the *stil rustique* was the use of shells, both in their natural form and in imitations in more precious material. An idea of the importance accorded to shells, described as *indianische Schneggen* (literally 'Indian snails') can be gathered from Phillip Hainhofer's correspondence with Duke Philipp II of Pommern. Writing in 1610, Hainhofer informed him that the Duke of Württemberg had just bought a quantity of Indian snails for 1200 florins cash and observed further that if they had not already been sold, the Duke of Bavaria would have been prepared to pay 1500 florins for them. He goes on to say that he has a large number himself and that they were suitable for decoration, and would look well on the table or go in a collector's cabinet, or even decorate a grotto. Finally he states that the Dutch States are said to have presented the King of France with 6000 florins worth of snails, and the Emperor himself has had a room decorated with them.[8] While such shell-decorated rooms no longer survive from this period, the grotto which is attached to the south east corner of the Antiquarium in the Munich Residenz represents the effect well enough. Drinking cups mounted with shells, usually either nautilus- or trochus-shells still survive in large numbers from the Mannerist period. The catalogue of the Dresden Grünes Gewölbe, the collection of the Wettin rulers of Saxony, includes no fewer than fifty-two such vessels.

Typical of the somewhat perverse sophistication of the period is the practice of producing a readily available natural form in another material, preferably one that was extremely difficult to work. The more sophisticated taste preferred to the natural shell a shell-like shape that had with infinite labour been carved from a piece of hardstone, such as the lapis lazuli cup illustrated in pl. 332 or the surprisingly early red agate shell cup made for Markgraf Georg von Brandenburg-Kulmbach in 1536 (pl. 275). This delight in metamorphosis, which is typical of Mannerist taste, can also be found in the designs for goldsmiths of Giulio Romano (pls. 63, 67, 73) which show silver vessels wrought in the form of a fish, vine leaves or basket work. A typical expression of this fashion is the Proserpina ewer, a rock-crystal vessel carved by Annibale Fontana for Duke Albrecht V of Bavaria about 1570-1575.[9] This ewer is furnished with mounts of enamelled and jewelled gold, but the carver has imitated table-stones in large collets in the shaping of the rock-crystal. The greater the contrast between the material imitated and that actually used, the more the spirit of the time was satisfied. The most extreme versions of this fashion are the paintings of human figures composed of fruit, flowers and other artefacts that were invented by Rudolph II's court painter, Giuseppe Archimboldi.

Many of the finest and most characteristic expressions of Mannerist taste in the art of the goldsmith are found in the enamelled gold mounts of semi-precious hardstone vessels. Such vessels were known in classical antiquity and in the Middle Ages; the collection of hardstone assembled by Lorenzo de' Medici included a number of ancient vases which he had re-mounted in contemporary fashion. Whereas the earlier vessels are of restrained form, those created by the hardstone cutters of the second half of the sixteenth century were carved into the shapes of animals or monsters and were given far more elaborate decoration. In no field of the applied arts did Mannerism achieve so complete a manifestation as in the working of hardstone; this was because the natural shape of the unworked block often suggested some fantastic shape to the artist, much in the way that Leonardo da Vinci obtained inspiration from stains on walls or chance blots. Of the various hardstones used in the sixteenth century, rock-crystal was the most important. The elegance of the Mannerist style could be more readily expressed in this delicate material than in the coloured stones which were better suited to the vigorous and more masculine Baroque style. Again, rock-crystal was better adapted to the intaglio cutting technique of the sixteenth century, while the coloured stones gained from the plastic treatment of the Baroque. Nevertheless, jasper, lapis lazuli, bloodstone and various forms of agate were exploited by the Mannerist hardstone sculptors as well, and some of the richest mounts were devised for vessels of coloured hardstone.

The beauty of rock-crystal was such that one would expect it to have been displayed as effectively as possible when used in a drinking-vessel. A peculiar fashion, which is represented by a few surviving examples, preferred to conceal the crystal behind a cage of filigree which permitted only a glimpse of the precious material behind. Various explanations of this practice can be suggested; perhaps the most likely is the surprise provided by a vessel, apparently with pierced walls of filigree, which proved in use to be watertight. An example by an Augsburg goldsmith is illustrated in pl. 494. Another, also probably of German origin but dating from the mid-sixteenth century is at Clare College, Cambridge, where it goes by the name of the Poison Tankard, on the grounds that the rock-crystal would make it possible to recognise the presence of poison in the vessel.

In the production of sculptured hardstone vessels the goldsmith had to accept a secondary role. The form of the vessel was worked out by the sculptor by reference to the shape of the stone in its natural state and to the commission he had received. The goldsmith was thus required to produce mounts for a vessel the shape of which had already been determined. On the later hardstone vessels the role of the goldsmith became more important as not only the foot and the mouth rims were gold-mounted but the spout and handle were made separately and had to be attached by gold rings. The gold mounts of the foot and mouth were often of modest size but the handles of some of the Milanese and Florentine pieces were elaborately wrought and were the most important feature of the whole vessel (pl. V). The curious vessels in the form of exotic birds or monsters also required numerous gold mounts to hold together the various elements of which they were constructed. The mounts were often further enriched with precious stones, sometimes of large size and great value. The end product was a work of invention and ingenuity that has never been since equalled (pl. VI).

While hardstone vessels have survived in considerable number, often deprived of their precious mounts, there are few drawings that can be identified with certainty as designs for them. These are mostly the work of two masters, the Italian, Bernardo Buontalenti, who worked at the court of Grand Duke Francesco de' Medici in Florence, and the Flemish-born Erasmus Hornick who worked in Antwerp, in South Germany and finally in Prague. It is not always possible to be certain whether a drawing was intended to be executed in hardstone or entirely in precious metal and it is possible that some of the designs illustrated, which would appear to be best suited for execution in hardstone, were really meant for the goldsmith.

The decorative arts have always followed the lead of architecture, painting and sculpture with a more or less considerable time-lag and it was not until the late sixteenth and early seventeenth century, when the major arts were already experiencing a process of transition, that the greatest achievements of the Mannerist goldsmiths, particularly in the north were made. The goldsmiths of the mid-sixteenth century still made use of familiar Renaissance ornament and stressed the horizontal element in their compositions at a time when masters of ornament, such as Cornelis Floris in the Low Countries or Virgil Solis and Erasmus Hornick in Germany, had begun to reject classical forms altogether and to design vessels composed of a mixture of animal and vegetable forms. These designs date from the 1560's, but it was not until some twenty years later that the goldsmiths, who had probably been held back more by the conservatism of their clients than by the difficulty of creating such complex forms, began to execute them. Towards the end of the sixteenth century vessels appear in which vertical movement has replaced the horizontal structure of the Renaissance. The form of the foot now followed on through the stem and body up to the apex of the cover in a continuous unbroken rhythm, achieving that effect of unity, which was later a basic feature of the Baroque.

Italian fashion and precept were of great importance in the development of northern Mannerist goldsmiths' work. Quite apart from the circulation of Italian designs in the north, some of the most inspired of the northern goldsmiths spent some time in Italy between completing their apprenticeship and seeking admission as master-goldsmiths. Just as designers such as Androuet du Cerceau, Cornelis Floris, Cornelis Bos and Erasmus Hornick, went to Italy, so also did the leading goldsmiths such as Anton Eisenhoit of Warburg, Christoph Jamnitzer of Nürnberg, Paul van Vianen of Utrecht and Andreas Attemstett of Augsburg. Thus the northern style was constantly refreshed through contact with Italian masters, always so prodigal in new ideas.

The last development of Mannerist fashion in the sixteenth century was the auricular style, which persisted so long into the seventeenth century that it is sometimes regarded as belonging more properly to Baroque. Its origins date back to the mid-sixteenth century and it is best regarded as a form of northern Mannerism. It developed out of the earlier grotesque, which it presented in a plastic form, and made its first appearance in the northern Netherlands whence it spread to Germany and to England but not to the south. At first purely a form of surface decoration, it came in the work of the van Vianen family to determine the whole form of the vessel. The style was propagated in Germany and finally in Prague at the Imperial Court Workshop by the peripatetic artist, Paul van Vianen, but German essays in this manner, such as those of Anton Schweinberger (pl. 579) use its forms in a decorative rather than a structural manner.

While on the one hand Mannerism was an elegant and courtly fashion in which a high value was placed on novelty (*inventiones*), it had on the other hand, its darker side. In the northern courts Mannerist sophistication took a turn in the direction of the perverse and displayed a curious fascination in the less agreeable manifestations of nature, freaks, dwarfs and monsters. It is not easy to determine how far such interests were motivated by the new-born search for knowledge of the human being and his place in nature, but one consequence was the cult of the ugly, which is a striking feature of the later phase of Mannerist art. Whereas most of the earlier manifestations of Mannerism, such as are seen in the designs engraved by Virgil Solis or Matthias Zündt (pls. 136 or 137) have grace and charm, the later designs, including many from the prolific pen of Erasmus Hornick, are repulsive and seem, like so many creations of twentieth-century art, to have been intended to shock and disturb (pls. 151-3). The delight in exotic materials manifested by the patrons of the Mannerist goldsmiths was not inspired exclusively by aesthetic motives. Such princes as the Emperor Rudolph II were greatly influenced by superstition and attributed magical powers, particularly in relation to the recognition of poison, to certain materials. This applied especially to the unattractive bezoars, gall-stones from the bladders of animals that were mounted with such splendour in enamelled gold. At a time when deaths that could not readily be accounted for by natural causes were attributed to poison, there was much interest in the exploitation of any means of recognising poison in the cup before it had been absorbed into the system. Even so relatively common a material as serpentine was credited with such powers. A silver mounted serpentine cup and cover in an English private collection is inscribed *'Serpentin Heiss Ich Alle Gift Vertreib'* (I am called Serpentine and I banish all poison).

Sixteenth-century patrons of the goldsmiths looked far and wide for splendid objects to enrich their treasuries and maintained agents abroad who searched for both finished vessels and raw materials that could be worked up in the court workshop. Two of the most enthusiastic collectors of the latter half of the sixteenth century were the Emperor Rudolph II and Duke Wilhelm V of Bavaria, followed by the Archduke Ferdinand of Tirol, who, however, devoted most of his energies to assembling a great collection of armour in his castle of Ambras outside Innsbruck. Vessels of rock-crystal and of lapis lazuli were obtained from Florence, of rock-crystal, agate and jasper from Milan; carved coral from Genoa, in particular from Battista Negrone Viale; mother-of-pearl, both carved and in the rough, came from Italy; bezoars from Spain and Peru; amber from the Baltic coast; river-pearls from the Danube and precious stones from a variety of sources, including the Far East and South America. Duke Wilhelm employed the banking family of Fugger with their worldwide network of agents, while the Holy Roman Emperor made use of his diplomatic representatives in his search for rarities. Among the most active of these agents was Jacopo da Strada (see p.46), who worked for the Holy Roman Emperor, the Duke of Mantua, the Duke of Bavaria and for a time for Pope Julius II.

The contents of a princely *Kunstkammer* were not by any means confined to goldsmiths' work. Every conceivable material was included, though, where appropriate, mounted in precious metal. A picture of a typical *Kunstkammer* is given by the inventory of the collection of the Archduke Ferdinand of Tirol, prepared after his death in 1596. This collection was contained in eighteen large cupboards which were set up in his castle of Ambras. It is significant that objects of precious metal were put in the first three cupboards; one cupboard contained vessels of rock-crystal with enamelled gold mounts, many in the form of fantastic animals, others carved from semi-precious hardstone including presents from other princes, the most important being the four pieces given by King Charles IX of France: the Cellini Salt, the onyx ewer, the cup with figure of the Archangel Michael on top and the so-called Burgundian Court Beaker. The second cupboard contained vessels of gold and silver including quite a number of medieval pieces. There were many mounted pieces, including griffins' claws, rhinoceros horns, ostrich-egg and coconut cups, articles decorated with casts from nature, and a garniture composed of ewer, basin and candlestick of exotic shells in silver-gilt mounts (pls. 466-7). The third cupboard contained *Handsteine*, while in the others were a multiplicity of objects illustrating every activity of mankind, various freaks of nature and other natural forms. The *Kunstkammer* of the Archduke Ferdinand of Tirol occupied a large chamber, but similar collections were put together in Augsburg on a miniature scale. During the early decades of the seventeenth century the diplomat art-dealer of Augsburg, Phillip Hainhofer, specialised in devising, composing and marketing cabinets (*Kunstschränke*) which were fitted with innumerable drawers containing a vast number of articles illustrating the whole range of human activity, but with special reference to scientific discoveries. The most famous of these cabinets, the *Pommersche Kunstschrank,*[10] which was designed by Hainhofer for Duke Philipp of Pomerania, was destroyed after the Second World War, though its contents survive in the Berlin Kunstgewerbemuseum. They illustrate classical mythology and Humanist philosophy as well as material objects. The latter numbered some hundreds, including a musical-box, toilet articles, a chemist's outfit with boxes, scales, mortars and presses, medical and surgical equipment, writing materials, instruments for drawing, measuring, reading and weighing, implements for eating and drinking, games of all kinds and a wide range of tools. The contents were not intended for use; this is made clear by the magnificence of the cabinet in which they were contained, but rather to provide a summary of the whole range of human knowledge. The frivolous side of Mannerism is well represented in some of the contents, in particular, the set of twelve silver and parcel-gilt heart-shaped dishes.[11] Hainhofer mentions these in his detailed description of the contents in the following terms: 'In the drawers on the right hand side of the cabinet are six heart-plates, and the dishes are made in the shape of hearts so that one can arrange them in sets like a star, rose, cross, etc. and place the square candlesticks and complete dishes between them in an attractive pattern.'[12] A host of Augsburg artists and craftsmen worked on the cabinet and the range of its contents was discussed at every stage with the Duke who was to own it. Finally, the Augsburg painter, Anton Mozart, painted an imaginary scene of its being handed over to the Duke in the presence of all those who had worked on it. Other less elaborate cabinets have survived in the University of Uppsala (presented to King Gustavus Adolphus of Sweden by the city of Augsburg) and in the Palazzo Pitti, Florence, the latter without its original contents.

Apart from these *Kunstschränke,* the most typical productions of the Mannerist goldsmiths were vast table-centres usually combined with a fountain (pl. 127). Like the cabinets, these also had a didactic purpose. While they might be constructed around some mythological scene which was presented in the round as on a stage, they included supporting features that were intended to provide a visual summary of human knowledge. The most ingenious creator of these table-centres, not one of which survives in its entirety, was the Nürnberg master, Wenzel Jamnitzer. The most ambitious of those made by Jamnitzer was originally commissioned by the Emperor Maximilian II in 1556. Only the figures that supported it now survive, but a description of the whole complex was made by a German student who saw it in 1540.[13] Unfortunately his powers of description were limited and the result is somewhat confused. It is, nevertheless worth quoting a summary of his account, as it gives a unique picture of these ambitious mechanical artefacts in whose manufacture goldsmiths, mathematicians, scientists, humanists and philosophers combined. The table-centre is described as being ten feet in height and five in width. Its form as a whole was based on that of the imperial crown, symbolising the supreme terrestrial power. It was supported by four large bronze figures representing the seasons (the only parts that survive). Spring was represented by Flora, summer by Ceres, autumn by Bacchus and winter by Vulcan, each figure holding its appropriate attribute in its hand which was stretched out in the direction of the next figure, thus symbolising the continuity of the Seasons. Between each of the figures was a lion holding a shield with the arms of Austria and Burgundy. Next came a platform which constituted the main support of the table-centre. This was divided into two regions representing the elements of earth and water respectively. The Earth was presided over by the crowned goddess, Cybele, around whom were hills and mountains composed of gold and silver-bearing ores and fields in which grew all kinds of grasses and herbs, also cast in precious metal. The element of water was represented by Neptune standing on a shell and accompanied by all kinds of sea-monsters. His crown was a fully-rigged ship and he held a trident in his hand. The four chief rivers of Europe, the Danube, Rhine, Elbe and Tiber, flowed from their source on this platform. The source was guarded by a nymph and as the rivers ran off the platform they operated a miniature grinding-mill, sawmill, hammer-mill and stamping-mill, thus representing human industry. Above this platform was the Element of Air, represented by Mercury hanging from a golden star. The air was filled with many birds and with clouds, upon one of which were the Four Winds. Further up again were four angels holding laurel wreaths and ribbons bearing legends. In the air around were birds occupying the space between the clouds. All these were within the area enclosed by the crown, above which was a celestial globe which represented the transit of sun and moon across the heavens. This in turn was surrounded by four archangels, between whom flew young eagles with sceptres representing the younger princes who would rule the empire in the future. A larger eagle perched on top of the globe symbolised the monarchs and the ruling princes and, by strangling a basilisk with its claw, symbolised their function on earth of punishing and frustrating sin. Finally the figure of Jupiter seated on the back of the eagle represented at the same time the Emperor himself and by the thunderbolt in his hand the Element of Fire.

Yet another part of the centre-piece illustrated the history and nature of the imperial rule. This was not placed inside the crown nor over the celestial globe but probably around the arches of the crown. The four monarchies of history were represented by Ninus, Cyrus, Alexander the Great and the ruling Holy Roman Emperor, Maximilian II. Then came the seven Electors of the Empire, four Dukes, four marquesses and so on, through all ranks and classes of the Empire down to cities, villages and even the peasants, represented by their appropriate chains, orders and coats-of-arms. Four stars moved around the heads of the monarchs and were probably driven by the same clockwork that moved the celestial sphere. Finally, when an appropriate lever was moved, two dances, entitled *Rolandt* and *Pickelhering*, were played on cymbals operated by water-power.

It would be difficult to find an object which displayed more comprehensively the elaborate philosophical programme of Mannerist goldsmiths' work. As the German student observed, it allegorised not only the imperial regime but also 'Physica, Metaphysica, Politica and many fine Philosophical and Poetical ideas as well'.

A feature of German goldsmiths' work that calls for further consideration is the long persistence of the Gothic style in the sixteenth century. It is not surprising that Albrecht Dürer, who had so important a part in the dissemination of the Italian Renaissance style in northern Europe should have continued in the later years of his life to produce designs in Gothic as well as Renaissance taste. His design for a double cup of Gothic lobate form in the Albertina, Vienna,[14] dates from 1526, only two years before he died. Moreover, the *Akeley Pokal* continued in use as the Nürnberg masterpiece throughout the sixteenth century and must have exerted a significant influence in maintaining Gothic tradition alive in the goldsmiths' shops. There must have been a period, however brief, about the middle of the century when Gothic style cups, other than the masterpiece cups, ceased to be fashionable, but an indication to the contrary can be found in the Gothic double cup from the collection of James de Rothschild which bears the arms of the Counts von Salm and the date 1549.[15] In spite of its Renaissance frieze this cup was probably made some years before 1549, but the very fact that the family arms should have been engraved on it in that year indicates that the cup was not considered to be excessively *démodé*. If the Salm Cup should be regarded as a Gothic survival, then the cup made by Wenzel Jamnitzer for the Tucher family (pl. 425) must be a manifestation of the Gothic revival. It is a typical late Gothic double cup bearing that date 1564; even the frieze engraved round the rim is composed of Gothic thistle foliage instead of the Renaissance ornament usually found at this point on Gothic revival cups. It is, however, possible that Wenzel Jamnitzer was commissioned to provide a replica of an earlier cup that no longer survives, in which case it would not rank as an anticipation of revived Gothic. It was during the last quarter of the sixteenth and the first of the following century that the Gothic revival exercised the strongest influence. Leading Nürnberg masters, such as Hans Petzoldt, Peter Wiber and Hans Beutmüller, all produced cups in revived Gothic style. Three main types can be distinguished: firstly, lobate cups (pl. 550) in which both Gothic and Renaissance elements can be recognised, but in which one or the other predominates: secondly cups that are close reproductions of late Gothic prototypes (pl. 483): and thirdly, what are now called 'pineapple cups', though contemporary inventories describe them as 'bunch of grapes cups' (*Trauben Pokal*) (pl. 480). These were not known in the fifteenth century and do not constitute a true revival, though the form was evidently influenced by late Gothic taste.

This neo-Gothic revival in Germany might be interpreted as another bizarre Mannerist reaction against the formal classicism of the Renaissance. There is, however, one circumstance that throws doubt on this interpretation; this is the fact that the revival seems to have been confined to Nürnberg and to a lesser degree the northern towns of Hamburg, Lüneburg and Lübeck. It had little influence in Augsburg, where only the pineapple cups became popular. It has been suggested that the revival may have been connected with the Counter Reformation, in which case it might be explained as marking a return to the more godly style that had preceded the pagan intermission of the Renaissance.[16] There are two good reasons for rejecting this explanation: firstly, it was most strongly represented in the productions of the predominantly Lutheran city of Nürnberg, and, secondly, it was, in Germany at any rate, more marked in secular than in ecclesiastical plate. In England, where a Gothic revival appears in church plate of the Charles I period, this was a manifestation of the Laudian reaction against Puritanism. An alternative solution is that the revival should be regarded as a precocious manifestation of the nascent Baroque. Though some of the neo-Gothic vessels were highly complex in form, the general effect was more unified than in the case of typical Mannerist work. The *Trauben Pokal* made in large numbers by Hans Petzoldt (pl. 480) which were composed only of embossed lobes, achieved, for instance, an integrated effect. The beauty of their form and ornament can be appreciated at a glance: there is no need to turn them round and round to follow curving and interlacing elements or to read figure scenes of arcane significance. These are features that contradicted the eclectic and diffuse effect of Mannerism but reflected the unified and dramatic effect of Baroque, for which the theorists of aesthetics of the late sixteenth century were already preparing the way. Revivalism was not restricted to the craft of the goldsmith. In their search for articles for inclusion in the *Kunst und Wunderkammer,* the antiquarians commissioned copies to be made of reliefs by Dürer and other early sixteenth century masters.

Possibly the best explanation is also the simplest, namely that there was no true revival because the Gothic cup never went out of fashion. It remained a standard form for wedding presents and the addorsed coats-of-arms of husband and wife are often found on such cups; the Gothic tradition was also preserved in the form of the *Willkomm* cup, an important possession that recalled the history and status of family or guild. Such cups were made in the traditional manner that was considered appropriate for solemn occasions long after the fashion that originally had determined their design had been abandoned.

1 For a discussion of the minimal interpretation, see J. Shearman, *Mannerism*, London, 1967 and J. Bialostocki, *Umeni*, Prague, XVIII, 1970, p.105 'Two types of international Mannerism, Italian and Northern'. For the opposite interpretation see the exhibition catalogue *De Trionf van het Manierisme*, Amsterdam, 1955.

2 Berliner, Band I, pls. 134-8. It is significant that Thiry is described as *Peintre excellent* in the dedication of the Jason Series, see Berliner, Textband, p.151, note 1.

3 The same design was re-used by Jamnitzer as the title-page of his *Perspectiva Corporum Regularum*, which was engraved by Jost Amman after Jamnitzer's drawings and published in Nürnberg in 1568.

4 Fontainebleau II, cat. no. 245.

5 Baader, p.34.

6 For a general account see J. v. Schlosser, *Kunst und Wunderkammer der Spät-Renaissance*, Leipzig, 1908.

7 See Kris, 'Der Style Rustique', *Jahrbuch des Kunsthist. Museums*, N.F.I., Wien, 1926.

8 Doering, p.8-9.

9 ill. Thoma, pl. 73.

10 For the literature of the *Pommersche Kunstschrank*, see Pechstein I, cat. no. 110.

11 ill. Pechstein I, cat. nos. 112-123.

12 '*In der schubladen zur rechten Hand dess tisch ligen 6 hertzschisslen und 6 herzteller, und sein die schisslen darumb in forma cordium, damit man khunde zugweiss, wie stern, rosen, Creutz und dergleichen machen, und die vierekhete leichter und complet schusselen fein darzwischen setzen'.*

13 Reproduced in full by Lhotsky, p.325ff.

14 Kohlhaussen, fig. 520.

15 ill. E. A. Jones, *Baroness James de Rothschild Collection*, London, 1912, pl. III.

16 See O. von Falke, 'Die Neugotik in deutschen Kunstgewerbe der Spätrenaissance', *Jahrbuch der Preuss. Kunstsammlungen*, Vol. 40, p.76ff. and R. Franz-Berdau, 'Der so-gennante Lutherbecher der Universität Greifswald, ein Werk der Neugotik um 1600' *Zeitschrift für Kunstwissenschaft*, 1960, Berlin, p.127.

CHAPTER SEVEN

Italy

THE range of activity of the Renaissance artist knew few limits and it is not surprising that many of the most prominent Renaissance masters should have been more or less closely associated with goldsmithing. Masters such as Francesco Francia of Bologna (1450-1517) and his son, Giacomo Francia, continued throughout their working careers to combine the crafts of painter and goldsmith. Others, among them Antonio Pollaiuolo, Pierino da Vinci and Francesco Salviati, were trained as goldsmiths and continued to provide designs for the craft after they had themselves abandoned the hammer in favour of the brush or the rule. Drawings of goldsmiths' work were produced by Michelangelo Buonarotti, Cosimo Tura, Baldassare Peruzzi, Perino del Vaga, Giulio Romano, Giorgio Vasari and Marco Marchetti of Faenza, to mention only a few. With the exception of Pollaiuolo and Peruzzi, whose designs were firmly anchored in the Renaissance, all these masters adopted in their goldsmiths' designs to a greater or lesser degree the more adventurous forms of Mannerist art during the second quarter of the sixteenth century.

Despite the presence in Italy of many northern craftsmen, especially goldsmiths, there are clear distinctions between Italian and northern goldsmiths' work. The Italians preferred a more architectural and restrained manner and were less inclined to follow the fantastic suggestions of the designers. Unlike Spain where the Counter-Reformation was accompanied by a new and appropriately sober style, there is no trend towards severity in Italian work of the last third of the century. Original graphic designs by Italian masters have survived in large numbers, but few printed pattern books intended for the goldsmith are known. This suggests that it was the custom in Italy for the more important vessels to be made, not after pattern-book designs, but from an original drawing by the goldsmith himself or by an artist commissioned to provide one. Before considering the few extant examples of Italian Mannerist silver, it seems best to look briefly at the large quantity of drawings surviving beginning with those produced in Rome, though not necessarily by masters born there. Artists of all kinds were frequently on the move in sixteenth-century Italy. The distances involved were not great and it was often necessary to flee from enemies, the law, creditors or the plague.

Michelangelo Buonarotti

As might be expected, one of the earliest datable Mannerist designs for goldsmiths' work is from the hand of Michelangelo. This is the highly original salt-cellar[1] with cover which he drew for Francesco Maria della Rovere, Duke of Urbino, in 1537 (pl. 49). The correctness of the traditional attribution to Michelangelo is confirmed by a letter written to the Duke on July 4, 1537, by his agent in Rome, Girolamo Staccoli.[2] This refers to several features of the drawing, including the paw feet, the festoons and masks around the top of the vase, and the figure modelled in the round which surmounts the cover. Michelangelo doubtless produced other designs, and the Roman goldsmith, Gentile da Faenza, had in his possession casts and models by Michelangelo and other masters.

Classical vases play an important part in the architecture of the *Sagrestia Nuova* of the monastery of San Lorenzo in Florence. In this famous chamber, which contains Michelangelo's Medici tombs, the corners are occupied by pairs of niches, surmounted by pediments. The bases of each pair of jambs are carved in low relief with two-handled vases with tall necks. There are eight of these niches and each pair of vases differs in detail, though the profile as a whole is consistent. There seems to be no reason to question that all these vases were designed by Michelangelo himself.

Michelangelo also made a model for a salt-cellar that had been commissioned by Cardinal Alessandro Farnese from the Roman goldsmith, Manno di Sbarri. Two alternative versions of the salt were offered to the Cardinal, a drawing and a model of terracotta. It is clear from a letter written by Tommaso de' Cavalieri, a mutual friend of the sculptor and goldsmith, that the model had been prepared by Michelangelo. It is not known which of the alternatives was chosen; but the model was supported by four tortoises placed in niches and surmounted by a single figure.

Polidoro Caldara

The most fantastic and the most remote from practical possibility of the Italian Renaissance versions of classical Roman vases are those designed by Polidoro Caldara da Caravaggio and painted by him on the facade of the Palazzo Milesi in Rome.[3] Caldara died in 1543, but his extraordinary vase designs seem to belong to the age of Baroque rather than to the Renaissance. They had, however, little significance for the goldsmith at the time they were created. They were intended to be seen from below and, in order to achieve an effect from a distance, their ornament was designed in extremely high relief. This relief, the elaborately figured friezes and the complex handles could not be achieved by the goldsmith except by a lengthy and expensive process of casting from a large number of models. They were not engraved until the latter part of the sixteenth century, first by Cherubino Alberti in 1582, then by Aegidius Sadeler in 1605 and again by Galestruzzi in 1638. Versions exist cast in bronze or modelled in majolica, but all seem to date from the seventeenth century; they are recognisable by the characteristic drooping lip which Polidoro favoured and which had, indeed classical precedent (pl. 50). Judging by the very large numbers of copies extant, it must have been one of the standard tasks of apprentices to make drawings of the Polidoro vases. Whether all, or indeed any, of these copies were made in goldsmiths' workshops is uncertain; they were probably done by apprentices to painters as exercises in perspective and foreshortening. That this was often the practice is shown by the fact that similar vessels appear in sixteenth-century *grottesche* frescoes and in paintings of such popular subjects as 'Balshazzar's Feast' or 'The Marriage at Cana'.

Perino del Vaga

One of the most influential masters in the field of decorative art was Pietro Buonaccorsi, known as Perino del Vaga, because he served his apprenticeship with an obscure Florentine painter of that name. He was born in Florence in 1501, left for Rome at the age of about sixteen and remained there until the sack of the city in 1527, when he went to Genoa in the service of Andrea Doria, where he is said to have designed ornaments for the poops of Genoese galleys. He spent ten years there and was present when Doria received the Emperor Charles V and entertained him on his magnificent barge.[4] On this occasion a complete new service of plate had been ordered in the design of which del Vaga probably played an important part. Unfortunately nothing remains of this service. In 1537 Perino returned to Rome where he became Court Painter to Pope Paul III. He was one of the most imaginative interpreters of the Mannerist style and though he did not outlive the first half of the century, having died as early as 1547, his drawings display the fully evolved *Maniera*. His designs show great elegance as in the superb tazza with snake handles and foot composed of mermen and putti (pl. 53) or the boat-shaped vessel with a frieze of sea-creatures along the side (pl. 54). Typical of Perino are tall graceful figures with small oval faces and finely drawn features. His designs are usually very stylish but he was certainly assisted by a workshop, and some of the workshop productions in his manner show the contemporary tendency to sacrifice aesthetic considerations in the search for novelty (pls. 55-7).

Perino's designs were among the most advanced of their time and they foreshadow the whole Mannerist development of the second half of the sixteenth century. The covered tazza (pl. 53) with its low wide bowl anticipates the manner of the Florentine court designer, Buontalenti (see p.151) while the intermingled bodies that constitute the foot and stem can be seen at the end of the century in the work of the Augsburg goldsmiths, Johannes Lencker (pl. 502). The *horror vacui* of Mannerist design also appears in some of Perino's drawings, in particular in the fine drawing of a basin or, perhaps, tazza bowl in the British Museum (pl. 58).

The fortuitous preservation of a series of letters relating to Perino's designs for the carved rock-crystal panels in the Farnese casket (pls. 321-7) throws an interesting light on the artist's status and on the methods of commissioning such work.[5] In 1532 Michelangelo presented his friend, Tommaso Cavalieri, with two drawings of Tytius and Ganymede respectively, to these he subsequently added another showing the subject of the Fall of Phaeton. These drawings, which were much admired and frequently copied in engravings and bronze plaquettes, were seen by Cardinal Hippolito de' Medici, who commissioned the seal-cutter and rock-crystal carver, Giovanni dei Bernardi, then in the service of the Roman Mint, to cut rock-crystal plaques after them. After the death of the Cardinal, Bernardi's plaques fell into the hands of Duke Pier Luigi Farnese who determined to have them mounted in the walls of a casket. The three plaques were insufficient for this purpose and Tolomei, the Duke's secretary, approached Perino del Vaga and asked him to supply the remaining designs. When Perino saw the crystal plaques, however, he declined the commission for fear of offending Michelangelo and, thereafter, as he put it, suffering a fate similar to that of the unhappy Phaeton. Eventually, he agreed to supply sketches but not finished drawings for the additional plaques. The procedure of commissioning rock-crystal intaglios is shown to have been a lengthy one. First a humanist, in this case Pier Luigi's secretary, Tolomei, produced the idea of the subject; this was then translated into a sketch by Perino del Vaga. This sketch had then to be turned into a working drawing to scale, from which the rock-crystal carver could work. In some cases, though not in that of Giovanni dei Bernardi, the carver could himself produce the final working drawing; the number of stages involved was then reduced to three. Bernardi's rock-crystal plaques after the Perino sketches were eventually incorporated in the Farnese casket (see p.149).

As Perino supplied drawings for panels to be inserted in caskets, it is very likely that he designed caskets as well, though not necessarily the Farnese casket, which is attributed with more probability to Francesco Salviati (see p.143). Among Perino's drawings is a design for a casket in the Uffizi at Florence (pl. 59). This is one of the earliest versions of a type that remained in fashion throughout the century and was still being produced by masters such as Matthias Wallbaum and Boas Ulrich of Augsburg in the early seventeenth century. Vasari relates that Perino was prepared to design a wide variety of hangings, costume, porches and every kind of small object.[6] Presumably his goldsmiths' designs were included in the last category. According to Vasari,[7] he was closely associated with the goldsmith, Giovanni di Baldassare, commonly known as *il Piloto*, who was a friend of Benvenuto Cellini and worked in Florence, Rome and Venice until his death in 1536. It was Piloto who took Perino from Rome to Florence, a move which brought him in touch with Manno Fiorentino, the actual maker of the Farnese casket, for which he supplied the sketches. Perino del Vaga was assisted by Luzio Romano, and the goldsmiths' designs in the British Museum, formerly attributed to Perino, have now been provisionally assigned to this assistant.[8] If this change of attribution is correct, it would follow that several of the drawings here given to Perino del Vaga should also be given to Luzio Romano, including some of those illustrated (pls. 52-60).

Typical features of Luzio's manner are small but lively human figures with long bodies and tiny heads which turn in unexpected directions, just the same type that is associated with Perino. Luzio Romano is well represented in the Italian drawings in the Royal Collection at Windsor.

Enea Vico

Among the masters who published books of engraved ornament, the most forward-looking was undoubtedly Enea Vico, whose earlier work has been described above (p.82). He was born in Parma about 1520, worked in Rome and died in Ferrara in 1570; his life thus covers the period of the birth and development of Mannerist ornament. In his designs the attenuation of form, the lengthening of the body and the reduction of the foot of a vessel to an impracticably small circumference, in order to enhance the elegance of effect, are already strongly manifest. Vico introduced figures of satyrs as handles and stems and also applied them either in relief or in the round, to spouts, both characteristic features of Mannerist goldsmiths' work (pls. 13, 14, 51). His designs, especially his satyr figures, were copied by Cornelis Floris of Antwerp and also by Androuet du Cerceau in Paris, so that he had an important influence on northern Mannerism. Vico's use of the human figure was carried to its logical conclusion by artists such as Giulio Romano and Perino del Vaga who designed whole vessels in human or animal form (pls. 56-7). The later masters such as Christoph Jamnitzer or Daniel Kellerdaler, whose style bridged the transition between Mannerism and Baroque, supremely imaginative as they were in exploiting the sculptural possibilities of silver, never surpassed the inventiveness of these early Italian masters. In 1552 Enea Vico produced four quite original designs for candlesticks of which one is illustrated (pl. 51). Their style is curiously anomalous in that, while some classical elements are retained, the general effect is decisively anti-classical. There is no evidence to show whether these highly original designs of Vico were ever executed by the goldsmiths of his time.

Giulio Romano

One of the most prolific designers of goldsmiths' work was Giulio Romano, who, as his name suggests, was of Roman origin, though he spent the years from 1524 to 1546 in Mantua in the service of the Gonzaga Dukes of Mantua. He was born about 1492 and was the chief assistant of Raphael in Rome until the latter's death in 1520. He completed some of Raphael's paintings before leaving Rome to take up his court appointment in Mantua. In the course of the twenty-two years he worked at Mantua he and his assistants produced a considerable number of designs of silver and gold vessels for the ducal table. The standard work[9] on Giulio accepts no fewer than eighty-four silver designs as autograph and a far larger number from his workshop survive. Many of the former are annotated that they were prepared for the Duke himself or for a member of his family. One cannot claim great artistic merit for many of these designs; one gets the impression that the master sought to get his ideas on paper as quickly as possible, presumably intending that they should be drawn out more carefully by an assistant. In spite of their summary character, they were much admired and were copied repeatedly by subsequent generations. They provided a source of ideas for a number of lesser masters who followed him, foremost among whom was Jacopo da Strada. (See p.47).

Born in Mantua in 1507, da Strada was trained as a goldsmith and worked in the city in that craft until 1546 when, on the death of Giulio Romano, he left Italy to seek his fortune north of the Alps. He must have been closely associated with Giulio for he wrote a manuscript account of the Palazzo del Te which is still preserved in the Vienna Nationalbibliothek. He succeeded in purchasing from Giulio's son, Raffaello, all of the former's drawings, of which there was a vast quantity, mostly topographical but including antiquities as well.[10] When Vasari visited Mantua for four days in 1542, Giulio showed him 'the plans of the ancient edifices of Rome....and of all the best antiquities of which one has memory, drawn partly by him and partly by others'. Jacopo da Strada seems to have taken these drawings with him when he left Italy and in his new career as art expert to have sold them to the northern princes who were building up collections of antiquities.[11] A good set of drawings of vases and ewers in the classical style after originals by or in the manner of Giulio Romano is preserved amongst a much larger number of similar drawings by other Italian and German masters which is now in the Victoria and Albert Museum, having once formed part of the collection of the Emperor Rudolph II. Da Strada was *Hofantiquar* to the Emperor and it seems, therefore, probable that it was he who supplied these Giulio drawings to the Imperial *Kunstkammer*.

Another group of twenty-four drawings of vases in the manner of Giulio Romano is preserved in the Berlin Kunstbibliothek, most of these with inscriptions claiming quite untruthfully that they represent antique Roman vases dug up in or near Rome.[12] Two further volumes of designs are in the Oesterreichisches Museum, Vienna,[13] and the Fitzwilliam Museum, Cambridge,[14] containing eighty-two and a hundred drawings respectively. These also are mostly copied from originals by Giulio and together give a very complete idea of his range as a designer of goldsmith's work. The volume in Vienna, was, according to the title page, drawn by Ottavia da Strada, Jacopo's son and successor as Court Antiquary to the Emperor Rudolph II '*di mano propria*'. It is implied that they were da Strada's own inventions but this does not appear to be true of any one of them. The majority are copied after Giulio Romano (pls. 70-3), but a few ewer designs may be taken from Polidoro da Caravaggio. While it is not important to know who actually copied the drawings, it is surprising to find them being re-issued as new designs in 1597, the date of the Vienna title-page, fifty years after the death of their original author. The volume of drawings at Cambridge bears no name on the title-page, but seems to date from the same period as that produced by da Strada. Thirty-three of the drawings are common to both volumes and two others appear in only slightly variant versions. It follows that both go back to a common source, probably originals by Giulio Romano or from his workshop. Presumably Jacopo da Strada did not dispose of all the Giulio Romano drawings and bequeathed the remainder to his son, Ottavio. It is possible that Jacopo himself worked on some of the vessels which according to annotations on the drawings were intended for the Gonzaga court at Mantua. Taking the four sets of drawings, together with the many others preserved in Print Rooms throughout the world, we are as well informed about Giulio Romano's goldsmiths' designs as those of any other contemporary master.

Federigo II Gonzaga, who was Giulio Romano's patron in Mantua, followed the custom of his family in his enthusiasm for building palaces and filling them with works of art. Giulio was entrusted with a variety of tasks ranging from the construction of great palaces such as the Palazzo del Te, of churches, villas, public buildings, funeral monuments, pageants and festivities down to vessels of precious metal and majolica. Among all these tasks his designs for goldsmiths' work cannot have ranked very high; in his study of the master, Frederick Hartt dates the designs for the minor arts to the short period between Giulio's arrival in Mantua in 1524 and his beginning to work on the Palazzo del Te in 1526. The great range of these designs, extending from conventional *cinquecento* themes derived from classical Rome to others of highly fantastic and naturalistic character, would seem to predicate a longer period of production than the mere two years suggested by Hartt. The designs were intended not only for Duke Federigo but for other members of the family (pls. 61-2); extant drawings bear inscriptions linking them with Ercole and Ferrante Gonzaga as well as Vincenzio Guerrieri. There is, however, a letter from Francesco to Federigo Gonzaga dated November 1525 in which the writer refers to Giulio's design for a salt-cellar;[15] this does establish that the production of designs for silver was amongst Giulio's first duties at Mantua. As a designer of plate Giulio Romano was adventurous and quite prepared to sacrifice grace of form in the pursuit of originality. His fertile imagination created a great variety of vessel forms, many of them of quite impractical shape (pl. 66). His drawings are, nevertheless, important as the most forceful and extreme expressions of Mannerist taste. Unfortunately they often lack that stylish quality which is the most attractive feature of Mannerist art and merely display a brutish ugliness. Like Enea Vico he anticipated the Dutch seventeenth-century Baroque masters by his soft treatment of surfaces into which mollusc-like forms dissolve (pl. 65).

As might be expected of a master who was predominantly occupied as an architect and as a fresco painter in the grand manner, some of his designs have a monumental character more suited to objects of a larger scale than table silver. This applies, for instance, to the salt-cellar or tureen in the form of a Roman sarcophagus surmounted by a half putto emerging from foliage and holding an ewer, which he designed for Don Ferrante Gonzaga (pl. 61). Giulio employed the same putto again in the lively design for a tureen in the Victoria and Albert Museum (pl. 66). The sarcophagus was also used by Cellini, who made a salt-cellar of sarcophagus form when he was working for Giovanni Firenzuola, a Roman goldsmith who specialised in large vases.[16] Many of Giulio's ideas subsequently became part of the common vocabulary of goldsmith's design. A salt-cellar in the form of a scallop-shell supported on a dolphin's tail was still popular three hundred years later, as was a fruit dish composed of naturalistic vine-leaves and tendrils (pl. 67), while the ewer in the form of a dolphin with wide-open mouth, (pl. 63) an Urbino majolica version of which is in the Bargello Museum in Florence, has been revived in the present century in pottery. Original as are such designs as the double-spouted ewer (pl. 64) they lack the elegance of contemporary drawings by Perino or Salviati.

Typical of Mannerist fashion was Giulio's practice of using silver to imitate other materials, such as the wicker in the ewer design (pl. 71) or the vine-leaves in pl. 67. He did not always produce new ideas; and the same elements might be adapted to serve as candlestick, table-fountain or base of a salt. Shells, dolphins or marine creatures are rarely absent from his designs, even in the case of an article so completely remote in its function from the sea as a lamp (pl. 69). Of all Giulio's designs Hartt singles out as the most original that of a large basin (pl. 68). Not one of the vessels depicted in these lively drawings seems to have survived, but we do not know how many of them were ever carried out. It is curious that the vessels represented in his paintings, as in the *Marriage Feast of Psyche* in the Sala di Psyche of the Palazzo del Te, are far more restrained and elegant than the extravagant forms he proposed to the Gonzaga Dukes.

Papal Patronage

The city of Rome exercised an almost magnetic attraction on Renaissance artists. The Popes were the source of vast patronage and constantly required a supply of precious objects for presentation to foreign sovereigns and their ambassadors. One such was the golden binding which Cellini was commissioned by Pope Paul III to make for a Book of Hours, which the latter wished to present to the Emperor Charles V on his return through Rome from his successful expedition to Tunis. This binding was enriched with enamel and precious stones and decorated with foliate scrolls; it does not seem to have survived. The office of supplier of seal-dies for the Papal Mint was also sought after by Italian goldsmiths; amongst the masters who cut dies either for medals or coinage for the Mint were Benvenuto Cellini, Gian Giacomo Bonzagni and Andrea Casalino. This last master was appointed Court Goldsmith to the Farnese Dukes of Parma in 1572 and in the following year was sent to Rome to improve his art under the guidance of two masters from the Roman Mint. This does not imply that he was found to be an incompetent goldsmith, but rather that he was required to cut medal dies for the Farnese Dukes. This was a task somewhat on the fringe of normal goldsmiths' work and he doubtless found that he required technical instruction. One of his two masters was the famous Guglielmo della Porta, who wrote to Duke Ottavio Farnese on March 15, 1573,[17] 'I have received your Excellency's letter recommending your ingenious goldsmith . . . and I am and will be most ready to serve you. I have already shown your man various works in silver and in other gilt metal and various newly invented designs that are relevant to his art'. The second Roman master was Federigo Bonzagni, who wrote in similar terms but without giving any interesting information.

Tobia da Camerino

Cellini's main rival in Rome was Tobia da Camerino, whose presence in the city is recorded from the year 1521. Cellini particularly disliked the Milanese and mistakenly thought that Tobia, who owned property there, was of Milanese birth.[18] He had other grounds for grievance against Tobia since Tobia's design for the mounting of an unicorn's horn, that was to be presented by Pope Clement VII to King Francis I of France, had been preferred to his own. He describes the affair as follows:[19] 'The Pope meant to give it (the horn) to King Francis, but first he wished it richly set in gold, and ordered us to make sketches for that purpose. When they were finished, we took them to the Pope. That of Tobia was in the form of a candlestick, the horn being stuck in it like a candle, and at the base of the piece he had introduced four little unicorn's heads of a very poor design. When I saw the thing I could not refrain from laughing gently in my sleeve. The Pope noticed this, and cried; "Here show me your sketch". It was a single unicorn's head, proportioned in size to the horn. I had designed the finest head imaginable; for I took it partly from the horse and partly from the stag, enriching it with fantastic mane and other ornaments. Accordingly no sooner was it seen than everyone decided in my favour. There were, however, present at the competition certain Milanese gentlemen of the first consequence, who said "Most blessed Father, your Holiness in sending this magnificent present into France; please to reflect that the French are people of no culture, and will not understand the excellence of Benvenuto's work; vessels like this one of Tobia will suit their taste well, and these can be finished more quickly'."

As Benvenuto was still engaged on a chalice for Clement VII, he was enjoined to carry on with it and the commission for the unicorn mount was given to Tobia. Cellini mentions in a later passage Tobia's work on the unicorn mount, and it appears subsequently in the inventory of the vessels and jewels of the French *Cabinet du Roi* prepared at Fontainebleau in 1560 and 1562,[20] as Item no. 1. *'Une grande licorne emorcée par le bout, garnie d'or et soustenue sur trois testes de licorne d'or par le pied, etc.'* In the years between 1537 and 1540 Tobia also made a number of papal golden roses which were presented annually to those sovereign princes who had done most to further the cause of the Christian Church. Like many an Italian goldsmith he employed two German assistants, through whom he was involved in an accusation of fraud.[21]

The skill peculiar to the seal die-cutter can be seen in the silver hammer made for the Jubileum of Pope Julius III (1550-1555) in the year 1550 (pls. 308-10). So fine is its finish that one is tempted to attribute the piece to Cellini himself, who did, in fact, go to Rome during the papacy of Julius III. He relates[22] that 'One of the first things I did was to go and kiss the Pope's feet; and while I was speaking with his Holiness, Messer Averardo Serristori, our Duke's envoy arrived. I had made some proposals to the Pope which I think he would have agreed upon and I should have been very glad to return to Rome on account of the great difficulties which I had at Florence. But I soon perceived that the ambassador had countermined me.'

The Jubileum of Pope Julius III had been planned by Paul III, but he died in that year and the celebration was taken by his successor. It seems, however, reasonable to assume that the hammer must have been commissioned by Paul rather than, at the last moment, by Julius. Of the various seal die-cutters employed by the Vatican in 1550, the most likely seems to have been Gian Giacomo Bonzagni of Parma; this master was commissioned by Julius III in 1551 to supply the sword presented by the Pope on the occasion of the Feast of the Nativity.[23] In 1552 Bonzagni supplied the sword, belt and hat awarded in that year. The production of a sword would seem to be most closely related to the making of a hammer, though this depends largely upon the manner in which the former was made. Sometimes the hilt was constructed of embossed sheet bent around an iron core, a method quite unrelated to the casting and chasing of the hammer. Another master who might have been awarded this task is Manno Sbarri; a comparison between the detail of the Farnese casket and the hammer reveals many similarities.

Antonio Gentile

While in Florence and Milan the *Maniera* was explored and developed to so elegant a conclusion, in Rome a pre-eminent goldsmith was, even towards the end of the sixteenth century, still working in a Michelangelesque manner. This was Antonio Gentile, who was born in Faenza in 1519 and first settled in Rome in 1550. He married there in 1561 and held various offices in the Goldsmiths' Guild. In 1584 he was appointed an assayer to the Papal Mint, an office which he held until 1602, when he was succeeded by his son. He died in Rome in 1609. In his time he was one of the leading Roman goldsmiths and, had he left an autobiography of comparable interest, might have been as famous as Cellini. He is described by his biographer, Baglione, as 'a worthy artificer of gold plate, who worked for great princes and fashioned two metal torch-holders that burn day and night in front of the most Holy Sacrament, worked with many bizarre ornaments, grace-ful to the highest degree; with little figures, animals and diverse decorations, extraordi-narily noble and delightful to see; and he made many designs, especially for graceful fountains'.[24] This description of his manner, in particular the reference to bizarre orna-ments, little figures and animals, is surprising, suggesting rather the work of Wenzel Jamnitzer than the architectural designs of Gentile with their broken pediments and *ignudi* in striking *contrapposto*. One is, however, forced to judge Gentile's manner on the strength of only one major work. His first important commission was a set of twelve reliquaries ordered by Pope Pius V in 1570. These were to be made from designs by Guglielmo della Porta, a personal friend with whom he collaborated on other occasions. He also made a silver and rock-crystal reliquary for the Jesuits in 1578, a cross for the Certosa at Naples, a silver reliquary for the skull of St. Petronilla at St. Peter's and a silver deposition of Christ, again from a model by Guglielmo della Porta. As might be expected of a leading Roman goldsmith, he was mostly occupied with ecclesiastical commissions. His greatest work was the altar set of cross and two candlesticks (pls. 305 and 307) that were commissioned by Cardinal Alessandro Farnese at a cost of 13,000 scudi and presented by him to St. Peter's. Gentile himself published an engraving of the cross accompanied by the following text:[25] 'This is the design of the very rich silver cross in the base of which are four oval plaques, and the circular plaques in the ends of the cross are of crystal engraved with the subjects that you can see. The base of the cross is of lapis lazuli of the same size and there are two similar candlesticks; they were given by Cardinal Farnese of happy memory to the altar of St. Peter's in Rome during his lifetime in the year 1582.' The altar set was subsequently completed by the addition of four further candlesticks made to match by Carlo Spagna in 1670 and 1672 at the expense of Cardinal Francesco Barberini. The design of the Gentile silver candlesticks and cross in the Vatican was followed in the pair of large pricket altar candlesticks presented to Milan Cathedral by Cardinal Frederico Borromeo in 1626, and dated as having been completed in that year.[26] The modelling of the figures that decorate these candlesticks is attributed to G. Andrea Biffi, chief sculptor of the *Opera del Duomo*, Milan.

Gentile is believed to have had a hand in another pair of altar candlesticks in the Vatican. These are of gilt-bronze, and were formerly attributed to Pollaiuolo, later to Andrea Riccio of Padua. They date from two different periods, the beginning and the end of the sixteenth century.[27] In order to make the candlesticks more important, addi-tional elements were inserted, but the author of the additions, if it was indeed Gentile, did not endeavour to adapt his style to match the earlier parts and the sticks now have a rather incoherent appearance.

Besides two reliquaries in St. Peter's, Rome, a few other works by or attributed to

Opposite page
Plate XIII
Trochus-shell ewer, with enamelled and gilt mounts by Wenzel Jamnitzer. Nürnberg, about 1570.

Plate XIV
Watercolour drawing by or after Wenzel Jamnitzer. Nürnberg, third quarter of 16th century.

Gentile survive. These include a set of knife, fork and spoon in the Metropolitan Museum, New York (pl. 306). Their attribution to Gentile is based on the existence of a drawing, now also in the Metropolitan Museum, either for this set or for a very similar set of cutlery, inscribed, apparently at a later date, with the name 'Gentile da Faenza'.[28] Another work by Gentile is the silver binding of the *Hours of Cardinal Alessandro Farnese* in the Pierpont Morgan Library, New York; of somewhat conventional design, this was commissioned by Cardinal Odoardo Farnese, who had inherited the Book of Hours from Cardinal Alessandro. It was made in about 1600 and is described in a Farnese inventory of 1653 as the work of *Il Faenza*.

A group of seven unpublished drawings in the Victoria and Albert Museum, acquired from a source in Rome, can be attributed to a follower of Antonio Gentile or his workshop. They comprise three ewers, a flask, a table-fountain, an incense-burner and a version of the pair of altar candlesticks in the Vatican Sacristy. Two of the ewer designs (pl. 52) bear the arms and initials of Alessandro Farnese, for whom they must have been intended. The influence of Michelangelo is most strongly evident in the three ewers and, of course, in the candlesticks, but the lack of coherence in the former as opposed to the latter supports the view that the candlesticks are probably based on a lost Michelangelo drawing. Michelangelesque features play an equally important role in the work of Manno Fiorentino, who was working in Rome at the same time as Gentile and, but for the presence of the drawings of the candlesticks in the group, one would be tempted to attribute them to him. Alessandro was also a patron of Manno and commissioned the Farnese casket from him (pl. 321).

Less original is the set of six gold reliefs of mythological subjects after plaquettes by Guglielmo della Porta set against a background of lapis lazuli enriched with bosses of red cornelian, which Gentile made, probably as adornments for a piece of furniture or, perhaps, simply as objects for a collector's cabinet.[29] The oval plaquettes were popular at the time and many examples in bronze have survived, but the Gentile versions, now in the Sculpture Collection of the Staatliches Museum, Berlin,[30] are the most opulent.

A contemporary reference to Gentile as *Argentarius in urbe* has been interpreted to mean that he was also a retailer of silver articles made by other masters. This does not necessarily reflect upon his status or skill, as the artist craftsman of the sixteenth century was often hard put to it to find the wherewithal to feed his family, although he worked in so intrinsically valuable a material, and could not afford to miss any legitimate source of income.

Francesco Salviati

Of equal importance to the Roman master, Perino del Vaga, as a source of goldsmiths' designs was the Florentine painter, Francesco Salviati (1510-1563) who was ten years his junior. Vasari[31] tells us that he was much inclined to design and as a boy received no little assistance from his cousin called Diacceto, a young goldsmith, who had a passing good knowledge of design, in that he not only taught him all that he knew but also furnished him with many drawings by various able men. Subsequently Salviati was set to learn the craft of the goldsmith in the shop of his uncle 'by reason of which opportunity for design Francesco in a few months made so much proficience that everyone was astonished'. Vasari also relates that Salviati became a member of a group of young goldsmiths who went round Florence on feast-days drawing the most famous works. Among them was Francesco di Girolamo da Prato, to whom he was very well disposed. This master is described by Vasari as a man of 'most beautiful genius' who drew better than any other goldsmith of his time, and not inferior to his father Girolamo, who executed every kind of work with silver plates better than any of his rivals.[32] It is possible that some of the many drawings in the manner of Salviati, which for one reason or another one hesitates to attribute to him, may be the work of this Francesco da Prato. Though Salviati's life was mainly devoted to the art of painting, he always maintained his association with members of the goldsmith's craft and, according to Vasari, his dearest friend was Manno Fiorentino, the distinguished pupil of Benvenuto Cellini and creator of the Farnese casket (pls. 321-7).

The only designs for goldsmith's work by Salviati that were published as prints are two sheets, each with two knife-handles (pl. 82). These were sufficiently popular to be re-issued within a few years by Cherubino Alberti (1553-1615). The few other gold-smiths' designs that can be attributed to Salviati's own hand are both lively and original. The drawing of a ewer (pl. 76) in the Ashmolean Museum, Oxford, is surely one of the most beautiful of its kind in existence. Less finished, but of lively invention, is the drawing of a covered tazza (pl. 77), which can also be attributed to Salviati himself. In this case the linked figures around the cover and the skilfully composed group on top suggest his hand. Of original design, but perhaps not entirely from Salviati's hand, is the combined table-centre and salt-cellar (pl. 78). The arrangement of the sides of the base provides a link with a large group of drawings that show clear signs of Salviati's influence. The protuberant bosom of the female satyr on the ewer (pl. 76) and the female half-figures with linked hands on the tazza (pl. 77) will also be encountered in these Salviati school drawings.

In view of the considerable number of the goldsmiths' designs of the Salviati school in existence, the fact that several versions of some individual drawings exist, and, finally, their wide distribution (they are well represented amongst the drawings believed to have belonged to the Emperor Rudolph II, see p.245) they are of greater importance in the context of this book than the more versatile drawings from Salviati's own hand such as pl. 79. The school drawings can be further divided between those that might be originals from his workshop and others that are copies after designs by a master who worked in his manner. It is these that are the most numerous. Among the former is a pair of dishes intended to be embossed with friezes of nymphs and tritons while the centres show figures of Neptune and Amphitrite respectively drawn on chariots of sea-horses and dolphins (pl. 80). The pairs of amorous nymphs and tritons and of fighting tritons depicted in the border are met with repeatedly in the Salviati school drawings. While the original drawings of masters such as Salviati or Perino tend to be left as sketches, the Salviati school designs are usually carefully finished (pl. 81). The most complete set of goldsmiths' designs in the Salviati manner was purchased in Bologna in the 1920's by a Swedish collector, Dr. Perman, but it has since been dispersed. The set consisted of twenty-four sheets covering almost the whole range of the goldsmith, including candle-sticks, dishes, tazzas, salt-cellars, caskets, flasks, cruets, spoons and forks. Thirteen of the designs are repeated amongst a group of eighteen by the same hand, preserved with the drawings from the *Kunstkammer* of Rudolph II in the Victoria and Albert Museum. This collection seems to contain the largest number still remaining together, but single drawings from this workshop are to be found in many of the print-rooms of Europe and America.[33] The existence of not only one but of several replicas of the same design, often showing signs of routine production, can probably be explained by their being turned out in sets for sale to goldsmiths, as were printed sheets from designs by Agostino dei Musi or Enea Vico. There may have been valid economic reasons for employing apprentices to produce series of copies of designs rather than go to the expense of having them engraved on copper plate and printed.

All the known drawings belonging to this group appear to be copies; the originals, which would presumably have been distinguished by a more competent and lively hand, have not yet been recognised, if indeed they are preserved at all. Some differences in quality can, however, be found; the design for a large basin (pl. 81) with its numerous alternative suggestions is certainly by a better hand than the salt in pl. 83 or the oval dish in pl. 87. The most mechanical hand is that represented in the drawings from the Perman collection (pls. 86, 89, 90). In these designs most of the ideas that could be derived from antiquity are exploited, but without the extremes of fantasy that were a feature of northern Mannerism. Some of the drawings are annotated in Italian but the comments (pl. 83) do not give information of much interest. One of the tazzas (pl. 90) and one of the salts (pl. 83) follow the galley form that is so often encountered in sixteenth-century Italian hardstone sculpture. Perhaps the most original of all these drawings is the galley-like vessel in the Victoria and Albert Museum (pl. 88).

The Salviati school designs frequently include friezes derived from Mantegna or, perhaps, directly from Roman sarcophagi; they are composed of numerous human or semi-human figures whose bodies are intermingled in combat or amorous embrace (pl. 80). Such friezes were adopted as the standard treatment for the borders of rose-water basins and dishes, not only in Italy but throughout western and northern Europe until well into the seventeenth century. The drawings also exploit with considerable imaginative resource the stock of marine life, crabs, shells and so on, which are already to be found in the prints of Enea Vico or Agostino dei Musi. Other favourite devices are pairs of winged terms or sphinxes set back to back (pl. 83) and cartouches with rolled-over borders enclosing a single recumbent nude male or female figure, usually in a suggestively erotic pose (pl. 89). In the figure subjects the same theme is often repeated, a bearded recumbent man and a group of a triton embracing a nereid appear frequently. The stressing of the erotic element in these designs accompanies rejection of the classical ideal; instead of the logical architectonic construction of the earlier decades of the sixteenth century, these vessels are composed of living swelling forms, while the detail of the friezes approaches the orgiastic. Considered as a whole the productions of this prolific workshop are composed of a limited number of elements which are repeated in a variety of combinations. In comparison with some of the Flemish drawings discussed below, these Italian designs are restrained, lacking altogether the grotesques and dominating strapwork so characteristic of northern Mannerism. Strapwork and rollwork is confined to the framing of the cartouches; its full potentialities were first recognised and developed by the Italian masters working at Fontainebleau.

While no silver vessels made after these designs are known to me, a number of closely related bronzes exist (pls. 716, 717). This does not mean that the designs were exclusively intended for the bronze-founders but that only those made in base metal have survived. Among other bronzes that derive from the same source are a pair of inkstands attributed to Tiziano Aspetti in the Judge Untermyer Collection[34] and a pair of candlesticks in the Victoria and Albert Museum. All date from the third quarter of the sixteenth century, when Mannerist design was strongly manifested in Italian decorative art. The survival of so many drawings emanating from this particular workshop and in so many identical or slightly variant versions points to their widespread use in Italy. They could, in fact, be executed equally well in precious metal, bronze or majolica, though it was difficult to render the subtle movement and delicate detail of the drawings in so coarse a material as clay. Nevertheless they can frequently be recognised in Urbino wares of the middle of the century. The boat-shaped salt-cellar from the Walters Art Gallery (pl. 718) recalls such designs as the salt-cellar base in the Salviati manner (pl. 83). Numerous other comparisons could be cited.

Marco da Faenza

A number of designs for vases, ewers and candlesticks have been attributed to Marco Marchetti of Faenza (?-1588), a fresco-painter who is known to have worked under Vasari on the decoration of the Palazzo Vecchio in Florence. No positively documented drawing by this master is known, but the goldsmith's designs attributed to him, including the ewer (pl. 85) show him to have been a typical Mannerist with an inexhaustible force of imagination in creating decorative forms. These drawings display the influence of Salviati, so much so that it is difficult to distinguish between them. On the other hand, a drawing showing two alternative designs for a tall altar candlestick in the Royal Library at Windsor, which has been attributed to him, is strikingly close to the pair of gilt-bronze candlesticks (see p.140) in the Treasury of St. Peter's, Rome, which were first constructed by Andrea Riccio and then brought up to date and enlarged, probably by Antonio Gentile da Faenza, in the second half of the sixteenth century. Gentile's most famous altar candlesticks (pl. 307) are Michelangelesque in design but it is tempting to think that his older contemporary from Faenza may have provided the design for the remodelling of the Riccio candlesticks. Both Marchetti and Gentile are known to have been working in Rome in the 1570's. In a somewhat different manner from the vases rapidly executed in brown wash is his design for a large basin in the Turin Gallery.[35] Whereas a drawing of a ewer or a vase may have been intended as a sketch for a detail in a painting, one can be reasonably sure that a detailed basin design must have been meant for a goldsmith or potter.

Pierino da Vinci

Another member of the Florentine school of goldsmiths was Pierino da Vinci (1530-1553) who was born in Vinci and brought to Florence to be trained as a goldsmith at the age of twelve. He subsequently went to Pisa to work for his rich patron, Luca Martini, but died from fever at the early age of twenty-three. According to Vasari he made a silver vase and two beakers for his patron but these have not survived. A number of bronzes have been attributed to him; these are mostly in the manner of Michelangelo. The most convincing attribution is a small bronze base in the British Museum;[36] this corresponds to a design in a collection of Pierino drawings, consisting mainly of decorative details presumably intended for execution in bronze, some of them of typically bizarre invention.

Benvenuto Cellini

In his writings, Benvenuto Cellini reveals himself as one of the creators of Mannerism. He introduces conceptions that are fundamental to Mannerist philosophy: the duty of the artist to express noble and beautiful ideas, the importance of the conception (concetto) underlying the work of art and the conviction that by the exercise of virtuosity and intellect the rugosity of Nature could be transmuted into a form that was 'bella e graziosa'.

After the first publication of Cellini's autobiography in 1728, his name acquired such a romantic aura that almost every sixteenth-century piece of goldsmith's work of outstanding quality was attributed to him. Such unscholarly attributions have long been abandoned and there has even been a tendency to suggest that he was but one of a number of equally-skilled goldsmiths of his time. In this connection it would, however, be wrong to ignore the evidence of Vasari, who was cordially disliked by Cellini and not likely to have praised him beyond his merits. In the Vite Vasari states of him,[37] 'When he applied himself to goldsmiths' work in his youth he was unequalled....he set jewels and decorated them with marvellous collets composed of figures of such fine workmanship and sometimes of such original and capricious design that one could not imagine anything better. Mooreover the medals that he made in his youth in gold and silver were executed with such incredible skill that it is impossible to praise them enough.'

Cellini learnt the goldsmith's craft in Florence where, between the ages of thirteen and eighteen, he worked for a number of different masters. In 1519, he went to Rome and there worked for a year in the employ of a certain Giovanni de Georgis of Firenzuola. Both this master and another Roman goldsmith, Lucagnolo di Jesi, for whom he worked, specialised in making the huge ewers and companion basins that were the standard prestige productions of Italian Renaissance goldsmiths and were so often represented in contemporary paintings. Of the latter master, Cellini writes in the Vita [38] 'He executed large plate only, that is, vases of the utmost beauty, basins and such pieces.' Cellini worked with Lucagnolo from 1523 to 1524 and it was at this time that he secured his first important commission, from the Spanish Bishop of Salamanca to whom he obtained an introduction through one of Raphael's pupils, Giovanni Francesco Penni. The order was for a pair of candlesticks, presumably altar candlesticks, but he only informs us that they were very richly decorated. Although Cellini does not mention this, it is probable that Penni provided a drawing for the sticks, as he did on another occasion for the same client. In 1524 he left Lucagnolo and joined the workshop of Giovan della Tacca and soon after opened his own shop. He then received the second commission from the Bishop of Salamanca, this time for a 'large water-vase' (i.e. ewer) once again designed by Penni. This vase took three months to make, mainly because Cellini was occupied with other interests. He describes it at some length.[39] It was made 'with little animals and foliage and masks, as beautiful as one could imagine...amongst other ornaments this vase had a handle made all of one piece, with most delicate mechanism, which, when a spring was touched, stood upright above the mouth of it'. Shortly afterwards, Cellini made a similar but larger ewer for Cardinal Cibo Malaspina, Archbishop of Genoa and thereafter he received commissions from three other cardinals, Cornaro, Salviati, and Ridolfi, as well as lesser prelates.

In one passage of the *Vita* Cellini mentions what sounds like one of the first experiments in the Mannerist style in the field of the goldsmith. He tells us that a wealthy physician, Maestro Giacomo da Capri.[40] 'chancing to pass one day before my shop, saw a lot of drawings which I had laid upon the counter, and amongst them were several designs for little vases in a capricious style, which I had sketched for my amusement. These vases were in quite a different fashion from any which had been seen up to that date. He was anxious that I should make one or two of them for him in silver; and this I did following my own caprice'. It appears that earthenware (majolica) copies of these vases were subsequently made in Ferrara and were shown to Cellini there. After Cellini's release from imprisonment in the Castel Sant Angelo in 1540 through the good offices of the Cardinal of Ferrara, he began to make a ewer and basin for him of which the ewer 'was designed with figures in the round and with bas-reliefs. The basin was executed in a similar style, with figures in the round and with fishes in bas-relief. The whole had such richness and excellence of style that everyone who saw it expressed astonishment at the fame of the design and the beauty of invention.'[41]

Cellini himself tells us little of his activities as a goldsmith in Italy but is more informative about his stay in France from 1540 to 1545. Shortly after his arrival there he states that[42] 'we brought to completion the little vase and oval basin, which had been several months in hand. Then I had them richly gilt, and they showed like the finest piece of plate which had been seen in France'. These were handed over to the Cardinal of Ferrara who presented them to the King.[43] Subsequently in 1543 he made 'several little things for the Cardinal of Ferrara and a small silver vase of rich workmanship which I intended to present to Madame d'Etampes.'[44] In the end, when Cellini visited the lady, who was the official mistress of the French king, he was kept too long in her waiting room, and losing patience, presented the vase to the Cardinal of Lorraine instead. Apart from the King, for whom he made four large silver vases and a life-size figure of Jupiter in embossed silver sheet, intended to serve as a *torchère*, Cellini did not obtain many commissions from the French nobility. At all events, the clients to whom he refers in the *Vita* were Italian, namely Signor Piero Strozzi, the Count of Anguillara, the Count of Pitigliano, the Count of Mirandola and many others. While in Paris he also made three silver vases of which the largest was 'richly decorated with a variety of ornaments and figures'. When he left France two further vases were still in hand in his workshop; these were finished by the two assistants who remained behind, Ascanio di Tagliacozzo and Paolo Romano. Though many such vases can be seen in paintings by Salviati, Vasari and their Mannerist contemporaries, examples made of precious metal and dating from the sixteenth century are almost unknown. Pls. 610 and 404 illustrate one of a pair and another single vase in the treasury of Seville Cathedral; these seem to be the only surviving examples of the great vessels that once gave such splendour to the sideboards of popes and princes. Cellini describes them as being intended *per pompa di credenza di cardinale*. 'They were egg-shaped, a little over a forearm in height, with narrow necks above and with handles very richly worked with foliage and various animals.'[45]

The most important example of the art of the Mannerist goldsmith is the golden salt made by Cellini for King François I (pl. 311-20). Judging by the lengthy descriptions he gives of it in both the *Vita* and the *Trattati,* it must have been the most ambitious piece he ever made and its fortunate survival makes it possible to arrive at an independent judgement of Cellini's skill as a goldsmith. In fact, the salt narrowly escaped destruction in 1562 when it was almost consigned to the melting-pot. It left France forever in 1570: it was presented to Archduke Ferdinand of Tirol by King Charles IX when he acted as proxy for the King on the occasion of his marriage to Elizabeth of Austria. It has remained ever since in the Austrian state collections. According to his own account, Cellini originally designed the salt for the Cardinal Ippolito d'Este in the last months of 1539 or the beginning of 1540 in the period between his release from imprisonment in the Castel Sant'Angelo and his departure to France. When the Cardinal first commissioned the salt, two Florentine humanists, the poet Luigi Alamanni and the philosopher, Gabriele da Cesano, made suggestions for an appropriate design. Alamanni proposed that the main figures should be Venus and Cupid while Cesano preferred Amphitrite and the tritons. Cellini dismissed their proposals, pointing out that many things, while fine enough in words, did not turn out so well in practice.[46] The eventual design was entirely his own. The final commission to make the salt came not from the Cardinal but from King Francis I after Cellini's arrival in Paris. When, twenty years later, Cellini was writing his *Vita* he described the piece very fully and one cannot do better than quote his own account of it.[47]

'I first laid down an oval framework, considerably longer than half a cubit — almost two thirds, in fact; and upon this ground, wishing to suggest the intermingling of land and ocean, I modelled two figures, considerably taller than a palm in height, which were seated with their legs interlaced, suggesting those lengthier branches of the sea which run into the continents. The sea was a man, and in his hand I placed a ship, elaborately wrought in all its details, and well adapted to hold a quantity of salt. Beneath him I grouped the four sea-horses, and in his right hand he held his trident. The earth I fashioned like a woman, with all its beauty of form, the grace and charm of which my art was capable. She had a richly decorated temple firmly based upon the ground on one side; and here her hand rested. This I intended to receive the pepper. In her other hand I put a cornucopia, overflowing with all the natural treasures I could think of. Below this goddess in the part that represented the earth, I collected the fairest animals that populate our globe. In that quarter presided over by the deity of the ocean, I fashioned such choice kinds of fishes and shells as could properly be displayed in that small space. What remained of the oval I filled in with luxuriant ornamentation.'

Cellini's other important goldsmiths' works were mainly large vases. When one sees the large number of gold vessels that are listed in the Medici *Guardaroba* inventory of 1587, it becomes evident that the number of pieces mentioned by Cellini in his works is quite small in comparison with the output of the other goldsmiths at the time. this was presumably because Cellini became more interested in sculpture after his return to Florence from France. Cellini himself must have produced a great many drawings of goldsmiths' work but none have hitherto been identified with certainty. Attributions have been made in the past, such as that of the drawing in pl. 92, but until something more is known of his manner of handling the pencil these must remain conjectural. An idea of his prolific production of designs can be gathered from the account of the works he executed for Benedetto Accolti, Bishop of Ravenna.[48] This includes a payment of 100 scudi made in September, 1540, in respect of three hundred designs of various works. The same account refers to a number of wax models made for the Cardinal; evidently he was not satisfied with the impression given by a drawing alone and wanted to see the effect in the round. This is hardly surprising if the article was to be made of gold. The models include a horse with rider above and three figures below, a large and rich galley, a basin and ewer with many figures and two tazzas with figures in high relief. Cellini also refers to designs he made for Duke Cosimo de Medici for vases that were eventually produced by goldsmiths of Venice and elsewhere, and, in a letter addressed to Grand Duke Francesco de' Medici dated 9 December, 1564, he mentions designs he made for the banker, Piero Salviati of Lyons.[49]

The most important piece of ecclesiastical plate made by Cellini, the chalice commissioned by Pope Clement VII in 1531,[50] was also accepted by the Pope on the basis of a model made of wood and wax, presumably wood for the basic construction and wax for the ornament. Cellini gives a description of this chalice: it seems that the knop was decorated with three figures of Faith, Hope and Charity, each in the round, while on the foot were three low relief scenes of the Nativity, The Resurrection and the crucifixion of Peter. His failure to complete the chalice for the Pope led to his loss of papal favour and he was eventually instructed to abandon work on it and deliver it to the Pope in its unfinished state. This he refused to do and the Pope had to have him arrested in order to secure sight of the chalice. It was returned to Cellini who still had not completed it when Pope Clement died. The goldsmith eventually took it with him to Florence where it was pledged for 200 gold scudi. Subsequently redeemed by Cosimo de' Medici, it was given to Niccolo di Francesco Santini to complete and in 1569 was presented to Pope Pius V by Cosimo when he was crowned Grand Duke of Tuscany. According to Vasari it was wrought by Cellini with 'the most marvellous craftsmanship' (con artifizio maravigliosissimo).

Manno di Sebastiano Sbarri

The Farnese casket (pls. 321) of the Florentine goldsmith, Manno di Sbarri (1520-1586), has been unjustly overshadowed by Cellini's golden salt. It has at least an equal claim to rank as the finest surviving Italian Mannerist work in precious metal. Its design has been attributed conjecturally to either Perino del Vaga or to Salviati. Both were acquainted with Manno and Perino is known to have delivered sketches for the rock-crystal panels with which the sides are mounted. Perino died in 1546 and Manno started work on the casket for Cardinal Alessandro Farnese in the following year, so there is nothing inherently improbable in the suggestion that the former was responsible for its design. One writer has pointed out a similarity in the composition of the casket to a drawing in the British Museum and thus strengthened the Perino attribution.[51] Both Salviati and Perino worked in a very similar idiom and their designs have to be distinguished by idiosyncrasies of drawing rather than difference of style. Perino may well have sketched out certain ideas for the casket, but on the whole Salviati's claim to authorship seems to be the stronger, the more so as Vasari described Manno as Salviati's 'dearest friend.' That it was made by Manno we know from Vasari's account[52] in which he states 'Wishing to have an extremely rich casket of silver made, the same Cardinal entrusted the work to Manno, a Florentine goldsmith'. Although, or perhaps because, Manno was his equal as a goldsmith, Cellini refers only once to him in the Vita and then in the course of a disagreeable story about Giorgio Vasari, whom he cordially disliked. Manno was subsequently employed by a cardinal who is not more precisely named, but who was probably the same Alessandro Farnese. In 1548 he started work on a second casket which was still not finished ten years later. It must have been finished by 1561 when Manno was trying to obtain payment for it. In 1556 he made a pair of basins and ewers for the same cardinal and in 1567 he sent him a drawing together with a terracotta model of a salt-cellar. This last had been made by Michelangelo, presumably at the request of the cardinal. Manno was also employed by Pope Julius III (1550-1555) and Paul IV (1555-1559). He delivered to the Basilica of St. Peter a gilt altar cross, two figures of St. Peter and St. Paul and a pair of large altar candlesticks.[53]

In general the Farnese casket owes more to Michelangelo than anyone else and, in particular, to his tomb of Lorenzo de'Medici in the sacristy of the Church of San Lorenzo. Of Michelangelesque derivation are the form of the broken pediment that surmounts the casket, the modelling of the figures placed in its deep recesses on each side instead of on top, the bold volutes which form the inner terminals on each side, the brackets that support the base and the figures at each corner representing Mars, Minerva, Diana and Bacchus. The seated figure of Hercules that surmounts the casket also shows the powerful muscular development typical of Michelangelo's male sculpture. In one respect it differs from a Michelangelo design, namely in its extreme richness. Whereas the recesses of the Medici monuments are plain, in the casket they are elaborately ornamented, though the insertion of rock-crystal intaglios in the sides does help to lighten the effect of the whole. The costly nature of its materials, silver-gilt, lapis lazuli and rock-crystal does in any case call for elaborate treatment. Every part of its surface both inside and out is finished with the utmost care and attention. The Farnese casket represents the culminating point in magnificence of design and execution of a type of casket which was well-known in Italy. Earlier examples are illustrated in pls. 244 and 247.

Annibale Carracci

Towards the end of the sixteenth century Cardinal Odoardo Farnese commissioned a tazza and a bread-basket to be made for him.[54] The name of the goldsmith who executed them is not known and only the engraved plaque from the centre of each piece has survived. Each is engraved with the same subject, namely a bacchanal with the drunken Silenus sitting up and supported by a kneeling satyr while another pours wine from a goatskin into his mouth. The survival of the two silver plaques is due to the fact that the engraving was both designed and executed by Annibale Carracci himself. Several Carracci drawings of the scene on the tazza at various stages of being worked out survive. The tazza and the basket were brought to Naples with the remainder of the Farnese heirlooms after the death of the last Farnese duke and the plaques must have been cut out as late as some time in the eighteenth century. Evidently Annibale Carracci did not think it beneath him to engrave silver as a side-line for, in addition to the two pieces already mentioned, there is also at Naples a *Pietà* engraved on silver by him. A contemporary writer, G. Mancini, said of him 'he engraved excellently with the burin, as one can see from a number of tazzas belonging to Giulio Cesare Abbate.[55] This additional piece of information is valuable in that it establishes that Carracci did not accept the commission from Cardinal Farnese purely on account of his high position in the church but was prepared to execute similar work for less distinguished clients.

The Medici Court Workshop

Three rulers of Tuscany in succession were great patrons of the goldsmiths' art: Cosimo I (1537-1574), Francesco I (1574-1587) and Ferdinand I (1587-1609). Besides employing Benvenuto Cellini after his return from Paris in 1545, Cosimo also engaged Cellini's two assistants: Gian Paolo and Domenico Poggini. Cellini records[56] some of the commissions he executed for the Duke, none of which, however, survive: 'I was glad to pass my time in the Duke's Wardrobe with a couple of young goldsmiths called Gianpagolo and Domenico Poggini, who made a little golden cup under my direction. It was chased in bas-relief with figures and other pretty ornaments, and his Excellency meant it for the Duchess to drink water from. He furthermore commissioned me to execute a golden belt, which I enriched with gems and delicate masks and other fancies. The Duke came frequently into the Wardrobe, and took great pleasure in watching me at work and in talking to me.' He also furnished a number of designs for vases for the Duke, but these were made by other goldsmiths, presumably because Cellini was by this time more interested in sculpture. References to the Poggini brothers in the Medici *Guardaroba* archives dating between 1546 and the mid-1550's show them carrying out a variety of tasks from the more humble, such as cleaning silver figures, to making a dagger, a belt and silver candlesticks.[57] Like his son after him, Cosimo employed a number of foreign goldsmiths at his court, both Germans and Flemings. An entry[58] in the *Guardaroba* accounts for 1569 refers to the provision by Matteo di Nicolo di Ratisbona (Regensburg) of two scorpions and five serpents of silver. These were presumably castings from nature of the type that had been perfected at the Jamnitzer workshop in Nürnberg (see p.68, n.25). One may assume that the indigenous Italian goldsmiths had not succeeded in mastering this particular technique.

Like other Renaissance princes Cosimo collected vessels of rock-crystal: his accounts contain many references to the purchase of hardstone vessels from Milan which was then the undisputed centre of the glyptic art. The earliest relates to the delivery in 1544 of crystal vases by Dionigi de Ripalta, a Milanese goldsmith, to Eleonora di Toledo, Cosimo's wife.[59] A more important Milanese artist who worked for Cosimo was Jacopo da Trezzo; in 1550-1 he made a large rock-crystal vase and a beaker of the same material for the Duke and in 1552 he wrote asking for payment of the sum of 850 scudi for a crystal vase 'made a long time before'.[60] A few years later in 1557 Cosimo summoned to Florence another Milanese goldsmith, Giovanni Antonio de Rossi (c.1517-1575), the maker of the famous onyx cameo carved with portraits of the Medici family.[61] Few of the hardstone vessels made for Cosimo retain their original mounts and it is not, therefore, possible to give an adequate account of them. There is, however, in the Kunsthistorisches Museum, Vienna, a jasper bowl with its original enamelled gold mounts, which is recorded in the 1570 inventory of the Medici *Guardaroba* but which was presented to the Emperor Ferdinand II in 1628.[62] While the jasper bowl is likely to be of Milanese origin, the handles, composed of the intertwined bodies of snakes, and the foot appear to be the work of a Florentine goldsmith.

Most of the Florentine goldsmiths of Cosimo's reign are but names to us but a little more is known of Michele di Battista Mazzafirri, who was born in Florence about 1530 and worked for the Medici family until his death in 1597. He is best known as a medallist and became head of the Florence Mint. A few goldsmith's works have been tentatively attributed to him; these include the figure of Hercules on the cover of a jasper vase in the shape of the Hydra in the Medici Collection.[62a] This little golden figure is modelled in the round and is the equal of the superb figures that surmount contemporary Milanese vessels such as the vase (pl. V).

Bernardo Buontalenti

The chief arbiter of taste at the court of Cosimo's son, Francesco I, was Bernardo Buontalenti, who was born in Florence and acquired his knowledge of painting and architecture in the circle of Salviati, Bronzino and Vasari. He designed and possibly had a part in the construction of ebony cabinets enriched with precious stones and mounted in silver for the Grand Duke, but his most important commission was that of building the Casino di San Marco as his city residence. This was begun in 1568 and completed in 1574, immediately after the Duke's accession. It was in this building that Francesco gathered his most talented artists until the workshops were transferred to the ground-floor of the Uffizi in 1588. A panel painting by Alessandro Fei in Francesco's *studiolo* in the Palazzo Vecchio, depicting a goldsmiths' workshop (pl. 1) shows the scene that might have been observed in San Marco. Indeed the fact that the goldsmith in the right-hand corner of the picture is working on the Medici crown suggests that the artist meant to represent the Grand-duke's goldsmiths at work. Another painting in the *studiolo*, representing the sacking of a city and painted by Niccolo Betti, shows in the foreground a general and a soldier looking at a pile of gold and silver vases and tazzas all of characteristic Mannerist shapes. The large vases are probably the same type which Benvenuto Cellini wrought for the Bishop of Salamanca (see p.147). The Grand Duke Francesco I was a great patron of the goldsmiths, though recent research has shown that much of the Renaissance plate in the Palazzo Pitti (*Museo degli Argenti*), formerly thought to have belonged to the Medici family, derives in fact from the treasury of the Archbishops of Salzburg and did not reach Florence until the beginning of the nineteenth century. Nevertheless, the Medici *Guardaroba* inventories record many important commissions from the Grand Duke, who was so fascinated by the craft that he took up the goldsmith's hammer himself. The 1589 inventory of the *Tribuna* lists '*Un monte di madre perlle con più gioe e duo figurini d'argento dorato d'un Cristo che è tentato del diavolo tutti di mano del Serenissimo Francesco Medici felicie memoria*', while a letter from the court goldsmith, Biliverti, to the Grand Duke, dated 28 November 1584, discusses a large emerald which Francesco wished to have made into a small vase and promises to send a wax model of the proposed design. Biliverti also asks for instructions concerning the working of a piece of ruby in the rough. The whole tone of the letter shows that Francesco took an active part in guiding the programme of work of the court hardstone sculptors and goldsmiths.[63]

Buontalenti was responsible for the construction of the *Tribuna* on the top floor of the Uffizi which took the place of the *studiolo* in the Palazzo Vecchio as the repository of Francesco's most precious treasures. Around the walls were set the series of Labours of Hercules cast in silver after models by Gian Bologna and in the centre was a magnificent cabinet of ebony in the form of a temple, also designed by Buontalenti.[64] This must have been an object of the greatest splendour, for a group of jewellers and cabinetmakers worked on it for four years from 1584 to 1588. In front it was decorated with a series of bas-reliefs by Gian Bologna of gold set against grounds of amethyst and jasper illustrating events from the life of Francesco; the cabinet has disappeared and all that remains are the gold reliefs, now in the Museo degli Argenti.[65]

Giacomo Biliverti

While the main designer at the court of Francesco I was Bernardo Buontalenti, many of the craftsmen who executed his designs were foreigners. The foremost of these was Giacomo Biliverti (or Jacques Bylivelt) who was known in Florence as Giacomo Delfe, because he came from Delft in Holland. He was born there in 1550 and left his native city at the age of twenty-two, going first to Antwerp and Augsburg, where he spent several months, and finally to Florence. A month after arriving in Florence he was rewarded with ten scudi from the Grand-ducal treasury for making the journey; this incident suggests he came at the Grand Duke's invitation. When he arrived in 1573 he brought with him several German workmen, probably from Augsburg. The names of nine assistants who worked with him from time to time between 1581 and 1587 are recorded.[66] All are German. The presence in the Florentine Court Workshop of so many German craftsmen at a time when such famous goldsmiths as Cellini, Manno di Sebastiano Sbarri, Domenico Poggini and many others were at work in the city of Florence is another proof of the mobility of craftsmen in the luxury trades in the sixteenth century and of the high reputation of the German goldsmiths. Biliverti also had Italian assistants; the Milanese Gianbattista Elmi is known to have worked for him from 1575 until at least 1590. One wonders whether these foreign goldsmiths from north of the Alps assimilated the Florentine court style or continued to work in their native manner.[67] Northern influence is, for instance, strongly manifested in the silver and parcel-gilt mounts of the sardonyx vase from the collection of Lorenzo the Magnificent (pl. III). This classical Roman vessel was remounted in the latter part of the sixteenth century in a typically Flemish manner and can reasonably be attributed to one of Biliverti's northern assistants.

Biliverti was appointed *Proveditore della real galleria* by Grand Duke Francesco I at the salary of 20 Florentine scudi, which was double the amount granted to Buontalenti. Six days after his arrival in Florence, Biliverti received 35 scudi in gold to make a pendant for the Duke and his account book during the first few years in Florence records work on pendants, rings, watches, lapis lazuli and crystal vases. Biliverti's most important commission was to make the new crown, the right to which had been conferred on Cosimo I by Pope Pius V in 1570. Biliverti's account book shows that he started work on it on May 29, 1577, and finished it six years later. This magnificent crown, the jewels of which were valued at 275,000 scudi in a seventeenth-century inventory, was destroyed by order of the Austrian Grand Duke Leopold I in 1789. The best record of it is the watercolour drawing in the Victoria and Albert Museum, which is annotated as being the *Corona di Casa Medici*.[68] This shows both sides of the rays which.were an individual feature of the Grandducal crown. The mauresques, masks, animal heads and flowers which decorate it are of northern inspiration and probably reflect Biliverti's own contribution to the design. He was still working in Florence in 1593, twenty years after his first arrival there, so that his oeuvre covered the whole range of later Mannerism. When in 1588 after the accession of Ferdinand I de'Medici the various court workshops were concentrated in the Uffizi under the control of the *Soprintendente,* Emilio Cavalieri, such was the status accorded to Biliverti that he was exempted from the terms of the order. W. Fock's researches in the Medici archives have thrown much light on the work of the Florentine court goldsmiths and, in particular, on Giacomo Biliverti. An oval lapis lazuli vase in the Museo degli Argenti that was mounted by Biliverti retains only its enamelled gold foot mounts, but the superb vase in the Kunsthistorisches Museum (pl. 334) and the vase with chains in the Museo degli Argenti (pl. IV) both retain in their full splendour the mounts Biliverti made for them. In each case the richness of the mounts contrasts with a comparatively simple vessel form. The most impressive of the newly discovered works of this supreme goldsmith is the house-altar of rock crystal with enamelled gold mounts which was commissioned by Grand Duke Ferdinand de'Medici for the Tribuna, but which also ended up in the Kunsthistorisches Museum, Vienna, as part of the Habsburg Imperial Treasury. Fock has pointed out the influence of Gian Bologna, who then played a dominating role in Florentine sculpture on the modelling of the caryatids that support the architrave of this altar. Biliverti is known to have worked from Bologna's designs and in November, 1590, received payment for seven silver figures for the *studiolo* after his models. Like the goldsmiths of Augsburg and Nürnberg the Medici workshops also produced ebony caskets with mounts of precious metal. One of the finest was presented to the Emperor Rudolph II in 1591. Filled with sweetmeats, perfume or scent, they were a standard form of gift to foreign notabilities.

A recent attribution to Biliverti[69] is the shell-shaped cup in the Metropolitan Museum, New York (pl. 328). This enamelled and jewelled gold cup was acquired from the Rospigliosi family, but it is not known whether it was originally commissioned in the sixteenth century by a Prince Rospigliosi or obtained subsequently by gift or marriage. It was once thought to have been the work of Benvenuto Cellini, but contemporary inventories show that many such vessels once existed. There must have been many goldsmiths competent to produce them, among them some of the numerous rivals to whom Cellini refers.

Odoardo Vallet

Biliverti died in 1603 and was succeeded in his post as *Proveditore* by his former assistant, Odoardo Vallet, a goldsmith of French origin who had spent thirty-three years of his life in the employ of the Medicis.[70] He was evidently more skilled as a goldsmith than jeweller for, after Biliverti's death, the most important jewellery commissions went to a goldsmith in Frankfurt am Main. There is little to show for Vallet's long period in Florence but he is known to have made the mounts of the slender rock-crystal vase (pl. 340), which ranks as one of the finest creations of the Florentine court workshop. Whoever designed the crystal vase had overcome the sixteenth century taste for profuse ornament; its sophisticated form displays an original conception that can hardly be paralleled among the many hardstone vessels from the Medici collection. It was probably designed by Buontalenti some years before 1618, when Vallet mounted it. Such vessels were not necessarily mounted at the time they were made; there may have been an interval of many years between the carving of the rock-crystal and the making of the mount. Other vessels were remounted in a style more in accord with changing taste. This circumstance imposes some discretion on the dating of individual pieces. In view of the many years he spent in Florence, Vallet must have worked on many other pieces besides the vase (pl. 340), but none can now be recognised, nor can the works of other goldsmiths of French origin whose names are mentioned in the Medici *Guardaroba* accounts.

Hardstone cutting in Florence

Under Francesco's patronage the Florentine Court Workshop became one of the chief

European centres of hardstone cutting and engraving. During the second half of the century certain workshops acquired a reputation for specialising in the working of particular materials, presumably because the raw materials were readily obtainable. Vessels of lapis lazuli, (pls. 330-4) which seems to have been available in larger quantity in Florence, were a speciality of the Medici court workshops, but Milan was always the chief Italian centre of rock-crystal working. This does not imply that coloured hardstones were not carved there, but they were never so plentiful in Italy as they were in Prague which drew on the mountain ranges of Bohemia. Towards the end of the century an important advance was made in the technique of working rock-crystal and other hard-stones, which made production of vessels of these materials less time-consuming. This was the practice of lathe-turning, which was particularly well suited for solid pieces such as stems, feet and covers. It is known to have been employed in Florence and was presumably followed elsewhere at about the same time.

The hardstone-cutting workshop was first established in Florence in 1572 when Cosimo I brought two brothers, Stefano and Ambrogio Caroni, from Milan. Three years later, after Cosimo's death, they were joined by Giorgio Gaffuri, another Milanese artist. Subsequently Francesco summoned Giorgio's elder son, Cristoforo, who arrived before 1586, and then his two younger sons, Bernardino and Giovanni Battista Gaffuri. With Buontalenti to make the original designs, the Milanese masters to cut the jewels and hardstones and Biliverti, assisted by Mazzafirri and Lorenzo della Nera to provide the gold mounts, Francesco had a highly qualified team and was freed from the irksome and expensive necessity of ordering precious vessels from Milan. The hardstone cutters and goldsmiths did not stay for long in the Casino di San Marco, for by a decree of 1588, their workshops were transferred to the ground floor of the palace of the Uffizi, joining the other Grandducal workshops which were already installed there and creating an institution that was capable of producing a wide range of applied art. Under Francesco's successor, Ferdinand, emphasis was transferred from producing vases to religious articles such as the great hardstone altar for the Capella dei Principi, attached to the church of San Lorenzo. Ferdinand also commissioned hardstone mosaics rather than vases from his hardstone cutters and it was for these artefacts that the Florentine masters were most famed during the seventeenth century.

Most of the Milanese craftsmen who worked in Florence are no more than names to us, but Fock's researches in the Medici archives have shown that some of the major pieces were the work of Stefano Caroni, who had a considerable reputation in Milan before he went to Florence and was paid the same salary as Biliverti, and of Giorgio Gaffuri.[71] Between them the Florentine hard-stone cutters and goldsmiths produced some of the most exquisite examples of goldsmiths' work in the Mannerist fashion, in which the emphasis was directed more towards beauty and inventiveness of form than extravagance of decoration. It would be impossible to find the sophisticated sense of style of Mannerism better represented than in the Florentine vessels of lapis lazuli mounted in enamelled gold preserved in the Kunsthistorisches Museum, Vienna[72] and in Florence itself (pls. 330-4). The sheer beauty of the material employed called for the most subtle handling of the decorative mounts, which are sometimes quite restrained though others are of the greatest richness. The lapis lazuli vase, after a Buontalenti design, which was presumably sent to Vienna as a present from Francesco to the Holy Roman Emperor (pl. 334), had a swing handle of most complex form in which animal and vegetable elements merge into one another, with scales developing into foliage and the foliage into plumage. The attenuated forms favoured by Buontalenti display a refinement of taste that contrasts strikingly with the elaborately ornamented vessels favoured at the northern courts.

The Buontalenti drawings for hardstone vessels preserved in the Uffizi in Florence are very sketchy in character; it was probably unnecessary to finish them in more detail as they would have been executed under his own direction in the Casino. It has been suggested that Buontalenti was himself a carver of rock-crystal and hardstone vessels, but there seems to be no evidence to justify this, and he was fully occupied in other directions.[73] Buontalenti was first and foremost an architect and his architectonic sense is revealed in the excellent design of the superb vessels made at the Casino and subsequently in the Uffizi. His drawings cover a wide range from the rather old-fashioned design of a font bearing the Medici arms (pl. 93) to the curious wavy-edged two handled vase in pl. 91. It is not clear from this last drawing whether the handles were meant to be applied separately or carved out of the solid stone. On the later pieces the handles were often applied separately, but the bowl and handle of the small cup from the Gutman collection (pl. 332), which may well go back to a Buontalenti design, are cut entirely from one piece. Buontalenti conformed to contemporary Mannerist taste in preferring a foot of very small size; in some cases this was so small and impracticable that it has been necessary to add a ring at a later date to give the cup more stability (pl. 331). While some of the vessels he designed are of restrained form with elongated egg-shaped bodies, others seem already to anticipate the crumpled writhing forms associated with the style of the van Vianen family of Utrecht.

Milan

It would be difficult to exaggerate the importance of the Milanese rock-crystal and semi-precious hardstone carvings produced during the second half of the sixteenth century. The two workshops of the Miseroni and Saracchi families are as significant in Italian applied art as that of the Jamnitzer family in Germany or of the enamelling workshops in Limoges in France. Unlike the Florentine Court Workshop, which was exclusively occupied with commissions for the Medici Grand Dukes, the Milanese shops accepted orders from most of the courts of Europe. Some of the most able Milanese masters left the city, some temporarily, others permanently, and set up workshops at the courts of princes both north and south of the Alps. The vases they produced numbered some of the most attractive and original achievements of Italian Mannerist art. Not only were vessels of all the conventional shapes, that were then fashionable, carved from rock-crystal, but also a variety of other forms which were unknown to the goldsmith were created. Most characteristic of Mannerist taste were vessels in the form of monstrous birds and animals. These could not be made from a single piece of crystal; instead the head, neck and wings were carved from separate pieces which were then attached to the main body of the vessel by enamelled gold mounts (pl. VI).

The form and richness of decoration of the enamelled gold mounts of sixteenth-century hardstone vessels was determined by the importance of the commission. As a rule rock-crystal vessels were more sparsely mounted while those carved from coloured hardstones, such as jasper, heliotrope or lapis lazuli, were set with enamelled and jewelled mounts. The mounts of hardstone vessels were usually of gold, though some of German origin (pls. 463-4, 492) were mounted in enamelled silver. Those which now have mounts of plain silver or gilt-bronze have almost certainly been deprived of their original gold mounts, which were replaced in a cheaper metal when they were no longer considered fashionable. The large numbers of rock-crystal vessels made in Vienna during the nineteenth century in Renaissance style usually have mounts of enamelled silver.

The identification of the place of origin of enamelled gold mounts is difficult, but it is possible to recognise some of those made in Milan. The mounts of the less extravagant Milanese vessels were decorated with a simple arabesque design, usually executed in black enamel with only slight use of other colours such as red, blue and green (pl. 338). The more important pieces were further enriched with numerous table-cut precious stones set in large square collets; the more modest ones had imitation jewels executed in coloured enamel within a gold frame resembling a collet. The finest pieces, such as those made for Duke Albrecht V of Bavaria and still preserved in the Munich Schatzkammer, were provided with gold mounts that combined superb modelling with polychrome translucent enamels and gemstones of great size and value (pl. V). Their makers are mostly anonymous, two of the five Saracchi brothers worked as goldsmiths: the only other named master was Giovan Battista Croce who, according to Morigia,[74] worked for many years for Duke Emanual Filiberto of Savoy and then subsequently for his son Duke Carlo. He left Milan and went to live in Turin, and he is thought to have provided the mounts for some of the rock-crystal vessels that the Dukes of Savoy ordered from Milan, among them those of the Madrid casket (see p.157). The mounts of Milanese hardstones were not always executed there; they were often exported unmounted to be finished by the goldsmith appointed by the customer abroad.

The chief families of hardstone sculptors in Milan were the Miseroni and the Saracchi. In the present state of our knowledge it is difficult to distinguish with certainty between the earlier works of the two. Both used the same mythological subjects to ornament their vases and no clear distinction can be recognised in the gold mounts that were used to assemble their pieces.

The Miseroni Family

The first generation of the Miseronis consisted of the two brothers, Gasparo and Gerolamo, who were trained in their art in Milan by Jacopo da Trezzo and Benedetto Poligno. Gasparo became one of the most sought-after masters of his day: he was assisted by his brother, Gerolamo until 1564, when the latter followed Jacopo da Trezzo to Spain. Gasparo worked for Pope Paul IV (1555-59) and for the Emperor Maximilian II, receiving payment for rock-crystals supplied in 1565 and again in 1571.[75] He was also employed by Cosimo I de' Medici and in 1556 made a large heliotrope vase, two rock-crystal vases and a beaker, all mounted in gold for him. Of these only the heliotrope vase survives;[76] it is of extremely restrained form but the sobriety of its present appearance is due to the loss of its enamelled gold mounts. In 1561 he supplied a tazza with gold handles and foot mount, another vase with gold-mounted foot for placing in a niche and a beaker 'alla tedescha' with a low foot entirely of rock-crystal (perhaps shaped like a German Setzbecher). These vessels have yet to be identified among the large number of rock-crystals in the Museo degli Argenti, if any of them do indeed survive there. On the whole it can be said that the earlier the rock-crystal vessel, the less obtrusive the gold mounts, as more importance was attached to the delicacy of the intaglio-cut ornament. Gerolamo was also employed by Cosimo de' Medici for in 1575 his son, Giorgio Ambrosio Miseroni, received 350 scudi in his father's name for making a lapis lazuli vase in the shape of an urn at Milan to the order of His Most Serene Highness, the Grand Duke.[77]

The Saracchi Family

The Saracchi family, unlike the Miseroni, remained in the city of their birth, whence they supplied vases as remarkable for the quality of their intaglio cutting as for their enamelled gold and jewelled mounts. The first generation of the family was made up of the five brothers: Giovanni Ambrogio, Simone, Steffano, Michele and Raffaello Saracchi. Duke Albrecht of Bavaria tried to persuade three members of the family to come to work at his Munich court and entrusted his ambassador and art adviser in Milan, Prospero Visconti, with the task of conducting the negotiations.[78] These seem to have come to nothing, but the proposed agreements throw some light on the workshop practice of the rock-crystal carvers. It seems that Steffano Saracchi carried out the rough shaping of the vessels, the design of which had been provided by Giovanni Ambrogio, who also finished them in their final form. The actual intaglio decoration was then carried out by a third brother, Simone, who received a higher salary than his brothers for this delicate and important task. The Emperor Rudolph commissioned rock-crystal vessels from the Saracchi as well as the Miseroni and records survive of payments to Ambrogio in 1665/6. The second generation of the family, Gabriello, Gasparo and Pietro Antonio Saracchi, crystal-workers and goldsmith respectively, joined the family workshop before seeking their fortune abroad. Between them they supplied rock-crystals to the Duke of Mantua, to Grand Duke Ferdinand I of Tuscany and to Duke Emmanuel Filibert of Savoy.

The name of Saracchi is often associated with the winged dragons on tall baluster feet, such as that illustrated in pl. VI. Another type of vessel that was much admired was shaped like a galley.[79] This ship form derived from the medieval nef, but unlike the latter was purely a sideboard ornament and served no useful purpose. One of the most splendid of these galleys was made in Milan by the Saracchi workshop for Duke Albrecht of Bavaria and still survives, though in despoiled condition, in the Munich Schatzkammer. This vessel is described at length by Morigia as follows 'The galley was constructed with poop and prow of a single very large piece of rock-crystal all carved intaglio with mythological subjects and mounted in gold and with jewels and fully armed like a real galley, and so it had Moorish slaves, two each on nine benches on each side, and captains, soldiers, officers, under-officers, gunners and various pieces of artillery which fired and with masts and sails and with the arms of the said Duke of Bavaria.'[80] This galley and the Neptune vase (pl. V) in 1579 cost 6000 gold gulden and in addition a special gratuity of 2000 imperial lire.

Annibale Fontana

This master was certainly the equal of any of the Miseroni or Saracchi. After spending some years in Palermo, he returned to Milan in 1574 and it is from the period between this year and his death in 1587 at the age of forty-seven that his rock-crystal vessels must date. Of these the finest are the Jason Vase, the so-called Albertinische Casket, both of which were made for Duke Albrecht of Bavaria,[81] and a second casket constructed of rock-crystal panels of exceptional size, which was presented in 1593 by the Infanta Caterina, wife of Duke Carlo Emmanuele of Savoy to her sister, the Infanta Isabella, daughter of Philip II of Spain, where it still remains in the treasury of the Royal Palace, Madrid.[82] It is decorated with nine rock-crystal panels of which some are by Fontana, whereas others are attributed to members of the Saracchi family, a circumstance which points to a close association between them. The cutting of the rock-crystal ewer in pl. 336 is attributed to Fontana.

The Tortorino Family

Two members of this Milanese family of craftsmen are known to have carved hard-stones. The better known of them is Francesco Tortorino, who worked for the Emperor Maximilian II, an important patron of the Milanese masters. He is represented by signed pieces in both Vienna and Florence. The 'large crystal glass' for which he received payment in 1569 by order of the Emperor Maximilian can, however, hardly be the extremely attractive but small tazza on a tall foot that bears his signature in the Kunsthistorisches Museum, Vienna.[83] Giovanni Maria Tortorino was employed as a hardstone cutter by the Farnese Dukes of Parma and Piacenza. The 1588 inventory of the Farnese *Guardaroba* lists a number of vases and other vessels cut from hardstones found within the ducal territories.[84]

Gasparo Mola

This goldsmith was one of the most outstanding of his day, but his extant works are nearly all of base metal and date from the very end of our period. He was born in the village of Coldre in Canton Ticino at some time in the 1570's:[85] a typical Renaissance master in that he was highly skilled in working all kinds of metal, he travelled from court to court and was patronised by numerous princes. . His earliest work dates from 1592 and his first court appointment was in Florence where he assisted the Florentine court gunmaker, Anton Maria Bianchini. He was also required to produce a series of crucifix figures after a model by Gian Bologna and in 1597 is referred to as *Orefice sul corridore*. In the same year he succeeded Michele Mazzafirri as Die-Cutter to the Medici Mint (*Intagliatore della Zecca*) and subsequently worked on the bronze doors of the cathedral of Pisa. Leaving Florence after a dispute about his pay, he was much in demand as a medallist and is recorded as Master of the Mint in Turin in 1607. From 1608 to 1609 he was back at the Florence Mint; later he worked for the Este court at Modena and also at Guastalla. He returned to Florence after 1614 and stayed there in the employ of Cosimo II until 1623, when he was appointed to the Papal Mint in Rome, where he remained until his death in 1640. It was during his later stay in Florence that he produced the finely decorated arms for which he is most renowned (see p.321). While he was in Florence he came to the notice of Philipp Hainhofer, through the latter's brother, who was a resident in the city. In one of his letters Hainhofer refers to his outstanding skill, the equal of which cannot be found far or wide (*fürtreffliche Kunst seinsz gleichen soll weit und breit nit sein*). Mola's most famous and, indeed, only surviving work entirely in precious metal is the magnificent silver-gilt dish he made to commemorate Pope Gregory XIII's reform of the calendar in 1583.[86] This dish probably dates from the 1630's when Mola was in Rome; it belongs to a transitional phase between late Mannerism and Baroque, though the delicacy of the ornament seems to foreshadow the capricious manner of rococo.

The Medici Inventory

Most of the surviving examples of Italian sixteenth-century goldsmiths' work are mounted hardstones, but the Medici inventories show that there was no shortage of vessels entirely of precious metal. The following extracts are representative:[87]

A vase of solid gold, the body in the form of a nautilus, on tall foot the cover surmounted by a figure of Neptune seated on a sea-horse.

A silver-gilt basin of large size divided into compartments with sea-snails, fish and grotesques, in the middle within a circle of grotesques, compasses, masks and festoons, a figure with a harp, the border with compasses and figures within ovals.

A silver-gilt salt-cellar in the form of a sarcophagus with four lion feet, the whole body decorated with arabesques and the cover surmounted by a figure of a river-god with the Medici arms.

A silver-gilt oval flask wrought with foliage, the handles two dragons with the arms of Medici and Austria, the cover surmounted by a horse's head.

A mother of pearl flask mounted in silver-gilt with rubies or garnets and pearls, the foot decorated with grotesques, spout formed as a dragon and a horse's head, the handle a dragon with two cartouches, the cover with three turquoises and a large spinel ruby within [one of the few pieces surviving in the Museo degli Argenti].

A silver lamp chiselled with foliage with its chain and cover.

A silver-gilt beaker with foot in the form of a windmill with a man climbing up a stair.

A silver-gilt tazza with tall foot decorated with terms, chiselled in the middle with Actaeon and Diana.

Two salt cellars of lapis lazuli with tripod feet and cover of gold enamelled with arabesques.

Study of the Medici inventory makes it clear that its contents were of varying origin. The dynastic marriages of the Medici dukes had brought vessels from north of the Alps, in particular that of Francesco I with the Archduchess Giovanna of Austria.

Turning to surviving Italian goldsmiths' work, the survival rate, as might be expected, becomes higher towards the end of the century. Just as the most important drawings of the period represent ewers and basins, so also are these the most frequently surviving pieces. Made of gold, silver-gilt or white silver, they not only occupied the most important position on the sideboard, but, so long as forks were not used, fulfilled an essential function during the meal. The ewer and basin were carried around between courses by two servants and a little water was poured from the one into the other, rinsing the fingers of each guest. The basin was not deep enough for the fingers to be dipped into it as is sometimes imagined. Ewers and basins were usually made *en suite* but it is doubtful whether any great importance was attached at the time to such congruence between the

Plate XV
Watercolour drawing by a follower of Wenzel Jamnitzer. Nürnberg, third quarter of 16th century.

Plate XVI
Gilt cup and cover. Augsburg, about 1570.

two vessels. The ewer and basin illustrated in pl. 348-9, though they appear to have formed part of the same service of plate, are not in fact decorated en suite. One reason for the survival of a relatively large number of Italian ewers and basins is that they had a use in church, the ewers as baptismal vessels, the basins for collecting offerings. The great vases, which are so often represented in Renaissance paintings, have disappeared without trace, but the form can be seen in the smaller vase for Holy Oil of 1560 in the treasury of Cagliari Cathedral.[88]

When Plon wrote his pioneer study of Cellini and Italian sixteenth-century gold-smiths' work, he included several ewers or basins that have since proved to be of Flem-ish or German origin, but a number of Italian examples that were unknown to him have now been identified. It is probable that others exist, preserved in private collections or inaccessible church treasuries. It is, however, still necessary to exercise great circum-spection in attributing such vessels to Italian masters, even when they have been preserved in Italy. It is known that many foreign masters were working in Italy and it seems reasonable to assume that goldsmiths who had been trained in the Italian Renais-sance tradition would have avoided the extremes of northern Mannerism in their designs. Of the various sets of ewers and basins associated with Italy, either because of their marks or armorial bearings, three, illustrated in pls. 341, 344; 342, 345 and 348-9, are here attributed to Iberian goldsmiths. One set is certainly, another possibly, by Antonio de Castro who worked in Genoa, while the third (pls. 341, 344) was probably wrought in Spain. Of the remaining sets three are Venetian, three are Genoese, while the others are unattributed. The ewer bodies are egg or plum-shaped, but variety is achieved by the differing forms of handle and spout; the basins are circular with wide depression and high central boss over which the base of the ewer fitted. The whole surface is decorated with concentric rings of ornament, usually including cartouches with figure subjects. Most of the northern Renaissance ewers have wrought bodies, the decoration being beaten out of the metal of the sides. This process was more difficult to carry out in the case of those with egg-shaped bodies and small necks, and the finest of the Italian ewers appear to have cast bodies. These must have been assembled from a number of castings, but the bodies have been worked up so carefully that the vertical or horizontal joints cannot be seen. The companion basins seem always to have been embossed, whether of northern or southern European origin. Ewers dating from the end of the sixteenth or the early seventeenth century often have their ornament arranged in long vertical panels set within cartouches instead of the horizontal friezes of the sixteenth century. By arranging the decoration in this way an effect more in accord with the Baroque principle of unity was achieved.

Genoa

The earliest surviving Italian ewers and basins are those by Antonio de Castro, a gold-smith of Portuguese origin who worked in Genoa in the second half of the sixteenth century.[89] The contract for making them is dated May 11, 1565; this is of great value in establishing a system of dating for such pieces. It will be seen (pls. 342, 345) that strapwork cartouches play an important part in their design, perhaps more so than would be the case in the work of a native Italian. The profuse employment of strapwork was more closely associated with northern goldsmiths' work, although its first development and exploitation was the achievement of the Italian colony at Fontainebleau.

Immigrant goldsmiths seem to have played an important part in the development of the craft in Genoa. Apart from Antonio de Castro there was a large Flemish colony of goldsmiths. One of the most splendid productions of their art in Genoa is the great silver shrine of the Corpus Christi in the treasury of the Cathedral of San Lorenzo.[90] This huge piece took many years to make; of the five goldsmiths who were first called on in 1562 and 1563 to work upon it, four were described as *fiamminghi*: Tomas Opluten, Raniero Fochs, Baldassare Martinez and Davide Scaglia. The only Italians involved were Agostino Groppo and Luca Cambiaso, the painter who produced the designs. The list of Flemish works does not end there; the great silver altar frontal of the cathedral was executed by Melchio Suez, while silver plate was made for Andrea Doria by Enrico Fiammingo. Genoa continued to attract Flemish goldsmiths in the seventeenth century and a magnificent embossed dish, now in the Stockholm National Museum, is signed and dated 1674 by the Flemish goldsmith, Carel Bolcool of Genoa.

A service of silver-gilt vessels dating from the third quarter of the sixteenth century in the Wallace Collection (pls. 348-9, 351) is Portuguese in style and may have been made in part by de Castro. The pieces are not marked and are evidently the work of more than one goldsmith, though not necessarily more than one workshop. The service consists of a ewer and basin, a standing cup, a salt-cellar and a single cover, perhaps from another vessel now missing from the service. The standing cup, which is severely damaged, is decorated with the same castings on both foot and body as the ewer and must have come from the same workshop. The ewer and basin have been tentatively attributed to de Castro on the grounds of their similarity to the signed Lercaro pieces[91] (pls. 342, 345). They are certainly similar, but not to such an extent that the identification can be accepted as more than conjectural. Similar stylistic resemblances can be found in silver objects of about the same date made by goldsmiths working in different German cities.

Genoese silver of a somewhat later period (the first quarter of the seventeenth century) is particularly well represented. In the Museo Nazionale of the Palazzo Spinola in Genoa are a large basin and a pair of vases or ewers, since converted for use as ice-pails, which appear to have been made in Genoa during the first half of the seventeenth century, but already in a style that can properly be described as Baroque. These pieces commemorate the departure of Christopher Columbus from Palos en route for America. They have been attributed to Lazzaro Tavarone (1556-1641)[92] but an alternative theory suggests that they may be the work of the Antwerp goldsmith, Matthias Melin (active 1627-1636), who is thought to have worked for a time in Genoa. The Columbus theme is also the subject of a superb dish showing him receiving gifts from Amerindian natives; this is signed and dated *Gio. Aelbosca Belga Ge^a. 1626*, once again the work of a goldsmith from the southern Netherlands.[93]

The most impressive surviving service of Genoese silver vessels is the set of three ewers with their companion basins, (pls. 356-62). This service was made for a Genoese noble family, probably that of Lomellini, whose arms appear on each piece (pl. 360). It consists of a single ewer and basin of exceptionally large size, the latter with a frieze embossed with subjects relating to the maritime rivalry between the cities of Genoa and Venice (pls. 361-2), and a pair of smaller ewers and basins, the decoration of which is identical (pls. 356-7, 360). The repetition of ornament down to the smallest detail on large and important pieces of plate is quite exceptional at this date. The central friezes are decorated with the usual nymphs and tritons, while the borders are embossed with recumbent figures in cartouches alternating with bunches of fruit (pl. 357). The smaller vessels are dated 1619 and the larger 1621. Following the usual Italian practice, the ewers are assembled from cast elements while the basins are embossed in heavy metal. The modelling of the figures is superb, especially that of the cast-work around the neck and foot. The treatment of the handle of the larger ewer as a triton wrestling with a faun is both original and of great sculptural merit (pl. 359).

Although these pieces date from the end of the second decade of the seventeenth century, they still belong to the Mannerist epoch. Whereas the Baroque feeling for unity required the decoration of a basin to be set in one plane so that it could be appreciated at a single glance, in these there are still two concentric rings which can only be understood by turning the piece round in a full circle (pl. 357).

Another magnificent silver basin in an Italian private collection, traditionally made for the Genoese family of Giustiani-Longhi, also follows the sixteenth-century scheme. This basin is of exceptional interest because the original sketch for it by the Genoese Baroque master, Bernardo Strozzi, still exists in the Ashmolean Museum.[94] While Strozzi's painting with its dramatic chiaroscuro is Baroque in manner, the silver dish, which probably dates, like those described above, from the second decade of the seventeenth century, is more conservative. The border design is broken up by strapwork cartouches enclosing figure subjects, while the intervening spaces are filled with putti engaged in various activities. The inner frieze is filled with a battle subject between horsemen. The Baroque force of Strozzi's design is lost in the low relief of the figures, but this is to some extent inevitable, as the technique of embossing in heavy gauge metal seriously limited the height of relief. The battle subject, though an original design by Strozzi, owes much to the engravings of similar subjects by Tempesta.[95] The existence of so many important vessels made in Genoa: namely four complete sets of ewer and basin, the basin after the Strozzi design, the Columbus dish in the Spinola collection and the (attributed) Wallace Collection service, suggests that Genoa must have been one of the most important centres of the goldsmiths' art in Italy. Genoa was also famous in the second half of the sixteenth century as a source of coral, either already carved or in its natural state. As a wonder of nature the material was much in demand, and in Germany a branch was often mounted on the cover of a cup as a finial. It was also employed to make handles for cutlery. The Bavarian court of Duke Albrecht V ordered quantities of coral from Genoa; it was supplied by the coral-carver and dealer, Battista Negrone Viale.[96]

Venice

During the fifteenth century the Venetian goldsmiths came under strong German influence, due in part to the presence in the city of German immigrant masters. Whether this influence continued in the following century is not known as so little Venetian silver has survived the destruction caused by changing taste, wars and forced contributions of occupying powers. Among the few documented pieces is the silver binding of the breviary of Doge Antonio Grimani in the Biblioteca Nazionale, Venice. This was completed in or before 1574. Its design, which is attributed to the Venetian sculptor, Alessandro Vittoria, is in the purest Renaissance taste, the borders of both covers being embossed with acanthus scrolls interrupted by circular frames enclosing decorative medallions, while in the centre of the top cover is an embossed medallion head of Doge Grimani.[97]

One of the finest of the Italian Mannerist vessels is the basin, no longer accompanied by its ewer, in the Museum of Trapani, Sicily.[98] This once belonged to the Grimani family and is, therefore, probably of Venetian workmanship, though there is no mark which would justify a definite attribution. The outer border of this basin is embossed and chased with eight recumbent figures symbolising the Virtues set within oval cartouches and separated by oval cartouches. The inner frieze is embossed with pairs of nymphs and tritons, also enclosed by oval cartouches. The figures have long elegant bodies in conformity with Mannerist taste. Another basin of analogous design, formerly in the treasury of the Basilica of Santa Barbara at Mantua was removed by French troops in 1796 and presumably destroyed. A fine pair of basins, formerly in the Rütschi collection, Zürich, were attributed to Venice; the bowls are embossed in fairly high relief with nymphs and tritons in a vigorous manner suggesting the nascent Baroque of the early years of the seventeenth century.[99]

The Venetian ewer and basin illustrated in pls. 354-5 illustrate the new fashion of the decorative panels being arranged vertically. It will also be seen that the cartouches enclosing the figure subjects show the fleshy forms that foreshadow the Baroque instead of the crisp leatherlike outlines of the de Castro pieces. A second version of this ewer and basin was also executed to the same design and by the same master but in gilt-copper instead of gilt-silver. An English goldsmith would not have been permitted by his guild to produce such a piece in base metal, but the Italian goldsmiths had more freedom in this respect.

The treasury of St. Mark's, Venice, which is so rich in Byzantine goldsmiths' work, has curiously little to show for the sixteenth century and the Renaissance ecclesiastical plate preserved there does not approach the importance of the splendid late Gothic pieces. Our knowledge of what must have been one of the finest Venetian basins is based upon a drawing of, or for, it in the Düsseldorf Kunstmuseum (pl. 94). The subject matter of the ornament relates to the defeat of the Turks by the Venetians at the battle of Lepanto. The basin was made for the Doge Alvise Mocenigo (1570-1577) or for a later member of his family. The original design may well go back to the circle of Veronese; it must have been much admired, for it was copied by masters working north of the Alps. The version illustrated has been attributed tentatively to the Augsburg painter, Rottenhammer. So little Venetian sixteenth-century silver survives that it is impossible to gain an adequate idea of its merit, but the combination of so admirable a design with craftsmanship, such as one sees on the contemporary Genoese pieces, would have produced an object of outstanding importance.

Two Italian ewers that are no longer accompanied by their basins are illustrated in pls. 346-7 and 350. Although the detail of the ornament of the first is derived from prints by Etienne Delaune, the bold modelling of neck, lip and handle suggest the work of an Italian master, though a French origin cannot be excluded. The whole vessel is constructed of cast elements but the detail of the ornament is so finely finished that at first it gives the impression of embossed and chased work. The second ewer (pl. 350) appears on grounds both of construction and design to be Italian and of the early seventeenth century. Though now in Museo degli Argenti in Florence, it did not form part of either of the collections of the Medici Grand Dukes of Tuscany or the Archbishops of Salzburg, but was acquired more recently.[100] The design shows a restraint in the use of ornament that is more likely to derive from an Italian than from a northern goldsmith.

The treasury of the cathedral of Cagliari in Sardinia contains a ewer and basin by two different masters.[101] The ewer is a rather coarse piece, probably of local manufacture, but the basin is of the highest quality. It is embossed with a continuous frieze of the triumph of Galatea on the rim, while the interior is embossed with stopped flutes, centering on a plaquette also embossed with Galatea. The introduction of an almost plain area between the central medallion and the outer frieze is quite unusual at this period and achieves a calm and pleasing effect.

Also dating from the early seventeenth century is the pair of basins and a single ewer presented by Archbishop Bonciani to the cathedral of Pisa in 1618.[102] The embossing of these vessels is executed in a somewhat summary manner on a rather large scale, indicating a decline in standards of craftsmanship in comparison with the Mannerist period. This set of a ewer and pair of basins is exceptional in that it was intended for use at the altar, whereas others preserved in cathedral treasuries were originally secular and given subsequently to the Church by some pious donor. The scenes embossed in the cartouches are taken from the New Testament. Their arrangement follows the usual Mannerist scheme. The ewer and basin illustrated in pls. 352-3 conform to the same pattern, but in this case the execution is of the highest quality. These two vessels are embossed and chased with scenes from the lives of Pompey and Julius Caesar respectively, subjects perhaps more familiar to Italian than to German artists. In the past the fact that they are preserved in the Schatzkammer of the Munich Residenz has led to their attribution to a German goldsmith but they reached Munich as part of the bridal gift of the Polish princess, Constanza, the daughter of Sigismund III; Poland had at this period strong connections with Italy as well as with Germany. A second ewer and basin *en suite* with those in pls. 352-3 have survived in a Paris private collection. They are decorated with scenes from Roman history and must also have belonged to Sigismund III of Poland. Their giant size gives an idea of the great wealth of the treasuries of Renaissance princes.

While so many ewers and basins have survived there appear to be no comparable drinking-vessels of Italian origin extant, with the possible exception of the small tazza in the Untermyer collection.[103] The series of drawings of drinking-vessels in the Fitzwilliam Codex (see p.25) which is the best source of information on the subject, shows that two forms were in use; either a wide-bowled tazza (pl. 74) or a goblet on baluster stem with a tall, tapering bowl (pl. 75). In comparison with the other designs in this codex the drinking-vessels are unexciting, a fact which may explain their subsequent destruction.

A unique set of twelve silver-gilt tazzas (pls. 363-5), dating from about 1580 and formerly thought to be of German origin, can with better reason be identified as Italian.[104]

The whereabouts of nine of these tazzas are known, the remaining three are now missing, presumably in private collections. They were originally made at some time in the last quarter of the sixteenth century for an unknown person, from whom they were either purchased or inherited by a Cardinal Aldobrandini. They later passed to Prince Giovanni Battista Pamphili and a manuscript[105] list of his property dated March 2, 1710 includes the entry 'Twelve large dishes with tall bases, with low relief historical scenes and a standing figure of an Emperor on each. They weigh 109 pounds and eight ounces.' In the nineteenth century the set was in the collection of the Marquis of Scarisbrick, but it was sold by auction in 1861 and subsequently split up. Six of the tazzas passed into the possession of the Paris dealer, Frédéric Spitzer, who for some reason substituted highly wrought Spanish bases, probably removed from a contemporary set of monstrances, for their fluted bases. They are described in Christie's auction sale catalogue of 1861 as 'the celebrated Aldobrandini Caesar *Tazzas,* the stems and feet fluted; each tazza surmounted by a beautiful figure of a Roman Emperor, attributed to Cellini'. The remaining six retained their original stems and bases, which are decorated only with fluting in a manner better suited to the bowls than the busy detail of the Spanish ones. The Spitzer Collection included a manuscript account of the dishes giving the names of the Emperors and identifying the scenes embossed on the bowls, but this is now lost.

These tazzas have been attributed to Augsburg on the following grounds;[106] firstly that one of the scenes on the bowl of the example now in the Victoria and Albert Museum, which depicts the Emperor Domitian's German conquests, shows German troops holding a banner bearing the device of a pine-cone, the emblem of the city of Augsburg (pl. 364), and secondly because much of the decoration on foot and stem of the second set can be paralleled in German pattern-books. It has also been suggested that the figures of the Emperors themselves are closely related to the engravings of Roman Emperors by the Nürnberg master, Virgil Solis, but this is not correct as they wear carefully observed Roman classical armour and not the peculiar mixture of medieval and Roman armour of the Virgil Solis engravings. One thing is certain; they show no similarity to German tazzas of the same period. These survive in large numbers; there is a set of no fewer than fifty-four in the Palazzo Pitti (see p.233), formerly in the Salzburg Schatzkammer, and another set of twelve is in the British Museum (Waddesdon Bequest). All these German examples were made in Augsburg and conform to a single type (pl. 443), quite different in proportion and form from the Aldobrandini set. Despite the later alterations to which six of them have been subjected they constitute the most impressive single monument of Italian and perhaps of European goldsmiths' work of the sixteenth century. The same type of interlaced strapwork border of the tazzas is also found on the Italian rock-crystal incense boat with silver-gilt mounts (pl. 366). Apart from the religious inscription which runs around the top, there are no features that suggest its liturgical function.

A 'poor man's' silver furniture was produced in Italy during the second half of the sixteenth century; few examples have survived, doubtless because of their flimsy construction, but there is a table in the Rijksmuseum and a table-top in the Victoria and Albert Museum. The method of manufacture seems to have been to press silver foil over a mould and then to fill the back with plaster or some mastic material. The panels were then applied with the silver face uppermost to the object to be decorated. The result was effective, but the foil was so thin that it was soon worn through and showed the plaster beneath. The table-top in the Victoria and Albert Museum is of interest in the context of this book as the scenes moulded on it are taken from well-known paintings by Raphael including his *Triumph of Galatea* and *Judgement of Paris.* While the composition is copied faithfully enough, the figures have been elongated in order to correspond to the Mannerist ideal, a liberty that later ages would have hesitated to take. In the following century small ebony cabinets with drawers covered with silver foil pressed with foliate or other ornament were made in the Low Countries.

1 There is a contemporary copy of this drawing in the Victoria and Albert Museum.

2 Quoted *Vasari*, Milanesi Vol. VII, p.383
The text is as follows:
In resposta de una de V.S. di vinti due del passato, gli dico che piu mesi fa essere finito il modello della saliera de rilievo, e principato de argento alcune zampe de animali, dove se ha a possare il vaso della saliera, e a torno di esso vaso ci va certi festoni con alcune mascare, et in nel coperchio una figura di rilievo tutta, con alcuni altri fogliami, secondo Michelangolo ordino et secondo appare nel modello finito detto de sopra.
(In reply to your letter of the 22nd of the past month, I inform you that the model of the salt-cellar in relief was finished several months ago, and certain animals' paws upon which the vase of the salt is to be placed have been begun in silver, and around this vase go certain festoons with some masks, and on the cover is a figure modelled completely in the round, with other foliage, as Michelangelo ordered and as can be seen in the completed model mentioned above.)

3 See A. Marabottini, *Polidoro da Caravaggio*, Rome, 1969.

4 E. Pandiani, 'Vita privata genovese nel Rinascimento', *Atti Soc. Ligure di Storia Patria*, Vol. XLVII, p.222-57.

5 Kris I, Vol. I, p.64-5.

6 Vasari, Vol. V, p.629 *'Lavoro drapelloni, sopraveste, portine, et ogni minima cose d'arte'*.

7 Vasari, Vol. V, p.603.

8 Pouncey and Gere, pps. 110-112, pls. 156-8. See also B. F. Davidson, Exhibition Catalogue, *Perino del Vaga e la sua Cerchia*, Florence, 1966. Blunt also attributes some of the Perino-style drawings at Windsor to Luzio Romano.

9 Hartt, Vol. I, cat. nos. 48-132.

10 Giulio Romano had bequeathed the collection to his son, who sold them before his death in 1562. The collection is referred to by da Strada in his preface to the seventh volume of Serlio which he published in Frankfurt in 1573.

11 See J. F. Hayward, 'Ottavio da Strada and the Goldsmiths' Designs of Giulio Romano', *Burlington Magazine*, Vol. CXII, p.10.

12 See J. F. Hayward 'Some spurious antique vase designs of the sixteenth century' *Burlington Magazine*, 1972, Vol. CXIV, p.378ff.

13 *Libro di dissegni per far Vasella da Argento et Oro per servitio della Credenza e tauola per un gran Principe....Dissegnati di mano propria di Ottavia Strada, Cittadino Romano et Gentilhuomo della Casa di Rudolpho II Imp. 1597.*

14 Inv. No. P.D.6-1948. For these drawings see also Chapter I, p.25.

15 A. Bertolotti, *Arti Minori alla corte di Mantova*, Milan, 1889, p.69.

16 Cellini I, I. cap. 14.

17 Quoted by A. Ronchini, 'L'orefice Andrea Casalino' *Periodico di Numismatica e Sfragistica per la Storia d'Italia*, Vol. IV, p.228 *'Ho gia mostrato diversi lavori d'argento, et d'altro metallo indorato, et varie invenzioni di dissegni al suo huomo, che sono pertinente all' arte sua'*.

18 He did, however, work for two years as assistant to a Milanese goldsmith, Paolo Arsagno, in Rome, see Bertolotti, *Artisti Lombardi a Roma*, Milan, 1881, p.242.

19 Cellini I, I, 60. *Volendolo il papa donàre a il re Francesco, lo volse in prima guarnire riccamente d'oro, e commesse a tutti a dua noi che fascessimo i detti disegni. Fatti che noi gli avemmo, ciascun di noi il portò dal papa. Era il disegno di Tubbia a foggia di un candeliere, dove a guisa della candela si imboccava quel bel corno, e del piede di questo ditto candeliere faceva quattro testoline di liocorno con semplicissima invenzione: tanto che quando tal cosa io vidi non mi potetti tenere che in un destro modo io non sogghignassi. Il papa s'avvide e subito disse: Mostra qua il tuo disegno. Il quale era una sola testa di liocorno. A corrispondenza di quel ditto corno avevo fatto la più bella sorte di testa che veder si possa; il perché si era che io avevo preso parte della fazione della testa del cavallo e parte di quella del cervio, arrichita con la più bella sorte di velli e altre galanterie, tale che subito che la mia si vide ognuno gli dette il vanto. Ma perché alla presenza de questa disputa era certi milanesi di grandissima autorita, questi dissono: Beatissimo Padre, vostra santita manda a donare questo gran presente in Francia: sappiate che i franciosi sono uomini grossi, e non cognosceranno l'eccellenzia di questa opera di Benvenuto ma si bene piacerà loro questi cibori, li quali ancora saranno fatti piu presto.*

20 Plon, App. VII, p.387-392.

21 Bertolotti, *Artisti Lombardi a Roma*, Milan, 1881, Vol. I, p.298. Their names are recorded only as Rafaele and Roberto.

22 Cellini I, II.81. *In prima era ito a baciare i piedi ai papa; e in mentre che io ragionavo col papa, sopraggiunse misser Averardo Serristori, il quale era imbasciadore del nostro duca. E perché io avevo mossi certi ragionamenti con el papa, come e'quali io credo che facilmente mi sarei convenuto seco e volentieri mi sarei tornato a Roma per le gran difficulta che io avevo a Firenze; ma 'l detto imbasciatore io mi avvidi che egli aveva operato in contrario.*

23 Plon, App. IX, p.393.

24 G. Baglione, *Vite de' pittori, scultori et architette*, Roma, 1733, p.109 and also 103 *'Egli era valente orefice grossiere, e modellava da scultore eccelente siccome le sue belle opere dimostrano. Fece belli getti d'oro e d'argento, e per tirar piastra e formar figure non trovassi pari che in quel genio l'eguagliasse.'*

25 *Questo e il disegno della richissima croce d'argento nella quale vi sono di quatri ovati del posamento et i tondi delle teste de la croce sonno di cristallo intagliati con le istesse istorie che si vede. Et il piano de la croce e di lapis lazaro dell' istessa grandezza a punto che è l'opera con due candellieri simili, la quale dono a l'altare di Sa Pietro di Roma l'Illmo Card. Farnese di felice me. in vita sua nell'anno 1582.*

26 ill. Catalogo, *Argenti Italiani*, Museo Poldi Pezzoli, 1959, pl. XVII.

27 W. F. Volbach: 'Antonio Gentile da Faenza and the large candlesticks in the Treasury of St. Peters', *Burlington Magazine*, Oct. 1948, p.281. In this same article the writer illustrates a number of drawings of candlesticks from the Chigi Codex P. vi, in the Vatican Library and attributes them also to Gentile. They appear, however, to date from the eighteenth century and, if they have any connection with Gentile, they can only be later copies of his designs.

28 G. Sangiorgi, 'Antonio Gentile', *Bollettino d'Arte*, 1932, p.220. R. Berliner in 'Two contributions to the Criticism of Drawings', *Art Bulletin*, 1951, p.51 rejects the attribution of the drawing to Gentile and considers the set to be earlier in date. Gentile da Faenza was not, however, particularly famous in the eighteenth century and the inscription on the drawing must have derived from an old tradition.

29 L. Avery, 'Sculptured Silver of the Renaissance' *Bulletin of the Metropolitan Museum*, 1946-7, p.252. See also W. Gramberg, 'Guglielmo della Porta, Coppe Fiammingo und Gentile da Faenza' *Jahrbuch der Hamburger Kunstsammlungen*, 1960, p.31.ff.

30 Inv. Nos. 2909-2914. See also W. Gramberg 'Vier Zeichunugen des Guglielmo della Porta zu seiner Serie mythologischer Reliefs' *Jahrbuch der Hamburger Kunstsammlungen*, 1968, p.69.

31 Vasari, Vol. VII p.5-43.

32 ibid. p.43.

33 Among them the Metropolitan Museum, New York and the National Gallery of Canada, Ottawa. See Popham and Fenwick, *European Drawings*, Toronto, 1965, nos. 188-190.

34 Y. Hackenbroch, *Bronzes, other metalwork and sculpture, Untermyer Collection*, London, 1962, figs. 69 and 70.

35 Bertini, *I Disegni italiani della Biblioteca Reale di Torino*, 1958, cat. no. 241, a quadrant section of a basin, embossed with a scene of nymphs and sea-centaurs. Formerly attributed to Cellini.

26 U. Middeldorf, 'Notes on Italian Bronzes', *Burlington Magazine*, Vol. LXXIII 1938, p.204, pl. 1d and e.

37 Vasari, Vol. VII p.621ff.

38 Cellini I, I, 19 *'Lavorava solamente di grosseria, cioe vasi bellissimi, e bacini, e cose tali'.*

39 Cellini I, I.24 *'con tanti belli animaletti, fogliami e maschere, quante immaginar si possar . . . era infra gli altri belli ornamenti un manico tutto di un pezzo a questo vaso, sottilissimamente lavorato, che per virtu di una certa molla stava diritto sopra la bocca del vaso.'*

40 Cellini I, I.28 *'Passando un giorno a casa dalla mia bottega, vide a sorta certi disegni che io avevo innanzi, in fra' quali era parecchi bizzarri vasetti che per mio piacere avevo disegnati. Questi tali vasi erano molti diversi e vari da tutti quelli che mai s'erano veduti insino a quella età. Volsi il ditto maestro Iacomo che io gnene facessi d'argento; il quali io feci oltra modo volentieri, per essere sicondo il mio capriccio. Con tutto che il ditto valente uomo molto bene me gli pagasse, fu l'un cento maggiore l'onore che mi approtono; perche in nella Arte di quei valenti uomini orefici dissono non aver mai veduto cosa piu bella ne meglio condotta.'*

41 Cellini I, II.1 *'Il quale era composto di figurine tonde e di basso rilievo; e similmente era composto di figure tonde e di pesci di basso rilievo il detto bacino, tanto ricco e tanto bene accomodato che ognuno che lo vedeva resteva maravigliato, si per la forza del disegno e per la invenzione.'*

42 Cellini I, II.14 *'In mentre che io davo ordine a queste cose, si finiva il vasetto e il bacino ovato, i quali ne portono parecchi mesi. Finiti che io gli ebbi, gli feci benissimo dorare. Questa parve la piu bell' opera che mai si fosse veduta in Francia.'*

43 They must in fact have been the same ewer and basin referred to above.

44 Cellini I, II.20 *'Ancora avevo fatto parecchi operette al cardinale di Ferrara: di piu un vasetto d'argento riccamente lavorato avevo fatto, per donarlo a madama de Tampes.'*

45 Cellini II, cap. XXII *'in forma di uovo, alto piu di un braccio qualcosa, con le bocche strette di sopra, e con i lori manichi...richissimamente lavorati di fogliami e di animali diversi'.*

46 Cellini I, II, 1. *'molte cose son belle da dire, che faccendole poi non s'accompagnano bene in opera'.*

47 Cellini I, II, 2.*'Io feci una forma ovata, di grandezza di più d'un mezzo braccio assai bene, quasi dua terzi, e sopra detta forma, sicondo che mostra il Mare abbracciarsi con la Terra, feci dua figure grande più d'un palmo assai bene, le quale stavano a sedere entrando colle gambe l'una nell'altra, si come si vede certi rami di mare lunghi che entran nella terra, E in mano al mastio Mare messi una* *nave ricchissimamente lavorata: in essa nave accomodatamente e bene stava di molto sale; sotto al detto avevo accomadato quel quattro cavalli marittimi: in nella destra del ditto Mare avevo messo il suo tridente. La Terra avevo fatta una femmina tanto di bella forma quanto io avevo potuto e saputo, bella e graziata; e in mano alla ditta avevo posto un tempio ricco e adorno, posato in terra, e lei in sun esso s'appoggiave con la ditta mano: questo avevo fatto per tenere il pepe. Nell'altra mano posto un corno di dovizia, adorno con tutte le bellezze che io sapevo al mondo. Sotto questa iddea, e in quella parte che si mostrava esser Terra, avevo accomodato tutti quei più bei animali che produce la terra. Sotto la parte del Mare avevo figurato tutta la bella sorte di pesci e chiocciolette, che comportar poteva quel poco ispazio: Quel resto dell'ovato, nella grossezza sua feci molti ricchissimi ornamenti....*

Cellini I, II, 36 gives a further account of the salt as follows:—

'*la quale, si come io ho detto di sopra, era in forma ovata, ed era di grandezza di dua terzi di braccio in circa tutta d'oro, lavorata per virtùdi cesello. E si come io dissi quando io ragionai del modello, avevo figurato il Mare e la Terra a sedere l'uno e l'altro, e s'intramettevano le gambe, si come entra certi rami del mare infra la terra, e la terra infra del detto mare: cosi propiamente avevo dato loro quella grazia. A il Mare avevo posto in mano un tridente in nella destra; e in nella sinsitra avevo posto una barca sottilmente lavorata, in nella quale si metteva la salina. Era sotto a questa detta figura i sua quattro cavalli marittimi, che insino al petto e le zampe dinanzi erano di cavallo; tutta la parte dal mezzo indietro era di pesce. Queste code di pesce con piacevol modo s'intrecciavano insieme: in sul qual gruppo sedeva con fierissima attitudine il detto Mare: aveva all'intorno molta sorte di pesci e altri animali marritimi. L'acqua era figurata con le sue onde; di poi era benessimo smaltata del suo propio colore. Per la Terra avevo figurato una bellissima donna, con il corno della sua dovizia in mano, tutta ignuda come il mastio appunto; nell'altra sua sinistra mana avevo fatto un tempietto di ordine ionico, sottillissimamente lavorato; e in questo avevo accomodato il pepe. Sotto a questa femina avevo fatto i più belli animali che produca la terra; e i sua scogli terresti avevo parte ismaltati, e parte lasciati d'oro. Avevo da poi posata questa ditta opera e investita in una basa d'ebano nero: era di una certa accomodata grossezza, e aveva un poco di goletta, nella quale io avevo compartito quattro figure d'oro, fatte di più che mezzo rilievo: questi si erano figurato la Notte, il Giorno, il Graprusco e l'Aurora. Ancora v'era quattro altre figure delia medesima grandezza, fatte per i quattro Venti principali, con tanta puletezza lavorate e parte ismaltate, quanto immaginar si possa*'.

48   Plon, p.166.

49   Cellini III, p.611.

50   There are repeated references to this chalice and to the long delay in making it in Cellini I, I, caps. 56, 58 and 60 to 73 inclusive. For its further history, see Cust. Vol. I, p.238 n. 1.

51   Pouncey and Gere, cat. no. 167, p.98.

52   Vasari, Vol. V, p.373 '*Volendo poi fare il medisimo cardinal Farnese una cassetta d'argento ricchissima, fattone fare l'opera a Manno Orefice fiorentino*'. For a detailed account of this casket see de Rinaldis 'Il cofanetto farnesiano del Museo di Napoli', *Bolletino d'Arte*, 1923, p.145.

53   C. de Fabriczy, 'Manno, orefice fiorentino', *Archivio storico dell' Arte*, 1894, p.149. See also Ronchini, *Atti e Memorie di Storia patria per le provincie modenesi e parmensi*, Vol. vii, 1873.

54   O. Kurz, 'Engravings on Silver by Annibale Carracci' *Burlington Magazine*, Vol. XCVII, 1955, p.282.

55   Quoted Posner, *Annibale Carracci*, London, 1971, Vol. II, cat. no. 113.

56   Cellini I, II.58, '*ai quali io facevo fare un vasetto d'oro tutto lavorato di basso rilievo, con figure e altri belli ornamenti; questo era per la duchesa, il quale sua excellenzia faceva fare per bere dell'acqua. Ancora mi richiese che io le facesse una cintura d'oro; e anche quest' opera richissimamente, con gioie e con molte piacevole invenzioni di mascherette e d'altro, questa se le fece. Veniva a ogni poco il duca in questa guardaroba, e pigliavasi piacere grandissimo di veder lavorare e di ragionare con esso meco*'. A note of Cellini preserved in the Bibliotheca Riccardiana gives a further description of this cup '*un vaso d'oro per bere acqua, il quale si dette a finier a Poggini in guardaroba di Sua Excellenza, che quivi lavoravano. E detto vaso era cominciata assai bene innanzi, e feci tutti i disegni e modelli d'esso, quale fu cesellato di mezzo rilievo, con due figurine tutte tonde, e molte altri ornamenti; e ogni giorno vi lavoravo di mia mano qualche ora*'.

57   Plon, p.385.

58   Supino, p.54.

59   Supino, p.54.

60   ibid. p.54.

61   ill. Morassi pl. 25.

62   C. W. Fock, 'Der Goldschmied Jacques Bylivelt aus Delft und sein Werken in der Medicieischen Werkstatt in Florenz', *Jahrbuch* Band 70, 1974, pls. 88-90, p.113. Mazzafirri was also entrusted with the task of casting in silver the four *Labours of Hercules* which had been modelled by Gian Bologna for the Medici court.

62a   ill. Piacenti, pl. 21.

63 Fock, p.95 and Heikamp and Grote, Vol. II, passim.

64 For a contemporary description, see Berti, p.134. For Buontalenti's designs see the exhibition *Disegni di Buontalenti,* Uffizi, Florence, 1968, cat. no. XXVIII.

65 ill. Piacenti, pls. 25, 26.

66 Supino, p.43, states that Bilivert brought a whole group of German workmen with him from Augsburg: '*Col Bylevelt vennero a Firenze gli orefici Giovanni de Visser, Francesco Linderer, Hans Müller, Hans Schultz, Zacharia Veis, Erhart Heisller, Hans Kiefert, Laurent Camper, Bartolomeo Durnhauer*'. Subsequent research by C. W. Fock, *Oud Holland,* 1970 p.197-209 'The Medici Crown: Work of the Delft Goldsmith Jaques Bylivelt', shows that the goldsmiths named by Supino worked for Bylivelt over a period of seven years, two or three at a time.

67 Among those mentioned in the Medici archives (see Supino, p.54) are a Fleming, Peter Coster, who delivered a silver cup in 1558, Matteo di Nicolo from Regensburg, Michel Cheppel (in 1560) and Rinaldo Wolfe (in 1561), the last two presumably of German origin. For a detailed study of the Medici court goldsmiths see Fock, passim.

68 See J. F. Hayward, 'An Eighteenth-century Drawing of the Grand-ducal Crown of Tuscany, *Burlington Magazine,* 1955, p.311 and C. W. Fock, *Oud Holland,* 1970, p.197-209.

69 Y. Hackenbroch, 'Jacopo Biliverti and the Rospigliosi cup', *Connoisseur,* Vol. 172, p.175.

70 C. W. Fock, 'Goldsmiths at the Court of Cosimo II de'Medici', *Burlington Magazine,* Vol. CXIV p.11. See also K. Piacenti, 'Two jewellers at the Grand Ducal Court of Florence' *Mitteilungen des Kunsthist. Inst.* Florence, Vol. XII, 1965-6, p.107-124.

71 Agostino del Riccio, a Dominican Friar who visited the Casino di San Marco states that the Grandduke Francesco I surrounded himself with *virtuosi forestieri*' amongst them Maestro Giorgio the Milanese and his sons...Maestro Ambrogio, Maestro Stefano... since they were reliable men and of rare skill in making animals and doing other things with crystal', see Zobi: *Notizie storiche,* Firenze 1853. The *forestieri* referred to are Giorgio Gaffuri and Ambrogio and Stefano Caroni.

72 ill. Fock, pls. 81-6, 91-2.

73 See Morassi, p.25. Vasari is not quite clear on this point. He mentions that Buontalenti discovered a method of fusing rock-crystal and purifying it, further that he made vases of various colours with this material. He also states that Buontalenti made porcelain and did stupendous things with several kinds of clay. Finally he designed and worked on semi-precious hardstone *commessi* tables.

74 Morigia, Lib. V, p.295.

75 *Jahrbuch,* Band VII-2, Reg. no. 4982, 5169, 5260.

76 ill. Morassi, pl. 32.

77 Supino, p.55 '*per fattura di uno vaso di lapis lazzuli a modo d'urna fatto in Milano per ordine nostro et a noi consegnato qui*'.

78 Kris I, Vol. I, p.116.

79 Cellini had already made a model of one of these galleys for the Cardinal of Ravenna in the 1540's. (see p.148).

80 Morigia, Lib. V, p.292.

81 For the Jason Vase see Thoma, pl. 69, and for the Albertinische Casket see Thoma, pls. 66-8.

82 ill. Kris I, Vol. II, pls. 498,499.

83 ill. Kris I, Vol. II, pls. 336, 337.

84 Ronchini, *Periodico di Numismatica e Sfragistica per la Storia d'Italia,* p.234: '*Un vaso d'agata delle montagne di Parma, ovato. Un boccale di pietra mischia con il collo et il piede, quali sono in quattro pezzi. Un Bicchiero con il piede alto, legato con argento dorato, di diaspro delle montagne di Parme Un bacile di agata della montagne di parma, di assai grandezza, ovato*'.

85 K. Piacenti 'Artisti alla Corte Grandueale' *Antichita Viva* 1963 Vol. II no. 1, and Guinta di Roccagiovine '*Un artista troppe volte dimenticato*', ibid. Vol. II, p.57-63.

86 ill. Catalogo, *Argenteria Italiana,* Museo Poldi-Pezzoli, Milan, 1959 pl. XIX.

87 For the Italian text, see Berti, p.54.

88 ill. Lipinsky, pl. 9.

89 de Castro is described in the contract for making these pieces as '*Lusitanus, faber argentarius*'. See Morazzoni, p.45.

90 ill. Morazzoni, pl. 97.

91 See *Coloquio,* Lisbon, March, 1959, R. dos Santos and I. Quilho '*Ourivesaria Portuguesa no Estrangeiro* p.8ff.

92 Morazzoni, p.45.

93 This unpublished dish is in a private collection in Paris.

94 ill. H. Macandrew, 'A silver basin designed by Strozzi', *Burlington Magazine,* Vol. CXIII, p.4ff.

95 For a discussion of the Tempesta precedents for the Strozzi design see Macandrew, op. cit.

96 Stockbauer, p.111; in 1580 a certain Alessandro Tossignani of Bologna informed the Duke that he had mastered the secret of dying coral to different colours.

97   E. Steingräber, 'Opere occidentali dei secoli xv e xvi', *Il Tesoro di San Marco,* Venezia, 1971.

98   ill. Plon, pl. XXXV.

99   For a cast of the Mantua basin see Plon, pl. XXIX. For the Rütschi basins see the sale catalogue O. v. Falke, Zürich, 1928, nos. 287-8, pls. 69, 70. These are now in the collection of the Abegg-Stiftung, Bern, where they are identified as Genoese, beginning of the 17th century. The central plaques are engraved underneath with the addorsed arms of the Spinola and De Mari families. One is illustrated in M. Stettler, *Abegg-Stiftung in Bern,* Bern, 1973, pl. 44. The presence of the arms of two Genoese families confirms the attribution to Genoa rather than Venice.

100 Morassi, no. 53, described as probably Salzburg; this attribution was presumably based on the mistaken assumption that the ewer had formed part of the plate of the Archbishops of Salzburg.

101 ill. Lipinsky, pls. 5 and 9.

102 ill. Lipinsky, pl. 4.

103 Y. Hackenbroch, *Catalogue Irwin Untermyer Collection,* New York, 1969, no. 201.

104 See J. F. Hayward, 'The Aldobrandini Tazzas', *Burlington Magazine,* Vol. CXII, p.669ff., where all the relevant literature is quoted. Since this article was published the two tazzas, there described as missing, have been traced to a Paris private collection.

105 *Archivio di Stato,* Roma, Not. Acc. 2661. The pages of this inventory are not numbered.

106 Y. Hackenbroch, 'The Emperor Tazzas', *Bulletin of the Metropolitan Museum,* March 1950, p.197. Some support for the identification of these tazzas as German can be found in the four figures of Roman Emperors which form the finials of a tower-clock (inv. no. 1968-409) dated 1569 in the Württembergisches Landesmuseum, Stuttgart. The modelling of the figures and their frontal treatment does recall those of the tazzas, but Roman Emperors were an obvious solution when a series of related figures were needed.

CHAPTER EIGHT

France

THE frequency with which sumptuary laws, prohibiting the manufacture of vessels of gold and restricting the production of those of silver to a maximum weight, were repeated in sixteenth-century France suggests that there was no lack of custom for the French goldsmiths. So large was their number in Paris that in 1571 an *Arret de la Cour des Monnaies* established a maximum figure of three hundred. The work of French sixteenth-century goldsmiths is now better represented by vessels with mounts of enamelled gold than by those of silver. While most of the silver vessels belonging to the Crown and nobility were melted by order of Louis XIV, many of those made of semi-precious stones dating from the sixteenth and seventeenth centuries survived not only that holocaust, but also the French Revolution and the dynastic changes of the nineteenth century. They are now preserved in two separate collections: in the Galerie d'Apollon of the Louvre and in the palace of the Prado, Madrid.[1] The Spanish collection came from the inheritance of the Grand Dauphin, son of Louis XIV and father of Philip V of Spain. The vessels that compose it originally formed one collection with those still in the Louvre which they resemble. In view of the considerable number of pieces surviving from the royal collection, one would expect that there would be no great difficulty in giving a coherent account of French work in gold of the sixteenth century. Unfortunately this is not the case; many vessels have lost the enamelled gold mounts, which alone would make possible the definite recognition of their origin. These have been replaced with later and inferior mounts of silver or even base metal. Furthermore, the majority of the hardstone vessels are of Milanese origin or wrought in an international Mannerist style and cannot be exactly located. These two collections, in spite of their extent, present, therefore, almost as difficult a problem as if they had been assembled by a nineteenth-century collector. Because of this it is necessary to turn first to other sources of evidence.

Much information about fashion in silver is to be found in the innumerable representations of cups, vases and ewers of Mannerist taste in the paintings of the Fontainebleau school. In these almost every variety of form known to the Mannerist goldsmith, and many that could never have been executed by him, are shown. The masters of the first school of Fontainebleau were not, however, for the most part French and many of those paintings that seem most typically French have proved to be the work of Italianate Flemings. Some of the graphic masters who engraved the designs of the Italians at Fontainebleau were of French origin and the famous painting by the French artist Jean Cousin le Père (circa 1490-1561) of *Eva Prima Pandora*,[2] which dates from the middle of the century, already shows a vase of altogether bizarre form. The Fontainebleau style was essentially decorative and could readily have been assimilated by the French goldsmiths, but Mannerism long remained an alien style in France and they were slow to accept it.

In discussing French Mannerist silver one has to rely on a very small number of surviving pieces, which do not necessarily represent the most interesting aspects of the style. It is in the designs rather than in the extant pieces that the most dynamic expression of the *Maniera* is to be found. One of the earliest dated French goldsmiths' designs in an evolved Mannerist style is also attributed to Jean Cousin; it survives in an etching dated 1545 by an anonymous master, who signed with the initials N.H. This design is of such splendid proportions that the catalogue of the Fontainebleau exhibition suggested it must have been a sketch for a monument.[3] Nevertheless, it could well have been executed on the small scale of a vessel of precious metal, perhaps a perfume-burner, a use which is suggested by the flaming ball that surmounts the cover. Alternatively, it could have been a salt. The combination of confronted satyrs, straps developing into volutes, claw feet, masks and a cover of architectural form place this design in the forefront of French Mannerism, and would justify us in attributing a significant role to Jean Cousin.

Benvenuto Cellini

The most important surviving monument of Mannerist goldsmiths' work is the golden salt (pl. 311-20) that was begun in Italy by Benvenuto Cellini and completed in Paris for François I. The fact that the king troubled to secure Cellini's release from a papal prison and bring him to Paris, some eight years after work had begun on the decoration of the great gallery and chambers of Fontainebleau, implies that the indigenous goldsmiths did not readily adopt the imported style. This may have been because it was regarded as predominantly architectural. Although the engravers had done much to popularise the style, it may well be that the ease with which it could be applied to the small scale of goldsmiths' work was not yet appreciated.

In his *Trattato dell'Oreficeria*[4] Cellini relates how the French king first came to hear of him. He had been commissioned in 1528 by a Florentine gentleman, Federigo Ginori, to make a medal; this he had done with such success that his design had been preferred to that of Michelangelo. After Ginori's death the medal came into the possession of Luigi Alamanni, who subsequently emigrated to France and there presented it to François I. It seems that the king was so taken with the jewel that he decided to take Cellini into his service. The king took the keenest interest in goldsmiths' work; according to Cellini,[5] it was François I who gave him the opportunity to evolve: 'I can indeed and with good conscience affirm that all that I am, whatever of good and beautiful quality I have produced, all this must be ascribed to that extraordinary monarch'.

Cellini took only two assistants with him on his journey to France, Paolo Romano and Ascanio di Tagliacozzo, but once established in the spacious apartments of the Chateau de Petit Nesle which the king allotted to him, he engaged a large body of workmen. The contrast between his situation in Italy and in France can be measured by the fact that when he first set up on his own in Rome he employed five workmen, by 1537 when he was established in Florence he had eight, whereas in Paris in 1540 he employed no fewer than thirty. They were of various nationalities and he says of them 'They belonged to several nations Italian, French and German; for I took the business well. These select craftsmen I worked to the bone with perpetual labour. They wanted to rival me; but I had a better constitution. Consequently in their inability to bear up against such a continuous strain, they took to eating and drinking copiously; some of the Germans in particular, who were more skilled than their comrades and wanted to march apace with me, sank under these excesses, and perished.'[6] While Cellini seems to have considered the French goldsmiths inferior in skill to the Germans, the French nobility do not appear to have shared their king's enthusiasm for the style practised by his chosen goldsmith. Apart from those emanating from the king, most of Cellini's commissions came from Italian noblemen resident in Paris.

The letters of naturalisation granted to Cellini by François I in July, 1542 describe him as royal goldsmith (*orfèvre du roi*) but political circumstances were not favourable to the settlement of foreign goldsmiths in France. The outbreak of war between France and the Holy Roman Empire was followed by a decree ordering the expulsion of all aliens. This decree was issued in 1542 and was repeated in the following year, but by a letter dated 29th July, 1542 the king specifically excepted from the effect of the decree those Germans who were employed by his goldsmith, Benvenuto Cellini.[7] The same exception applied to those employed by the royal armourer. The decree of 1543 allowed exemption only to those who had acquired letters of French naturalisation and had also married in France. Cellini had not fulfilled the latter condition, but he was specifically exempted by another letter signed by the king.[8] As in other countries the guild was not prepared to admit foreigners, even when invited by the king himself. Nearly all the names of masters (maîtres orfèvres jurés) admitted to the Paris guild (corporation) at this period are French.

Cellini's first meeting with François I was at Fontainebleau where, after thanking him for procuring his release from prison, he presented the ewer (described in the Vita as 'a vase') and basin which he had made for the Cardinal of Ferrara. Cellini mentions these pieces on two occasions. On the first he stated that they 'showed like the finest piece of plate that had been seen in France'. He was prone to such hyperbole, but the two vessels probably impressed on account of the originality of their style and the excellence of their workmanship. His second account of this occasion in the Vita[9] tells us that the king 'took the vase and basin' and exclaimed 'Of a truth I hardly think the ancients can have seen a piece so beautiful as this. I well remember to have inspected all the best works, and by the best masters of Italy, but I have never set eyes on anything which stirred me to such admiration'.

Cellini's first commission from the French king was for a set of twelve silver torchères in the form of gods and goddesses modelled in the round. As they were to be life-size the commission was a very important one: this explains why he was allowed to establish so large a workshop in Paris. He was paid five hundred crowns on account to cover the cost of the precious metal alone.

In the Vita he relates how he set to work on the models in the house of his protector, the Cardinal of Ferrara: 'There I began to work in God's name and fashioned four little waxen models, about two thirds of a braccia each in height. They were Jupiter, Juno, Apollo and Vulcan. During this time the king returned to Paris whereupon I went to him at once taking my models with me and my two apprentices, Ascanio and Paolo. On perceiving that the king was pleased with my work, and being commissioned to execute the Jupiter in silver of the height given above I introduced the two young men.'[10]

A second account of François I's commission is given in a letter sent by Giulio Alvarotto, the Ferrarese ambassador to the French court, to the Duke of Ferrara on 29 January 1545.[11] He reported that 'the King wished him to make twelve statues of life-size, preferably a little more rather than less, which according to his Majesty's wish should each hold a torch, some in the left and some in the right hand to serve as floor candlesticks to be placed in the galleries of Fontainebleau. Each was to have a gilt-metal plinth and to be supported on a certain kind of ball-bearing which served to make them easy to move around. Benvenuto made one which he calls Jupiter, it is a little larger in size than the king himself and everyone considers it to be very beautiful.' The only figure that was completed was the Jupiter, and when he took it to Fontainebleau to show the king he had already been working for him for four years with a large body of assistants. The king was greatly displeased with him and, according to Cellini's account said 'I remember that I gave you express orders to make me twelve silver statues; and this was all I wanted. You have chosen to execute a salt-cellar, and vases and busts and doors and a number of other things which quite confound me, when I consider how you have neglected my wishes and worked for the fulfilment of your own.'[12] According to Cellini the king had been pushed into this complaint by his mistress, Madame d'Etampes, but, whatever the reason, it was not long before Cellini abandoned France and left his workshop with all his models in the charge of his two assistants.[13]

Only three of the works executed for the king by Cellini during his stay in France are known to have survived. These are the golden salt (pl. 313), the bronze nymph of Fontainebleau and the bronze model for the candlestick figure of Juno, the drawing and the model for which are illustrated in pls. 97 and 713-14. So little French goldsmiths' work of the period remains that it is impossible to assess Cellini's influence on his French contemporaries. Not one of the silver vases, which, according to Cellini, were such a speciality of the Parisian goldsmiths, is left; neither are the two wrought by the gifted youth which weighed twenty pounds of silver each (see p.86), nor the two which he describes in the last chapter of the *Trattato* as follows:[14] 'I set to yet greater labours still. I took thirty pounds of silver of my own money and gave it to two of my workmen, with the designs and the models to make two large vases of it. As it was a time of the great wars I had asked no money of the King and left untouched six months of my salary. Setting to work lustily at my own vases, I finished them in a month's time, and set out to find the King who was in a city called Argentana. When I gave him the vases he made a great fuss of me.'

When Cellini left Paris in 1545, his workshop in the castle of Petit Nesle was carried on until 1556 by his two Italian assistants, Ascanio Maria di Tagliacozzo, who later became goldsmith to Henri II, and Pietro Paolo Romano. The royal accounts for payments to them from 1549 until their departure survive and show that they were not only ordered to complete those works that had been started but also given new commissions. Thus in November, 1546, a Parisian joiner, Pierre Coussinault, was paid for supplying a walnutwood model of a square vase to contain sweetmeats, and in the previous month the two Italian goldsmiths received a payment sufficient to cover the cost of the purchase of 51 marcs of silver required to make 'A large vase of silver in the form of a square table, set upon four satyrs, also of silver, to contain sweets and *confitures* as desired by the said lord and according to the sketch which he has had made of it.'[16] François I died in 1547, but the Italians continued to work in the Chateau de Petit Nesle, assisted by a third craftsman, a German named in French documents as Pierre Bauduc or Baudulc. On another occasion they received payment for 'two silver-gilt cups, one large and one small and for a gilt caddinet dish complete with spoon, knife and fork and surmounted by a small casket serving as a salt-cellar, upon which lies a figure of Diana'.[17] In 1552 they supplied for King Henri II a silver gilt basin containing 'a *nef* from which come all manner of fish, a vase, a cup of assay and another cup flat-wrought.'[18]

These two masters also continued to work for the Cardinal of Ferrara after the departure of Cellini. The Cardinal's accounts show that between July 1548 and May 1549 they supplied 'four triangular salt-cellars; four triangular candelabra decorated with escutcheons and cornices; an altar cross-foot decorated with foliage and with a lantern in the middle; a basin and ewer; a flat cup and cover; a covered drinking-cup; a chalice; a gilt cup, the cover with medallions and the foot with foliage and escutcheons; two large water vases for the sideboard; the base, rosaces and enamels for a gilt pax; the framework of an old Venice basin restored and two others for two Portuguese basins.'[19]

Rosso Fiorentino

Italian influence on French goldsmiths' work was the result not so much of the achievements of Cellini and his assistants as of the use of prints after the designs of the Fontainebleau school. The most important source of such designs was Rosso Fiorentino, the creator of much of the stucco decoration of the Galerie François I at Fontainebleau. According to Vasari, Rosso designed a whole sideboard of plate for François I. In his life of Rosso he refers to the 'numberless designs that Rosso made for salt-cellars, vases, bowls and other things of fancy, all of which the king afterwards caused to be executed in silver; but these were so numerous that it would take too long to mention them all. Let it suffice to say that he made designs for all the vessels of a sideboard for the king'.[20] None of the plate designed by Rosso for François I and mentioned by Vasari has survived, but we can gain an excellent idea of its appearance from a set of nine engraved sheets of goldsmiths' work based upon them.[21] One could accept the engravings as exact reproductions of the Rosso drawings, but for the fact that none of them show any of the royal devices which one would expect to find on the table plate of the King of France. They include salt-cellars, ewers, (pl. 99-101), vases, tazzas (pl. 98), a fountain (pl. 103) and a nef (pl. 102); precisely the range of articles necessary for the French king's table. One object alone survives that seems to be based on one of Rosso's tureen designs; this is the stone urn carved by Pierre Bontemps to contain the heart of François I.[22] It was ordered by Philbert Delorme in 1550 and completed in 1556. Originally placed in the church of the Abbey of Hautes-Bruyères, it is now in the cathedral of Saint Denis. The urn is supported on four lion-paws and is decorated with four oval cartouches carved in low relief with subjects symbolising Astronomy, Music, Song and Poetry, while on the plinth are four others representing Architecture, Sculpture, Painting and Geometry. The treatment of these groups enclosed in their strapwork cartouches is closely related to similar subjects embossed on the bowls of silver tazzas. The design of this monument is utterly unlike anything else of earlier date in French funeral sculpture and there seems little doubt that its designer, whether Delorme, Bontemps or another, must have been familiar with the Rosso drawings or with engravings based on them.

In the designs for goldsmiths' work, believed to have been engraved after Rosso's drawings, the whole repertoire of Mannerist design is exploited. Crabs, frogs, tortoises and shell-fish, rendered in relief or the round, support the bases or adorn the covers; bunches of fruit and of fish are embossed in the walls and scrolls terminating in grotesque heads are applied to the stems. The designs follow Cellini in their ambitious use of figure sculpture; figures modelled in the round are set on the covers of tazzas and of salt-cellars. While those on the covers are sometimes allowed freedom of movement, those on the stems are often imprisoned within heavy strapwork of almost architectural solidity. The gesticulating figures encircled by monstrous straps recall the human forms squeezed uncomfortably into a heavy framework of scrolls and straps in the borders of Rosso's Fontainebleau decorations. In these designs the Mannerist obsession with sexual symbolism is present, sometimes expressed explicitly as in the case of a standing salt with stem composed of a man and woman united in intercourse,[23] or in the table-fountain (pl. 103) in which the figures of putti are urinating. The standing salt is one of two in the series, one surmounted by a female figure symbolic of the Earth, the other by Neptune symbolising the Sea.[24] The figures are shown reclining in a position that is evidently derived from Cellini's salt, in which, however, both are combined on the one vessel. These are the only known instances of a direct quotation from Cellini's salt in French goldsmiths' designs. The attribution of the original designs for these engravings to Rosso has not been accepted by all writers on the subject,[25] but they certainly show an originality of conception that was unrivalled at the time. They cannot all have been invented by Rosso, for the two designs based on the Cellini Salt cannot be his, nor can he have seen the salt inasmuch as he died in 1540, the year that Cellini arrived in Paris. Two other engravers have been suggested as the authors of these prints, René Boyvin and Pierre Milan, both of whom worked in Paris during the middle decades of the century. Boyvin was born in Angers in 1525 and worked for a time in the Angers Mint; thereafter he went to Paris where he is still recorded in 1580. He was not a contemporary of Rosso, who died when he was only fifteen years old. Boyvin produced a large number of engravings, not only after Rosso, but also after the other Fontainebleau masters, Primaticcio, Luca Penni and the Roman Mannerist, Giulio Romano. The attribution to Rosso of the engravings of silver for François I dates back to Robert Dumesnil, but the catalogue of the Fontainebleau exhibition, after mentioning Pierre Milan as a likely author, includes them under the heading of the *Anonymes*.[26] Pierre Milan was the principal Parisian engraver towards the middle of the sixteenth century; he was slightly older than Boyvin and possibly his master, for Boyvin's style was very similar. Yet another attribution has been made by Zerner,[27] who put forward the name of Antonio Fantuzzi, one of Primaticcio's chief assistants at Fontainebleau and, like his master, a native of Bologna. Amongst his prints are two sheets each etched with five fantastic vases, including a male and a female term vase and another with body in the form of a lively satyr.[28] Others are variations on the more familiar classical types and were probably copied from representations of vases and ewers in the frescoes of the Galerie

François I at Fontainebleau. Others reappear among the series of vases engraved by Androuet du Cerceau. It is not possible to determine which master, if either, was their inventor. All these engravers had close associations with the goldsmiths. They might be called upon either to design a vase or to engrave the ornament upon one and had often learnt their skill originally when working in a goldsmith's shop as an apprentice or journeyman.

The three ewers illustrated in pls. 99-101 show that the followers of Rosso lost touch with the reality of the goldsmith's craft in assembling and re-assembling the typical elements of Fontainebleau ornament. The surface is so lost in the convolutions of straps, masks, bunches of fruit and the rest of the vocabulary of Mannerist ornament that it is difficult to decide exactly where it should lie. That shown in pl. 100 is perhaps the work of an assistant after an idea of Rosso; an ovoid body has been stretched to an original but ugly and quite impracticable shape. In other designs from the same group we find ewers with bodies of almost square section which would have presented the working goldsmith with almost insuperable problems should he attempt their manufacture. The influence of Rosso's designs can be recognised in the enamelled gold mounts of the Venetian glass ewer illustrated in pls. 367-8. Two other ewers in the Galerie d'Apollon and the Kunsthistorisches Museum respectively dating from the third quarter of the sixteenth century provide further examples of the introduction of Mannerist ornament into French goldsmiths' work. The first, like so many vessels of semi-precious stone, has an earlier body remounted in the sixteenth century (pl. 371). The second, the onyx ewer (pl. 372) presented to the Archduke Ferdinand of Tirol in 1570 together with the Cellini Salt and the St. Michael Cup, has retained its original form unaltered.

Jacques Androuet du Cerceau

Du Cerceau's earlier designs for goldsmiths have been discussed in Chapter V. In his later designs he exploited the Mannerism of Fontainebleau and published a wide range of decorative designs, including a book of mauresques, which appeared before 1540, and two books of grotesques published in 1550 and 1556 respectively. The introduction to the last of these runs *'pourra servir aux orfèvres, paintres, tailleurs de pierres, menuisiers et autres artisans, pour esveiller leurs esprits et appliquer chacun en son art, ce qu'il trouvera propre'*. It is significant that the goldsmith takes first place amongst those for whom the prints were intended. Although a Protestant, du Cerceau went to Rome between 1531 and 1533 and doubtless studied the grotesques which decorated the Loggie of the Vatican; nevertheless, his grotesques of 1550 are more closely related to the heavier style of Fontainebleau. A set of eleven etched sheets by du Cerceau, each with three or more designs, dating from the mid-century, explores a favourite Mannerist theme; the rendering of vases and ewers in the form of the human body. These follow Italian prototypes, such as two drawings attributed to Perino del Vaga or his school in pl. 57, but in exaggerated form. The salt (pl. 106) attributed to du Cerceau[29] is of more pleasing design; the stem is formed as a figure of Diana, a treatment that was particularly favoured during the second half of the sixteenth century.

The most influential of du Cerceau's engraved designs, both in France and beyond her frontiers, seems to have been the set of ten engravings of the inside and outside of tazza bowls.[30] These were originally intended for the Limoges enamellers and were much used by them, especially those composed of interlacing strapwork. Other designs in the set introduce friezes peopled by satyrs, sea-creatures (pl. 104) or triumphs (pl. 105), evidently derived from Italian prototypes. In considering du Cerceau's designs one is struck by the great variety of themes, but the width of his range can also be explained by the freedom with which he drew upon the work of his predecessors.

Though far less prolific than du Cerceau, another engraver of the Fontainebleau school, who worked at Lyon and signed his sheets with the initials CC, has left a few designs of original form in which highly naturalistic detail is combined with classical forms. They mostly represent the interiors of dishes, but the design illustrated in pl. 107

Plate XVII
Detail of the house altar of Duke Albrecht of Bavaria, enamelled gold. Augsburg, about 1573-4.

Plate XVIII
Gilt cup and cover. Lübeck, late 16th century.

shows a cup and cover. In some of these designs an extreme of fantasy was reached that would not be found in the work of contemporary Italian masters, in which some contact, however tenuous, was kept with classical sources. In German sources one must look back further, even to the beginning of the century, for a similar combination, as in Albrecht Dürer's table-fountain design in the Ashmolean Museum, Oxford.[31]

Enamelled gold vessels decorated with mauresques

Mauresque ornament played an important role in northern European goldsmiths' work, particularly in France. Of the various vases and other vessels of semi-precious hard-stone with gold mounts enamelled in typical French manner formerly in the collection of *Joyaux de la Couronne,* five are known to survive. These are the ewer in Vienna (pl. 372), two vessels in the Galerie d'Apollon of the Louvre and two in the Prado, Madrid. The first three may have formed part of a service decorated en suite; the material used in each case is a dark onyx, while the mounts are enamelled with gold mauresques against a black ground within interlacing white strapwork. The two pieces in the Louvre are a small ewer, the foot of which is decorated with mauresques while the stem is composed of *Rollwerk* and bunches of fruit, the handle of the intertwined bodies of snakes, and a vase which is now a mere fragment of what must have been one of the treasures of the French royal collection. The tapering cylindrical bowl of onyx is mounted with gold, enamelled with the typical French mauresques; the jewels that originally enriched it are all missing, as is the enamelled and jewelled gold foot-rim. This piece has a peculiar history as it was once in the collection of Cardinal Mazarin, but was not acquired by Louis XIV when his jewels were sold. It subsequently went to Germany and was purchased for the French royal collection from a Frankfurt am Main dealer in 1685. A drawing of it had been sent to Paris and this, preserved in the Bibliothèque Nationale, shows it in original condition with jewels and all its rich mounts.[32]

One of the vessels in the Prado (cat. no. 74: Steingräber pl. 36) is a covered vase or jar of rock-crystal, the mounts enamelled with the same type of black and white mauresques and retaining their original jewelled enrichment. The lip mount and cover are of enamelled gold decorated with strapwork cartouches enclosing jewels set in high collets and with garlands of fruit on which are seated *amorini,* all wrought in high relief. The generous use of strapwork makes this a typical production of French goldsmiths under the influence of Fontainebleau. The vase itself is cut with spiral gadroons and oval bosses in a manner similar to the Holbein cup in the Munich *Schatzkammer* (pl. 647). The second vessel is a rock-crystal ewer with handle composed of a cornucopia and figures.[33] The design of the enamelled mauresques on all these pieces is strikingly consistent; however, it differs from that of the mauresques on the Holbein cup which has been included by one writer in this group of French gold-mounted rock-crystals.[34] Two of the rock-crystal vessels in the Rijksmuseum, a low bowl and a ewer (pls. 337 and 339) have gold mounts that can be identified as French by reason of the mauresque enamels that embellish them. Similar mauresques in white and gold against a black ground are a regular feature of Limoges painted enamels of the second half of the sixteenth century; this constitutes valuable support for the identification of this type of decoration on mounted rock-crystals and hardstones as French.

Among the treasures of the former Dukes of Württemberg in the Stuttgart Museum is an ivory beaker with cover, the body of which is surrounded by three bands of typical French mauresques (pl. XI). The cover is set with a *verre fixé* plaque bearing the Danish royal arms and the date 1558. It is tempting to claim this vessel also as French, but enamelled mauresques were used by goldsmiths in other countries, particularly by Hans Reimer in Munich (see p.226) and its origin is, therefore, uncertain. Another vessel of partly French origin is the Italian rock-crystal tazza with enamelled gold mounts in pl. 373. This can be dated with certainty to the reign of Henri II (1547-1559), as the cover, which must have been added in France, is pierced with the interlaced initials H and C, or less probably D, according to whether the monogram is interpreted as that of the King and his Queen, Catherine de' Medici, or his mistress, Diane de Poitiers.

Etienne Delaune

More important than any of the graphic masters mentioned above is Etienne Delaune, who dominated French goldsmiths' design in the second half of the sixteenth century. He was a contemporary of Boyvin, having been born, probably in Orléans, in 1518 or 1519. He worked for five months as an engraver at the royal Mint in Paris, just as so many of the Italian goldsmiths found their way into the employment of the papal Mint in Rome, after which he seems to have specialised in medals and jewellery designs. He was of Huguenot faith and is believed to have left Paris after the St. Bartholomew's Day massacre in 1572 and to have gone to Strassburg and subsequently to Augsburg. He returned to Strassburg in 1580 and finally to Paris where he died in 1583. He was an immensely prolific master and left a great many designs for medals and jewellery (Ashmolean Museum, Oxford) and for embossed armours, which were probably made in the French royal workshop in Paris. The large number of small prints he produced were used by jewellers for execution in enamel, by cabinet-makers and gun-stock makers for inlay work in engraved bone or ivory and by armourers for chiselling in iron or damascening in gold or silver on iron (pl. 116).

In addition to Delaune's small prints for jewellery, his engraved oeuvre includes eight sheets of designs for hand-mirrors (pl. 108), in which the *Maniera* received its most complete expression in France, and six for the undersides of tazzas, evidently intended for the use of Limoges enamellers. Finally, his set of loop handles for furniture shows great ingenuity in applying familiar elements of ornament and constitutes an apotheosis of this domestic article.[35] A number of drawings for silver vessels also exist scattered throughout the Print Rooms of Europe and America. In the Louvre are three drawings, originally part of a larger series, of tazza bowls, of which two represent scenes from the life of Moses and a third one from the Life of Samson (pl. 113). At Chantilly there is a superb drawing of a standing mirror, the frame of which is composed of human figures with elongated, elegant bodies, and also two curious designs for standing cups and covers. The decoration of each of the cups relates to bees and bee-keeping, the stems being formed as beehives and the bowls and covers being embossed with panels showing human figures engaged in tasks associated with the culture of bees. Among the best of Delaune's drawings of goldsmith's work is the ewer at Windsor Castle (pl. 109) the ornament of which illustrates the legend of Apollo and Daphne, and two covered cups in the Royal Collection, Windsor and the Victoria and Albert Museum (pls. 110-111). The last drawing illustrates a trend, increasingly noticeable near the close of the century, towards treating the whole surface as a single area to be decorated instead of dividing the subject into separate scenes enclosed with cartouches.

Delaune's drawings have an elegance and refinement that show him to have been one of the chief exponents of the Mannerist style. The large number of his prints surviving proves how much they were admired and used at the time. He is known to have gone to Augsburg, for in 1576 he published two engravings showing the interiors of a goldsmith's shop, each signed *Stephanus f. in Augusta 1576* (pls. 2, 3). It has usually been assumed that he left France to escape persecution as a Huguenot, but it also possible that he went in the train of the French king, Henri III who, with his queen visited both Augsburg and Munich in that year. Etienne Delaune had a son, Jean, whose drawings are hardly to be distinguished from those of his father. Jean Delaune accompanied his father to Augsburg and in 1578 and in 1580 Etienne executed two engravings after designs by his son. Further evidence of Jean's activities in Munich is provided by a reference in the 1598 Inventory of the Munich Kunstkammer to a book of illustrations to the Old and New Testament executed by him in 1576.[36]

One of Delaune's innovations was his return to a more naturalistic presentation by freeing the figure subjects from the encroachment of the heavy strapwork preferred by Flemish masters of ornament. In Delaune's designs the strapwork is reduced to its proper function of providing a frame for the figure subject. He also revived the grotesque in the manner of the Raphael Loggie; using them mainly for his small prints intended for jewellery and for Limoges enamels. Here again he was returning to Italian sources rather than following Flemish interpretations of them. These minute prints, though intended for jewellery, could also be executed on a larger scale and we find them used to decorate a wide range of objects from backs of pendants to large dishes (pl. 384) and even armour.

The influence of Delaune's style can be recognised in some of the most splendid pieces produced by Augsburg or Munich goldsmiths for the court of the Dukes of Bavaria during the last quarter of the century. Among these are the great house-altar of the Flagellation,[37] in which the posture of the figures recalls his manner and, more strikingly, the mirror-shaped pax in[38] the Reliquien-Kammer of the Reiche Kapelle of the Munich Residenz. This is thought to have been originally a secular mirror which was given to the chapel by its pious owner for conversion into a reliquary. Its plan appears to derive from one of Delaune's mirror designs such as pl. 108.

Surviving French sixteenth-century silver vessels are mostly dishes or tazzas, though a few miscellaneous pieces also exist. Among the former, one of the most interesting, because it derives directly from a du Cerceau print, is the gilt basin in pl. 376. This is thought to date from 1560, but it is difficult to distinguish with certainty between Paris date-letter series and the year mark may be a whole series, that is twenty three years, later in date. Of about the same date is the dish in the Wernher Collection, its French origin being indicated not by marks, but by the Limoges enamel boss and the repeated use of dolphins in its decoration (pl. 377). The dolphin was used in a patriotic sense in France, referring to the title of Dauphin of the heir to the French throne.

One of the most imposing remaining examples of French sixteenth-century goldsmiths' work is the huge silver-gilt basin in the Louvre (pls. 378-9). This vessel seems to be based on an original design; no print showing the exact scenes has been discovered. Whereas most of the surviving basins of this period, irrespective of country of origin, are decorated with the familiar themes of nymphs and tritons or with the 'Triumph of Neptune and Amphitrite' derived from classical Roman sarcophagi fronts, through the medium of Mantegna's prints,[39] here at last is a different subject, namely battle scenes. The great size of the dish is also exceptional; other examples of the period are not too large to serve a useful purpose, but this one is of such proportions that it could only have served as a sideboard display piece.

Delaune's engravings were widely distributed and were exploited by goldsmiths and by masters of engraved ornament working in other countries. It follows that ornament taken from Delaune's prints does not necessarily imply that the vessel upon which it appears is of French origin. His influence is particularly evident in the work of the French pewterer, François Briot, the master of the Temperantia ewer and basin (pl. 736), see p.328. The pewterers usually followed contemporary silver design and many dishes of precious metal similar to the Temperantia must have been made. One such was produced by the Nürnberg goldsmith, Martin Rehlein, and is now in the Hermitage Museum, Leningrad.[40] There are in existence quite a number of silver vessels decorated with subjects taken from Delaune's prints, but as stated above, they cannot be identified as French for this reason alone and without further consideration, unless, of coure, they happen to bear French marks. One such, the superb ewer in pl. 347, is of uncertain origin and is here tentatively attributed to an Italian master. On the other hand, the basin in pl. 383 and the ewer and basin in pls. 380-2 are more probably French. While the composition of the basin (pl. 383) follows Briot, the scheme of ornament is taken directly from Delaune.[41] Those few scenes that do not follow directly from Delaune's prints imitate his manner so precisely that it is tempting to attribute its design to him. Its earliest possible date is given by the scenes of the Labours of the Months around the border. The Delaune print for January of this set bears the date 1568. In favour of a French origin is Benvenuto Cellini's comment on his experience in Paris:[42] 'I have seen the most marvellous pieces that you could possibly imagine in the world made by those skilled Paris masters'.

Also derived from prints by Etienne Delaune are the ewer and basin illustrated in pls. 380-2. The ewer is somewhat squat if compared with the form usually preferred at this period but this is probably due to some later alteration. It appears to be entirely of cast work while its basin is wrought and chased, though in considerably heavier metal than the basin in pl. 383. The handle of the ewer is of bold design, formed as a triple-headed dragon whose tail terminates in a bunch of serpents' heads. The workmanship is superlative and the basin is embossed with no fewer than sixteen Old Testament scenes. These are mostly worked from the front with only slight embossing from the back. Neither vessel is marked and, as the print with the original owner's arms has been removed, the attribution to a goldsmith working in France can be no more than conjectural. Of comparable quality is another gilt basin which was formerly in the Pierpont Morgan collection, but has been lost sight of since. It was exhibited in London in 1901[43] and since it bore a Paris maker's mark and the date letter B, probably for 1576, there is no doubt as to its French origin. The whole surface of the well is embossed with scenes from the life of Joseph in a manner closely resembling the two basins illustrated in pls. 380 and 383. Though a number of basins and tazzas have survived, French ewers are rare. The very fine ewer in the Fitzwilliam Museum, Cambridge (pl. 387) which again is unmarked, seems to follow the usual international Mannerist style, but there are some features that indicate its French origin. The design owes much to Etienne Delaune, as will be seen if it is compared with the Delaune drawing in pl. 109. Similar compositions of oval cartouches embossed with figure subjects and surrounded by compositions of masks and bunches of fruit can be found among the Delaune armour designs for the French court, and on some of the armours that were actually made.

Study of paintings and drawings of French silver and of the extant pieces makes it clear that the standard piece of plate was not, as in the northern countries, a tall standing cup but instead a covered tazza.[44] The shape of this tazza differed from that usual in the northern countries; instead of the wide shallow bowl it had a deep bowl of almost semicircular section. The cover was more elaborately treated than would have been that of a Dutch or English tazza: some of the most adventurous designs for goldsmiths' work by French artists are for these tazza covers. (pls. 98, 107, 110 and 111). The surviving French tazzas correspond to the designs of du Cerceau and his school and of Etienne Delaune, though the imaginatively modelled covers are nearly all lost. The most attractive tazza cover is that of silver-gilt and enamel, pierced with the French royal devices, which was made for an Italian rock-crystal bowl (pl. 373). Other tazzas are illustrated in pls. 375, 385, 388-9 and 392. As was the custom elsewhere in the case of finer quality pieces, the lower side of the embossed bowl was covered with a separate plate, but in France this was usually soldered to the bowl instead of being held in position by a screw passing through a hole in the centre. The underside of a tazza bowl of 1560 is illustrated in pl. 386: its ornament is derived from Delaune. The tazza illustrated in pl. 388, with stem composed of two melusines with twisted tails set back to back and with rather heavy shell covering the underside of the bowl, seems to be French, though the marks are not identifiable as such. It may be of provincial make as is the simpler example in pl. 385 with the Orleans mark. The stem and foot are engraved with the almost ubiquitous mauresques of international Mannerism, as is another foot in the Louvre (pl. 375) which supports a superb jasper bowl, that may once have been more splendidly mounted.

A service of plate bequeathed to the Convent of Santa Cecilia in Trastevere in Rome by a member of the Sfondrati family includes a set of six covered bowls or deep tazzas by two different makers and with the Paris date letter for 1606. It has been suggested that they are of later date, but as they are believed to have belonged to Cardinal Paolo Emilio Sfondrati, who was created Cardinal by his uncle, Pope Gregory XIV, in 1590 but died in 1618,[45] the identification of the date letter as 1606 is the most convincing. The decoration of these tazzas (pls. 392-393) is of German inspiration and the small plaquettes inside the lids, to which were formerly attached the screws that held the finials on top of the covers, are actually cast from German models. [46] When the tazzas were no longer used for secular purposes and were converted by the nuns into reliquaries, crosses replaced the finials and the plaquettes were no longer required. They are, however, still preserved in the Vatican where the whole service is now displayed. A second tazza, also from the Sfondrati service, is illustrated in pls. 394, 395. The bowl is decorated in distinctly German style with a recumbent Bacchus filling a bowl from a wine fountain while putti collect the grape harvest in the foreground. On the cover putti gather grapes and form a triumphal procession with a goat-drawn cart and infant fauns. It is not known how this service of plate came into the possession of Cardinal Sfondrati, but the occasion may have been similar to that which provided Bishop Maffeo Barberini, Apostolic Nuncio in Paris, with another service when he left Paris on his return to Rome in 1607.[47] He took with him *un buffet de vaiselle d'argent vermeil, doré pesant environ quatre cens marcs duquel nous* (Henri IV, King of France) *luy avons faict dons'.* Unfortunately this service has not been preserved.

While several French tazzas survive, there are hardly any of the tall standing cups which were made in great numbers in Germany, the Netherlands and England. The famous St. Michael Cup must now be regarded as originating in Antwerp and the only standing cup that bears a Paris hall-mark is the curious double cup illustrated in pl. 396, which was presumably made to special order. This is of pure Germanic form and might have been copied from one of the pattern sheets of Matthias Zündt, but for the fact that the profile does not conform exactly to the contemporary German fashion. Another standing cup which may have been of French origin was given by the Nürnberg City Council to the Emperor Matthias on July 3, 1612 on his journey through the city after his coronation.[48] The cup no longer survives, but a drawing of it (pl. 115) in the Nürnberg Stadtarchiv shows a vessel that probably dates from the third quarter of the sixteenth century. It was described at the time as having come from France (*so aus Frankreich herausgekommen*); of silver-gilt it was set with twenty-five precious stones. According to the evidence afforded by the du Cerceau album in Berlin, this type of cup was regarded as German, and the statement that it had come from France may perhaps refer only to its immediate source and need not imply that it was wrought by a French goldsmith. In the sixteenth century it was the practice of the citizens of the larger towns to offer a gift in the form of some piece of goldsmiths' work to the king when he visited the town. Vessels given by the larger cities were of great magnificence, but few records of their appearance remain. One has been mentioned above and a pictorial record of another presented to King Charles IX by the City of Paris is preserved in the engraving by Olivier Codoré illustrated in pl. 112.

A design by Etienne Delaune or one of his followers was probably the source of the frieze of classical soldiers in combat that surrounds the body of the silver-gilt vase clock illustrated in pls. 397-399. A number of German vase-shaped clocks with cases of gilt-copper exist, but this seems to be the only recorded French example with a silver case. A splendid enamelled and jewelled gold cup in the Vienna Kunsthistorisches Museum was described in the 1730 Inventory of the Schatzkammer as 'an old-fashioned beaker with four bands of Paris work',[49] though it is of distinctly German form. It is tempting to add this vessel to the small number of identifiable examples of French goldsmiths' work, but even if the 1730 inventory is interpreted as meaning that the cup was made in France, and not that the particular type of enamelling was then regarded as a Parisian fashion, it is possible that it is the work of a German immigrant.

The taste of Fontainebleau did not hold exclusive sway in France during the latter part of the sixteenth century. There were foreign goldsmiths at work in Paris and probably in Lyon, which was then the artistic centre outside the capital. At the same time an almost rustic taste for heavy, robust forms, quite different from the exquisite and sophisticated pieces discussed above, persisted in France and was even represented at the French court. This fashion for plain silver of massive proportions and bold profiles is well represented in the plate of the chapel of the Order of the Saint Esprit (pl. 400) founded by King Henri III in 1578. It is possible that the commissioning of these pieces came from an ecclesiastic and not from an officer of the court. It is a commonplace that ecclesiastical silver is of more conservative design than that for secular use. This is also indicated by the reticent design of a large pair of altar candlesticks of silver-gilt and rock-crystal bearing the Paris hall-mark for 1560-1 (pl. 401). The plain gadrooned bases and baluster stems show no awareness of contemporary Mannerist fashion. The taste for massive forms can also be seen in a ewer in the Musée des Arts Décoratifs bearing the Paris date-letter for 1603.[50] Like the Saint Esprit ewers this has a handle of rectangular profile that offers an effective contrast to the rotund form of the body. Another example of this somewhat brutalist trend in French design is the large tureen in the Vatican that forms part of the service of Cardinal Sfondrati. This bears the Paris date-letter for 1586 (pl. 398).

Among the foreigners working in France was Henri III's own goldsmith, Martin de Malines, who is recorded between the 1570's and 1612, but of whom nothing further is known. Elias Lencker the Elder of Nürnberg worked in Paris for seven years and Wenzel Jamnitzer's eldest son met his death there in 1572 on a journey trying to sell some important silver. This fact is known from a letter written by the City Council of Nürnberg to the King of France on 10 October, 1572, see p.215.[51]

The numerous portraits of the Fontainebleau school showing ladies at their toilet suggest that mirrors with frames of precious metal were fashionable at the French court. A design showing two alternative schemes of decoration of a mirror frame in the Berlin Kunstbibliothek, illustrates the influence of Fontainebleau. It combines figures with pilaster ornament at the sides and a series of roundels, probably intended to contain medallions of lapis lazuli. It has been attributed to the otherwise obscure Maître Guido.[52]

The Jamnitzer basin in the Louvre (pl. 421) formed part of the *Ancien Trésor de la Couronne* and was, therefore, presumably acquired during the sixteenth century. Whether it formed part of a gift of plate to the king or was actually commissioned from the Nürnberg master is not known. The first supposition is the more likely, but there was a fashion for vessels decorated with insects and reptiles cast directly from nature in France though no French silver of this type has survived. This was exploited to the full by the Huguenot potter, Bernard Palissy (about 1510-1589-90) who specialised in the production of dishes and bases decorated in high relief with casts taken from nature and enamelled in natural colours.[53] As the casts were executed in clay and then covered with a ceramic glaze the effect was far coarser than that achieved by the German goldsmiths. Palissy enjoyed considerable success in France and was protected by powerful patrons, among them, Anne de Montmorency, *Connétable de France,* for whom he erected a grotto in the garden of the Chateau d'Ecouen. One might expect that the fashion would have extended to the French goldsmiths, but there is little evidence to support this assumption. Some of the tazza designs engraved after Rosso or Thiry, however, introduce rockwork, naturalistic foliage and small animals which illustrate a trend towards the *stil rustique.* While much of Palissy's work was original he was followed by others who were content to take their inspiration from contemporary goldsmiths' work, even to the extent of taking moulds directly from originals of precious metal. These are well represented in the Louvre, where there are Palissy school dishes with plaquettes in their centres moulded from known models in precious metal. The Fontainebleau exhibition of 1972 showed such dishes as well as a candlestick of columnar form that was evidently based on a silver model.[54] Also in the Louvre is a pair of ewers modelled in the form of dolphins which derive from the Giulio Romano design illustrated in pl. 63. When reproduced in a material so coarse as faience and covered with a thick tin glaze, the fine detail of the original was all but lost, a loss for which the polychrome of the painting did little to compensate. The sources used by the potters seem to have been Flemish and Italian rather than French. Considering the decisive influence of Flemish and Italian decorative art in France at the time, this is not surprising. More closely related to contemporary French goldsmiths' work is the rare Saint Porchaire or Henri Deux ware. Not only do the shapes derive from silver but the all-over decoration of mauresques follows silver precedent.

The second half of the sixteenth century was marked in France by the desperate struggles for political supremacy between Catholics and Huguenots culminating in the final tragedy of the massacre on the night of St. Bartholomew. The constant wars and destruction of works of art did not provide a propitious background against which a luxury trade could flourish and the poverty of the few remaining pieces of French silver of this period may be due not so much to the destruction of the finer examples as to a general decline in standards and to the absence of important commissions. This situation was not remedied until the signing of the Edict of Nantes and the accession of Henri IV to the French throne.

1 A large part of the French royal collection of mounted hardstones, including many of those now in the Louvre were originally acquired by Cardinal Mazarin and were purchased by Louis XIV for the French Crown after his death. An inventory of Mazarin's collection prepared in 1661 after he died listed a hundred coloured hardstones and one hundred and sixty one rock-crystals. While many of these were made in the seventeenth century others were certainly of earlier date. The inventory descriptions of those vases that cannot be recognised among surviving pieces are reproduced by D. Alcouffe, 'The Collection of Cardinal Mazarin's Gems', *Burlington Magazine*, Sept. 1974, p.514. Unfortunately no indication is given in the inventory of the country of origin of the individual pieces, though one, bearing the monogram of the Emperor Rudolph II, must have been made in Prague, ill. Alcouffe, no. 314. For the Prado collection, see Steingräber, p.29-34 and D. A. Iniguez, *Catalogo de las alhajas del Delphin*, Museo del Prado, Madrid, 1944. Much of the collection of the Dauphin was remounted or otherwise altered when acquired by him and care must be exercised in drawing conclusions from the pieces in it. The Prado collection includes a number made for Philip II in the sixteenth century. One or two pieces from the Mazarin collection are now in Madrid.

2 ill. Fontainebleau II, cat. no. 56. Cousin seems to have been a goldsmith, for he was one of the signatories of a remonstrance addressed to the King against a decree of 1540 by the goldsmiths of Paris.

3 ibid. cat. no. 401.

4 Cellini, cap. XII, Lavorare de Minuteria, p.699-700.

5 Cellini I, II, 73, '*E sappiete, signor mio, per certissimo, che tutte le grandi e difficilissime opere chèio ho fatto in Francia sotto quel maravigliossimo re Francesco, tutte mi sono benissimo riuscite solo per il grande animo che sempre quel buon re mi dava con quelle gran provvisione e nel compiacermi di tanti lavoranti quanto io domandavo. Che gli era talvolta chèio mi servivo di più di quaranta lavoranti, tutti a mia scelta*'.

6 Cellini I, II, 18, '*Erano questi lavoranti, italiani, franzesi, todeschi, e tal volta n'avevo buona quantità, sicondo che io trovavo de'buoni; perché di giorno in giorno io mutavo, pigliando di quelli che sapevano più, e quelli io gli sollecitavo di sorte che, per il continuo affaticarsi, vedendo fare a me, che mi serviva un poco meglio la complessione che a loro, non possendo resistere alle gran fatiche, pensando ristorarsi col bere e coi mangiare assai, alcuni de quei todeschi che meglio sapevano che gli altri, volendo seguitarmi, non sopportò da loro la natura tale ingiurie, che quegli ammazzò*'.

7 *Archives de l'Art Français*, Documents, 2e Serie, 1862, p.6-7.

8 *Archives de l'Art Français*, Documents, 2e Serie, Paris, 1862, p.15.

9 Cellini I, II 9 '*prese il vaso e il bacino, e poi disse Veramente che tanto bel modo d'opera non credo mai che degli antichi se ne vedessi; perche ben mi sovviene di aver veduto tutte le miglior opere, e dai migliori maestri fatte di tutta la italia, ma io non vidi mai cosa che mi movesse piu grandemente che queste*'. François I reacted with comparable enthusiasm, though perhaps with more reason when he saw Cellini's golden salt.

10 Cellini I, II, 12 '*E quivi cominciai in nel nome di Dio a lavorare, e feci quattro modelli piccoli di dua terzi di braccio l'uno di cera: Giove, Junone, Appollo, Vulgano. In questo mezzo il re venne a Parigi; per la qual cosa io subito lo andai a trovare, e portai i detti modelli con esso meco, insieme con quei mia dua giovani, cioe Ascanio e Pagolo. Veduto che io ebbi che il re era sodisfatto delli detti modelli, e m'impose per il primo che io gli facessi il Giove d'argento della ditta altezza. Mostrai a sua maestà che quelli dua giovani ditti io gli avevo menati di Italia per servizio di sua maestà*'.

11 L. Dimier, 'Benvenuto Cellini à la cour de France' *Rébue Archéologique*, Paris, 1902, p.85ff. Giulio Alvarotto's report is written in strangely spelt Italian: '*Benvenuto nha fatta una che la chiama un giove la quale e qualche coseta magiore della persona del Re, la quale della maggior parte e giudicata molto bella, formitala lha condotta a fontana bleo e fattolo intendere al Re soa Maesta di volerla vedere un doppo desinare*'.

12 Cellini I, II, 44 'Io mi ricordo avervi commandato espressamente che voi mi facessi dodici statue d'argento; e quello era tutto il mio desiderio: voi mi avete voluto fare una saliera, e vase, e teste e porte, e tante altre cose, sche io sono molto smarrito, veduto lasciato in drieto tutti i desideri delle mie voglie, e atteso a compiacere a tutte le voglie vostre'.

13 The original model for the figure of Earth from the gold salt is said to have been in Vienna before the Second World War and to have been sold through Dr. Planiscig of the Kunsthistorisches Museum to an American private collector.

14 Cellini, *Trattato della Scultura*, VIII, 'Io mi messi a maggior fatiche, et operai piu della meta che io non avevo si maggiormente delle fatiche. Cosi presi trenta libbre d'argento di mia danari, e queste detti a dua miei lavoranti con disegni e modelli, dei quali se ne fece dua vasi grandi. E perchè le guere erano grandissime, io non gli avrei domandato denari, che ne restavo d'avere di piu di sei mesi di mia provisioni. Cosi attesi sollecitssimanente a tirare innanzi i du gran vasi, e quali in un mese gli ebbi finiti, e con essi me ne andai a trovare Sua Maestà, il quale era a un citta vicina al mare, che si domandava Argentana. E presentato a Sua Maestà li du vasi, e mi fece gran carezze'.

15 Plon, p.66 'A Pierre Coussinault, menuysier, demourant à Paris, la somme de treize livres dix sols tournois à luy ordonnée, le vingtiesme jour de novembre mil cinq cens quarante six, pour avoir par luy fourny et livré, de sondict mestier, ung vaze de boys de noyer, en forme de table carrée, à mettre dragées et confitures selon le devis qui en a esté faict au plaisir du Roy'.

16 ibid. p.66 'Auditz Paul Romain et Ascaigne, la somme de sept cens soixante huict livres huict sols tournois, à eulx ordonnée dix-neufviesme jour d'octobre mil cinq cens quarante six pour l'achapt de cinquante et ung marc six onces, deux gros d'argent á ouvrer, pour convertir et employer à faire un grand vase d'argent, en forme de table quarrée, posé et assis sur quatre satires, aussi d'argent, pour mettre dragées et confitures au plaisir dudict seigneur et selon le devis qui en a esté par luy faict avec les ouvriers'.

17 ibid p.68 'A Paul Romain et Ascaigne Desmarry, la somme de six vingt dix neuf livres seize sols six deniers tournois à eulx ordonnée par le Roy pour argent blanc et or par eulx employé, tant en deux couppes d'argent dorées, dont l'une est grande et l'autre petite, que pour une assiette à cadenatz garnye de cuillier, cousteau et fourchette avec ung petit coffre au dessus servant de salière, sur lequel est couché une Diane et pour la doreure desdictes deux couppes et assiette livrée par lesdicts ouvriers audict seigneur le quinziseme jour de ce présent mois de novembre mil cinq cens cinquante ung'.

18 ibid p.68 'A Paul Romain et Ascaigne Desmariz, orfeuvres italiens, besongnans de leur dict mestier pour le service du Roy en son hostel de Nesle, la somme de trois cens quinze livres deux sols neuf deniers tournois, à eulx ordonnée par le Roy, pour l'or et argent par eulx fourny et employé en ung bassin d'argent doré, dedans lequel y a une nef figurée de laquelle sort toutes sortes de poissons, en ung vase, en une coupe plaine avec l'essay et en une autre couppe platte ouvrée, le tout livré au dict seigneur'.

19 See Plon, p.68, note 2.

20 Vasari, vol. V, p.170.

21 Robert-Dumesnil, nos. 171-179.

22 Illustrated and discussed in Fontainebleau II, no. 508, p.378-9.

23 Robert -Dumesnil, *op cit* no. 173, ill. Jessen, p.73. In his *Vie des Dames Galantes* (Librairie Générale Française, 1962, ed. Pascal Pia, p.62) Pierre de Bourdeilles, Abbé de Brantôme, gives account of a somewhat similar cup, which is believed to have been made for the Duc d'Alençon. His account begins in the following terms 'J'ai conneu un Prince de par le monde qui fut bien mieux, car il acheta d'un orfèvre une très belle coupe d'argent doré, comme pour un chef d'oeuvre et grant speciauté, le mieux elabourée, gravée et sigillée qu'il estoit possible de voir, ou estoyent tailées bien gentiment et subtillement au burin plusieurs figures de l'Aretin, de l'homme et de la femme, et ce au bas estage de la coupe, et au dessus et au haut plusieurs aussi de diverses manières de cohabitations de bestes,….Cette coupe estoit l'honneur du buffet de ce prince; car comme j'ay dit, elle estoit très belle et riche d'art, et agrèable à voir au dedans et au dehors'.

24 See M. Leithe-Jasper 'Der Bergkristallpokal Herzog Philipps des Guten von Burgund' *Jahrbuch der Kunsthistorischen Sammlungen*, Band 66, Wien, 1970, p.241.

25 See Fontainebleau II, cat. no. 438, p.332-3.

26 Fontainebleau II, cat. no. 438.

27 Zerner, cat. nos. AF54 a, b.

28 Zerner, pl. AF 53.

29 Geymuller suggests that du Cerceau may have copied this design from Cellini, but it is attributed to du Cerceau in the catalogue of the *Cabinet des Dessins* of the Bibliothèque Nationale.

30 Geymuller, p.321.

31 ill. Kohlhaussen, fig. 400, p.260.

32 For an illustration of the onyx cup as it is now and of the 1685 drawing, see Alcouffe, 'The Collection of Cardinal Mazarin's Gems', *Burlington Magazine*, Sept. 1974, fig. 20.

33 Prado, cat. no. 77.
34 Krempel, p.112.
35 Ill. *Oeuvres de Bijouterie et Joallerie de la Renaissance à Louis XVI* ed. Guérinet, Paris, n.d. pls. 136-141.
36 Thieme-Becker, *Künstler-Lexikon,* article on Etienne Delaune.
37 ill. Krempel, pl. 35.
38 ibid. pl. 27.
39 Bartsch, *Le Peintre-Graveur,* Vol. XIII, 17, 18.
40 Inv. No. E 8756.
41 The subjects are copied either directly or with minor modifications from Delaune prints, the Robert Dumesnil concordance is:
Labours of the Month, RD 185-196.
Central ring, Jupiter, RD 359, Venus 420, Saturn 94⅞, Hercules 373 Apollo 419, Diana 418, Mars 416, Mercury 421; the intervening figure of Bellona is based on 417.
Inner ring, Earth, Air and Fire, 104, 105, 106. Water apparently from another source.
42 *Trattato dell'Oreficeria, XII 'Io ho visto in Parigi fare da quelli pratichi uomini le piu mirabil cose che si possar imaginar al mondo'.*
43 ill. Burlington Fine Arts Club, *Catalogue of Silversmiths' Work,* 1901, cat. no. J 12, pl. LXXX.
44 A number of French Mannerist vessels are illustrated in French still-life paintings, though the latter were painted in the seventeenth century; they are well represented in the paintings of Meiffren Conte (1630-1705), see *La Nature Morte en France,* Michel Faré, Geneva, 1962, pls. 194-208.
45 Cardinal Sfondrati owned a collection of paintings and antiquities of sufficient interest for it to be the subject of a report to the Emperor Rudolph II from his agent in Rome, Rudolph Corraduz, see Lhotsky, p.278.
46 A few plaquettes of bronze or lead have been tentatively identified as French but do not differ in any essential feature from contemporary German types. Two examples in the Louvre are cast with the Conversion of St. Paul and a Marine Triumph respectively.
47 F. Haskell, *Patrons and Painters,* London, 1963, p.26.
48 The entry in the Nürnberg archives states *'als Kaiser Matthias beneben dero Kais. gemahlin nach empfangener crönung zu franckfurt als ein Römischer Kaiser das erste mal...eingeritten'.* See Kris III, p.22.
49 *'ain ganz altväterischer Becher mit 4 Pariser arbeith geschnitzen Raiflen'.* See Kris, III, cat. no. 34, p.100.
50 ill. *Les Grands Orfèvres,* Paris, 1965, p.53.
51 Frankenburger, no. 71, p.17-18.
52 ill. Berkenhagen, *Die französischen Zeichnungen der Kunstbibliothek,* Berlin, 1970, p.36 Hdz 45.
53 Kris II, p.175ff.
54 Fontainebleau II, cat. nos. 621-4. There is also a Palissy version of the Briot Temperantia dish in the Louvre.

CHAPTER NINE

Spain and Portugal

Spain

so profuse and unrestrained was the decoration of Spanish Renaissance silver that the impact of Mannerist fashion was less dramatic in Spain than in northern Europe. Mannerist ornament came to Spain both directly from Italy and also indirectly through the southern Netherlands. Many of the leading Italian Mannerist artists came to Spain to work on the interior decoration of Philip II's palace of the Escorial, amongst them Federigo Zucchero, Pellegrino Tibaldi, Luca Cambiaso and Bartolommeo Carducci. The Spaniard, Gaspar Becerra of Baeza, who was appointed Court Painter to Philip II in 1563, had even worked under that arch-Mannerist, Giorgio Vasari, on the decoration of the Palace of the Cancelleria in Rome. There had been close commercial relations between Flanders and Spain since the fifteenth century. Both Flemish artists and Flemish prints came to Spain, and the entrapped satyrs that appear in the engraved ornament of Cornelis Bos and of Cornelis Floris can be found even on Spanish ecclesiastical plate of the second half of the sixteenth century. Striking evidence of the rapid spread of Flemish pattern-books in Spain can be seen in a design by Gomes Alonso for a saltcellar or cup in the *Llibros de Passanties* of the Barcelona Instituto de Historia de la Cuidad.[1] This drawing, which was submitted as a masterpiece in 1556, is copied exactly from a Cornelis Floris print in the series illustrated in pls. 196-9. Even on their ecclesiastical plate Spanish goldsmiths associated grotesques derived from Italian Renaissance sources with lecherous satyrs of northern origin, though not necessarily in a prominent position. Thus an altar cross by Juan Franci of Toledo in the Victoria and Albert Museum has panels on the arms embossed with mermen chasing mermaids,[2] while an altar cruet in the same Museum (pl. 405) is of purely secular design, with a winged dragon spout and an S-scroll handle to which a satyr is bound. Alongside such pieces, which show an awareness of developments elsewhere in Europe, we find vessels of about the same date wrought by the same makers, but in which conventional Renaissance design is still dominant, as in the circular basin by Juan Franci illustrated in pl. 409. Towards the end of the sixteenth century a purer style was introduced in which the elegance of Mannerism was rejected in favour of a characteristically Spanish severity and monumentality.

So little Spanish domestic silver survives from the sixteenth century that we cannot be sure whether the vessels upon which our conclusions are based are representative. Two Mexican ewers dating from the second half of the sixteenth century in the Amsterdam Rijksmuseum (no. 1955.1) are more extravagant in style than extant examples made in the mother country, but may nevertheless represent a type that was widespread at the time. The Spanish goldsmiths worked in rather heavier plate than was usual in the northern countries, doubtless because of the plentiful supply of the raw material. It is difficult to emboss so finely in heavy-gauge plate and for this reason some Spanish wrought work seems to be less carefully finished than similar work by northern masters. The Spanish goldsmiths were nevertheless great masters of the art of embossing silver in high relief; an example of ecclesiastical silver with ornament in high relief is shown in pl. 412, while secular pieces of outstanding merit are illustrated in pls. 407, 411 and 341-4. Typical of the coarser work is the pair of huge silver vases (pl. 404) in the treasury of Seville Cathedral, which have been attributed to Fernando Ballestaros the Younger, a master who subsequently worked with Juan d'Arfe on the Seville custodia. Such vases are among the rarest of all sixteenth century plate; their impracticable size condemned them to the melting pot and it is only their chance presence in a Spanish cathedral treasury that has preserved them.

It is hazardous to suggest exact dates for individual examples of Spanish silver; few pieces are marked and the natural conservatism of the Spanish people is such that styles changed very slowly. Some indication can be derived from the presence or absence of strapwork ornament. This was probably introduced about the middle of the century and is present on the rim of the Juan Franci basin (pl. 409). Spanish secular silver must have existed in great quantity, for precious metal was being imported in increasing amounts throughout the period. It is to this plentiful supply of bullion that the vast proportions of Spanish custodias can be attributed. Even embossed pieces were wrought in heavier metal than was used elsewhere. The cracks, which are so often seen on German or Dutch silver as a consequence of working the metal too thin, are not to be found on Spanish sixteenth-century vessels.

There are many references to Spanish silver in contemporary inventories. That prepared at Valladolid[3] for Prince Philip, later Philip II of Spain, dated 11 April 1554, refers to large quantities of plain vessels and then lists a number of more imposing cups and dishes presented to him by Flemish cities, including Brussels, Antwerp, Maastricht and Louvain. The Prince's strongest suit was, however, his series of gold-hilted swords, all the work of his personal goldsmith, Juan de Soto of Barcelona (see p.317). The Tudor royal inventory, while it contained a large number of *Almain* vessels, seems to have been poorly off for Spanish silver, though the following two cups must have been handsome objects:[4]

> Item 199 one Spanish cup of silver and gilt all over wrought with divers men hunting and a man in the top kneeling and a hart with a crucifix between his horns before him and twelve ragged pearls hanging at it.   116 oz.

> Item 226 one Spanish cup gilt all over wrought with a cover like a coronet with divers flowers enamelled.   80 oz.

Two other items, nos. 296 and 297 are described by the inventory clerk as being either Portuguese or Spanish; these were gilt cups with white silver borders.

One of the most frequent references in non-Spanish inventories[5] is the term *'façon d'Espagne'*. Thus the inventory of Charlotte, Duchesse de Valentino, wife of Cesare Borgia, dated 1514, lists three cups and a basin for washing made *'à la façon d'Espagne'*. That of Margaret of Austria, of 1523 likewise has a small basin and ewer with a handle *'fort bien ouvré a la mode d'Espaigne'* as well as many other items described in a similar way. A later inventory of 1560 of Queen Mary Stuart lists large numbers of buttons also in the *'façon d'Espagne'*. In this case it seems likely that enamelled mauresque ornament is meant. This cannot, however, apply to the earlier inventories which antedate the introduction of this type of decoration to the jewellers' shops. Unfortunately such inventory descriptions cannot always be trusted. In this connection it is worth quoting the comments of Kris[6] on the use of the description 'Spanish' in the Habsburg imperial inventories: 'in the inventory made after the death of the Emperor Matthias in 1619 a large number of cameo mounts are described as 'Spanish' or of Spanish workmanship. This description seems to have been quite indiscriminately, inasmuch as it is lacking in the case of certain mounts that are identical with those described as Spanish. This fact very much reduces the value of the description. Some of the settings described as 'Spanish' can indeed be attributed to the Rudolphine workshop. This is not necessarily a contradiction, as it is very likely that the term 'Spanish work' referred, not to the origin of the piece, but was a standard description in the goldsmiths' shops of the period for a particular technique of ornament. It is not unusual to find such terms employed in the history of the applied arts. This explanation is supported by descriptions as, for instance: a medallion surrounded by twenty-five Spanish enamelled roses (*25 spanische geschmölzte reslein*) dating from about 1569. This is made even clearer in the French inventory of the *Joyaux de la couronne de France* at Fontainebleau in 1560[7] in which some of the smaller goldsmiths' works are described as being in the '*façon d'espaigne*'. In the present state of our knowledge we cannot explain these terms.' In 1577 and 1561 in the Austrian records[8] we find the terms *französischer Arbeit* (French work) and *alla francese* (in the French manner).

From the first half of the sixteenth century there was a close relationship between the Habsburg court and Spanish goldsmiths. As early as 1538 a bill of a Spanish goldsmith rendered to Queen Anna is recorded. The Emperor Maximilian II occasionally had work carried out in Spain and a Spanish goldsmith, Juan Maczuelos, is listed amongst his court artists. In 1589 Rudolph sent a goldsmith of the same name to his ambassador in Madrid, and also in 1589 the Emperor ordered some gold buttons in Spain. The imperial envoy, Khevenhüller, was always a warm supporter of the Spanish craftsmen; in 1575 he wrote to the Archduke Ferdinand of Tirol to the effect that Madrid goldsmiths' work was finer and more durable than could be obtained in any other place; he sent a sample at the same time to prove his point.[9]

The discovery of the wreck of the Spanish galleass, *Girona,* one of the many ships of the Spanish Armada lost on the northern and eastern coasts of Ireland in 1588, led to the recovery of quantities of silver vessels, but unfortunately nearly four hundred years of battering by the waves left little to show of their former splendour. The cups and dishes, of which there must have been a great store, were broken up into hundreds of fragments, and although their decoration made it possible to assemble them to some extent, no complete pieces could be found.[10] The drinking-vessels were decorated with mauresque ornament or with the type of marine subject often found on vessels connected with liquids, while the candlesticks, of which a number survived without their bases, had plain baluster stems and cylindrical sockets. The quantity of silver carried on this ship was evidently large, perhaps because plate had been transferred to it from other ships that had been wrecked earlier.

The Barcelona *Llibros de Passanties*[11] is of great use in illustrating the types of domestic vessels of which no examples have survived. On the whole the vessel forms follow a few standard types, usually a vase, ewer or salt. One of the best is the ewer design decorated with dancing putti, fruit and garlands and with a tall handle modelled as a lion, which was submitted in 1551 by Juan Pery Pockh,[12] the same goldsmith who left Spain and obtained the court appointment to the Empress Maria, the consort of Charles V. He subsequently worked for Maximilian II: the sword-hilts commissioned from him by this Emperor are discussed in Chapter XVI. His ewer design of 1551 shows such strong Italian influence that one suspects he must have had access to the ewer designs of Agostino Veneziano or, perhaps, the copies of them by the French engraver, Androuet du Cerceau.

Ewers and Basins

Three distinct ewer forms were made in sixteenth-century Spain. The designs submitted as masterpieces to the Barcelona guild were mostly of the type illustrated in pl. 405. This particular vessel is actually an altar cruet, not an ewer, and consequently of small size, but there was at the time no difference, other than size, between ewer and cruet so it can be accepted as representing the former type. No full-size ewer of this type seems to have survived. A second type, shaped like a helmet, is by far the best represented amongst surviving Spanish secular plate. This continued in use on into the seventeenth century, though the later examples lack the elaborate ornament of those in High Mannerist fashion. The ewer (pl. 402) can be dated fairly accurately as it conforms almost exactly to a design by Antonio Maltes of Barcelona in the *Llibros de Passanties* of that city.[13]

The drawing is dated 27th May, 1564 and differs only in lacking the engraved ornament of the extant ewer. The design is, in fact, somewhat conservative; similar vessels of English origin, but some twenty years earlier, are known. The engraved ornament also is in strictly Renaissance style. A ewer of similar form but much more adventurous design is illustrated in pl. 403. This shows Spanish Mannerist taste in an extreme form. Ewers of northern European origin of the same period commonly have handles composed of mixed human and animal forms, but it would be difficult to find one that achieved quite this shock effect. The third type corresponded to the international form, which had been evolved in Italy. It is this type which is the most difficult to identify; in this case the body is egg-shaped and tapered sharply towards the stem. A design for a ewer of this form dated 1597 is illustrated in pl. 117 while an example of about the same date is shown in pl. 408. That the type was established in Spain as well as elsewhere is proved by the inclusion of a version of it by Juan de Arfe in his treatise *De Varia Commensuracion para la Esculptura y Architectura*. An imposing ewer of this third type was formerly in the Pierpont Morgan Collection, and was exhibited in London in 1901. The present whereabouts of this ewer and its companion basin are not known.[14] Like much Spanish silver of the period the decoration, though lively and vigorous, is somewhat coarse and does not stand up to close inspection. Heavily embossed with strapwork enclosing cartouches and lion masks, they follow contemporary Italian fashion. The ewer handle in the form of a grotesque monster with wings and convoluted tail is particularly imaginative. The most fantastic Spanish ewer ever devised is surely that shown in the painting *The Last Supper* by Alonso Vasquez in the Museo Provincial, Seville. It probably derives from Giulio Romano; parcel-gilt and enriched with rubies and pearls, its spout has figures of tritons sitting on hippocamps. It is represented in such precise detail as to suggest that the artist had the original in front of him.

Juan de Arfe

The introduction of this classical style owed much to Juan de Arfe, the last goldsmith member of the famous family, but its development was encouraged by patronage from the royal court and it is sometimes called the Philip II style. In the years 1585 to 1587 Juan de Arfe published in Seville a verse treatise entitled *De varia Commensuracion para la Esculptura y Architectura,* which rejected the Mannerist elements of ornament introduced from Italy and the Netherlands and called for the adoption of a pure Renaissance style in silver. The style he proposed was basically architectural and he actually described himself as *platero de maconeria* (goldsmith-architect). Like the earlier members of his family, he was responsible for the design of several splendid custodias, including those of the cathedrals of Avila and Seville. Of these, the former (pl. 412) was built between 1564 and 1571 and the latter between 1580 and 1587.[16] This was the largest custodia built by the Arfe family. It weighs over a thousand pounds and is over ten feet high. The design of four tempietti of diminishing size, set one above the other, conforms to Juan de Arfe's architectural principles; the ornament as a whole is restrained, but if one looks more closely at the custodia, one is aware of much rich detail, especially around the base. The columns supporting the peristyle of the base are exquisitely wrought with twining grape-vines, inhabited by cherubs. The complex iconography was supplied by an eminent theologian, Francisco Pacheco, while much of the figure sculpture was from Juan de Arfe's own hand. These custodias are, as one would expect of their architect-creator, of purer Renaissance style than those made by Juan's father, Antonio. The details display Juan's familiarity with the works of Vitruvius, but the most impressive feature is without doubt the sculpture, both low reliefs and figures modelled in the round. Juan de Arfe drew attention to his sculptural skill when he described himself as *escultor de oro y plata* (sculptor in gold and silver). These huge custodias took many years to build and whole workshops were engaged on them. Though Juan de Arfe usually went to work in the city for which the custodia upon which he was working was destined, parts might be made elsewhere. Thus the relief panel on the base of the Avila custodia illustrated in pl. 412 bears the town and assayer's mark of the city of Valladolid, where Juan de Arfe had his headquarters.

Philip III also employed Juan de Arfe; in 1599 he received payment for a ewer and basin for the King which have not survived. They were made of enamelled and gilt silver and further decorated with relief figures of divinities. The commission cost the large sum of 4,054 ducats,[17] implying that they must have been magnificent. Such elaborately enriched vessels seem to have been the exception during the latter decades of the sixteenth century. Typical Spanish silver of this period, while of excellent proportion, was of uniform design with simple forms divided horizontally by plain mouldings and vertically by buttress-like ornaments. Besides Juan de Arfe, another goldsmith, Francisco Merino from Jaen, had considerable influence in developing the Herrera style. He was mainly employed by the chapter of Toledo cathedral; his manner achieves a combination of rich ornament with an austerely architectural construction. He did not adhere to Juan de Arfe's strictly correct classicism.

Jacopo da Trezzo

Philip II gathered round him a group of Italian immigrant artists and craftsmen whose main task was the creation of the vast palace-monastery of Escorial. The first to enter his employment was the Milanese architect and hardstone sculptor, Jacopo da Trezzo (1514-1589). This master was one of the few Renaissance artists who were accepted almost as noblemen by the princes who employed them and were accorded a dignified station at court. After working in Milan as a sculptor, he entered the service of Philip II as a young man and in 1554, at the age of thirty, followed the king to the Netherlands, where he produced coin and medal dies. The historian of Milan, Morigia,[18] describes him in the following terms, *'Del valoroso e immortale Giacomo da Trezzo, inventore del intagliare il diamante, raro nell' intagliare il cristalla et altre pietre, e inventare di altre virtu'*. In his reference to *Invention* Morigia puts his finger upon da Trezzo's main quality. His activities at the court of Philip II were manifold; he acted not only as a general adviser on artistic problems but also as a designer, as an inventor of the machinery needed to cut and shape the hardstones for the tabernacle and custodia of the Capilla Mayor of the Escorial and finally as a craftsman: as jeweller, goldsmith, medal die-cutter and sculptor.[19]

The finest of all the sixteenth-century ewers and basins, irrespective of country of origin are the set in the Metropolitan Museum, New York (pls. 341, 344). These are both struck with a Rome hall mark of later date, but there is no maker's mark and they can be attributed to a Spanish master working either in Spain or in Italy. The decoration of the ewer is arranged in horizontal bands, one above the other; while the neck and stem are cast, the frieze of a Roman triumph which runs round the middle is embossed and chased. A feature of this ewer, also found in the Agostino Veneziano designs of 1531 (pl. 12) and in many other Mannerist ewers, is the attachment of the lower end of the handle to the upper part of the body. In order to leave enough room to insert the hand, it was necessary to carry the handle well up above the level of the lip and to provide a link element between the latter and the top of the handle. This takes the form of a lion on this Spanish ewer and of an eagle on the Venetian ewer (pl. 354). The basin is constructed in an unusual manner, the outer border being set with twelve plaques each embossed and chased with a different subject, the workmanship being of the highest order. These are attached to the rim by screws. The circular frieze around the central boss is chased with hunting scenes, including one of a man being chased by a bull of distinctly Spanish build. The underside of the basin is engraved with lively scenes of acquatic monsters, with the exception of the central frieze which is embossed and of which the underside is exposed. It is possible to give a precise date *post quem* for these pieces, as the frieze on the ewer includes a representation of a rhinoceros. The majority of such representations derive from Albrecht Dürer's woodcut of 1515, which was not anatomically correct; this ewer derives from another source, which must have been another rhinoceros brought to Lisbon in 1579. After the death of King Sebastian in battle and the accession of Philip II to the throne of Portugal, the animal was transferred to Madrid and put on display in 1584. In the following year Juan de Arfe published a print of it in his *Varia Commensuracion* and it must be from this work that the rhinoceros was taken.

This ewer and basin combine unusual construction, the finest chasing and exquisite engraving. Nothing is known of secular plate by Juan d'Arfe but this ewer and basin are of the quality one would expect from his workshop. The tazza on low foot illustrated in pl. 411 is, perhaps, the work of the same master. The last ewer type before the full development of Baroque is illustrated in pl. 410. The applied buttresses belong to the severe style associated with the Counter Reformation in Europe, but the subtle profile of the piece and the elegant handle look back to sixteenth-century courtly taste.

Spanish and Italian basins and ewers of this period are so alike that it is difficult to determine the origin of unmarked specimens and it is sometimes necessary to rely on such evidence as the degree of finish given to the vessels. The frequent exchange of goldsmiths between the two countries adds to the difficulty of distinguishing between their productions. While basins with scenes embossed in relief running in concentric friezes around a central boss were popular throughout western Europe, and for that matter, even further afield in central and eastern Europe, an individual type with scalloped border seems to have been a speciality of the Iberian Peninsula. The large dish in pl. 407 from Seville Cathedral is, in view of its present location, more likely to be Spanish, whereas another, formerly in the Rothschild collection,[15] is probably Portuguese. A considerable number of basins of much simpler design has survived; no fewer than fifteen are in the Museo Lazaro Galdeano, Madrid, of which five are still accompanied by their original helmet-shaped ewers. These all date from the very end of our period, and are generally of uniform design. They have or originally had central prints with an engraved or enamelled coat-of-arms. The borders, which are either engraved with strapwork or foliations or left plain, are usually gilt to match the gilding of the central print. They are mostly serviceable pieces and are not relevant here.

During the last quarter of the sixteenth century, Spanish silver took a turn that was not paralleled elsewhere in Europe and, while northern goldsmiths were still producing Mannerist designs, a monumental style that anticipated some features of Baroque was adopted. During the first half of the century, there had been a close relationship between architectural design and goldsmiths' work, but the architects had derived their plateresque ornament from the goldsmiths, now the reverse was the case and the goldsmiths followed the severe and reticent classical style that was introduced by the Spanish architect, Juan de Herrera (1530-1597). In architecture the busy ornament of plateresque was abandoned and decoration reduced to a minimum. In adapting the Herrera style to the material in which they worked the goldsmiths preferred massive architectural elements to the crowded figures and lively surface treatment of the plateresque. Vessel surfaces were either left plain or wrought with bas-relief scrolls and then decorated with applied oval bosses enriched with translucent enamels in a restricted colour range. The great basin in the Metropolitan Museum, New York (pl. 406), which dates from about 1600, well illustrates the use of these applied enamel plaques. Of gold and polychrome translucent enamel, they confer great splendour upon an otherwise conventional design.

After two years in the Low Countries, da Trezzo moved to Spain, where he established his workshop in Madrid, with, subsequently, another in the Escorial. He was at first mainly employed as a goldsmith and hardstone sculptor; an account for his work for the court during the period November 1558 to December 1562 shows that in this period he was working on seals and producing large numbers of cameos for mounting in buttons. He also supplied three rock-crystal cups, one of which was described as being engraved with marine monsters. He must have made or supervised the making of large numbers of these rock-crystal and other hardstone vessels, but none can now be identified. Besides those he made for the court of Spain, he sold others to Cosimo I, Grand Duke of Tuscany;[20] a Spanish jasper flask (pl. 335) in the Palazzo Pitti has also been conjecturally attributed to him. The following description of a rock-crystal vessel

Plate XIX
Parcel-gilt coin cup. Worms, 1571.

Plate XX
Gold and enamel flask. Made by Hans Karl, Salzburg, dated 1602.

believed to have been made by Jacopo da Trezzo, taken from an inventory of the property of Philip II,[21] resembles typical Milanese productions of the last quarter of the sixteenth century:

A crystal drinking vase, made like a serpent with wings, the body carved and around its neck a golden mount set with two cameos and two rubies, and between the wings, above the body, another gold mount with a small crystal cover, and with the serpent's beak mounted with gold; on the stomach a figure of Bacchus with a garland of leaves and a vine trail of gold, holding in his right hand a small gold cup and in his left a bunch of grapes with a vine leaf, all of gold. The vessel has the foot mounted in gold and set with eight stones in gold collets, four rubies and four cameos. Upon the foot is attached a crystal serpent from which rises the baluster stem that supports the vase. At the point of juncture there is another gold mount set with two rubies and two cameos. There is a cover to which the wings and the tail are attached and also a finial on top of all in the middle; these parts are also held by gold mounts set with ten stones: six small rubies and four cameos. Contained in two boxes covered with gold tooled blue leather and lined with red velvet.

This vessel corresponds in type to that illustrated in pl. VI.

The great collection of vessels of semi-precious hardstone in the Prado derives for the most part from the treasury of the Dauphin brought from Paris by the Bourbon king, Philip V, but includes a number of earlier rock-crystal vessels dating from the period of Philip II. These cannot be distinguished from contemporary Milanese work; this is not surprising as they were the work of Milanese *emigré* craftsmen. A fine ebony casket set with engraved rock-crystal panels in the treasury of Burgos Cathedral seems to be of Milanese origin, as is the superb casket in the Escorial.[22] The small group of rock-crystal vessels presented by the Spanish ambassador to Robert Cecil, and still preserved in England at Hatfield House in Hertfordshire, were presumably made in Spain and may well have been carved in the workshop of Jacopo da Trezzo. A standing cup in the Museu Nacional, Lisbon, with rock-crystal bowl and knop in the stem, and with silver-gilt foot and baluster stem is of Spanish origin, but whether it was intended for secular use or to serve as a chalice is uncertain. The ornament is devoid of religious subjects; this is not unusual on Spanish ecclesiastical plate, and the form and profile of the cup correspond to a chalice.

It is known that da Trezzo produced the high altar for the chapel of Philip II's palace of the Escorial. In order to assist him in this and other commissions, da Trezzo recruited two further masters from Milan, Giulio and Hieronimo Miseroni, who arrived in 1582 and 1584 respectively. Thus by the end of the century members of the Miseroni family were to be found in the main rock-crystal working centres of Europe. Jasper was found in quantity in Spain and in 1572 da Trezzo, who, by the standards of the time, was already an old man, sent six pieces of the precious material from Spain to Grand Duke Francesco I of Tuscany.[23] Three years later in 1575 he wrote[24] from Madrid to the Duke asking him to choose the form and subject of the work he wished to make for him before he died. It has been suggested that the jasper flask composed of two shell-like forms in a jewelled gold mount (pl. 335) may be the piece he made on this occasion. His most important work in Spain was the custodia he made for the Escorial; it was of jasper mounted in gilt-bronze and still survives, but a smaller one inside of silver-gilt was destroyed by the French troops during the Napoleonic Wars. This custodia took seven years to make and was produced in a workshop at the Escorial that da Trezzo shared with another Milanese artist and architect-sculptor, Pompeo Leoni, who had first arrived in Spain in 1556. Both masters were given the title of *Escultor de Su Mayestad* and worked together for many years, but not without friction.

Pompeo Leoni

Pompeo Leoni was another of those Renaissance men whose range included architecture, sculpture and goldsmith's work. He seems to have competed with da Trezzo in the production of rock-crystal vessels. A warrant by Philip II dated 2 May 1590[25] provides for the payment to Pompeo Leoni, court sculptor, of the sum of 200 ducats for a rock-crystal mirror with its frame, on the frame sixteen ornaments set in gold and enamelled in different colours with a little ruby in each, and above foliage with a silver ring. The fact that payment was made to Leoni does not, however, necessarily mean that he had worked on the piece himself. Philip II also took into his service the Florentine goldsmith, Gianpaolo Poggini, a former assistant of Cellini, who is mentioned in Cellini's *Vita* as having worked with his brother, Domenico, on the reliefs of a gold cup for Eleonora, Grand Duchess of Tuscany. He went to Brussels in 1555 and worked there until 1559 making medal and coin dies; subsequently he settled in Spain where he remained until his death in 1602. He also was appointed an *Escultor del Re* in 1563, but does not seem to have been employed on goldsmith's work in Spain.[26]

Portugal

During the first half of the sixteenth century, Portuguese goldsmiths were conservative in their choice of decoration and therefore vessels of the latter part of the century can easily be mistaken for those of earlier date. After the death in battle of King Sebastian in 1580 Portugal became part of Spain. Like Spanish silver so also Portuguese silver was not always submitted for assay and marking which makes it difficult to distinguish between them, the more so as fashion in the two countries was determined by the taste of the same monarch.

Portuguese secular silver of the second half of the sixteenth century[27] is less rare than Spanish silver of the same epoch. The most frequent survivors are the salvers standing on low feet known as *fruiteros*. They are decorated with concentric rings of ornament, usually groups of figures in high relief, divided into compartments by half-columns or pilasters. These were originally made in sets and are well represented in the Palacio Nacional de Ajuda, Lisbon.[28] Plainer salvers of more international type are decorated with incised strapwork derived from some northern pattern-book. These salvers resemble the Spanish type with low foot. It is difficult to distinguish between them with absolute certainty, but the Portuguese examples are more frequently struck with hall-marks. Portuguese work seems on the whole to be coarser than contemporary Spanish silver, but there were doubtless exceptions. The finest examples extant, the Lercaro ewer and basin (pls. 342,5) and the service (pls. 348-9) were probably both made by *emigré* Portuguese masters, the former by Antonio da Castro, who went to work in Genoa. Typical of Mannerist show plate, they point to the supreme skill of this Portuguese master of the second half of the century. This service with its crowded friezes worked in high relief, particularly that of the innermost ring, is distinctly Portuguese in style, showing a lack of sophistication in design when set against contemporary Italian pieces. It is a curious circumstance that Portuguese silver of this period, much of which is provincial in taste, should have survived while most of the Spanish secular silver of the period is lost.

1   ill. Muller, pl. 39.
2   ill. Oman I, pl. 75-77.
3   Davilier, p.148ff.
4   Collins, pps. 319, 325.
5   Davilier, p.148ff.
6   Eichler-Kris, *Die Kameen im Kunsthistorischen Museum*, Wien, 1927, p.31, n.1.

7   *Inventaire des Joyaux de Fontainebleau*, p.334ff.

8   *Jahrbuch*, Wien, Band XIV, Regest no. 10674.

9   ibid. Band VII, Regest nos. 5375, 1577.

10 For illustrations of silver recovered from the wreck of the Girona, see R. Stenuit, *Les Trésors de l'Armada*, Paris, 1971, pps. 224-5.

11 Davilier, passim.

12 ill. Muller, pl. 83.

13 Oman I, pl. 199.

14 Burlington Fine Arts Club, *Catalogue of Silversmiths' Work*, London, 1901, pl. lxxxii.

15 F. Luthmer, *Schatz des Freiherr Karl von Rothschild*, Frankfurt am Main, 1883, Vol. I pl. 23.

16 See also A. M. Johnson, *Hispanic Silverwork*, New York, 1944, figs. 70, 71 and Babelon, p.19.

17 Davilier, p.224. For the Arfe family see also C. Justi, 'Die Goldschmiedefamilie der Arphe', *Miscellanea aus drei Jahrhunderte*, I, 1908, p.271ff.

18 Morigia, Lib. II, cap. ix, p.43 'the noble and immortal Giacomo da Trezzo, inventor of diamond cutting, of rare expertise in cutting crystal and other stones, and inventor of great virtuosity'.

19 Morigia, lib. II cap. ix. 'This miraculous Trezzo invented for the King a mill by means of which one could saw all kinds of jasper and all the finest veined stones, rock-crystal and other fine marbles with water power. Moreover he used water-power to operate four huge hammers for working iron'.

20 Babelon, p.23, quotes the Medici *Guardaroba* accounts for 1550-1 in which da Trezzo is mentioned as creditor in respect of a rock-crystal vase. Kris I, Vol. I p.102, n.16 quotes a letter from P. Luigi Manlilio to the Grand Duke Cosimo dated 11.xi.1564 referring to a rock-crystal bought from Jacopo da Trezzo.

21 Quoted by Babelon, p.253.

22 Kris I, figs. 498-503.

23 ibid. p.274.

24 ibid. p.276.

25 Davilier, p.218. A warrant for the payment of 200 *ducats* and 11 *reals* in addition to the 273 *reals* already paid to Leoni, is dated 10.8.1564; this relates to a silver reliquary head which he had fashioned for the King.

26 ibid. p.216.

27 For illustrations of Portuguese ecclesiastical silver of the sixteenth century, see J. Couto and A. Gonçalve, *Ourivesaria em Portugal*, Lisbon, 1960.

28 Dos Santos, pls. 53, 54.

CHAPTER TEN

South Germany

So vast was the production of the goldsmiths in the region of Teutonic culture and so numerous are the surviving examples of their work that it is necessary to divide the subject into three, and to deal with each in a separate chapter. First must come South Germany, in which Nürnberg and Augsburg were the main centres. These two cities were in the sixteenth century the most important sources of style and fashion throughout the German-speaking world and their influence was felt from as far as Strassburg in the west to Krakow in the east.

In the second half of the century there was close relationship between the engravers and the goldsmiths; many of the former were by profession goldsmiths. The traditional German art of the woodcut gave way to engraving on copper and many of the engravers working in Germany in the latter years came as emigrés from the Low Countries, whence they were driven by religious persecution. Some went to the Protestant refuge at Frankenthal, others to Augsburg, Munich and especially Prague where religious freedom was guaranteed by the tolerant Emperor Rudolph II.

The output of engraved designs for the goldsmith from the Nürnberg presses increased in volume as the century advanced and it is possible to find a graphic source for both the general design and the detail of the ornament of much of the plate of this period produced in the Teutonic cultural region.

Nürnberg

Nürnberg goldsmiths' work of the mid century conforms to the manner developed by Brosamer of Fulda, whose designs have been discussed above as representing German Renaissance style. While generally adopting the rigid structure of contrasting vertical and horizontal accents in the vessels he designed, he did not adhere to the classical Renaissance standards of proportion and of propriety in the use of ornament. Some of the forty designs in his *Kunstbüchlein* introduce complex profiles and bloated forms which, while lacking the sophistication of Mannerism, are far removed from Renaissance ideals. While Brosamer cannot, therefore be described as a Mannerist, some of his designs indicate a tendency to reject Italian forms and to revert to a style which had its roots in native German tradition. Brosamer describes himself on the title-page of the *Kunstbüchlein* as *Maler* (painter) and he was probably identical with the portrait painter who signed with the initials HB and a griffin's head.[1] His status as a portrait painter would, of course, explain his limited output as a master of ornamental design and also his individual manner in rendering Renaissance forms.

Another master, Augustin Hirschvogel (1503-1533), by origin a Nürnberger, who settled in Vienna in 1542, was more adventurous, particularly in his sixteen designs of vessels (pls. 28, 29), which look forward to a mature phase of German Baroque. Some of his designs were taken up and developed by Hornick but as a whole they were too impracticable to have much influence. Hirschvogel was, however, familiar with the mauresque, which he first plagiarised from a Flemish source, but subsequently in 1547 developed from his own resources. German Mannerism did not spring from the coarse and rustic manner of these masters but was developed in a highly refined and self-conscious style by Wenzel Jamnitzer and the Nürnberg engravers who followed him.

The characteristic production of the sixteenth-century goldsmiths of Nürnberg was the columbine-cup (*Akeley Pokal*) (pls. 413-415), which was also one of the masterpieces required from aspirants to admission as master-goldsmiths to the guild. It was a refined version of the lobate cup (*Buckel Pokal*) which had been introduced in the fifteenth century and had remained the standard form of the Renaissance. In spite of its Gothic derivation the columbine-cup continued to be the set masterpiece throughout the sixteenth and on into the following century.[2] At first the aspirant to mastership had to produce both design and cup, but after 1535 this was not longer necessary and the goldsmith was permitted to obtain his design from a graphic artist. It was not until the 1540's that the young goldsmith would have been able to find his model in a printed pattern-book and even then there were no printed designs that correspond precisely to the Nürnberg columbine-cup. It was, presumably, to remedy this situation that in, or shortly before, 1572, Wenzel Jamnitzer commissioned the *Punzenstecher*, Georg Wechter, to design a columbine-cup in a style more in accord with the fashion of the second half of the century. From this design Jamnitzer made — or had made — a model which was passed on to the Nürnberg goldsmith, Martin Rehlein, who wrought the pattern cup for submission to aspirants for admission to the guild.[3] This last cup has tentatively been identified with that now in the Victoria and Albert Museum (pl. 413) because its weight — 333 grams — corresponds closely with the 338.7 grams given in the bill as the weight of the Wechter-Rehlein cup. If on the other hand, this model cup was given out to journeymen to be copied, it could hardly have survived in so pristine a condition as the Museum example. That the model cup was worn out is indicated by the fact that it was from time to time renewed (pl. 178), the last being produced for the Nürnberg guild in 1631. The columbine-cup in the Victoria and Albert Museum (pl. 413) is one of three that remained in the possession of the guild until 1868, when the whole collection of silver was sold for the benefit of the widows and orphans of members. The two others were acquired by the Germanisches Nationalmuseum (pl. 415). These three cups show certain features that distinguish them from most others of the period. They are of white silver instead of being gilt, as was practically every South German cup of good quality at this time. Furthermore, they bear neither town nor maker's mark, thus contravening the fundamental rules of the guild. The suggestion that they were all three intended to be shown to candidates for admission to the guild can be rejected, as they appear to be of approximately the same date, and we know that payment was made in 1571 for one cup only. Nor do these three columbine-cups stand alone; another similar, but slightly later, unmarked white cup is in the British Museum and yet another (pl. 515) is in the Victoria and Albert Museum. A list compiled by Rosenberg in 1885 includes several others. There are, in short, too many for them to be explained as model cups. In a manuscript note in the Department of Metalwork of the Victoria and Albert Museum, Rosenberg suggested that some might be masterpiece cups which were sold without being marked because they had been produced under the direct control of the wardens and marking was, therefore, superfluous. This explanation is unacceptable as the wardens were unlikely to flout their own regulations in this way. It is just conceivable that some goldsmiths kept their masterpieces instead of selling them and that in this way the cups escaped assay and hall-marking, but this would surely have been exceptional as a young master would not normally be able to afford to do so. Rosenberg put forward this last suggestion in relation to the cup (pl. 515) which was then accepted as being the masterpiece of Christoph Jamnitzer (see p.221). It is, however, not the work of Jamnitzer alone and would not therefore, have fulfilled the conditions applicable to masterpieces. The problem of these unmarked white columbine-cups cannot be said to have been completely solved. It follows from the foregoing that none of the surviving columbine-cups was an original creation of its maker. The form was determined by a guild tradition that held good for many generations, not only in Nürnberg but in many other German towns as well. Nevertheless the finest examples all seem to be the work of Nürnberg goldsmiths. Although the candidate for admission to the guild had to adhere to the pattern laid down, his ability to vary that form by an original plan of decoration was a matter of some importance and no two columbine-cups are identical. The guild regulations were quite definite in this respect; the candidate was free to improve the cup according to his ability (*besser zu machen, wo er kann*) and everyone could apply the decoration in whatever way or whatever design he wished (*es steht auch in einer jeden Willkühr die zierd auf ein andere weys oder Arth zu machen*).

Wenzel Jamnitzer, his Workshop and Followers

The credit for introducing international Mannerist fashion to the goldsmiths of Nürnberg must be given to Wenzel Jamnitzer, the first of three generations of goldsmiths, who contributed more than any other single family to establish Nürnberg as the chief centre of design and production for nearly a hundred years. Although Jamnitzer did not leave an autobiography as did Cellini, the archives of the city of Nürnberg contain much information about him and, unlike Cellini, many splendid examples of his work survive. He was born in Vienna in 1508 and went to Nürnberg at a date that is not recorded, but must have been prior to his admission as a citizen on 23 May, 1534. He was a fully qualified master-goldsmith when he settled in Nürnberg, but it is not known where he served his time as a journeyman.[4] Within four weeks of the grant of citizenship, his marriage to Anna Braunreuch was celebrated in the Nürnberg church of Sankt Sebaldus on 22 June.[5] Nearly ten years later he received his first official appointment in the city, that of coin and seal die-cutter. It is significant that the entry in the city register relating to his appointment described him as *kunstreich,* a term that implies both skill and artistic sensibility.[6] He lived on in Nürnberg occupying various honourable city offices until his death at — for that time — the advanced age of seventy-seven. He worked in his shop in the Zistelgasse, at first with his brother Albrecht and subsequently with his sons and sons-in-law, of whom three sons and two sons-in-law became goldsmiths in Nürnberg. During much of his life he must have been in charge of a large workshop and we have his own evidence that he was overwhelmed with business.

Like Cellini, Wenzel Jamnitzer enjoyed the patronage of the most powerful and cultured princes of his time. He worked for four Holy Roman Emperors in succession, Charles V, Ferdinand I, Maximilian II and Rudolf II. He made the Sword of State of Charles V[7] (pls. 218, 219, 220) and we know from his sketch-book that he designed and possibly produced the jewel of the Order of the Golden Fleece for Ferdinand I. He was commissioned to make a huge and complicated table-fountain for Maximilian II and as *Kaiserlicher Hofgoldschmied* to Rudolf II he received frequent commissions. He also worked for the Archduke Ferdinand of the Tirol and his niece Elizabeth, widow of Charles IX of France. Other clients included Duke Philip of Pomerania, Duke Albrecht of Bavaria, the Elector August of Saxony, Wratislaus von Bernstein, Chancellor of Bohemia[8] and Cardinal Granvella, Minister of State to Charles V and Philip II of Spain. After his death his assistants were among the leading goldsmiths of their generation: his sons, Hans and Abraham (the Wenzel, eldest, having met with an early death) his son-in-law Hans Straub, Nikolaus Schmidt, Jonas Silber and Matthias Zündt.

In the course of so long a working life Wenzel Jamnitzer practiced many different styles and his works cannot be dated with certainty on the basis of stylistic criteria as the progressiveness or conservatism of his designs must have depended to some extent on the taste of his client. One of the most important documents that has survived concerning him is a sketch-book[9] which he seems to have used between the years 1545 and 1546, that is, in the earlier part of his career. This sketch-book shows him to have been more concerned with ornament than with form, but it is of particular significance as it shows us his ideas directly as they came to mind, before they had been worked up into a more finished form. The book, now preserved in the Berlin Kunstbibliothek, consists of seventeen sheets with thirty-four pages of drawings; originally there were more pages, but the more finished ones have presumably been extracted. The designs are not worked out in detail, but are mostly rapidly executed records of ideas, including, rather unexpectedly, a number of sketches of watch movements. Several ewers are depicted, all with the egg-shaped body that is seen on the ewer by Jamnitzer in the church of Santa Maria presso San Celso, Milan,[10] and in an ewer drawing that has been attributed to him (pl. 129). There are also a number of sketches of ornament for the borders of basins (pls. 123-4), which show the same type of decoration as the basin and cup illustrated (pls. 421, 426). The human figure plays little part in the various designs whereas the mauresque, then a new fashion, is of great importance, providing the ornament for borders, friezes and even the whole body of ewers. The collection of plaquettes from the Jamnitzer workshop in Basel complements the designs in this sketch-book to a remarkable extent and, between the two, we have the full range of Jamnitzer's early production. The book establishes beyond doubt that Jamnitzer was, at any rate at this early period in his career, responsible for the design as well as the fashion of his vessels. The lion mask which appears so frequently in his sketches was also the mark of the family and introduces a personal note in the book.

Jamnitzer was a typical Renaissance man with a wide range of skills and interests. Apart from goldsmithing he was a jeweller, possibly a watchmaker, and he had mastered the art of bronze casting. A fine mortar in the Berlin Kunstgewerbe Museum is attributed to him and others of the same design are recorded.[11] Among his other special achievements were the study of the sciences of perspective, geometry and astronomy, the development of the art of casting insects and grasses directly from nature, the exploitation of etching as a form of decoration for silver, the application of the mauresque as an important element in the repertoire of ornament and finally the introduction of the collector's cabinet, known sometimes as a *Kunstschrank*, though he seems to have preferred the term *Kunstlicher Schreibtisch*. Wenzel Jamnitzer was also proficient in the manufacture of scientific instruments and the Nürnberg historian, Johann Doppelmayr,[12] gives an account of his achievements in this field. He seems to have produced the whole range of instruments then known, many of them made of silver-gilt. This may account for their disappearance, whereas those made of the more usual gilt-brass or copper have mostly survived. Extant examples by Jamnitzer include the celestial globe dated 1566 in the Germanisches Nationalmuseum[13] and the *Mess-scheibe* in the Mathematisches Salon, Dresden, which was made in 1578 for the Elector August of Saxony, who was greatly interested in scientific instruments and devoted much time to efforts to invent a practicable hodometer. The celestial globe called not only for scientific knowledge but for the ability to design and cast the stand and to engrave the constellations on the surface of the globe. The engraving on the Dresden *Mess-scheibe* is thought to have been executed by Jost Amman, who engraved Jamnitzer's designs during the later years of the goldsmith's life. According again to Doppelmayr, who was writing one hundred and fifty years after Jamnitzer's death, the goldsmith also made a striking clock which included calendar and astronomical work. In 1568 Jamnitzer's experiments in the science of perspective received recognition from the City Council, which ordered that he should be awarded the sum of forty florins *Ehrengeld* (honorarium) for his *Kunstbücher,* presumably the *Perspectiva Literaria* which he had published in Nürnberg in 1557.[14] Jamnitzer was not the only goldsmith interested in the study of perspective. His contemporary, Hans Lencker, published his own *Perspectiva Literaria* in 1567, ten years after Jamnitzer. He was subsequently summoned to Dresden to instruct the Elector Christian in the science.

Apart from his sketch-book Jamnitzer is represented by a sufficiently large number of drawings for us to be able to arrive at a fair estimate of his skill with pen and wash.[15] There seems to be no reason to doubt his responsibility for the manner which appears consistently both in his drawings and in so much extant goldsmiths' work. His drawings cover a wide range from the rapidly-noted ideas of the sketch-book to highly detailed designs, such as those for the Sword of State of the Emperor Charles V at Weimar (pls. 218, 219, 220), for the table-fountain in the Veste Coburg (pl. 127) or for the Merckel table-centre in the Germanisches Nationalmuseum (pl. 132). Jamnitzer's earliest dated drawings, a design for the bowl of a cup decorated with mauresques enclosing a lion's mask in the Berlin Kunstbibliothek,[16] and the Weimar sword design, both of 1544, are carefully finished, as is the slightly later drawing of a cup, perhaps half a double cup (pl. 125). This last design is in itself quite unremarkable and, but for the master's initials W.I., one would have attributed it to lesser hand. In his later years Jamnitzer would hardly have had time to produce such finished drawings as those in pls. 132 or 127 and would have had to hand such work on to an assistant. That he did produce drawings for publication we know from the evidence of his unpublished book entitled *Kunstlicher Schreibtisch* in the Victoria and Albert Museum, and from the introduction to his *Perspectiva Corporum Regularicum,* published in 1568, in which he states that he had himself produced the drawings which were then engraved by Jost Amman.[17]

An interesting feature of the two drawings of 1544 is that both introduce panels of mauresque ornament. This was not, however, the first recorded use of such ornament in Germany. In 1534 and 1535 the pattern-carver, Hans Schwarzenberger of Augsburg had already issued two books of mauresque designs, both copied from Italian sources. Mauresque panels can also be seen in German architectural ornament, as, for example, on the entrance porch of the *Rathaus* of Marienberg in Saxony,[18] but Jamnitzer must still have been one of the earliest, if not the first, to exploit this new form of ornament.[19] At first the mauresque tended to sweep all before it, replacing ornament of classical derivation. Important standing cups or ewers, as that shown in a drawing attributed to Wenzel Jamnitzer himself,[20] relied mainly and sometimes exclusively on the mauresque. Soon, however, the more traditional forms returned and the mauresque was confined to the border of foot or bowl. On vessels of German origin the mauresque was either engraved or etched; etching being particularly favoured by German goldsmiths, but little used elsewhere.

Drawings by or attributed to Wenzel Jamnitzer are preserved in the Library of the University of Erlangen[21] and also in the Victoria and Albert Museum. The latter group consists of fourteen pen and colour-wash drawings which were formerly bound in a codex with a large number of other goldsmiths' designs by Erasmus Hornick and his contemporaries, though they were probably associated with those by Hornick at some later date (see p.245). Whether they are the work of Wenzel Jamnitzer himself, or Matthias Zündt or some other follower or assistant can hardly now be determined. An assistant in the workshop might well have mastered the style of Wenzel Jamnitzer so completely that a drawing from his hand, which elaborated a sketch by the master, would hardly differ from a finished drawing done entirely by Jamnitzer. A comparison between some of these drawings and those by Zündt in the *New Kunstbuch* or the *Kraterographie* establishes the close relationship between them; thus the pilgrim flask (pl. 135) from the latter and the drawing (pl. XV) are strikingly similar. The ornament of these two flasks and perhaps of the ewer and companion basin designs (pls. XV, 130), consisting of an arrangement of strapwork centering on a human figure, often a bound satyr, and enclosing birds and animals within its convolutions, was probably taken over by Zündt from Jamnitzer. From the same Jamnitzer workshop as the drawings, but not necessarily from the same hand, is the design for a basin (pl. 131). This is a working drawing, one of the rarest types of sixteenth-century goldsmiths' designs. It will be seen that the drawings illustrated in plates 126 to 131, all of which are attributed to the Jamnitzer workshop, are less fantastic than the engraved pattern-book designs. The artist who was preparing designs for a pattern-book that would be used as a source of ideas by other masters, could allow his imagination free rein without concerning himself unduly about problems of execution. He could leave it to the working goldsmith to omit impracticable detail. On the other hand, drawings such as that on pl. 131 were intended to be copied literally by the goldsmith and the design must be kept within the bounds of practicability. Nevertheless, the success with which sixteenth-century masters translated the grotesque and often contorted forms devised by the masters of ornament into vessels of gold and silver has never been equalled. Jamnitzer did not publish a pattern-book himself and, apart from his extant works, his style is best represented by Zündt's *Kratero-graphie*.

Virgil Solis and Matthias Zündt

How far Jamnitzer was himself the inventor of some of the innovations in design that he introduced is difficult to ascertain. Mannerist ornament was made available to German goldsmiths in general through the publication in Nürnberg of a series of pattern-books by Virgil Solis (1514-1562) and by Matthias Zündt. Virgil Solis's numerous sheets are undated and, in view of their differing format, it is difficult to establish their chronology and relationship to each other. So large was Solis's *oeuvre* and so various the styles represented in it that he should probably be regarded, not as an original designer, but rather as an engraver of designs that had been thought out by other artists, some of whom were not sufficiently familiar with the burin to be able to cut their own designs in copper. Some two thousand prints by Solis are known, and it is unlikely that he could have been the inventor of them all. Like his contemporaries, he put his monogram on prints that he had copied from other sources, thus recording that he had executed the engraving, but not necessarily claiming any title to the design. The article on Solis in the Thieme-Becker *Künstler Lexikon* lists no fewer than eighteen masters whose work he reproduced, among whom were the Antwerp engraver, Cornelis Floris, and his fellow citizens, Wenzel Jamnitzer and Matthias Zündt. The engravings bearing Solis's name should not, therefore, be regarded as representing the ideas of a single master, but constitute a collection of designs which were thought by him or by Nürnberg artists to be saleable to goldsmiths and to other craftsmen of the time.

The engravings for goldsmiths' work published by Solis fall into two groups which appear to date from two distinct periods. The earlier group, probably dating from the 1540's, shows vessels of conventional Renaissance design, as one might expect to find in the late 1530's in the work of Heinrich Aldegrever of Soest or of Hans Brosamer. However, one must guard against the mistake of ascribing too early a date to such pattern-books, for they were sometimes issued at a time when one would expect their style to be quite unfashionable. There was always a time lag between taste in the larger cities and the provincial towns and what might appear unacceptable in Nürnberg could still be fashionable in Danzig. Thus a third edition of Brosamer's *New Kunstbüchlein* was published in 1570, thirty years after its first appearance, and at a time when sophisticated Mannerist taste was ruling in the northern courts.

Some designs engraved by Solis show an awareness of the dramatic sculptural effects that the Italian engravers, such as Enea Vico or Agostino dei Musi, had taken over from classical antiquity (pl. 122). Solis was also the first to introduce in his prints of ornament the crowded style that determined German design during most of the second half of the sixteenth century (pls. 118-21). This manner was derived from the prints of ornament published by the Antwerp engravers, Cornelis Floris and Cornelis Bos: its introduction to Germany should probably be attributed to Wenzel Jamnitzer. He was, in fact, long regarded as its originator but was later excluded on the grounds that he had merely followed the fashionable style of the period. The credit for designs such as those in pls. 118-121 and 128-131 was given partly to Solis and partly to Zündt, because their names appeared on the prints which popularised the style. Solis can be excluded as the author of the second group, since he was primarily an engraver and not a draughtsman to the goldsmiths' trade. Matthias Zündt is a more likely candidate. The first we know of him is that he was a journeyman in Jamnitzer's workshop when in 1551 he published his *Kraterographie*, the most comprehensive exposition of the Jamnitzer style. In 1554, when he applied for but was refused citizenship of Nürnberg he was described as a hardstone cutter (*Steinschneider*). Two years later in 1556 he was through Jamnitzer's influence admitted as citizen and in 1560 he became a master-goldsmith. In 1559 when he was negotiating with the Archduke Ferdinand of Tirol about a table-fountain he called himself a *Bildschnitzer* (carver). It seems, therefore, that his activities in the goldsmith's shop were directed more towards designing and model-carving than to working the precious metal. This is confirmed by the fact that he produced a large number of engravings on copper during his lifetime in addition to the goldsmiths' pattern-book.

The prevailing feeling in Zündt's *Kraterographie* is that of overcrowded ornament (*horror vacui*) in which the eye is given no opportunity for repose. The profile of his vessels is as complicated as their surface treatment; they are encumbered with numerous projections: brackets, medallion busts, figures and applied castings from nature of small animals, insects and flowers (pls. 133, 134, 136). With the exception of a few ewer designs, whose very function required them to be asymmetrical (Pl. 134), Zündt adhered to exact symmetry. While in the designs engraved by Solis, presumably after Jamnitzer, a standing figure of a satyr (pl. 137) or a group of figures forms the stem of the cup, Zündt followed the Renaissance system of piling one horizontal element on another to form the base and stem. Another feature that occurs in the Solis, but not the Zündt, engravings is the combination of several different purposes in a single vessel, usually a large standing cup (pl. 137). This design provides only for a cup, a bowl and a salt but others incorporate a candlestick, a beaker, a dish, a pepper-sifter and a small clock. The ingenious device of concealing one element within another is a characteristic expression of Mannerism and can be paralleled in Mannerist literature.[22]

Multiple-purpose Vessels

Such combined vessels were exported from Germany, probably finding a market abroad because of their unusual character. In July 1553, when John Dudley, Duke of Northumberland, was thrown into the Tower of London before his attainder and eventual execution, some ten thousand ounces of plate were taken from his various residences and confiscated.[23] Among the articles seized were two combined cups and candlesticks. The inventory description, made when the confiscation took place, runs as follows 'ij almon bolles wt candlesticks in the bottome all gilt'. Their weight was sixty-two ounces. The same two vessels appear in the 1574 *Inventory of the Jewels and Plate of Queen Elizabeth I* with a slightly more detailed description: 'two Almaine bolles chasid with vine knottes on thone side and likewise within and fyve studdes a pece with womens heddes ther feete to serve for Candlestickes'. They are also listed in subsequent royal inventories, but like the rest of the Tudor plate were melted or sold during the reign of James I or Charles I. The use of the term 'Almaine' in the English inventories makes it clear that the pieces were of German origin and a few German examples have survived, though in an incomplete state.[24] A standing cup in a private collection consists of three parts, a drinking-bowl, a socket candlestick and a small tazza. All three can be assembled to form a cup, the tazza screwing into the foot of the cup.[25] The piece appears to date from about 1570-80 and bears the Nürnberg town mark with an unidentified maker's mark, a spray of three leaves within a shaped shield. A second example is of strikingly similar design but is the work of another goldsmith (pls. 442, 445-6). This belongs to a travelling set of which several parts survive, though they are no longer all preserved together. There is a pair of candlestick cups, without, however, the tazza in the base, a pair of footed tazzas and a single cover. The pair of candlestick cups and the single cover remain together, while the pair of tazzas have found their way into another collection and their present location is unknown to me. Presumably the various pieces in this set were originally supplied in a fitted box such as that illustrated in pl. 185, but large cups were also made, into which a number of other vessels were inserted. The first three items in the 1574 *Inventory of the Plate of Queen Elizabeth I* under the heading 'Cuppes of silver guilt'[26] are of this type; no. 192 is described as follows:

> Oone Double Antique Cup guilt embossed containing therin xij Spones guilt twelve knives thauftes wodde tippid with siluer guilte foure Goblettes guilt two Saultes and xij Trenchers parcell guilt the foote being two Chaudellours with a paire of Nippers and twelve Forkes guilte poiz togethers . . . . ccvj oz.

Wenzel Jamnitzer, his Extant Works

Among Jamnitzer's inventions was his use of castings taken directly from natural objects. His skill in preparing these was such that some of the vessels he decorated in this way rank amongst the most remarkable creations of the Mannerist goldsmiths. His finest essay in this manner was his inkstand, presumably made for the Emperor and now in the Kunsthistorisches Museum, Vienna.[27] The top and sides of this are decorated with the most lifelike castings of beetles, shells, moss and the like. The silver bell (pl. 423) is decorated in the same way and with a comparable mastery of casting technique. Jamnitzer perfected his method of casting at a comparatively early date in his working life, and his earliest extant design, that of Charles V's state sword (pl. 220), already shows, surprisingly enough, applied figures of newts. His technical skill in making these castings was greatly admired by his contemporaries and the Nürnberg writing master, Johann Neudörfer, who was also a personal friend, left an account of Wenzel and his brother, Albrecht, in which, after praising their piety towards their elderly parents, he continues 'They both work in gold and silver, are masters of proportion and perspective, cut coats-of-arms and seal dies in silver, stone and iron. They enamel in the most beautiful colours and have brought the technique of silver etching to the highest pitch of excellence. Their skill in making castings of little animals, worms, grasses and snails in silver and decorating silver vessels therewith has never been heard of before and they have presented me with a whole silver snail, cast with all kinds of flowers and grasses around it; and the said flowers and grasses are so delicate and thin that they move when one blows on them'.[28] The minute figures of reptiles and insects introduced by Jamnitzer became one of the standard features of German goldsmithing, not only in Nürnberg, but in Augsburg and other cities influenced by Nürnberg fashion.

Jamnitzer's standing in the city of Nürnberg was such that already in 1549 he was commissioned by the council to produce his most remarkable extant work, the great centre-piece (pls. 416-420) known as the *Merckelsche Tafelaufsatz* after the Nürnberg merchant who bought it at the auction sale of the city silver treasure in 1806 and so saved it from destruction by melting.[29] It was doubtless intended to be presented to some important visitor to the city, perhaps the Emperor himself, but, for some reason unknown to us, remained in the possession of the city. A blank escutcheon on the base was presumably meant for the armorial bearings of the eventual recipient. Its character was such that it can hardly have been suited to the needs of the fathers even of so rich a city as Nürnberg. In the same year, 1549, a silver table was also purchased by the city council from Wenzel Jamnitzer, but this has not survived, probably because it was, in fact, presented. In considering Jamnitzer's significance as a goldsmith this table-centre constitutes an important starting-point, as, despite its early date, it already illustrates an advanced state in the development of Mannerist art. As a rule the designers of goldsmiths' work were ahead of the craftsmen in ideas, but in this case it was the working goldsmith whose ideas had outstripped the designers. The centre-piece is based on a philosophical programme. The foot (pl. 416) represents the earth from which life springs; this idea followed the contemporary architectural conceit of treating the base of a building with rock-faced rustication to symbolise the living rock from which it sprang, while the upper stories were built of wrought stone. In this centre-piece Jamnitzer has followed a consistent programme, but in some of his work there is a fundamental contradiction in his combination of carefully composed classical ornament with grasses and flowers cast from nature. It was a curious practice of some sixteenth-century goldsmiths to decorate their vessels with cartouches etched or engraved with Latin verses, which explained the purpose or the intellectual programme of the piece or gave the requisite historical background to the subject represented on a panel or frieze. This was entirely in accord with the characteristic Renaissance love of asserting classical knowledge, even in the most unlikely context. In the case of Jamnitzer's centre-piece the comments explain how all the necessities of life spring from Mother Earth. Other examples are the Holbein cup with its verses relating to sobriety and to inebriation (pls. 645-7) and the

Strassburg cup (pl. 547) in which the Latin verses explain the scenes drawn from Roman history.

Among the notable features of the centre piece is the circular plaque that fills the centre of the bowl (pl. 420). This has been ingeniously composed from details of Renaissance ornament, picked out from the pilaster designs of Daniel Hopfer or one of his German contemporaries after an Italian source. The cornucopiae, putti, eagles and trophies of arms are all of Renaissance type and combine with the enamelled roundels they enclose to produce an extremely rich effect. It would be hard to parallel this panel in contemporary German goldsmiths' work; in it we see Wenzel Jamnitzer at the height of his powers. The plaque is surrounded by an etched overlapping leaf border, a technique of ornament that was then an unfamiliar element in German decorative art. The centre-piece is, moreover, one of the earliest Renaissance show pieces constructed with such an elaboration of ornament that it could hardly have served any practical purpose. Medieval inventories make it clear that complex decorative objects intended purely for show had then adorned the sideboards and cupboards, but none survive. According to the programme explained in the verses, the centre-piece should have born the fruits of the Earth in the bowl, but this is so delicately enamelled and the grasses that surround it so fragile that it would be difficult to fill the bowl without damaging it. This was not the only occasion when Jamnitzer introduced decorative detail that seriously interfered with the apparent function of a vessel. This applies in particular to the grasses and minute insects with which he liked to adorn his works; one example is the silver, parcel-gilt, basin in the Louvre (pl. 421) while another even more strikingly impracticable is the basin with its companion ewer in the cathedral treasury of Dubrovnik. In the latter case the shells and other natural growths spring so luxuriantly from the lower part of the body of the ewer that its profile is obscured and grasses project so far from its spout that it could hardly be used for pouring water. The basin is so full of similar growths that it could contain but little liquid.[31]

Typical of Wenzel Jamnitzer's exploitation of casts from nature as ornament are the silver table bell in the British Museum (pl. 423) and its counterpart in the Munich Schatzkammer.[32] There is a drawing for one or other of these bells in the Berlin Kunstbibliothek. In the past both have been attributed to Wenzel's son, Hans Jamnitzer, although they in no way resemble the latter's identified works. The attribution was founded on an entry in the Vienna accounts of the year 1558 recording the payment to Hans Jamnitzer of the sum of 54 gulden and a free livery in respect of a silver table-bell he had made for the Emperor Ferdinand I.[33] The reference to payment gives no further detail about the bell but it must have been a piece of great ingenuity or splendour to justify so high a price. In 1558 Hans was, however, still a journeyman aged twenty and it was not till five years later, in 1563, that he was admitted master. The most probable explanation is that the clerk who recorded the payment made a mistake in the Christian name of the artist and wrote Hans instead of Wenzel.[34] An examination of these bells illustrates the difficulties encountered in taking casts from the fragile wings or legs of insects. Many of them are imperfect. Great skill must also have been needed to give an appearance of life to the newts and other creatures which had to be killed before being prepared for casting. The fashion for decorating silver vessels with figures of insects and reptiles cast from nature persisted into the seventeenth century and the bases of both vessels and figures continued to be profusely adorned with them. There is an interesting contemporary reference to such decoration in a letter[35] written by Phillip Hainhofer, the Augsburg diplomat and antique dealer, to his customer and patron, Duke Philipp of Pomerania, in which he states that the Augsburg goldsmith, Christoph Lencker, 'still has a large snake cast entirely of silver, and a number of little lizards which were cast by old Lorenz....he paid 8 florins for a lizard and refuses to sell any of them, looking on them as a treasure: there is no chiselled work on these reptiles and grasses, but they are entirely cast from life'.

The Lorenz referred to by Hainhofer must have been the Augsburg goldsmith, Lorenz Dhem, who had produced the castings needed for a fountain commissioned by

Duke Wilhelm of Bavaria. For this he had made a huge tortoise and six crabs as well as a quantity of snakes, lizards, frogs etc. Though the casting of such creatures is usually associated with the name of Wenzel Jamnitzer, the skill was soon acquired by other masters.[36] Vessels decorated with castings from nature by Jamnitzer or his followers also found their way abroad where they were copied. The basin from the French royal collection and another complete with its ewer in the cathedral of Dubrovnik have already been mentioned, while a third piece of the same type, but of far greater importance, is recorded in the *Inventory of the Plate of Queen Elizabeth I.* It was purchased in 1583 from Sir Richard Martin, a London goldsmith who subsequently became Lord Mayor of London. This was of vast proportions, weighing no less than 404 ounces. It is described in the list of accessions for 1583[37] in the following terms:-

'Item oone faire great standing Cup guilt with a Cover the body garnisshed with sundrey vermen as Snakes Ewetes (newts) Frogges and others the said body and foote also laide with sundrey collours the cover garnisshed with sundrey men and beastes hunting with a Stagge in the toppe thereof bought of the saide Alderman Marten poiz.ccciiij oz.'

The same cup was noticed in the following year by a German traveller who commented on the masterly modelling and natural colouring of the reptiles. Such large showpieces were acquired by the Crown to serve as gifts when the occasion arose and this cup may have been purchased because of its great size and value rather than the original character of its ornament. At all events it was passed on in 1594 as a present to James VI of Scotland at the christening of his eldest son, Henry.

Wenzel Jamnitzer is one of the few German sixteenth-century goldsmiths of whose work we know enough to form a coherent idea of his style and development. In his long lifetime he witnessed the rejection of Renaissance principles and their replacement by a variety of fashions. Most of these fashions are reflected in his works which range from orthodox Renaissance to Gothic Revival and extreme Mannerism. The mounted jasper cup (pl. 422) is typical of his more conservative manner, while his neo-Gothic manner can be seen in the *Doppel Pokal* which he made for the Tucher family (pl. 425). The fashion introduced or re-introduced by Jamnitzer with this piece was followed in the later decades of the century by so many others that one can without exaggeration speak of a Gothic Revival (see p.131).

Documentary sources show that Jamnitzer received many important commissions from the Habsburg family. In 1556 he was commissioned to make a large combined centre-piece and table-fountain for the Emperor Maximilian II and at about the same time Archduke Ferdinand of Tirol ordered another from him. The first was not completed and delivered until 1578, when Maximilian had already been succeeded by his brother Rudolph II (see p.130). The second fountain was never completed and was finally abandoned. Some idea of the appearance of these table-fountains can be gained from a large-scale drawing of one, of which slightly differing versions exist in the Veste Coburg (pl. 127) and the Basel Kupferstichkabinett. In the production of these huge fountains Jamnitzer needed a technical understanding of the uses of water-power and a knowledge of history and mythology that could hardly lie within the capacity of one man. In the planning of their complex philosophical programme he was probably helped by contemporary humanists.

Table-fountains were by no means new inventions; several drawings by Albrecht Dürer show that they were familiar items on the table of the nobility. On the other hand, Wenzel Jamnitzer does seem to have been the first to introduce the large caskets which also extended the range of the goldsmith into the world of philosophy. Eventually they became one of the most important lines of the leading Nürnberg and Augsburg goldsmiths, but the earliest recorded was one made by Jamnitzer in 1570, now preserved in the Convent of the Descalzas Reales at Madrid.[38] Of several surviving caskets by Wenzel Jamnitzer this is the most imposing. It was presented to the convent for use as a reliquary by Anna of Austria, Queen of Philip II. She had probably received it as part of her dowry on her marriage to Philip II from her father, the Emperor Maximilian II, who was a regular patron of Wenzel. It is signed in unusually explicit manner on a cartouche '1570 Noric. aurifaber Venclaus Gamnitzer ista Aeterni fecit ductus amore boni'. A preliminary drawing for this casket was formerly in the Stieglitz Museum, Leningrad.[39] Though of large proportions and very elaborate, it is still less rich than the version that was finally executed. The casket is basically of ebony with silver-gilt mounts. The sides are embellished with figures set in niches and with rectangular plaques engraved with grotesques against a red enamel ground. In its construction much use has been made of borders stamped or pressed with the machine invented by Jamnitzer himself. The models for much of the cast ornament on this casket can be found amongst the lead patterns from the Jamnitzer workshop in the Basel Historisches Museum (see p.60). Jamnitzer had worked out his designs for frames enclosing niches with figures of the type that decorate the sides of this casket long before 1570. Two etched designs of such frames signed and dated 'Wenzl Gamniczer 1551' are in the Berlin Kupferstichkab-inett.[40]

Other caskets by Jamnitzer in the treasuries at Munich (pl. 427) and at Dresden were presumably made for the ruling houses of Wittelsbach and Wettin.[41] While the general effect of these caskets is splendid, not least on account of their polychromy, this was achieved with a certain economy of means. In the case of the Jamnitzer casket at Dresden, while the triglyph and metope frieze is cast, the six panels decorated with strapwork are stamped from sheet silver. The most elaborate of the caskets at Dres-den (pl. 428), though corresponding in style to those bearing the mark or signature of Jamnitzer, is struck with the mark of Nikolaus Schmidt, who was not admitted master until 1582. It was a present from the Elector Christian I (reigned 1586-1591) to his wife and the precise share in its production taken by Jamnitzer and Schmidt respectively is uncertain.[42] The design as a whole is very similar to the signed Jamnitzer casket in Madrid, and it seems that the main credit for its production should be given to Jamnitzer, though the presence of Schmidt's mark probably means that it was not finished until after the former's death. During his lifetime Wenzel Jamnitzer would surely have taken responsiblity for and stamped his mark on all pieces issuing from his workshop. Although the Jamnitzer workshop produced some fine caskets after Wenzel's death, among them that bearing the mark of Hans Jamnitzer illustrated in pl. 444, by the end of the century the goldsmiths of Augsburg were pre-eminent in this particular line, the leading masters being Boas Ulrich and Matthias Wallbaum.

The Jamnitzer caskets followed a type that had been created during the first half of the century by Italian goldsmiths, but silver reliefs were substituted for the rock-crystal intaglios preferred in Italy. The sixteenth-century caskets did not approach the dimen-sions of those designed by Philip Hainhofer and made by Augsburg goldsmiths for his clients in the seventeenth century (see p.229). These, with their multiplicity of drawers containing objects representing the whole range of natural forms and of human creative activity, were intended to serve as a microcosm of the universe and had thus a didatic purpose. The Jamnitzer caskets, though smaller in size, were richer in their ornament and, in character with the spirit of their time, seem to have had no special function apart from having a splendid appearance and being obviously expensive. Some may have held jewels and an inscription inside the casket by Hans Jamnitzer (pl. 444) indicates that this was its purpose. Whereas the later Augsburg caskets were produced by a number of craftsmen working in concert, it is probable that those from Nürnberg were made by just two masters – the goldsmith and the cabinet-maker.

After the Merckel table-centre the most splendid of the existing works of Wenzel Jamnitzer is the huge and imposing Kaiser Pokal (Imperial Cup), which is believed to have been presented to the Emperor Maximilian II on the occasion of his first entry into the city of Nürnberg on 7 June, 1570 (pls. 424, 426). The Kaiser Pokal is, as the solemn occasion demanded, of fairly traditional form, though if one looks into the detail of the ornament, it will be seen that its creator has drawn on a wide range of sources. In com-plete contrast is the extraordinary ewer at Munich (pl. XIII) which is, unfortunately, no longer accompanied by its companion basin. Dozens of sixteenth- and seventeenth-century shell cups survive, but none equals in ingenuity and fantasy this achievement of Wenzel Jamnitzer. While the influence of Cornelis Floris must be admitted (pls. 196-7), Jamnitzer has surpassed his source.

The *Kunstkabinett* of the Basel humanist, Basilius Amerbach, has preserved for us a record of another imperial commission of which all other trace has been lost.[43] This is the silver saddle made for the Emperor Maximilian, probably for his coronation in 1564. All that remains is a somewhat damaged plaster cast for the front plate of the saddle. These repeat the typical Jamnitzer manner but on a rather larger scale: the front takes the form of a figure of Charity with an infant on each side beneath whom is a globe or hemispherical heraldic shield flanked by strapwork clasps from which emerge bunches of fruit. This composition was evidently a favourite of Jamnitzer for it is also found on a small model in the same Amerbach collection and on a series of silver vessels. These include a bowl in the Basel Museum, for which it serves as handle, two similar bowls in the Kunsthistorisches Museum, Vienna[44] and the National Museum, Budapest, and the two table-bells already mentioned in the Munich Schatzkammer and the British Museum (pl. 423) respectively. The most unexpected appearance of the model is, however, its use as a handle for the Holy Water Bucket made by the Warburg goldsmith, Anton Eisenhoit (see p.258) for the Bishop of Paderborn.[45] The plaster cast of Wenzel Jamnitzer's saddle-mount is related to a group of six drawings of designs for saddle-plates, three for front plates and three for rear plates (pl. 160), in the Erlangen Universitätsbibliothek. These do not appear to be in Jamnitzer's hand, but the style with its crowded ornament set within a framework of straps with *Rollwerk* ends shows his influence. Extant saddle-plates of this type are all wrought in iron and it is not certain whether these designs were meant to be in precious or in base metal. The survival of the cast from the Emperor Maximilian's saddle does, however, suggest that silver was used for saddle-plates.

In the nineteenth century Wenzel Jamnitzer was credited with almost superhuman powers but pieces bearing his mark show considerable variation in quality, doubtless because his workshop was large and not all the pieces issuing from it received his personal supervision. As a man of the Renaissance, he was greatly interested in science and in the perfection of methods of manufacture, including the substitution of the machine for hand-production. The tools he invented were used by other goldsmiths, the most popular being a roller stamp and the model for the frieze of triglyphs and metopes. This is found on the Elias Lencker desk and on the Nicholaus Schmidt casket already mentioned, on the Hans Jamnitzer casket in Stuttgart (pl. 447), on another by Hans Straub in the Berlin Kunstgewerbe Museum[46] and on a cup by Hans Petzoldt in the Hamburg Museum für Kunst und Gewerbe.[47] All these masters worked in Nürnberg. Panels of ornament composed of low relief strapwork surrounding a central figure of the type introduced by Wenzel Jamnitzer became very popular in the goldsmiths' shops of the second half of the sixteenth century. A large number of cups, ewers and basins decorated in this way survive. Most were made in Nürnberg (pls. 436, 483) but the style was also known in other cities and countries (pl. 554). This ornament was probably preferred by the less skilful goldsmiths because it was easier to execute, and by the customer because it was fashionable. Instead of being embossed by hand it was cast from moulds made from patterns which were supplied by other goldsmiths. The production of these patterns was a speciality of the Nürnberg masters; a large collection of them (pls. 429-35) mostly from the Jamnitzer workshop, is preserved in the Amerbach *Kunstkabinett*. These lead patterns, which were produced in the goldsmiths' own workshops, should be distinguished from the cast bronze or brass patterns (*Patronen*) made by the *Patronschnitzer* and *Patrongiesser*. The latter were only roughly modelled and were used as patterns upon which silver plaquettes were pressed or hammered.

Like Benvenuto Cellini before him, Jamnitzer tried his fortune in France, but, instead of going himself, sent his eldest son, also called Wenzel. In this case the result was disastrous; Wenzel Jamnitzer the Younger went to Paris in 1572 on the occasion of the wedding of Henri of Navarre, later Henri IV of France, and Margaret of Valois, daughter of King Henri II, taking with him a fine silver table, a mirror and other items, pro-

Plate XXI
Pair of parcel-gilt dishes. North German or Baltic, last quarter of 16th century.

Plate XXII
Gilt tankard. Made by Sebastian Liebhardt, Pressburg, late 16th century.

bably making up a complete toilet service. He presumably hoped that it would find a purchaser among the princes or nobility attending the occasion and that it would be given as a present to the royal pair. Unfortunately Wenzel the Younger either died or was killed in the St. Bartholomew's night massacre in Paris and, according to French law, the whole of the deceased's property devolved upon the French king. With the help of the *Bürgermeister* and of the City Council of Nürnberg his father tried to recover his property on the grounds that it had belonged to him and not to his son and that its loss would reduce him to penury.[48] Unfortunately the outcome of this critical affair is not recorded but the incident throws an interesting light on commercial practice among the wealthy goldsmiths of the time, since it suggests that Jamnitzer could afford to make on his own account and hold in stock pieces of sufficient importance to be worthy of presentation to a royal bride. There may, however, be another explanation; the pieces could have been commissioned for another client who had died before taking delivery, thus leaving them on Jamnitzer's hands. Jamnitzer ran a comparable risk in 1553 when Duke Philip Magnus of Braunschweig was killed in battle after having placed a large order for silver to a total value of some 4800 florins.[49] All work was stopped on the order, but in this case the commission was acknowledged by Philip's successor, Heinrich Julius of Braunschweig, and the order was completed. That Jamnitzer had other commercial connections with France is indicated by the existence of Limoges enamels mounted in silver-gilt by him. There is a Limoges ewer with companion basin dated 1562, the mounts of which bear Wenzel Jamnitzer's mark, in the Germanisches National-almuseum,[50] and another almost identical but unmarked, in the Munich Schatzkammer.[51] The former is part of a service of Limoges enamel vessels ordered by the Tucher family of Nürnberg and bearing their arms. It is possible that the Tuchers procured the enamels and gave them to Jamnitzer for mounting but the existence of a second ewer apparently mounted by him suggests that he may well have ordered and imported them himself.

Hans Jamnitzer

Three of Wenzel Jamnitzer's sons became goldsmiths; the eldest also called Wenzel, predeceased him, but two others, Hans and Abraham, were admitted masters in Nürnberg in 1563 and 1579 respectively. What survives of Abraham's work is not remarkable by Nürnberg standards,[52] but Hans was a goldsmith of considerable stature. Like many other leading German goldsmiths he went to Italy as a journeyman and in 1558 was working for the Duke of Ferrara. After his return to Nürnberg and admission to the guild he followed in his father's footsteps and in 1569 was appointed seal die-cutter to the city. His appointment to this office shows that he was exceptionally skilled in the technique of die-cutting and hence of chasing, but within a few weeks he was dismissed for swindling his fellow goldsmith, Christoph Lindenberger, out of two drinking-cups.[53] In 1571 he was commissioned by the Emperor Maximilian II to supply two seals and at the same time he supplied a quantity of small animals cast from nature — a well-known speciality of the Jamnitzer workshop. He was in trouble with the city authorities again in 1582 when he was warned against making enamelled medals (*Schaugroschen*). According to Wenzel's will, Hans had borrowed money from him on more than one occasion, but by 1584, the year of the will, he had resumed a respectable life and Wenzel was well satisfied with him.[54] In his later years he was, like his father before him, nominated a member of the Great Council (*Grosser Rat*) of Nürnberg. He died in 1603.

Hans Jamnitzer is thought to have been the master of many finely-chased tazza bowls — altogether over twenty tazza bowls or plaquettes after such bowls have been attributed to him.[55] He seems to have had more than average sculptural skill and it has been suggested that he may have carved the boxwood models for the reliefs of the figures of the Planets on the silver-gilt mounted lapis lazuli casket struck with Hans Straub's mark in the Kunstgewerbemuseum, Berlin.[56] His hand has also been recognised in the modelling of the figure of the risen Christ which is set in the base of the foot of the Jonas Silber *Weltallschale*.[57] Only one major piece bearing Hans Jamnitzer's mark, as opposed to his monogram, is known: this is the mother-of-pearl casket with jewelled silver-gilt mounts (pl. 447) from the *Kunstkammer* of the Dukes of Württemberg, now in the Württembergisches Landesmuseum, Stuttgart. This piece conforms to the type introduced by Wenzel Jamnitzer, but is less spectacular in size and splendour, though the colour combination of gilt and mother-of-pearl is very attractive. The casket does not fit into the picture of Hans Jamnitzer as a master who specialised on embossing and chasing since much of the ornament of the borders has been applied with a revolving stamp, but it may have been made immediately after he had left his father's workshop and was still following his style.

There are two reasons for the attribution of so many plaquettes to Hans Jamnitzer: firstly his known skill in relief work, and secondly the fact that a group of four plaquettes exist each bearing the initials H.G. together with a date. One of these (pl. 438) is chased in silver, the others are cast in base metal (pl. 440), but derive from a boxwood or silver original by Jamnitzer. The initial letters G and J were almost interchangeable in the sixteenth century and the records of the Nürnberg guild show Jamnitzer's name spelt with either initial letter. The four plaquettes are dated between 1569 and 1572 and therefore fit well into Jamnitzer's known period of activity. On the other hand, the initials are not unusual and there is no definite proof that any of these plaquettes should be attributed to him. On the strength of the signed H.G. plaquettes a number of features have been identified as characteristic of Hans Jamnitzer's style. These include the very careful rendering of foliage of different types of tree, the piling up of the background with many-towered cities and high mountains and the treatment of clouds like rolls of cotton-wool pulled out to a point at each end (pl. 438-9). These details appeared in the lead patterns (pl. 440) that the goldsmiths copied and are therefore likely to be found in tazza bowls, or in casts from them, by other masters. His patterns were derived from graphic sources, usually prints after paintings by fashionable masters such as Joseph Heinz, Bartholomäus Spranger, Hendrik Goltzius, Christoph Schwarz or H. Bol. The original prints were often engraved in circular form to make the work of adaptation easier but sometimes the goldsmith had to adapt a rectangular print to the circle of the tazza bowl himself.

There is a great variation in quality in the embossing of the figure subjects on tazza bowls and few German examples equal the quality of those produced by Dutch masters, in particular by the Van Vianen family of Utrecht. If, Hans Jamnitzer was, in fact, the master of the H.G. tazzas, then he must rank as the first of the German masters in this respect, followed by his son, Christoph, who in his turn became one of the most skilled chasers of his time (pls. 509-514). Presumably he would have learnt this skill under his father's guidance. The whole subject of the authorship of embossed scenes on tazzas is a difficult one as most of them are not signed and individual hands cannot be distinguished with certainty.

Barthel Jamnitzer

Barthel, the son of Wenzel's brother, Albrecht, must rank as a minor master of the Jamnitzer family, though he is represented by a series of nautilus-cups with silver-gilt mounts in the Grünes Gewölbe, in Stuttgart and in the Rothschild collections. Perhaps his finest extant piece is the glass tankard with pierced silver-gilt mounts in the Rijksmuseum: the same museum has a gilt ewer with embossed body by him that maintains the highest standards of the Jamnitzer family.[58]

Jonas Silber

A slightly younger contemporary of Hans Jamnitzer, Jonas Silber, who came to Nürnberg from Kulmbach, was another leading designer and maker of plaquettes for goldsmiths. A large number, decorated with figures and animals after the manner of Peter Flötner, have been attributed to him or his workshop. Like most of his contemporaries he made use of prints as the source of his compositions. In addition to plaquettes he produced a large number of designs in the dotted technique (see p.238) for the guidance of goldsmiths working in relief. For the most part he seems to have worked for other goldsmiths rather than on his own account, but he was the creator of one of the most important Mannerist vessels, the covered tazza called the Weltallschale[59] (pls. 474-5). He was first apprenticed to a goldsmith in Bern and then subsequently to Wenzel Jamnitzer. He was admitted master in 1572 and, after two years as Court Goldsmith to the Elector Palatine in Heidelberg and a period of uncertain length as a coin die-engraver in Danzig, he returned to Nürnberg where he was established before 1589, the year in which he completed the tazza. According to the history of the piece given when it was presented to the King of Prussia by the Jewish community of Halberstadt in 1703, it was originally made for the Emperor Rudolph II, who was said to have worked out its programme himself.[60] Whether the tradition is true or not, there can be no doubt that its quality made it worthy of the Imperial Treasury, and the complex symbolism of its design would surely have appealed to the melancholic and introspective Emperor. One would expect so important a commission to have gone to the Jamnitzer workshop, but it is possible that Silber was employed by Wenzel Jamnitzer after his return to Nürnberg and took on the commission after Wenzel's death. Despite its small size and the limited area available for conveying its message, this vessel was intended to symbolise nothing less than the history of the world. It would be difficult to imagine a more characteristically Mannerist example of the goldsmith's art; not only could it not be used, but it could only be understood if it were picked up and each part studied with care. Starting with Christ the Redeemer on the base, one passes by the Continents that have yet to be saved, through the Old and New Testaments to the world as then constituted with the political system on the underside, and the geographical distribution of power on the upper side of the bowl. The cover illustrates the history of Germany and on the underside celebrates her power, while the heavenly bodies are represented above and, finally, Christ is shown ruling over all. The theme of this tazza is, therefore, much the same as that of the large table-fountain made by Wenzel Jamnitzer described on p.130 but it is represented on a minute scale. Without the help of a written explanation of its meaning even a person learned in history and science might find it difficult to comprehend. This concentration of a wide range of abstract ideas within the compass of a small piece of domestic plate is a typical manifestation of the Mannerist delight in conceits and prodigies of ingenuity. No other comparable work by Silber is known and if the suggestion that it was devised by the Emperor Rudolph is correct, it may indeed have stood alone in his *oeuvre*. So alike are the plaquettes by the Nürnberg masters of the second half of the sixteenth century that it is difficult to attribute them with certainty. Later research may add to the number of Silber's recognised works.

Nikolaus Schmidt

Another Nürnberg goldsmith who was trained in Wenzel Jamnitzer's workshop and subsequently produced outstanding work was Nikolaus Schmidt, who became a master in 1582. Strangely enough, his masterpiece was rejected by the guild when first submitted and it was only as the result of Jamnitzer's personal intervention that he was allowed to try again. He collaborated with Wenzel Jamnitzer on the Dresden casket and is represented both at Vienna and at Dresden by vessels that rank among the finest of their time. Among other pieces by him, both these cities have a magnificent ewer and basin (pls. 476-8). So original is the design of the Dresden ewer (pl. 476) that it has been attributed to Wenzel Jamnitzer's grandson, Christoph, rather than the master whose mark it bears. As has been explained above, the mark on a vessel is not necessarily that of the master who made it, but, in the absence of compelling grounds to the contrary, one is bound to accept it. The Vienna ewer (pl. 478) conforms to the Renaissance type but its decoration is highly original. Once again mother-of-pearl plays a major part in its design, but its most striking feature is the splendid sculptural ornament. Both ewers are accompanied by their original basins. While the ewers differ considerably, the basins are of similar design, even to having the same figures of river-gods in high relief applied to their borders (pl. 477). No decoration has been given to the mother-of-pearl plaques. In view of the comparatively small value of this material, it may seem strange that it was considered worthy to adorn such magnificent pieces of gilt plate, but its attractive colour and inherent appropriateness to vessels intended to contain water explain its use. Both basins are further decorated with many small figures of reptiles cast from nature. Like other goldsmiths trained in the Jamnitzer workshop, Nikolaus Schmidt took a somewhat naive pleasure in these cast figures and introduced them wherever possible, irrespective of their relationship to other elements of ornament of the same object. There is reason to think that Schmidt may have looked outside his own workshop for some of the sculptural details he used. There is a definite contrast in style between the female figures on the Vienna ewer, which are of German derivation, and the recumbent male and female figures on the borders of the two basins, which seem to derive from a master familiar with Venetian late sixteenth-century sculpture. One of Nikolaus Schmidt's most eclectic creations is an elaborate nautilus-shell cup (pl. 473). In this case the sculptural detail is masterly, though the design as a whole gives a somewhat disorganised impression. By the last years of the sixteenth century, the period of this piece, the use of shell was becoming more common; of the various shells available the nautilus and after it the trochus were the most admired and sought after, and consequently, the most richly mounted.

Jakob Fröhlich

A significant innovation in German design was the introduction during the third quarter of the sixteenth century of the decoration of the bowls of cups with a continuous frieze. This had been adopted earlier in Antwerp but probably did not become usual in the German workshops until after the mid-century. It offered an attractive alternative to the panels of grotesques derived from Wenzel Jamnitzer (pl. 436). The type is illustrated in the standing cup of the London Broderers' Company (pl. 483). In this the lobed border which was to become so dominant a feature of late sixteenth-century neo-Gothic cups is confined to the lip of the bowl. The body is cylindrical, composed of two cast plaques, the points of junction of which can clearly be seen. The need to find space for a frieze of mythological, historical or hunting scenes inhibited the freedom of the designer and such cups tend to follow a standard pattern. Several by Jakob Fröhlich, the maker of the cup illustrated, survive. Admitted master to the Nürnberg guild in 1555, he died in 1579; during the intervening years he produced cups of conventional Renaissance form as well as lobate cups and others wrought in the form of animals. He is represented here by the unusual covered beaker set with *verre fixé* panels and enriched with enamelling (pl. 486).

Hans Petzoldt

One of the most famous and most prolific Nürnberg goldsmiths of the second half of the sixteenth century was Hans Petzoldt, who was born in 1551, admitted master in 1578 and died in 1633.[61] He was fortunate inasmuch as he enjoyed the patronage of the Nürnberg City Council which regularly covered its needs for presentation plate from his workshop. In the period between 1595 and 1616 for which records are available, no fewer than eighty-four silver vessels were purchased from him for presentation to important visitors or to other persons who had rendered some service to the City that could not be rewarded appropriately by a cash payment.[62]

In view of the large number of pieces produced by Petzoldt within a fairly short space of time, nearly all large standing cups (pls. 479-482, 484), it is not surprising that he should have repeated himself and that some of his most handsome productions, such as the splendid nautilus-cup illustrated in pl. 479, exist in several identical or almost identical versions. Two of these, identical in every respect are in the *Kunstkammer* of the Dukes of Württemberg, while a third is in the Museum of Decorative Art, Budapest. In this respect he seems to have been an exception amongst the Nürnberg goldsmiths; his contemporaries, even when making use of the same casting patterns, usually assembled them in a different manner in order to avoid exact repetition of the same design. One of Petzoldt's cups, purchased in 1610, was presented to none other than Christoph Jamnitzer himself in recognition of certain services he had rendered to the City Council. This took the usual form of a bunch of grapes (pl. 480). Petzoldt resembled Jamnitzer in his mastery of sculptural detail or, perhaps in his success in finding first rate modellers. The figures that crown the covers of his cups are of larger size and higher sculptural pretensions than the small figures of one or other of a few standardised patterns that are found on most cups of the period. The original device of decorating the cover of a nautilus-cup with a large demi-figure (pl. 479) enabled him to add a plastic dimension to the piece and to give it a more interesting profile. Petzoldt is of particular interest on account of his enthusiastic adoption of the revived Gothic style (pl. 482). A high proportion of the cups purchased from him by the Nürnberg Council are described as *knorret,* that is to say, they were decorated with lobes in the Gothic manner. His exploitation of Gothic revival forms had greater influence on his contemporaries in the Nürnberg guild than did the more original style of his rival, Christoph Jamnitzer, who, instead of looking back to the first half of the century, anticipated the germinating Baroque. Petzoldt's influence was doubtless due, on part, to his favoured position *vis à vis* the City Council. It was natural that the style favoured by the City Fathers should have been followed by other customers and other goldsmiths, and as a result this archaising style of Petzoldt persisted until late in the seventeenth century. It may indeed have contributed to the decline of Nürnberg and the emergence of Augsburg as the chief centre of the art of the goldsmith in South Germany, which took place about the end of the sixteenth century. Like other prominent Nürnberg goldsmiths, Petzoldt also received a summons from the Emperor Rudolph to go to Prague to work for him.[63] His first visit there was in 1604 when he worked upon a silver fountain, a commission for which he received the sum of 3166 gulden paid in three instalments in June, July and August, 1605.[64] Writing in 1730, the historian of the city of Nürnberg, Johann Gabriel Doppelmayr,[65] stated that Petzoldt had been engaged on the repair of a fountain and one is tempted to identify it with that delivered by Wenzel Jamnitzer to the Emperor Rudolph in 1578. The amount seems, however, large if no more than repairs were called for. A note made in the account books referring to these payments mentions a further 3693 gulden due to Petzoldt for other goldsmiths' work he had completed, indicating that he must have received a number of major commissions at this time. The considerable sums mentioned do not seem to have sufficed to cover the total cost of Petzoldt's work for the Emperor, for in 1608 he received a further 1087 gulden towards his bill for the fountain and other works.[66] In 1616 the Emperor Matthias requested the City Council of Nürnberg to allow Petzoldt to visit Prague again, but we do not know what his commission involved. His bill on this occasion amounted to 1500 thaler.

Some forty cups by Petzoldt have been identified, an exceptionally high rate of survival for a sixteenth-century goldsmith. This can be explained by the nature of his business: he specialised in the production of fine presentation cups which for the most part entered the treasuries of reigning monarchs or of the nobility, persons who were not likely to be compelled by financial need to convert them into specie and who could afford to purchase new plate in the latest fashion without having to melt down earlier pieces. By contrast, some of Jamnitzer's greatest achievements were of immense size and value and were more likely to be melted. This applies particularly to his famous table-fountains, which had the disadvantage that, when they had ceased to be fashionable, they were difficult to maintain in working order and no longer had any use.

The Nürnberg *Stadtrat* resolutions reveal a curious disagreement between Petzoldt and his fellow citizens. In 1597 he moved to a new house and asked for permission to construct an oriel window in it. Such luxuries were confined to members of the patrician class and his request was refused. Nevertheless he built it, only to have it demolished by order of the *Stadtrat*. He rebuilt it and it was demolished a second time. Even though he had been elected to represent the goldsmiths on the *Stadtrat* in 1591, he was unable to circumvent its decisions.

Hans Petzoldt's chief emulators in Nürnberg were Hans Beutmüller who, having been admitted master in 1588, was almost a contemporary, and Peter Wiber, who was first admitted as master in 1603. Both are represented by a large number of surviving pieces, not all of equal quality. On the whole Wiber, whose work is well represented in the Dresden Grünes Gewölbe,[67] maintained a more consistently high standard. The Gothic Revival style cups made by these masters (pl. 487) are distinguishable from their fifteenth-century predecessors by their tall stems and the detail of the engraved borders which adheres to the Renaissance style. The fashion for neo-Gothic and for other aspects of Mannerism did not completely oust the Renaissance style even in Nürnberg. Cups constructed on the plan of horizontal divisions were not necessarily produced by more conservative masters; they may have been commissioned by clients who preferred the earlier style.

By the close of the sixteenth century important presentation cups were given quite extravagant proportions by the German goldsmiths. Their height was increased without a corresponding increase in breadth, giving them a slenderness that corresponded to contemporary taste.[68] Such tall and slender forms were particularly well suited to the neo-Gothic manner to which they most frequently conform.

Hans Keller

Among the outstanding Nürnberg masters ranking with Hans Petzoldt and Christoph Jamnitzer, was Hans Kellner or Keller, who was admitted master in 1582 and died in 1609. The comparatively large number of his works that have survived show him to have possessed a wide range of talents. That his skill was appreciated by his contemporaries is proved by the presence of his work in the Saxon Electoral treasury in the Grünes Gewölbe, Dresden, and other formerly princely collections. Two examples show that he was equally skilled in the techniques of embossing and modelling. One is the table-centre[69] in the form of a group of St. George killing the Dragon in the Grünes Gewölbe, which displays his mastery of a complicated composition and his skill in embossing single figures. Typical of the period is the fact that this superbly modelled group was intended also to serve as a *Trinkspiel* (drinking jest) and the three figures are each wrought as drinking vessels with removable heads. Keller was also the creator of the silver mounts of the *Geschlechtsbuch* (family record) of the Tuchers of Nürnberg. This achievement is described by E. W. Braun in the following terms: 'One of his chief works is the making of the decorative mounts of the famous Tucher book which he executed in superb cast and chased silver-gilt strapwork. The designer of the mounts, as indeed of the whole work, was the greatest Nürnberg master of design of the second half of the century, namely Jost Amman.....That Hans Keller was the maker of these wonderful castings is shown by the fact that his mark, a sceptre, is struck twice upon them. Apart from the excellence of the figures, the clarity of the elaborate strapwork which surrounds them is remarkable.' The original binding is in the Germanisches National-museum, Nürnberg, but a set of lead plaquettes cast from the mounts at the time they were made is preserved in the Berlin Kunstgewerbemuseum.[70]

Christoph Jamnitzer

The most gifted member of the Jamnitzer family after Wenzel was his grandson, Christoph, the eldest son of Hans Jamnitzer. Born in 1563, he was admitted master in Nürnberg in 1592 and lived on there until 1618. Like his father and his uncle, Abraham Jamnitzer, Christoph received numerous commissions from the Holy Roman Emperor for splendid show vessels and, although he was never a regular member of the *Hofwerkstatt* in Prague, he travelled there several times on business relating to Imperial commissions. His surviving work is varied in style. A columbine-cup in the Victoria and Albert Museum (pl. 515) has been identified as his masterpiece but there are good grounds for rejecting this, as the stem and other parts of the cup are signed *BEN.CER.* and with the initials B.C. in stamped letters, presumably for some Italian goldsmith working in Jamnitzer's employ: one of the biblical subjects engraved around the rim is also signed *Jakob Scheib*. While the style of the cup is certainly in the manner of Christoph Jamnitzer, two other craftsmen worked upon it and he may have been responsible only for the design. It is, therefore, more likely that this is one of the pattern cups made for the Nürnberg goldsmiths' guild (see p.202).

A lobate cup and cover by Christoph in the Moscow Kremlin is so convincingly Gothic in style that, but for the applied brackets with beaded rat-tail ornament, it might have been taken from a design by Albrecht Dürer. Another cup in the Germanisches Nationalmuseum, Nürnberg, is, however, in a rather half-hearted Gothic manner, and suggests that this archaistic style did not come easily to him. Other vessels by Christoph are decorated with numerous minute plaques of mother-of-pearl in the manner adopted by Elias Geyer or Friedrich Hillebrand,[71] though their design is so ungainly that they could only belong to the epoch of Guiseppe Archimboldi and his melancholic imperial patron. Characteristic of Christoph's designs is his treatment of the foot of a vessel as a composition of intertwining scrolls from which the stem develops without interruption. This feature can also be found in a series of drawings attributed to Christoph Jamnitzer, but which are more probably by a workshop assistant, in the Kunstbibliothek, Berlin. They are certainly in his manner and some of the figure drawings are very stylish, but others show a failure to understand the principles of perspective that is difficult to reconcile with Christoph's high standing as a goldsmith.[72] The figure drawings in this set show that he or his assistant had completely mastered late Mannerist fashion. Whereas other goldsmiths were often satisfied to set figures taken from a standard pattern that was available to the whole craft on top of the vessels they made, Christoph worked out individual designs for this purpose. The drawing of a combined dish and centre-piece from this series (pl. 175) is surmounted by a figure of Mercury, apparently derived from that most popular of all Mannerist sculptures, the Mercury of Giovanni da Bologna, a master whose work also influenced Christoph's chief rival in Augsburg, Christoph Lencker. In designing a finial figure Christoph thought out the effect from various points of view, a practice that enabled him to achieve the Mannerist ideal of the *linea serpentinata*. The scrolls and brackets that constitute so important an element in these drawings appear in an inexhaustible variety in his printed pattern-books. In 1610 Christoph Jamnitzer published a series of sixty etchings in three sections, each with a different title; the *Neuw Grotteskenbuch*, *Der Schnecken Markt* and *Der Radesckisch Radesko Baum* — the term *Radeskisch* presumably relating to arabesques. These prints consist of scrollwork inhabited by animals, children at play, and even tournament scenes as well as elements composed of a fantastic mixture of shell, scroll and insectlike forms, displaying an originality of invention that has hardly been equalled in the history of goldsmiths' ornament (pls. 168-172). The manner reflected in these prints does not derive from his grandfather, but looks back to the fantasies of Bosch and Brueghel, or among contemporary sources to the *Architectura* of Wendel Dietterlin.

Christoph's most important work was the Triumph Ewer and Basin made for the Emperor Rudolph II. These vessels (pls. 511-4) are characteristic of the Prague *Hofwerkstatt* style, but the basin bears the Nürnberg town mark and was, therefore, submitted for assay and, presumably, made there. The exact date of manufacture is not recorded but it is probable that they were made shortly before 1603, as Jamnitzer received payment in that year of the very large sum of 4,014 florins through the Nürnberg City Council on the instructions of the Emperor Rudolph.[73] In this basin and ewer

Christoph Jamnitzer created one of the most impressive monuments of the last and most sophisticated phase of Mannerist goldsmiths' work. The design of the ewer is no mere compilation of elements drawn from various pattern-books, but is an original composition based on a masterly appreciation of contemporary Italian and Flemish Mannerist art. In its composition Jamnitzer has overcome the usual tendency of goldsmiths to stress the horizontal, inherited from Renaissance tradition, and the form continues upwards without interruption. The basin (pl. 511) is embossed in such high relief that it could hardly ever have served its practical purpose of holding water and its border of openwork scrolls is so delicately constructed that it has suffered damage in the past, although it appears to have been used only at coronations of the Emperor. While the scenes embossed on the ewer and basin owe much to Italian sources, it will be noticed that the whole vocabulary of Renaissance ornament — the friezes, brackets, lion masks and acanthus foliage — has been abandoned and a new range of decorative motifs introduced. For the sheer fantasy of its design the Vienna ewer is rivalled only by another work by the same master, the Dresden ewer (pl. 516). It is a measure of Christoph Jamnitzer's status as goldsmith and artist that he signed his work like a painter or sculptor with his name in full. The Triumph Basin is signed *Christoforo Jamnitzer fezit;* the rest of the family, including the great Wenzel, had been satisfied to use the lion's mask alone. The basin that accompanies the ewer is not just a vessel but is rather a frame for a pictorial representation of the Triumph of Cupid, to whom emperors and heroes are shown to be captive. While the centre is embossed in high relief, the border is decorated with delicately stippled scenes of the story of Atalanta and Hippomenes, the original drawings for which have survived in the Victoria and Albert Museum (pl. 173). Christoph Jamnitzer's painterly approach to his art can be recognised in his treatment of the Triumph scenes in which he is creating sculpture rather than decoration. The scene representing the Triumph of Death (pl. 514) includes a number of portraits of those great masters whose fame would be immortal, among them Petrarch, Dürer, Michelangelo and two others, less certainly identifiable, but probably representing Wenzel Jamnitzer and the Prague Court Painter, Hans von Aachen. His sculptural skill is also well illustrated by the figures on the cover; the Leda has shed the almost peasantlike heaviness that can be recognised in the Earth figure on the stem of the Wenzel Jamnitzer table-centre (pl. 416) and displays all the elegance of Mannerist sculpture. In the same way the putti surrounding the neck show that Christoph Jamnitzer had broken with the tradition of the Vischer workshop that had so long imposed a note of Teutonic realism on the style of the Nürnberg sculptors.

Christoph Jamnitzer is known to have been in Prague in 1609 and most of his later works follow the pictorial style associated with the Rudolphine court, among them the ewer in the form of an elephant (pl. 517), the companion dish of which does not survive. The idea of an elephant ewer was not new (see pl. 189 for a comparable work by Jakob Mores) but the Jamnitzer version makes use of ornament that belongs to the seventeenth rather than to the sixteenth century.

Christoph excelled both in embossing in low relief and modelling in high relief. His finest surviving works in the former technique are the series of four tazza bowls in the Hermitage, Leningrad. These have lost their original bases and stems; the inside of the bowls are wrought with four scenes from the story of Phaeton, of which two are illustrated (pls. 509-10). His representation of the wide landscape receding into the far distance on the tazza top showing Phaeton driving the chariot of the sun (pl. 510) is masterly. Working in higher relief and a different technique he modelled a series of single figures and groups,[74] intended to be cast and chased. These groups which, though not signed, are convincingly attributed to him, are modelled with great liveliness and originality and finished with crisp precision, the exaggeration of their postures well reflecting the taste of the time. They were originally intended to adorn caskets but are now usually found as separate detached fragments. Christoph Jamnitzer's works show so many reminiscences of contemporary Italian sculpture that a period of study in Italy can be assumed in his case. A drawing of a globe-cup with stem in the form of a figure of

Hercules derived from a Sansovino bronze which has been convincingly attributed to Christoph Jamnitzer is actually annotated in Italian.[75] Three silver versions of this group, in which Hercules is shown taking the place of Atlas in supporting the globe of the world, by Christoph Jamnitzer are known, the best being the one in the Rijksmuseum, Amsterdam.

Christoph Jamnitzer had a younger brother, who was named Wenzel after his grandfather. No piece of silver has been attributed to him but he went to work in Italy and stayed there for, when he died in Rome in 1618, he was described as goldsmith to Cardinal Farnese, 'aurifex Ill. et Rev. Dom. Cardinalis Farnesii'.

Hans and Elias Lencker

In the region of Teutonic culture the art of translucent enamelling on precious metal was a speciality of the city of Augsburg but one of the most splendid monuments in this technique bears the mark of two members of the Nürnberg family of Lencker. This family played a particularly important rôle in the sixteenth-century goldsmiths' art as it consitutes a link between the two great centres of Augsburg and Nürnberg. The first of the line was Hans Lencker, who was admitted master in Nürnberg in 1550 and subsequently worked for the ducal courts of both Hesse and Bavaria. He was assisted by his brother, Elias Lencker, in the production of the magnificent writing casket in the Munich Schatzkammer (pl. 491) which is decorated in translucent enamel with hunting scenes and panels of grotesques inhabited by birds and animals. A less expensive alternative to translucent enamel was to set panels of verre fixé or Hinterglasmalerei (inappropriately known in England as verre eglomisé) in the top, base or walls of a vessel. Elias Lencker struck his mark on a rock-crystal standing cup[76] in the Kassel Museum, the foot of which is set with a circular panel, painted with a peacock surrounded by flowers against a gilt ground. One might be tempted to think that Elias Lencker was particularly drawn to such polychrome ornament in view of the brilliant colour effect of his writing casket in the Munich Schatzkammer. Chance survivals do not, however, provide adequate evidence for such a conclusion and, in any case, polychrome decoration was originally applied to a great many pieces of German silver in the form of Kaltemail, which has since disappeared. A particularly colourful example is the Nürnberg covered beaker (pl. 486). Another work of Elias Lencker is the double cup made for the Holzschuher family (pl. 489). The idea of setting one cup on top of the other so that the upper one functioned as a cover seems to have originated in Germany. This device certainly had the advantage of economising in space on the sideboard but the effect was far from graceful. Though the example illustrated is by Lencker, such vessels were made by most of the leading German goldsmiths of the time. The two halves have often become separated, but a cup that was originally part of a double one can be recognised as the lip is vertical instead of being splayed out slightly.

Elias Lencker was one of the Nürnberg goldsmiths who did not keep a shop from which he retailed his wares but entrusted one of his fellow goldsmiths with the task of finding customers for him. His agent was Wolf Mair, the brother-in-law of Hans Jamnitzer. These goldsmiths acted much the same role as the Krämer, but had the advantage of being accepted as members of the goldsmiths' guild. They travelled round, visited possible clients, offered their goods and obtained commissions as and when they could.

Gold and Gold-mounted Hardstone Vessels

Neither Nürnberg nor Augsburg rivalled Milan, Florence or Prague as centres of the glyptic art, but there were certainly hardstone-carvers in Nürnberg. When on April 9, 1591, Hans Petzoldt was appointed to the City Council, (Grosser Rat), the two other appointments were Hans Gruber, the watchmaker, and Hans Vollandt, stone-cutter (Steinschneider).[77] A considerable number of standing cups or bowls with foot, stem and cover of rock-crystal mounted in silver-gilt exist; these date from the late sixteenth and first half of the seventeenth century. The mounts are usually modest in character and unmarked. They are often attributed to Freiburg-in-Breisgau but considering the fame of the Nürnberg glass-engravers, such as Georg Schwanhardt, it seems likely that some of them were produced entirely in Nürnberg for mounting. It was not till the seventeenth century that Nürnberg became the centre of glass-cutting in Germany, but the craft developed out of the earlier one of rock-crystal engraving which was already established there.[78] The cups mounted in south Germany were usually of shell shape, carved with a mask or head at one end and corresponding to the type believed to have been made in Prague by Ottavio Miseroni. Subsequently similar cups of rock-crystal, but not of coloured stones, were carved in Freiburg and it is not easy to distinguish between them, though the Freiburg hardstone cutters did not equal those of Prague in skill.

Among the few German examples illustrated, the agate cup (pl. 492) bears the mark of the Nürnberg master, Jörg Ruel, while the mounts of the amethystine quartz bowl in pl. 464 bear the Augsburg town mark together with the mark of an unidentified maker. The rock-crystal cup in pl. 463 was mounted by an Augsburg goldsmith. Whether the hardstones were cut in the towns where they were mounted or obtained by goldsmith of patron from elsewhere, it is not at present possible to determine. The rock-crystal beaker with enamelled gold mounts (pl. 575) is possibly of Nürnberg origin; in this case the cutting of the crystal suggests Nürnberg more strongly than the somewhat unsophisticated design of the gold mounts.

Of quite a different class from the silver-mounted hardstones vessels discussed above are those mounted in enamelled gold; these were mostly commissioned by members of the ruling families from their court goldsmiths and were embellished with precious stones of great value. Those made for the Bavarian Wittelsbach family can be attributed to identified masters (see p.226) but others such as the exquisite rock-crystal cup from the *Kunstkammer* of the Dukes of Württemberg can only be attributed approximately to some unknown Augsburg master. This little cup (pl. 457) well expresses Mannerist taste, being made up of elements that do not blend together perfectly, the colours of the hardstone composing the foot, body and cover being different and the stem formed of a Baroque pearl surmounted by the demi-figures of a merman and mermaid, which was probably originally a pendant jewel before it was converted to this use. The cup as a whole is indeed a jewel rather than a vessel.

Vessels made of gold and precious stones were not normally marked and it is, therefore, rare for such pieces to be ascribed to a named master. There was, however, in the Mannheimer collection and later in an English private collection, a tankard of glass set in a frame of enamelled gold enriched with jewels, that can be attributed with some confidence to Christoph Jamnitzer. The tankard is close enough in design to another of silver-gilt in the Museum at Schwerin bearing Christoph Jamnitzer's mark, to be ascribed to the same maker.[79] The gold-mounted tankard is set with three panels of *verre fixé* painted by the Swiss master, Jacob Sprüngli, who was for some time working in Nürnberg. The painted decoration of the tankard has suffered considerably in the course of time, but the original effect of the brilliantly coloured *verre fixé* panels against the enamelled gold mounts must have been imposing. The existence of this single piece by Christoph Jamnitzer does, however, suggest that many superb vessels of gold were made by leading masters which have since been sacrificed to the melting-pot. The question arises whether the examples that are now so much admired really represent the finest works of the sixteenth-century masters, it may be that we are only seeing the second best while the finest pieces were too valuable intrinsically to survive. While the court goldsmiths of the Dukes of Bavaria produced vessels of gold for their patrons, there is less evidence of such luxury articles being made by the Nürnberg goldsmiths. Apart from the Jamnitzers the only Nürnberg masters known to have worked in enamelled gold are Melchior Baier, to whom the gold Pfinzing Cup in the Germanisches Nationalmuseum[80] is attributed and Hans Karl, who left Nürnberg for Salzburg and, subsequently Prague. For obvious reasons the percentage of survival of gold objects is considerably smaller than that of silver and the scarcity of examples remaining does not necessarily reflect the quantity that were made. Judging by what survives, the main centres of production were Spain and Italy and many of those made elsewhere were the work of *emigré* Spanish and Italian masters.

Many of the gold-mounted vessels that do survive are of very small size, in marked contrast to the huge silver-gilt cups made by Hans Petzoldt for presentation to distinguished visitors. This is explained by the vastly greater value of gold in the sixteenth century. On the whole, gold was a material for Princes rather than City Fathers.

The Goldsmiths of Augsburg

Although Nürnberg has been discussed before Augsburg there was during the second half of the century little to choose between the reputation of the goldsmiths in the two cities. No Augsburg goldsmith enjoyed quite the international fame of Wenzel Jamnitzer, but journeymen goldsmiths came from towns spread over the vast area of the Holy Roman Empire in order to seek training in Augsburg workshops. Valuable commissions from the Emperor and the Dukes of Bavaria were given to Augsburg masters. The goldsmiths' guild of Augsburg had so high a reputation for its excellent organisation of the craft that it received numerous inquiries from goldsmiths' guilds of other cities, including a request from Nürnberg itself in 1540. The number of goldsmiths at work in Augsburg rose rapidly during the second half of the century. The rate books show that in 1555 there were sixty-three goldsmiths in the city. By 1573, when the Wardens protested that the number was excessive, there were a hundred and sixty. By 1588 the number rose to a hundred and seventy and in 1594 there were two hundred. To this last figure must be added three hundred journeymen on their travels, twenty-four foreign journeymen employed in Augsburg, a hundred Augsburg-born journeymen and a hundred apprentices, making seven hundred and twenty-four in all. During the Thirty Years War the number sank but rose again in the early eighteenth century.[81] Lavish orders for secular and ecclesiastical plate of precious metal for the wealthy court of the Dukes of Bavaria seem for the most part to have gone to Augsburg masters, who executed them in their own workshops. In the case of an exceptionally important commission, a goldsmith might be summoned to Munich to discuss the project, but as a rule the Bavarian orders were handled by the Augsburg banking house of Fugger. This firm had agents in the main European capitals and was well placed for obtaining rare materials from foreign parts. In cities such as Nürnberg and Augsburg in which the guilds had great power over their members it was unusual for silver to escape marking. One of the finest Augsburg tazzas (pl. 496, 497) has, curiously enough, only the Augsburg town mark but no maker's mark. The goldsmith, whoever he was, has shown ingenuity in adapting the rectangular print to the circular tazza bowl and supreme skill in chasing the scene with its many figures. The stem design corresponds to that of two tazzas by Ernzt van Vianen (pl.623) while the chasing of the bowl shows the influence of Paul van Vianen, another instance of the international character of the leading Mannerist goldsmiths' work. By the time this tazza was made, during the first quarter of the seventeenth century, Augsburg was already eclipsing Nürnberg as the chief centre of the craft in south Germany.

The major commissions came from the court and in considering the extant work of Augsburg goldsmiths it is best to study first those who worked for the Dukes of Bavaria, Albrecht V and his son, Wilhelm V.

Abraham Lotter

Abraham Lotter the Elder, of Augsburg,[82] has been credited with being the master of the great house-altar of Albrecht V, Duke of Bavaria, one of the most monumental of the combined works of goldsmith and cabinet-maker for which Augsburg later became so famous (pl. XVII), now in the Residenz Museum, Munich.[83] It is possible that this combination of the highest craftsmanship in precious metal and precious wood may have been one of the *Inventiones* to which Lotter referred in his petition to the Augsburg guild (see p.43). This house-altar, which was followed by several others of similar design (pls. 452, 453) also made for Albrecht V, is believed to have been in course of construction in the year 1573. Rather more is known about the production of a gold-mounted ebony shrine that was presented by Duke Albrecht to Philip II, King of Spain, but has since been lost and presumably destroyed.[84] The manufacture of this shrine, which was to contain a relic of Saint James of Compostella, the patron saint of Spain, was entrusted to the Augsburg banking family of Fugger, who not only advised on the choice of the master best suited to work on it, but also undertook the no less difficult task of locating and determining the authenticity of the relics it was to contain. In this case the cabinet-work was carried out by Hans Krieger and the gold mounts made by Ulrich Eberl, while the gold figure of the saint that crowned the reliquary was entrusted to the Flemish or Dutch immigrant goldsmith, Andreas Attemstett, then referred to as Hadrian von Friedberg. References in contemporary documents (see p.65) suggest that Attemstett was one of the most important of the goldsmiths employed at the Munich court, but hitherto no work from his hand has been identified. It is, perhaps, significant that among the most delightful and characteristic creations of south German Mannerist sculpture are the miniature figures of enamelled gold that decorate the house-altars of Albrecht V. They have a lilting elegance of movement that seems to anticipate the Rococo style. It may be that Attemstett, who was chosen to execute the figure on top of the St. James reliquary, was their master.

Hans Reimer

Rather more is known of another court artist who took the exceptional step of signing two vessels that have survived. This is Hans Reimer who submitted his masterpiece in 1555 and died in 1604.[85] If we can accept the evidence of what may be only a chance survival, the Munich court favoured the most luxurious of all materials for their commissions, namely enamelled gold. Both of the signed Reimer vessels, a standing cup and a tankard, are constructed of this material. Both display a mixture of classical and mauresque ornament and profuse enrichment with enamel and jewels. The standing cup (*Saphir Pokal*) conforms to Mannerist fashion with its small foot, complex form and mixture of classical and Near-Eastern ornament. Its form is basically that of the columbine cup (*Akeley Pokal*) but even the superb technique of its ornament hardly makes up for its unfortunate shape.[86] This cup is dated 1563, while the signed tankard is set with carved panels of narwhal horn in the drum and dated 1572.

The earliest of the attributed works of Reimer is a covered cup, also in the Munich Schatzkammer, which is dated 1562 (pls. 454-5). Unlike the later pieces this lacks the further enrichment of jewels; its body is decorated with mauresques in blue and white and bears the Bavarian arms in *Rollwerk* cartouches on each side. This profuse employment of enamelled mauresques is a marked feature of Reimer's style, but one should not regard it as in any way unusual. Similar mauresques can be seen on slightly earlier Parisian goldsmiths' work, though usually with a black ground, and on the Holbein bowl also in the Munich Schatzkammer. Reimer's works in enamelled gold have a splendour which is now lacking in the silver vessels of the period, but the contrast was less marked at the time as the *Kaltemail* decoration gave the silver vessels a polychrome effect that has long since been cleaned away. The original effect of *Kaltemail* ornament can best be judged from the Jacob Mores designs for the Danish court preserved in the Berlin Kunstbibliothek.[87]

Of the other court artists Georg Bernard has already been mentioned (p.41), while the Hungarian goldsmith Georg Zeggin was the creator of the magnificent enamelled gold binding in the Bayerisches Staatsbibliothek.[88] This is enriched with small translucent enamel panels like those on the big Cornelius Grosz cup in the Munich Residenz (pls. 468-70). It is possible that Zeggin was, like Altenstetter, a specialist enameller and carried out enamel decoration, such as that on the Epfendorfer cup, for other Augsburg masters.

A regular feature of German Mannerist ornament was the etched mauresque, either in bands or, less frequently, covering the whole surface of a vessel. Two gilt ewers with their companion basins by Augsburg masters show all-over etched ornament interrupted by applied cast medallions of biblical subjects. One of these, belonging to the Herberstein family and formerly in Schloss Herberstein near Graz, bears the maker's mark of the Augsburg master, Ulrich Schönmacher.[89] The second ewer and basin, decorated with exactly the same medallions, is in Spain in the Fundacion Lerma, Toledo.[90] It is exceptional to find sixteenth-century pieces of such importance decorated in identical manner. The design of both ewer and basin and the lay out of the medallions correspond closely to the Habsburg gold ewer and basin (pls. 564-7).

Elias and Cornelius Grosz

Most customers were satisfied with a conventional version of the current fashion, but more varied features were introduced by the goldsmith, should the commission be sufficiently generous to justify the extra expense. An example is the standing cup and cover of about 1570 by Elias or Cornelius Grosz in the Munich Schatzkammer (pls. 468-470). In the variety of its decorative themes this cup is one of the most extravagantly ornamented in existence. The decorative treatment is, however, somewhat disorganised and unsophisticated. The overpowering effect of the all-over decoration, which was so much admired during the second half of the sixteenth century has been exaggerated to satisfy the patron's wish for an exceptionally expensive piece. The same makers, Elias or Cornelius Grosz, were responsible for the highly original ewer and basin (pls. 466-7). So different in conception are the cup and this ewer and basin that it is at first difficult to accept the evidence of the maker's mark. It is possible that the ewer and basin were made by one goldsmith and submitted for assay by another, but it is the mark of a supreme goldsmith that he could design and work in different styles. Moreover, there may well be a gap of some twenty years between the manufacture of these pieces. Whoever designed and modelled them was a sculptor of more than average skill.

The Flemish influence that is evident in this ewer and basin can also be recognised in some of the finest south German silver of the third quarter of the century. The sources seem to have been the engraved designs of Cornelis Floris and Vredeman de Vries (see ps.283,7). An example is the imaginative snail cup from the Schweizerisches Landesmuseum (pl. 465). Floris's shell ewer (pl. 198) is also supported on the back of a satyr secured by bands around his belly, while a shell with snail's head emerging can be seen in de Vries's design for a *Hydria* (ewer) (pl. 208). Another Augsburg vessel, presumably meant for use as a salt, has a base of similar design but the stem is a merman satyr seated on a turtle (pl. 464).

David Altenstetter

During the first three-quarters of the sixteenth century, enrichment in translucent enamel had mainly been confined to vessels of gold, whereas silver or even silver-gilt vessels were decorated with cold-painted enamel. Translucent enamel was a speciality of David Altenstetter, who came to Augsburg from Colmar before 1570. He was described by his contemporary, Phillip Hainhofer, as one of the most skilled and most famous masters of enamelling (*under den geschicktesten und beruembtisten maistern . . . mit schmeltzwerckh*). In earlier books on German goldsmiths' work David Altenstetter is wrongly identified as the son of Andreas Attemstetter (see p.225) who was of Flemish origin, the confusion being caused by the similarity of their names. One of the earlier vessels, probably enamelled by David Altenstetter, is the great standing cup and cover bearing the mark attributed to Elias or Cornelius Grosz (pls. 468-70). The enamelled decoration of this cup is not signed, but the monogram of Altenstetter appears on the silver and partly-gilt case of a table-clock supplied by the same gold-smiths to the Emperor Rudolph II. This clock, now in the Kunsthistorisches Museum, Vienna,[91] is first recorded in the inventory of the property of Rudolph II of 1611, but was doubtless produced towards the end of the sixteenth century. As Altenstetter worked with the Grosz brothers on the clock, it is very likely that they had also secured his help in decorating the cup. Altenstetter also signed the enamelled silver plaques that cover the stock of the extraordinary wheel-lock rifle[92] made by Munich court gunmak-ers and later presented to the Emperor Rudolph. His panels, decorated with delicately enamelled swags of drapery, insects, animals and birds, were in demand for the most extravagant commissions of the time, such as the *Pommersche Kunstschrank* or the ivory casket made by Angermaier for Duke Wilhelm of Bavaria. Two cups, illustrated (pls. 471 and 472) can also be attributed to Altenstetter, at least so far as the enamelling is concerned. The first (pl. 471) was probably only decorated by him, but the little goblet (pl. 472) may have come in its entirety from his workshop, for without the enamel it would be of little consequence. Translucent enamel showed up well against a white silver ground and it will be noticed that several of the pieces referred to above are of white silver, even if the enclosing framework is gilt. Pattern-books of ornament intended specifically for execution in translucent enamel were published in Augsburg by Daniel Mignot and the style adopted by Altenstetter was followed by many of his contemporaries in Augsburg and elsewhere towards the end of the century. The backs of pendant jewels were commonly enriched in this way.

The Masters of the HANS and HS Monograms

One of the most original Augsburg masters of the third quarter of the sixteenth century used as his mark the letters *HANS* in monogram. He made the unusual cup with bowl embossed with animals' heads[93] (pl. XVI) and the colourful ewer and basin in the Munich Schatzkammer (pls. 459-61). The frieze running around the depression of the basin is similar to some of Hornick's designs (pl. 200) and it is perhaps significant that this basin and ewer were made about 1570 when Hornick was resident in Augsburg. The only figure common to the Hornick design and the decoration of the basin is the Neptune standing on a shell drawn by four seahorses and holding a trident (pl. 460). This group was not an invention of Hornick, since it appears on a rock-crystal intaglio by Giovanni Bernardi, after which a number of bronze plaquettes are known. It also appears as the central panel of a design for a dish by, or in the manner of, Salviati in the Victoria and Albert Museum and its origin can be traced back even further to an engraving by Mark Antonio Raimondi.[94] The monogram *HANS* is also struck on a rock-crystal cup (pl. 463) with silver-gilt mounts in the Grünes Gewölbe, Dresden, which is further enriched with enamelled decoration in blue and green. The fact that this master should be represented in the Munich and Dresden treasuries suggests that he enjoyed a considerable reputation at the time. Rock-crystal vessels were of such great value that they were only entrusted to a highly skilled goldsmith for mounting. The name of this maker has not been discovered, but a contemporary master who used a similar mark, the monogram *HS*, has been identified as Hans Schebel of Augsburg.[95]

Schebel's controversy with the Augsburg guild has been described already (see p.40). His mark appears on the so-called *Landschadenbundbecher* in the Graz Johan-neum. This huge cup (pl. 462) was commissioned by the Munich court as a gift to the Archduke Carl of Steiermark on the occasion of his marriage to the Archduchess Maria of Bavaria in 1571. The same mark appears on two standing cups of identical design in the Grünes Gewölbe, Dresden. The reason for attributing these vessels to Hans Schebel is that a design for a standing cup which was supplied by Hans Schebel to Duke Wilhelm Johann of Sachsen-Weimar (pl. 165) shows a similar lip decorated with etched mauresques and also the same knop adorned with three harpies between faun masks. The presence of the same form of knop does not, however, provide final proof that the maker of the cups and the author of the design was one and the same, since the model in question may have been available to more than one goldsmith from a *Formenschneider*. A very similar knop can be seen on the Rappolsteiner cup (pl. 546) which was made in Strassburg some years before. The *Landschadenbundbecher* and the two cups in Dresden are of interesting design because of the arrangement of the foot and stem in alternate zones of relief and flat ornament. The foot and the knob are cast, the bowl and the reliefs embossed, the mauresques on the lip etched, while the base of the knop, the bowl and the figure on the cover are enriched with bands of enamel.

Matthias Wallbaum

The difficulties experienced by Matthias Wallbaum, who came to Augsburg from Kiel in north-west Germany before 1579, in satisfying the Augsburg goldsmiths' guild have already been mentioned (p.41). Eventually he built up a highly successful business specialising in ebony cabinets, caskets, monstrances and frames, all profusely mounted in silver.[96] At least fifty pieces from his workshop have been identified. Production was large because the silver mounts were cast and even stamped in quantity according to a variety of patterns which could be applied to different objects. The extent of his repertoire of mounts made it possible to achieve various effects on similar objects. His work was not confined to silver mounts for cabinets, for his mark appears on several of the superb groups of Diana mounted on a stag (pl. 508). Wallbaum worked for the Prague *Hofwerkstatt* and received commissions from sources far from Augsburg; the ebony and silver altar of Cardinal Scipio Borghese, which still stands in its original position in the Villa Borghese − is a creation of his workshop. Not all his work was marked and it is difficult − if not impossible − to distinguish it from that of his Augsburg contemporary, Boas Ulrich. While he was certainly a gifted master, one cannot credit the invention of these cabinets to him, for they were, in fact, less expensive versions of those produced during the third quarter of the century by Wenzel Jamnitzer. Nevertheless, as a sculptor in silver, Wallbaum ranks amongst the leading masters of his time; he worked with as much skill in low relief as in modelling figures in the round. As a sideline to his cabinets, he also produced many small house-altars. These followed a fairly standard architectural form and were constructed of ebony with silver or silver-gilt mounts, corresponding to those on the cabinets but with a religious flavour. Such house-altars seem to have become popular during the last quarter of the sixteenth century, probably as a consequence of the Counter Reformation, which was then at its peak.

Wallbaum's most important work was in the construction of the *Kunstschrank* that was designed by Phillip Hainhofer for Duke Philipp von Pommern. This remarkable creation was one of the major losses of German applied art in the Second World War, though most of the contents of its numerous drawers survive in the Berlin Kunstgewerbe museum. The cabinet, which can best be described as a *Kunstkammer* in miniature, occupied some twenty Augsburg craftsmen for seven years between 1610 and 1617 and was the subject of constant correspondence between Hainhofer and his patron during these years. A painting showing portraits of the various artists who had collaborated on it was set in the base, among them that of Matthias Wallbaum. Two other similar cabinets made to Hainhofer's design exist, one belonging to the University of Uppsala in Sweden, the other in the Museo degli Argenti, Florence, the latter robbed of its contents and all its silver enrichment. Philipp of Pommern was a major customer of the Augsburg goldsmiths in the early seventeenth century; he ordered through Hainhofer two further elaborate confections, neither of which survives. One was the *Nähkorb* (sewing-basket), the other the *Maierhof,* a miniature version of a south German farmhouse and farmyard, rather similar to a child's toy but made of precious metals instead of lead.

Silver Flowers

One of the most admired achievements of Wenzel Jamnitzer was his skill in casting flowers and grasses of extreme delicacy in silver. Silver blossoms and grasses made in this way were very fragile and few examples have survived, the most remarkable being those that decorate Jamnitzer's own *Merckelsche* centre-piece. Silver flowers constructed from cut and shaped silver sheet were stronger; of this type were those presented by the Pope in a gilt or golden vase to those ladies, usually or royal rank, who had performed some special service to the Catholic Church. The best example of these golden roses is preserved in the Museo del Opera del Duomo of Pisa. During the second half of the century a bunch of flowers of cut silver sheet, sometimes finished in cold enamel, became the standard finial for the cover of a cup. The vase of silver flowers illustrated in pl. 490 is recorded in an inventory of 1596[97] and shows how effectively they were used by the end of the century. Their production became a specialised branch of the craft but little is known of their makers as they were not normally marked. Only one Nürnberg goldsmith marked the flowers he made; this was J. Rauwulff who was a journeyman in Nürnberg in 1603 and worked subsequently in Fürth.[98] The first goldsmith to introduce the making of silver flowers in Augsburg was Erasmus Hornick (see Chapter XI); he was remembered for his skill in producing them long after he left the city. Thus a petition in the Augsburg archives dated 15 June, 1592, by two Augsburg goldsmiths, Christoph Epfenhauser and Bartolme Lotter,[99] states that the art of making small flowers had been developed by the late Erasmus Hornick (spelt Hornung). The document goes on to state that on the old vessels the flowers were so exquisitely made that it would require all the art and skill of the petitioners to copy them.[100] The practice of making these flowers and setting them in silver vases led to trouble between the Augsburg goldsmiths' guild and some of its members. Hornick had made flowers that weighed four Lot and could be marked. Subsequently other goldsmiths made lighter flowers and were fined for omitting to have them marked.

Embossed Plaques and Tazzas

Among the outstanding achievements of the South German goldsmiths, and, in particular, of those of Augsburg was their mastery of the technique of embossing and chasing landscapes and narrative scenes in the flat surfaces of tazzas, basins and dishes. A valuable contemporary opinion on the relative merits of the leading Augsburg goldsmiths is given in a letter written by Hainhofer to Duke Philipp von Pommern in October, 1610.[101] The Duke wished to commission some panels embossed with scenes from the Passion – probably a set of Stations of the Cross – and Hainhofer reports as follows:-

> There are three highly skilled goldsmiths here who produce very fine, excellently embossed and chiselled work; they are, however, extremely expensive. One is called Bayr; he has executed some very fine work for the Emperor and especially for the Duke of Bavaria. It is a pity that he is so devoted to the bottle and he drinks quite a number of glasses of wine with Rottenhammer who provides designs for him. The other is de Vos who comes from the Low Countries and who understands the art very well. He cast the descent of Christ from the cross after a wax model by Michelangelo Buonarotti for his Majesty the Emperor.[102] He also did another version of it in secret for the present Duke of Württemberg, almost as large in size as half a cubit *(Bogen)*. The work was extremely fine and carried out with great care and skill. I believe he was paid 500 florins for it. The third goldsmith is called Lencker, in fact, father and son. The son is still young and unmarried but diligent and reserved. If your Grace will send me the engravings of the Passion which you wish to have made, I will show them to each goldsmith separately and find out how quickly each would make them before I reply. There will certainly be no lack of diligence and skill in making them, but one must establish the price with the maker beforehand.

In a subsequent letter to the Duke, Hainhofer states that he has consulted Rottenhammer about the matter of the embossed silver plaques and the latter's opinion is that, while Bayr and de Vos are certainly very good, Lencker, who does a great deal of this sort of work, is still the best. Hainhofer suggested either giving the whole commission to

Plate XXIII
Gilt cup and cover. Antwerp, about 1560.

Plate XXIV
Enamelled gold morion of King Charles IX of France. Made by Pierre Redon, Paris, before 1572.

Lencker or splitting it between the three goldsmiths and seeing who worked best and most speedily. Of the three goldsmiths mentioned by Hainhofer, the two Lenckers are doubtless Christoph and his son, Zacharias, who are discussed below, see p.234. Bayr is Hans Jakob Bayer, to whom Rosenberg attributed a large number of pieces, including four vessels in the form of stags.[103] Johann de Vos came to Augsburg from Cologne and was apprenticed there to his cousin David Altenstetter at some time before 1582. His only known surviving work is a silver relief double portrait of Duke Philipp II and his wife, Sophie von Pommern, now in the Herzog Anton Ulrich Museum, Braunschweig. Like so many skilful goldsmiths of this period he was summoned to Prague and appointed *Kammergoldschmied* to the Emperor Rudolph II on 1 January, 1605.

By the middle of the second half of the sixteenth century the decorative plaques by Peter Flötner were beginning to seem old-fashioned and a number of masters in Nürnberg and Augsburg created a complete new stock of designs for goldsmiths. Unlike the plaquettes of Flötner these were first produced in the form of embossed and chased tazza bowls from which lead casts were taken. Where the silver bowl no longer survives its form is often preserved in lead plaquettes and no class of German goldsmiths' work is better represented than that of low relief chasing. So large is the number of tazzas surviving from the later decades of the sixteenth and early seventeenth centuries (pls. 441,3, 474-5, 496-7) that it is not possible to refer to more than a few of them. In addition there is a number of large dishes enriched in a similar manner. Of these one of the most spectacular, because of its polychrome effect, is that presented to the city of Bern in 1583 together with two other large vessels, a standing cup and a figure of a bear wrought in the round, by a grateful German merchant in recognition of the grant to him of an extended lease of some salt mines near the city (pl. 495). The dish is enriched with forty-five coats of arms painted behind glass and the embossed ornament is further decorated with cold enamel that is remarkably well preserved.[104]

The large pair of gilt dishes (pl. 500) in the treasury of the Munich Residenz has been attributed to various masters, including Paul van Vianen,[105] working in Munich as a court goldsmith, to Nikolaus Schmidt of Nürnberg and to the Augsburg master, Paul Hübner. They appear in a Munich inventory of 1598 and the absence of a maker's mark implies that they were made by one of the court goldsmiths of the Dukes of Bavaria, but an attribution to a named master is not possible. The problem of the recognition of the authors of such reliefs is particularly difficult as one cannot assume that the goldsmith who marked a piece had executed the chasing. The only circumstances in which one can be certain is when the relief is signed with the artist's name.

Paul Hübner

The largest single group of Augsburg vessels in existence is the silver-gilt service ordered by or for Archbishop Wolf Dietrich von Raitenau of Salzburg (1587-1612).[106] Of the original service, which was probably larger, two basins with ewers and fifty-four tazzas are preserved in the Palazzo Pitti, Florence. One ewer with its companion basin and forty-eight of the tazzas bear the mark of Paul Hübner, while the other ewer and basin and the remaining six tazzas bear a mark tentatively identified as that of Kornelius Erb. Both basins are decorated with the same subject, Orpheus charming the wild animals, but, whereas Erb has treated the scene in a more modern manner so that it could best be seen when the dish was set upright on the cupboard, Hübner has placed the figures in a continuous band running around the central boss. The fifty-four tazzas were purchased for the Archbishop on two separate occasions; first three dozen, all by Paul Hübner in 1590, and the remaining eighteen in 1594. Of the last, he bought six by Cornelius Erb from his own treasurer, Paul Endris, and twelve by Paul Hübner from the Augsburg merchant, Bartholomäus Fesenmayer, at the Regensburg Reichstag in 1594.[107] The Hübner sets are made up as follows: twelve Old Testament subjects, twelve Months, two sets each of eight Cardinal Virtues and two each of the Four Elements. The Erb set is composed of three Virtues and three Seasons; these may have formed parts of larger sets, as it is unlikely that a goldsmith would have composed a set in so incoherent a manner. It can be taken as axiomatic that tazzas ran in sets of at least half a dozen and the many single examples now encountered originally formed part of a set decorated *en suite*. Although the names of Paul Hübner and Cornelius Erb have been mentioned as their makers, the chasing of the narrative scenes in the bowls would have been the work of a specialist who was probably employed by more than one goldsmith. Another similar set of twelve tazzas, all but one by Paul Hübner, is preserved in the British Museum (Waddesdon Collection). Here again there are eight dishes embossed with Cardinal Virtues and four with the Elements. In view of the close similarity of these tazzas (altogether sixty-six, counting those in the British Museum) it seems probable that they were ordered to a standard design by an Augsburg merchant (perhaps the Bartholomäus Fesenmayer who sold one set to the Salzburg Archbishop) from different goldsmiths and made up into sets according to the client's wishes. Fesenmeyer evidently operated on a quite considerable scale, for in the years between 1593 and 1601 the payments made to him for purchases on behalf of the Bavarian court totalled no less than 14,614 florins.

Writing of the Hübner tazzas, I. Weber has pointed out the curious fact that, while the same graphic sources have been used for the two sets of Cardinal Virtues, a distinction exists in their presentation. In those intended for the Archbishop the bodies of the female figures are draped, while in the British Museum set, which was destined for a secular patron, Count Thun, they are shown with bare breasts.

In discussing Mannerist goldsmiths' work, it has been mentioned that the decoration was often so profuse as to render the vessel useless for any practical purpose. This applies less to tazzas which seem to have had a dual purpose, serving either as drinking vessels or for setting out desserts on the dining table. A painting by the Antwerp master, Antoni Baiis, dated 1578, in the castle of Policka, Czechoslovakia,[108] shows an aristocratic company seated at a long table on which stand a number of tazzas containing fruit, while others, of the same size and shape, are used by the noblemen present as drinking cups. With their wide circumference and shallow bowls they must have been awkward vessels from which to drink. The large sets in which they were made suggests that one was placed before each guest at a banquet.

Christoph and Johannes Lencker

Two later members of the Lencker family who worked in Augsburg in the late sixteenth and early seventeenth century developed a style that verged on the Baroque. The more important was Christoph who received numerous commissions from the Habsburg court and died in 1613. Johannes lived on until 1637, well into the Baroque period. Both brothers produced sets of ewer and basin in which the ewer was modelled in the round as a group of Europa being carried off by Jupiter in the form of a bull, while the basin was decorated with reliefs of the same subject. Unfortunately no complete set survives; there are a drawing for a basin (pl. 167), a basin by Christoph Lencker of similar but not identical design and at least two ewers, both by Johannes Lencker. The Christoph Lencker basin in the Kunsthistorisches Museum, Vienna (pls. 498-499) is the finest surviving work by this master. When it was listed in the inventory prepared by order of the Emperor Matthias in 1620, its ewer was still extant but it is now missing. It presumably corresponded in general form to the two ewers by Johannes Lencker, one of which is in the collection of Prince Fürstenberg, while the other, now lacking its figure of Europa, is in the Hamburg Museum für Kunst und Gewerbe. The design of the Vienna basin has been the subject of some discussion. Kris thought that Christoph Lencker had arrived at it by combining details from various sources. More recently Professor Müller[109] has suggested Hans von Aachen or Hans Rottenhammer as the source. Neither was aware of the existence of the superb drawing of a basin in the Germanisches Nationalmuseum, Nürnberg (pl. 167). This drawing, which shows the same subject as the Lencker dish, may be a preliminary but rejected design for it. It may, on the other hand, have been a design for one of the missing basins which must once have accompanied the ewers by Johannes Lencker and which would also have been embossed with subjects from the story of Europa. Before its connection with the Lencker dish was recognised, the drawing was attributed to Friedrich Sustris, but it may now be attributed with more likelihood to Christoph Lencker himself or to the Augsburg painter, Hans Rottenhammer. The drawing could be attributed to Lencker without qualification but for the fact that Philip Hainhofer states that Rottenhammer provided the designs for Lencker.[110] On the other hand, Lencker is said to have made both designs and wood models for the six statues of Muses which were used to decorate the *Kunstschrank* of Duke Philipp of Pommern, constructed in the years 1610 to 1617. Another drawing in the manner of and perhaps by Christoph Lencker is illustrated in pl. 166. A design for decorating a tazza bowl, it is less finished than that in pl. 167, but shows a flooded landscape unencumbered by the oppressive detail of contemporary Mannerist fashion.

Christoph Lencker was assisted by his son Zacharias, who was one of the most gifted chasers of his time. He worked as a journeyman with his father but never registered a mark, as he died prematurely in 1612.[111] His work is seen, signed only with his initials, on four embossed plaques on the silver altar of the Marienkirche in the North German town of Rugenwalde. This ambitious creation, mainly the work of a Stettin goldsmith named J. Körver was decorated with no fewer than forty embossed plaques illustrating the Passion of Christ. In addition to the Vienna basin, which must have been an Imperial commission, Christoph Lencker supplied the ewer (pl. 501) and companion basin formerly used as baptismal plate in St. Aegidius Church in Nürnberg; the presence of the Habsburg arms on the boss of the basin shows that these pieces also were made for the Emperor, but originally for secular use.

Johannes Lencker was the maker of the silver-gilt mounts on the peculiar drinking cup once thought to be composed of petrified palm-wood but actually made of an unusual striated agate (pl. 502). This does not mean that he was necessarily the author of the superbly modelled figure that supports the bowl. This may be the work of Christoph Lencker, who was certainly a sculptor. A magnificent ewer and basin in the Munich Schatzkammer, both unmarked, (pls. 352-3) were attributed to Johannes Lencker by von Falke[112] under the mistaken assumption that they bore his mark. They are not in fact marked and are difficult to identify. They follow the international late Mannerist style but are more probably the work of an Italian goldsmith.

Figure Sculpture in Silver

During the latter years of the sixteenth and early seventeenth-century German goldsmiths, in their search for more ambitious and complex subjects, turned to Italian bronzes as their source. Where they found these bronzes to copy is uncertain, but they may have had access to the *Kunstkammer* that were being formed by German princes and noblemen. The models were sometimes followed with great fidelity, sometimes amended according to the taste or whim of the goldsmith, but the silver sculpture they produced is the equal of anything made elsewhere on a comparable scale. The variety of sources drawn on was remarkably wide; Gian Bologna, the Venetian masters, all were known and reproduced in precious metal. Some of the finest silver figures made after bronze originals bear the marks of Christoph and Johannes Lencker. The 'Europa and the Bull' groups they made have already been mentioned. They are derived from one or other of the 'Rape groups' by Gian Bologna.[113] Perhaps the best of Johannes' achievements is the nymph and sea-centaur ewer illustrated in pl. 507, though the unmarked group of a nude woman being abducted by a horse in the Louvre, which probably came from the same workshop, is of comparable merit. One of the problems in constructing such ewers was to provide a sufficiently strong joint between the slender stem and the base. In the case of the Europa and the Bull ewer, the spout, instead of proceeding from the mouth of the animal, emerged from a sea wave which extended upwards from the base between the bull's legs, thus providing a firm support. Ewers designed by Erasmus Hornick in the form of struggling monsters are discussed in Chapter XI. Among his essays in this vein is one in the form of a horse upon the back of which a lion has sprung (pl. 153). Apart from the tortoise base, this group is strongly reminiscent of the well-known bronze by Gian Bologna, in which however, the horse has sunk to the ground. Hornick's ewer is probably derived, not from Bologna, but from the classical Roman marble of the same subject in the garden of the Palazzo dei Conservatori in Rome. Whether Hornick's ewer was ever made is not known, but the type was certainly admired, not least because of the difficulties encountered in making it. An unpublished bronze group in the Württembergisches Landesmuseum, Stuttgart, formerly in the ducal *Kunstkammer,* and attributed to an Augsburg sculptor, comes nearest to Hornick's drawing.

Towards the end of the sixteenth century the fashion for drinking-vessels in the form of human beings, animals or monsters became more widespread and they were made in large numbers in the main German centre of goldsmithing. They were wrought with a hollow body and removable head so that they could be used as drinking-vessels, but are for the most part so little suited to this purpose that they should rather be regarded as manifestations of Mannerist virtuosity. Examples illustrated include figures of a musketeer and of a huntsman with a boar-spear by Nürnberg goldsmiths and a bear from Augsburg (pls. 505, 506, 504). The most popular of all seems to have been the owls many of which have survived, often with bodies composed of coconut-shells. Ostrich cups were also made, in which case the body was an ostrich egg (pl. 584). As sculpture, the finest creations were stags, (pls. 508, 568), bulls or bears; this fashion continued during the seventeenth century and some of the most ambitious and monumental examples date from the Baroque period. Besides more or less naturalistic animals, fantastic creatures were also produced, their bodies of nut, shell, precious metal, or some semi-precious hardstone (pl. 563).

Some of the most curious cups and ewers formed as animals or humans can be seen among the designs of the Hamburg goldsmith, Jakob Mores, in the Berlin *Kunstbibliothek*. These include an elephant cup (pl. 189) and even two drinking-cups modelled in the form of the Holy Roman Emperor and the Empress. As an example of the interest shown in silver sculpture, the gifts taken to Moscow for presentation to the Tsar Boris Godunow may be cited.[114] In 1603 a delegation from the German Hanseatic cities took to Moscow for the Tsar: a large eagle, an ostrich, a pelican, a griffin, a lion, an unicorn, a horse, a stag, a rhinoceros and, for his eldest son, a small eagle with a gilt sceptre, a figure of Fortuna, another of Venus, a peacock and a horse, all being of silver-gilt. It is recorded that the total weight of the gift was 5338 Lot and that the goldsmith who accompanied the embassy had to work night and day to repair and assemble the pieces. The eagle bottle illustrated in pl. 518 may have formed part of this particular gift.

Certain Nürnberg masters specialised in making these figures, among them Meinrad Bauch and David Lauer. Rosenberg lists no fewer than thirteen vessels of this type by Bauch. One of the most imposing of the surviving silver vessels is the huge eagle made by Christoph Jamnitzer,[115] which was originally presented to King Christian IV of Denmark by his subjects. It was pawned during the Thirty Years War and was eventually acquired, together with many other silver vessels from the Danish Royal treasury, for the Russian Imperial Treasury in the Moscow Kremlin, where it still remains. In contrast with most of the other works bearing Christoph Jamnitzer's mark, this eagle is not very finely worked. It was intended to serve as a wine cistern and weighs no less than twelve kilos.

Besides the single figures described above, larger groups composed of several figures were made. These also had removable heads so that they could, at least in theory, be used as drinking-vessels. In practice they were regarded as table ornaments. The most popular was the Diana seated on a leaping stag (pl. 508). A number of Augsburg goldsmiths made this particular model; the majority bear the marks of Matthias Wallbaum, Jakob Müller the Elder or Joachim Fries.[116] It is, of course, possible that all were produced by a single master who worked to the order of other goldsmiths who then put their marks on the finished article. Alternatively, they may have been made from the same patterns which circulated from one goldsmith to another according to need. Although there are variations in the small accompanying figures that decorate the bases of these groups, the cast parts of the larger figures are so similar that some form of co-operation must have existed. Some twenty to thirty of these groups are known and it has been suggested that they may have been commissioned for some special occasion,[117] perhaps to be given as tournament prizes at the celebrations which accompanied the coronation of the Emperor Matthias at Frankfurt am Main in 1612. Apart from their evident aesthetic appeal, these groups had the additional attraction to the contemporary observer in that they had a clockwork movement built into the base which, when wound, moved them along the table. One of the most remarkable surviving vessels of this kind, made by a Breslau goldsmith, belongs to the Mercers' Company of the City of London, having been presented to them in 1573. It takes the form of a triumphal car (pl. 559), the whole surface of which is covered with etched mauresques. It is accompanied by another piece, a miniature barrel with a tap set on a circular base, which could be placed on the platform between the front and rear parts of the carriage. Presumably the person in front of whom the carriage stopped could turn the tap and refill his glass.

Nürnberg and Augsburg Designs of the Last Quarter of the Sixteenth Century

At a time when it was the fashion to decorate the whole surface of objects made by the goldsmith, there was a constant demand for new ideas or for the new combinations of old ideas from the masters of engraved ornament. The Nürnberg City Council made special efforts to attract competent engravers to the city for this purpose. Just as in 1559 they granted honorary citizenship to Erasmus Hornick of Antwerp so also in 1577 the privilege was granted to the Zürich engraver Jost Amman (died 1591). This master had arrived in Nürnberg in 1561, the year before the death of Virgil Solis, who had been so prolific a supplier of sheets of engraved ornament. As Hornick left Nürnberg in 1566, Amman inherited Solis's position and played an important role in inventing designs himself and also in recording those by other masters as he did those of Wenzel Jamnitzer in or before 1568. The resolution of the City Council which granted him citizenship described him 'als Maler und Kupferstichreisser mit seiner Kunst so beruhmt und trefflich' (so famed and excellent in his art as painter and engraver). Amman was an excellent draughtsman; his woodcuts and engravings were widely used by the Nürnberg and Augsburg goldsmiths as sources of decorative design,[118] as also by bronze-founders, gunmakers and gunstock-engravers.[119] A number were published posthumously: in 1592 his *Kunstliche Wohlgerissene Figuren von allerlei Jagd-und Waidwerk*, and in 1599 his *Kunstbüchlein*, which was a collection of the various woodcuts he had issued during his lifetime. Of the many goldsmiths' designs that have been attributed to Jost Amman such as the cup in pl. 176 or the large dish in pl. 190 it is probable that most are based on his woodcuts rather than actually from his hand. Details taken from his prints of figures in elaborate costume of the time will frequently be encountered in engraved or cast friezes of the late sixteenth or early seventeenth century.

During the last decades of the century a new version of the familiar strapwork was introduced. Instead of the high relief developed by the Fontainebleau masters, strapwork was now rendered in a flat manner almost without relief (*Schweifwerk*). This seems first to have been introduced by the Nürnberg painter, Georg Wechter, who published a book of designs in 1579. In this book he offered forms that came readily within the scope of the competent goldsmith; his style, composed of all-over strapwork enclosing masks and flowers, is well represented by the ewer design (pl. 177).

At about the same time the new technique of dotted prints (*Punzenstiche*) was adopted by the masters of ornament for the use of goldsmiths. It was borrowed from the process followed by goldsmiths in preparing to emboss ornament on wrought plate. Before the metal was embossed the areas to be decorated were marked out with a fine punch, producing a dotted outline. It was usual to take a rubbing of these outlines in order to keep a record of the design employed and no great labour was required to transfer the design to a copper plate from which a pattern sheet could be printed. The masters of the dotted prints set the dots more closely together than the goldsmith, creating a continuous effect when the sheets were printed. These prints were not so ambitious as the drawings of Erasmus Hornick or the engraved designs of Matthias Zündt, but kept well within the bounds of the capacity of the working goldsmith. They represent the average production of the period and not the exotic fantasies intended to appeal to the imagination of a sophisticated prince.

The flat strapwork of Georg Wechter was taken up by three practitioners of the dotted print: Bernard Zan, Jonas Silber and Paul Flindt, all of Nürnberg. The first of these was a journeyman in Nürnberg; in 1580 he published a set of twelve designs for the bowls of cups and beakers entitled *12 Stick zum verzaichnen.* In the following year he published in Ansbach forty designs of complete vessels under the title *Allerley gebuntz-wierte Fisierungen* (all kinds of dotted designs) (pl. 181).

Between 1581 and 1590 Jonas Silber, who was himself a goldsmith of considerable standing, produced a large number of sheets of designs for tazza bowls, border patterns and panels of landscapes with antique figures, which were sometimes inspired directly by Zan's prints, from which they little differ. Four examples of surviving vessels decorated with designs based upon or similar to those found in the dotted prints are illustrated; a standing beaker (pl. 458), a tankard (pl. 503), a ewer (pl. 520) and a standing cup with pear-shaped body (pl. 521). Of these the last three represent typical Augsburg or Nürnberg production of the late sixteenth century, whereas the standing beaker of the Augsburg Butchers' Guild (pl. 458) is of outstanding quality.

Paul Flindt

The most prolific engraver of dotted prints was Paul Flindt, who signed his sheets P.V.N., i.e. *Paulus Vlindt Norimbergensis.* His first two sets of designs were published in Vienna in 1592 and 1593, but his third appeared in Nürnberg in 1594. Thereafter he produced a series of similar sets until his death after 1631, the total number of his prints reaching over two hundred. His designs cover the whole range of the goldsmith's art with the exception of jewellery. They include typical Nürnberg columbine-cups, designed for those about to submit their masterpiece (pl. 178), altar plate and altar candlesticks, all kinds of cups and beakers, among the latter a curious type with high domed cover shaped like a beehive, giving an acorn-like profile to the vessel. He also designed some more adventurous forms such as the nautilus shell cup (pl. 180) or the curious cup in the form of a standing woman in contemporary dress (pl. 182). Nautilus-shell cups remained in fashion well into the seventeenth century and as the sea routes became less difficult they were less expensive to provide. A late sixteenth-century example by a Nürnberg maker is illustrated in pl. 522, while a drinking-cup of similar construction to that of pl. 182 is shown in pl. 525. In his later series, published after the turn of the century, the auricular forms of early Baroque play a substantial role. As might be expected of so prolific a master, Flindt derived many of his ideas from other sources, in particular from the *Kunstbüchlein* of his Nürnberg fellow-citizen, Jost Amman. He seems to have been a practising goldsmith and is credited with a set of plaquettes as well as making the new masterpiece pattern cup for the Nürnberg guild.[120]

Boas Ulrich

This Augsburg goldsmith produced cast silver mounts for ebony caskets and reliquaries in a manner that is almost indistinguishable from his rival and contemporary in Augsburg, Matthias Wallbaum. It is unlikely that he supplied the finished articles; he would have sold mounts by the dozen that were used by the cabinet-makers as and when they required them. Boas Ulrich is believed to be the master of a number of drawings signed with the monogram BV which are preserved in the Veste Coburg. In style they show the influence of the contemporary *Punzenstecher,* such as Bernard Zan or Paul Flindt, and date from the last decades of the sixteenth century. This would correspond to Boas Ulrich's working life, as he was admitted master about 1576 and died in 1624. The initials are not, however, unusual and the drawings may be the work of another master. They correspond closely to the type of vessel that was then being made; this suggests that they are the work of a practising goldsmith rather than a graphic artist, who would have been more tempted to indulge his imagination. The drawings (pls. 183-4) show only the bowls of the cups, and not the stems. This is because the feet and stems would have been cast from existing patterns and original designs would only be required for the embossing or engraving on the bowl.

A book of drawings of figures intended to surmount standing cups or similar vessels in the Berlin Kunstbibliothek is also attributed to Boas Ulrich. The title-page is inscribed *Ein schönes Kunstbuch daryan mancherley figguren aufs des Berspektyff.* It shows that Ulrich was a competent draughtsman, if the attribution is indeed correct. Finial figures on south German cups are less various than those of the late fifteenth or early sixteenth century. The goldsmiths were apparently content to use again a figure for which a model was available rather than go to the trouble of carving and making a mould for a new one. Figure finials cast from the same pattern are found on South German cups of the second half of the century made by different goldsmiths.

The recorded *oeuvre* of most of the Nürnberg *Kleinmeister* and of such masters as Jost Amman, Bernard Zan and Paul Flindt does not represent anything like a lifetime's work, even allowing for the loss of a number of their prints. It is known that Paul Flindt decorated vessels for goldsmiths and it seems reasonable to assume that others did likewise. It is rarely possible to attribute the embossed, engraved or chased ornament on a piece to an individual, but the designs of the *Punzenstecher* correspond so closely to the ornament on surviving pieces of the period that they can be credited with carrying out the ornament on them as well as providing the designs.

The South German goldsmiths preferred to decorate their wares with embossed and chased ornament rather than engraving but there were exceptions. The most usual recipient of engraved ornament was the small beaker on low-foot (*Satzbecher* or, if made in a set of twelve engraved with scenes representing the labours of the months, *Monatsbecher*). Few sets survive but the many individual beakers are engraved in a masterly manner that betrays the hand of the professional engraver. One of the most spectacular surviving examples of such engraved ornament is the ewer (pl. 519) and companion basin by a Nürnberg goldsmith using the mark BI. The large number of biblical scenes on these vessels are derived from such familiar sources as Virgil Solis and Bernard Salomon's Lyon Bible. The effect of the engraved ornament on these as on other engraved vessels of this period, was enhanced by gilding the panels and leaving the surrounding ground white. For engraved ornament of comparable extent it is necessary to look to the work of contemporary Dutch or English goldsmiths.

1 See 'Hans Brosamer und der Meister H.B. mit dem Greifenklau', *Zeitschrift für Kunstwissenschaft,* Vol. XIV, Berlin, 1960, p.68.
2 The Berlin Goldsmiths' Guild specified a columbine-cup as masterpiece in 1597, the Dresden goldsmiths in 1607. A columbine-cup in the Leipzig Kunstgewerbemuseum was submitted as a masterpiece in Leipzig as late as 1676. See R. Graul, *Alte Leipziger Goldschmiedearbeiten,* Leipzig, 1910, p.xxviii.
3 For a detailed discussion of the Nürnberg masterpiece cups, see M. Rosenberg, *Kunst und*

Gewerbe, Vol. XIX, Wien, 1885, p.298 and, by the same author 'Die drei sogenannten Jamnitzer-becher', *Der Kunstwanderer,* 1920, p.351. The guild regulation specified *ein Trinckgeschirr, seines Namens ein Ageley-Plumen von Silber von fremden Patronen vor...mit sein selbst hanndt on meniglich hilf unnd zuthun'* (a drinking vessel known as a columbine flower of silver made to a foreign pattern...by his own hand without human help or assistance). It is interesting to note that Wechter published a columbine cup-design in his 1579 pattern-book; this was probably a repetition of or an adaptation of his design for the 1571 Nürnberg guild pattern cup. It is strikingly similar to a columbine-cup in the Victoria and Albert Museum.

4   Pechstein III, p.240 suggests that he probably learnt in the south-west in either Basel or Strassburg.
5   Frankenburger, p.1.
6   ibid. p.3.
7   Schenk zu Schweinsberg, *Jahrbuch der Preuss. Kunstammlungen,* Berlin Vol. XLVII, 1926, p.38ff.
8   Frankenburger, p.20-1.
9   Fully discussed by Pechstein III, p.240ff.
10 ill. Rosenberg II, pl. 34.
11 Pechstein IV, cat. no. 8.
12 J. G. Doppelmayr, *Von den Nürnbergischen Mathematicis und Künstlern,* Nürnberg, 1730 p.205-6.
14 For Jamnitzer's significance as a mathematician, see I. Franke 'Wenzel Jamnitzer's Zeichnungen zur Perspectiva' *Münchner Jahrbuch der bildenden Kunst,* 1972, p.165.
15 Pechstein, II, p.81ff.
16 ibid. p.83, fig. 2.
17 The exact wording is *'Welchs ich erstlich alles selber mit meiner schweren handt gestellt und gemacht und darnach durch den kunstlichen Jobst Amman von Zürich aus demselben ins Kuppfer reyssen lassen'.*
18 ill. J. Sponsel, 'Flötner Studien IX', *Jahrbuch der Preuss. Kunstsammlungen,* 1925, p.60ff.
19 The enamelled standing bowl by Melchior Baier of Nürnberg, believed to have been made about 1545 for King Sigismund I of Poland, in the Munich Schatzkammer (Brunner no. 45) has an engraved mauresque frieze around the lip.
20 Pechstein II, p.89.
21 Elfried Bock, *Die Zeichnungen in der Universitätsbibliothek Erlangen,* Frankfurt a. Main, 1929. The group of eight drawings in this collection which bear Jamnitzer's initials W.I. are so various in manner that it is impossible to accept them all as his work. It follows that the signature is in each case a later addition. Some, may, nevertheless, be by him or from his workshop.
22 G. R. Hocke, *Die Welt als Labyrinth, Manier und Manie in der Europäischen Kunst,* Hamburg, 1957, passim.
23 Collins, p.367, no. 458.
24 Duke Johann VII of Mecklenburg owned a similar combination vessel. The inventory of his effects made after his death in 1592 includes *'Zwey getriebene verguldete Leuchter mit aufgeschobenen Trinchgeschirren und Confectschalen'* quoted Hüseler, p.12.
25 See J. F. Hayward, 'Candlestick Cups', *Connoisseur,* 1961, vol. 148, p.17ff.
26 Collins, p.371.
27 Kris II, pl. XXII.
28 *Quellenschriften zur Kunstgeschichte,* Vienna, Band X, p.126 'Johann Neudörfer, Nachrichten von Künstlern und Werkleuten daselbst aus dem Jahre 1547'.
29 For the best account of this piece, see Kris II, pps. 147-152.
30 A mauresque design by Jamnitzer in the Berlin Kunstbibliothek, signed and dated 1546, resembling the mauresques of the centre-piece is illustrated Rosenberg I, pl. 74.
31 ill. Kris II, p.157, 158.
32 Brunner, cat. no. 614.
33 *Jahrbuch,* Vienna, 1888, Vol. VII, Reg. no. 4953.
34 This attribution to Wenzel instead of Hans is due to K. Pechstein, see 'Wenzel Jamnitzer's Silber-glocken mit Naturabgüssen', *Anzeiger des Germ. Nationalmuseums,* 1967, p.36.
35 Doering, p.79.
36 In 1601 the Nürnberg goldsmith, Bernard Goldschmidt, was given leave by the City Council to go to Bamberg for two years to cast silver reptiles and grasses for the Bishop of Bamberg.
37 Collins, p.578.
38 Pechstein III, p.265ff.
39 ill. Rosenberg II, pl. 9.
40 ill. Rosenberg II, pls. 7, 8.
41 See Brunner, cat. no. 565 and Sponsel, Vol. 1, p.122, pl. 24.
42 Menzhausen, pl. 30, p. 31. The author credits Jamnitzer with the production of 'many of the cast parts' only.

43 The 1586 inventory of the collection describes it as follows: *Ein sattelbogen mit einer Caritas und hinder theil eines sattels mit gybs (von Keiser Maximilian sattel, so Gamnitzer ze Nournberg in silber gemacht) abgossen'.*

44 ill. Kris III, cat. no. 52.

45 ill. Kersting, fig. 85.

46 ill. Pechstein I, cat. no. 88.

47 ill. Böhm, pl. XIX.

48 The letter from the Nürnberg Council is printed in full by Frankenburger, p.17.

49 Frankenburger, nos. 32-40, pps. 8-12.

50 ill. Rosenberg II, pl. 15.

51 Brunner, cat. nos. 568-9.

52 One of Abraham Jamnitzer's best works, if it is indeed by him, is the gilt figure of Daphne with a large coral branch growing out of her head in the Grünes Gewölbe, Dresden, ill. Menzhausen, pl. 54. This figure is almost identical with another, now in the Cluny Museum, which bears the mark of Wenzel Jamnitzer. It is difficult to account for the difference in the marks on the two pieces. For the Cluny piece, see the poor drawing reproduced in Rosenberg II, pl. 4.

53 Frankenburger nos. 61, 63, p.16.

54 ibid, p.30.

55 See E. Kris and O. von Falke, 'Beiträge zu den Werken Christoph und Hans Jamnitzers' *Jahrbuch der Preussischen Kunstsammlungen,* Vol. 47, 1926, p.196ff. The conclusions reached in this article have been questioned by I. Weber, 'Fragen zum Oeuvre des Meisters H. G.', *Münchner Jahrbuch der bildenden Kunst,* Band XXII, 1971, p.133ff. Not only does the writer reject many of the Falke attributions but she also questions whether the identification of Hans Jamnitzer as the *Meister H. G.* is correct.

56 See K. Pechstein, 'Neu-entdeckte Arbeiten von Hans Jamnitzer', *Berliner Museen,* N.F. XX p.61.

57 ill. ibid, fig. 8.

58 Inv. nos. 17008 and RBK 1966-8 respectively.

59 For a detailed study of this tazza see A. Schönberger, 'Die Weltallschale Kaiser Rudolfs II', *Festschrift Theodor Müller,* Munich, 1965, p.253.

60 This description was destroyed in the Second World War.

61 See Böhm, passim.

62 ibid, p. 80ff.

63 On one of his visits to Prague Paul van Vianen produced a medal with a profile portrait of him. The medal is signed with Vianen's monogram and dated 1609, see H. Modern, *Jahrbuch,* Vol. XV, 1894, p.94.

64 *Jahrbuch,* Vol. X, 1889, Regest No. 5641.

65 Quoted by Böhm, p.56.

66 *Jahrbuch,* Vol. X, 1889, Regest No. 5672.

67 Sponsel, Band II, pl. 14.

68 These huge cups are still best represented in the Moscow Kremlin, though some, sold in the 1930's, returned to Sweden and Denmark whence they had been sent as gifts in the seventeenth century.

69 ill. Menzhausen, pl. 56.

70 ill. Pechstein IV, nos. 217-20.

71 See Rosenberg II, pls. 64, 66.

72 For evidence of his draughtsmanship see the two cartouches from his hand illustrated by Kris and Falke, figs. 6 and 7.

73 *Jahrbuch,* Band X, Regest No. 5909 (11 April 1603).

74 See Kris and Falke, passim.

75 See Weihrauch II, pps. 268-271. The drawing of a casket illustrated in Rosenberg II, pl. 72 is also annotated in Italian, though whether in Christoph's own hand has not been established.

76 ill. F. H. Dreier, 'Hans Jacob Sprüngli aus Zürich als Hinterglasmaler', *Zeitschrift für Schweiz. Archäologie* Band 21, 1961, pl. 7 a, c.

77 Hampe, no. 1091.

78 E. Meyer-Heisig, *Der Nürnberger Glasschnitt,* Nürnberg, 1963.

79 Both tankards are illustrated by O. von Falke 'Aus dem Jamnitzerkreis' *Pantheon,* 1937, Band XIX, p.13-17.

80 ill. Kohlhaussen, pl. 669.

81 Weiss, chap. vii, passim.

82 For a fuller account of Lotter see Krempel, p.138ff.

83 ill. Krempel, figs. 29-31.

84 Stockbauer, p.96ff.

85 For Hans Reimer, see Krempel, p.126ff. for the *Saphir Pokal,* figs. 12, 13.

86 ill. Krempel, figs. 12, 13.

87 A. Winkler, Die Handzeichnungen des Jakob Mores in Berlin, *Jahrbuch der Preuss. Kunstsammlungen*, 1890, p.108.

88 ill. Krempel, p.133, figs. 25-6.

89 Illustrated on the cover of the Exhibition Catalogue, *Goldschmiedekunst*, Landesmuseum, Joanneum, Graz, 1961, cat. no. 47.

90 *Carlos V y su ambiente*, Toledo, 1958, Exhibition catalogue, pl. CCXXI.

91 ill. Catalogue, *Sammlung f.Plastik u. Kunstgewerbe*, II Teil, Vienna, 1966 pl. 53.

92 ill. J. F. Hayward, *The Art of the Gunmaker*, Vol. I, 1965, Colour PL. III.

93 The same scheme was used by Daniel Kellerdaler of Dresden in the decoration of the body of the ewer he made in 1629 to accompany the basin embossed with the contest between Apollo and Marsyas before Midas, now in the Grünes Gewölbe, though in this case the heads project even further. See Sponsel, pl. 51.

94 Bartsch XIV, p.264, no. 352.

95 See H. W. Seling, 'Hans Schebel, ein unbekannter Augsburger Goldschmied des 16ten Jahrhunderts', *Kunstgeschichtliche Stüdien für Kurt Bauch*, 1967, p.145. When Schebel died in 1571 two writing desks (*Schreibtische*) were found in his workshop, intended for his patron, Duke Albrecht V of Bavaria. One was decorated with biblical and the other with Roman histories.

96 See *Jahrbuch des Schleswig-Holstein Museums*, Schleswig, 1959, p.128 and, for Herzog Philipp von Pommern's commissions to Augsburg goldsmiths, Bethe, *passim*.

97 '*Ain schoner kunstlicher krueg, der grund desselben vergult und darüber durchaus mit durchbrochner silberner arbait mit zwaien vergulten henden, auf dem krueg gar kunstliche steudl und pluemen; hat nit gewegen kunden werden und aber gestanden 700 gulden*'.

98 Rosenberg I, no. 4152, see also ibid, Band III, pps. 192-3.

99 Weiss, p.156.

100 Stadtarchiv Augsburg, *Goldschmiedeakten*, Band III, p.127 '*Dann es weist und sicht meniglich, daz an den allten Geschüren so herrlich und zierlich Bluemenwerckh gesehen würdt, daz inen alle Khunst und Hürn sollche nachzemachen, zerinnen wurde*'.

101 Doering, p.50, letter dated 17-27 October, 1610.

102 This is preserved in the treasury of Klosterneuburg, Niederoesterreich, see K. Drechsler, *Goldschmiedearbeiten in Klosterneuburg*, 1897, pl. XII.

103 Rosenberg I, nos. 383, 384.

104 See E. v. Rodt, 'Berner Kunstdenkmäler', *Berne Artistique*, Band I, Bern 1902, Bl. 3.

105 Thoma, pl. 51. Brunner, cat. nos. 589-90, p.248, where the previous attributions are listed.

106 For a detailed study of these pieces and their graphic sources, see I. Weber, p.360.

107 Rossacher, nos. 50-109.

108 ill. O. Sronkova, *Fashion through the Centuries*, London, n.d. p.98.

109 T. Müller, *Pantheon*, Vol. XVIII, 1960, p.16.

110 Rottenhammer is credited with a number of designs for silver, including a drawing of the Rape of the Sabines within a roundel intended for a silver tazza bowl (see I. Weber, 'Rottenhammer Entwurf für ein Goldschmiedrelief', *Pantheon* Vol. XXVII-4, 1969, p.328) and also those for a crucifix figure ordered from Christoph Lencker by Duke Wilhelm V of Bavaria and the figures of the Nine Muses and the Pegasus for the *Pommersche Kunstschrank*. Other works by Rottenhammer are the models for H. Bayr's Eichstädter Monstrance and the design for the openwork cross made by Christoph Lencker for the *Heilige Kreuzkirche* in Augsburg.

111 A gilt-bronze plaque chased with the 'Lamentation over the Dead Christ', and signed by Zacharias Lencker about 1610 is in the Amsterdam Rijksmuseum (not in Rosenberg I).

112 O. von Falke, 'Die Augsburger Goldschmied Johannes Lencker', *Pantheon*, I, 1928, ps. 12 and 18. See also *Exhibition Catalogue*, 'Der Trionf van het Manierisme', Rijksmuseum, Amsterdam, 1955, no. 433, p.200.

113 See Weihrauch II, p.276-7.

114 See Hach, p.38.

115 B. A. Rybakow, *Der Moskauer Kreml, Die Rüstkammer*, 1962, Prag, pl. 104.

116 See G. Axel-Nilsson, 'Falk Simons Donation 1949, I. Diana auf dem Hirsch', *Arstryck 1950*, Rösska Konstslöjd Museet, p.41-65 and ibid 1957, p.55-58.

117 ibid. 1950, p.62.

118 For the use of Amman's prints by Augsburg goldsmiths of the late sixteenth century, see Weber, 'Bildvorlagen', The series of 54 tazzas and two large basins provides the most fruitful field for the study of the sources of designs used by German goldsmiths.

119 See J. F. Hayward, 'Designs for Ornament on Gunstocks', *Livrustkammaren*, Stockholm, 1951, p.109.

120 E. W. Braun, *Archiv für Medaillen und Plakettenkunde I*, 1913-14, p.21.

CHAPTER ELEVEN

Erasmus Hornick

ONE of the most prolific designers of goldsmiths' work was Erasmus Hornick, who lived in Nürnberg for several years from after 1559 to 1566. During this time he proved himself to be among the most daring and imaginative exponents of Mannerism in the goldsmiths' art. He came to Nürnberg from Augsburg where he had already practised as a goldsmith. He arrived there from Antwerp, probably as a master goldsmith, in the early 1550's and ended his days in Prague as a member of the court workshop of the Emperor Rudolph II. So large is the number and so wide the range of his drawings and prints that his career justifies closer study.

Most of Hornick's drawings date from the latter part of his career, after he had left Antwerp, but a number can be attributed to his first period on account of their resemblance to Antwerp vessels made at the time he is believed to have been working there. Assuming that he was born about 1520, he would probably have completed his apprenticeship and been working as a journeyman by the 1540's. In that case he would have been admitted master, presumably in Antwerp, before 1550. It is significant that, whereas the designs of architects such as Cornelis Floris and Hans Vredeman de Vries (see p.283), seem to have had a restricted influence upon contemporary goldsmiths' style, the drawings of Erasmus Hornick can be paralleled without difficulty amongst surviving marked Antwerp silver of the mid-sixteenth century. It is not, however, likely that Hornick was himself the creator of this mid-century Antwerp style. He only spent the earlier years of his working career in the city and his drawings may be copies of pieces he had seen or elaborations of familiar themes. In his later drawings Hornick can be credited with great originality but his early ones are mostly derived from the work of other masters. In many of them he introduced the familiar marine symbolism that has already been noticed in designs attributed to the workshops of Salviati or Androuet du Cerceau. Often he arranges his aquatic elements in a rather confused manner (pl. 200) but in the borders of larger basins the combats between tritons show a dynamic sense of rhythm in their composition (pl. 201). Another manner adopted by Hornick is seen in the drawing of a standing cup (pl. 205). In this case the surface of the vessel is covered with strapwork enclosing panels of arabesques with lions' masks and grotesque heads at regular intervals. These Hornick drawings are best studied in comparison with contemporary Antwerp silver vessels of which a representative series survives (see Chapter XIV).

Hornick's significance as a designer or as a working goldsmith in Augsburg is difficult to estimate as he spent much time away from the city. By his marriage with Afra Haug on 27 July 1555, he not only gained the privilege of citizenship of Augsburg but allied himself with one of the leading families of the city. Two inferences may be made from this alliance; firstly that he must have been a well-known figure in Augsburg by 1555 and secondly that he was resident there for some years before. The earliest reference to him in the Augsburg rate books dates from 1558, three years after his marriage. The absence of his name in the intervening years probably means that he was temporarily employed outside Augsburg at one of the German courts. He left Augsburg in about 1559, but must already have acquired a considerable reputation in Nürnberg, since he was admitted to citizenship there without payment of the customary fees, as was another foreigner and master of ornament, Jost Amman, some years later. The resolution of the City Council[1] is recorded in the following terms:-

> 'Erasmus Hornay (Hornick) of Antwerp, inasmuch as he is an outstanding artist in the goldsmiths' craft, to be admitted citizen and to be given the rights of citizenship free of charge'.

We do not know what prompted the City Fathers of Nürnberg to treat him so generously, but their action was exceptional. At that time Wenzel Jamnitzer was the most influential goldsmith on the City Council and he would doubtless have had a say in the matter.[2] It is also possible that Jacopo da Strada, who was associated with the Jamnitzer workshop in 1559 (see p.47) and who subsequently appears to have had dealings with Hornick, may have been the connecting link between him and Nürnberg. The German craft guilds were generally extremely jealous of their privileges and did not lightly agree to the granting of citizenship and the consequent right to practise his craft in the city to a foreign master. It was not until four years later, on 6 November, 1563, that we find the record of Hornick's admittance to the Nürnberg Goldsmiths' Guild in their *Meisterbuch*.[3] On this occasion the fee was not waived and he had to pay the considerable sum of ten florins.

Erasmus Hornick was a designer of both goldsmiths' and jewellers' work; so numerous are the drawings attributed to him that it is doubtful whether he can often have laid down the pencil to take up the tools of the goldsmith. However, had he not practised his craft with exceptional skill and diligence he would not have been described as an outstanding artist in it, and still less would he have received in 1582 the appointment[4] of *Kammergoldschmied* to the Emperor Rudolph II, one of the most lavish patrons of the craft of all time. The key to the identification of the large number of drawings by Hornick that survive is to be found in the series of pattern-books of designs which he published in Nürnberg and, perhaps, elsewhere during the 1560's. The earliest appears to have been the set of twenty designs for jewellery including needle-cases, scent-bottles and mounts for flea-furs (*Flohpelze*) which is signed and dated 1562. In 1565 Hornick published two further pattern-books in Nürnberg; the first was a set of twenty jewellery designs, most of which showed the then fashionable type of pendant composed of figures within arched niches, and the second, a set of vases, ewers, etc., consisting of a title-page and eighteen sheets.

The second set is signed and dated *Erasmus Hornick, Nürnberg, 1565*. A curious feature is the lay-out of the title-page in the form of the stretched-out skin of an ass (pl. 138) suspended by the head and the four hooves by ribbons. The macabre device of using a flayed skin for his title-page had been used by the master once before and it provided an appropriate frontispiece to the fleshy forms he used so freely. Hornick published two further sets of designs of which complete or nearly complete examples survive.[5] Each consists of ten medallions enclosing figures, similar to those which are frequently included on his vessel designs. These last are undated and their place of publication uncertain. Finally, three single sheets are known which bear his signature or monogram, presumably belonging to two other pattern-books that have not survived in their entirety. These comprise a fine engraving of a ewer (pl. 142) and two sheets showing candlesticks, fork, spoon, knife and snuffers.[6] In view of the very large number of drawings by Hornick that seem to have been meant for publication in pattern-books, there can be little doubt that these isolated engravings also belong to complete pattern-books. Hornick's printed designs are extremely rare, perhaps because they were used in the goldsmiths' shops until they were worn out and thrown away. Alternatively they may have had little success so that few copies were ever printed. A client who chose one of Hornick's designs for a ewer or a vase must have been a thoroughly committed follower of the *Maniera* in the goldsmiths' art.

The largest group of drawings by Erasmus Hornick is preserved in the Victoria and Albert Museum.[7] These illustrate the whole range of the goldsmith's craft with the exception of jewellery, which was covered in the two printed books published by Hornick in Nürnberg. The drawings were formerly bound together with a codex containing 275 sheets, by no means all of which were by Hornick himself. Among the sheets are four designs for title-pages; the presence of these makes it clear that at least some of the designs were intended for pattern-books, which these title-pages would have preceded. The first title-page is dated 1560 (pl. 139). In the centre of the lion's skin is a passage from Seneca and, written in a later hand, *Sunt Figurae num 275 Rudolfi Caesaris Thesaurus Delineat* (There are 275 Designs representing the Treasury of the Emperor Rudolph). Whoever made this annotation knew nothing of Hornick, but, knowing that Rudolph II had accumulated a large collection of vessels of precious metal, assumed that the drawings constituted a pictorial inventory of the Imperial Treasury. If he had looked a little more closely he would have realised that the repetitious nature of the drawings made his theory untenable. He was not, however, far out in his guess, since Hornick was eventually appointed *Kammergoldschmied* to the Emperor Rudolph. Furthermore, two of the other groups of Hornick drawings in existence can also be connected with Vienna: a group of thirteen drawings in the Oesterreichisches Museum für angewandte Kunst, and a codex formerly in the Liechtenstein library. It is very probable that all these drawings, now widely distributed, were originally together and constituted the material for a series of pattern-books of which only a few were ever published. The reference to the Emperor Rudolph on the title page (pl. 139) gives a hint as to the identity of the first owner of the drawings after Hornick's death in Prague in 1583. It is most probable that the Hornick drawings passed into the collection of the Emperor himself, who is known to have acquired designs for goldsmiths' work as well as the objects themselves.

The title-page with the lion's skin as its central feature (pl. 139) was probably intended to accompany a series of eighteen to twenty designs for vases or other goldsmiths' work, corresponding in arrangement to that published in 1565; it is, however, no longer possible to determine which. In the case of two other title-pages from the Victoria and Albert Museum codex one can recognise some of the designs they were intended to introduce. Neither is dated, but both seem to belong to Hornick's time in Nürnberg when he published so many pattern-books. The first (pl. 140) relates to the hunt, and, distributed between the various groups of Hornick drawings, are sixteen that were probably meant to accompany it. They represent hunting-swords (pls. 224-5), hunting-horns and other equipment for the chase. The second title-page (pl. 145) has once again a Latin tag, *Spes Alit Agricolas,* within a winged cartouche and shows a gardener at work. It was meant to introduce designs for flower vases (pl. 143). According to a typical Mannerist conceit the flowers were not intended to be natural but were to be made of silver. Vases with flowers cut from silver sheet are preserved in the Kunsthistorisches Museum, Vienna (pl. 490) and the Museum of the City of Dortmund.[8] Another can be seen in the background of the portrait of Wenzel Jamnitzer (pl. 5). The presence of a set of drawings of vases with silver flowers is only to be expected as Hornick was himself a specialist in their production. In 1592, ten years after his death, he is mentioned in the Augsburg *Goldschmiedeakten* as having taught the art of making them and in the same year, there is a reference to a bunch of flowers (*Blumenwerk*) of unusually large size which derived from a design (*Invention*) by Erasmus Hornick.

Three groups of drawings by Hornick have been mentioned above: one in the Victoria and Albert Museum, one in the Oesterreichisches Museum, Vienna, and one in the Liechtenstein Collection, since dispersed. Three other codices containing Hornick drawings survive. One was formerly in the collection of the Earl of Warwick but has been lost sight of since its sale to the U.S.A. between the wars. The title-page of this last mentioned codex consists of a *Rollwerk* cartouche (pl. 141) dated 1569 and brings us to a period when Hornick was no longer resident in Nürnberg. The *Bürgerbuch* of the city records that he surrendered his citizenship on 27 February, 1566.[9] The second codex containing drawings by Erasmus Hornick is preserved in the Bayerische Staatsbibliothek, Munich, and was already recorded in the catalogue of the manuscripts in the library of Duke Albrecht V of Bavaria, prepared in 1582.[10] It is there described as *Vascula antiqua von Jac. da Strada abgerissen,* but, as I have demonstrated elsewhere,[11] all the drawings it contains are in the highly individual manner of Hornick and can with confidence be attributed to him. There are in all sixty sheets of drawings in the codex showing vases, scent-flagons, drinking-cups, including a peculiar type without foot, known in England as stirrup-cups, candlesticks, egg-cups, tazzas (pl. 144), cutlery and hand-bells. These drawings repeat some which are included in other groups by Hornick; there are, indeed, as many as three or four versions of the same design distributed amongst the various groups into which the Hornick drawings are now divided. If we were to accept the entry in the Munich Library catalogue of 1582 as correct, we should also have to accept that Jacopo da Strada found time, despite his numerous commissions from the Emperor, the Duke of Bavaria and the Fuggers, to undertake the tedious work of producing large numbers of copies of designs by Erasmus Hornick. Although no other evidence connecting da Strada with Hornick exists, they can hardly have failed to meet each other. Hornick was admitted a master of the Nürnberg Goldsmiths' Guild on 6 November 1563 and da Strada was resident in the city from 1546 until about 1565. In the later years da Strada was often abroad but, as both were working goldsmiths, they must have had every occasion to meet. Two years before Hornick's arrival in Nürnberg, da Strada had received the sum of 100 thaler and 54 gulden from the Archduke Ferdinand of Tirol as an honorarium. This figure enables us to compare the relative importance of the two men, for, at the current rate of exchange (one thaler equals one and a half gulden), da Strada was paid on this occasion as much as Hornick would have earned as a member of the *Kaiserliche Hofwerkstatt* in thirty-four months. Da Strada was evidently too important a person to have assisted the newly-arrived Erasmus Hornick and the relationship must have been quite the opposite. Presumably at some time between 1565, when he went to work for Duke Albrecht V, and 1582, when the inventory was made, da Strada offered to provide the Duke with a collection of drawings of antique vases and similar metalwork to round off the ducal collection of antiquities, and, remembering his former Nürnberg colleague, who had been granted honorary citizenship on account of his skill as a draughtsman, commissioned him to supply them. In this commission the emphasis was placed on the antiquity of the vessels represented, not on originality, and hence Hornick was content to exploit once again his familiar stock of ideas. It is, of course, possible that da Strada passed off the drawings as his own work, or that the clerk who prepared the inventory, knowing that the codex had been supplied by da Strada, mistakenly assumed that he must also have executed the drawings.

The third codex referred to above is in the Berlin Kunstbibliothek. In this case the style is rather more evolved than in those already described; the drawings could be the work of an assistant of Hornick or they may be a late work of Hornick himself. There are a hundred drawings covering much the same range as the other Hornick codices. While the profile of the vessels shown corresponds more or less closely to those in his other groups of designs the ornament is more florid (pl. 147) and introduces more foliate detail. The circular salt from the Berlin codex, illustrated in pl. 146 belongs to a type that does not otherwise appear in the Hornick *oeuvre.*

In 1566 Erasmus Hornick left Nürnberg,[12] presumably returning to Augsburg, though he may have found employment for a time elsewhere. He subsequently turned his hand to other matters than the art of the goldsmith. An entry in the minutes of the Nürnberg City Council[13] shows that he embarked upon military affairs. According to a decision of the Council of 24 May, 1578, Wenzel Jamnitzer was required to write to Erasmus Hornick, citizen and goldsmith of Augsburg, in reply to the offer he had made of certain new inventions relating to artillery and other warlike equipment and inform him that, as the city had no need of such armament, he should offer them elsewhere. None of his known drawings relates to military matters, so we do not know what manner of invention he had devised. His name appears in the Augsburg *Steuerbuch* for 1568 and he is described as a goldsmith in an entry in the *Pflegschaftsbuch*[14] for 23 October, 1570. In November 1570 he remarried and he was then described as a *Freykunstler*, meaning that he was not a member of a guild but was self-employed, finding commissions for work wherever he could, probably for the most part outside Augsburg at the court of one or other of the many ruling princes of Germany. Unfortunately we know practically nothing of Hornick's activities in Augsburg apart from his effort to obtain employment in Nürnberg as a military engineer. The title-page of the Warwick set of designs is dated 1569, after Hornick's return from Nürnberg. He must, therefore, have continued to produce designs for goldsmiths, and the fact that he was called to the Imperial Court Workshop of the Emperor Rudolph in 1582 implies that he was then considered to be a leading goldsmith.

To assist in distinguishing the periods of the very large number of extant drawings by Hornick we have the evidence provided by the pattern-book of eighteen sheets of vases published in 1565. These show six ewers, three sauce-boats, three ewers or buckets of a type that could either be suspended from a swing handle or stood on a circular foot, three two-handled vases with covers, a pilgrim flask, a standing cup and cover and a scent-flask. The book does not include any of the candlesticks, salts, peppers or basins of which Hornick produced so many designs. Not all of these reflect the sophisticated taste of the fashionable Mannerist style. Two distinct styles can, in fact, be recognised in the pattern-book. The first is conservative and looks back to that which was fashionable in Antwerp in the 1540's when Hornick is believed to have been working there. The vessels in this group have their surface divided into small panels by a symmetrical arrangement of straps (pl. 148). While the form of the vessels is of an international northern type, the decoration can be identified as specifically Flemish.

The second style represented in these prints is more advanced and introduces an attitude of mind that rejected previously accepted standards of beauty and proportion (pl. 149). Instead of applying ornament to vessels of conventional form, as he had done in his Antwerp designs, Hornick adopted a sculptural approach and treated his vessels as forms that could be moulded to suit his fantasy without consideration for their ultimate purpose. Italian artists such as Giulio Romano or Perino del Vaga had anticipated him in giving human or animal form to drinking-vessels, but Hornick displayed an imaginative power in devising monstrous forms that was unparalleled in northern Europe. In some of his drawings the strapwork takes on a fleshy guise, merging into the living forms it confines, so that it is difficult to determine where the limbs end and the straps begin. No space, however small, is left undecorated, and tails, legs, arms, breasts, masks and draperies are mingled in a confusion that seems to ignore the decorative purpose of ornament and to delight in fantasy alone (pl. 150). Masks develop at frequent intervals out of these intertwined limbs and scrolls, and while some display the cold stare of classical art others glare at us with vicious, sadistic intent (pl. 151). In such designs Hornick displays a perverse delight in the creation of repulsive forms and unnatural associations that recall the pictorial experiments of the Emperor Rudolph's court painter, Archimboldi. A typical drawing shows the intertwined bodies of a male monster and a mermaid supported by a dragon.[15] With a concession to propriety by no means typical of Mannerist art, the male and female figures are not confronted but set back to back or side by side (pl. 152).

Hornick's drawings invariably reproduce the Mannerist ideal of the female form with small head and long elegant body. His method of modelling is idiosyncratic; muscles are represented by a large number of small blotches which at first sight look like wounds or bruises (pls. 150, 157). His obsession with muscular development derives, of course, from Michelangelo. Neither male nor female nudes often played a dominant part in the Hornick designs; the figures were usually too crowded by surrounding animal and vegetable forms to stand out. A favourite device copied from designs of the school of Giulio Romano or of Francesco Salviati was to place a female figure in profile under the spout or handle of a ewer. The sauce-boat (pl. 150) is one of the few in which the figures are allocated sufficient space to form a satisfactory composition. His placing of figures sometimes redeemed the profile of what would otherwise be a graceless object, but Hornick was usually quite ready to sacrifice shape in the interest of dramatic effect. Many of his designs, especially those of ewers, are of an ugliness that can have been acceptable only at a time when Renaissance standards were no longer respected (pls. 150-6).

It is probable that Hornick's style was fully evolved when he left Nürnberg in 1566. It would certainly be difficult to achieve a higher degree of fantasy than his 1565 pattern-book. It does, in fact, represent most of the various treatments and styles found among his hundreds of extant drawings. The large number associated with the title page dated 1569, that is from after his return to Augsburg, cover much the same range of ideas. The 1565 pattern book differs from the other collections of Hornick drawings in one significant respect. This is the narrowness of its range, for it is confined to seven vessel types, whereas the drawings cover the whole field of production with the exception of church plate. The absence of this is curious, for the Church was at the time one of the most important sources of commissions for goldsmiths' work and the other sets of drawings referred to above, such as those in the Salviati manner, include a number of church pieces.

While the range of Hornick's invention is so great, there are few, if any, vessels in which function is treated as of equal importance to display. This is not surprising, for the working goldsmith did not require the aid of an original artist in the production of useful wares, the design of which followed an established pattern. Some of the vessels depicted are of so fantastic a form that they can hardly have been capable of execution. We do not, however, know in what medium Hornick intended them to be made. During the second half of the sixteenth century great interest was shown in the use of exotic materials and semi-precious hardstones, and it is probable that Hornick, who must have hoped for commissions from wealthy princes or nobles, would have intended such materials to be used in their production. Many designs, including some of the sheets in the 1565 pattern-book (pls. 148, 149) show elements that suggest the spiral form of the nautilus- or trochus-shell, others seem meant to be composed of panels of mother-of-pearl in a silver framework (pl. 148) Others again are of a form that could best be executed in rock-crystal or some other semi-precious hardstone (pls. 155, 156). Hornick never gives any indication on his drawings of the material intended, but examples such as those illustrated in pls. 147, 155-6 were probably meant to be mounted in gold. The delicate arabesques indicated on drawings such as that in pl. 156 would be well suited for rock-crystal and the pendant jewels that complete the design imply that the mounting was to be of gold. The theory that some of Hornick's designs were meant to be cut in semi-precious stone is supported by the evidence of the last phase of his life. The Emperor Rudolph was an enthusiastic and generous patron of the glyptic art and his recruitment of Erasmus Hornick into the Prague *Hofwerkstatt* may well have been motivated by his appreciation of the master's skill in devising vessel forms appropriate for sculpture in hardstone.

In Hornick's later designs there is evidence of Italian influence. This is only to be expected of an artist working in the north during the third quarter of the sixteenth century, but the influence is so strong that one is tempted to assume that he actually went to Italy. This would not be a daring assumption. Two of his Flemish predecessors, who designed for the goldsmith's craft, Cornelis Bos and Cornelis Floris, spent some time there and in the second half of the sixteenth century there were usually a number of Flemish artists at work in the Italian princely courts, including Giacomo Delfe, who was one of the leading masters at the court of Francesco I, Grand Duke of Tuscany (see p.152). The earliest mention of Hornick in Germany is his marriage in Augsburg in 1555, so his stay in Italy, if it took place, would probably have been in the early 1550's. The Hornick Codex in the Victoria and Albert Museum includes drawings that seem to have been copied by him or by an assistant from Italian originals as well as a number of original Italian drawings. Unfortunately we do not know if the codex was assembled by Hornick or by a later collector; even if all the drawings in it did belong to him, we also do not know whether he acquired them during a visit to Italy or bought them from an itinerant vendor in Nürnberg, Augsburg or Prague. Of these Italianate drawings at least twenty seem to derive from Guilio Romano or Francesco Salviati, either workshop replicas of their designs or original drawings produced under their influence but not after their design. Several versions of some of these exist, for the most part as single sheets which are distributed among the Print Rooms and private collections of Europe and America.

Some of the most impressive of designs of the Salviati school are for salt-cellars and two of the best of Hornick's drawings also represent them. The importance of the salt in the sixteenth and seventeenth centuries was due to its position on the dining-table in front of the lord of the house, displaying his wealth and social status. The symbolism upon which both the Italian and the Hornick designs are based is somewhat naive. They are decorated with themes relating to water, though not necessarily salt water; a figure of Neptune in his chariot drawn by sea-horses surmounts one Hornick design (pl. 158) while in another Amphitrite is in a shell pulled by dolphins. Hornick seems to have been familiar not only with Italian goldsmiths' work but also with Italian majolica, for a number of his designs must surely have been based upon a ceramic original[16] (pl. 157). Something of his weakness as a designer can be appreciated if his drawing of a table-centre, or perhaps an ink-stand (pl. 159) is compared with the Italian design (pl. 83). Both have a sarcophagus-like base, but, whereas Salviati's drawing is well composed, Hornick's is built up layer-wise. While the winged sphinxes of the salt-cellar provide a solid base for the whole composition, those of the Hornick table-centre are insignificant.

The survival of so large a number of drawings from the Hornick workshop is not easily explained. Most of them depict vessels of great complexity of form and elaboration of ornament that would have required much time and labour to produce. Hornick could hardly have received a sufficient number of commissions to necessitate the preparation of so many designs and, in any case, he frequently repeated himself with only the slightest variation of detail and sometimes without variation. Such identical drawings cannot have been intended for inclusion in the same pattern-book, nor would there have been a demand for pattern-books that contained closely similar designs, for the goldsmith himself would have been able to improvise such minor changes of detail. It is conceivable that Hornick set his assistants the task of producing variations on his themes, but all these versions seem to proceed from one and the same hand. Another possibility is that Hornick himself may have produced several sets of designs which were not intended for printing and publication but for direct sale to other goldsmiths, just as plaquettes after models by the Nürnberg *Formenschneider*[17] were sold all over northern Europe. I have suggested that this may also explain the existence of numerous versions of some of the Salviati school drawings. If this theory is correct, it would appear that Hornick had little success, as so many drawings seem to have remained in his possession. Not all his drawings were intended for the working goldsmith; some at least were meant to be offered to German princes and noblemen as representations, not of contemporary goldsmiths' work but of antique vases, as was actually done by Jacopo da Strada when he planted Hornick's drawings on the Duke of Bavaria. In fact the designs had only the remotest resemblance to those of classical antiquity, but his clients were not competent to judge this.

While the number of drawings of vessels intended to be made of gold or silver that can be attributed to Erasmus Hornick runs into several hundred, no sixteenth-century piece remains that can with confidence be identified as his work. There are, indeed, very few pieces that even show much similarity to his style at all. His designs for jewellery, published in two pattern-books in Nürnberg in 1562 and 1565 respectively, seem to have had much more influence than his silver designs and it has been shown that a number of jewels based on them still survive.[18] Though no evidence exists to show whether he actually made jewellery himself, it is probable that some of these came from his workshop. The recognition of such jewellery is made more difficult as his designs were printed and were, therefore, available to any of his contemporaries. Moreover, they were not so outstandingly original that pieces based on them can be distinguished with certainty from those based on similar designs by Hans Collaert of Antwerp, Virgil Solis or Matthias Zündt of Nürnberg. The book published by Hornick in 1562 is the more interesting of his two jewellery pattern-books. It includes among other objects some imposing mounts for plumes to be worn in the hat (aigrettes) and fan-handles (pl. 154). In studying these one is impressed by the various skills of the sixteenth-century goldsmith and jeweller. Hornick's designs give the craftsman every opportunity to display his virtuosity, even at the cost of crowding one decorative feature against another. As compositions, his designs for pendants are the more successful; in these he offers lively asymmetrical groups unencumbered by the heavy frames of the fan-handles or aigrettes. His figure subjects evidently derive from prints after contemporary Mannerist paintings.

Hornick's appointment in Prague dates from 1582 and his death was recorded in the following year. It seems unlikely that there could be much to show for this brief period. Among the Hornick drawings in the Victoria and Albert Museum is a group of nineteen sheets (pls. 191-3) which I attribute to an anonymous master, who was an assistant or, in any case, a contemporary of Hornick. The possibility must not, however, be excluded that they are by Hornick himself and belong to his last stage when he altered his style to conform to current fashion. The reason for associating these drawings with the Prague Court Workshop is that some of their features appear in Prague pieces. Their ornament is more closely packed and more rigidly symmetrical in arrangement than in Hornick's earlier designs, and there is also a difference in execution. While the earlier designs are mostly drawn with a light and delicate touch, these are executed in a firm thick line. Further, the panels of mauresques, which are a standard feature of the earlier drawings, are now replaced by bold acanthus foliage. The association between Hornick and the anonymous master of these drawings must have been close, for he made an exact copy of at least one of Hornick's own designs. The drawing of a ewer belonging to this group in the Victoria and Albert Museum is copied from one by Hornick in the Oesterreichisches Museum, Vienna.[19] The fact that one copied from the other suggests that their relationship was that of pupil to master, but this must remain uncertain. Although there seems to be no doubt that these designs date from the last quarter of the century and are, therefore, later than the Hornick designs discussed above, they are in some respects more conservative and do not show quite the same fantasy. The vase (pl. 191) with profile dominated by female half-figures recalls the Italian drawings discussed above and may indeed have been copied from Giulio Romano (see p.136). A feature of these designs is the treatment of the foot as an assemblage of writhing forms; a typical example is the drawing of a standing cup (pl. 192). The closest parallel to these forms in foot and stem can be found in Augsburg goldsmiths' work of the late sixteenth century, as, for instance, the foot of the Johannes Lencker ewer (pl. 502) or that of the strange ewer made for the Emperor Rudolph by the Augsburg-born goldsmith, Anton Schweinberger (pl. 579).

1   Hampe p.545. '23 November 1559: Erassmussen Hornay vonn Andtorff alls einen treffenlichen Künstler ufm Goldschmidthanndwerckh zu Bürger annehmen und ime das Bürgerrecht schennken'.

2   A definite resemblance can be traced between some of Jamnitzer's and Hornick's drawings. Hornick's designs for scent-bottles recall the Jamnitzer drawing in the Erlangen University Library (Bock, cat. no. 537), while his designs for cups can be related to that of a columbine-cup by Jamnitzer (Bock, cat. no. 536).

3   Hornick's name appears in the Augsburg Steuerbuch for 1562; he may not, therefore have taken up the offer of citizenship of Nürnberg until 1562 or 1563.

4   Jahrbuch, Band VII, Regest n. 5436.

5   Katalog der Ornamentstichsammlung der Staatl. Kunstbibliothek, Berlin, 1939, nos. 622, 623, p.94.

6   The only examples of this set known to me were included in the Gilhofer und Ranschburg, Luzern, catalogue no. XVII, 28.XI.1934, no. 417, p.53.

7   Dept. of Prints and Drawings, nos. 5131-5406.

8   ill. R. Fritz, *Gold und Silber,* Dortmund, 1965, no. 32, maker, R. Laminit, Augsburg, about 1570.

9   Staatsarchiv, Nürnberg, *Bürgerbuch,* 1534-1631, Bo. 201.

10 *Katalog der deutschen Handschriften,* Sign. M. S. Teutsch, St. 1, no. 2.

11 J. F. Hayward, 'The Goldsmiths' Designs of the Bayerische Staatsbibliothek reattributed to Erasmus Hornick', *Burlington Magazine,* 1968, p.201ff.

12 Hampe, no. 4093, 25.ii.1566.

13 Frankenburger, no. 84, p.21.

14 A record of persons responsible for the care of minors.

15 This seems to be the only Hornick design of which a version executed in silver exists, though it was made much later. The ewer in question was modelled by C. B. Birch A.R.A. for Messrs. Garrards of London and was presented to the Worshipful Company of Goldsmiths in 1900.

16 An Urbino majolica service in the National Museum, Stockholm, which was probably made for the Emperor Charles V and formed part of the war booty taken from Prague in 1648 by the Swedish army, includes pilgrim bottles that might have provided the inspiration for Hornick's Italianate designs. These bottles have some of the ornament modelled in relief and might even have been seen by Hornick when he was working for the Prague *Hofwerkstatt* of the Emperor Rudolph II.

17 The term *Formenschneider* is here used to refer to the various masters who carved models in stone, wood or other materials from which moulds were made either for casting bronze plaquettes or for making lead or pewter patterns for sale to goldsmiths.

18 Y. Hackenbroch, 'Erasmus Hornick as a Jeweller', *Connoisseur,* Vol. 166, 1967, p.54-63. This study attributes to Hornick himself a number of jewels that appear to be derived from his engraved prints of ornament.

19 See J. F. Hayward, 'Christoph Jamnitzer and his Contemporaries', *Connoisseur,* July 1968, p.164, fig. 6.

CHAPTER TWELVE

North and Western Germany: Switzerland: Saxony

IN this chapter the German speaking regions outside the Habsburg hereditary provinces are discussed, with particular reference to the goldsmiths of Lübeck, Lüneburg and Hamburg in the north, Strassburg, Freiburg and Stuttgart in the west, Zürich in Switzerland and Dresden and Leipzig in Saxony.

North Germany

So little North German silver has survived in comparison with that made in Nürnberg and Augsburg that one might be led to think that those cities had almost a monopoly of fine goldsmiths' work in the sixteenth century. It is only the fortunate survival in the Berlin Kunstgewerbemuseum of a large part of the treasure of the City Council of Lüneburg (*Lüneberger Ratsschatz*) that has demonstrated the importance of North German production, especially in the first half of the sixteenth century. Only twenty-nine out of the three hundred vessels which belonged to the city of Lüneburg about 1600 still survive, but most of these are of great size and splendour, giving a picture of wealth and, to a lesser degree, of taste that would not otherwise have been expected of a city that did not rank amongst the major centres of German culture. This treasure was intended to be displayed upon a buffet on ceremonial occasions rather than for use. The vessels that survive are mostly in late Gothic or early Renaissance style, but, partly on account of their size, they lack the sophistication of design and finish that one finds on the best of contemporary south German work. Some recall the manner and finish of Hungarian goldsmiths' work.

During the second half of the sixteenth century both Lübeck and Lüneburg gradually lost ground to Hamburg, which became the main centre of the craft in North Germany. As long as trade with the Baltic had been of prime importance Lübeck had retained its position as the leading Hansa town but as trade with Asia and Africa increased in scope and volume, Hamburg took its place. The profitable commissions from the court of Denmark and Sweden that had previously gone to Lübeck were now transferred to Hamburg and, in particular, to Jacob Mores the Elder. By the seventeenth century Hamburg apprentices no longer went to Lübeck to learn their craft and instead the reverse was true.[1]

Dirich Utermarke

There were, nevertheless, outstanding goldsmiths in both Lüneburg and Lübeck during the second half of the sixteenth century (pls. 527-9). Two of the leading Lüneburg goldsmiths were not members of the goldsmiths' guild of the city; these were Luleff Meyer and Dirich Utermarke. The former belonged to the brewers' guild, while the latter broke the regulations of the goldsmiths' guild by working as a journeyman gold-smith for Meyer without being a member of the guild. In spite of this irregularity Meyer was on the best of terms with the City Fathers of Lüneburg, who in the course of a period of twenty years bought over twenty drinking vessels from him. These were intended as gifts for important visitors and only one of them, which was purchased in 1599, has remained in the Lüneburg *Ratsschatz*.[2] Utermarke was less fortunate, for when in 1592 he sought admission to the goldsmiths' guild his application was rejected, in spite of the fact that he was a native and had offered to present the city with a piece of plate worthy of the *Ratsschatz*.[3] He left Lüneburg in the same year and went to seek his fortune in the more flourishing city of Hamburg. During his first few years in Hamburg he worked as an independent master (*Freikünstler*) outside the guild but in 1595, when the number of goldsmiths allowed to set up shop was increased in order to keep up with the greater prosperity of the city, he finally obtained admission as master of his craft. Subsequently, like Meyer in Lüneburg, he enjoyed the patronage of the City Fathers and supplied a large number of presentation cups as well as a complete service, consist-ing of seventy-five pieces and twelve gilt spoons, for the use of the City Council.[4]

Meyer and his journeyman, Utermarke, collaborated in the creation of a mirror frame that ranks among the greatest achievements of German Mannerist goldsmithing. The actual share of each master in its production is uncertain. The most recent account of the contents of the Grünes Gewölbe, Dresden,[5] where it is displayed, attributes it to Luleff Meyer alone without any reference to his assistant, whereas Schröder,[6] in his study of the mirror, gave the whole credit to Utermarke, regarding Meyer as merely its retailer. It is difficult to arrive at a definite answer to the problem of responsibility, inasmuch as the few surviving works by the two masters show little resemblance to the mirror frame and certainly do not approach it in quality. The frame (pls. 527-9) was made for Sophia, the consort of the Elector Christian I of Saxony, but it was not delivered until 1592, a year after she had been widowed. According to the 1610 inventory of the Dresden *Kunst-kammer* the mirror was purchased from a citizen of Lüneburg, presumably Luleff Meyer himself. It was shown in 1629 to the Augsburg diplomat, Phillip Hainhofer, who in an account of his visit relates that it had cost many thousands of gulden and was supposed to have been made in Lüneburg. Its design was derived from one of the monumental epitaphs of the second half of the sixteenth century that can be seen in north German churches commemorating noblemen or wealthy merchants. This taber-nacle form was also exploited by the jewellers of Germany and the Low Countries and is found in the engraved designs of jewellery by Hans Collaert of Antwerp or Erasmus Hornick of Nürnberg. The figures and groups are set within a superbly modelled frame-work of scrolls terminating in volutes from which hang swags of drapery, the design of which owes much to, and possibly derives from some of those of Hornick. It is signifi-cant that Sponsel,[7] who was the first to investigate the history of the mirror in depth, pointed out the influence of the Flemish *Rollwerk* style on its design. Many of the details of ornament can be found repeated in Hornick's prints, but as he died in 1583 he can hardly have provided the original design for a mirror that was not begun until about 1587; on the other hand it seems probable that its makers were familiar with some of his prints or drawings. Among these details are the monsters' heads in profile with swags of drapery hanging from their mouths (pl. 527), the oval bosses with flutes radiating out-wards, the trophies of arms and, finally, the treatment of the figures, especially the bearded warriors in classical armour. It would be difficult to find a more typical example of Mannerist fashion than this mirror in which every possible form of ornament is con-centrated over a confined space and executed in relief that varies from figures in the round to engraved detail. The crowded effect is increased by the addition of so many jewels and heraldic shields to a design that was complete without them, illustrating the additive treatment which is one of the less acceptable aspects of Mannerism. For its date the framework of vertical and horizontal is more strongly marked than one would expect. The monumental mirror was not an exclusively German conception, as the Ital-ian example in the Victoria and Albert (pl. 737) shows. The Utermarke mirror gives some idea of the magnificence of the toilet mirror taken by Wenzel Jamnitzer the Younger to Paris and confiscated by the French Crown after his death there (see p.212). Judging by the cup bearing the mark of Luleff Meyer from the Lüneburg *Ratsschatz*[8] he was less gifted than his assistant Utermarke. Though competently made, the casts from nature which are applied to the base are introduced in a casual manner without any convincing relationship to the design of the vessel.

A number of presentation cups by Dirich Utermarke are in the Moscow Kremlin; like those of Jacob Mores the Elder described below, they are of great size. One of the best examples of Utermarke's later style is the huge gilt cup now in an English private collection (pl. 526). This was presented to the Lüneburg *Ratsschatz* in 1602 by a member of the patrician family of Töbing and remained in the city until 1706 when it was given to the Elector of Hannover, in whose possession it remained until after the First World War. It is significant of the declining status of the Lüneburg goldsmiths that in 1602 a citizen of the town should have chosen to present a vessel made in Hamburg. The cup is so different in style and taste from the mirror frame that, but for the mark, one would not think of attributing them to the same master. The discrepancy can best be explained by assuming that the complex design of the mirror frame was worked out by another artist.

A standard North German vessel of the second half of the sixteenth and the early seventeenth century was the tall flagon, known as a *Hansekanne* on account of its popularity with the wealthy merchants of the Hanse towns. Whereas the *Wilkomm* cups, such as that made by Dirich Utermarke (pl. 526) usually followed contemporary south German fashion, the *Hansekanne* was an exclusively northern type. While the South German tankards usually tapered upwards, the *Hansekanne* tapered downwards (pls. 531, 534, 535). These vessels were produced over a wide area from Hamburg and Bremen in the west as far as Riga in the eastern Baltic. Though the basic form was a truncated cone, these flagons were given a great deal of ornament, either engraved, embossed or cast and applied, according to the taste and skill of the goldsmith. The most elaborate treatment was reserved for the handle, which was surmounted by a large pierced thumb-piece and terminated below in a profuse arrangement of volutes ending in shells or ball-flowers.

A typical *Hansekanne* in the Statens Historiska Museum, Stockholm, made by Dirich Utermarke is illustrated (pl. 531-3). The large size of the vessel gave the goldsmith an excellent opportunity to exploit the all-over low relief ornament then fashionable. An indication of the popularity of these flagons can be gained from a broadsheet advertising a lottery which took place in Hamburg in 1614.[9] The sheet illustrates all the prizes offered, which took the form either of silver plate or coins. While fifteen standing cups of various types are shown, there are no fewer than thirty-two *Hansekannen* with weights varying between 240 and 18 Lot. Several of the surviving examples were made, not in Hamburg or Lübeck, but in Riga; the style of the latter suggests that they were probably made by goldsmiths who had emigrated from Lübeck or had learnt their craft there.[10] The examples illustrated show three different methods of decoration: embossing and chasing, engraving, and piercing against a gilt ground. In each case the elaborate treatment of the base of the handle with spiral coils terminating in buds or hips is a distinguishing feature. Of the great numbers of *Hansekannen* that must have been made in Lübeck in the late sixteenth and early seventeenth centuries, only isolated examples (pl. 534) now survive. The destruction of Lübeck silver took place in two stages, firstly the ecclesiastical plate at the time of the Reformation and, secondly, the secular plate of the city and the corporations during the Napoleonic Wars. To judge the skill of the Lübeck masters it is necessary to rely on the very few examples preserved outside the city.

The *Hansekanne* served equally well for domestic or ecclesiastical purposes, but in some north German areas a tankard was used instead of the larger Communion flagon for the service of the altar. This did not differ from the secular tankard used for beer-drinking, except that the decoration on the body was usually of a religious nature, such as that of the Pressburg tankard (pl. XXII). The presence of religious themes on a

tankard can be accepted as fairly certain evidence that the piece in question was originally intended for the service of the altar.

Jakob Mores

Among the very few goldsmiths who have left both extant works and signed or attributable drawings is the Hamburg master, Jakob Mores, who was born in the decade
between 1540 and 1550 and who died in Hamburg shortly before 1612. He was admitted
as master in 1579 and almost immediately received commissions, which were frequently
repeated, for large and expensive cups destined for presentation to visiting dignitaries.
His success in Hamburg was soon followed by the patronage of the northern courts,
especially that of King Frederick II of Denmark (1559-1588) and of Duke Johann Adolf
of Schleswig-Holstein. The presentation cups of the late sixteenth century were of giant
proportions and give the impression that weight of precious metal was of more importance than design or workmanship. Three cups made by Jakob Mores for presentation to
Christian IV of Denmark (1588-1648) were subsequently pawned by the king and eventually found their way to the Moscow Kremlin where they still remain. Two are a metre
each in height, while the third is even taller. The largest cup appears to have been that
made for Johann Adolf, Duke of Holstein Gottorp; this was as tall as a man. Mores'
annotation to the drawing, which survives in the Berlin Kunstbibliothek, states 'und is
eines Mannes lengede oder hoechte gewesen' (this was the same length or height as a
man). The surviving cups give but a faint picture of Mores' activity in comparison with
his designs or drawings. There are two collections of these, firstly a volume of designs
for jewels, most of which were intended for the Danish court, though they include the
drawing of a jewel presented by King Gustavus Adolphus of Sweden to his cousin,
Margaretha Elisabeth of Mecklenburg on the occasion of her marriage in 1608. This
volume is preserved in the Hamburg Museum für Kunst und Gewerbe.[11] The other
collection consists of eighty-seven unbound drawings of vessels, which were formerly
in the Brandenburg *Kunstkammer* and are now in the Berlin Kunstbibliothek.[12] The
Hamburg volume does not concern us further here since with one exception only jewellery is shown; the variety and magnificence of the pieces depicted does, however, provide impressive evidence of the scale of Mores' business. The Berlin drawings are, on
the other hand, of exceptional interest. Their attribution to Mores is confirmed by the
fact that one of the drawings bears his signature. They are of importance less on account of
their aesthetic quality, which is not high, than the information they give about his business
and his customers. Thirteen of the drawings bear the name of the prince for whom they
were executed, while others have the customer's coat-of-arms or the weight of the piece.
Most show the object in its actual size, some measuring a metre or more in height; they
are, moreover, coloured to show the areas that should be gilded or decorated with *Kaltemail* of which much use is made. The drawings do not show alterations of plan and
appear to be records of pieces made rather than designs for submission to clients. The
presence of such details as names of clients and weights shows that the vessels were
actually executed. The vessels shown in these drawings are so various as to raise the
question whether all were made or merely supplied by Mores. The fact that there is no
record of his taking on any apprentices implies that he was mainly active as a dealer.
Goldsmiths who received a large number of orders were forced by the guild to put their
work out to other masters and thus became retailers and merchants, if they had enough
capital to support the position. One of Mores' major commissions was the supply of a
great silver altar piece for the chapel of Frederiksborg castle; this remains in position
and investigation has shown that parts of it bear the mark of other masters as well as that
of Mores. In this case Mores probably struck his mark as a form of approval, performing
the same rôle as a town-mark elsewhere. One of his most successful designs was for a
travelling service consisting of dishes, spoons, candlesticks, ewer and basin, etc. (pl.
185). According to a note at the bottom of the drawing he supplied similar services to the

Elector of Saxony, the Duke of Holstein, the Archbishop of Bremen and the Count von Schauenberg.

Drinking-vessels wrought in the form of human figures, monsters or animals seem to have enjoyed particular popularity in the North German provinces. Jakob Mores produced many drawings of such vessels: of the eighty-seven drawings in Berlin of goldsmiths' work which are attributed to him or his workshop, twenty-four depict vessels of this type, some of quite fantastic design. Two are even constructed in the form of figures of the Holy Roman Emperor and the Empress respectively. A great deal of technical ingenuity was required to make a lion ewer such as that illustrated in pl. 186. It had to be built up of numerous pieces, some wrought, others cast. While some of the Mores designs appear to be original, others are evidently derived from south German prototypes such as the printed pattern-book of Matthias Zündt. The ostrich-egg illustrated in pl. 188 corresponds to the standard south German type of the second half of the sixteenth century and might have been made by any competent German goldsmith. The table-centre in the form of an elephant (pl. 189) is so similar to that bearing the mark of the Nürnberg goldsmith, Christoph Jamnitzer, in the Berlin Kunstgewerbemuseum (pl. 517) that one would have been tempted to attribute both to the same master. In fact, More's design must be some twenty years earlier in date than the Jamnitzer piece. Christof Ritter of Nürnberg seems to have specialised in this amusing conceit and Rosenberg records three elephants by him, of which one is now in the Amsterdam Rijksmuseum. The idea is an earlier one, for a drawing by Polidoro da Caravaggio dating from the first half of the sixteenth century shows an elephant supporting a circular dish, while its saddle-cloth bears the Medici arms. The form of the vessel would, however, be more suitable for majolica rather than precious metal.[13] Jamnitzer's elephant was intended to serve as a ewer and was originally accompanied by a basin, whereas a note on the Mores drawing describes it as a *Wilkomm*, a cup in which the health of distinguished visitors could be drunk. Both the Mores and the Jamnitzer elephant ewers probably go back to some common prototype, but it would not be correct to think that Mores was a purely derivative artist. This is shown by his original ewer design (pl. 187) the form of which differs from the usual German fashion of the time, though it does show reminiscences of earlier designs such as those of Hans Brosamer.

Another group of drawings, which probably derive also from the Mores workshop, depict sword and dagger-hilts; some were probably intended for King Frederick II of Denmark (see p.316). After the death of Jakob Mores his business was carried on by his two sons, Jakob Mores the Younger and Hans Mores. Like their father they acted as agents rather than as working goldsmiths, securing commissions from the northern courts for objects made by other masters.

Rupprecht Müller

Another Hamburg goldsmith, Rupprecht Müller, left his native city in 1606 and was appointed Court Goldsmith in Stockholm, where he is still represented by important works that show him to have been an outstanding master. He not only made the crown of Queen Christina the Elder, but also a magnificent mount for an aigrette for the coronation of King Charles IX in 1607 and a set of saddle plates with elaborately worked scrolls, figures and jewels for the coronation of King Gustavus Adolphus in 1617, all of which remain in the Swedish Royal Armoury.[14] In the design of the saddle-plates, which are of silver-gilt with applied decoration in enamelled gold, Müller has followed contemporary jewellery design, but has increased the scale to suit the size of the objects he was making. The attraction of Mannerist ornament lies to a large extent in its delicacy, but in spite of the change in scale this quality has in this case not been sacrificed.

Königsberg

One of the chief patrons of the goldsmith's art in Northern Germany was Duke

Albrecht von Brandenburg-Ansbach who summoned to his court at Königsberg leading masters from Nürnberg, Basel and Ulm. Their main achievement was the production of his silver library, a set of twenty volumes of theological subjects, with bindings of silver set with plaquettes or engraved with religious themes.[15] The finest are the work of Cornelis Vorwendt who came to Königsberg from Nürnberg, others were by Jobst Freudener from Ulm, who also made the Duke's Sword of State, and probably the fine cup in the Berlin Kunstgewerbemuseum.[16] The bindings all date from the period between 1550 and 1560. In none of these pieces can one find anything that could be described as a Königsberg style; their masters worked in the South German manner that was familiar to them and were uninfluenced by local taste. So much is this so that the cup in Berlin attributed to Jobst Freudener has also been claimed as a Nürnberg production.

Western Germany

Anton Eisenhoit

The attribution of the Dresden mirror (pl. 527) to Luleff Meyer and to Dirich Utermarke is a comparatively recent development; it was long held to be the work of another prominent goldsmith who resided in North-west Germany, namely Anton Eisenhoit of Warburg in Westphalia[17] (born 1553 or 1554, died 1603). There is, however, a marked contrast in the styles of the two masters; while Utermarke followed northern sources, Eisenhoit was much more susceptible to Italian and South German influence.[18] This can be explained by his residence for some five years in Rome. Few of Eisenhoit's works have survived; the most important are the nine pieces from the set of altar plate he made between 1598 and 1600 for Dietrich von Fürstenberg, Prince Bishop of Paderborn, and a cross foot for the church of St. Patroclus at Soest. Eisenhoit's main claim to fame lies in his exceptional skill in embossing figures in low relief; in this respect his art has with good reason been compared with that of Paul van Vianen. All his surviving works are characterised by superbly modelled figures, especially nude females in the current Mannerist fashion with long elegant figures often turned in complex poses. The Soest cross foot (pls. 537-9) which was made to support an earlier cross, is perhaps the most Italianate of Eisenhoit's works; strapwork is conspicuously absent from the design. In his altar set now at Schloss Herdringen, strapwork is present but does not dominate the figure subjects, which always constitute the main feature. His most distinguished achievement is the silver binding he made for a Cologne missal;[19] in this he combines recumbent and seated nudes with two circular reliefs of the Last Supper and its Old Testament prototype in charming compositions. It was only in the full flood of Mannerist art that figures of such elegant sensuality as those symbolic of the Seasons could have been associated with the Last Supper on a missal cover.

Eisenhoit was never a member of a goldsmiths' guild; he signed and dated his works but they bear neither hall-mark nor assay-mark. The fact that so gifted a master should have been content to stay in the little town of Warburg can only be explained by the patronage he enjoyed from the wealthy family of Fürstenberg. In general the great goldsmiths of the sixteenth century worked in the large cities. Eisenhoit was also an engraver, though his engravings do not reach the same standard of quality as his silver reliefs. Most of these were derived from contemporary graphic sources and it was probably as an engraver that he gained such familiarity with the work of other masters both in Germany and elsewhere.

Cologne

Towards the end of the sixteenth century, at about the same time as the tall neo-Gothic style cups were being made, another type was revived that also originated in the late Gothic period. These were cups with stems constructed in the form of naturalistic branches; they seem to derive from those with bowls in the form of fruit — apples or pears — designed by Albrecht Dürer and made in Nürnberg in the Krug workshop. In the late sixteenth century versions, the bowl did not necessarily take the form of a fruit, but there is a particularly fine covered cup with pear-shaped bowl by a Cologne master in the Berlin Kunstgewerbe Museum,[20] the engraved decoration of which is probably the work of a professional engraver rather than a member of the goldsmith's workshop. The city of Cologne was the most important centre of the craft in the west after Strassburg. A number of coconut-cups mounted by goldsmiths of Cologne have been recorded,[21] suggesting that the goldsmiths of the city may have specialised in mounting them. This may, however, be due to the chance survival of a larger number of Cologne coconut-cups than of those made elsewhere. The Cologne pilgrim flasks mounted with coconuts carved with biblical subjects certainly rank amongst the finest extant examples (pl. 541). The bourgeoisie of the Rhineland cities did not provide many major orders for their local goldsmiths, who, moreover, lacked the access to wealthy ruling princes that was enjoyed by their rivals in southern Germany. It was only rarely, therefore, that they had the opportunity to display the full range of their skill. The Cologne master, Gilles Sibricht, had the good fortune to be commissioned to produce a pair of handsome standing cups for presentation to the city of Wesel in 1578 by the Protestant refugees from the southern Netherlands, who had been granted refuge there in their hour of need.[22] The cups are somewhat conservative in style in comparison with contemporary south German work but no whit inferior in quality. The coin-cup made by a Worms goldsmith for a local collector of coins (pl. XIX) illustrates the high standard of workmanship attained by a provincial master who had the good fortune to receive an important commission.

Strassburg

Little Strassburg silver survives to show the skill of its goldsmiths, who were among the best of their time. The ultimate in German Mannerist design was, however, the achievement of a Strassburg master, Wendel Dietterlin (1550-1599), whose five books of architecture were published in parts in 1593 in Stuttgart and in 1594 in Strassburg. These books were based on the five orders of architecture, Tuscan, Doric, Ionic, Corinthian and Composite. None of the plates were designed with the goldsmith in mind, but there are chimneypieces, window frames, doorways, epitaphs and fountains, many of which could be adapted for works in precious metal. Mannerist vases also appear as decorative adjuncts in them. Dietterlin's designs show an unequalled exuberance of invention; his pilasters are equipped with as many mouldings and volutes as the wildest fantasies of Christoph Jamnitzer, whose contemporary he was. A fountain design (pl. 122 of the Nürnberg edition of 1598) already shows the mollusc-like forms exploited by the van Vianens and some at least of his table-fountains, elaborate as they are, could well have been executed by the goldsmith. He exploits the openwork bracket that was so much used by the early seventeenth century goldsmiths to decorate stems of cups, but preferred the high-relief scrollwork of the Fontainebleau masters to the flat German *Schweifwerk*. His sources seem to have been as much Dutch as German and he still plays with the entrapped ferocious satyrs of the Antwerp masters, though Vredemann de Vries is his main source. The neo-Gothic fashion of the last decades of the century is also represented in his designs. There is even an elephant with warriors in the castle on its back, recalling those designed by Jakob Mores (pl. 189) and Christoph Jamnitzer (pl. 517), though Dietterlin seems to have intended his design to serve as a stove.

South German influence is evident in Strassburg goldsmiths' work and but for the town mark, some of the vessels made there would be accepted as typical of Nürnberg or Augsburg, as would the Linhardt Bauer cup in pl. 542. While the design derives from Matthias Zündt, the detail of the cast ornament seems to have been taken from Nürnberg patterns after Peter Flötner and Wenzel Jamnitzer. The Strassburg town mark was changed from time to time and marked pieces can, therefore, be dated within certain limits. The mark was changed in 1534 and again in 1567, but this change is of no more than marginal assistance in dating as there was much stylistic development between these two years. If the average production of the Strassburg masters followed south German example, there were, of course, occasional pieces of original form. Foremost amongst these is the Rappolstein Cup in the Munich Schatzkammer. (pls. 544-7). If the traditional dating of this vessel is accepted, then its maker, Georg Kobenhaupt, must have anticipated Wenzel Jamnitzer in the exploitation of Mannerist ornament. Kobenhaupt was first admitted master in 1540 and his cup bears the Strassburg town mark for 1534-1567. All the editions of the Munich Schatzkammer catalogue since 1931[3] state that the cup was made from a rich vein of silver discovered in 1530 in a mine on the property of the von Rappolstein family. The precise date of manufacture is not recorded but the cup is said to have made its first appearance in 1543 on the table at the wedding feast of Georg von Rappolstein and Elizabeth von Hellfenstein. The 1931 catalogue does, in fact, point out the discrepancy between the stylistic character of the cup and the early date suggested for it, but observes that the master might, if he had been familiar with the graphic ornament of the school of Fontainebleau, have been in a position to produce it before 1543. The cup does not appear to be an early production of Mannerist taste; it combines all the known techniques of ornament and represents a mature stage of the fashion. I would, therefore prefer to reject the traditional dating and to regard it as a creation of the third quarter of the century. The improbability of the usual dating is made clear if one compares the cup with those (pls. 284, 285) which can with confidence be attributed to the 1540-50 period.

A favourite form of table ornament of the second half of the sixteenth century was the galley, usually made of rock-crystal. This was sometimes fitted with a superstructure resembling a ship with sails, but the material of which the vessel was made inhibited any seriously realistic treatment. The goldsmith was not subject to such limitations, and the Strassburg galley (pl. 548) shows a degree of realism that could not be achieved by the hardstone sculptor. This and the few other Strassburg vessels remaining from this period point to the excellence of the goldsmiths of the city. Erasmus Krug, a member of the famous goldsmith family of that name, who had gone to live in Strassburg as early as 1506, was succeeded by his son, Diebolt, who was admitted to the goldsmiths' guild in 1545. He is best known for mounting rock-crystal vessels, a material that was readily available from Freiburg im Breisgau. Two of his finest pieces are illustrated in pls. IX and 549. It will be noticed that, whereas the mounts of a hardstone vessel are often of little significance, Diebolt Krug designed them to play an equal part with the semi-precious stone. Vessels made of rock-crystal were mounted by goldsmiths in other German cities, wherever, in fact, the local prince or merchants were sufficiently rich to acquire the precious material and had sufficient confidence in their goldsmiths to entrust them with the commission.

Freiburg im Breisgau

The main source of carved rock-crystals was Milan, where skilled carvers had been at work for generations. There were, however, rock-crystal carvers in the Germanic cultural area, in the cities of Nürnberg, Freiburg im Breisgau and probably elsewhere. The identified Nürnberg pieces date, however, from the seventeenth century and the earliest signed Freiburg piece is dated 1633. Even the presence of a German town mark on the mounts of a rock-crystal does not indicate that the crystal was cut in the town in which it was mounted. Hardstones were imported from Italy and mounted by German goldsmiths. There is regrettably little to go on when endeavouring to identify German carved hardstones. In his study of earlier Freiburg rock-crystals Legner[24] came to the conclusion that the carvers of that city confined themselves to facetting or fluting their material, but did not engrave figures or scenes. He has assembled a sufficient number of rock-crystal standing cups and candlesticks with Freiburg-marked silver mounts to give us an idea of the scope and nature of Freiburg rock-crystals. Their creators were content to have mastered the art of cutting and shaping the crystal and did not attempt to rival the greater skill of their Milanese contemporaries. That this was also the contemporary view is shown by a letter from Hainhofer to Duke Philipp of Pomerania written in January 1611 in which he says that no rock-crystal was available in Augsburg, but it might be obtained more easily in Freiburg im Breisgau; it could also be cut there as they had water-power with which they could work the crystal more cheaply, but, he concludes, the work is not the finest.[25]

The Freiburg type is represented by the tall covered cup (pl. 551). In the seventeenth century more ambitious work was done though the Freiburg carvers did not succeed in rivalling the achievements of the Saracchis in Milan or the Miseronis in Prague. A dragon bowl in the Württembergisches Landesmuseum, Stuttgart, might well be taken for a Milanese piece were it not so clearly signed and dated *Friburggensis Brisgoius 1633.*[26] In spite of its late date this vessel corresponds to the fashion of the late sixteenth century; only the enamelled mount, painted with hunting subjects, is in a later style. Among other rock-crystal vessels that may be of Freiburg origin is the superb tankard (pl. 549) and the standing cup (pl. 456) which was probably mounted in Augsburg by one of the goldsmiths working for the Bavarian court.

The goldsmith had only a limited rôle to play when he came to mount a hardstone vessel and one must look to pieces entirely of precious metal in order to appreciate the merit of the Freiburg masters. A measure of their skill is given by the ewer and basin of Abbot Jodocus Singeisen of Muri in Switzerland (pls. 552, 554). As is often the case with vessels made by German provincial goldsmiths, the models used for the decoration of the depression of the basin and the cast band round the body of the ewer are from the Jamnitzer workshop. The Abbot purchased these pieces at second-hand from a Jewish dealer in 1635. They can hardly be later than about 1600 and, but for the beaded border of the ewer spout, would be assigned to an even earlier date. If the abbot had commissioned a new ewer and basin he would surely have employed one of the skilled masters then working in Zürich or Basel.

The Württemberg Kunstkammer

During the latter part of the sixteenth century, Friedrich I, Duke of Württemberg (1593-1608), established a *Kunstkammer* in his Stuttgart *Residenz*. Much of his collection remains in the Stuttgart Landesmuseum, and it is in Stuttgart that the work of the Freiburg rock-crystal cutters can best be studied; not only the earlier facet-cut pieces but also the more ambitious ones shaped as monsters and carved with scrollwork and figures in the Milanese manner. His son, Johann Friedrich (1608-1628) extended the collection and also gave full-time employment to a hardstone carver, Hans Kobenhaupt, who is thought to have been the son of the Strassburg goldsmith, Georg Kobenhaupt. The records of the Stuttgart court contain many references to payment to Kobenhaupt in respect of jasper and agate cups. Only a few examples of his work remain in Stuttgart as the ducal Kunstkammer was plundered during the Thirty Years War, but there is a superb red agate cup with enamelled gold mounts signed by him in the Castle of Rosenborg, Copenhagen. On the cover is a figure supporting the arms of Johann Friedrich who probably gave the cup to Queen Anna Catherina, his wife's sister-in-law. A similar cup in the Vienna Kunsthistorisches Museum, also attributed to Kobenhaupt, was probably part of the loot taken by the Imperial troops from the Stuttgart Kunstkammer. Fleischhauer[27] has suggested that a number of other cups in Vienna may have been carved in Stuttgart, but the resemblance between the work of Kobenhaupt and some of the Prague masters is so close that it is not possible to be certain on this point. Kobenhaupt would not have mounted the vessels he carved; this was probably the work of two brothers, François and Claude Guichard, who were goldsmiths to the Stuttgart court.

Switzerland

In the sixteenth century the main centres of the Swiss goldsmiths' craft were in the German-speaking regions and Switzerland is therefore here discussed as part of the Teutonic cultural area. Swiss vessel types conform to contemporary German fashion and their ornament was drawn from German sources. In the sixteenth century patronage in Switzerland came from the guilds, monasteries and the wealthy merchants; much of the guild plate survives and points to a flourishing corporate life providing plenty of commissions for the craft. A few goldsmiths, foremost amongst them Abraham Gessner, achieved international fame.

Abraham Gessner of Zürich

Towards the end of the sixteenth century Zürich was the main centre of goldsmithing and no fewer than seventy masters were at work there, of whom the most outstanding was Abraham Gessner (1552-1613). This master is famous for the globe-cups in which he specialised, following the example of his fellow-citizen of the previous generation, Jakob Stampfer, who made the earliest known globe-cup in or shortly before 1539 (see p.104). Abraham Gessner's globe-cups corresponded in design to those made by Stampfer. Eight globe-cups by him[28] are are known to exist and, if one takes into consideration how small a proportion of the life's work of any one sixteenth-century goldsmith survives, it would seem that he must have produced a great many. All are constructed as double cups, a form dictated by their nature. The geographical theme was often continued on the foot, the surface of which was finely chased with four cartouches enclosing figures emblematic of the Four Continents. Globe-cups by or attributed to Gessner with bases of this type are in the Schweizerisches Landesmusem, Zürich, and in the Historisches Museum, Basel. They provide yet another example of the determined quest of the Mannerist goldsmith for some new conceit to amuse and, in this case, to instruct his client. Globe-cups were highly regarded and the one presented by Queen Elizabeth I to Sir Francis Drake was also the work of Abraham Gessner (pl. 556). This cup rests on a conventional vase stem, but Gessner sometimes used a figure of Atlas at this point, as in the case of the globe cup in the British Museum.[29] This piece conforms to the usual Gessner type, but has in the past been attributed to a French goldsmith on the grounds that the map engraved on the globe is based upon one by the French cartographer, Oronce Finé, whereas Gessner copied the map devised by Abraham Ortelius. There were not, however, so many maps of the world available at the time and Gessner may have chosen a French map in this case. Abraham Gessner was equally famous as an embosser and chaser and ranks as one of the best masters of his time. A number of tazzas and tazza bowls wrought by him survive. His method of chasing was extremely fine, working on a minute scale with much detail; his manner makes the average Augsburg tazza bowl seem coarsely worked. Many of the tazzas he made have been broken up and melted and only the relief from the centre of the bowl survives[30] (pl. 555).

Hans Jakob Sprüngli

Colour has always been an attractive adjunct of goldsmith's work and it was never more appreciated than in the sixteenth century. The most satisfactory solution of the problem of giving colour was for the vessel to be made of pure gold, enriched with translucent enamels and finally set with jewels. Only a limited number of clients could commission such costly pieces and an alternative method of providing colourful effects but at less expense was to decorate the piece with painting under glass. This appears early in the century, usually in the form of the owner's coat-of-arms either on top of or underneath the cover. Some of the spice-plates[31] listed in the inventory of the plate of Queen Elizabeth I were decorated in this way: items 750 to 752 all refer to 'pictures of

Christall'. No. 752 reads: 'Item foure Disshes or Spiceplates of silver guilt with a brym plated on of silver guilt and white rabaske worke and vi pictures upon the same brymes under glasses'.

The Zürich-born master, Jakob Sprüngli,[32] produced under-glass paintings of sufficiently large size to decorate the whole top surface of a tazza or the barrel of a tankard; some are so ambitious as to reduce the goldsmith's work to the provision of a mere skeleton frame for the painted subjects. Sprüngli was born in 1559 and learnt the art of glass painting but became free of the *Zimmerleute* (Carpenters) in 1579. He went to Prague in 1598 and made frequent visits to Nürnberg between 1596 and 1610, thus achieving a reputation that went far beyond the place of his birth. His glass paintings were mounted by Nürnberg goldsmiths of the rank of Hans Petzoldt and Christoph Jamnitzer. Two splendid tankards with bodies painted by him and mounted by Christoph Jamnitzer survive, one in the Schwerin Museum, the other in an English collection.[33] Like many of his contemporaries he did not devise his own design but copied them from prints by Virgil Solis or after the fashionable Mannerist painters of the time such as Tintoretto or Bartolomäus Spranger. His close connection with Prague doubtless explains his choice of sources. He also made use of the prints of his fellow-countrymen, Meyer and Ringli, both of Zürich.

Swiss designers for glass painting such as Jost Amman or Tobias Stimmer were perfectly capable of providing goldsmiths with appropriate drawings. One fine drawing which introduces a large number of subjects from Ovid derives from the circle of one or other of these masters but could also be the work of either Daniel Meyer or Christoph Murer (pl. 190). The latter master was working in Strassburg between 1580 and 1586. Drawings such as this serve to remind us of the magnificent embossed dishes that were made during the sixteenth century but have since been destroyed.

Basel

Basel silver vessels of the second half of the century are remarkable more for the fineness and precision of their finish, especially their engraved borders, gilt while the remainder is of white silver, than for originality of form. As a whole Basel goldsmiths followed South German precedent closely. Many of the small beakers, known as *Satzbecher* (or *Monatsbecher* when they were made in sets of twelve engraved with scenes illustrative of the labours of the months) survive. They cannot be distinguished from contemporary German vessels of similar construction except by the marks. The type survived in Switzerland until well into the seventeenth century, whereas it had a shorter life in the German cities.

One would expect the predominantly bourgeois customers of the Swiss goldsmiths to be more conservative in their taste than their South German or Flemish contemporaries. This is born out by the superbly proportioned but somewhat old-fashioned standing cup of 1558 by a Bern maker (pl. 557). Its creator has endeavoured to move with fashion in one sense in that, instead of setting the owner's arms on the flat top of the finial, these are placed inside and an attractive figure of Eve of Mannerist fashion crowns the cover. One of the finest cups of Swiss — or presumably Swiss — origin (pl. 555) bears the mark of the small town of Sitten (Sion). As the mark is struck on a ring that has been added to the foot subsequently, the attribution to Sitten is conjectural. It was, however, made for a Swiss family and bears no other mark.

Saxony

The wealth of the twin duchies of Saxony was largely based upon the great deposits of silver which were mined in the Annaberg, the Marienberg and the Schneeberg. The Dukes received their share of the proceeds and splendid palaces at Meissen and Dresden bore witness to their riches.

Judging by what has survived of their collections, the Electors of Saxony patronised the goldsmiths of Nürnberg until late in the sixteenth century, when they turned to those working in their own capital city of Dresden. Amongst the earlier Dresden pieces are cups and tankards of serpentine with mounts of silver-gilt.[34] The serpentine was obtained locally from the mines of Zöblitz and was much exploited during the last quarter of the sixteenth century. Many vessels were mounted by the Dresden master, Urban Schneeweiss, but they were also exported unmounted and even found their way as far as England for mounting. Serpentine is itself an uninspiring material and the mounts designed for it seem always to have been correspondingly unassuming.

Hans and Daniel Kellerthaler

The most ambitious example of sixteenth-century goldsmiths' work by a Dresden master is the great jewel — or medal — cabinet made by Hans Kellerthaler in 1585.[35] This corresponds in design to, but is apparently of earlier date than, the numerous examples that were made in Augsburg by Matthias Wallbaum and Boas Ulrich. The splendour of the piece lies mainly in the figure sculpture that decorates it. This, like other ambitious productions of the time, is based upon a philosophical programme. At the top is a group of 'Truth triumphing over Envy and Hate', while on successive stages below are the kings of the four ancient empires, the four continents and the chief metals and, at the bottom, the four main rivers of the world. The sculpture shows the influence of Sansovino, particularly in the river gods, and should probably not be attributed to Hans Kellerthaler himself.

When Hans Kellerthaler died in 1611 the workshop was carried on by his equally gifted son, Daniel Kellerthaler, who was admitted Master in 1608. Daniel stands alongside the Nürnberg masters, Christoph Jamnitzer, Nikolaus Schmidt and Hans Petzoldt as one of the most inventive of the late Mannerist masters. His lifetime extended on into the Baroque period, but with the conservatism typical of the craft he was still exploiting Mannerist themes in the second quarter of the seventeenth century. His ewer of 1618 shows a dignity of form and harmony of treatment which confer on it a sense of repose and unity that would have been out of place a few decades earlier; this was, however, intended for church use and his most famous works, the great Midas ewer and basin of 1629 (pls. 558, 560) are, in spite of their late date, Mannerist in style. The dish presents certain problems, for the central scene is pictorially handled and apparently intended to be looked at when set up vertically. On the other hand the border friezes face inwards, implying that the basin must be laid down horizontally; moreover, the complex profile with cast shells projecting so far beyond the border prevents it being set upright. The variant scale of its ornament, some of which has to be examined closely in order to be appreciated is not in conformity with the Baroque ideal. The treatment as a whole seems to be derived from the Triumph Basin made by Christoph Jamnitzer for the Emperor Rudolph, but it is uncertain whether he ever had the opportunity to study the vessel in question. He would, however, have known the silver-gilt and mother-of-pearl basin made by Nikolaus Schmidt which was then in the Saxon treasury (pl. 477). The border of this basin is decorated with three cast figures of nymphs and river gods in reclining-poses that may well have suggested to Kellerthaler the similar composition of the figures on his basin. The companion ewer (pl. 560) seems at first sight far more Baroque in conception; but the modelling of its body as a group of struggling wild animals has a precedent in an earlier Augsburg standing cup (pl. XVI). Kellerthaler's other works include the ewer and basin from the Dresden Domkirche, and a most remarkable sculptural achievement; the modelling of a ewer for the Saxon ruling family of Wettin in the form of a baptism group of Christ and St. John, which can claim to rank as one of the most ingeniously devised and executed goldsmiths' works of its period.[35] It has been described as early Baroque in style but the extreme ingenuity of its construction, which succeeds in concealing effectively its actual function, is typical of Mannerist artifice. All too little is known of Kellerthaler; the wide range of his achievement suggests that he had studied the work of other masters and in fact he mentioned in a statement to the Elector of Saxony that he had undertaken long journeys, though he does not say where he went.

Valentin Geitner

Valentin Geitner or Greffner, who is believed to have added the *verre fixé* plaques to the Utermarke mirror at Dresden, must have been a man of diverse skills, for he seems to have been a gunmaker as well as a goldsmith and enameller. He not only supplied the plaques for the mirror but was the master of one of the most handsome standing cups in the Dresden collections; it is enriched with fifteen plaques enamelled in translucent colours with the various arms of the Saxon ruling family.[37] His most peculiar production is a so-called 'Griffin's Claw', actually a cow-horn, mounted in a purely medieval style.[38]

Elias Geyer

Perhaps the most prolific master of monsters and animals modelled in silver (pl. 562) or of shell mounted in silver was the Leipzig goldsmith, Elias Geyer,[39] who was born about 1560 and admitted master in Leipzig in 1589, where he was active until his death in 1634. He enjoyed the patronage of the Saxon court and a *Kunstkammer* inventory dated 1 Aug. 1610 enumerates seven ostrich-egg cups, three others decorated with mother-of-pearl, a silver mounted mother-of-pearl casket and five drinking cups in the form of mermen, mermaids or tritons. Most of these vessels are still preserved in the Grünes Gewölbe, Dresden. Geyer evidently attracted court patronage by reason of his mastery in this fashionable genre; he supplied figures in groups of two or four at a time for use as table decorations. Some of his productions show a vigour of modelling that belongs to the period of transition between Mannerism and Baroque. Apart from the hippocamps, tritons and mermaids, ingeniously formed from silver and trochus- or nautilus-shells, Geyer produced a range of typical sixteenth century plate. Characteristic of Mannerist taste is his set of four three-sided cups, the bowls mounted on each side with a nephrite panel. In these cups he has created a form of drinking-vessel that could hardly be less well adapted to its apparent purpose. One of the commissions he received from the Saxon court was to mount in silver-gilt a casket and a large basin of Near-Eastern workmanship decorated in mother-of-pearl. Each is constructed of wood covered with intarsia of mother-of-pearl set in a black composition to a mauresque pattern.[40] Geyer's mounts are quite restrained and he has done no more than provide a frame for the highly decorative black and white mauresques. To complete the basin he supplied a ewer of conservative Renaissance design, the body of which is set with two rows of convex oval mother-of-pearl plaques (pl. 561). By adding the ewer, Geyer made it clear that the basin was intended to hold water, as it doubtless would for a while, but in frequent use it would have warped and become damaged. It should, therefore, be regarded as another Mannerist conceit. In the case of the casket he allowed himself more freedom in his additions and provided elaborately pierced borders and, following medieval tradition, set the whole piece on four lion feet. Geyer's most important extant piece is a great gilt basin in the Grünes Gewölbe,[41] the depression of which is embossed with scenes from the hunt, mostly embossed in low relief with some of the detail cast and applied. This vessel already conforms to the Baroque fashion in that the scene is viewed from one side instead of running round the central boss. The boss, which is oval, following the outline of the dish, is wrought with shells and corresponds in lay-out with the 'Europa and the Bull' basin by Christoph Lencker in the Kunsthistorisches Museum, Vienna, (pl. 498).

1 Hüseler, p.6.
2 This cup is decorated with casts from nature of grasses and grasshoppers in the manner associated with Wenzel Jamnitzer.
3 Scheffler, Vol. II, p.907.
4 Scheffler, ibid Vol. II, p.912.
5 Menzhausen, no. 64, p.89.
6 'Dirich Utermarke, ein Hamburger Goldschmied der Renaissance,' *Ehrengabe des Museums für Hamburger Geschichte,* 1939, p.94-113.
7 Sponsel, Vol. II, p.83-91.
8 Pechstein I, cat. no. 17.
9 ill. Hüseler, pl. I.
10 e.g. the flagon by Hans Relowes of Riga in the Victoria and Albert Museum, no. M 31-1961.
11 R. Stettiner, *Das Kleinodienbuch des Jakob Mores,* Hamburg, 1916.
12 A. Winckler, 'Die Handzeichnungen des Hamburger Goldschmiedes Jakob Mores', *Jahrbuch der Preuss. Kunstsammlungen,* 1890, p.111ff. See also B. Olsen, *Die Arbeiten der Hamburger Goldschmiede Jakob Mores Vater und Sohn,* Hamburg, 1903.
13 For the Jamnitzer centre-piece, see Pechstein I, cat. no. 102; for the Ritter elephant centre-pieces, see Rosenberg I, no. 3880; for an illustration of the Polidoro drawing, now in the Louvre, see M. Winner, 'Raffael malt einen Elefanten', *Mitteilungen des Kunsthist. Instituts,* Florence, Vol. XI, 1969, p.101, fig. 26.
14 ill. C. Hernmarck, 'Hamburg und der schwedische Hof während des 17 Jahrhunderts', *Festschrift f. Erich Meyer,* Hamburg, 1957, p.273.
15 See A. Rhodes, *Goldschmiedekunst in Königsberg,* Stuttgart, 1959.
16 Pechstein I, cat. no. 47.
17 Sponsel, Vol. II, p.83.
18 Kesting, *Anton Eisenhoit, ein Westphälischer Kupferstecher und Goldschmied,* p.10.
19 ibid, pls. 58, 59.
20 Pechstein I, cat. no. 48.
21 R. Fritz, 'Ein geschnitzter Kokonusspokal der Spätgotik und andere Kölner Kokonusspokale', *Miscellanea pro arte, Hermann Schnitzler zur Vollendung des 60. Lebensjahres 1965,* Düsseldorf, 1965, p.163ff.
22 ill. *Rheinische Goldschmiedekunst,* exhibition catalogue, Cologne, 1975, pl.140.
23 *Schatzkammer der Münchner Residenz, Amtliche Führer,* 1931, no. 141.
24 See A. Legner, 'Freiburger Werke aus Bergkristall: Kristallschliff der Spatgotik und in den Jahrzehnten um 1600'. *Schau ins Land,* 75 Jahresheft, 1957.
25 Doering, p.89-90.
26 ill. Landenberger, pl. 47.
27 W. Fleischhauer, 'Hans Kobenhaupt' *Pantheon,* Vol. XXVIII, 1970, p.284.
28 Two are in the Zürich Landesmuseum, three in the Historisches Museum, Basel, one in Rappoltswiler and one in the collection of Fürst Waldburg-Wolfegg, while there are two in English collections. illustrated in pls. 556 and 557.
29 ill. Read and Tonnochy, *Silver Plate, medieval and later,* British Museum, London, 1928, cat. no. 70, pl. XXXIV.
30 For a list of detached plaques from tazza bowls, see the article on Gessner in the *Thieme-Becker Künstler Lexikon.*
31 Collins, p.417.
32 F. Dreier, 'Hans Jakob Sprüngli aus Zürich als Hinterglasmaler,' *Zeitschrift für Schweizerische Archäologie und Kunstgeschichte,* 1961, Heft, pl. 3 d and b.
33 ibid. the attribution of the mounts in this case was made by von Falke.
34 For Dresden goldsmiths' work, see Holzhausen, *passim.*
35 Holzhausen, pls. 12-15.
36 Sponsel, Vol. II, pl. 48.
37 ibid. Vol. II, pl. 11.
38 Holzhausen, pl. 18.
39 See J. Menzhausen, *Der Goldschmied Elias Geyer,* Dresden, 1963.
40 Sponsel, pl. 29.
41 J. Menzhausen, op. cit., pl. 40.

CHAPTER THIRTEEN

The Habsburg Family Dominions: Hungary and Poland

Vienna

So few identifiable examples have survived from the sixteenth century that it is impossible to give a connected account of Vienna goldsmiths' work. The widespread destruction can be attributed to the incessant Turkish Wars and, perhaps even more, to the Liberation War against Napoleon when vessels of precious metal had to be surrendered for melting if the owner did not pay a special tax to secure exemption for his plate. The records of the Vienna goldsmiths' guild[1] provide the names of many goldsmiths, among them relatives of Wenzel Jamnitzer, who was of Viennese origin, but a mere handful of them are represented by extant pieces. The main commissions of the Emperor Ferdinand I (1558-1564) went to goldsmiths in Augsburg and Nürnberg, but his successor, Maximilian II (1564-1578) patronised the goldsmiths of Vienna more frequently, giving them orders for important presentation pieces. Maximilian's own *Kammergoldschmied*, Juan Maczuelos, was a Spaniard, but he is believed to have returned to Spain in 1570.[2] He was paid a salary of 10 gulden a month, which put him amongst the better paid artists at the Imperial court. Maximilian's Empress, Maria, who was a daughter of Charles V, also had a Spanish goldsmith, Juan Pery Pockh, attached to her household. He received a monthly wage of ten florins and seventy-five reales. His only recorded surviving work is the sword and dagger with enamelled gold hilts at Dresden (pl. 703). An appointment to the Empress did not, of course, imply that he was employed exclusively on commissions for her personal use.

Mazuelos was succeeded as *Kammergoldschmied* by the Vienna goldsmith Marx Khornblum, who worked regularly for the court from about 1575 to 1591, when he was followed by his younger brother, Mang (Magnus) Khornblum. Only one vessel by him is in the Kunsthistorisches Museum, Vienna.[3] It is not of outstanding quality and is probably hardly representative of the Imperial goldsmith's best work.

Among the most sumptuous examples of goldsmiths' art in Mannerist style are the enamelled gold ewer and basin (pls. 564-7) presented by the *Stände* (nobility) of the Province of Carinthia to Archduke Carl of Inner Austria and his spouse, Maria of Bavaria, as a wedding present in 1571. Contemporary inventories record the presence of many large vessels of pure gold in royal treasuries, but these are unique survivals. They have long been used as baptismal plate by the Habsburg family and are known to have served this purpose as early as the seventeenth century. The most recent publication[4] that refers to these vessels describes them as North Italian, but gives no reason for the attribution. It is difficult to establish the origin of unmarked plate in the International Mannerist style; one would, however, have expected the donors to have commissioned the vessels either from a Vienna court goldsmith or from one of the south German masters in Nürnberg or Augsburg. If they were made in Vienna then one of the Spanish goldsmiths, either Juan Pery Pockh or Juan Mazuelos, employed at the Imperial court at the time, might have been their creator. The applied medallions of enamelled gold are of a type that was supplied by Augsburg goldsmiths, such as David Altenstetter, as well as being fashionable in Spain. The enamelling of the medallions is noticeably finer than that of the embossed masks, but this is due to the different technique employed, namely champlevé. Our knowledge of gold objects made by Spanish masters is at present confined to sword-hilts (see Chapter XVI) and jewellery, but in the light of present knowledge, an attribution to a Spanish goldsmith seems to be the most acceptable. Enamelled work such as that on these two vessels is referred to in contemporary Austrian inventories as 'spanische Arbeit'.

An imposing set of chalice, mass cruets, dish and altar cross of gold and translucent enamel dated 1625 in the treasury of the monastery of Klosterneuburg[5] bears the signature of Hans Melchior Sibmacher, *K. K. May. Hofgoldarbeiter in Wien* (Imperial court goldsmith in Vienna). The enamelled ornament corresponds to the manner of David Altenstetter. Sibmacher was evidently related to the engraver of the same name who published a series of pattern-books for goldsmiths in Nürnberg in 1592, 1596 and 1599. These show details of ornament for vessels rather than complete pieces. Nothing further is known of this Vienna court goldsmith, but the enamelled gold ewer (pl. 574) in the Weltliche Schatzkammer, usually attributed to Prague, might be his work.[6]

From the point of view of court patronage the situation in Vienna became less favourable to the local goldsmiths after the accession of the Emperor Rudolph II (1578-1612), as he maintained a great court workshop in Prague and fewer orders came to the Vienna masters. The very fact that the Vienna goldsmiths are so poorly represented in the former Imperial Collection can only mean that their work as a whole did not equal that of their South German rivals, though it should be mentioned that some of the unmarked pieces in the Vienna collections may be unrecognised productions of local goldsmiths. A stag cup by a Vienna master is illustrated in pl. 568.

Salzburg

Of the other Habsburg Residence cities, Graz, Innsbruck and Salzburg, the last is best represented by extant pieces.[7] The Salzburg goldsmiths might have expected numerous commissions from their wealthy archbishops but their patronage went either to their own court goldsmith or to South German masters. The Salzburg goldsmiths specialised in mounting the horns of mountain goats with precious metal, but they hardly achieved more than a provincial status and do not call for further treatment here. The curious ewer in the form of a fish from the treasury of the Archbishops of Salzburg has been conjecturally attributed to a Salzburg master (pl. 563); the companion basin, now lost, was almost certainly a South German piece.[8] The most enthusiastic patron of the goldsmiths' craft was Archbishop Wolf Dietrich von Raitenau (1587-1612), who purchased new sets of plate both for his own table in the Residence and the cathedral altar. Two of the leading goldsmiths of their time, Paul van Vianen and Hans Karl, were summoned to Salzburg to work for him.

Hans Karl

The most important of the Salzburg court goldsmiths was Hans Karl who came from Nürnberg to work for the Archbishop Wolf Dietrich von Raitenau. He made a set of enamelled gold cups,[9] which, like so many of the finest achievements of sixteenth century goldsmiths, were long thought to be Italian and were, therefore, attributed to Benvenuto Cellini. The attribution was strengthened by the fact that they were preserved in the Palazzo Pitti and were assumed to have been made for one of the Tuscan Grand Dukes. A flask belonging to this set is dated 1602 (pl. XX), but one of the cups (pl. 571) bears the arms of Archbishop Wolf's successor, Marcus Sitticus, who did not accede until 1612. By this date Hans Karl had left Salzburg and gone to work for the Emperor Rudolph II in Prague, so one must assume that he delivered the cup and possibly finished it, when already in imperial pay. The flask of 1602 displays the all-over decoration of the sixteenth century, but the ornament is laid out with exact symmetry and there are no disturbing changes of scale nor a combination of antithetical elements. The enamelled ornament of the bowls in the set is restrained and leaves much of the surface free from decoration. There is another two-handled cup of enamelled gold of very similar design in the Munich Schatzkammer. This was made for Prince Janusz VII Radziwill, whose arms it bears. It is probably a work of Hans Karl, dating from the period when he worked in Prague (pl. 572). The Salzburg gold cups were delivered to Archbishop Wolf Dietrich and his successor, Marcus Sitticus, according to the terms of an agreement between the Archbishop and the lessees of the gold-mines at Gastein. This provided for an annual tribute of an enamelled gold cup in recognition of the Archbishop's forgoing certain taxation. Five gold cups are recorded in the 1612 inventory of the Salzburg treasury, but only three survive.

Paul van Vianen

Another goldsmith of great distinction who worked in Salzburg was Paul van Vianen who came there after leaving the employ of the Elector Maximilian of Bavaria. He was present in Salzburg only for the short period between 1602 and 1603 but while there a son was born to him, at whose christening the Archbishop acted as godfather. This indicates that he was accorded recognition as an artist of exceptional skill. Only one work has been attributed to his Salzburg period; this is the group of the crucified Christ flanked by the Virgin Mary and Saint John, which, like most of the Salzburg treasure, is now in the Palazzo Pitti.[10] The three figures are of pure gold, that of Christ cast in five parts and joined, the others wrought from sheet. The expressive Mannerism of the Low Countries can, as Rossacher has pointed out, be recognised in their modelling. The pathos of pose and of facial expression implies a sculptural skill of the highest order and it has convincingly been argued that van Vianen is their most likely author. Most of his identified work is in low relief, but the gold mounts of the jasper ewer (pl. 580), which are of equal merit to the Salzburg figures, are also wrought in the round.

Goldsmiths working in Salzburg, the residence of an archbishop, received important commissions for church plate. Some remains in Salzburg Cathedral, some was removed to Florence, but a particularly fine pair of altar sticks is now in the Bayerisches National Museum.[11] These also show the widespread influence of the Jamnitzer workshop since the cast borders appear to derive from Jamnitzer models.

The Habsburg Court Workshop, Prague

The emergence of the city of Prague as one of the chief European artistic centres was due to the personal influence of the Emperor Rudolph II, whose residence was the palace of the Hradschin on Mala Strana, on the opposite side of the river from the old city. There is curiously little goldsmiths' work of Prague origin surviving from the period prior to the establishment of Rudolph's court there. Among the few interesting pieces are the chalice of 1575 in Gothic Revival style in the Berlin Kunstgewerbemuseum[12] and an ostrich-egg cup (pl. 583) in the British Museum, both by the same maker.

The Emperor Rudolph was tormented by melancholia and one of the duties of his court artists was to devise conceits to distract him. A dominant interest in his life was his *Kunstkammer,* in which he accumulated a vast quantity of natural objects and artifacts made by the many artists employed in his court workshop. The wonders of nature fascinated him, but even more so the skill of man shown in transforming natural materials into other forms. The ability to produce splendid vessels out of shells and human or animal figures out of hardstones was admired as a manifestation of the triumph of human ideas over nature.[13] The skill and fantasy of his goldsmiths transformed precious metals in much the same way as the court painter, Archimboldi, created human portraits out of assemblages of fruit or domestic objects. His interest was not confined to the end product, we are told that 'he goes every day to see the painters at work, painting himself sometimes, and goes to see the goldsmiths, the masters of mosaic and the hardstone engravers at their labours'.[14] He paid a special retainer to one of the goldsmiths in return for instruction in using the tools of the craft.

The Emperor took quite a different attitude towards the acquisition of works of art from his predecessors and also most of his contemporaries. In the course of his long reign from 1578 until 1612 he was not just motivated by the need to provide an adequate stock of expensive presents for other rulers or the desire to amass treasure in convenient form. While his collection undoubtedly included a large number of what we should now regard as curios, one can surely allow him some credit for the original ideas that were developed by goldsmiths at the Prague Court Workshop. His main love was for precious and for semi-precious stones, which he admired not only for their intrinsic qualities but also for the magical powers he believed them to possess. His personal physician, Anselm Boeth de Boot, published in 1609 a book entitled *Gemmarum et Lapidum Historia* in which he recorded all the wondrous qualities with which precious stones were credited. Rudolph himself recognised in such materials a reflection of the Deity himself. De Boot gives an account of the Emperor's attitude: 'the Emperor was not attracted to them (precious stones) in order with the help of their lustre to increase his own importance and majesty (the latter was in any case so great that there was no need for help from elsewhere) but to understand through the medium of precious stones the grandeur and infinite power of God, who was able to combine in such minute particles the beauty and the force of all other things on earth, and in this way to have before his eyes a permanent reflection of the brilliance of the Deity.'

In 1588 Rudolph issued an edict instructing his subjects in all the lands of the Bohemian crown to search for precious stones; and two years later he published a patent to the hardstone sculptor, Matthias Krätsch, entitling him to purchase precious stones for the Emperor in all the territories of Bohemia. The Emperor was not satisfied with the local hardstone cutters and he is said to have instructed his ambassador in Madrid, Hans von Khevenhüller, to ask the advice of Jacopo da Trezzo before he appointed the Milanese artist, Ottavio Miseroni, as his court hardstone cutter.[15] The family was already known to Rudolph, as Gasparo Miseroni had supplied a quantity of rock-crystal beakers to his father, Maximilian II. The appointment of Ottavio Miseroni was followed by many others, until Rudolph established in Prague a court workshop covering the whole range of applied art. His idea of retaining court artists and paying them regular salaries was not a new one, but this had never been done on so large a scale. In addition to commissioning new works of art, he also made every effort to recover for the Imperial treasury precious objects from the estate of his father that had passed to other members of the family. His love of superb goldsmiths' work and finely-mounted vessels of hardstone attracted many of the leading craftsmen from other European courts, but most of them are known only from documentary references. While the Miseroni family came from Milan, many of his goldsmiths came from the Low Countries: Jan Vermeyen, Paul van Vianen, Erasmus Hornick, Jost Gelle and Hans de Vos. The engraver, Aegidius Sadeler, and the court painters, Hans von Aachen and Barthlomäus Spranger, also came from the same region. Some of the most famous goldsmith families can be recognised in the names of the German masters working for Rudolph; Georg Lencker, Philip Holbein, Benedikt Krug and Christoph Jamnitzer.

The term *Kaiserliche Hofwerkstatt* (Imperial Court Workshop) should not be interpreted to mean a co-operative undertaking in a large joint workshop. The various masters doubtless specialised in their own individual skills, so that a vessel wrought or cast by one master might be passed on to another for engraving, but for the most part they would have worked independently. There was no uniform Prague court style, except in the case of the enamelled gold mounts of some of the hardstone vessels, in which the goldsmith played a subsidiary role. Moreover, the goldsmiths were allowed to work on their own account as well. They used to offer their wares for sale in the great Wlasdislaw Hall of the Hradschin Palace, a scene that has been preserved for us in an engraving by

Aegidius Sadeler.[16] Nevertheless it is possible to recognise certain common features in the creations of the Prague workshop: they date from a moment when the Mannerist version of classical art was being superseded by the Baroque version and we find a combination of the two styles, on the one hand elaborate and ingenious ornament, on the other the higher relief and increased pathos of the Baroque. This manner was by no means confined to Prague; the great dish of Christoph Jamnitzer (pl. 511) which represents it at its best can be paralleled by two others made in the early years of the seventeenth century by Elias Geyer of Leipzig and by Daniel Kellerthaler of Dresden, both in the Grünes Gewölbe.

Although some of the best goldsmiths in Europe had been engaged to work there, the Prague workshop was unable to satisfy all Rudolph's orders and he gave commissions to many other masters working elsewhere, including Christoph Jamnitzer and Niklaus Schmidt in Nürnberg, Abraham Lotter and Christoph Lencker in Augsburg and the Vienna goldsmiths, the brothers Khornblum. Finally there were numerous and often extremely expensive purchases from merchants, mostly in Augsburg. Many of the purchases made from sources outside the court workshop were intended for presents.

Much has been written above about Erasmus Hornick, who was appointed in 1582 *Kaiserlicher Majestäts Hofgoldschmied und Juwelier* in Prague. The only reference to him there, apart from the record of his death in 1583, is the complaint he addressed to the Nürnberg City Council in March, 1582, alleging that he had left a silver-gilt mounted mirror with a certain Nürnberg citizen, from whose possession it had been removed by Philip Scherl, against whom he asked for redress.[17] The outcome is not recorded, perhaps because of his death.

Ottavio Miseroni

Ottavio Miseroni[18] was aged about twenty when he was appointed to the Imperial Court Workshop; the document appointing him was dated 23 December 1589 but his pay was back-dated to the beginning of 1588. He remained in the Emperor's employ until his death in 1624 and ranks as one of the most important personalities in the history of the Prague workshop. He was also entrusted with various offices in the Imperial treasury and was perhaps eventually put in charge of it. He certainly enjoyed the Emperor's favour and, according to Sandrart,[19] was granted the rank of *Freiherr*, provided with an estate appropriate to the title, and granted the right to farm salt (*Salzmeisteramt*). Though he signed some of the cameos and inlaid hardstone plaques (*commessi*) that he produced, none of the bowls of semi-precious stone that constituted his main work bears his signature. An idea of the extent of his work is given by a petition which he addressed to the Emperor Matthias in 1621. In this he lists fifteen completed drinking-vessels and nine others that were still in the process of manufacture. He was joined in Prague after 1600 by two brothers, Giovanni Ambrogio and Alessandro, but it is not known what they produced there. Their names appear in the Prague records for the last time in 1612. Five other hardstone-cutters are mentioned in the records, Giovanni and Cosimo Castrucci, Caspar Lehmann, Mathias Krätsch and Hans Schweiger.[20] Of these the two Castrucci worked on landscapes executed in hardstone mosaic, Caspar Lehmann was a glass-cutter and Mathias Krätsch was mainly engaged in searching for and procuring supplies of hardstones. It seems, therefore, that the Miseroni family was responsible for most of the hardstone vessels produced in the Prague workshop.

In contrast to the earlier Milanese rock-crystals which were decorated with intaglio-cut figure subjects, Ottavio Miseroni seems to have concentrated on vessels of fantastic form carved from coloured stones such as smoky quartz, topaz, heliotrope or jade. Those hitherto attributed to him are of oval form with a figure or grotesque mask growing out of one end. Prague mounts can be identified by the type of champlevé ornament they bear. As they mostly date from the very end of the sixteenth or from the seventeenth century, enamel plays a more important role than on the earlier Milanese rock-crystals. In any case the coloured hardstone called for more polychrome mounts. The late sixteenth-century type can be seen on the heliotrope cup in Florence (pl. 569) or the rock-crystal vase (pl. 570). The presence of a Prague cup in the Medici collection can presumably be explained by an exchange of gifts between sovereigns; some of the finest extant lapis lazuli vases from the Florentine Court Workshop are for the same reason now in Vienna. As might be expected in a workshop directed by a Milanese master craftsman, the rock-crystal vessels carved in Prague were cut with festoons, floral ornament and birds but not, apparently, with the figure subjects that had been a speciality of the masters working in Milan. Where the enamelling of the gold mounts is not in the typical Prague style, it is difficult to distinguish with certainty between Prague and Milanese work.

Various types of gold mount were employed by the Prague goldsmiths. The most elaborate can be seen on the ewer and companion basin in pls. 576, 577. In this case the gold mount is overlaid with enamelled gold scrollwork which is set with precious stones. With this type of mount more elaborate cutting of the rock-crystal is usually found. In a second type, which appears towards the beginning of the seventeenth century, instead of the gold forming the ground, as in pls. 569-70, the enamel, usually white, formed the ground while the detail of the strapwork and cartouches was reserved in gold (pl. 578). The effect resembles that of cloisonné enamel though the technique was, in fact, champlevé.

During the first quarter of the seventeenth century the formal Renaissance ornament composed of festoons and bunches of flowers gave way to a more naturalistic type, now known as pea-pod ornament in reference to the natural form from which it derived. This was much exploited by the Prague enamellers, carried out in polychrome translucent enamel against the gold ground of the mounts. The Prague goldsmiths did not confine themselves to hardstone vessels that had been cut by their fellow workmen; like the Florentine masters employed by Lorenzo de' Medici a century earlier, they used whatever came to hand. Amongst the exotic objects mounted at the time is the Fatimid rock-crystal bottle illustrated in pl. 570. The simple mount provided for this piece indicates that it was not at the time considered to be of great importance. The Prague goldsmiths usually mounted hardstone vessels in enamelled gold; the handsome two-handled bowl with silver-gilt mounts illustrated in pl. VIII may have been carved and engraved in Prague but was perhaps mounted elsewhere.

The development of Baroque taste was already manifest when Ottavio Miseroni was in charge of the hardstone cutting workshop, but it is rather with his son, Dionysio, that the typical Baroque vessels are associated. Carving on these was executed in higher relief and at the same time their forms became more fantastic, derived more directly from the natural shape of the stone from which they had been cut (pl. 578). The enamelled enrichment became more profuse with the bunches of fruit and flowers executed on a larger scale with a wider range of colour until, towards the middle of the century, the gold of the mounts disappeared beneath a covering of painted enamel.

Hardstone vessels from the Prague *Hofwerkstatt* were not all mounted there. Many of those in the Kunsthistorisches Museum have gilt mounts struck with a maker's mark, the letters HC. It is not known whether this master was active in Vienna or Prague. Other vessels were probably purchased by noblemen or merchants who had them mounted elsewhere according to their own individual taste. Even in the early seventeenth century hardstones from Prague were mounted in gold or silver-gilt set with rows of garnets in traditional Bohemian manner.

Anton Schweinberger

This master was born in Augsburg and followed a course similar to that of Hornick, passing from the city of his birth to Prague where he was appointed to the *Kaiserliche Hofwerkstatt* in 1587, four years after Hornick's death. His monthly salary was fixed at ten gulden, not a high one, though better than the six gulden which was all that Hornick received. Schweinberger is one of the few goldsmiths in whose work one can recognise something of Hornick's style as reflected in his later drawings. He evidently enjoyed the full trust of the Emperor, for, when Rudolph wished to work at the bench himself, it was one of Schweinberger's assistants who was paid the rather generous sum of thirty gulden for instructing him in the use of the goldsmiths' tools.[21] Schweinberger worked in Prague for sixteen or seventeen years until in 1603 he was succeeded as *Kammergoldschmied* by Paul van Vianen. Few pieces have been attributed to him, the most important being the ewer illustrated in pl. 579, a peculiar cup with the cover modelled in the form of a boar's head,[22] while the body is cut from rhinoceros horn, and a rock-crystal cup with enamelled silver-gilt mounts in the Metropolitan Museum, New York. The ewer and the boar's-head cup have a number of common features: first, the foot composed of mermen with writhing tails, secondly, the superbly modelled human demi-figures that embellish the handles of the ewer and enclose the body of the cup, and, finally, the helmets composed of scrollwork worn by the figures, Auricular details more typical of Baroque art make their appearance in these vessels, but are restricted to a decorative function and cannot be said to anticipate the more advanced ideas of Paul and Adam van Vianen, whose vessels were composed of purely auricular forms.

Paul van Vianen

The earlier stages in the career of the most outstanding goldsmith at the Rudolphine court, Paul van Vianen, are dealt with elsewhere (see p.269 and p.292). Like many of the great sixteenth-century master goldsmiths, he moved from one court to another, thus acquiring an international reputation which finally gained him the appointment to the Prague Court Workshop. Unlike those goldsmiths who were members of their guild, van Vianen did not strike his pieces with a mark but signed them like an artist, either with his full name or his initials or in monogram. He was, in fact, a painter as well as goldsmith and contemporary documents refer to him sometimes as *Hofmaler* (court painter). A painting signed by him was once in the picture collection of Charles I of England, while there is a self-portrait showing him holding a piece of goldsmith's work: a finely modelled figure of Venus.[23] His skill as an artist did not equal that as a goldsmith and, when he was appointed to the Hofwerkstatt in Prague in 1603, he was given the office of *Kammergoldschmied*. He was granted a salary of twenty gulden a month, which was equal to that enjoyed by Jan Vermeyen, the chief Rudolphine goldsmith, and twice as much as the other Prague goldsmiths received. He held this position until his death, which took place as a result of the plague in either 1613 or 1614. A final proof of his exceptional status is that five of his works are listed in the inventory of the Rudolphine *Kunstkammer,* while no other goldsmiths are mentioned by name.

His Prague period is the best documented in his life, as a number of signed and dated pieces made there survive. Most are reliefs of rectagular or circular form, the latter originally intended to decorate tazza bowls. The silver plaques have often been destroyed and we have now only a base metal version of bronze or lead. Like his German contemporaries he probably took moulds from the reliefs that he embossed and lead patterns taken from these were sold as models to other goldsmiths. These plaquettes also found much favour with collectors, for whom the bronze casts were intended. The bronzes were, however, sometimes cast from badly worn lead plaquettes and so give no adequate idea of the quality of van Vianen's original. The best known of his plaquettes are those illustrating scenes from the legend of Argus. This set is mentioned by Sandrart: many after-casts exist and the individual plaquettes were copied in silver by contemporary Dutch masters. He did not confine himself to making small plaquettes of tazza bowl size. He also produced a series of rectangular plaques, the larger dimensions of which gave him more opportunity to display his skill. While most of his plaquettes were executed in silver, he did not disdain to work in copper which was afterwards gilded. One of his best compositions, the Resurrection, exists in two versions, silver and gilt-copper.[24]

Brass patterns (*Patronen*) were also made from original reliefs by Paul van Vianen;

these were only intended to give a rough outline and the detail was put in by the gold-smith, but they saved him a lot of trouble in working out the composition. A set of sixteen such patterns depicting the Crucifixion of Christ and the martyrdom of various saints, each signed with van Vianen's monogram, has survived in the form of plaster casts or electrotype reproductions.[25] As these patterns served as the foundation upon which silver sheet was hammered, they give no indication of the skill of their master. Presumably van Vianen must also have wrought a finished set which formed the model for the *Patronen,* but these have not survived.

The list of major works attributed to van Vianen has been greatly reduced as a result of the re-attribution of the great Triumph Ewer and Basin (pls. 511, 512, 513) to Chris-toph Jamnitzer and of the four gold panels that decorate the side of the *Hauskrone* of Emperor Rudolph II to Jan van Vermeyen or to an anonymous goldsmith working under his direction. These plaques represent the crowning of Rudolph as Holy Roman Emp-eror, as King of Hungary, as King of Bohemia and as the victor in battle against the Turks. The attribution of these plaques, which was made by Kris, was questioned in the later editions of the catalogue of the Weltliche Schatzkammer because the crown is dated 1602 and Paul van Vianen did not arrive to take up his position in Prague until the following year.[26] He was, however, already working within the Habsburg dominions in 1602 and the possibility should not be ruled out that he was commissioned to execute them before he took up residence in Prague. The crown of the Emperor Rudolph is one of the most magnificent objects of its kind ever made and was certainly not the unaided work of Jan van Vermeyen, the chief court goldsmith from 1597 till his death in 1606. At present one can only regard the plaques as the work of an unknown member of the *Kaiserliche Hofwerkstatt.*

The most colourful and individual work by Paul van Vianen of his Prague period is the brown jasper ewer in the Kunsthistorisches Museum (pl. 580), for which he supplied the gold handle, lip and foot mounts. This superb vessel illustrates a significant aspect of his achievement; that he was less interested in vessel design than in creating sculpture, or at any rate, sculptural ornament. That he thought of himself in this light is indicated by the fact that he was never a member of a guild, that he signed with his name instead of with a stamp and finally by the portrait which shows him holding a statue of Venus. It is unlikely that this ewer is the only hardstone vessel he mounted, but no other has been recognised in the large collection of mounted vessels in Vienna. A gold cup dated 1610 and signed with his full title *S. Caes. Mtis. aur. Paulus de Viana* (Paul van Vianen goldsmith to his imperial Majesty) is now in the collection of the Prince zu Wied to whom it is believed to have descended from Heinrich Julius, Herzog von Braunschweig and Bishop of Halberstadt, a medal of whom is set inside the cover.[27] This Prince and prelate was often in Prague between 1610 and 1613 and is known to have shared the Emperor's collecting enthusiasm. Although made at an early date in the seventeenth century this vessel already shows some Baroque features. The bowl is embossed with the subject of Diana and Actaeon, the original drawing for which survives in the Frank-furt am Main Kupferstichkabinett.[28] Paul van Vianen repeated this composition on several occasions; besides the cup of 1610, it is seen on the basin of 1613 (pl. 632) and on a plaquette dated 1612.

Whereas in his earlier period Paul van Vianen used engravings by other masters as source material for his designs, in his later life he worked out his own compositions and even supplied other masters, among them Georg Schwanhardt the Elder, the glass engraver and, incidentally, his personal friend, with drawings. Besides the Diana and Actaeon drawing a number of others from his Prague period have survived. They include landscapes of the surroundings of Prague and a series of drawings for a silver tazza bearing the date 1607, which is now in the Rijksmuseum.[29] In 1610 Paul obtained permission from the Emperor to return to Utrecht for four months and he may have taken some of his drawings back with him on that occasion. Others may have been returned to the family workshop after his death. It is at any rate certain that they were returned, for they were copied by his brother Adam and by other assistants in the

Utrecht workshop (see pl. 634 and 637).

In the course of his life Paul van Vianen's manner as a chaser developed; he rendered his figure subjects in higher relief and gave them more importance while his landscapes were wrought in very low relief. His finest work was his last: the splendid ewer and basin in the Rijksmusem (pls. 630-2). In comparison with the ewer wrought by Adam van Vianen in the following year (pl. 628) Paul's ewer is distinctly conservative, though the development of the Dutch auricular style can be recognised in the modelling of the foot and lip which seem to be composed of living tissue. It is interesting to observe that, although he was an employee of the Imperial Court Workshop, he was allowed enough freedom of action to work out this fundamentally Dutch style there. The dish that accompanies the ewer is exceptional in that the central plaque, which is embossed with the meeting of Diana and Actaeon, is backed by another decorated with the death of Actaeon, so that the piece can be looked at from either side. It was not unusual to set another plaque underneath the bowl of a tazza to conceal the unsightly underside of the embossing, but to treat in this way a dish which can rarely have been turned over shows an altogether exceptional concern for excellence of finish.

Owing to his premature death Paul did not develop his style as far as his brother Adam van Vianen and the most imaginative essays in the auricular manner are the work of the latter. Whereas Paul remained satisfied with traditional vessel shapes and experimented with the new form of ornament, Adam went further and created altogether new vessel forms. Paul is best to be judged as a creator of plaquettes, in which, after adopting the manner of the great Nürnberg masters, he eventually developed a personal style. In this he displayed an acutely pictorial sense which more aptly justifies his title of *Hofmaler* than his paintings. In some of these later plaquettes he inserts landscape backgrounds apparently based on drawings he made himself of views in the neighbourhood of Prague.[30]

Andreas Osenbruck

Some reference has been made above to the crown of Rudolph II; this together with the orb and sceptre of his brother and successor, Matthias, is the most important creation of the Prague *Hofwerkstatt*. The imperial regalia have been dealt with at length in specialist publications[31] and do not require detailed discussion here, though they certainly constitute the finest goldsmiths' achievement of the period. While the masters who produced Rudolph's crown are unknown — the names of Jan Van Vermeyen for the goldsmithing, of Paul van Vianen for the embossing and chasing, and of Hans Karl for the enamelling being no more than possibilities — the sceptre is signed by its maker, Andreas Osenbruck, *Kammergoldschmied* of the Emperor Matthias, and dated 1615. The orb was formerly attributed with confidence to van Vermeyen on account of its stylistic relationship to the crown, and it was only after it was recognised as having been made long after his death that it also was attributed to Osenbruck. Of comparable quality to the regalia is the small gold ewer (pl. 574) which has been used as an alternative to the large ewer (pl. 565) at Habsburg christenings. Whereas the latter ewer is known to have been secular in origin, the small one is decorated with winged cherubs' heads, a standard ornament of ecclesiastical plate. Its designer has achieved a pleasing balance between its constituent elements and given it a most graceful profile. Like most vessels of gold it is not marked and cannot be attributed with any certainty, though the name of Osenbruck should be mentioned as a possibility.

Hungary

In the sixteenth century the silver mines of Hungary were the most productive in Europe and many goldsmiths were kept busy, especially in the northern region of the Siebenbürgen. The most characteristic productions of the first half of the century were tall beakers splayed out towards the lip and of evidently Gothic derivation. They correspond to the type made in South Germany, and Hungarian goldsmiths' work throughout the century shows strong German influence, partly because young Hungarian goldsmiths went to south Germany during their period of training as journeymen and partly because, at any rate in the latter part of the century, German pattern books and lead models from Wenzel Jamnitzer's workshop (pl. 582) were used by Hungarian masters. Little is known of the Hungarian goldsmiths unless, like Georg Zeggin from Szegedin,[32] they came to work at one of the German courts, or have left drawings or pattern-books. The recognition of sixteenth century Hungarian or Bohemian silver vessels is rendered more difficult as they were frequently unmarked. A few survivals, such as the huge but curiously shaped ewer and basin from the Esterhaszy Collection now in the Iparmuveszeti Museum, Budapest,[33] which was made in 1548 by a Koloszvar goldsmith, or the series of *Handsteine* attributed to Bohemian goldsmiths in the Kunsthistorisches Museum, Vienna, provide evidence of central European production. Further evidence of Bohemian interest in vessels decorated with silver mining scenes is found in the attractive drawing by Concz Welcz of Joachimstal (pl. 36). A nationalistic trend common enough amongst art historians has led to some vessels of apparently German origin, such as the Krug workshop cup (pl. 269) being claimed as Hungarian.[34] On the other hand, many unmarked pieces that are in fact of Hungarian make have been described as German because they so closely resemble contemporary South German work. The tankard by Johann Lippai of Kassa (pl. 582) would certainly have been called South German had it not been marked. There is even a prejudice in the antique trade against describing a piece as Hungarian as this may diminish its value. There was a distinct time-lag between fashion in the chief south German cities and the towns in the Siebenburgen. A striking example is the Nagyszeben Flagon, formerly in the Figdor Collection,[35] which is set with coins and decorated with mauresques in the manner of the mid-sixteenth century, though its actual date is given by an inscription as 1640. It would not, however, be correct to regard Hungarian goldsmiths' work as a mere provincial copy of South Germany. It is notable for the outstanding quality of the embossing and chasing; both the tankard chased with 'The Fall of Man in the Garden of Eden' (pl. XXII) and the standing cup (pl. 581) by the Leutschau master, Sebastian Aurifaber, are the equal of the best contemporary south German work. The magnificent enamelled gold cup[36] presented in 1598 by the religious orders of Niederoesterreich to Miklos Palffy, in commemoration of his victory over the Turks in the battle of Gyor, is included in the most recent work on Hungarian goldsmiths' work, but is more likely to have been made by one of the Vienna court goldsmiths. The enamelled gold tazza (pl. XII), a piece of more provincial character, is perhaps of Hungarian origin.

A favourite decorative treatment during the latter part of the sixteenth and early seventeenth centuries was to emboss the walls of beakers or flagons with a tear-drop pattern which was gilt against a white silver ground. This practice was not confined to Hungary, but unmarked pieces decorated in this way are likely to be of Hungarian origin. The Gothic Revival associated in Nürnberg with Hans Petzoldt was much in evidence in Hungary and the goldsmiths of Siebenburgen went on producing a decadent type of lobed cup[37] (*Buckelpokal*) well into the eighteenth century. These were used as communion cups and their ecclesiastical rôle may account for their extreme conservatism of design.

Poland

In the sixteenth century Poland was a large and powerful country and its capital city, Cracow, a flourishing cultural centre, whose prosperity was stimulated by the royal residence in the castle of Wawel. Many German craftsmen had come to live in the Polish cities and, in particular, to Cracow in the later Middle Ages, and some had adopted

Polish speech and way of life. The presence of the court also brought foreign artists to the city to execute special projects, but most returned once their commissions had been completed.

Like Spain, Poland is rich in ecclesiastical plate, but very little secular plate has survived. The most important commission for church plate, that for the chapel of Sigismund I in the cathedral of Wawel, went, not to local goldsmiths but to Nürnberg. Apart from the altar frontal mentioned above (p.100), the great pair of candelabra of 1536[38] and also the golden reliquary of Saint Sigismund were made in Nürnberg after designs by Peter Flötner. The state sword of 1540,[39] which was carried by King Sigismund Augustus, the last king of the Jagellon line, and ceremonially broken at his funeral was also made in Nürnberg. The handsome cock trophy dated 1565, which was presented by Sigismund Augustus to the Cracow Shooting Confraternity, is perhaps the work of a local goldsmith.[40] This king also employed an Italian goldsmith, Jacopo Caraglio of Verona, and a curious portrait in Cracow, attributed to Paris Bordone, shows the goldsmith receiving a golden chain from the king who is represented in the guise of the Polish white eagle. Caraglio is shown standing by his bench and working on a silver helmet of classical form.

One Polish goldsmith who has been adequately researched is Erasmus Kamyn of Posen.[41] There were two generations of goldsmiths of this name in Posen; the elder, Benedict Kamyn, emigrated from Germany, perhaps from the town of Kammin in Pomerania. His son, Erasmus, published in 1552 a book of designs for goldsmiths consisting of a title-page and twelve sheets. The designs are clearly derived from contemporary Nürnberg pattern-books but while the title page follows the manner of Matthias Zündt, the sheets show mauresques in the manner of Virgil Solis. A further series of designs was issued by Erasmus Kamyn in 1592. The title page, which is printed in Polish, describes the designs as being re-issued (*Teras nowo*) so the gap between the two publications was less than would at first appear. The later book shows a considerable change in style and follows the manner of the Flemish engraver, Theodor de Bry. Though far from original, it is clear that Kamyn's designs were well up-to-date. No goldsmiths' work by either of the Kamyns has been identified, but the Posen archives show that Erasmus was a busy, if somewhat unreliable goldsmith, who employed a large number of apprentices.

The keen personal interest shown by Renaissance princes in the goldsmiths' craft has been mentioned above. The Emperor Rudolph received instruction from a member of his workshop, but King Sigismund III of Poland (1587-1632) went further and actually worked at the bench as a goldsmith. The *Kammergalerie* Inventory of the collection of Duke Maximilian I of Bavaria included under no. 35 'a gold spoon which Sigismund III, King of Poland, had made with his own hands'.[42] This piece has not survived in the Munich Schatzkammer, but there is an enamelled gold bowl set with four translucent enamelled plaques bearing the arms of Poland, Sweden, Lithuania and Vasa, which is believed to have been the, doubtless not unassisted, work of Sigismund.[43] It is of somewhat naive design with four panels of narwhal tusk alternating with the armorial plaques and, though not attributed in the Schatzkammer inventories to Sigismund, there is no reason to question the tradition. This bowl came to Munich together with a number of precious objects as part of the dowry of Princess Anna Catherina Constanza, the daughter to Sigismund III, who married the *Pfalzgraf* Philip Wilhelm in 1642. Of the surviving pieces from her dowry only two others have been identified as Polish, a pair of enamelled gold salt-cellars,[44] one of which is now incomplete. These are set with diamonds and rubies and enamelled with the impaled arms of Sweden and Poland and the monogram of Sigismund. Their attribution is based on their resemblance to the bowl of Sigismund and to the presence of his arms. They are the work of an unidentified court goldsmith, who was not necessarily of Polish nationality.

More likely to be of native Polish make are the ambitious ewer and basin (pls. 585, 586); the profile of the ewer is lacking in grace and points to a somewhat provincial master, but the programme of ornament of the basin is highly original, so much so that the piece ranks as one of the most interesting extant from its period. The arms on the centre of the basin are those of a later owner and it was eventually given to Wawel Cathedral by Bishop Potkanski (1753-86) for use in the annual ceremony of washing the feet of the poor. There is no ecclesiastical allusion in the decoration of either.

1   V. Reitzner, *Alt Wien Lexikon für Oest. und Suddeutsche Kunst*, III, Vienna 1952 and also J. H. Sausterman, '600 Jahre Wiener Gold und Silberschmiede' *Zeitschrift der Öst. Uhren und Schmuckwirtschaft*, Mai, 1967, p.17.
2   Lhotsky, p.170.
3   See Camillo List, 'Wiener Goldschmiede und ihre Beziehungen zum kaiserlichen Hof', *Jahrbuch* Vol. 17, 1896. For a frame for a gold relief by Marx Khornblum, see K. Drexler, *Goldschmiedearbeiten in Klosterneuburg*, 1897, pl. XI.
4   Fillitz und Neumann, p.19, no. 45.
5   ill. Drexler, op. cit.
6   Fillitz and Neumann, cat. no. 46.
7   K. Rossacher, *Der Schatz des Erzstiftes Salzburg*, Salzburg, 1966.
8   Rossacher, ill. pl. 55, p.141.
9   Rossacher, cat. nos. 113, 117, p.148-50.
10 Rossacher, p. 21-22, cat. no. 121.
11 Museum nos. 13-43, 44; Rossacher, cat. no. 46, illustrated.
12 Pechstein I, cat. no. 34.
13 For a detailed study of the Emperor and his collecting, see R. J. Evans, *Rudolf II and his World*, Oxford, 1973.
14 R. Alidosi, *Relazione di Germania e della corte di Rodolfo II*, ed. Modena 1872 'va a veder dipingere, dipingendo ancor lui proprio maestri d'orioli, ed intagliatori de pietre'.
15 Lhotsky, p.249.
16 ill. Lhotsky, *Zweite Teil, Zweite Hälfte*, fig. 36.
17 Hampe, nos. 587, 589, 15.III.1582.
18 For the Miseroni family see Kris I, p.137ff. and B. Bukovinska, 'Anmerkungen zur Persönlichkeit Ottavio Miseronis', *Umeni* 2, Prague, 1970, p.185ff.
19 Sandrart, p.117.
20 For the hardstone-cutters of the Prague Court Workshop see E. Eichler and E. Kris, *Die Kameen in Kunsthist. Museum*, Vienna, 1927, p.23ff.
21 Lhotsky, p.252.
22 ill. Kris II, pls. 53, 55.
23 See H. Modern, 'Paulus van Vianen', *Jahrbuch*, Vol.15, 1894, p.60-102 and, for the self-portrait, pl. V. This study is out of date in many details.
24 ill. Frederiks, Vol. IV, pls. 79, 79a.
25 For a detailed discussion of these patterns, see H. Habich, 'Treibarbeit', *Münchner Jahrbuch der bildenden Kunst*, 1927, p.334 and also Frederiks, Vol. I, p.147, cat. no. 87.
26 Fillitz und Neumann, p.21, see also A. Weixlgärtner, 'Die Weltliche Schatzkammer in Wien', *Jahrbuch*, 1928, N.F.III, p.267ff.
27 Frederiks, Vol. I, p.151.
28 Duyvené de Wit Klinkhamer, 'Diana en Actaeon door Paulus van Vianen', *Nederlandsch Konsthistorisk Jarbok*, Vol. VI, 1955, p.185.
29 For Paul van Vianen's landscape drawings, see O. Benesch, *Zeichnungen der Niederländischen Schulen*, Vienna, 1928, cat. no. 291; for his designs for the Rijksmuseum tazza see Duyvené de Wit Klinkhammer, 'Een drinkschal van Paulus van Vianen', *Bulletin of the Rijksmuseum*, 1954, p.75.
30 Frederiks, Vol. I, cat. nos. 76, 77.
31 H. Fillitz, 'Studien zur Krone Kaiser Rudolphs II', *Kunstmuseets Äarskrift*, Copenhagen, 1950, p.79, ibid *Die oesterreichische Kaiserkrone*, Vienna, 1959.
32 Krempel, p.132-4.
33 Ill. E. Koszeghy, *Merkzeichen der Goldschmiede Ungarns*, Budapest, 1936, no. 985, pl. IV. These pieces were seriously damaged during World War II.
34 Mihalik, p.85, n.14 maintains that the arms on this cup are those of Istvan Zapolyi, who died in 1499, and that the cup could not possibly have been made by Krug. Study of the cup and comparison with other Krug pieces suggests that a date about 1530 is more likely to be correct.
35 ill. M. Rosenberg, 'Studien uber Goldschmiedekunst in der Sammlung Figdor in Wien', *Kunst und*

Kunsthandwerk, Vienna, 1911, p.387, fig. 112. For another flagon of sixteenth century form but later date, see Kolba and Nemeth, pl. 37, also from Nagyszeben. In this case the decoration is already Baroque.

36 ill. Kolba and Nemeth, Pl. III.

37 See Mihalik, p.64-85.

38 Kohlhaussen, figs. 658, 659.

39 ibid. figs. 660, 661, 662.

40 Exhibition cat. *L'Art à Cracovie* 1350-1550, National Museum Cracow, 1964 pl. 90.

41 A. Warschauer, 'Die Posener Goldschmiedefamilie Kamyn' *Zeitschrift der hist. Gesellschaft für die Provinz Posen,* Vol. IX, 1894.

42 *'Ein guldener Löffl, welchen Sigismund der dritte diss namens, König in Poln, selbst mit aigner Handt gemacht hat'.* A silver-gilt reliquary and an enamelled gold chalice formerly in the Franciscan Convent of St. Anton, Warsaw, and the cathedral treasury of Wawel respectively, both now lost, are believed to have been made by King Sigismund.

43 Brunner, cat. no. 593.

44 ibid. cat. no. 626-7.

CHAPTER FOURTEEN

The Netherlands

The Southern Netherlands

The city of Antwerp enjoyed a period of great affluence during the third quarter of the sixteenth century and its goldsmiths set the fashions that were followed by their competitors in the other cities of the southern provinces. Such was the predominance of Antwerp as a centre of the arts and so numerous were the goldsmiths there that the goldsmiths' work of the whole region can be covered by studying the productions of this one city. So extensive was the international trade of Antwerp that over one thousand foreign merchants are said to have resided there about 1560. This golden age was brutally interrupted in the years 1576 by the massacre, known as 'the Spanish Fury', when the city was sacked by its Spanish garrison, some six thousand of its inhabitants slain and vast damage done. This disaster was followed on 17 January 1583 by a similar outbreak on the part of the French troops that were then occupying the city. A further stage in the decline of the city followed its long siege and final capture by Spanish troops under the Duke of Alba in 1586. This was accompanied by the introduction of the Spanish Inquisition with the result that the Protestant communities abandoned the city, among them the diamond cutters who emigrated to Amsterdam and to London. Antwerp masters had gone to seek their fortune elsewhere before, but what had been a trickle became a flood after 1586 — almost comparable with the emigration of artists after the Sack of Rome in 1527. Instead of foreign craftsmen seeking permission to work in Antwerp, as had previously been the case, the city was abandoned by all who could obtain work abroad.

Writing in 1557 of the various industries that flourished in the city, Lodovico Guicciardini stated,[1] 'There are one hundred and twenty four goldsmiths, without counting a large number of lapidaries and other cutters and engravers of precious stones; these produce works of great beauty and marvellous quality and undertake great enterprises and make most marvellous and incredible purchases. There is a larger number of such craftsmen in this one city than in several large Provinces'. He goes on to list the main recipients of the silver worked in Antwerp as Spain, Portugal and England. Confirmation of Guicciardini's figures can be found in the tax registers for the city of Antwerp for the year 1584 to 1585: these record 121 names, distributed as follows, 80 goldsmiths, 7 goldbeaters, one gold wire-worker, 2 gold workers and 31 silversmiths. It is no longer possible to determine what was the difference between goldsmiths and silversmiths.

Antwerp was as famous for its jewellers as for its goldsmiths, but, owing to the lack of makers' or town marks on jewellery, it is impossible to distinguish the work of the Antwerp jewellers from that made in other European centres. As Antwerp was the main centre of the European diamond cutting industry, it is not surprising that many commissions for jewels mounted with precious stones should come to the Antwerp goldsmiths. On the occasion of the wedding of Duke Wilhelm V of Bavaria with Princess Renata of Lothringen in 1568, gold chains and natural pearls were obtained from Antwerp, as was also what was described as a *Welsche* (Italian) fan.[2] In this case the term *Welsche* presumably applies to the fashion rather than the town of origin. At the same time, clocks and a gilt dog, probably a clockwork toy, were bought in Augsburg, while silver salt-cellars etc. came from Munich. The Fugger banking family had their own representative, Karl Fugger, in Antwerp, who acted for both the Habsburg and the Wittelsbach ruling families. An idea of the variety of articles available in the Antwerp trade can be gathered from Fugger's offer in February, 1575, of the following for the *Kunstkammer* of Duke Albrecht of Bavaria: 'a gold bowl with cover, in which were set 36 small antique gold heads (presumably Roman coins) and in the centre a fine medal of 1416, at a cost of 1000 florins, 13 large gold medals at 2500 florins, six tall antique silver-gilt jugs at 4000 florins'. The duke acquired the first two items.[3]

Like Nürnberg in Germany, Antwerp also attracted journeymen from other countries who came to study the style and technique of the goldsmiths there. Among them was Peter Holtswijller, whose career followed the international course typical of the Mannerist goldsmith.[4] He was born in London, the son of Hendrik Holtswijller, who had come there from Düsseldorf. He was probably apprenticed to his father in London and was admitted master to the Guild of St. Lucas in Antwerp, where he became a citizen in 1540. He subsequently went to Stockholm as court goldsmith to the splendour-loving Eric XIV. He is represented by a few drawings, of which the most interesting is that of a covered cup in the Berlin Kunstbibliothek. This drawing, which is dated 1565, points to no more than a modest competence as a draughtsman; the most important goldsmith's work with which he was associated was a silver throne for the Swedish king, which no longer survives, if indeed it was ever executed. Antwerp was not only the centre of a flourishing goldsmiths' industry, but also of design, and the engravers working there produced pattern books of goldsmiths' ornament that found a ready market throughout northern Europe. These masters were indeed one of the main channels by means of which Italian Mannerist design was transmitted to the north. Artists such as Cornelis and Jacob Floris, Hans Collaert and Hans Vredeman de Vries, who were born in the second or third decades of the century, were between them largely responsible for the creation of the northern Mannerist style. The influence of Antwerp design was carried on by Adriaen Collaert in the following generation. The Mannerist style peculiar to the goldsmiths of the Spanish Netherlands drew both directly on Rome, through the Flemish masters who went to study there, and also indirectly through those who joined the Italian colony working under Primaticcio on the decoration of Francis I's palace at Fontainebleau. Among the latter is the somewhat obscure figure of Léonard Thiry who, after working at Fontainebleau, returned to Antwerp where he died about 1550.

Léonard Thiry

Thiry,[5] whose name is probably a gallicized form of the Flemish Dirck, is of particular interest because he has been credited with assisting Rosso in his designs for goldsmiths' work, including the series of silver vessels that were probably engraved by René Boyvin (see p.175). Among his signed work the best known is the set of tapestry designs illustrating the legend of Jason and the Golden Fleece (pl. 96), These were engraved by René Boyvin and published in Paris in 1563. In view of his early death one hesitates to attribute much influence outside Fontainebleau to Thiry during his lifetime.

Cornelis Bos

The first of the Flemish masters of ornament to make a version of the Italian Mannerist decorative style available to northern masters was probably Cornelis Bos,[6] who was born in 'sHertogenbosch in 1510 and went to Rome at an early age to work in the studio of Marcantonio Raimondi. He returned to the Low Countries in the 1540's and published a set of designs for panels bearing dates between 1545 and 1548. In these he not only mastered the possibilities of strapwork, but developed it in an original manner.

He also engraved designs for friezes, the curved shape of which is intended for the borders of tazzas or basins or the feet of cups; these may have been intended for silver vessels but would also have served for Limoges enamels or majolica. His straps, which sometimes seem to have the weight and solidity of masonry, firmly enclose within their convolutions as disreputable a set of satyrs as Renaissance imagination ever created (pl. 194) In spite of their predicament they leer suggestively through the gaps left between the imprisoning bars. In some of Bos's later designs the strapwork frames are so massive that only the heads, hands and feet of the satyrs and their companion nymphs emerge through the intersections.[7] Bos's treatment of these figures is typically Mannerist: it is impossible to give any rational explanation of their position, either how they got into such a situation and what they are doing there. Though Bos owed much to the Roman *grotteschi*, he introduced so much of the rustic Netherlandish humour into his versions that they acquired a character of their own. His prints had much influence in Germany and were the source of the characteristic Jamnitzer ornament to which frequent reference has been made. Netherlandish influence is particularly manifest in the prints of Virgil Solis (pl. 120). The chapter headings in Wenzel Jamnitzer's *Perspectiva* also derive from designs by Bos.

Cornelis Floris

Flemish Mannerism usually, but not altogether justly, goes by the name of the Floris style, after the Antwerp-born sculptor and architect, Cornelis Floris, though he had little to add to the manner that Bos had elaborated. Floris, like Bos, went to Rome and it was on his return to Antwerp that he took up and developed his countryman's style. From our present point of view his most interesting set of designs is the series of twenty engravings of ewers (pls. 196-9) that he published in 1548.[8] At first sight of striking originality, they prove on investigation to owe a great deal to the vase designs published by Enea Vico in 1543. A number are, in fact, direct copies from the Vico plates. Among those thus borrowed is that of a nautilus-shell, supported on a peculiar stem in the form of a bearded man holding a large goose under each arm (pl. 196). One of Vico's favourite themes, taken over and elaborated by Floris, is the fleshy auricular scrollwork that was later to become so important an ingredient of Dutch Mannerism (see p.289). While Vico introduced these forms without exploiting them further, Floris developed them with untiring inventiveness and in so doing anticipated many of the ideas of Adam van Vianan and Jan Lutma. In his panels of ornament Floris followed the path already indicated by Cornelis Bos and introduced satyrs and nymphs imprisoned within straps. His designs must surely rank as some of the ugliest and least graceful that emerged in the whole history of Mannerist goldsmiths' art. The profile of his ewers is confused, the gross humour of his satyr figures (pl. 199) seems inappropriate for the precious material in which they were intended to be executed. Nevertheless he exploited his limited stock of ideas to the full and few, if any, of his contemporaries rivalled him in the creation of fantastic vessel forms. Two of the examples of Antwerp goldsmiths' work illustrated in this book derive from the designs of Cornelis Floris (pls. X and 609).

The designs of artists such as Cornelis Floris were often too exaggerated for use by the working goldsmith. The translation of a printed design into a form that could readily be executed has always been a problem for the craftsman, particularly when he worked in an intractable material. The artist could easily create original and imaginative forms with his pencil, but was not able to consider the practicability of executing them in every material. A number of original drawings of goldsmiths' work in the Victoria and Albert Museum show close resemblance to the surviving Antwerp silver of the period. I have attributed these to the Antwerp master, Erasmus Hornick, and discussed them in Chapter XI.

Antwerp silver was usually marked with town and maker's mark and also with a date letter. The identification of these date letters has hitherto been uncertain, as the information given in Rosenberg is erroneous, but a convincing interpretation has now been worked out by M. Baudouin of Antwerp.[9] As in other countries some of the more important vessels made in Antwerp were not marked. Furthermore, whereas it was the practice in most other countries to strike both town and maker's mark on the exterior of a piece where they could readily be seen, the Antwerp masters frequently marked their work on the bottom. The ewer (pl. 587) is even marked on a circular plate sprung into the underside of the base to conceal the back view of the embossed ornament, should the cup be held up on high; this plate could easily become detached and all evidence of the date of the piece lost. This appears to have happened in the case of the cup (pl. XXIII) where the original base plate has been removed at a later date and replaced by another.

The survival of a series of Antwerp vessels either with date letters of the middle decades of the sixteenth century or attributable to this period greatly assists our study. The earliest is the ewer (pl. 590) of 1544-5 originally made for the Aspremont Lynden family.[10] All the decorative features, floral scrolls, bunches of fruit, snakes, monsters, entrapped satyrs, are typical of northern Mannerism; nowhere were they so consistently exploited as in Antwerp goldsmiths' work. A second Antwerp ewer (pl.587) and companion basin (pls. 588, 589) which are signed and dated 1559 and 1558 respectively, are decorated with figure subjects, the ewer with *The Rape of Helen* after Raphael. The handle is modelled as a figure of Pan. Just as it was in the handle designs that the Italian engravers departed furthest from their classical models, so also the goldsmiths of the sixteenth century allowed their imagination free rein in designing handles. Even the pattern-books of the time hardly anticipated the fantastic forms of the handle and spout of the ewer (pl. 590).

Each of these ewers has an egg-shaped body of less extravagant form than the nautilus-shell shape favoured by Cornelis Floris. Comparable designs can be found amongst the early drawings of Erasmus Hornick; in some of these both the all-over grotesque decoration and the frieze of figures around the body are represented. The drawing of a ewer (pl. 202) has a mask under the handle, another under the spout and a frieze of figures around the body, as does also the Antwerp ewer (pl. 587) Following Italian precedent, Hornick shows in his designs a foot of great elegance but impracticably small size. This treatment was not invariably followed by the goldsmith, the two ewers illustrated are provided with feet of larger diameter. Each is accompanied by a basin. The basin (pls. 591-2) associated with the ewer (pl. 590) cannot have belonged to it originally, for not only is it two years later in date (1546-7) but it also bears a different maker's mark. There is, moreover, no relationship between the ornament of the two vessels. The basin (pls. 588-9) belonging to the other ewer is oval; it bears the same maker's mark and must, therefore, have been made en suite. The oval shape is, however, quite unusual for the sixteenth century; it is more typical of the second half of the seventeenth.

The silver-mounted glass goblet in the Rijksmuseum, Amsterdam (pl. 593) is an Antwerp-made piece of 1546-7; as a rule rock-crystal was preferred to glass for mounting in precious metal, but such rare materials were not always available and in this case the more modest material of glass was used. Sixteenth century inventories list numbers of silver-mounted glass vessels, especially flagons, but the fragility of the material combined with its small value has resulted in the destruction of nearly every example. Whereas the glass vessel corresponds to simple Renaissance fashion, the silver mounts already show in the curled-over straps of the finial features of Mannerist design. The tazza of about 1550 is one of the finest surviving Antwerp pieces (pls. 594, 595). It was presented to Emmanuel College , Cambridge by its Founder, Sir Walter Mildmay, in 1584 and the two addorsed shields of the arms of Mildmay which form the finial were presumably added by an English goldsmith; in other respects the tazza is in original condition. Again many of its features can be paralleled on one or other of the Hornick Antwerp period drawings. That of a tazza (pl. 207) has a similar profile and a knop of almost identical form, while that of a basin (pl. 201) shows tritons engaged in combat with each other in a manner similar to the frieze embossed inside the bowl of the tazza (pl. 594). Another Hornick drawing of a vase decorated with crayfish, mussels and scallop shells (pl. 203), resembles the similar details which are embossed on the shell which covers the underside of the tazza bowl.

The most important of these mid-century Antwerp vessels are the ewer and basin (pls. 596, 597, 602) made for, or by order of the Emperor Charles V. They bear the Antwerp mark for 1558-9; this was the year in which Charles V died and it is, therefore, unlikely that he ever received the two vessels. As, however, they commemorate the successful expedition of the Emperor in 1535 against the Barbary pirates of Tunis, it is difficult to conceive that anyone else would have commissioned them so long after the event to which their decoration refers.[11] Though this basin and ewer are contemporary with the other pieces already discussed, they fall outside the usual range of the Antwerp designers. Thus the neck of the ewer in the form of the head and bust of a young woman seems to derive from a design such as that attributed to Perino del Vaga (pl. 55). While the Italian drawing shows the same treatment of the spout as a female head and bust, the Antwerp goldsmith has introduced even more fantastic features in this ewer.

The surface of the basin is embossed and chased with a minutely detailed representation of the siege of Tunis by the Imperial army perhaps designed by Jan Vermeyen, court painter to Margaret, Regent of the Netherlands and aunt of Charles V. Whoever the designer was, he introduced a new fashion of pictorial representation in the art of the Netherlandish goldsmith. Vermeyen is known to have designed the set of twelve tapestries illustrating the Tunis engagements that were woven in Brussels by William de Pannemaeker. It seems very likely that Vermeyen would have been entrusted with the design of the ewer and basin as well. Destrée, comparing the tapestries with the basin and ewer, comments 'the details of the landscape, the style of the buildings, the costumes of the figures, the concentration on exactness of detail reveal the same spirit and the same approach'.[12]

The standing cup in the Munich Schatzkammer (pl. 611) bears the Antwerp date letter for 1557-8. It is stylistically related to the Emmanuel College tazza and its finely embossed frieze, depicting the Triumph of Amphitrite and Neptune, seems to have been chased by the same master who decorated the inside of the tazza bowl. The large attached S-scroll brackets terminating in lion masks are typical Antwerp details. As has frequently been the case, some uninformed servant in the past has mixed up the cover of two different cups and a Cologne cover (not illustrated) from another cup is now associated with it.

Another fully marked vessel is the Falcon Cup at Clare College, Cambridge, an altogether different type superbly wrought in the form of the bird of prey seated on a rectangular plinth engraved with scrollwork enclosing, within a laurel wreath, the bust of a Roman emperor (pl. 599). This dates from 1561-2 and demonstrates the ability of the Antwerp masters to compete in an area that the German goldsmiths had made peculiarly their own. The last of the cups dating prior to the Sack of Antwerp illustrated here is that presented by King Frederick II of Denmark to the Guild of St. Knud of the Swedish city of Malmo in 1566. It bears the date letter for 1563-4 and was, therefore, almost new when it was given. Its design is advanced for so early a date and it seems at first sight to belong to a later stylistic phase; with its tall stem and vase-shaped knop it corresponds to the type introduced in Germany towards the end of the sixteenth century (pls. 606, 607).

A number of Flemish sixteenth-century cups and ewers are unmarked and can only be attributed on grounds of their similarity to other pieces that are marked. So pronounced was Antwerp's domination of Flemish goldsmithing that it seems reasonable, in the absence of compelling evidence to the contrary, to regard such unmarked vessels as the work of Antwerp masters. We are assisted in dating them by the printed pattern-books of the period, particularly that of Vredemann de Vries of 1563. The earliest of these unmarked vessels is the cup bequeathed in 1551 by Maximilian of Burgundy, first Marquis of Veere, to the small Dutch town from which he took his title.[13] It has been preserved there ever since. The bowl is chased with a frieze and with a descriptive legend commemorating an exploit of Maximilian of Egmont, Count of Buren, in the war against the League of Smalkalden. This exploit was the successful crossing of the Rhine together with a large body of troops to link up with the Imperial army at Ingolstadt under the command of the Emperor Charles V on 15th September, 1546. The cup is believed to have been commissioned by the Emperor as a gift for the Count. It passed from the latter to his cousin, the Marquis of Veere, and through him to the town. The cup can be dated on internal evidence to the years 1547 to 1550. The embossed and chased frieze on the bowl represents the reception of Count Buren and his troops by the Emperor. A feature of the frieze is the depiction of bodies of mounted knights with their lances held upright, giving a honeycomb-like effect, above which a few banners project. The same characteristic is repeated on the large basin, which was also made for the Emperor Charles V (pl. 597). It seems very likely that both were decorated by the same Antwerp chaser.

A second unmarked Antwerp cup, in an English private collection, is illustrated in pls. XXIII and 601. It appears to date from the decade immediately following the Emmanuel College tazza. Its composition adheres to the same vertical and horizontal system, the vertical being in this case more emphasized than in the tazza. Among the Hornick drawings, which seem to date from his Antwerp period, is one of a standing cup (pl. 205); this has much in common with the cup just mentioned, not least its *horror vacui*. The drawing follows the Floris engraved designs more closely than the cup and, instead of a frieze of figure subjects, it shows the body of the cup divided by strapwork into panels enclosing mauresques or lion masks. The Hornick design presumably dates from an early stage in his career when he was more dependent on the engraved ornament of other masters for ideas. The Antwerp tazza (pl. 595), the standing cup (pl. XXIII) and the Hornick designs (pls. 205-7) all share one distinctly Flemish feature, namely the treatment of the knop on the stem as a wicker basket containing fruit, to which are applied either lion masks, free-standing scrolls or both.

Also unmarked, but cast from the same models and, presumably, made by the same goldsmith as the cup just mentioned, is the nautilus-shell cup (pl. 608). The design of the foot and stem corresponds almost exactly and the form is so original that it can hardly be the work of another master.

The most spectacular of these unmarked cups attributed to Antwerp (pls. 600, 603-4) was formerly in the English royal collection, but became part of the Hanoverian plate after the transfer of much of the former to Hanover by order of George II. Like other Antwerp cups it shows the rather heavy treatment of the stem but in other respects it is of outstanding merit. The composition shows striking similarity to the English Bowes cup of 1554 (pl. 652) but the finish is far superior. In view of the complete dispersal of the English royal plate during the Civil Wars, it cannot have been in continuous royal possession since the sixteenth century, nor can it be identified in the Tudor royal inventory.

A fifth unmarked Antwerp cup (pl. 605) has the body embossed with three cartouches enclosing figures of the Virtues, the intervening spaces being filled with a network of straps interspersed with birds, fruit, masks, etc. These standing cups have a common constructional feature that the bowl consists of an outer and an inner member, the inner being plain, while the outer is a sleeve which slides over it. This cup has an interesting history. It was presented to the Magistrature of the City of Emden by the Merchant Adventurers' Company of London in 1598.[14] It appears that in the year 1564-5 the Company had moved their agency temporarily from Antwerp to Emden and in 1598 the City of Emden sent a special delegation to London to invite them to return. The request was refused but this gilt cup was sent as a gesture of goodwill; the figure on the cover bears a shield with the arms of the Company and of the City of Emden. The cup was, of course, over thirty years old when it was given but such presentation pieces were reckoned more by weight than by elegance of fashion.

Two shell cups (pl. X and 609) are both derived from a print by Cornelis Floris. The former, the stem of which follows Floris exactly, is exceptional because the bowl is carved from quartz in imitation of a Trochus shell, a virtuoso performance that is rivalled only by the Nürnberg cup (pl. 275) and very few others. The nautilus-shell cup (pl. 609) has no date letter, but is by the same master as the ewer (pl. 590) and the standing cup (pl. 611). The rich appearance of the nautilus-cup has been enhanced by the painted garlands of fruit and flowers on the shell, an example of Mannerist additive treatment. The satyr who composes the stem, instead of carrying a pair of geese (pl. 196) or two dolphins (pl. X) is more logically supporting the shell on his back. Such shell cups were an indispensable feature of the princely *Kunstkammer* of the sixteenth century (see p.126). They subsequently became a speciality of the Dutch goldsmiths who devised the most original and extravagant mounts for them. The marks of the Antwerp masters have yet to be identified but one or two masters are represented by a group of surviving pieces; in particular, the masters who used the mark of a pair of compasses (pls. 590, 609 and 611) and the pipes of Pan (pls. 598, 599 and two pieces in the Historisches Museum, Frankfurt, and Rosenborg Castle, Copenhagen, respectively). Reynier van Jaersvelt, the maker of the mounts of the glass beaker (pl. 593), is represented by three other pieces, two of them made for the abbey of Averbode.

The most exceptional survival amongst Southern Netherlandish, probably Antwerp, silver is the great double-spouted vase in the treasury of Seville Cathedral (pl. 610). This was probably originally of secular origin: there is certainly nothing ecclesiastical in its decoration. It is presumably what Cellini meant by the large vessel he described as an *acquareccia*. Its designer has, in a manner not unusual for this date, shown slight regard for the problem of reconciling differences in scale.

Hans Vredeman de Vries

Turning to the pattern-books of goldsmiths' work published in the 1560's, the first is the series of twelve sheets of various types of vessel by Hans Vredeman de Vries issued in 1567. This master was born in Leeuwarden in the Northern Netherlands about 1527. He learnt his art in his birthplace in Campen and in Malines and is recorded in Antwerp, in Malines and in Friesland between 1549 and 1570. He was City Architect of Antwerp from 1577 to 1585 and lived on until the great age of ninety-six or more. His pattern-book represents quite a variety of contemporary styles and seems to have been borrowed from the works of other masters rather than to have proceeded from his own fantasy. The repulsive vulval style of Cornelis Floris is recalled by the ewer (pl. 208). In this particular design de Vries experiments with the fleshy forms that were at the same time attracting Hornick (pl. 151). On the other hand, the tazza design (pl. 210) is closely related to current Antwerp production and does not differ greatly from the Antwerp tazza (pl. 595). The scrolled brackets which are so regular a feature of Antwerp stem design have here taken over the task of supporting the dish and the central stem is omitted altogether. Three of his designs show salt-cellars; these are clearly of Italian inspiration[16] and their prototypes can be found in the drawings associated with Salviati or his workshop (pls. 209 and 83).

Balthasar Sylvius

Balthasar Sylvius, who took his name from the Latin form of his birthplace, the town of 'sHertogenbosch, was born in 1518 and was active in Antwerp from 1543, where in 1551 he was admitted master. He is best known on account of his three sets of designs of mauresques, the plastic quality of which suggests contact with Fontainebleau or with engraved designs after the Fontainebleau decorations. In 1568 Sylvius published a pattern-book for goldsmiths entitled *Un Livre de grosserie et des flacons et boîtes de poivre et du sel*. The twenty designs[17] consist for the most part of scent-bottles decorated with powerfully modelled strapwork and masks set rather incongruously in architectural niches (pls. 211-2). Similar scent-bottles were designed in great number by Erasmus Hornick during his period of activity in Nürnberg and Augsburg, but very few examples have survived to the present day. Two scent-bottles of the type designed by Balthasar Sylvius are known, one in the collection of Judge Untermyer, New York,[18] the other in the Victoria and Albert Museum (pl. 649). His two designs of a standing cup and a tazza correspond precisely to Antwerp fashion of the third quarter of the sixteenth century (pls. 213-4).

Adriaen Collaert

Two generations of the Antwerp family of Collaert produced designs for jewellery and goldsmiths' work. The elder member, Hans Collaert, is credited with the jewellery designs, of which the last series was published in 1581, while the set of four insides of dishes superbly engraved with marine subjects are signed by his son, Adriaen Collaert.[19] One of these last designs (pl. 195) seems to have inspired the English engraver of the set of spice plates, of which one is illustrated (pl. 660). Adriaen Collaert also engraved a set of six rectangular panels each of which showed one of the figures from the Judgement of Paris set within a border of delicate grotesques and scrolls (*Schweif-werk*) against a black ground,[20] in a manner that was to be much exploited in the engraved ornament of early seventeenth-century goldsmiths' work.

During the years that followed the Sack of Antwerp by the Spaniards in 1576 the production of silver in Antwerp seems to have declined. Whereas the period between 1540 and 1575 is represented by a series of splendid vessels, the last quarter of the century has left far fewer examples. This may also be due to the chance of survival. The collections of silver of the Antwerp guilds seem to have survived until the end of the eighteenth century, when they had to be melted in order to pay the fines imposed by the armies of the French Revolution. An idea of the rich plate owned by the Antwerp Guild of Saint Luke, which included some goldsmiths as well as painters, can be gained from the portrait by Cornelis de Vos of Abraham Grapheus the Elder in the Antwerp Museum voor Schone Kunsten. Grapheus was Steward of the Guild and his portrait, which is dated 1620, shows him with a selection of fine gilt cups, including one presented to the Guild in 1549. The temporary loss of wealth did not, however, accompany any decline in skill; the period after the Sack is represented by the fine parcel-gilt tazza (pls. 612, 616). This shows that a change in fashion had taken place and this becomes clear if the tazza is compared with the de Vries engraving in pl. 210. The terminal figures linked with draperies that support the bowl and the applied or embossed straps that were so prominent a feature of earlier Antwerp vessels and are also seen in the engraving are omitted from the stem of this tazza. Its restrained character, which contrasts so strongly with earlier Antwerp goldsmiths' work, can be explained in part by change in fashion but also in part by the fact that the original commission from the client was less generous.

In the seventeenth century Antwerp recovered to some extent its former importance as a centre of goldsmithing. The leading master was Matthias Melin who specialised in the Baroque technique of embossing in high relief. He is represented by a set of five silver plaques embossed with scenes from the life of the Spanish General, Giovanni Battista Spinola in the Rijksmuseum, Amsterdam, and by a large basin dated 1627 in Toledo Cathedral.

The Northern Netherlands

To follow the further progress of goldsmiths' work in the Low Countries it is necessary to turn to the northern provinces, and in particular to the cities of Amsterdam and Utrecht. During the third quarter of the sixteenth century, vessels wrought by goldsmiths of the northern Netherlands were hardly distinguishable from those of the south. This is well illustrated by the two cups (pls. 613 and 614), made by a s'Hertogenbosch master in 1561 and by an Amsterdam master in 1569 respectively.

The most imposing Amsterdam drinking-vessel of the third quarter of the century is the great drinking-horn of the Guild of St. George of 1566;[21] this is supported on a large pedestal of oval section upon which almost the whole range of Mannerist ornament is represented. The group of St. George killing the dragon which surmounts it is intensely dramatic in effect and ranks as one of the major examples of late Renaissance gold-smiths' work. It shares with most Dutch silver of the second half of the century an extreme fineness of finish in the embossing and chasing of the borders and other detail. This standard of finish was achieved by the leading goldsmiths working elsewhere, but in Holland it was the general rule rather than the exception. The Dutch goldsmiths were influenced by the fashion of the surrounding countries, by Germany in the north and by the southern Netherlands. At the same time they also had some influence abroad, parti-cularly in England. The Dutch standing cup (pl. 615) is very similar in composition to the Booth Cup of St. John's College, Cambridge, (pl. 665) which bears the London hall-mark for 1616. This may merely be an example of Dutch influence, but the resemblance might also be explained by the latter having been made by a Dutch immigrant to England.

In relation to the size of the country a very large quantity of Dutch silver has survived from the second half of the sixteenth century onwards. Particularly numerous are the tazzas with bowls embossed in high relief. Their popularity is indicated by the frequency with which they appear in contemporary Dutch still-life paintings. In making them the Dutch masters showed a skill which was equal to the best achieved anywhere else. A remarkably large number of Dutch goldsmiths were capable of producing pictorial scenes on tazzas. Though such work was to some extent confined to specialists, there seem to have been in each town one or more highly skilled chasers. Though they were evidently popular in Holland amongst the few who could afford them, they were not produced in such large sets as were made for German princes (see p.233). The Dutch standing cups of the late sixteenth century, while following the general lines of the southern Netherlandish vessels of the mid-century, had somewhat slimmer lines, con-forming to Mannerist taste. Their decoration is usually small in scale but profuse, cover-ing the whole surface of the vessel. Amongst the finest surviving examples are the four unmarked cups that formerly belonged to the city of Zwolle and are now in the Dutch Reformed church there. These date between 1583 and 1605 but in spite of the date span conform to the same type with thistle-shaped bowls and baluster stems.[22]

As a leading seafaring nation the Dutch had an ample supply of the exotic shells and similar curiosities of nature that collectors liked to place in their cabinets. In Holland the nautilus-shell seems to have been the favourite natural form and they were mounted in lavish and highly imaginative manner in considerable numbers. The goldsmiths of Delft, Rotterdam (pl. 619) and Utrecht (pl. 618) specialised in them, and during the last quarter of the century a great deal of ingenuity was employed in devising fantastic mounts for these shells. The stem often took the form of a figure while the volute of the shell was rendered as the gaping jaws of a sea-serpent.[23] Perhaps the best illustration of these Dutch shell-cups is the painting by an anonymous master of the treasure of the Paston family (pl. 688).

The Auricular Style in the Northern Netherlands

The proper definition of the Dutch auricular style has been the subject of much dis-cussion between Dutch and English scholars. Whereas the former have regarded the style as an altogether new development for which the name of proto-Baroque has been suggested, the latter have preferred to treat it as a natural development of Mannerist art in the late sixteenth century. In favour of the second point of view is the fact that its origins can be recognised in early Italian Mannerism, as for instance, in the curiously flaccid spouts of some of the Polidoro da Caldara ewers (pl. 50), and even more emphat-ically in Enea Vico's candlestick designs (pl. 51). The fleshy lip of this piece would not look out of place in the pattern-book of design by Adam van Vianen which was first published a century later. The same spirit can be seen in Italian architectural design, notably in the doorway which Federigo Zuccari designed for the Palazzo Zuccari in Rome.[24] The beginnings of the auricular style can also be found in the engravings of Hans Vredeman de Vries, as for instance in the peculiar ewer illustrated in pl. 208.

There seems, therefore, good reason to recognise the style as the final phase of Netherlandish Mannerism and it is so treated here. The style played an important part not only in the goldsmiths' shops but in the whole field of decorative art. In Holland it was brought to its most advanced form by the Amsterdam goldsmith, Jan Lutma, towards the middle of the seventeenth century. Outside Holland it can be found in the work of the Hamburg goldsmiths and it was introduced by Christian van Vianen to England, where it persisted into the second half of the seventeenth century.

The van Vianen Family

The auricular style was created by two members of the Utrecht goldsmithing family of van Vianen. Four goldsmiths of this name are recorded: firstly, Willem Eerstenz van Vianen, of whom nothing is known apart from Sandrart's description of him in his *Teutsche Academie*[25] as a gifted silversmith of Utrecht (*ein sinnreicher Silberarbeiter zu Utrecht*). This master had two sons, Paul and Adam, about whom Sandrart has much more to say. They were, he tells us, 'considered to be very diligent in designing, modelling in wax and embossing in silver, to such an extent that both became very famous.' Sandrart discusses the younger brother Paul before dealing with Adam, but as the former spent most of his working life outside Holland, it is more appropriate in the present context to reverse the order. Sandrart states that Adam followed 'the same profession as his brother of working silver and was no less admired for he was just as skilled in embossing with the hammer from a single piece of silver in the so-called grotesque or *Schnakkerey* manner hand basins, bowls, salt-cellars, knife-handles and other decorative objects. These he made for collectors in Amsterdam and all over Holland and so acquired special fame. Just as Paul was skilled in depicting figure subjects, pictures, animals, landscapes and indeed everything that could be represented in narrative form, so also was Adam predominant in embossing a piece of silver with any kind of grotesque theme.'[26]

Adam van Vianen is more closely associated with the development of the auricular style; not because he was necessarily the first to introduce it but because Paul's emigration and premature death in Prague in 1613 reduced his significance as a Dutch goldsmith. Though the style was to become a basic element in northern Baroque art, it was during the early decades of the seventeenth century almost a monopoly of the van Vianen family. Other Netherlands goldsmiths continued to make the established type of Dutch cup with thistle-shaped bowl decorated with strapwork cartouches, baluster stem and vase knop until well into the seventeenth century. The earliest piece which displays some details of auricular ornament is the tazza of 1607 (pls. 626-7) made by Paul van Vianen; in this vessel the style is employed in a restrained manner that does not go much further than Enea Vico's candlestick design (pl. 51). Most of the earlier pieces from the van Vianen workshop adhere to the conventional vessel forms of the period and the auricular motifs, while adding a certain irregularity to the surface, are confined to the function of ornament, either forming cartouches enclosing figure subjects or heraldic bearings or masking the junction of handle and body. The most interesting development of the van Vianens was the gradual appreciation of the plastic possibilities inherent in the auricular style. The first move in this direction can be seen in the foot of a ewer made by Paul in Prague in 1613, the last year of his life (pl. 630). Thereafter it was Adam who was the prophet of the new style, and he developed vessel forms that exceeded in strangeness the most extreme fantasies of all his sixteenth-century predecessors. The term 'conceit' which has been used above in relation to Mannerist taste best describes these curious objects. In the words of one writer[28] they conformed to 'that taste of the late sixteenth and early seventeenth centuries which pressed ingenuity and conceit in the arts to the utmost limits. The unpractical design of these and other pieces as well as their audacity of form and ornament, proves that they were conceived solely as works of art, function being recalled in their general forms, only to be denied in all their other aspects.'

Adam van Vianen

Adam van Vianen was born about 1565 and was probably made a master about 1593; he died in 1627 and had an unusually long working life for the period. It was not until a comparatively advanced stage in his career that he began to use the fleshy auricular forms and, as late as 1612, he was still following international Mannerist fashion, as in the tazza (pls. 624,5) in the Victoria and Albert Museum.[27] The auricular style is particularly associated with Adam because the pattern-book of designs (pl. 217) which was published in Utrecht by his son, Christian, attributes them to him as follows, 'Modelles Artificiels de divers Vaisseaux d'argent..... Inventées et desseignées du renommé Sr. Adam de Viane...mis en lumière par son fils Christien de Viane à Utrecht, 1650.' It is uncertain whether the son was correct in his attributions or was moved by filial piety. It may well be that the book incorporates drawings by Paul van Vianen which were returned to the Utrecht workshop after his death abroad. Once he had adopted the style, Adam took it to extreme lengths. Combining auricular ornament and plastic forms, he produced a sort of sculpture in silver that was evidently derived from familiar vessel forms, most of which, if not obviously functional, could nevertheless be made to serve their purpose. Quoting the same source[28] 'All rigid segregation of individual parts is abandoned for the sake of overall unity; the firm outlines of the Renaissance are dissolved into contours of softly capricious irregularity in which scroll forms or less definite motifs may suddenly curl into lobe-like shapes or swell with unexpected curves. The inside of the bowl is no longer temperately decorated with a classical scene, but descends in a succession of swirls until it is metamorphosed into a huge mask, only perceived to be such because of two eyes which appear on either side of a ridge. The result is a style in which the traditional architectural approach to design is abandoned in favour of a sculptural manner whose subtle modulations of relief and plastic freedom are as nearly akin to modelled effects as medium and technique permit.' Typical of such pieces are the tazza of 1618 in the Rijksmuseum and that of 1628 formerly in the collection of the Duke of Hamilton, which, though dated the year after Adam's death, was probably made under his direction.[29]

Though he still continued to work in his more conventional manner, Adam van Vianen had completely mastered the auricular style by 1614, in which year he produced the extraordinary silver ewer and cover (pls. 628-9) which is referred to by Sandrart in his notes on Paul van Vianen. He relates that 'the city of Amsterdam commissioned to be made to his (Paul van Vianen) memory an ewer about one and a half spans high which was entirely embossed out of a single piece of silver, and composed of grotesque or Schnakkerey, as it is called, and this piece was considered to be a rare and wonderful achievement'. Sandrart does not actually mention that it was Adam van Vianen who received the commission to commemorate his younger brother and he seems also to have been mistaken in thinking that it was the Municipality of Amsterdam that commissioned the ewer, when it must, in fact, have been the goldsmiths' guild of the city. This most eccentric piece was, as Sandrart commented, regarded as a weird and wonderful thing and for this reason it was repeatedly represented in still-life paintings by Dutch seventeenth century masters.[30] The fact that it belonged to the Amsterdam Goldsmiths' Guild presumably meant that it was more readily available for copying than another piece that had gone into private possession. It also appears as Plate 42 in Christian van Vianen's publication of his father's designs but makes its appearance in Dutch paintings long before the book was published. The earliest pictorial representation known is dated 1616, only two years after it was made. Though Adam van Vianen subsequently produced or designed many other vessels in the same grotesque vein (pl. 217) none quite equalled the fantasy he expressed in this, his first, whole-hearted experiment in this extraordinary manner.

Adam van Vianen sometimes combined his auricular style with pictorial subjects embossed and chased in low relief with much delicately executed detail in Mannerist taste. The contrast between the bold lobate forms of the frame and the exquisite reliefs seems curious to modern eyes. This trend is well illustrated by the monstrous ewer (pl. 638) or the pair of wall-lights (pls. 633-4). In the latter case the pierced borders are of exceptional extravagance with human figures and animals developing into auricular scrolls while the classical scenes they enclose show the delicate manner associated with the earlier style of the van Vianens. At no other time and by no other master was so eccentric and idiosyncratic a form of Mannerism developed as that of Adam and his brother Paul van Vianen. His manner was followed by his son, Christian, who was commissioned to produce a set of plate for the royal chapel of St. George at Windsor Castle. That Christian continued his father's style is demonstrated by the dish he signed and dated 1635, which is now in the Victoria and Albert Museum. It is skilfully composed of fishy shapes that merge into each other and at the same time form the border of a pool realistically embossed with water and with partially submerged dolphins.[31]

Paul van Vianen

Paul van Vianen was born in Utrecht between 1565 and 1570, a few years after Adam. Little is known of his earliest work and it is thought that he left his native city at an early age. He is known to have been working in Munich from 1596 until 1601, then subsequently in Salzburg and finally in Prague. Sandrart has much to say about him: 'Paul was particularly interested in producing pictorial and historical subjects, and sought to acquire the fullest knowledge about them. For this reason he went to Rome and there extracted from the antique the purest knowledge. With the aid of his embossing hammer alone he worked with the greatest taste and decorative and graphic skill from one single piece of silver complete pictures, large vessels and splendid basins, such as the Bath of Diana with numerous nude female figures, animals and landscapes so that with good reason he was honoured as the originator of this particular technique. The many representations of the Virgin Mary, poetic themes, the story of Argus and other subjects cast from his models that are now to be seen bear witness to his popularity. He was of excellent disposition and made himself liked by all, nevertheless he was quite unjustly out of envy of his great success considered to be an infidel and as a result held prisoner in Rome by the Inquisition for several months. He was eventually released on condition that he never left Rome. As a result of the intervention of the Ambassador of the Holy Roman Emperor he was allowed to enter the service of the Emperor Rudolph in Prague, where he produced his finest work, which was held to be priceless and provided excellent models for those who wished to learn his craft.'

Paul van Vianen's earliest works are plaquettes;[32] there are a number of these which are not particularly original in manner but seem to derive from similar ones produced by the Nürnberg masters, such Hans Jamnitzer or Jonas Silber in the 1570's and 1580's. Most of these plaquettes are of lead, the original silver reliefs having been destroyed. They conform to the contemporary Mannerist style with much fine detail covering the whole surface of the plaquette. The landscape is given great importance and the figure subjects are rendered on quite a small scale in the foreground. They are modelled with the small heads and long elegant limbs of the period. The precise date of Paul van Vianen's Italian journey is not known nor has any piece of silver been attributed to his Italian period. This is not surprising as he would have been employed in the workshop of a Roman goldsmith, probably embossing and chasing figure subjects and landscapes on basins and dishes, and his productions, if any have survived, would have followed the style of his employer. This journey to Italy must have brought him into closer touch with Italian Mannerism; it is certainly a fact that a change in style is apparent in his later work. The German influence which is so apparent in his earlier work becomes less evident later. In place of the crowded detail of the early plaquettes, the figures now play a more important role, and the background is no more than a frame for the figure subject.

According to Sandrart it was the Emperor Rudolph who saved Paul van Vianen from a Roman prison. It is difficult to reconcile this with the fact that he was employed in Munich between 1596 and 1601 and thereafter was in Salzburg and Prague, except for a return journey to Utrecht in 1610. He must have gone to Rome before 1596, in which case one would expect that it would have been the Duke of Bavaria and not the Emperor whose ambassador intervened to secure his release. Paul spent five years from 1596 to 1601 in Munich and in this time he evidently enjoyed the special favour of the Duke, for it was at the latter's special request that in 1599 he was admitted master goldsmith to the Munich guild without having to submit the usual masterpieces. His work for the Bavarian court was doubtless important but the few objects in the Munich Schatzkammer formerly attributed to him (pl. 500) have since been ascribed to German goldsmiths. It seems unlikely that nothing by him remains in Munich and future historians may yet rediscover his work there. Apart from a number of plaquettes (pl. 639) there is little to show for what was probably a highly creative period. Paul must have left Munich shortly after May 18, 1601, the date of the Order in Council that gave him permission to leave the city. From Munich he went to Salzburg where in 1602 and 1603 he was employed as court goldsmith by the Archbishop Wolf Dietrich von Raitenau. It was during this period that he made the gold crucifixion group now in the Museo degli Argenti, Florence — if, that is, its attribution to him is correct.[33] His status in Salzburg is indicated by the fact that the Archbishop himself was godfather to a child born to him during his residence in Salzburg. For his subsequent career as a member of the Court Workshop of the Emperor Rudolph II in Prague, see p.273.

The van Vianens introduced a new style of embossing: instead of treating each detail in the degree of relief appropriate to its position in the picture, they brought out the main figures in high relief and left the rest in a relief so low that they are no more than indicated, thus increasing the plastic effect. No other goldsmiths rivalled them in the delicacy of this low relief. The van Vianen designs were used by other masters as well as Adam and Paul. Evidence of this can be found in the Utrecht ewer and basin (pls. 635-7) These are embossed with subjects recorded on plaquettes or other works by Adam or Paul van Vianen but the basin bears the monogram of another goldsmith not as yet identified, whose skill as an embosser and chaser approached that of the van Vianens.

Paul van Vianen's fame long survived his premature death; this is shown by a curious incident that took place in Amsterdam in 1637.[34] It appears that a Dutch gentleman, Maerten Snouckaert van Schauburg, owned a ewer and basin made by Paul van Vianen, which he valued at no less than one thousand pounds sterling. When Snouckaert went on a journey to England before 1637 he deposited the ewer and basin with a certain Marten van den Heuvel, who passed it on to the Amsterdam goldsmith, Servaes Cocq, for a copy to be made. This copy was, it seems to be taken to Danzig for sale to the king of Poland. Whether the sale actually took place is not recorded. The copy was made without the permission of the owner, who, hearing of the affair, took legal steps to establish the facts. It is through the testimonies that were made at the time that we know of the incident. It appears further that, in order to make the copy, a mould had been made from the original van Vianen ewer and basin. This would seem to imply that the copy by Cocq was cast and not wrought. The van Vianen originals are believed to be those dated 1613 which are now in the Rijksmuseum, Amsterdam (pls. 630, 631, 632).

One further member of the family remains to be mentioned, Ernszt Jansz. van Vianen. This master specialised in embossing and chasing: he must have had close connections with the goldsmiths of Haarlem for he executed the chased decoration on the St. Martin Cup of 1604 which was made for the city.[35] Two tazzas that are attributed to him both bear the maker's marks of other goldsmiths (pl. 622, 623). The decoration is in each case exceptionally rich and the form of the stems is individual, differing from the usual Dutch baluster. The exact relationship of Ernszt to Adam and Paul is not known but the fact that the scene chased on the tazza decorated by Ernszt in the Rijksmuseum[36] is derived from a drawing by Paul proves that there was a close connection.[37]

Arent van Bolten

Next to the brothers van Vianen in renown as a master of relief work in silver is Arent van Bolten, who was born about 1573 in the small town of Zwolle in the province of

Overijsel[38] and died before 1633. Three of his works are signed with the initials AVB in monogram, namely three plaquettes[39] embossed with the Adoration of the Magi, the Crucifixion (pl. 641) and the Entombment, respectively. Our knowledge of Arent van Bolten's *oeuvre* is mainly due to the survival in the British Museum of his sketch-book. This contains some two hundred drawings and is dated 1637, presumably having been bound together after his death. The drawings cover a wide variety of objects and figure subjects, but include amongst the goldsmiths' work twenty three designs for ewers and sauce-boats, three standing cups in the style of the early seventeenth century and one chalice.[40] There are also a number of drawings of grotesque monsters, half animal, half bird, and a group of bronzes apparently deriving from these drawings have been conjecturally attributed to him. Several tazza bowls and plaquettes have also been accepted as his work, though none of these is signed. The plaquettes already show a more Baroque approach in their bolder handling and higher relief, while Mannerist details such as the small heads, long bodies of human figures and crowded backgrounds are absent. Van Bolten also treated foliage in a less detailed manner than Paul van Vianen, clustering leaves together in fanlike forms. A dramatic accent is given by his setting bare tree-branches against a plain background. His treatment of clouds is also idiosyncratic, with banks of cloud worked in low relief looking more like drapery. A sheet of five engraved designs for spoons decorated with auricular ornament after drawings by van Bolten was published, but otherwise his designs do not seem to have reached a wider market. Many of van Bolten's contemporaries produced plaquettes, dishes and tazza bowls embossed with figure subjects, but these are characterized by a height of relief and dramatic force that belongs to the age of Baroque rather than Mannerism and they do not call for consideration here.

Theodor de Bry

During the last decades of the sixteenth and the early seventeenth centuries the insides of dishes or tazza bowls were usually embossed with a pictorial subject, copied from some more or less well-known print. An alternative treatment was to engrave the scene using the same technique that had been employed to produce the print that served the engraver as a source. Presumably any competent engraver would have been capable of copying a print on to a flat or nearly flat surface, but only a small number of artists, mostly Dutch or Flemish, are known to have practised their art on silver vessels. In some rare cases the silver tazza bowl was itself the original and only version of the subject, but this was an exception.[41] Towards the end of the sixteenth century, Adriaen Collaert had engraved designs that were suitable for copying on to tazza bowls (pl. 195) but it was the achievement of the de Bry family of Liège to provide a wide range of prints for this purpose. Theodor de Bry was born in Liège but he abandoned his native country in 1570 to escape religious persecution and went to live in Frankfurt am Main, where he died in 1598. He was accompanied by his son, Johan Theodor de Bry. Their work is discussed here as it remained Netherlandish in character. He engraved a series of designs for tazza bowls, two of which must date from the period he was working in Liège.[42] These represent William of Orange and the Duke of Alba, described as the Captain of Wisdom and the Captain of Folly respectively. Of similar size and possibly belonging to the same series are two others representing Pride and Folly and Charity respectively, the latter dated 1578. Each of these four designs consists of a central subject set in a circular frame, surrounded by a wide border of grotesques, the detail of which has some bearing on the subject of the central panel. Finally, each has a concentrically arranged exterior border engraved with inscriptions in French and Dutch. Another set of four engraved roundels show portrait heads of Roman emperors, with three on each tazza, making a set of twelve in all.[43]

The most important surviving example of Theodor de Bry's engravings on silver is the mirror in the Grünes Gewölbe, Dresden.[44] The wood frame is covered with sheets of pierced and engraved silver-gilt candelabrum ornament and strapwork interrupted by four oval medallions and a fifth in the centre of the mirror cover, two of which are signed with two signatures in mirror writing *QMAS* and *TB fe* respectively. The TB signature is evidently that of Theodor de Bry whereas the other may refer to the original source of the designs, which represent human figures fighting animals with the help of mirrors. The fact that the signature is executed in mirror writing suggests that the silver plates were originally intended for printing. Another example of the elder de Bry's engraving on silver is the silver-mounted ebony inkstand in the Victoria and Albert Museum, (pls. 642-3). This is not signed, but the technique is closely similar to that of the signed mirror frame. The theme of the decoration in this case is religious.

Johann Theodor de Bry

Of even greater importance as an engraver of silver vessels was Johann Theodor de Bry, (1561-1623), the son of Theodor de Bry. Born in Liège, he seems to have spent most of his working life in Frankfurt am Main. His speciality was the engraving of tazzas and two letters preserved in the archives of the Habsburg Archdukes of Tirol in Innsbruck written by de Bry himself to the Archduke Maximilian of Tirol, Grand Master of the Order of Teutonic Knights, relate to these tazzas.[45] The first letter, though couched in terms of fitting humility, is directed to the Archduke himself, a circumstance which suggests that in October, 1604, when the letter was written, de Bry was a person of some standing in his art. The letter informs the Archduke that the writer was, in accordance with the Archduke's wish, releasing one of his assistants in order to work exclusively for him. It goes on to say that the Commander of the Teutonic Order's House in Frankfurt. a certain Eberhard von Karpfen, had told de Bry that the Archduke was particularly fond of finely-engraved dishes and intended to order a dozen of such dishes to be made. De Bry relates that he had, by chance, just completed a dish of this sort and could not refrain from making a present of it to the Archduke. He begged him to condescend to accept the gift, and, doubtless with an eye on the possible commission for a dozen, assured him that he was always ready at any time to execute his wishes for further dishes of a similar nature. The gesture of offering a dish as a gift was not misunderstood by the Archduke, for a further letter from Eberhard von Karpfen to the Archduke, dated November 2nd 1604, acknowledges the latter's instructions to pay de Bry for the dish.[46] The letters refer only to one dish, but until the present century two dishes, known as *Kredenzschalen*, each signed by Johann Theodor de Bry were preserved in the treasury of the Order of the Teutonic Knights in Vienna.[47] The dish which de Bry actually presented to the Archduke can be recognised from the inscription below the label with an extract from *Genesis* describing the subject of the engraving. It reads in translation 'Given to the most reverend and illustrious Prince and Lord, the Lord Maximilian, Archduke of Austria, Duke of Burgundy, Grand Master of the Order of Teutonic Knights, Count of Habsburg and Tirol, to his most clement Lord'. The fact that there was a pair of dishes shows that de Bry's hopes of securing further commissions were not entirely disappointed. Within two years of acquiring them, the Archduke presented them along with a quantity of plate to the Order. Their subsequent history included their being stolen from the Treasury of the Order at Mergentheim and being damaged before they were recovered. They are now in a Dutch private collection.

At least four other dishes of corresponding design to the two from the treasury of the Teutonic Knights are known to survive, two in England, where they were long used as patens in the parish church of Egham, Surrey,[48] and two in the Musée d'Art et d'Histoire at Geneva, (pl. 640). The bowls of these dishes are all so similar that they can certainly be ascribed to about the same period, that is, the early years of the seventeenth century. It is not, indeed, impossible that they belonged to the same set originally. De Bry may, in anticipation of the Archduke's expected order for a dozen dishes, have gone ahead and produced the remaining ten, and then, having been disappointed by his patron, had to dispose of the others elsewhere. While size, shape, choice of subject and its disposition correspond in these six dishes, it must be remembered that they were popular articles and were produced by other goldsmiths, particularly in the Low Countries and West Germany. De Bry may have had other patrons as well as the Archduke Maximilian. The two dishes in the Geneva museum do, in fact, differ slightly from the remaining four in that the border around the engraved scene is decorated with six ornaments composed of dotted scrollwork, while the exterior of the bowl also has a dotted border. The feet and stems also differ but appear to be later alterations. Although the engraved dishes are signed with the de Bry's monogram (two only) or with his full name (four); this does not mean that he was the author of the design. In fact all are derived from contemporary engravings by Jan Sadeler after paintings by Italian or Dutch masters.

De Bry was not himself a goldsmith and it follows that he must either have been commissioned by a goldsmith to engrave the dishes or have purchased finished undecorated vessels from a goldsmith and then engraved them for his client. We know that in the case of the dishes of the Archduke Maximilian of Tirol it was his own idea to decorate the dishes. It is probable that in the course of his long life (1561-1623) he must have engraved many more of these dishes than the six mentioned above. At least eight roundels suitable for copying on to tazza bowls were engraved by him and issued as prints. [49] These are copied from paintings by fashionable Mannerist artists of the late sixteenth century, such as Joseph Heinz, one of Rudolf II's court painters, Abraham Blomaert, Hieronymus Franken, Marten van Heemskerk and Martin de Vos. There are, in the Victoria and Albert Museum, London, four pulls from engraved tazza bowls that can be attributed to Johann Theodor de Bry. [50] They can be identified as pulls from engraved dishes by reason of the folds which can be seen around the circumference of the impressions. In order to fit the flat surface of the paper to the curved surface of the dish, it was necessary to fold it around the edges and the creases so made now show white. That the pulls were made in the engraver's shop and not later is proved by the fact that two of the tazzas were unfinished, with blank labels left, presumably for further inscriptions according to the taste of the customer who eventually bought them. The impressions must have been made either as a record of work done by the engraver or as proofs to show a potential customer. In the illustration (pl. 215) the impression has been printed in reverse in order to show the appearance of the original dish; the inscriptions appear, therefore, the right way round.

The subjects of the four dishes have been copied with the slight modifications, necessary to adapt them from rectangular to circular format, from engravings by contemporary masters after well-known paintings. One of the four also exists as a print by de Bry and was probably adapted by him from Egidius Sadeler's engraving after Joseph Heinz's painting of *Diana and Actaeon*. [51] The impression from the dish is twice the size of the print; in other respects they correspond line for line, though the text of the labels differs. The remaining dishes are engraved with the *Rape of Proserpine* after Heinz, *Perseus and Andromeda* after Goltzius and *Man receiving the Gifts from the Five Senses* after Martin de Vos. None of these impressions is signed and the attribution to de Bry is, therefore, based on stylistic grounds. The most striking evidence in his favour is the practical identity between the impression of the *Diana and Actaeon* from the dish and his signed print of the subject. By means of a transfer it would have been possible to reproduce de Bry's print almost line for line, but this cannot have been done as the impression is twice as large. Further evidence of his hand is to be found in the detail of the engraving. He used the burin with masterly skill, and the great variety of tone achieved by him can also be recognised in the impressions, in spite of their evident imperfections as prints. De Bry's skill as an engraver was superior not only to that of other goldsmiths, but also to that of many of the Dutch and German engravers of his time. Many of the engravings of the Sadelers, which he copied, seem coarse and heavy-handed in comparison with his versions.

A contemporary of de Bry, Hans Bol, who was born in Malines in 1534, also engraved tazzas. Like so many Flemish engravers, he left his home town in search of religious toleration, going first to Heidelberg, subsequently to Antwerp, and finally to Amsterdam where he died in 1593. His *oeuvre* [52] includes a large number of circular prints, landscapes and biblical subjects, which were suitable for copying either by engravers or embossers on silver tazza bowls. His manner is very close to that of de Bry and the numerous texts in various languages typical of de Bry are also found in his prints. A tazza engraved by him (pl. 644) is of small size and the subject, a family in a typical Dutch interior saying grace before their meal, is treated in minute detail. Two circular plaques cut from tazza bowls and signed with his monogram are in the Württembergisches Landesmuseum, Stuttgart.

It is significant that the number of engraved tazzas of the end of the sixteenth and early seventeenth centuries does not approach that of the embossed ones. The main reason was doubtless that few goldsmiths were sufficiently skilled with the burin to execute so ambitious a work as the inside of a tazza bowl. The very fact that so outstanding an artist as Johann Theodor de Bry undertook the engraved decoration of silver vessels suggests that such work was beyond the competence of the average goldsmith. Embossed ornament on the other hand gave the goldsmith greater opportunity to exploit the intrinsic qualities of the metal in which he worked. However skilled the engraver might be, it cannot be claimed that engraved scenes were well suited to the decoration of tazzas. These were intended to be displayed on the dinner table or on a side table, but the quality and the detail of the engraving could not be appreciated unless the dish could be held close to the eye. In short, the nature of the ornament did not accord with the purpose of the object to which it was applied. There was, however, a considerable fashion for engraved silver articles in Holland during the first half of the seventeenth century: marriage medals, caskets, beakers and wedding knives, mostly anonymous works inspired by the engraved ornament of one or other of the Dutch masters of ornament. In comparison with other objects decorated with engraving, few engraved tazzas survive. They began to go out of fashion in Holland soon after the death of de Bry himself; later examples do not stand comparison with his works.

1 Lodovico Guicciardini. *Description de tout le Pays Bas*, Amsterdam, 1609 edition, p.117-8.
2 Baader, p.34.
3 For the purchases of goldsmiths' work for the Munich court, see Baader, p.248-265.
4 Pechstein, 'Zeichnungen des Antwerpener Goldschmiedes Peter Holtswijller', *Berichte aus den Berliner Museen*, 1973, p.55.
5 Jessen, p.72-3; see also Fontainebleau II no. 438, p.333.
6 Berliner, nos. 151-2 For an exposition of Cornelis Bos's importance, see S. Schele, *Cornelis Bos, a study of the origins of the Netherlands Grotesque*, Uppsala, 1965.
7 Schele, pls. 37-9.
8 The complete set is reproduced by R. Hedicke, *Cornelis Floris und die Florisdekoration*, Berlin, 1913 Vol. II, pls. IX, X.
9 I have to thank M. Baudouin of the Sterckshof Museum, Antwerp, for communicating to me his interpretation of the Antwerp date-letters.
10 For a fuller account of this ewer end basin see J. H. de la Croix, 'La Célèbre Aiguière Aspremont Lynden', *Bulletin des Archives Verviétoises*, Verviers, 1969.
11 The history of these vessels is discussed by J. Destrée 'L'aiguière et le plat de Charles Quint', *Annales de la Societé d'Archéologie de Bruxelles*, Vol. XIV, p.33ff.
12 ibid. p.47.
13 See J. Destrée, 'La Coupe de la Ville de Veere de 1546', *Oud Holland*, Vol. XLIX, p.97ff.
14 See. J. Stracke, *Das Emder Rathaus*, Emden, 1963, p.43-4. The cup was valued at the time at 299 gulden and sold by the Bürgermeister to the city for that amount.
15 Berlin, *Ornamentstich Katalog* no. 1004.
16 The Italian prototypes of these salts are discussed by Charles Oman, 'The base-metal Goldsmiths' work of the Italian Renaissance'. *Connoisseur*, Vol. 144, p.218.
17 Berlin, *Ornamentstich Katalog* no. 1005.
18 Illustrated Hackenbroch, cat. no. 77.
19 Berlin, *Ornamentstich Katalog* no. 1008.

20 One of these is illustrated in Jessen, pl. 69.
21 ill. *Dutch Silver*, Gans and Duyvené de Wit Klinkhamer, London, 1961, pl. 3.
22 Frederiks, Vol. IV nos. 45-48, pls. 58, 59.
23 Such as Frederiks, Vol. IV, no. 16, pl. 20; see also T. Duyvené de Wit Klinkhamer, 'Een Hollandse Nautilusbeker', *Bulletin Rijksmuseum*, 2, 1954.
24 ill. F. Württemberger, *Mannerism*, Vienna, 1962, p.96.
25 Sandrart, p.222.
26 ibid. p.223.
27 ill. Frederiks, Vol. I, no. 49, p.78-9.
28 R. W. Lightbown, 'Christian van Vianen at the Court of Charles I', *Apollo*, Vol. 87, 1968.
29 ill. Frederiks, Vol. I nos. 53, p. 90 and 174, p.270.
30 See T. Duyvené de Wit Klinkhamer, 'Een Vermaarde Zilveren Beker', *Nederlands Kunsthistorisch Jahrboek*, 1966, p.79-103. The author also reproduces on p.102 a drawing by Adam van Vianen of the border of a salver showing typical auricular scrollwork.
31 ill. Frederiks, Vol. I, cat. no. 171, p.266.
32 See R. Verres, 'Die Plaketten des Paulus van Vianen', *Pantheon*, I, 1928, p.291.
33 K. Rossacher, 'Eine goldene Kreuzgruppe des Paulus van Vianen', *Anzeiger des German Nationalmuseums, 1964, p.71ff.*
34 H. E. van Gelder, 'Paulus van Vianen's Zilverwerk nageboostet in 1637', *Oud Holland*, 34, 1916.
35 Rosenberg II, Vol. IV, no. 7713, p.416; Frederiks, Vol. IV, no. 12.
36 Rosenberg II, Vol. IV, no. 7712, p.415; Fredericks, Vol. I, no. 10.
37 See T. Duyvené de Wit Klinkhamer, 'Zilver uit de verzameling Dreesmann', *Rijksmuseum Bulletin*, 1960, p.85ff.
38 See T. Duyvené de Wit Klinkhamer, 'Werk van den Zilversmid A.V.B., *Oud Holland*, LXIII, 1940.
39 See I. Weber, 'Three hitherto unpublished reliefs by Arent van Bolten, the Master A.V.B.', *Burlington Magazine*, pps. 207-9, Vol. CXIII, 1971.
40 There are also 56 drawings of handles and frames, 40 of various mounts, many of them showing auricular detail.
41 For a full discussion of engravings on metal that were intended for decoration only and not for subsequent reproduction as prints, see Weixlgärtner, 'Ungedruckte Stiche', *Jahrbuch*, Vol. XXIX, 1911, p.259, see also J. M. Fritz, *Gestochene Bilder*, Cologne, 1966.
42 Hollstein, IV nos. 178-181.
43 Hollstein, IV,nos. 191-194.
44 ill. Sponsel, Vol. II, pl.43.
45 See *Jahrbuch*, Band XVII, Part 2, Regest No. 14562. As printed, the letter is addressed to the Archduke Ferdinand, but this must be a copying error as the context makes it clear that the Archduke Maximilian must be meant.
46 *Jahrbuch*, Band XVII, Part 2, Regest No. 14564.
47 ill. Bela Dudik, *Kleinodien des deutschen Ritterordens in Wien*, Vienna, 1865.
48 See J. F. Hayward, 'Engraved Silver Dishes', *Apollo Miscellany*, 1950, p.35ff. Both are now on loan to the Victoria and Albert Museum.
49 Hollstein, IV, nos. 1, 3, 4, 9, 10, 13, 14, 22.
50 All four are illustrated in J. F. Hayward 'Four Prints from engraved Silver Standing Dishes attributed to J. T. de Bry', *Burlington Magazine*, Vol. XCV, p.124.
51 Hollstein, IV, no. 10.
52 Hollstein, III, nos. 1-27.

CHAPTER FIFTEEN

England

THE death of Henry VIII must have greatly limited the volume of orders for plate of precious metal from the court. During the succeeding reigns of Edward VI, Mary I and Elizabeth I the tendency was to reduce the quantity of royal plate rather than to add to it. Mannerism was a style that flourished in the precious atmosphere of some of the Continental courts, but the more austere character of the English court during the reigns of Henry VIII's children was less favourable to its expression. Alongside those pieces, which display the influence of Mannerist fashion, many others were produced in which no awareness of it was manifested. Such pieces were not by any means the humblest: among them is the cup presented in 1598 by the Earl of Essex to the University of Cambridge of which he was the Chancellor.[1]

Hans Holbein the Younger

The most important surviving example of Tudor goldsmiths' work in Mannerist taste is the enamelled gold and rock-crystal bowl now in the Munich Schatzkammer[2] (pls. 645-7). Though no drawings that can be associated with it survive, there is good reason to think that it was designed by Hans Holbein. It was originally made for Henry VIII and it appears in the manuscript inventory of his treasury, compiled after his death by order of his successor. It reappears in all the subsequent Tudor inventories including that of 1574.[3] The text of the 1574 entry is as follows:

> Item oone Bolle of Christall the foote and bryme garnisshed with golde the foote also sette with thre smale Diamoundes and six pearles and cartaigne writinges in thre places vpon white enamelid vpon brym thereof is cartaigne Antique works of golde enamlid wherin is set a goodly Rubie and an Emeraude in collettes of golde being very curiously wrought and garnisshed with fyve roses of Diamoundes and v places written enamelid white the top of the Couer being a Christall and golde garnisshed with a Rubie and a Diamounde an Emeraude and thre perles in the top of the same is two pearles in oone and oone great pearle lower set in golde and thre smale pearles pendaunte at the same poiz togethers xxxviij oz. iij quarters.

The last reference to this bowl among the English inventories appears in the list of articles still remaining in the Upper Jewel House of the Tower of London in August 1649.[4] Its description, though briefer than the previous ones is unmistakable 'a broad christall bowle, and cover garnished with gold and pearle and other stones; 5 mottoes enamelled on the cover, and 2 about the foot, poiz. 3 lb. 2 oz.1½ (i.e. 38 1½ oz. oz.)'. There is a discrepancy in the number of enamelled mottoes on the foot; the description refers to two whereas there are in fact three. It is possible that one motto had become dislodged and has since been restored, but the error might easily have been made by a clerk copying out the inventory. The 1649 inventory was completed with valuations and this piece was valued at the very considerable sum of £120. The articles were sold and two lists of buyers exist, but unfortunately both omit this particular piece. There can, however, be no doubt that it was sold.

A gap of twenty-nine years follows, as the next appearance of the bowl dates from 1678, when it featured in a still-life painting by the Amsterdam master, Willem Kalf. This picture is in the Copenhagen Gallery but the bowl was painted by Kalf on at least two other occasions, one picture, dated 1680 is in the Weimar Schlossmuseum, while the other is in a private collection. The representation of the bowl in Kalf's paintings (pl. 648) is very detailed and there is no difficulty in identifying it with one described in the English royal inventories and now in Munich. There is, however, a significant difference in the cover. Whereas it now has a small button finial, the finial shown in the painting corresponds to the inventory description: two pearls in one surmounting one great pearl from which hang three pendant pearls. Another particularly interesting difference is that in Kalf's painting at Copenhagen the enamelled plaque on the foot, instead of bearing an inscription about drinking, is signed *Holbeen Fe*. The attribution to Holbein is not, in fact, mentioned in any of the English royal inventories, but this is hardly surprising as the clerks who prepared them were not interested in the names of artists. None of the three panels now on the foot appears to be a restoration; it seems, therefore, that Willem Kalf substituted the Holbein signature for the inscription in order to place on record an interesting fact about the authorship of the bowl.

The next description of the rock-crystal bowl appears in the *Inventarium über die in dem kurfürstlichen Schilderei-Cabinet befindlichen Pretiosa und anderer rarer Sachen* which was prepared by order of the Elector Palatine and dated 14th August 1711.[5] It runs as follows:

'*Nr. 28 Eine Schale mit einem Deckel von Cristallo di Montagna, mit gramalierter Arbeith und in Gold eingefasst, auch mit Diemanten, Perlen, Rubinen und Smaragden gantz kunstlich besetzt, welche von dem König Henrico 8vo v. Engelland an desz Königsz von Schottland Sohn Jacobum vor eine Tauff-gifft ist gegeben worden, durch Hans Holbein ordinirt und gezeichnet von dessen Bruder, den Goldschmied, aber gemacht worden.*'

(A bowl and cover of rock-crystal mounted in gold and enamelled work, and artfully set with diamonds, pearls, rubies and emeralds, which was given as a Christening present by Henry VIII of England to the King of Scotland's son, James, commissioned from and designed by Hans Holbein but made by his brother, the goldsmith).

The connection with Holbein is thus repeated and to it is added a new detail of its having been a christening gift to the King of Scotland's son. This prince, son of James V of Scotland and his queen, Mary of Guise, was born on 22 May, 1540, and, as the first born son and heir to the throne of Scotland, might well have received a gift of great splendour. Nevertheless, the story must be devoid of foundation, inasmuch as the bowl appears consistently in all the royal inventories between 1550 and 1649, and if one accepted the eighteenth-century Düsseldorf account, it would be necessary to find an explanation for the return of the bowl to the English Treasury within three years of its being sent to Scotland. The bowl remained in the Palatine treasury until 1802 when it was transferred with other objects to the Munich Schatzkammer.

The statement in the Düsseldorf inventory concerning the part played by Hans Holbein's brother is also unreliable. His only brother, Ambrosius, died in 1526 and was in any case a painter and not a goldsmith. The claim that it was designed by Holbein is more convincing. Inasmuch as the bowl was made for the king, one would expect its design to have been provided by his court artist. Furthermore many of its features correspond to details in existing designs by Holbein. The original finial, shown in the Kalf paintings, in the form of a series of tiers with pendant pearls is similar to that on the covered bowl Holbein designed for Hans of Antwerp (pl. 37). The female terms about the base and the border running around it, as well as the cartouches within mauresques on the cover (pl. 645) can all be paralleled on one or other of Holbein's original designs for goldsmiths' work. The design probably dates from Holbein's last years, for numerous Mannerist features can be recognised. A medieval rock-crystal bowl has been used as its foundation. The dissolution of the monasteries and confiscation of their treasures had led to the destruction of a great many reliquaries made of rock-crystal with mounts of precious metal. While the mounts were removed and melted, the rock-crystal elements were sometimes re-used, as in the case of the Stonyhurst Salt (pl. 670). The five roundels of rock-crystal set in the cover of the Holbein bowl may also have come from a reliquary. A silver-gilt bowl on tall stem formerly in the treasury of the Cardinal of Brandenburg[6] and illustrated in the pictorial inventory has five such roundels set in the cover to enable the faithful to have a sight of the holy particle. Apart from the use of an earlier bowl, another Mannerist feature is the wilful lack of consideration for function. The towering finial was so delicate that it broke off when used to raise the cover and had to be replaced by a more serviceable but less elegant one. When this magnificent bowl was being made for King Henry VIII, Benvenuto Cellini must have been at work on the infinitely more sophisticated gold salt-cellar for Francis I in Paris. Holbein's design seems to belong to an earlier generation than Cellini's salt, but does not lag behind contemporary northern fashion. A simpler and evidently earlier version of the Munich bowl is the standing mazer of the Barber-Surgeons' Company (pl. 300). This was presented to the Company by Henry VIII in or after 1543 and it also was probably designed by Hans Holbein for the Tudor treasury.

The death of Holbein in 1543 was followed, four years later, by that of the King. The death of both the great designer and his royal patron meant a set-back for the progress of English silver design and fashion became thereafter more insular. Though some of Holbein's silver designs were in advance of those of his German contemporaries such as Hans Brosamer, his influence in England was limited: in the first place because he had worked for an exclusive court circle and, secondly, because his designs were never made available to a wider public in the form of a pattern-book. As a result, the goldsmiths of English birth adhered to Renaissance fashion at a time when their Continental rivals were experimenting with more adventurous forms.

Alien Goldsmiths

During the third quarter of the century foreign immigration into England built up again as a result of renewed religious persecution on the other side of the Channel. The most important movements that brought many goldsmiths to this country took place in 1567 and 1569 following upon the Duke of Alba's campaign in the Spanish Netherlands culminating in the Sack of Antwerp, and then again in 1572 after the Massacre of Saint Bartholomew's Night in France. During the reign of Elizabeth I a hundred and fifty Dutch, German and Flemish goldsmiths were at work in London, while during the reigns of Elizabeth and James I sixty-three French goldsmiths have been noted.[7] The activities of these foreign goldsmiths were severely limited by the influence of the London Company of Goldsmiths, but many of the foreigners succeeded in evading guild control by settling in the former precincts of the dissolved monasteries of Blackfriars, Westminster and Saint Martin's le Grand. Before the Reformation the monasteries had claimed certain 'liberties' which had freed their denizens from guild control and the subsequent legal rights of the matter had never been cleared up. In 1545 the Court of the Goldsmiths Company resolved to sue the Secretary of State about 'goldsmiths living in sanctuaries' and claiming therefore, to be exempt from guild control. The return of aliens resident in London, which was prepared in 1571,[8] shows that most of them came from Holland, Flanders, France and Germany. The city of Hamburg also appears frequently, but the most important single town of origin was Antwerp in the Spanish Netherlands. Among the pieces with London marks that show Antwerp influence and may, therefore, have been made by an immigrant from there, is the now sadly defective standing cup in the Victoria and Albert Museum (pl. 651). Many of the aliens did not work as independent masters, but were employed as journeymen by native English goldsmiths. Silver vessels made by them would, of course, be submitted for assay by their English employer who alone had the right to do so and would be struck with his mark after assay. In later periods it was a frequent complaint on the part of some London goldsmiths that others would for a fee take a piece made by a foreigner to Goldsmiths' Hall for marking and assay and so encourage foreigners to set up on their own instead of seeking employment under an English master. While a great many foreign goldsmiths were active in London during the second half of the sixteenth century, it is difficult to identify their work. The mark plates of the Worshipful Company of Goldsmiths, which would have given the names appertaining to each maker's mark, have not been preserved. Amongst the prominent foreigners was John Spilman, goldsmith to Queen Elizabeth. He was of German origin from Lindau on the Bodensee. On the assumption that his mark must have been the initials IS, two gilt cups with conventional floral engraving have been attributed to him, one belonging to the Armourers' and Braziers' Company, the other in a private collection.[9] If they are his work they must be workshop productions, for their quality is not above average.

It seems reasonable to assume that those pieces that bear a London hall-mark but are clearly Continental in style are the work of the immigrant goldsmiths. Judging by the general character of English silver surviving from the second half of the sixteenth century, the foreign immigrant goldsmiths had little influence on the indigenous masters. It is not possible to parallel in English silver the more extreme fantasies of contemporary German work. There are, however, striking contrasts in London-made pieces of this period. Vessels of severely conservative design, such as the little two-handled cup of 1555 given by Archbishop Parker to Corpus Christi College, Cambridge (pl. 304) or the Inner Temple pomegranate-cup of 1563 (pl. 650), which might well have been based on a Dürer drawing, were made about the same time as the Bowes Cup of the Goldsmiths' Company of 1554 (pl. 652) or the Gleane Cup of 1565 (pl. 653), both of which show a familiarity on the part of their makers with contemporary Netherlandish fashion. The former cup, named after Sir Martin Bowes, Lord Mayor of London in 1545, is one of the few convincing examples of foreign influence on the work of London goldsmiths. A comparison between it and the contemporary, unmarked, but very probably Antwerp cup illustrated in pl. 600 shows striking resemblances. There are, however, many differences of detail and it seems likely that both cups derive from a common source rather than that the English goldsmith used the Flemish cup as his model. In each case the stem and body of the cup are composed of semi-precious hardstone or of crystal and the profile also follows the same lines. There is, however, one significant difference, namely in quality. The question arises whether the London-marked Bowes Cup should be attributed to a native English or to a Flemish immigrant goldsmith. It is unlikely that Sir Martin, with his long history of service in various public offices, including that of representing the City of London in Parliament, would have patronised one of the immigrant goldsmiths, and even less likely that he would have commemorated his year of office as Prime Warden of the Goldsmiths' Company in 1558 by presenting a cup made by one of the foreigners whose competition was so much resented. Bowes's own career shows that great riches were within the reach of native-born goldsmiths with a developed business sense. In 1559 his tax assessment for his property in Cheapside and Lombard Street was no less than £700.[10]

There were doubtless exceptions, but the average level of achievement in chasing and embossing by English goldsmiths of the second half of the sixteenth century did not equal that of the best continental masters. I may seem to be falling into the old mistake of unduly depreciating English craftsmanship in the applied arts, but one can I think, go further and say that the chasing found on some of the smaller pieces, such as salts, is of a quality below that found on any contemporary western European silver. Such outstanding work as the unmarked rock-crystal and agate cup illustrated in pl. 600 and here attributed to Antwerp could be the work of one of the immigrant Antwerp masters resident in London. Although the Goldsmiths' Company spared no efforts to compel the foreign immigrants to conform to their regulations and submit all their pieces for assay and marking, they were not uniformly successful. The Company also insisted that imported silver vessels should be submitted to the Hall and marked with the stamp of the goldsmith who had brought them into the country. This accounts for some of the vessels of Flemish or German fashion that are struck with full London hall-marks. Others were, of course, made in England to a foreign fashion by an immigrant goldsmith. One such is the standing cup of the parish church of St. Peter Mancroft, Norwich,[11] to which it was presented by Sir Peter Gleane in 1633 (pl. 653). The design shows both English and German features, a combination that can probably be explained by the fact that an immigrant German goldsmith employed an English engraver to execute the border around the lip of the bowl. Another English vessel that shows a combination of English and German decorative elements is the tazza of 1567 (pl. 658). In this case the embossed scene of the meeting of Eliezar and Rebecca is derived from a lead plaquette which is usually attributed to Hans Jamnitzer of Nürnberg. It is well known that South German lead plaquettes were in general circulation in northern Europe, but this seems to be the only recorded example of a Jamnitzer plaquette crossing the Channel and serving as a model for an English goldsmith. The embossing and chasing are competent, but do not equal the standard achieved by the skilled Dutch or German masters of the time. The artist who wrought it may have spent some time as a journeyman in the workshop of a German goldsmith, for such pictorial scenes are exceptional on English silver.[12]

During the sixteenth century a great deal of German plate must have been imported into England. The 1574 inventory of the Tudor plate lists forty items, mostly double cups, described as 'Almain' or in the 'Almain fashion'. An Act of Parliament of February 8, 1576 had re-enacted previous legislation making it an offence for any goldsmith to 'make, sell or exchange any wares of silver less in fineness than eleven ounces and two pennyweights, and the duty of ensuring that no sub-standard plate was offered for sale fell upon the Wardens of the London Goldsmiths' Company. Much German plate, including that made in Nürnberg, did not reach this standard of fineness and was, therefore, subject to seizure and destruction by the Company's officers. An unpublished incident recorded in the Minutes of the Company shows the lengths to which they went. On February 19, 1606, a certain Mr. Hampton was summoned before the Court of Wardens for selling four pieces of 'Norremberge plate' to Henry Chesshire, contrary to the ordinances of the Company and the statute laws of the realm, and was fined the sum of 20 nobles. Upon his refusing to pay he was committed to prison until the following day, when he apologised and paid his fine. One month later the same Court had to consider the case again as Henry Chesshire had prevailed upon Sir William Slingsby to mediate in his interest. It was now represented that the Queen's Majesty wished to view the plate, but the knight 'after he had been satisfied by the Company that the said plate was very deceitful and and not fit to be presented to the Queen's Majesty and that the Wardens had authority.....to break all kinds of deceitful plate offered for sale' could do no more than plead that the Company award some compensation to Henry Chesshire for the loss of his four cups. The Wardens went ahead with their decision to break the cups and compensated Chesshire by allowing him the sum of £5.13.4. However Chesshire did not get off completely, for it was decided that no plate, but only spoons, would be accepted for assay from him. In May 1607 at Court meeting, three further pieces of Nürnberg plate were presented, which had been discovered on a search by the Wardens, two cups from John Harris and one from William Ward. The Court decided once again to break the cups in spite of the fact that one of those taken from Harris was the property of Lord Hay, whereupon Harris 'grew into some forgettfullnes of himself and over boldly he alledged Mr. Warden Smythe that he since he was Warden had sold the like Norremberdge plate'. Harris escaped punishment for his impertinence after due apology; it is recorded that one reason for this was that Warden Smythe did not wish to pursue the matter - presumably because Harris's remark was not unfounded.

Some of the alien goldsmiths on the 1571 register are simply described as 'Dutch'. The most impressive London-marked cup that appears to be the work of a Dutch immigrant is the Booth Cup of St. John's College, Cambridge (pl. 665-7). In this case the design follows Dutch precedent so closely (compare the Dutch cup in pl. 615) that one is inclined to ask whether this is not an imported piece that was first marked at the London Goldsmiths' Hall by the goldsmith who brought it over.[13] This suggestion can, however, be dismissed inasmuch as the engraved lip is typically English.

Situated as England then was on the periphery of the civilised world it is probable that, apart from royal gifts, little English silver reached the Continent in the sixteenth century. That English fashion was not altogether unknown on the other side of the Channel is shown by an entry in the inventory made in 1595 of the treasury of the Comtesse de Sault, as follows:

67. *item 2 grands potz à anse d'argent doré façon d'Angleterre.*[14]

Among the English royal gifts to the court of France were the items numbered 104, 105 and 106 in the French royal inventory of 1560: two large tankards, two flagons with chains and a cup, all of gold and engraved with the arms of England.[15] The inventory does not, of course, tell us when they were presented. The curious English Wrotham ware jug with silver-gilt mounts in the Grünes Gewölbe, Dresden,[16] was also probably a royal gift. The mounts may in part be English, but further enrichment has been added in Saxony.

Engraved Silver

While the majority of English plateworkers were little influenced by Continental fashion, the artists who executed the engraved ornament were enabled through imported pattern-books to keep in touch with the course of fashion. Among many others the Drapers' Company Cup of 1578 (pl. 655) can be cited to illustrate this point. As an example of wrought plate the cup is unadventurous in design, but the engraving around the body makes use of the full vocabulary of Flemish Mannerist ornament. While the quality of the embossing on these Elizabethan cups varies, the engraved ornament is usually extremely attractive, introducing Tudor roses along with snails, insects and birds, recalling contemporary Elizabethan needlework. In another example of English engraving (pl. 679) the engraver seems to have composed the design himself, hence its somewhat naive and disorganised effect. The source is once again Flemish. This type of covered beaker seems to have been a specifically English form; it is now known as a Magdalen Cup because of its similarity to the cup borne by St. Mary Magdalen in sixteenth-century paintings. It is, in fact a development of the German *Satzbecher*.

An important group of English silver vessels dating from the 1560's and 1570's is decorated with engraved ornament alone. In view of the generally lower standard of chasing in England as against other European countries, the exclusive use of this particular technique is not surprising. The group consists of four sets of spice or fruit-plates, three of a dozen each and another of half a dozen; there is also a ewer with matching basin. They are curiously close in date to each other; one set bears the date-letter for 1567-8 (Fowler Coll. Los Angeles), a second set 1568-9 and 1569-70 (Duke of Buccleuch Coll.) a third 1573-4 (pl. 660), while the fourth set bears no date-letter but only a Strassburg mark, presumably meaning that they were wrought abroad though evidently engraved in England (Metropolitan Museum, New York). The ewer and basin bear London hall marks for 1567-8. The twelve plates in the Fowler Collection are engraved with eleven of the Twelve Labours of Hercules after Aldegrever, the twelfth by the same hand but with another classical subject. Three of the Fowler plates are signed by the artist with his monogram PM or MP and the same signature appears on both the ewer and basin and the set of plates in the Metropolitan Museum. The ewer is engraved with full-length portraits of English kings, while the basin is engraved with bust portraits of all the English sovereigns from William the Conqueror up to Elizabeth I, alternating with Old Testament subjects based upon the Bernard Salomon illustrations to the Lyon Bible of 1553. In his adaptation of the rectangular prints to the circular designs of the plates, the artist has shown great ingenuity. The problem of his identity has not yet been certainly solved. His use of Continental sources has given rise to the suggestion that he was probably one of the numerous Protestant immigrants who came to England at this period. He did not, however, rely exclusively on foreign sources, for he could have found no foreign print to serve as a model for the portraits of the English kings and queens. On the other hand, there were very few English-born engravers working at so early a date. He has in the past been tentatively identified with the Flemish-born master, Peter Maes, who is known to have been active in western Germany between 1577 and 1591, that is, after the period when he would have been in England. This identification has been questioned[17] on the grounds that he may be one and the same person as a certain Peirk Maas who was not apprenticed in Antwerp until 1572. There are other reasons for favouring Peter Maes, first, the fact that he copied Aldegrever on other occasions and secondly the existence of a print by him of Mary, Queen of Scots.

The set of plates in the Buccleuch Collection bears neither signature nor maker's mark, but is probably the work of the same engraver. The six plates in the Victoria and Albert Museum (pl. 660) are of somewhat different character and were certainly engraved by another hand. They are gilt and the centres are engraved with scenes of the parable of the Prodigal Son, while the inner borders show sea-monsters against a background of waves and the outer ones foliate scrolls inhabited by animals. The sea-creatures resemble similar subjects by du Cerceau, but they can also be found in the work of Erasmus Hornick. Others can be seen on a print by Adriaen Collaert (pl. 195) and this may have been the source from which the unknown engraver derived his ideas. As in the other pieces of this group, the execution of the engraving is of fine quality and certainly the work of a specialist. The survival of so many vessels decorated with all-over engraving from so early a period cannot be paralleled in the silver of any other European country.

Tazzas and Standing Cups

The tazza in England corresponded to the Continental type and, like some Dutch and Flemish examples, was completed with a cover. This meant there was less reason to decorate the interior of the bowl, which was only visible when the cover was removed. The gilt tazza and cover (pl. 659) has only a medallion embossed with a profile head in the centre of the bowl, and most of the decoration is on the cover. Though few survive, tazzas were much admired in England, no less than seventy-eight of them are listed as prizes in the State Lottery of 1567.[18]

It has, since the sixteenth century, been the practice in England for those officers of State who were entrusted with the Great Seal of England or Ireland to retain the seal on giving up their office. As the seal, which was of silver, had then to be defaced it was not worth keeping in its damaged form and, instead, a cup or tazza was made to commemorate the owner's period of office. The earliest extant examples of cups made from the Great Seal are the three which were made in 1574 for Sir Nicholas Bacon from the Great Seal of Mary Tudor and Philip II of Spain; one of these is in the Victoria and Albert Museum, another in the British Museum.[19] A cup made from the Great Seal of Ireland is illustrated in pl. 657. This practice does not seem to have been followed in any other country.

The goldsmiths of a maritime country such as England were well placed to obtain the exotic materials they required for mounting in precious metal. They used much the same ones as their medieval predecessors, mother-of-pearl, coconuts, nautilus- and trochus-shells and ostrich eggs, romantically known as 'griffin eggs'. One of the finest surviving English mounted cups of the period, the pelican cup of 1579 (pl. 654) was originally a nautilus-cup, the shell forming the body of the bird. Another English nautilus-cup (pl. 661) in the Fitzwilliam Museum, Cambridge, combines all the marine forms so frequently encountered on silver vessels of this period, but the various elements are set out in an irrational manner without any effort to set them in meaningful relationship. In this as in other goldsmiths' work of this period, this irrational treatment does not appear to be accidental. The boundaries between nature and fiction were purposely ignored and thereby a mysterious, even magical, quality was given to the object. This particular cup must have offered an exceptional fascination at the time it was made, for not only is the shell of an exotic species, but the engraved ornament on it is of Chinese origin, carried out by an artist in the remote and almost mythical Cathay. The ostrich was a creature so fantastic that the goldsmiths endeavoured to suggest its form in their design of cups mounted with ostrich eggs. The unmarked cup (pl. 662) belonging to Exeter College, Oxford, which probably dates from about the turn of the century, has the stem ingeniously formed as three ostrich-legs while the cover is surmounted by an ostrich; the Bohemian cup from Eger is modelled even more closely on the original (pl. 584). The two most popular types of standing cup of the late sixteenth and early seventeenth centuries were the gourd and the steeple cup. The former had the bowl of pear or gourd shape and the stem like a branch (pl. 656), often with the addition of a woodman chopping at it with an axe. This type originated in Germany, where it first appears – though without the woodman – in the first quarter of the sixteenth century. The English versions show German influence; the Leycroft cup which was presented to the Armourers and Braziers' Company in 1608 seems to be copied from one of the designs in the Paul Flindt pattern book published in Nürnberg (see p.238). The bowl is chased with strapwork enclosing landscapes in the Flindt manner, but the Englishness of the vessel is stressed by the tall pierced pyramid finial. The idea of rendering a standing cup in the form of a gourd with its twig as a stem, which in turn was attacked by a woodman had an evident appeal in this period of Mannerist fashion. The steeple cup was of exclusively English origin and had no Continental precedent. It had a tall trumpet-shaped foot, a short stem decorated with open brackets, an egg-shaped bowl, surmounted by a cover of corresponding form which terminated above in a tall pierced obelisk of triangular or rectangular section (pl. 664). This last feature helped to give importance by increasing the height without adding unduly to the weight and hence the cost of the cup. As a whole these steeple cups are ungraceful objects and introduce the decline that developed in English goldsmiths' work during the first half of the seventeenth century. In this respect there was a loss of taste and craftsmanship that was hardly paralleled on the Continent even during the terrors of the Thirty Years' War.

Standing Salts

The most typical, and at the same time most original, productions of the English goldsmiths of the middle years and second half of the sixteenth century were the large standing salts that occupied an important place on the dining-table. Whereas the purpose of the Continental salt was usually quite apparent from its design, the English makers liked to conceal the salt within an imposing architectural framework or, as we discover in the 1574 inventory of the Tudor royal plate, to incorporate it in a clock. This meant that the pattern-book designs for salts were not of much use to the English goldsmiths, who developed a series of original forms. The English type was not, however, entirely unknown on the Continent. There is in the Berlin Kunstbibliothek, among the drawings of the Hamburg master, Jakob Mores, a design for a salt in the English manner. An unmarked silver-gilt salt with rectangular boxlike body of English type in the Wallace Collection, hitherto regarded as French on account of the two Limoges enamel plaques which decorate two of the sides, is in fact, of uncertain nationality, as the plaques were added later, probably in the nineteenth century. There is no reason to think it English.

  Of the three gold and eight silver-gilt clock-salts listed in the Tudor inventory, the only one that has survived is of French make (pl. 251) and may have differed substantially from the English ones. The peculiar combination of salt-cellar and clock well illustrates one aspect of contemporary taste. Clocks and watches were then regarded as one of the wonders of the age. They were an indispensable feature of the *Kunst und Wunderkammer* and were often given a prominent position in portraits of noblemen or rich merchants. When combined with the salt the clock occupied a conspicuous position on the table and carried the mystery of the Chamber of Curiosities into the sphere of everyday life. A dominant aspect of life in the sixteenth century was the obsession with death and the clock provided a most graphic melancholic illustration of the rapid passing of Man's short span on earth.

Some of the earlier English silver salts recall the two designs drawn by Hans Holbein for Sir Anthony Denny's present to King Henry VIII (pls. 47-8). Two such salts are illustrated. The earlier (pl. 668) hall-marked in 1549-50, follows the first of Holbein's drawings fairly closely, particularly in the use of applied brackets terminating above in female busts. It may seem peculiar that the rock-crystal should form the body of a salt rather than the receptacle for it, but while rock-crystal was at this time extremely expensive, such cylinders of crystal could probably be obtained at a bargain price, being all that remained of some reliquary destroyed at the Reformation. The most interesting example of re-use of medieval rock-crystal fragments in an Elizabethan salt is the so-called Stonyhurst Salt in the British Museum (pl. 670). The second of the two salts, which is struck with the London hall-mark for 1562 (pl. 669), has a drum of similar design to that of the second Holbein drawing, but without the royal arms. The time-lag of twenty years between drawing and executed salt illustrates the slow pace of development in the goldsmith's craft after Holbein's death. The finest of these drum-salts is the so-called Queen Elizabeth Salt which forms part of the royal plate kept in the Jewel House of the Tower of London.[20] It is strange that this Elizabethan salt should have found its way into the royal treasury, as it must have seemed a very old-fashioned piece when it was acquired, presumably at or shortly after the Restoration of Charles II. There is no evidence that it formed part of the plate of Queen Elizabeth, and the only indication of royal ownership on it is the cypher of Charles II surmounted by a royal crown engraved on one of the feet. The body is embossed with figures of Hope, Fortitude and Faith within circular frames of laurel after Flötner's plaquettes of the Virtues,[21] while between each figure is applied a caryatid surmounted by a flat scroll-bracket with a female mask attached to the end. The cover is also embossed with the figures of Dido (?), Cleopatra and Lucretia within circular laurel medallions and it is surmounted by a knight. The salt is of advanced form for its date, inasmuch as the cover is held clear of the base and receptacle by four cast and chased S-scroll brackets which made it possible to take salt without removing the cover. This gave the salt a far more imposing appearance on the table. In view of the comparatively early date-letter of this salt — 1572 — it is possible that the brackets are a somewhat later addition. They are found on salts of the early seventeenth century such as that mounted with mother-of-pearl plaques (pl. 674).

When it became necessary to provide a set of regalia for Charles II in 1660, it was evidently difficult to find appropriate pieces at short notice. The royal goldsmith, Sir Robert Vyner, found two second-hand Continental ones for presentation by the cities of Plymouth and Exeter respectively. It is probable that the Elizabethan salt was another piece that happened to be available in London and was therefore supplied through the offices of Vyner. The other salts that were specially made for the coronation banquet are of inferior design and appear to have been produced in a hurry. Of the dozen or so English drum-salts surviving from the second half of the sixteenth century the most enterprising as a work of Mannerist art is that of 1562 in the Royal Scottish Museum, Edinburgh. The drum is embossed and chased with winged caryatids linked by ribbons and festoons, the chasing of unusually fine quality for English work of this period.

The clock shape can be recognised in another type of salt that was produced in England in the second half of the century. The Vintners' salt (pl. 672) belongs to this group, but the Vivyan Salt of 1592 in the Victoria and Albert Museum (pl. 673) is even more like a clock. The receptacle for salt is surmounted by a dome-shaped cover that recalls the form of the bell on which, in a clock, the hours were struck. One of the most original and elegant of all the surviving English salts is the Gibbon Salt of the Goldsmiths' Company[22] (pl. 671). As has been mentioned above, the rock crystal elements on Elizabethan vessels were sometimes taken from derelict Catholic reliquaries. In this case the unusual pentagonal shape of the rock-crystal cylinder makes this unlikely. The figure of a satyr imprisoned within strapwork is a familiar motif of Flemish Mannerist ornament, but the conceit of enclosing him within a rock-crystal cylinder shows an original sense of fantasy.

Just as the handsome Elizabethan standing cup developed at the close of the century into the ungainly steeple cup, so also the salt fashionable in the early years of the seventeenth century was surmounted by a small four-sided pyramid. In common with the trend of English taste at the time, ornament was omitted apart from the S-shape brackets which supported the two or more tiers that composed the salt (pl. 676). One or more of these could be removed and used separately. This ingenious arrangement was not an exclusively English invention; it is also found on Spanish salts of the same period.

The 1574 Inventory of the royal plate lists a great many salts of elaborate construction, but no indication is given of their nationality and the only one that has survived is French. Ambassadors to the English court were always bringing pieces of plate as gifts and a fair proportion of the royal plate is likely, therefore, to have been of foreign make. A salt that was probably of English origin is listed in the treasury of the Russian Prince Protector, Boris Godunov, in 1588, and had evidently been presented to him by one of the English ambassadors.[23] It is described as follows: 'Salt of English workmanship, cut glass mounted in silver with cover. On the cut glass of the lid stands a man on one leg drawing his bow, under him is a small basin around which are seven snakes. Amongst them stands a man with a spear: the lid is chased and has four pinnacles and at the corners four men with barrels sitting with goblets in their hands; and the salt has four siver buttons at the corners; under the salt are three brackets and on them sit leverets; the base is chased and rests on four small lions'.

The inventory of the goods of the Earl of Leicester made after his death in 1588 includes a particularly elaborate salt which may also have been of English make, though no English example of the kind now survives: 'A Salte ship-fashion, of the mother-of-perle, garnished with silver and divers workes of warlike engines and ornaments, with XVI pieces of ordinance, whereof ii on wheles, two anchers on the fore parte, and on the stearne the image of Dame Fortune, standing on a globe, with a flag in her hand'. A similar but simpler salt was amongst the royal pieces:[24]

Item oone Sault guilt of mother of pearle made Shippe fation garnisshed with conterfet stones poiz. xvij oz. quarters scant.

Ewers and Basins

Various forms of ewer appear in England during the second half of the sixteenth century; one apparently developed in England, the others of Continental derivation. The earlier English form (pl. 681) had a thistle-shaped body rising from a protuberant base with a short stem and a spreading foot below. A dramatic, almost barbaric, effect was achieved by opposing a large wedge-shaped spout, which jutted out like the prow of a ship, to an S-shaped handle with a shield-shaped terminal on the other side of the body. Two or more of the mauresque bands, which are rarely absent from vessels of English style and make of this period, decorate the body. The surviving examples mostly date from the 1560's and 1570's but there is one of 1602 in the Royal Scottish Museum, Edinburgh. The magnificent basin and ewer belonging to the Duke of Rutland (pls. 683-4) bear the London hall-mark for 1579-80 and were made by the same master who created the Gibbon Salt of the Goldsmiths' Company (pl. 671) three years previously. It would be difficult to imagine a ewer form that departed more radically from the classical Renaissance convention. The design has a strongly Continental flavour, with more than a suggestion of Antwerp influence. It is possible that these vessels also were made by one of the Flemish goldsmiths who sought refuge in England from Spanish persecution.

The Rutland ewer was not alone in departing from the conventions of the time. Two unmarked but apparently English ewers of fantastic construction exist; one in a London private collection is composed of mother-of-pearl plaques on a silver shell while the other, formerly in the James de Rothschild Collection, has snake handles and a shell spout while the body is decorated with applied lion-masks and embossed with a frieze of aquatic creatures.[25] By reason of its asymmetrical form, the ewer always presented a challenge to the goldsmith who was endowed with imagination as well as skill.

Though unmarked, the attractive ewer in the Victoria and Albert Museum has some claim to be accepted as English.[26] The body is composed of a fifteenth-century rock-crystal that has been cut down at the neck. This may be another relic of some monastic treasury. The quality of the goldsmith's work corresponds to that of the average English master during the second half of the sixteenth century, and many features of its design, including the precious stones, are also found on the Rutland Ewer. The Tudor royal inventories list a great many vessels garnished with stones, often of slight merit, and some of these must surely have been of English make.

The most usual type of Elizabethan ewer had an ovoid body with an applied mask under the spout and an S-scroll handle of Italian derivation, such as that of 1583-4 illustrated in pl. 687. The handle and some details of the ornament of the body are taken from the engraved design of Agostino dei Musi of 1531 (pl. 12). This is one of his most restrained designs and it is probably not just chance that this, rather than the far more adventurous conceits of Enea Vico (pl. 14) was chosen by the English goldsmith. More typical of the contemporary interest in novelty in design is the ewer of 1586 from the Rijksmuseum, Amsterdam, (pl. 685). While this is of complex construction and adventurous profile, the companion basin (pl. 686) follows the convention of the period with two embossed borders, one around the central boss, the other running around the rim. Usually the embossed decoration of both ewer and basin had marine associations but in this case, they are wrought with various kinds of wild animal, with, it must be admitted, more imagination than skill in working plate. The finest surviving English ewer with oviform body and accompanying basin is that bearing the Norwich hall-mark for 1617-18 which was presented later in the seventeenth century to the Corporation of the city of Norwich by the seventh Duke of Norfolk. These two pieces are struck with an unknown maker's mark and are of typically Dutch form and decoration (pls. 620, 621). They were either made overseas and marked in England or, perhaps, made in England by a Dutch immigrant; they are here included with Dutch goldsmiths' work (pls. 620, 621).

Flagons and Jugs

The Tudor royal inventories include a great variety of flagons and pots nearly all of which have long since been destroyed. One of the interesting items under this heading is no. 874 'one Lion being a Jugge of silver guilt'. Though cups and other vessels made in the form of animals or birds of German origin far outnumber those made elsewhere, two English examples of great size and splendour have survived; these are the huge pair of flagons modelled in the form of leopards that were sent in 1626 from London to Russia, where they joined many others that had previously been given by the Hanseatic League delegation (see p.236). The remain in the Kremlin[27] with much other Elizabethan and Jacobean silver and represent a type of English plate which, apart from a few nautilus shells in bird form, has all but disappeared. They bear the London hall-mark for 1601-2 and, prior to their sale to Russia, had formed part of the 'Great Gilt Cupboard of Estate' of the English royal household - that is to say, they were decorative plate for display on state occasions. In all eighty-two items were sold to Russia in 1626 from the Great Gilt Cupboard; presumably these were selected as being out of date, of impracticable size and of great value on account of their weight — 1184 ounces.

Such large vessels were only likely to be found in the wealthiest households, but silver-mounted pottery jugs had a wide distribution in England. Two main types were popular, both of German Rhenish origin, mottled brown stoneware from Cologne and white stoneware from Siegburg. They were of bellied form and were provided with silver-usually gilt-mounts to foot, rim and handle, while the cover was entirely of silver or silver-gilt. As the earlier specimens are not fully marked it is impossible to date them precisely, but they were certainly in fashion for a long period from about 1540 until the end of the century. The majority date from the last quarter of the century. The mottled stoneware jugs were quite unpretentious objects and were not thought worthy of anything more elaborate than a pewter mount in their country of origin. Why they should have been given such extravagant treatment in England has never been explained. Presumably the mere fact that they came from some foreign source gave them an exotic attraction and greater value. Judging by the large number of mounted examples that survive they can never have been rare. Curiously enough, no unmounted examples of the mottled stoneware jugs are known, whereas there are plenty of unmounted Siegburg jugs, but these may have been imported in subsequent centuries. The jugs exported to England differed from the usual German type, which was decorated with a relief head of a bearded man just below the neck — from which is derived the modern name of Bartmannskrug. The English type is devoid of decoration, relying for its effect on the attractive mottled glaze. English enamelled earthenware — Wrotham ware — was also mounted in silver, but few examples exist. While the majority of the stoneware jugs were mounted in London, a high proportion bear Exeter marks; the jugs have presumably been shipped direct to the ports of Plymouth or Barnstaple. Others were shipped to and mounted in Norwich. The mounts were either embossed with the usual ornament of grotesque masks alternating with bunches of fruit, or engraved with mauresques or, on the finer examples, with figure subjects. The embossing and chasing is usually of undistinguished quality or worse, whereas the engraving maintains a better level. In general one can lay it down that mounted vessels of this period represent the highest standard of craftsmanship, but these stoneware jugs constitute a curious exception. Most of them are simple pieces apparently destined for the bourgeois table. Similar mounts were provided for more valuable ceramic wares such as late Ming vases or bowls and the splendidly colourful jugs from Isnik in Turkey.

The form of the tankard was more dominated by function than most vessels and for that reason few are illustrated in a study concerned with the fantastic and the original in goldsmiths' work. The typical Elizabethan tankard had an upwards tapering cylindrical body strengthened by several widely projecting mouldings (pl. 680). Though the tankard was uniform in shape a variety of materials were used, ranging from precious rock-crystal and jasper to serpentine, alabaster, glass and ceramic wares. Rock-crystal was available in some quantity in England. Quite apart from the fragments which were obtained from dismantled medieval church plate, there must have been an import trade in rock-crystal; there are many Elizabethan cups and tankards with the London hallmark and bowls or bodies of rock-crystal. As a rule the rock-crystal must have been imported unmounted but the candlesticks illustrated in pl. 689 seem to have been remounted in England and made more important by the addition of larger bases and drip-pans. Very few English vessels have the rock-crystal parts engraved with figure subjects or even scrollwork; as a rule they are only shaped and facetted in the manner associated with Freiburg im Breisgau.

The Tudor royal inventories refer to another vessel of foreign origin, 'Hans Pottes'. These were presumably the large and richly ornamented flagons that are described above under the heading of *Hansekannen*. The 1574 inventory includes two of crystal, one each of alabaster and marble as well as a number of plain gilt ones.[28] Assuming that these Hans pots were in fact of Baltic origin, they had little influence upon English fashion in flagons, for the standard English type, still represented in many English churches where they were used as communion flagons, has a cylindrical body, sometimes finely engraved but usually roughly embossed. The type is well represented amongst the English plate in the Kremlin.[29]

The most readily obtainable and therefore the least costly of the exotic materials that were mounted by the goldsmith was shell or mother-of-pearl. This was much used by goldsmiths both in England (pl. 674) and on the Continent, as the amount of silver required to mount such vessels was small. They were often unmarked and identification of the country of origin is sometimes difficult, if not impossible. The attractive shell flask in pl. 690 was in England about the middle of the seventeenth century, but this does not necessarily prove that it was of English make. Its presence in England is indicated by a most important piece of evidence illustrating the taste and resources of an English East Anglian family in the seventeenth century. This is the painting of the silver treasure of the Paston family (pl. 688). Although painted towards the middle of the seventeenth century, most of the articles shown were made in the late sixteenth or early seventeenth century, and taken together, constitute a typical Mannerist *Kunst und Wunder Kammer*. Thirteen pieces of goldsmiths' work are included, of which only two are certainly English. The collection conforms to sixteenth-century practice in that so few of the vessels have much practical use. There are three nautilus-shell[30] and two strombus-shell cups, all decorative pieces; the large German cylindrical tankard in the middle of the picture, which dates from the middle decades of the century would be usable, as would the English flagon embossed with shell pattern held by the negro. The other shell cups are stoutly constructed, but would be inconvenient for drinking purposes. This leaves the three flasks on the right hand side of the picture; these might well be used for containing perfume. The presence of so much foreign silver can, perhaps be explained by the connections of the family with Norwich and trade with the Netherlands.

Few English goldsmiths of the sixteenth century are represented by a sufficiently large number of surviving pieces for any adequate account to be given of their style and progress. The most distinguished during the latter part of the century was the miniaturist, Nicholas Hilliard, who was admitted a Freeman of the Worshipful Company of Goldsmiths on July 29, 1569. His first miniature of the Queen is dated 1572, so his appointment as royal 'goldsmith, engraver and limner' probably dates from before that year. Unfortunately, the many references to Hilliard in the Minute Books of the Goldsmiths' Company appertain to jewellery and do not come within the scope of this book. There seems to be little doubt that he made some of the jewelled frames in which his miniature portraits were placed. Nicholas's father, Richard Hilliard, was an Exeter goldsmith and three of his works have been identified; one of these,[31] a font-shaped Grace cup has been dated to the period 1560-65, though, if this dating be correct, he must have been far behind his London colleagues as far as fashion is concerned.

One London goldsmith, who used the mark TVZ in monogram, is still represented by an important body of work. There are two tall covered cups by him in the Victoria and Albert Museum (pl. 663) and Christ's College, Cambridge, a rock-crystal cup and cover with gilt mounts in the church of Tong in Shropshire,[32] a large salt at Woburn Abbey,[33] a smaller vase-shaped salt in the Museum of Melbourne, Australia, and a vase-shaped pepper in the Victoria and Albert Museum. The two standing cups bear the London hall-mark for 1611-12; the remainder are unmarked. The fact that, out of six known pieces by this master, only two are marked shows how ineffective were the hall-marking regulations of the early seventeenth century. Their maker devised an original scheme of decoration, which is repeated on all these pieces, delicate scrolling and interlacing foliage with berries applied in relief to a matt ground. This group can be attributed to a single maker because of the individual treatment of ornament. Other unmarked vessels by him may well remain unrecognised because they are decorated in a different manner.

Among other makers who are represented by a fair number of marked pieces are two goldsmiths who specialised in the standard type of steeple cup that was so popular in England during the first half of the seventeenth century.[34] One, who marked with the letters AB in monogram, is represented by fifteen of these cups all made between 1602 and 1615, while the second, who marked with the letters FT or TF in monogram, is still represented by no fewer than twenty-five cups made between 1606 and 1639 (pl. 664).

1 ill. E. A. Jones, *Old Plate of the Cambridge Colleges*, 1905, pl. I.

2 For a fuller account see J. F. Hayward, 'A rock-crystal bowl from the Treasury of Henry VIII', *Burlington Magazine*, April, 1968, p.120-124.

3 Collins, p.285.

4 *Archaeologia*, Vol. XV, p.279.

5 *Badisches Generallandesarchiv*, Karlsruhe. Sig. 77-3889. See also Brunner cat. no. 40, where, however, the mounts are curiously described as French, an opinion since retracted in correspondence. It is true that mauresques in black and white enamel were much used by French goldsmiths, but the mauresque was not confined to France.

6 Halm und Berliner, pl. 93.

7 J. Evans, 'Huguenot Goldsmiths in England and Ireland', *Proceedings of the Huguenot Society of London*, Vol. XIV, 1933.

8 *Proceedings of the Huguenot Society*, Vol. X Part 1,19.

9 C. C. Oman, 'A Silver-gilt cup from Queen Elizabeth', *Burlington Magazine*, Vol. 59, p.194-9.

10 See T. F. Reddaway, 'Elizabethan London: Goldsmiths Row 1558-1645', *Guildhall Miscellany*, vol. II, no. 5.

11 Some old illustrations of this cup show it with an incongruous, and later, pineapple finial instead of the present one, which is a restoration based on an old print.

12 The suggestion in the catalogue of the exhibition *Silver Treasures from English Churches*, London, 1955, cat. no. 27, that the central plaque was an importation mounted in England is unacceptable as it is made in one piece with the border, which has typically English engraved decoration.

13 Compare also the Delft cup of 1604 and the Zwolle cup dated 1605, ill. Frederiks, Vol. IV, nos. 18 and 48 respectively.

14 *Inventaire des Bijoux et de l'Orfèvrerie appartenant à la Comtesse de Sault*, Paris, 1882.

15 Fontainebleau I, p.542, nos. 104, 5, 6.

16 Menzhausen, pl. 35.

17 Y. Hackenbroch, 'A Mysterious Monogram', *Bulletin of the Metropolitan Museum of Art*, vol. XIX, 1960.

18 Oman IV, p.65.

19 ill. Collins, pl. VI, p.587.

20 ill. E. A. Jones, *The Old Royal Plate in the Tower of London*, Oxford, 1908, pl. II.

21 K. Lange, *Peter Flötner*, Berlin, 1897, nos. 76-78.

22 This bears the mark of three trefoils within a trefoil, which may have been an earlier mark of the master of the standing cup of St. John's Cambridge, ill. pl. 664.

23 Oman II, p.25.

24 Collins, p.457.

25 ill. E. A. Jones, *The Collection of the Baroness James de Rothschild*, London, 1912, pl. XXII, there described as Flemish, early seventeenth century (?).

26 ill. J. F. Hayward, 'The Mannerist Goldsmiths: 4, Part II', *Connoisseur*, Vol. 164, p.23. The re-use of fragments of rock-crystal from medieval reliquaries is discussed by H. Tait, 'The Stonyhurst Salt', *Apollo*, Vol. LXXIX, p.270ff.

27 Oman II, ill. frontispiece, p.57-9.

28 Collins, p.440-442.

29 Oman II, pl. 26a, b.

30 Two of the nautilus-cups survive, one in the Rijksmuseum, Amsterdam and one in the Prinsenhof, Delft, the third was once in the collection of Horace Walpole at Strawberry Hill (Sale Catalogue 12.V.1842, no. 7). See also exhibition catalogue *The Orange and the Rose*, London, 1964, nos. 80, 141, 152.

31 ill. E. Auerbach, *Nicholas Hilliard*, London, 1961, pl. 170.

32 ill. *Silver Treasures from English Churches*, London, 1955, pl. XIII, no. 80.

33 ill. M. Clayton, *Dictionary of Silver and Gold*, London 1971, pl. 37.

34 See *Proceedings of the Society of Silver Collectors*, London, n.d. 'An Index of English Silver Steeple Cups.' by Dr. N. Penzer.

CHAPTER SIXTEEN

The Goldsmith as Armourer and Base Metal Worker

ONE of the side-lines of the sixteenth-century goldsmith was the production of sword-hilts and scabbard- and belt-mounts. The finest were of gold enriched with enamel and jewels, others were of silver, either plain or enamelled in translucent colours. A more functional type was basically of steel, damascened or overlaid with a sheathing of gold or silver. The ordinary sword-hilt maker, working in base metal to one or other of a number of established patterns, did not require much guidance as to design; the goldsmith, on the other hand, was required to produce hilts of great value and individual pattern and was, therefore, venturing into unfamiliar territory. He needed a design to guide him, hence the considerable number of original drawings of sword-hilts of this period which survive, all for pieces of great splendour intended for kings, princes or wealthy noblemen.

Sword-hilts wrought in precious metal by court goldsmiths are no less international in character than the drinking-vessels made at the same time, and the same difficulty exists in establishing their place of origin. They constituted a form of masculine jewellery and were subject to much the same rules of fashion as feminine jewellery. They were also among the first articles to be broken up when they ceased to be fashionable in order to recover the precious metals and jewels of which they were constructed. It follows that few swords with gold hilts survive; the largest group is that preserved in the Historisches Museum, Dresden, from the collection of the former Electors of Saxony. The surviving graphic designs for sword-hilts are with few exceptions of German, Italian, French and Spanish origin.

The German Cultural Region

Hans Holbein the Younger

The dagger type carried in Switzerland and, to a lesser extent, in Germany during the second and third quarters of the sixteenth century has in modern times been given the name of 'Holbein dagger'. The type was certainly not invented by Hans Holbein the Younger, but there is no doubt that he produced a number of designs for it. The typical 'Holbein dagger' had a scabbard with decoration running horizontally from locket to chape, indicating that it was intended to be worn almost at right angles to the body. The art of the goldsmith was expressed in the scabbard rather than the hilt, which was with few exceptions undecorated. The scabbard was cast from bronze or brass and pierced with one or other of a variety of subjects drawn from the Bible (pl. 691), classical history or legend (pl. 693) or with a purely decorative composition. A few made of silver-gilt survive, and there may once have been many more, but since destroyed to recover the precious metal. An original drawing by Holbein in the Basel Kupferstichkabinett shows a scabbard of this type decorated with the Dance of Death, which in turn was derived from a medieval wall-painting. Judging by the number of examples with this subject surviving, it must have been the most frequently made. Another Holbein drawing shows a Roman triumph; two slightly variant examples of this are recorded.[3] Holbein also designed dagger sheaths in which the ornament ran vertically.[4] German customers seemed to have preferred this construction to the Swiss version. There are three superb engraved designs for this type of sheath by Heinrich Aldegrever; the decoration is divided into panels of figures by three convex bands. The designs are dated 1536, 1537 and 1539 respectively.[5] Whereas the sheaths of Swiss daggers were constructed of panels, cast in two or three pieces and set into a framework, the German ones were usually embossed from sheet. A dagger with silver hilt and sheath of this type, unmarked but evidently of German origin and dating from the mid-sixteenth century, is illustrated (pl. 692).

During his residence in England Holbein designed a number of sword- and dagger-hilts for the court of Henry VIII. In these he made more adventurous use of Mannerist ornament than he had in his vessel designs. The most finished of his hilt drawings was prepared for Prince Edward, later Edward VI (pl. 222). Two other incomplete hilt designs by Holbein show an elaboration of figure ornament that would have made them, if they were ever executed, among the most splendid of their time. The finer (pl. 221) must also have been intended for Henry VIII. Of original form, the scabbard and hilt are peopled by innumerable minute figures of boys and monsters.

Wenzel Jamnitzer

It is only to be expected that so typical a Renaissance man, master of every aspect of his art, as Wenzel Jamnitzer should have designed presentation swords. One of his earliest designs is that for the Sword of State of the Emperor Charles V (pls. 218-20). The drawing is dated 1544 and the sword was actually made to Jamnitzer's design: it can be recognised in an inventory dated 1563,[6] prepared after the death of Charles V, and again in another inventory dated 1602. Thereafter it disappears from the Spanish royal inventories, presumably because it had been destroyed. The 1602 inventory gives a lengthy description of it:

'A sword, the blade engraved with the imperial eagles with the columns and with the motto *Plus Ultra;* the cross, the pommel, the grip and the scabbard are of silver-gilt, partly enamelled in black; the branches of the cross take the form of female figures and terminate in masks and the grip is worked with mauresques; the pommel is decorated with four female figures and the cross of the guard with four lizards, one of which is detached and on one side of the guard there is a mask. The portrait of the Emperor together with his motto *Plus Ultra* and the imperial eagles can be seen on the scabbard; there are also seven vacant spaces for rock-crystal escutcheons, which are now detached. The sword is in an open case covered with black velvet.'

It is probable that the series of sword- and dagger-hilt and sheath designs engraved by Solis about the middle of the century were also based on lost drawings by Wenzel Jamnitzer. The treatment of the scabbard locket (pl. 223) with a figure standing in a niche, was to become one of the most popular features of sword-hilt design of the second half of the sixteenth century. Whichever aspect of German mid-sixteenth century goldsmiths' work one chooses to examine, the influence of Jamnitzer is encountered. While there is no reason to think that the mounts of the swords (pls. 695-8) were either designed or made by Jamnitzer, it is evident that the artist who embossed them came within his circle.

Erasmus Hornick

The designs of the Flemish-born goldsmith, Erasmus Hornick, continue the fashion introduced by Wenzel Jamnitzer and Virgil Solis. Hornick is represented by a series of ten sheets of drawings in the Victoria and Albert Museum and in the Metropolitan Museum, New York: two of rapiers with their companion daggers, seven of scimitars and one of a powder-flask. There is also a number of drawings of purse mounts which may have been intended to form part of the same series and to be published in a printed pattern-book. The rapier-hilt designs show weapons that would have been quite service-able. The grips have the rather protruberant profile that also occurs in the Solis prints and on a group of extant hilts damascened with gold and silver, some of which are signed by the Spanish master, Diego da Çaias.[8]

The Hornick rapier-hilts could have been executed either in precious or in base metal. The proportions are correct and one feels that the artist had a good idea of how a sword should handle. From the aesthetic point they are no less satisfactory. While making use of the usual standing or reclining figures in niches, the designs achieve an interesting profile and are not over-decorated (pl. 226). Their construction is peculiar in that they lack the upper ring-guard, but this may have been omitted by the artist in order to display the ornament on the cross more effectively.

Hornick's seven scimitar designs are Italianate in style and may be copied from Italian sources. A number have pommels in the form of lion's or monster's heads (pl. 224) like the Orso designs; others are quite different with pommels ending in volutes (pl. 225). Another page of designs from the same series shows two knives, forks and spoons, two toothpicks and a pair of snuffers, all of unmistakably Italian type. Hornick was probably working in Nürnberg when he produced these designs; it is not, therefore, surprising to find, among the models attributed to the Jamnitzer workshop in the Historisches Museum, Basel, two lead patterns for a knife-handle (pl. 694) which correspond to Hornick's scimitar-handles. The most similar hilt surviving is not, however, of precious metal but of chiselled iron. This hilt has been attributed to Thomas Rücker of Augsburg, maker of the chiselled iron throne-chair presented to the Emperor Rudolph II by the city of Augsburg, but is, in fact, closer to the manner of the Munich master, Othmar Wetter.[9] Among the drawings from the Hornick codex in the Victoria and Albert Museum are two of a sword (pl. 227) and companion dagger that appear to be the work of another hand and are closer in style to the Virgil Solis designs. They correspond to the type of rapier-hilt that was fashionable during the 1560's and 1570's. These designs owe little to Italian prototypes; instead of the neatly arranged ornament of Hornick's scimitar-hilts, we have a busy composition that most closely resembles the enamelled gold hilt in the Munich Residenz (pl. 702) or those in the Historisches Museum, Dresden, which are here attributed to a Spanish goldsmith.

A rapier and companion dagger with enamelled gold hilts at Dresden are known to have been presented to the Elector August of Saxony by Duke Albrecht of Bavaria in 1567. The hilts (pl. 699) are enamelled with green snakes within bunches of fruit against a gold ground champlevé enamelled with black scrollwork. They were probably made by one of the goldsmiths attached to the Munich court. Also connected with Munich, and perhaps made there, are the sword and dagger with belt that are shown in the pictorial inventory of the Wittelsbach Treasure prepared by Hans Mühlich in 1570. The hilts are of gold, enamelled black and white and profusely set with precious stones (pls. 228-9). Their presence in the inventory is not a final proof of their German origin, but they differ considerably from the swords of Spanish type at Dresden. The knife which accompanies the sword scabbard has a handle of pilaster shape corresponding to those of a set of knife, fork and spoon of silver-gilt with translucent enamel in the Victoria and Albert Museum,[10] which bear the Augsburg town mark. Another sword, of which only a pictorial record survives, appears to be of German origin. In this case the hilt was to be decorated exclusively with scrollwork inhabited by mice executed in translucent enamel (pl. 230).

While many sixteenth-century sword-hilt designs are essentially impracticable, none quite equals the sabre from the collection of the Archduke Ferdinand of Tirol in the Kunsthistorisches Museum, Vienna, the hilt of which is formed from a single branch of coral, but a branch of such shape that it could hardly have been held in the hand. The coral was presumably supplied from Genoa, but the origin of the sword as a whole is probably German. It presumably occupied a place in the Archduke's *Kunstkammer* at

Ambras rather than in his Wardrobe.[11] The equestrian guard of the Elector August of Saxony were furnished with silver mounted equipment, comprising swords, daggers, pistols, priming and powder-flasks. Most of this equipment has survived in the Historisches Museum, Dresden, though some has been sold in the course of the present century. The silver mounts were supplied by Dresden goldsmiths and a few pieces bear their marks. They were etched with mauresques or engraved with scrolling foliage inhabited by birds with ruffled plumage. The Dresden Hofstallarchiv contains references to the ordering and delivery of silver mounted swords and other weapons by members of the Dresden goldsmith family of Unter den Linden.[12] The Dresden rapiers or *Panzerstecher* (literally armour piercer) with cross hilts sheathed in etched or engraved silver rank among the best designed weapons of their period. Twenty-nine swords, probably of this type, and their companion daggers were supplied by Wendel unter den Linden in 1587 for the guard of Christian I and a further twelve were supplied in 1604 for the guard of Duke Johann Georg who succeeded as Elector in 1611. One of these swords of *Panzerstecher* type, now in the von Kienbusch Collection, New York, has on the scabbard the mark attributed by Rosenberg to Wolf Paller, but according to Holzhausen of Wendel unter den Linden.[13] Most are unmarked, but the quality of the etched or engraved decoration on these weapons is invariably high. Another Saxon type of sword with broad blade and swept hilt (now described as a *Reitschwert*) was supplied with hilt and scabbard mounts plated with silver. In this case the precious metal was hatched on — i.e., hammered on to a surface prepared by cross-hatching.

During the second half of the century gilt bronze was introduced as a material for firearm mounts as well as sword hilts. This was an almost exclusively German fashion and the main centres of production were Augsburg, Nürnberg and Dresden. The fashion flourished with particular strength in Saxony and the gilt-bronze mounts found on Saxon swords, daggers and firearms were, like the silver mounts for which they were a less expensive alternative, made in Dresden. In the case of firearms the mounts took the form of butt- and pommel-caps, inlays in the stock, and plaques applied to lock-plate or barrel. Few hilts that could be described as goldsmiths' work were of gilt-bronze; the finest of the Dresden hilts is that made by Israel Schuech for the Elector Christian II.[14] It is superbly chiselled with figures within strapwork cartouches and is set with pearls, shell cameos and paste jewels (pl. 706). Both sword- and dagger-hilts and firearm furniture were also decorated with damascening in gold and silver and much of this work was carried out by goldsmiths.

Jakob Mores

A group of hilt designs associated with the Hamburg goldsmith and dealer, Jakob Mores, were perhaps intended for the court of Frederick II of Denmark.[15] His sister Anna married the Elector August of Saxony and, as a result, Saxon fashion was followed at the Danish court. There are five drawings, showing swords, daggers and belts. The two rapiers are typically Saxon and can be paralleled by others in the former Saxon Electoral armoury, though, being designed for a prince or nobleman, they are somewhat richer than those carried by members of the Electoral Guard. It was usual for persons of rank to own a garniture of edged weapons consisting of three, four or five pieces. In this case the rapier to the right of the drawing (pl. 232) probably went *en suite* with the hunting-knife in the centre and also with the dagger (pl. 231), the decoration of all three being closely related. An attractive feature of the drawings is the design of the scabbard mounts with either groups or single figures in classical costume. These are sketched with pleasing naiveté and recall another set of drawings, this time for the engraved staghorn panels on German wheel-lock firearms, in the Victoria and Albert Museum. Most of these derive from woodcuts by the Nürnberg master, Jost Amman.[16] Another drawing (pl. 233) shows a design for a dagger with an enamelled gold hilt set with rubies and diamonds, which does not this time follow Saxon fashion.

Spain

By far the most important enamelled gold sword-hilts are the group of five rapiers with companion daggers preserved in the Historisches Museum, Dresden. The Dresden inventories record their history. The earliest (pl. 700) was presented to the Elector August by Maximilian, later Emperor, but then King of Rome, at the Frankfurt election in 1562. The second (pl. 699), which has been discussed above, was presented to the same prince by Duke Albrecht of Bavaria in 1567, the third by the Archduke Ferdinand of Tirol on his return from Karlsbad via Dresden in 1574, once again to the Elector August, while the last two were presented by the Emperor Maximilian II in 1575 to the Elector (pl. 703) and to the young Prince Christian (pl. 701). The maker of the rapier and companion dagger presented to the Elector August on that occasion is recorded, since on June 2, 1576 the goldsmith of the Empress Maria, Pery Juan Pockh, received the sum of 399 gulden for the precious metal and 1000 Rhenish gulden for making them. Pockh (see p.267) had been trained in Spain and was a member of the Barcelona Guild of Goldsmiths, but his name suggests that his family was of German origin. He was admitted Master in Barcelona in 1551 and it seems likely, therefore, that his parents emigrated to Spain with the court of the Emperor Charles V. The swords presented by the Habsburgs to the Saxon ruling house are so similar that it is likely that all four were made by Juan Pery Pockh. The most striking feature of the sword known to have been made by Pockh (pl. 703) is the web of interlacing strapwork wrought in high relief that covers each element of the hilt, and through which snakes with enamelled blue scales make their way on both pommel and grip. Presented at the same time as this sword is the smaller one (pl. 701); the construction of its hilt, the decoration of its quillons, arms of the guard and ring-guard are so similar to pl. 703 that its attribution also to Pockh can be accepted.

Of the other Dresden swords that in pl. 700, which is, however, probably some ten years earlier in date, is very similar. It has the same form of quillon terminals while the treatment of the grip corresponds to that of pl. 703. Turning to the sword-hilt (pl. 705) it will be seen that it also corresponds closely in design to pl. 703, except that it has the additional feature of snakes amongst the straps.[17] Finally the Munich sword (pl. 702) is closely related to pl. 701, the main difference being in the treatment of the grip which is divided into compartments filled with figures, masks and bunches of fruit by low relief strapwork.

This group of enamelled gold hilts by or attributed to Pockh can be extended by three others. When the French troops captured Malta in the course of the Napoleonic Wars, they took as booty an enamelled gold sword and dagger,[18] of which, according to a tradition of uncertain date and origin, the sword had been presented to the Order of St. John of Malta by Philip II of Spain, while the dagger had been given by Pope Pius IV to Jean Parisot de la Valette, Grand Master of the Order (1474-1568). It is extremely unlikely that a sword and companion dagger of like design and make should have been presented by two different donors, and in view of the Spanish character of the hilts, these two pieces can be accepted as being of Spanish make. The third hilt is that of the sword in the Kassel Museum, which is of closely similar design. If we are correct in thinking that the four rapiers with their companion daggers at Dresden can be attributed to Pery Juan Pockh and that they do, in fact, represent Spanish fashion of the time, and that the Munich sword, the Kassel sword and the sword with companion dagger in the Louvre are also of Spanish origin, then the Spanish group becomes the largest and most consistent in design amongst all the surviving examples of hilts made by sixteenth-century goldsmiths. That there was an important production of gold-hilted swords in Spain is proved, firstly, by the presence of so many sword- or dagger-hilts among the masterpiece drawings submitted to the Barcelona Goldsmiths' Guild in the sixteenth century and, secondly, by the presence of a number of them in the inventory made by order of Philip II in 1554. Most of the swords listed in this inventory[19] were made by

Juan de Soto of Barcelona, but a particularly fine one was made for the king by another goldsmith named Rodrigo.[20] Contemporary portraits of Philip II show him wearing swords with enamelled gold hilts of this type, as for example that by Antonio Moro at Althorp, Northamptonshire, in which the hilt is shown in great detail. Spanish goldsmiths were famous for their jewellery and the manufacture of sword hilts of enamelled gold was a closely related activity. There appear, however, to be no sixteenth-century swords with gold hilts surviving in Spanish public collections.

The designs submitted to the Goldsmiths' Guild of Barcelona include several of sword-hilts. Those illustrated in pls. 234-6 date from the years 1537 and 1538. The rapier-hilt (pl. 235) corresponds in form to the gold hilts at Dresden which were constructed thirty years later; the ornament consists of minute arabesques presumably intended to be executed in black enamel against a gold ground. Much the same ornament is used for the dagger (pl. 234) and the ear-dagger in Venetian style (pl. 236), a type which persisted in Spain long after it had been abandoned elsewhere. The curious form of the quillons of the dagger in pl. 234 suggests that the goldsmith was unfamiliar with dagger construction and was relying upon his imagination.

Italy

Some of the finest surviving gold hilts are Italian and there are a good number of contemporary Italian drawings in existence. One of the most lively and original designs is that illustrated in pl. 237. Having been preserved in Florence, it has, almost inevitably, been attributed to Benvenuto Cellini. This attribution is highly speculative, but the drawing dates from the period when Cellini was employed by the Grand Duke Cosimo. It is more effective than the Spanish sword-hilts described above because undecorated areas are left between the sculptured details of the hilt.

Filippo Orso

An exceptionally complete picture of Italian mid-sixteenth-century sword-hilt fashions is provided by the album of drawings by the Mantuan artist, Filippo Orso, or Orsoni, in the Victoria and Albert Museum, London. The album was probably intended to be engraved and published, for it is preceded by a title-page on which its scope and the author's name are given. One of the sheets is dated 1554. Besides thirty-nine pages of hilt designs, it also has designs for pageant costumes, armours and horse-bits. Orso describes himself on the title-page as *Pictor Mantuanus;* this implies that he produced the drawings on behalf of a goldsmith or armourer. He is not likely to have furnished sword-hilts himself. The sword-hilt designs are introduced in the following terms 'Here begin the forty (actually thirty-nine) sheets on which are forty designs for garniture, furniture or hilts for swords for use on foot or in the saddle, also cutlasses for horsemen and scimitars for foot-soldiers, made with excellent design, and all different in chiselling and relief. They can be made by masters with skill in such arts, provided they are well rewarded' Each of the drawings is accompanied by notes recommending its merits in rather naive terms, the main interest of which lies in the suggestions as to the material from which each might be made. Some should be of gold or silver, but the majority were only intended to be of iron enriched with precious metal. Orso was very much a child of his days; in his hilt designs (pls. 238-40) he constantly introduces ornament in high relief without consideration for practical convenience. In the case of one hilt with a knuckle bow decorated with festoons of laurel, he does warn the hilt-maker that the points of the foliage must not be rendered in too high relief or they would tear the clothing and injure the hand.[22] Though on the whole the existing Italian sword-hilts are less prickly in appearance than those of Orso, he can be accepted as a good guide to the Italian mid-sixteenth-century sword. That he intended some of the designs for the goldsmith is proved by the fact that the first design of all (pl. 238) was to be decorated with silver or with both silver and gold.[23]

An Italian hilt design dating from the end of the sixteenth century (pl. 241) shows a gold base enriched with enamel, while the pommel is set with precious stones. The design is curiously similar to an extant sword which was presented in 1605 to the Elector Christian II of Saxony by Duke Carlo Emanuele of Savoy.[24] In this case, however, the basic structure of the hilt is of steel which is heavily gold-plated and enriched with rubies and diamonds. Over the surface of the bars of the hilt are applied panels of pierced scrollwork of gold enamelled white, red and blue, in typical Milanese style.

The most magnificent of all extant enamelled gold sword-hilts is that illustrated in pl. 709. Presented to the Emperor Maximilian II in 1549, it represents the very latest fashion in hilts.[25] The sword is recorded in the inventory of the Emperor Maximilian of 1550 and again in that of the Archduke Ferdinand of Tirol of 1596 described as Spanish and, in view of the established pre-eminence of the Spanish goldsmiths in making golden hilts, one hesitates to question this description. Nevertheless, as has been mentioned above (p.190) the term 'Spanish' was sometimes used to describe a particular type of decoration, such as enamelled gold, and there is at least a possibility that the inventory clerks who listed it in 1550 may have used the term in this sense. My reason for making this suggestion is that the design of the hilt does not correspond to Spanish fashion. It is closer to the Italian drawing (pl. 241) particularly in the formation of the quillons and their finials, allowance being made, of course, for the fact that the drawing must be some thirty years later than the Vienna sword. The closest parallel to the detail of the enamelled ornament with its cherubs heads can be found on some of the enamelled gold mounts of the hardstone vessels of about the same date which are believed to have been presented to the Emperor Maximilian II by Cosimo I of Tuscany. In hilt construction the most similar rapier is that presented to the Elector Christian II of Saxony by the Duke of Savoy in 1605: this constitutes another pointer towards an Italian origin. Though the sword at Dresden was not presented until 1605, it may well have been made some decades before. The splendour of the swords worn by the richer Italian princes can be gathered from the description of a garniture of sword and dagger delivered to the Medici Wardrobe in January, 1601, by the court goldsmith, Giacomo Biliverti; the hilts were of enamelled gold set with six hundred and eighty diamonds.[25a] Hainhofer, writing to his patron, Philipp von Pommern, in December, 1610, refers to another commission from the Grand Duke of Tuscany: a sword and dagger with gold hilts covered with diamonds. These were being made in Augsburg, together with a gold travelling service consisting of salt-cellar, bowl, spoon, knife and bodkin, each piece set with diamonds.

France

The most extravagant of the mid-sixteenth-century hilt designs are the set of six engraved roundels (pl. 242) and two larger sheets, each with a hilt and scabbard mounts, by Pierre Woeriot, an artist from Lorraine who worked in Lyon during the middle decades of the century. The six sheets were published in 1555; several sets have survived, which suggests that they must have been sufficiently successful to have been printed in quantity. As a result they are among the best known of their period. They follow the international Mannerist style and it is doubtful whether they really represent French hilt fashion of the time. Like the Spanish designs illustrated in pls. 234-6, they are the work of a goldsmith-designer who did not greatly concern himself with the practical problems of sword-hilt construction. The hilts are of such complexity and delicacy that it would have been extremely difficult to execute them at all in a metal less ductile than gold or silver. There is, however, in the Musée de l'Armée, Paris, a gilt-bronze hilt that is closely related to the Woeriot designs. The connection is most evident in the superbly modelled nude human figures that are bound to the quillons and the knuckle-bow (pl.

704). More remote from the Woeriot prints, perhaps because it is of wrought iron, is the hilt in the Bayerisches Nationalmuseum (pl. 707). In this case the base metal is almost completely covered by a thick plating of gold and silver, further enriched with polychrome enamel. Other comparable hilts are those of a sword of Philip II in the Real Armeria, Madrid,[26] a scimitar in the Musée de l'Armée, Paris,[27] and another in the Vienna Waffensammlung.[28] The small number of swords extant whose design is based on the Woeriot prints is probably due as much to the fact that they were made of gold and have suffered the usual fate of artefacts in that precious material as to the difficulty of executing them. No French hilts made entirely of gold are known to survive from this period; there is, however, in the Swedish Royal Armoury, Stockholm, a scimitar with a gold hilt enriched with translucent enamel and set with rubies and emeralds, which was made by Gilles Coyet, a goldsmith from Brabant who emigrated to Sweden to escape religious persecution (pl. 708).

The gold hilts described above were made of the most precious materials and intended to achieve the most sumptuous effect, but they nevertheless followed the design of the contemporary fighting sword and were entirely functional. They were equipped with the same type of blades and their balance in the hand was impeccable. Few as they are, they constitute a major achievement of the sixteenth century goldsmiths; their brilliant colour effect must have made a splendid contrast to the black court dress in the Spanish fashion and even have held its own against the richest of textiles.

Damascening

The goldsmith was required to master another skill, that of cutting dies for coins, medals or seals. The artists who cut dies for the papal mint were goldsmiths, among them Benvenuto Cellini, Gian Giacomo Bonzagni and Andrea Casalino; in Germany two generations in succession of the Jamnitzer family were die-cutters to the Nürnberg mint. Coin and medal dies had to be cut in steel and a goldsmith who had mastered the difficult art of cutting this hard metal would also be able to decorate the elaborately sculptured armour worn by Renaissance princes. Among these goldsmith-armourers the most distinguished were Leone Leoni, who made both a suit of damascened armour and a golden tazza for Ferrante Gonzaga, Duke of Mantua, and Jacopo da Trezzo, who combined the offices of sculptor, medal die-cutter and goldsmith to Cosimo I, Grand Duke of Tuscany, and subsequently performed the same tasks for Philip II of Spain. Even more varied was the range of Francesco di Girolamo da Prato, the friend of Salviati (see p.143). After being trained in the workshop of his father, whom, according to Vasari,[29] he equalled in skill, he turned to inlaying steel with precious metal. This he did with such excellence that he was commissioned to produce a complete damascened foot-armour for Duke Alessandro de' Medici. Subsequently he made medals, cast bronze figures, some of which were later acquired by Duke Alessandro, and cleaned and polished four bronze figures of gods that had been modelled by Baccio Bandinelli. Finally, however, finding the goldsmith's craft insufficiently interesting and lacking the resources to set up as a sculptor, he became a painter and so continued until his death in 1562. Cellini was also expert in the art of damascening and tells us something of it in the *Vita*.[30] He states that 'some little Turkish daggers fell into my hands . . . these were incised with steel tools with most beautiful foliations in the Turkish manner and then very neatly inlaid with gold. The sight of them stirred me to try my own skill and to work in a technique so different from the others I practised. As I was highly successful I made a number of them. Those I made were much more beautiful and more durable than the Turkish ones for various reasons. One was that I cut the grooves much more deeply and also undercut them, a process which the Turkish craftsmen did not use. The other was that the Turkish arabesques are composed only of arum leaves with a few small sunflowers; while these are not devoid of grace, they do not give as much pleasure as do the arabesques we use. In Italy we have various ways of designing foliage; the Lombards for instance produce most beautiful arabesques by copying the leaves of ivy and briony in exquisite spirals, which are most attractive. The Tuscans and the Romans make a better choice because they reproduce the leaves of the acanthus, called bear's foot, with its stalks and flowers which turn in various ways, and within these little birds and animals can be inserted, thus displaying the taste of the artist.'

In fact, the Italian masters of damascening (azziminia) practiced every variety of design from a strictly abstract mauresque of the type found on Persian arms to the naturalistic patterns in which figure subjects and even scenes were introduced. In the passage quoted Cellini distinguishes the so-called 'false damascene', practiced in Turkey and in India, from the true damascene, in which the gold was laid into undercut channels, practised in Persia and by himself.

The decoration of armour by goldsmiths seems to have been more generally practised in Italy than in northern Europe, presumably because of the more tolerant attitude of the Italian guilds. Among the prominent Italian armourers, who were also goldsmiths, was Bartolommeo Campi of Pesaro, who signed the armour of Charles V at Madrid in the following terms: *Bartholomaus Campi Aurifex*. His skill as a goldsmith and damascener can best be seen on the stirrups belonging to this suit of armour, now in the Victoria and Albert Museum.[31] Another was Giorgio Ghisi of Mantua, who signed the embossed and chased shield in the British Museum, and most important of all, Gasparo Mola. Though Mola was first and foremost a goldsmith, he executed some remarkable decorative work on arms and armour: the garniture of rapier, dagger and belt of steel decorated with panels of translucent enamel in the Musée de l'Armée, Paris,[32] a shield and helmet *en suite* for Grand Duke Cosimo II, decorated with gilt copper tracery[33] and, for the same Tuscan patron, the gold and silver encrustation on a number of iron-stocked wheel lock pistols.[34] Of the shield and helmet, which are still in Florence, a contemporary writer, Petrini, wrote 'The most famous alive today is Gasparo Mola, who has produced some pieces of marvellous quality, in particular a shield and helmet, which are now in the armoury of his Serene Highness; the surface of this is decorated with various figures, and with impressions of medals decorated with the signs of the Zodiac, and while this work is applied in chiselled and gilt silver, it is esteemed a most excellent thing.'[35]

Mola was particularly proud of the sword-hilt with dagger and belt, so much so that he gave detailed instructions about it in his will[36] which dates from about 1630. He bequeathed it along with his pictures, prints and books to the Hospitale di San Carlo al Corso in Milan, describing it as 'an enamelled sword guard, which is a work of exceptional quality and very great value and labour in making and worthy of any great king or emperor. It is a unique piece which perhaps no one will ever make again, and of a new type. The guard with its mounts for the dagger and belt and belt pendants is of enamelled iron; objects which money could not buy, no matter how much. In conclusion its true and honest price ought to be at least 3000 gold scudi. If one were to try to find a suitable person who had the spirit to attempt a similar work.....he would never accept to do it at such a price...and this should be taken into consideration by those great princes so that an honest price be paid. For this guard with its fittings the Grand Duke of Tuscany offered me 1500 scudi which I did not accept. I have given this brief account in order to warn the Superiors of this hospital against being deceived by the words of ignorant persons and selling it for an unworthy price.' Mola seems to have been correct in his statement that no one else would ever attempt to emulate his sword hilt which was worked in champlevé enamels on steel. The labour of cutting the recesses in the steel for the enamels was, of course, an immense one.

Embossing

It has been mentioned above that the same artist might execute the embossed decoration on both iron shields and silver dishes. There is confirmation of this in a passage from the historian of Milan, Paolo Morigia. Writing of the Milanese armourer, Lucio Picinino, he says 'In working both iron and silver in relief, either with figures, grotesques and other monsters, foliage and landscapes this master is most excellent and of rare skill in damascening'.[37] Lucio Picinino was but one among many craftsmen in Milan who produced embossed and damascened armour or plaques for attaching to furniture. The number of surviving pieces is so large as to suggest that the industry in Milan must have been an important one. Picinino was the master of one of the finest of the works of the armourer-goldsmith, the armour of Alessandro Farnese, now in the Vienna Waffen-sammlung.[38] Two other Milanese masters, who are known by name, are Giovanni Battista Serabaglio and Marc Antonio Fava: they received payment in 1560 for a magnificent armour for man and horse which they had made for the Archduke Ferdinand, of the Tirol. The whole surface of this armour, also in Vienna,[39] is embossed, chased and damascened in gold and silver, the relief-work being by Serabaglio and the damascening by Fava. Little is known of these masters, though Serabaglio is praised by two sixteenth-century historians of Milan, Paolo Morigia and Paolo Lomazzo.

The goldsmith or the designer of goldsmiths' work might also be asked to provide designs for the decoration of armour. The most interesting and extensive surviving group of French decorative designs of this period was intended for the armourer. It comprises one hundred and twenty drawings by a number of artists, probably both Italian and French, for François I, for his son, Henri II, and for the latter's sons also, Charles IX and Henri III. Most of them are in the Staatliche Graphische Sammlung, Munich, but others are in the national collections in England and the U.S.A.[40] Besides the drawings, many of the original armours have survived, though none from the reign of François I. The earlier designs, dating from the 1530's and 1540's, show how powerful was the influence of Fontainebleau on the French court workshop; it is possible that these designs were, as has been suggested by Bruno Thomas,[41] the work of Rosso himself. There seems no doubt that the earliest designs are Italian; they are dominated by a network of straps which are rendered more effective by the powerful relief in which they are shown. Similar designs pervaded by strapwork can be seen in the *oeuvre* of René Voyvin of about the same date (pls. 99, 102).

A change of emphasis is found in the later designs, dating from the reign of Henri II, who was a great patron of the armourers. Under the guidance of his taste, design became more classical, less fantastic and drawings were now provided by Etienne Delaune. Armours made to his design were produced in an almost indistinguishable manner in Paris and also in Antwerp. Neither the names of the masters who worked on them nor the exact situation of the French royal workshop are known, but one Antwerp goldsmith, who decorated some of the finest examples of the armourer's craft, is known, namely Eliseus Libaerts.[42] A finely embossed armour made in the French royal workshops for King Henri II, but apparently never assembled in his lifetime, was formerly exhibited in the Louvre in close proximity to the silver dish illustrated in pl. 378. A comparison of the two showed the most striking similarity in both execution and design, sufficiently close to suggest that the same workshop may have decorated both. Guild regulations would not have favoured their members working a base metal and iron was certainly much more difficult a material than gold or silver, but in the court workshops the guild could be ignored. The masters who embossed and chiselled armours in the sixteenth century showed a skill that equalled and sometimes surpassed that of most contemporary decorators of precious metal.

Many sumptuously decorated armours, helmets and shields from the Paris and the Antwerp workshops survive, but one shield (pl. 710) and helmet (pl. XXIV) stand out above the rest for the magnificence of their appearance. Both were made, or at any rate decorated, by the same artist, though they do not match each other exactly. They are believed to have been supplied shortly before 1570 to King Charles IX, whose cypher they bear, by a Parisian goldsmith, Pierre Redon, who was *Valet de Chambre* to Antoine de Bourbon, King of Navarre (reigned 1555-1562). Redon's widow received a payment of 5000 livres for the shield in February, 1572, giving a *terminus ante quem*. In shape the shield corresponds to many others based on Delaune's designs; of oval form, the central panel is embossed with a battle scene within an elaborate Fontainebleau-type strapwork border. Above and below are grotesque masks flanked by manacled prisoners, while the outer border is decorated with oval panels bearing the crowned monogram of Charles IX alternating with crossed laurel branches. The shield differs, however, from all the others of similar composition in that the whole surface is covered with a thick layer of gold, which is in turn decorated with translucent enamels. The morion, which has always been preserved with the shield, is decorated in the same way but with a different colour scheme, the ground being finished black. Once again the panels of battle scenes in the centre of the skull on each side are taken from designs by Delaune. Such splendid arms were not intended for use, but might be carried in front of the sovereign in a Triumph or tournament entry. Thus the shield of Henri II in the Wallace Collection,[43] though made of iron, has never had any carrying-straps and was, perhaps, intended to be hung upon the wall as a trophy, having lost its original function in the same way that in the following century the basin and ewer lost their purposes and became ornamental pieces for the sideboard.

The best-known German goldsmith who decorated armour was Georg Sigman of Augsburg; he was commissioned while still a journeyman to emboss and enrich with damascened ornament in gold a rich armour[44] that had been made by Desiderius Colman of Augsburg for Prince Philip, later King Philip II of Spain. This commission led Sigman into great difficulties with the Augsburg Goldsmiths' Guild, which rejected his claim that the two years between 1549 and 1550 he had worked on the armour should count towards the period he must spend as a journeyman goldsmith in the city before he might submit his masterpiece (see p.41). Subsequently Sigman wrought and embossed an iron shield but never completed it with the gold damascening that was envisaged.[45] He nevertheless signed it in full with his name, place of work and the date of completion: *GEORGIUS SIGMAN AURIFEX AUGUSTE HOC OPUS PERFECIT ANNO DOMINI MDLII MENSE AUGUST DIE XXVII.* His use of the term *Aurifex* (goldsmith) would presumably have been justified by the intended gold damascening. Ten years later in 1562 he signed a sword-hilt which, once again, has no enrichment with precious metal. By this time he had long been a master goldsmith of Augsburg, a position which presumably allowed him to overlook some of the guild regulations. That he was exceptionally skilled is shown by the fact that, when still a journeyman, he was allowed to put his mark twice on the armour of Philip II. His signature on the shield, put in a position where it could not be overlooked, is also unusual for the sixteenth century. In general it is probable that goldsmiths who practised the technique of damascening would not have wrought plate as well; that there were exceptions is proved by the case of Jörg Sigman.

During the second half of the sixteenth century, parade armours decorated with plaques of gilt-copper or even wrought entirely in this material became fashionable. As Sigman lived on in Augsburg until 1601 he may have had some part in their production as well. The earliest of these is the armour of the Emperor Maximilian II in the Kunsthistorisches Museum, Vienna,[46] which was made for him in 1557. In this case the gilt-metal decoration consists of vertical bands and strips following the borders. These are cast of gilt-bronze, and decorated with masks, fruit and figures within strapwork. Of about the same period is the gilt-copper shield in the Hermitage Museum, Leningrad (pl. 725), which is dated 1556 and embossed with concentric rings of ornament, the outermost with hunting subjects, the inner with battle scenes between horsemen, while the central boss shows a Roman general borne on the back of four of his defeated enemies. The shield is sufficiently close to the signed Sigman shield in London to justify attribution to Sigman himself or to his assistant, Jakob Knoll.

The most important assemblage of Augsburg armours decorated with appliques of gilt-bronze or wrought from gilt-copper is in the Historisches Museum, Dresden, and comes from the Armoury of the Electors of Saxony. Among them is a saddle which appears to be entirely Sigman's work. It is profusely decorated with grotesque ornament enclosing figures and roundels within elaborate strapwork cartouches.[47] Of the armours decorated with embossed and gilt copper appliques the most elaborate is that made for the Elector Christian II.[48] According to the 1606 inventory of the Dresden armoury it was purchased from a citizen of Augsburg in 1602, but it must have been completed by 1599, the date which is engraved on the sole of the left shoe. The name of the Augsburg goldsmith or merchant is not recorded; the armour differs from Sigman's accepted *oeuvre* in that the decoration is cast instead of being embossed. It is also rather different in style, the ornament being more profuse and its distribution less organised.

Goldsmiths did not mark their works in base metal; however, the gilt copper burgonet helmet in the Historisches Museum, Dresden (pl. 711) is marked on the silver border of the comb with the Augsburg town mark and with the house mark of an unidentified maker. A recent study of sixteenth-century armourers' work[49] has suggested that Sigman may have been responsible for objects in cast bronze as well. The pieces in question are the set of four pairs of stirrups believed to have been made in 1555 for the Emperor Ferdinand I and his three sons, Maximilian II, Archduke Ferdinand of Tirol and Archduke Carl II of Steiermark. These stirrups were orginally accompanied by a bit and a pair of spurs, but of these only one bit survives in the Vienna Waffensammlung. The suggestion has much to recommend it, for the decoration of the stirrups and bit are very similar to the relief ornament on Philip II's armour at Madrid. As Thomas points out, these stirrups unite the artistic possibilities of sculpture in iron, casting in bronze, etching and gilding.

Base Metal

Besides the manufacture of arms and armour there were other circumstances in which the goldsmith, at any rate in certain countries or regions, worked in base metal. One reason was economy, when objects usually of precious metal were instead made of copper, bronze or brass. Certain articles such as clock and watch-cases, which were usually of copper or bronze, were produced by goldsmiths for the clock-makers, whose sphere was confined to the movement: powder-flasks and mounts for scientific instruments fall in the same class. Finally, articles such as caskets, boxes or cutlery, which were wrought in iron or steel by the blacksmiths or cutlers, were often decorated with additional mounts of precious or base metal supplied by the goldsmith. Furthermore the process of fire- or mercury-gilding metals was a monopoly of the goldsmith, who was, therefore, constantly called in to complete the enrichment of objects made by other crafts.

The properties of bronze and copper are different, the former material being best suited to casting, whereas pure copper could be hammered, chiselled or engraved but not cast. Whether an object was cast from bronze or wrought from copper, once made it was worked with chasing tools in the same way that one of precious metal would be treated. In either case the article was finished by being heavily gilded. After the gilding had been polished, a base metal object could not be readily distinguished from a similar one made of gold or silver; at any rate, not by a purchaser who was ignorant of the technical processes involved. For this reason the guilds discouraged their members from working base metal and in England the Goldsmiths' Company prohibited it altogether. Though some Continental guilds were less strict, the use of base metal was a constant source of trouble between them and their members. Frequent offenders were journeymen-goldsmiths who turned to working base metal as a useful supplement to their income. A typical example is quoted by Neudörffer, the historian of the artists and craftsmen of Nürnberg.[50] The Emperor Maximilian I granted to Sebastian Lindenast, the leading Nürnberg coppersmith, the privilege of gilding or silvering copper, in spite of guild regulations prohibiting it. The guild protested but eventually yielded on condition that an ungilded area was left on each base metal object so that no deception could be practised and the purchaser prevented from thinking that he was buying an object of precious metal. The regulation was evidently more honoured in the breach than the reverse, but the Nürnberg guild persisted in trying to enforce it and in 1527 Sebastian Lindenast, in spite of his imperial patent, was fined for gilding small copper articles.[51] The abuse persisted and in March 1562 the Nürnberg City Council took firm steps against a certain Wolf Prüssel, who had made silver-plated copper beakers, and his wife and son who had sold them. All three were committed to prison.[52] When the object in question was made entirely of copper, such as the double eagle wrought by Christoph Jamnitzer in 1617 and set above the porch of the Nürnberg Rathaus, no problem arose.

A large enough number of articles made of copper, bronze or brass by goldsmiths survives to show that production was on a considerable scale, though the lower intrinsic value of the metal may have meant that the rate of survival has been higher than in the case of articles of precious metal. Extant examples cover almost the whole range of goldsmiths' work. Among German pieces coconut-cups mounted in and tankards made of silvered or gilt-copper are the most numerous. Even in a country such as Spain, where precious metal was available in ample quantity, copper was used as a substitute, as in the case of the magnificent monstrance from Castile or Aragon in the Victoria and Albert Museum (pls. 720, 722).

The first group - articles made of base metal instead of silver - includes a number of Italian pieces. Italian goldsmiths were less restricted than their northern contemporaries and seem to have worked in base metal without interference from the guilds. Owing to the almost complete destruction of Italian sixteenth-century vessels, other than ewers and basins, it is fortunate that it is possible to find base metal versions of at least some of the main types. Even these are few, as bronze and copper articles were also melted for the sake of the metal. Apart from a copper-gilt basin and ewer in Berlin,[53] nearly all the surviving Italian gilt-metal vessels are bronze salts. They range from the well-known model by Campagna in the form of a nude man bearing a shell on his bent back[54] to such splendid examples as the pair of Venetian salts (pl. 723) surmounted by figures of Jupiter and Amphitrite respectively. A simpler composition of three bearded tritons supporting three smaller shells (pl. 721) recalls the Giulio Romano design for a lamp (pl. 69) and strengthens my belief that such drawings found their way into the bronze founders' workshops. More typical of goldsmith's work, because it is partly wrought from sheet instead of being entirely cast, is the triple-tiered salt (pl. 719).

One of the very few examples of goldsmith's work executed in base metal that can be attributed to a known master is the gilt-copper and champlevé enamel beaker in the Walters Art Gallery, Baltimore;[55] this is of identical design to another of silver and enamel struck with the mark of Jakob Fröhlich, illustrated in pl. 486, and must therefore come from his workshop. In view of the position of Wenzel Jamnitzer as doyen of the Nürnberg goldsmiths, it is unlikely that his workshop actually made the little gilt-bronze goblet (pl. 726). It is, however, evident that the ornament of both bowl and foot derives from Jamnitzer models.

Clock-cases

Turning to the second group, some of the finest goldsmiths' work in base metal is on German sixteenth century clock-cases. It is probable that the plainer cases were produced by the clockmaker himself, but the assistance of a goldsmith was required on the decorated ones. The cases of Renaissance clocks were not only adorned with cast panels, they were also engraved with figure subjects and decorative borders. The clockmakers sometimes employed journeymen goldsmiths to assist them in the making and the decoration of the finer cases, but in so doing they offended the goldsmiths' guild, which frequently had to intervene, insisting that the clockmakers must commission a master goldsmith, presumably at greater expense. A successful clockmaker, such as Georg Roll of Augsburg, found that he had enough work to give full-time employment to a master goldsmith and his journeymen as well. This led to difficulties with the Augsburg Guild of Clockmakers, who objected to Roll employing members of another guild when he was not even a member of the Clockmakers' Guild himself.[56]

The maker of a clock-movement did not necessarily work in the same town as the maker of the case; this might well be made in one city and sent elsewhere for fitting with a movement. The situation is further complicated by the fact that bronze plaquettes made by Augsburg goldsmiths were exported elsewhere within or even outside Germany and made up into clock- or watch-cases. The same problem relates to fire-arm mounts; the finished piece usually bears the signature of the gunmaker who assembled its elements, but he was not likely to be the maker of them all. Little is known of the makers of the many fine clock- and watch-cases that survive from the sixteenth century. As a rule the signature on a case is that of the maker of the movement. On rare occasions the signature or monogram of the casemaker may be present as well, as on the case of a clock in the Berlin Kunstgewerbemuseum, which is signed by an Innsbruck clockmaker and by the Innsbruck goldsmith, Michael Kollinger.

The great astronomical clock constructed by Eberhard Baldewein and Hans Bucher for Kurfürst August of Saxony from 1563-7 was supplied with a case by the Giessen goldsmith Hermann Diepel. Furthermore the figures of the Planets drawn in triumphal cars which decorate two of the dials were engraved after drawings by the Antwerp master, Hans Collaert the Elder. The cast bronze reliefs that decorate the spandrels are similar to a set of four carved wood models for figures of the Arts preserved in the Germanisches National Museum, Nürnberg,[57]

Clock- and watch-cases were usually finished with engraved ornament, but some of the more important ones were decorated in relief. In this case, casting-patterns had to be carved from which moulds might be made. Of these a few examples have survived in addition to the clock-dial spandrels mentioned above. Perhaps the most remarkable is the set of four pearwood or limewood panels each carved in low relief with panels of grotesques in the manner of Matthias Zündt. Each panel (pl. 730) has a circular space reserved for the various dials of a rectangular table-clock. The carving is of the highest quality and reinforces the argument already set out above that much of the credit for the ornament of sixteenth-century goldsmiths's work belongs to the pattern-carver.

Scientific Instruments

During the sixteenth century great progress was made in the design and the accuracy of mathematical instruments. What had been mere curiosities, complicated automata that were little more than playthings, evolved into instruments capable of exact measurement, in the use of which ruling princes were anxious to be informed. However specialised, however scientific the function of the instrument, it was treated not only as a piece of technical equipment but received a programme of ornament that was almost as extensive as that of the cups and dishes intended for the princely table or sideboard. The most highly skilled pattern-carver, bronze-founders and goldsmiths of the day worked upon their production. The chief opportunity for the carver and goldsmith came in the making of the bases or stands for such instruments. The four figures emblematic of the Seasons that formed the base of Wenzel Jamnitzer's great table-fountain made for the Emperor Rudolph (see p.130) are typical of such work. The name of Wenzel Jamnitzer has long been associated with the superbly embossed and chased dial of a South German clock from the Fremersdorf Collection in the Württembergisches Landesmuseum (pls. 724,9). The chasing of the foliage, birds and animals on this dial constitutes one of, if not the finest example of such work in any material.[58] Somewhat similar work can be seen on a plaquette in the Berlin Kunstgewerbemuseum, which is not wrought but cast from a model.[59] Support for the attribution to Wenzel Jamnitzer can be found in the design of the upper side of the bowl of the Merckel Tafelaufsatz (pl. 420), the composition of which with interlacing branches inhabited by birds and masks could well be the creation of the same master. While the attribution to Jamnitzer is unproven, there is no doubt that he made scientific instruments and his sketch-book in the Berlin Kunstbibliothek includes drawings of clock- and watch-cases. Mathematical instruments made by Jamnitzer are preserved in the Dresden Mathematisch-Physikalisches Salon and in the Paris Observatoire Nationale,[60] while a bronze mortar and a balance in the Berlin Kunstgewerbemuseum[61] have also been attributed to him. As a rule scientific instruments and clock-cases were made of gilt-copper or, if cast, of bronze, but they were sometimes of silver or enriched with applied silver ornaments. This is indicated by the title of Wenzel Jamnitzer's manuscript study of scientific instruments dated 1588 and entitled *Ein gar kunstliche und wolgezierter Schreibtisch samt allerhant kunstlichen Silbernen und vergulten neuerfundenen Instrumenten so darin zufinden zum gebrauch der Geometrischen und Astronomischen auch andern schonen und nutzlichen Kunsten* in the Victoria and Albert Museum.[62] The work consists of two volumes and contains a detailed description of the various scientific instruments then known and an explanation of their purpose. It establishes beyond question Jamnitzer's understanding of both geometrical and astronomical sciences. The first volume shows on folio 38 an illustration of a standing cup, but it is of no aesthetic significance.[63] It is included to illustrate the method of reducing a drawing by the use of calipers.

Another Nürnberg goldsmith who also worked in base metal is Hans Epischofer. His signature appears on two globes in the Germanisches Nationalmuseum as well as on a series of instruments and a brass dish.[64] He signed either with his name in full or with his monogram alone, but when signing in full he used the term *Goldschmied*, as on the gunner's level in the Oesterreichisches Museum, Vienna, which is signed *1580 JAR ZU NORIMBERG IOHANNES EPISCHOFER GOLDSCHMID FACIEBAT.* It has also been suggested that Epischofer may have been the maker of the series of balances of gilt-bronze which have hitherto been attributed to Wenzel Jamnitzer. A feature of Epischofer's signed pieces is the excellence of their engraved ornament, but if the balances are also his work, then he must rank as a skilled sculptor as well, unless the credit belongs to a pattern-carver.

The leading maker of scientific instruments in Munich was Tobias Volkmer who in 1594 was appointed goldsmith and Mathematicus to the Bavarian court at an annual salary of 200 gulden.[65] Born in Braunschweig and admitted citizen and goldsmith of Salzburg in 1586, he always recalled his Braunschweig origin in his signature. He sought to set up open shop in Munich, selling his goldsmith productions, but like other court artists ran into difficulties with the goldsmiths' guild which raised objections. The Duke intervened pointing out the exceptional merit of a goldsmith who was master of his own craft and another as well. Tobias Volkmer and his son of the same name spent a whole year on the production of the mathematical instruments which were placed in a large *Kunstschrank* presented between 1616 and 1618 by Duke Maximilian to the Jesuit mission in China. This cabinet, which no longer survives, contained the usual assortment of small silver objects, drawings of European fauna and flora, automata, musical instruments, sweet-smelling essences, lamps, surgical instruments, writing-sets, watches and clocks and pictures of the Deity and Saints. Volkmer is well represented by the series of instruments he signed but nothing is known of his work as a goldsmith.

Among the few craftsmen working in base metal of whom something is known is Jakob Knoll, who first appeared in Augsburg in 1559. He obtained work in the following year with the goldsmith, Jörg Sigman, but committed the grave error of marrying before submitting his masterpiece and gaining admission to the guild.[66] As a result he was refused permission to do so and was debarred forever from becoming an established master of his craft. Instead he became a *Freykünstler*, a craftsman who did not belong to a guild but was restricted to activities which were not claimed as the exclusive province of a guild. His special field was working base metals: casting, embossing and engraving brass, copper and iron. He eventually came into conflict with the Augsburg Goldsmiths' Guild and in 1588 he was prohibited from gilding or silvering any objects other than clock- or watch-cases.

Iron and Steel Working

Besides cutting seals and decorating sword-hilts the goldsmith might make rings and mounts for caskets, purses or belts of iron, though this type of activity was also carried out by the iron chisellers (*Eisenschneider*) who were more likely to be members of the Armourers' Guild. The north Italian city of Milan was the most important centre of production of decorated iron work; not only armour but also cabinets, caskets, mirror-frames, chess-boards and even tables were decorated in this way. The larger pieces were constructed on a wood carcase that was covered with thin iron plaques embossed and damascened with gold and silver. Neither the making of the wood carcase nor the beating out of the iron plates was the work of the goldsmith, but the remaining operations were well within his competence. Iron was doubtless more difficult to work than the far more ductile silver, but the iron sheet used was quite thin and not too resistant to the embosser's hammer. Finally the object was likely to be adorned with mounts of either silver or gilt-bronze. Perhaps the most remarkable extant example of Milanese domestic metalwork is the extraordinary toilet mirror of iron damascened with gold and silver and further enriched with gilt bronze mounts and with figure sculpture in the Victoria and Albert Museum (pls. 737-9). The designer has made original use of the familiar features of Mannerist ornament; the base stands on a composition of free-standing straps, the mirror is flanked by elongated figures of gilt-bronze, surmounted by capitals composed entirely of projecting scrolls, but the most striking features are the two twisted human figures that link the side with the central finials. Typical of the period is the curious relationship between the figures and the niches, the latter being either too big or too small for the figures they contain. Though not made of silver this extraordinary mirror gives an idea of the splendour and originality of Italian goldsmiths' work that cannot be paralleled in any extant work in precious metal.

During the sixteenth century the pewterers produced copies of contemporary silver show-plate. Owing to the softness of the material such pieces decorated in relief with figure subjects were unsuitable for practical purposes and were intended only for display on the sideboard, providing an inexpensive substitute for the precious metal they imitated. The chief master of this type of decorative pewter (*Edelzinn*) was François Briot,[67] best known as the creator of the Temperantia ewer and basin (pls. 728, 736). He was born in Lorraine in 1550 but worked in the German town of Mömpelgard to which he emigrated, presumably in order to escape religious persecution. He was a die-cutter and pattern-carver (*Formenschneider*) and cut the copper moulds from which the pewter vessels were cast. The Temperantia Basin and its accompanying ewer are closely related to contemporary French silver vessels and it would seem likely that Briot would have made patterns for the goldsmith as well, but there is no evidence to support this. He may have, however, had a part in the decoration of ewers and basins in the style of Delaune such as those illustrated in pls. 380 and 381. The Temperantia Basin does not stand alone, though it is the finest in design. Others exist with similar relief ornament, also adapted from the engravings of Etienne Delaune or Aegidius Sadeler, their central bosses depicting figures of Mars, Hercules or the Temptation of Adam and Eve.[68] So fertile was Briot's imagination, or that of his source, that there is no repetition in his designs, not only does each mask on the Temperantia Basin differ from the others, but the arrangement of the recumbent or sitting figures within the cartouches show in each case a different composition. In Nürnberg, Caspar Enderlein copied the Briot basin, substituting his own signature for that of Briot. The mauresque ornament that was so much employed by the goldsmiths was equally effective on pewter, though in this case it was cast in a mould instead of being engraved or etched on the vessel.

1 For a comprehensive survey of Swiss dagger designs see C. Bosson, 'Les Dagues Suisses', *Geneva*, Vol. XII, 1964, p.167-198.
2 ill. Bosson, p. 172.
3 ill. Schmidt, Tafelband, figs. 75, 76.
4 ill. Schmidt, figs. 70, 71, 72.
5 ill. Bosson, p. 171.
6 See Schenk zu Schweinsberg, 'Ein Schwertriss Wenzel Jamnitzers von 1544', *Jahrbuch der Preuss.*

Kunstsammlungen, Vol. XLVII, 1926, p.30.

7   Davilier, p.157.

8   See C. Blair, 'A Royal Swordsmith and Damascener, Diego de Çaias', *Metropolitan Museum Journal*, Vol. 3. 1970.

9   ill. J. F. Hayward, 'Mannerist Sword-Hilt Designs', *Livrustkammaren*, Stockholm, Vol. 8, p.101, fig. 19.

10 Museum No. M618-1910.

11 The Archduke had more than one coral-hilted sword, another with hilt of more reasonable design is illustrated by H. Seitz, *Blankwaffen*, Vol. I, Braunschweig, 1965, pl. 274.

12 Holzhausen, p.xxii.

13 ibid. pl. 20, p.li.

14 Described in detail: J. F. Hayward, 'Israel Schuech's Rapier', *Art at Auction*, London, 1971, p.390.

15 For a detailed study of these swords, see J. F. Hayward, 'A Group of Sword-Hilt Designs attributed to Jacob Mores', *Livrustkammaren*, Vol. XIII, 1974, p.165-181.

16 See J. F. Hayward, 'Designs for Ornament on Gunstocks', *Livrustkammaren*, Vol. V, p.109ff.

17 Philip II also had a sword and dagger of gold with hilts decorated with serpents and ragged staves in relief. This was the work of de Soto. See Davilier, op cit. p.150.

18 ill. Laking, *Record of European Armour and Arms*, Vol. IV, figs. 1353, 1354.

19 Davilier, p.148-151.

20 Quoted by Babelon, from Simancas, Contaduria Mayor, 1.1053. 'A sword, in its case of black leather lined with blue satin, provided with five guards and a cross, with the pommel, grip and the end of the scabbard of gold, sculptured in relief, enamelled in all colours, with figures and masks on the grip, and on the crown of the guard, medals after the antique and four masks worked entirely in relief, with foliage like all the rest.'

21 '*qui comintia le quarante carte dove sono disegnade quaranta guarnimenti o fornimenti di o elssa de spade si da piede come da cavalo, e per cortelaci da cavalo o da piede, fate co beliss disegno, tutti variati dintalio e lavorieri, e si potrano fare co facilitade di maestri in tal arte esperti premiandolo.*'

22 Fol. EVII, '*questo guarnimento fatto a festoni....le punte delle folie bisognia siano base, perche havendo le punte levate straceria i vestimenti, e offenderia la mano*'.

23 Fol. CVI '*questo guarnimento da spada si potra fare piu piciolo.... adornandolo tutto, overo argentandolo, overo, oro e argento si come sovra si vedde*'.

24 ill. Haenel, pl. 50a.

25 For a full discussion of the sword, see H. Seitz, 'The Vienna Rapier with the Golden Hilt', *Livrustkammaren*, Vol. 4, p.376.

25a Fock, p.137.

26 ill. Valencia de Don Juan, *Catalogo*, Armeria Real, Madrid, 1898, no. G. 47, p.222.

27 ill. Mariaux, pl. III.

28 ill. Boeheim, *Album hervorragender Gegenstände*, Vienna, 1894, Vol. I pl. XX (3).

29 Vasari, Vol. VII, p.43.

30 Cellini I.I., 31.

31 ill. J. F. Hayward, *European Armour*, Victoria and Albert Museum, London, London, 1965, pl. 23.

32 ill. Mariaux, pl. XV. The grip shown in this illustration is a later restoration.

33 ill. Thomas, Gamber and Schedelmann, pl. 65.

34 ill. J. F. Hayward, *Kunst der alten Büchsenmacher*, Hamburg, 1968, pl. 64

35 '*il piu famoso che hoggi sia è Gaspero Moli, il quale ha fatto opere di gran meraviglie, massimo uno scudo, et un elmo il quale hoggi si ritrova nell'armeria dell' A. Ser.ma nel quale si è riportato sopra varie figurine, et impronte di medaglie con i dodici segni celesti, ben che sia tal ripporto d'argento dorato, e cisellato, nientedimeno e stimato cosa maravigliosa*'. From *L'Arte Fabrile* by Antonio Petrini, reprinted in *Armi Antiche*, Turin, 1962.

36 The complete Will is printed in *Rivista Europea*, Firenze, 1877, Vol. III. Fasc. II. A. Bertolotti, 'Testamenti ed Inventarii di Gaspare Mola.' The relevant passage runs '*una guardia di Spada smaltata, che per essere opera singolare et di grandissima spesa et fatica è degna d'ogni gran Re o Imperatore per essere opera unica che forse mai più ha per riuscire ad altri, et è opera noua, la quale guardia con suoi finimenti per il pugnale e la centura e pendagli con ferri smaltati, ogni cosa non si può fare per pagamento che sia, perchè non ci è danaro, che la paghi ma per terminare il suo giusto et honesto prezzo doueria essere almeno pagata 3 m. scudi d'oro, che se si farà proua di cercare se ci fosse persona idonea che gli bastasse l'animo di fare un opera simile, se colui che si sia non fosse un balordo non si obbligarà mai a farla per tal prezzo perchè se egli la facesse saria più tosto un stupore o merauiglia che cosa riuscibile, si come io che l'ho fatta con grandissimo tempo dico che anco ci sia concorso l'aiuto dal cielo et più tosto un miracolo che cosa sicura da potersi fare un altra uolta, et per cio sia messa in consideratione de'Principi grandi acciò sia pagata l'honesto prezzo della quale guardia e suoi finimenti dalle serenissime di Toscana me ne fu offerto mille e cinquecento scudi, che per non essere conueniente io non la uvolsi lasciare. Questa poca narratiua ho fatto per auertire gli*'

Signori Superiori di detto Hospitale a non lasciarsi ingannare dalle parole de pocchi intendenti et darla a uil prezzo.'

37 'Questo nel lavorar di rilievo in ferro, & in argento, si di figure come di groteschi, & altre bizzarie d'animali, fogliami, e paesi e molto eccellente, e rarissimo nella gemina'.

38 See. A. Gross, 'Vorlagen der Werkstätte des Lucio Piccinino', *Jahrbuch*, Band XXXVI. p.123-155.

39 ill. Thomas, Gamber and Schedelmann, pl. 44. For quotations from Morigia and Lomazzo see *La Storia di Milano*, Vol. XI, p.782.

40 These drawings are discussed at length by Dr. B. Thomas in a series of four articles published in the *Jahrbuch*, Vienna, 1959, 1960 1962 and 1965.

41 B. Thomas, 'Die Münchner Harnischvorzeichnungen im Stil François I', *Jahrbuch*, 1959, p.31ff.

42 See. B. Thomas, 'Neues zum Werk des Eliseus Libaerts', *Livrustkammaren*, Stockholm, Vol. IV77 14, p.011.

43 Catalogue, *European European Arms and Armour*, Vol. I, London, 1962, no. A. 320, pl. 86.

44 Valencia de Don Juan, Cat. no. A. 239, p.79.

45 See. J. F. Hayward, 'The Sigman Shield', *Journal of the Arms and Armour Society*, London, Vol. p.21ff.

46 ill. Thomas, Gamber, Schedelmann, pl. 35.

47 ill. J. F. Hayward, op cit. pl. X.

48 ill. Haenel, pl. 15, J. Schöbel, *Prunkwaffen*, Leipzig, 1973, p.61.

49 B. Thomas, 'The golden stirrups in St. Louis and related objects', *Museum Monographs, City Museum of Saint Louis*, 1970.

50 Neudörfer, p.37ff.

51 Hampe, p.135-6.

52 Hampe, p.561.

53 See C. C. Oman, 'Base metal goldsmiths' work of the Italian Renaissance', *Connoisseur*, Vol. CXLIV, p.218.

54 ill. Weihrauch, pl. 189.

55 ill. *Walters Art Gallery Picture-Book, Treasures and Rarities*, Baltimore, 1971, p.15.

56 M. Bobinger, *Kunstuhrmacher in Alt-Augsburg*, Augsburg, 1969, p.29ff.

57 H. J. Heuser, 'Drei unbekannte Risse Hans Collaerts des Alteren', *Jahrbuch der Hamburger Kunstsammlungen*, 1961, p.29-52.

58 P. Coole and E. Neumann, *The Orpheus Clocks*, London, 1972.

59 ill. Pechstein, IV cat. no. 184. In his catalogue of plaquettes, Pechstein describes the embossed and chased gilt-copper examples as *Goldschmiede-modellen* but the fact that they are gilt makes it clear that they formed part of some finished object and were not models.

60 Zinner, *Deutsche und Niederländische astronomische Instrumente des 11-18 Jahrhunderts*, Munich, 1956, p. 394-6.

61 Pechstein IV, cat. nos. 8 and 7. For a burning-glass stand in the style of Jamnitzer, see M. Rosenberg, 'Studien über Goldschmiedekunst in der Sammlung Figdor', *Kunst und Kunsthandwerk*, Wien, 1911; p.387, fi fig. 112.

62 'A most ingenious and finely decorated writing desk containing all kinds of newly invented and ingenious silver and gilt instruments for use in Geometry, Astronomy and also the fine and applied arts.'

63 Rosenberg II, pl. 43.

64 See Pechstein, 'Hans Epischofer-Der Monogrammist HE', *Anzeiger des Germ. National-museums*, 1970, p.96.

65 E. Zinner, *Deutsche und Niederländische Astronomische Instrumente*, Munich, 1956, p.574.

66 See. A. Buff, 'Urkundliche Nachrichten über den Augsburger Goldschmied Jörg Sigman', *Zeitschrift des hist. Vereins für Schwaben und Neuburg*, Vol. XIX, 1892, pp.149ff.

67 H. Demiani, *François Briot, Caspar Enderlein*, Leipzig, 1897.

68 An example of each of these dishes is in the Boymans Museum, Rotterdam, also a ewer decorated with a relief of Susanna and the Elders. There is a good example of the Mars dish in the Bargello Museum, Florence.

Part Two

CATALOGUE OF PLATES

Colour Plates

Plate I   page 33

Casket, the wood framework covered with mother of pearl scales, the gilt mounts enriched with jewels alternating with medallion heads against a blue enamel ground, a baluster column at each corner. This casket is one of a group of six objects dating from the decade of 1530 to 1540 and apparently made in the same Paris workshop, among them the ciborium and the salt (pls. 250-1). They represent the style fashionable in Paris before Cellini's influence was felt. The presence of the Ciborium and a pair of candlesticks from this group in the altar plate of the Order of the Saint Esprit implies that they were made by a court goldsmith. The casket was probably intended to contain jewels; many smaller French caskets of similar construction with baluster columns at the corners exist, some set with Limoges enamel plaques on top and sides. Paris, 1533-4, maker's mark the initial B. H. 29 cm. L. 40 cm.
Private collection, London

Plate II   page 34

Rock-crystal ewer with gilt mounts enamelled with naturalistic flowers in translucent colours, the lip and foot-mount borders with gilt mauresques against a black ground. While the form of the ewer is conservative, probably due to the re-use of late medieval rock-crystal elements, a brilliant effect is achieved by the polychrome enamels and the imaginative modelling of the sculptural detail: the twin snake handle, the faun that supports it and the melusine carrying the shell spout. Probaby Florentine, unmarked, mid 16th century. H. 26.5 cm.
Private collection, Switzerland

Plate III   page 51

Classical Roman sardonyx vase from the collection of Lorenzo the Magnificent; the parcel-gilt mounts are of later date and were presumably supplied by one of the immigrant, probably Flemish, Medici court goldsmiths. The foot is embossed with strapwork cartouches with rolled over ends in a typically Flemish manner, enclosing the Medici arms. Florence, late 16th century. H. 45 cm.
Museo degli Argenti, Florence

Plate IV   page 52

Lapis lazuli vase with enamelled gold mounts made by Giacomo Biliverti, master goldsmith at the court workshops of the Grand-dukes of Tuscany in the Casino di San Marco and subsequently in the Palazzo degli Uffizi, Florence. The design by Bernardo Buontalenti is preserved. The base is carved with the arms of Grand-duke Francesco I and dated 1583. The vase consists of four pieces of lapis lazuli: lid, neck, body and foot. A feature of this and other vessels created by Buontalenti and Biliverti is the natural way in which the handles and spouts seem to develop from the bodies. Such vessels were not intended for use but for display on the sideboard or in one of the cupboards of Francesco's Studiolo in the Palazzo Vecchio; the impracticable size of the handles and the foot was not, therefore, a serious disadvantage. H. 40.5 cm.
Museo degli Argenti, Florence.

Plate V   page 69

Rock-crystal vase of amphora form with enamelled gold and jewelled mounts by the Saracchi brothers of Milan, the body intaglio cut with the arms of the Wittelsbach Dukes of Bavaria and with a frieze of the Triumph of Bacchus after a print by Etienne Delaune. The handles of this vase, with their repeated change of theme from human to animal forms and back again, illustrate the Mannerist delight in metamorphosis. The cover is surmounted by a figure of Neptune holding his trident. This vase, together with a galley also of rock-crystal, was paid for in 1579 at a cost of 6000 gold gulden and a special honorarium of 2000 imperial lire. Morigia, writing in 1595, described this piece as 'a very large vase, bigger than any that had been wrought from rock-crystal, of egg shape and with a handle and engraved over all its surface with intaglio-cut figures.' The enamelled gold mounts are perhaps by Raffaello and Michele Saracchi, perhaps by an anonymous goldsmith of Milan. Before 1579. H. 51.5 cm.
Schatzkammer of the Residenz, Munich

Plate VI   page 70

Rock-crystal dragon ewer, enamelled gold mounts enriched with jewels, the body carved in relief with scales and wings; two feet each with three claws; the head with open mouth forming the spout, the tail ending in a curl. Each rock-crystal element is attached to the body by a gold ring decorated in champlevé enamel with black foliate scrolls; the cover carved with raised crest and two upstanding wings. Milanese, Saracchi workshop (?), late 16th century. Unmarked, H. 24.8 cm.
Sotheby's, London

Plate VII   page 87

Smoky quartz cup with enamelled gold mounts enriched with jewels, the bowl of shaped oval form turned over at the sides and carved with conventional foliage from which a grotesque mask emerges at the front. The stem carved in relief with leaves developing into scrolls, shaped oval foot carved *en suite*. Gold collars at each end of the stem and gold rim mount on the foot, set with openwork scrolls and flower-heads, enamelled white with points of green and blue, and enriched with table-cut rubies in square collets. Perhaps a late work of Ottavio Miseroni in Prague; the high relief of the carving on this cup marks the beginning of the Baroque. Unmarked, Prague, early 17th century. H. 14.5 cm.
Private collection, Switzerland

Plate VIII   page 88

Two handled rock-crystal bowl engraved with foliate scrolls developing into monstrous birds, the mounts of silver-gilt; those supporting the bowl in the form of openwork brackets terminating above in dragon heads, the mount below the bowl with four projecting male busts, the base of the stem also with openwork brackets. Unmarked, but probably Prague Court Workshop. About 1600. H. 29.9 cm.
Private collection, Switzerland

Plate IX   page 105

Rock-crystal two handled vase, composed of four pieces of crystal, foot, bowl, neck and cover held by silver-gilt mounts, cast and chased with strapwork, masks and mauresques. The bowl is secured by four term straps, the cover surmounted by a lion supporter for a shield which is now missing. The simplicity of the Freiburg facetted rock-crystal contrasts with the rich ornament of the mounts which are further embellished with cameos, intaglios and turquoises. The need to construct this vase from four separate pieces of crystal has imposed on the goldsmith a composition in which the horizontal is more strongly emphasized than the vertical, a feature of Renaissance rather than Mannerist design. Strassburg, Diebolt Krug (R³ 6968). Third quarter of the 16th century. H. 39.6 cm.
Württembergisches Landesmuseum, Stuttgart

Plate X   page 106

Standing cup carved in the form of a trochus-shell from quartz with brown inclusions and mounted in silver-gilt. The bowl surmounted by a satyr riding on a sea-horse and holding a cornucopia. The straps ending above in two lion masks and in the centre with grotesque mask. The bowl supported on the back of a satyr who bears a dolphin under each arm, after a print by Cornelis Floris (Hedicke, pl. X, 2). Circular base engraved with mauresques and with applied cherub's heads. The bowl carved like a shell from hardstone is a sophisticated Mannerist device, of which very few examples are known (pl. 275). Unmarked, Antwerp (?), about 1560-70. H. 25 cm.
Private collection, Switzerland

Plate XI   page 123

Ivory beaker and cover, the foot, girdle, rim and cover mounted with five gold bands, those on the body enamelled with mauresques against a black ground within white strapwork, those on the cover enamelled black only. The finial of the cover set with a *verre fixé* medallion bearing the arms of Denmark and the date 1558. Probably given by King Christian III to Duke Christoph V of Württemberg. The decoration shows exceptional restraint for its period. Mauresques, copied from du Cerceau's so-called *niello* series, were a favourite device of French goldsmiths at this time. Unmarked, French, dated 1558. H. 21.5 cm.
Württembergisches Landesmuseum, Stuttgart

Plate XII   page 124

Enamelled gold tazza, the bowl set with two concentric rows of twelve and one of six casts from antique gold coins, the spaces between the coins occupied by embossed and polychrome enamelled ornaments in the form of bunches of fruit and trefoil ended straps; a larger cast medallion is set in the centre. Baluster stem also set with enamelled bunches of fruit, the foot with six gold coins and six enamelled straps. The coins are cast from Greek *staters* and Roman *aureii* and Byzantine and Roman *solidi*. The central medallion is cast from a Roman Imperial period original. The origin of this tazza is uncertain; the simple design of the enamelled enrichment suggests a northern rather than an Italian origin. Comparable enamelled ornament is found on a gold bowl in the Munich Schatzkammer (cat. no. 593) which is believed to have been made by Sigismund III of Poland. Unmarked, Central European (?), mid-16th century. H. 11.5 cm. Diam. of bowl 18.5 cm.
Private collection, Switzerland

Plate XIII   page 141

Trochus-shell ewer with gilt and enamelled mounts, one of the most fantastic shell ewers ever made. Strikingly original is the treatment of the foot, which is composed of an eagle with wings outstretched perched on the back of and attacking the horns of a snail which, in turn, rests on a mass of writhing snakes. The framing of the two shells which are set together to form the body and the form of the C-scroll handle are ingenious, while the modelling of the harpy that forms the lower part of the spout predicates the hand of a sculptor of distinction. In this piece function is utterly ignored and the master has indulged his fantasy without restriction. Nürnberg, Wenzel Jamnitzer (R³ 3832t), about 1570. H. 33 cm.
Schatzkammer of the Residenz, Munich

Plate XIV   page 142

Pen and colour wash drawing of a ewer *en suite* with the basin in pl. 130 by or after Wenzel Jamnitzer. An unusual feature of this and a group of associated drawings from the Jamnitzer workshop is that they are coloured in red, green, blue and yellow, implying that the finished vessel was intended to be enamelled and gilt. Such drawings were presumably intended to be shown to a potential customer; had they been meant for workshop use they would not have been so carefully finished and if they had been meant for a pattern-book it would have been superflous to colour them. This ewer does not conform to the usual pattern of the mid century, having a pear-shaped, instead of ovoid body. Nürnberg, third quarter of 16th century.
Victoria and Albert Museum

Plate XV   page 159
Pen and colour wash drawing of a pilgrim flask by a follower of Wenzel Jamnitzer, probably Matthias Zündt. The composition with scrolling foliage and strapwork inhabited by hunters and wild animals points to the survival of late Gothic influence into the mid-16th century. The strapwork is apparently derived from one of the contemporary books of mauresques, as is the ornament of the low foot. It resembles, but is more adventurous than, the flask in the *Kraterographie* of 1551 (pl. 135). The drawing is coloured green, red, blue and yellow and was presumably intended to be decorated in cold enamel. Nürnberg, third quarter of the 16th century.
Victoria and Albert Museum

Plate XVI   page 160
Gilt covered cup; the form follows the conventional construction of the time, but the ornament is quite original. The stem is composed of two addorsed satyrs supporting a large vase on their shoulders, a theme derived from some Flemish prototype, the foot, bowl and cover are all embossed in high relief and with striking virtuosity with human, animal and grotesque masks. To achieve the startling effect of these often repulsive masks, the harmonious profile has had to be sacrificed. Projecting heads within circular frames are a familiar feature of the cups of this period; they were usually cast separately and inserted, but in this case they are embossed from the metal of the bowl and, far from being delimited by cartouches or frames, melt into each other in a manner that anticipates the auricular style of the end of the century. A long inscription around the top of the bowl consists of eight elegiac couplets extolling the virtues of sobriety, a theme that seems to be contradicted by the grape-vine trails running over the surface and, more forcibly, by the wild expressions of the masks. Augsburg about 1570, maker's mark the letters HANS in monogram (R³ 426). H. 42.5 cm.
Private collection, Switzerland

Plate XVII   page 177
Detail of upper stage, showing the Resurrection, of the house altar of the Archduke Albrecht V of Bavaria (for the whole altar see pl. 452), ebony and enamelled gold; the cabinet-work attributed to Hans Krieger, the goldsmith's to Abraham Lotter and the enamelling to Ulrich Eberl. Unmarked, Augsburg about 1573-4.
Schatzkammer of the Residenz, Munich

Plate XVIII   page 178
Standing cup and cover the foot, lower part of the bowl and cover decorated with a ring of gadroons (*Buckeln*) interrupted by masks or busts in relief. Around the bowl a frieze of Jamnitzer ornament, also interrupted by applied masks. The lip engraved with pendant mauresques, which are also repeated on the lower part of the foot. The rings on the vase knop intended for pendant coats-of-arms. Inside the cover a plaquette of a nymph seated by a vase against a mountainous background. On the cover a figure of a knight in armour holding a shield in his left hand and an unidentifiable object in his right. Lübeck, last quarter of the 16th century. Maker's mark, crossed maces or torches in a shaped shield. (R³ No. 3169). H. 46 cm.
Private collection, Switzerland

Plate XIX   page 195
Parcel-gilt standing cup made in 1571 for Christof Reinfart, Bürgermeister of Worms, a fact which is recorded in an inscription around the lip. The cover and body are set with 53 classical and Renaissance coins, each being surrounded by a strapwork cartouche of varying design. The cup had, as the inscription makes clear, a didactic purpose and over each coin is a label within the strapwork stating where it was current. Worms, maker's mark, two horns in a shield (R³ 4926), 1571. H. 40.5 cm.
Private collection, Switzerland

Plate XX   page 196
Enamelled gold flask by Hans Karl of Nürnberg, court goldsmith to the Archbishops of Salzburg, for Archbishop Wolf Dietrich von Raitenau, with whose arms it is enamelled. The flask belongs with four two-handled drinking cups to a service commissioned by Wolf Dietrich and by his successor in the See of Salzburg, Marcus Sitticus von Hohenembs. The flask and three of the cups bear the arms of the former, while the fourth bears those of the latter. The flask is signed and dated 1602; presumably the three bowls were made next and finally the fourth one with the arms of Marcus Sitticus who succeeded in 1612. 16th-century inventories show that most ruling princes owned such services of gold, of which this is a unique survival. Unmarked, Salzburg, signed by Hans Karl and dated 1602. H. 22.5 cm.
Museo degli Argenti, Florence

Plate XXI   page 213
Two matching parcel-gilt dishes, the centres set with medallions engraved with a merchant's mark and a coat-of-arms respectively accompanied by the initials LK and MK respectively, surrounded by embossed and chased strapwork, enclosing, on one, three roundels with allegorical figures and, on the other, three masks, the outer area of the dishes fluted. North German or Baltic, last quarter of the 16th century, maker's mark on the first dish only, a star. Diam. 14 cm.
Private collection, Switzerland

Plate XXII   page 214
Gilt tankard, standing on three cherub's-head feet, the body chased with the story of Adam and Eve and the Garden of Eden, the cover with a border of sea-monsters enclosing another of fruit and strapwork, surmounted by a figure of Judith with the head of Holophernes. The base inset with a plaquette embossed with the baptism of Christ, mermaid thumb-piece, Pressburg, late 16th century, maker's mark of Sebastian Liebhardt. H. 23.5 cm.
Private collection, Switzerland

Plate XXIII   page 231
Gilt standing cup, the wide frieze running around the bowl is embossed on one side with the Judgement of Paris watched by Jupiter and on the other with a river-god, referring to the purpose of the cup. The hair of the river-god takes the form of bullrushes, a detail also found in engravings of both Cornelis Bos and Cornelis Floris. The profuse cast and embossed ornament in the form of male and female caryatids, strapwork cartouches, human and lion masks and serpents that covers the surface of both cup and cover derives from contemporary Antwerp

engraved ornament. On the cover are four recumbent figures within elaborate strapwork cartouches, emblematic of the Elements (pl. 601). The pierced members of the stem and cover enclose rock-crystal cylinders. Unmarked, Antwerp, about 1560. H. 42.5 cm.
Private collection, London

Plate XXIV   page 232
Morion of steel covered with gold and enriched with polychrome enamel, made for King Charles IX of France. The helmet was doubtless wrought by an armourer but the enrichment with gold and enamel and perhaps the repoussé work as well was executed by the Paris goldsmith, Pierre Redon. It was made *en suite* with the companion shield illustrated in pl. 710. Such pieces of armour were probably intended to be carried in triumphal procession before the king. The helmet and shield were paid for in 1572 after the death of Redon. H. 32 cm.
Louvre, Paris.

Monochrome Plates

THE illustrations are divided into three groups, each arranged in approximately chronological order by countries: first, drawings and prints, then vessels of gold or silver or of other materials mounted in precious metal, thirdly objects of base metal and models of wood or other materials. The notes are not purely descriptive; they are intended to supplement the text of the book and to provide some historical background.

Many problems are encountered in establishing the local or national source of vessels made when style was so international; the identification of origin must sometimes be based on stylistic or typological analogy and may be no more than speculative. Where the identification is uncertain, the object is included in the group considered to be most likely, and alternative possibilities are mentioned in the catalogue.

Plate 1

Oil painting on panel by Alessandro Fei, depicting a goldsmith's workshop, apparently that of the court artists of Francesco I, Grand Duke of Tuscany, in the Casino San Marco. This painting is of exceptional interest because it illustrates so many activities of the craft. To the right, pinned to the base of a cupboard, are four drawings, showing, from right to left, a large altar candlestick with a small table stick at the side, next the Medici Grand-ducal crown, then, above, a standing cup with boat-shaped bowl and, below, another drawing, the design on which is concealed by the goldsmith's head. In the middle distance two men hammer dishes on a stake, while others mount stones at a table. In the far distance to the right are the furnaces for casting and annealing. At another table to the left a second group of men mount precious stones and a third group is at work in the foreground around a table. To the far left of this table, partly cut off by the picture's edge, is a papal triple tiara; next to this a royal crown and, in front, a coronet. Then come rings and stones for mounting and a workman holding up a magnificent golden ewer with pinched-in spout and loop handle ending below in a grotesque mask. On the table to the right of the workman are a pair of silver altar cruets, a perfume bottle and a gilt salt-cellar of sarcophagus shape. At the back another man works on the chasing of a basin, while to the right in front the master goldsmith holds in his left hand the most important object of all, the Medici crown, which he is finishing to the design fixed on the

cupboard in front of him. Further to the right a workman is chasing the base of a large candlestick or an altar cross. On a shelf above the drawings is a group of finished products: a pair of candlesticks, a large gilt helmet-shaped ewer, a scent flask, a gilt basin, a large two-handled vase embossed with acanthus foliage, a small jug, a gilt pilgrim flask, a table-centre composed of four dishes set one on top of the other with baluster stems between; and, finally, three gold chains which are looped around the feet of the vessels and hang down over the shelf, the fourth chain being part of the pilgrim flask.
Studiolo of Francesco I, Palazzo Vecchio, Florence.

Plates 2 and 3.

Two engravings of goldsmiths' workshops by Etienne Delaune, signed and dated in Augsburg 1576.
2. From left to right, drawing a wire, chasing an article held in a vice, chiselling a seal die, marking out a pattern and holding an object in the furnace with a pair of tongs prior to soldering. Hanging on the walls and placed on the tables are the various tools of the trade.
3. From left to right, using bellows to increase the heat of the furnace for refining and casting precious metal, chiselling the surface of an embossed basin, raising a beaker on the stake, and, in the rear, the master goldsmith in conversation with a client.
British Museum.

Plate 4.

Portrait by Titian of Jacopo da Strada; this shows him in his role as Court Antiquary to the Holy Roman Emperor and after he had abandoned the tools of the goldsmith. The marble Venus and the antique torso, as well as the gold coins on the table refer to his chief interests. The inscription on the cartouche in the top left-hand corner, together with the (restored) date 1566, are believed to be later additions made by his son, Ottavio.

Kunsthistoriches Museum, Vienna.

Plate 5.

Portrait by Nicolas de Neufchatel of Wenzel Jamnitzer of Nürnberg, presented by his son in 1600 to the Nürnberg City Council. It shows the sitter wearing a velvet robe, holding a pair of dividers in his right hand and in his left a silver rod of a type that was used to determine the weight of various metals. On the table in front of him is a sketch of a figure of Neptune and the completed figure of silver, an hour-glass and a pair of spectacles. In the niche behind him is a vase containing flowers and grasses cast from nature, a technique for which Jamnitzer was particularly famous.

Musée d'Art et d'Histoire, Geneva.

Plate 6.

Portrait of Christoph Jamnitzer of Nürnberg at the age of 34 in 1597 by Lorenz Strauch. The sitter is shown in fashionable dress holding the wooden base of a wax model of Bacchus on which he is working. A hammer and gravers lie on the table in front of him, while he holds a wooden modelling tool in his hand. The portrait shows that Christoph was himself responsible for the sculptural detail of his works.

Germanisches Nationalmuseum, Nürnberg.

Plate 7.

Panel of ornament engraved by Nicoletto Rosex or Rossi of Modena, executed after the year 1507, when he visited the classical Roman frescoes in the Domus Aurea of Nero. Besides monsters, bound captives and trophies of arms relating to warfare, the panel shows four different types of vase, while the warrior on the right of the central winged figure pours water from a ewer of antique form. This print, as well as others by the same master, was copied in the reliefs of the Fugger Chapel in Augsburg, completed in 1518.

Victoria and Albert Museum.

Plate 8.

Engraving of an antique vase and of another vase on a tripod base by Giovanni Antonio da Brescia. Influenced by Mantegna and by Marcantonio Raimondi, he was active in Rome during the second half of the first quarter of the 16th century. This print probably represents authentic antique bronzes and is one of the earliest Italian Renaissance representations of such vessels. Similar vessels are represented in pilaster panel designs by Giovanni da Brescia and other masters of

ornament of the period. About 1510-20.

Victoria and Albert Museum.

Plate 9.

Pen and wash drawing of a two-handled vase and cover; this elaborately composed vessel combines various classical elements arranged in horizontal order. The general effect is harmonious by reason of the excellence of the proportions, but if executed by the goldsmith the design would have to be much simplified. Paduan (?) early 16th century.

Victoria and Albert Museum.

Plate 10.

Drawing of a stand, perhaps intended for fruit; the design, which was formerly attributed to Baldassare Peruzzi, recalls the composition of the large Italian bronze altar candlesticks of the first half of the 16th century. Venetian (?) about 1520-40.

Cooper-Hewitt Museum, New York.

Plate 11.

Engraving of a vase in antique style from the set of twelve sheets of vases and ewers, dated 1530 and 1531 and inscribed *Sic Roma antiqui sculptores ex aere et marmore faciebant* (Thus worked the ancient Roman sculptors in bronze and marble), signed A.V. by Agostino dei Musi (also known as Agostino Veneziano). The body probably corresponds to a fragmentary excavated Roman original, but the handle is a conjectural restoration.

Victoria and Albert Museum.

Plate 12.

Engraving of a ewer in antique style from the same set as pl. 11 by Agostino dei Musi. This design is, with the possible exception of the lion handle, a convincing reproduction of a classical Roman vessel. It was produced in the 16th century in bronze and in majolica and there is even an English version in silver (pl. 687). Its popularity was probably due less to its authenticity than to the fact that, being a close copy of a piece that had been executed in metal, it offered fewer problems to the goldsmith than more adventurous designs in which the artist drew freely upon his own imagination. Dated 1531.

Victoria and Albert Museum.

Plate 13.

Engraving of a vase by Enea Vico, inscribed *Romae ab antiquo repertum* (found in Rome from the antique); both the irregular outline of the body and the curious handles, which develop from female figures, are far removed from classical antiquity. Signed AE.V. and dated 1543.

Victoria and Albert Museum.

Plate 14.
Engraving of a ewer by Enea Vico from the same series of designs as pl. 13; though derived from classical sources the resulting design is a Mannerist confection. The shell spout, the horned projection opposite the handle and the basketwork ring around the neck are unclassical features. Signed and dated 1543.
Victoria and Albert Museum.

Plate 15.
Drawing in pen and wash by Androuet du Cerceau of three designs for salt-cellars, two on baluster stems, the third on central baluster and four leaf-and-claw legs. About 1540.
Bibliothèque Nationale, Paris.

Plate 16.
Drawing in pen and wash by Androuet du Cerceau of a standing salt with cover, the design probably based on a table-fountain. The pendant swags around the central knop are a regular feature of du Cerceau's designs. The lively drawing of the figures on the cover suggests an autograph work of this master. From a codex bearing the arms of the King of England on the first sheet. About 1540-45.
Kunstbibliothek, Berlin.

Plates 17 and 18.
Drawings in pen and wash of two ewers by Androuet du Cerceau from the same codex as pl. 16. The medallion heads on pl. 18 are similar to those on the French ciborium and clock-salt in pls. 250, 251. The feathery fronds filling the spaces between the medallion heads on the body of pl. 18 are a favourite device of du Cerceau and his followers. The square profile of the handle of the ewer (pl. 17) is a French fashion that survives in the latter part of the 16th century on the ewers that formed part of the plate of the Order of *Saint Esprit*, founded in 1578. About 1540-45.
Kunstbibliothek, Berlin.

Plate 19.
Pen and wash drawing of a salt-cellar after du Cerceau. This appears to derive from an early work by du Cerceau in which a late Gothic form has been taken over and transformed by using Renaissance ornamental detail. The repeated use of the dolphin and the feathery frond fillings of the panels are typical of this master. About 1530.
Private collection.

Plate 20.
Pen and wash drawing of an altar candlestick after Androuet du Cerceau. This candlestick is of international type, but the dolphin form of the brackets around the central knop points to du Cerceau as the originator of this design. About 1530.
Private collection.

Plate 21.
Pen and wash drawing of a flask after Androuet du Cerceau, the lower part of the body gadrooned, the upper part decorated with leafy scrolls and dolphins. About 1530.
Private collection.

Plate 22.
Pen and wash drawing of a tazza after Androuet du Cerceau, the cover, bowl and foot with boldly modelled gadroons, finial flanked by dolphins. A less sophisticated version of this design was used by the English master of the pair of tazzas, pls. 297 and 298. About 1530.
Private collection.

Plate 23.
Pen and wash drawing of a ewer, from the same set as pls. 20-22; the body with four blank roundels, probably intended to be set with cameos or intaglios. Dolphins play an important part in its decoration; the leafy fronds on the upper part of the body develop into them and they are introduced in both handle and spout. About 1530.
Private collection.

Plate 24.
Pen and ink drawing of a standing cup by Androuet du Cerceau. This design corresponds to the type popular in northern Europe in the second quarter and middle decades of the 16th century. The inscription at the bottom *Couppe à la mode dallemaigne*, provides a valuable indication of mid-16th-century fashion. About 1540.
Bibliothèque Nationale, Paris.

Plate 25.
Etched design by Androuet du Cerceau of a candlestick on openwork base and four paw feet. This design dates from his middle period when he had mastered Italian Renaissance standards of proportion. The scrolling brackets that support the upper stage of the base are an early Mannerist feature. Mid-16th century.
Bibliothèque Nationale, Paris.

Plates 26 and 27.
Two etched designs of drinking-cups from a series of eighty by a master believed to be French, who signed with the monogram ACP or CAP. Their indifference to classical standards of proportion indicates an awareness of changing taste, but the consistent use of plain baluster stems and gadrooned borders can hardly be later than the mid-century. They are too uninspired to be attributed to Polidoro da Caravaggio, as was once thought, and they show a regard for the problems of manufacture that he did not need to consider. Features of later fashion that are apparent in these designs are the small feet and exaggerated bodies ranging from squat bulbous forms to excessively tall ones. It is prob-

able that some at least of these designs were intended for the glass-blower. Mid-16th century.
Victoria and Albert Museum.

Plates 28, 29.
Two etched designs of ewers from a set by Augustin Hirschvogel, published in Vienna in 1543. In this case the conception is so far removed from practical possibility that the artist was probably aiming at the print collector rather than the working goldsmith. The spout of the ewer is in each case the monster's tail which is brought round between his legs; in one case the handle is formed from the mantling of the tilting helmet, in the other it would appear to represent a long tress of plaited hair. The snail perched on one helmet and the bowl with a plant on the other are distinctly surrealist. Hirschvogel sets huge bodies on inadequate feet and these two designs of monsters, whose upper halves are composed of armoured knights, reach a degree of fantasy that is unrivalled in Mannerist art. Even more extraordinary is another ewer from the same series, which takes the form of a leg enclosed in a checkered stocking.
Kunstbibliothek, Berlin.

Plate 30.
Pen and wash drawing of a double cup dated 1526 by Albrecht Dürer. This design belongs to the transitional phase between Gothic and Renaissance. The thistle foliage is a Gothic survival, whereas the lobate form is typical of German Renaissance fashion. This appears to be a working drawing and the persistence of the Gothic at so late a date may have been due to the wishes of the customer who commissioned the cup.
Albertina, Vienna.

Plate 31.
Etched design for a cup with tazza-cover by Albrecht Altdorfer from a set of twenty-two designs for goldsmiths; the cover when removed can be reversed and stood up to form a separate cup. This device was popular in Germany throughout the 16th century. The feet and bowls gadrooned or fluted, the stems enclosed within acanthus leaves intended to be executed in cut and bent sheet. Altdorfer, a Regensburg painter, has shown in this set of designs a complete understanding of Renaissance proportion and has successfully translated Renaissance forms into a German idiom. About 1525.
Victoria and Albert Museum.

Plates 32, 33, 34, 35.
Etched designs of three standing cups and a flask by Hans Brosamer, published in Fulda in or about 1540. They show the fat putti so beloved of German Renaissance artists, medallions intended to enclose cameos, projecting masks modelled in high relief and the dolphins more frequently found in French Renaissance silver. The peculiar spiral bosses on the bowl and the complex profile of the stem of the cup in pl. 33 display

an element of fantasy that is lacking from the more classical French designs of the same period. The fat and heavy straps that compose the feet and the restless outline of the body of the flask (pl. 35) announce the beginning of the anti-classical trend that became evident towards the middle of the century. The central medallion of the flask shows a relief of the Judgement of Paris, always a popular subject in 16th-century art, because it gave the artist an excuse to represent both male and female nudes. The cup in pl. 34 is surmounted by a baluster finial with flat top in which the owner's arms would have been engraved or inserted.
Victoria and Albert Museum.

Plate 36.
Pen and wash drawing of a standing cup signed and dated *Concz (Kunz) Welcz 1532.* Welcz worked in the town of Joachimsthal in the Erzgebirge (Bohemia) but the design shows that he was aware of the latest Nürnberg fashion. The bowl is decorated with a frieze of female figures within niches, the cover with roundels enclosing profile heads, the lower part of the bowl also with roundels probably intended to be filled with cameos. Characteristic of Nürnberg fashion is the four-sided stem with a volute at the top and bottom of each angle. The foot is rendered in an original manner as a silver mine (*Erzstufe*) with buildings and minute figures of miners. Dated 1532.
Albertina, Vienna.

Plate 37.
Pen and wash drawing of a font-shaped cup by Hans Holbein. Running round the edge of the cover is the inscription HANS VON ANT(WERPEN), Following a practice usual at the time, Holbein has only drawn out half the design, which has been completed, probably at a later date, by damping and folding the paper to obtain a mirror impression. This is believed to be the earliest of Holbein's English designs for goldsmiths' work, and it is not particularly advanced for its presumed date, about 1532. It is no more than an elegant and sophisticated version of the font-shaped cups of which a number of English examples, dating from the second quarter of the 16th century, survive. While the form of this cup would not be unfamiliar to contemporary eyes, the composition of the ornament of the two bands that surround the foot and lip respectively shows a mastery of the Renaissance style that could not be paralleled on extant English goldsmiths' work of this date. Holbein has combined the usual Renaissance elements of acanthus foliage, dolphins, female terms and naked boys to form a harmonious and rhythmically flowing design.
Oeffentliche Kunstsammlungen, Basel.

Plate 38.
Pen and wash drawing of a tazza from Holbein's English sketch-book; the foot was apparently intended to be engraved or embossed with the design of a harpy holding up two cornucopias. The frilly collar, which can be seen on the slightly earlier English tazza (pl. 297), is here replaced by one engraved with *guilloche* orna-

ment. The bowl of this tazza could be unscrewed and supported on the rim foot which is shown on the drawing. About 1532-5.
Oeffentliche Kunstsammlungen, Basel.

Plate 39.
Pen and wash drawing from Holbein's English sketch-book of a covered salt. The baluster stem is surrounded by four early Renaissance columns surmounted by cherubs' heads attached to the foot of the salt receptacle. The basket-work chasing on the stem was a popular feature of the mid-16th century. About 1532-5.
Oeffentliche Kunstsammlungen, Basel.

Plate 40.
Pen and wash drawing of a salt from Holbein's English sketch-book. The circular receptacle is supported by three female caryatids, the lower parts of whose bodies terminate in long scrolls and volutes, resting on a circular gadrooned base. Between the scrolls is a panel of Renaissance ornament enclosing a female bust within a laurel wreath medallion. The cover is surmounted by a lively figure of Justice. About 1532-5.
Oeffentliche Kunstsammlungen, Basel.

Plate 41.
Pen and wash drawing by Hans Holbein of an enamelled gold and jewelled cup presented by Henry VIII to Jane Seymour, probably at the time of their wedding in 1536. Holbein's design conforms to the international northern type of the middle decades of the century, but in a particularly well-ordered version. The excellence of its composition becomes evident if it is compared with the two contemporary Antwerp cups illustrated in pls. 289 and 290. The mauresque ornament around the lip of the bowl is the earliest surviving exactly datable use of this motif on English goldsmiths' work. This magnificent cup was melted by order of Charles I in 1629, the gold being sold to the Bank of Amsterdam.
Ashmolean Museum, Oxford.

Plate 42.
Design for a glass or rock-crystal beaker mounted in enamelled gold, engraved by Wenceslas Hollar after the original drawing by Hans Holbein. Inscribed *H. Holbein olim delineavit pro Henrico 8 rege Angliae* (H. Holbein designed this long ago for Henry VIII, King of England). The importance of the royal commission in this case is indicated by the excellence of the design, which is more sophisticated than Holbein's earlier ones. The winged cherubs on the knop may seem out of place on what was apparently a secular object, but they were also used by Holbein on the salt shown in pl. 39. In spite of his tribulations as a husband and the stern justice he meted out to his errant wives, Henry was Supreme Head of the English Church and no one had a better right to such ecclesiastical details on his drinking-cup. The shields round the base take the form of the

supporters of the Tudor royal arms and were evidently intended to be enamelled with the various charges. Hollar has, in order to save space, made two separate engravings of this piece; these are set in their correct relationship to each other in the illustration.
British Museum.

Plate 43.
Pen and wash drawing by Hans Holbein from his English sketch-book of the table-fountain given in 1534 by Henry VIII to Queen Anne Boleyn. This design explains why Holbein was chosen to work for Henry VIII's court. It shows that he was familiar with up-to-date Flemish and French fashion and was ten years ahead of such German rivals as Heinrich Aldegrever, Hans Sebald Beham or Hans Brosamer. The design of the fountain with its figures of satyrs supporting the rim and resting on straps, which spring away from the body of the vessel before curling over and ending in split volutes, anticipates typical features of Antwerp silver of the following decades. The pendants joined by looped chains which hang from a girdle of foliage interspersed with medallion heads are another Flemish feature and can be seen on the Antwerp standing cup (pl. 289).
Oeffentliche Kunstsammlungen, Basel.

Plate 44.
Alternative design to pl. 43 by Hans Holbein for the table-fountain of Anne Boleyn or, perhaps, for another fountain made for her successor, Jane Seymour. This shows a wide basin standing on winged harpies from which the fountain rises like a wedding-cake in four tiers. At the top is a figure of Jupiter enthroned holding a thunderbolt. The satyrs that surround the bowl on the first design support brackets which continue above the brim and terminate in female winged figures bearing baskets of fruit on their heads, a detail from classical antiquity which is also found in the decoration of the Galerie François I at Fontainebleau. Each of the tiers above is decorated with numerous figures sculptured in the round. If it was ever made, this must have been one of the most splendid productions of the Tudor court goldsmiths. About 1534-5.
Oeffentliche Kunstsamlungen, Basel.

Plate 45.
Pen and wash drawing by Hans Holbein from his English sketch-book for a covered tazza of gold set with diamonds alternating with rubies. There is no royal device on this cup to indicate that it was a royal commission, but, in view of its costly nature, it seems likely that it is the preliminary design for the cup numbered 45 in the 1574 *Inventory of the Royal Plate of Queen Elizabeth I.* The drawing shows diamonds alternating with rubies, whereas the cup described in the inventory was set with diamonds only, nor is there any sign in the drawing of the black enamelled border on the foot (see p.111). However, such discrepancies might easily exist between a design and the vessel as completed by the goldsmith. In this case Holbein was evidently called upon to design a vehicle for the display of a large num-

ber of precious stones, probably over a hundred in number, and there was little opportunity to display his imaginative force. About 1536.
Oeffentliche Kunstsammlungen, Basel.

Plate 46.
Design for a standing bowl by Hans Holbein, engraved by Wenceslas Hollar after the lost drawing formerly in the collection of the Earl of Arundel. In this design the cover of a bowl of conventional shape is decorated above with mauresques while the bowl itself is treated as though it were made of wickerwork, a metamorphosis also found in the designs of Giulio Romano (pl. 71). The bowl is set on a stem of the oddest kind, composed of three philosophers' heads and three lion's legs and feet, with a moulded knop between. The base rests on three volutes and the finial takes the form of a pair of lovers embracing. Holbein seems to have made little effort to reconcile the various elements of this design, thus anticipating later Mannerist fashion.
British Museum.

Plate 47.
Pen and wash drawing of a combined sand-glass, compass and sundial intended to be presented by Sir Anthony Denny to Henry VIII on New Year's Day, 1545. The hour-glass rests on a drum-shaped base supported by male figures terminating in foliate scrolls and standing on scaly volute feet. Between the male terms is a circular panel, probably intended to be made of rock-crystal and to be transparent, like the cover of the enamelled gold and rock-crystal bowl (pl. 645). The alternative possibility that this panel was intended for a dedicatory inscription can be rejected as it was not the practice to record gifts in this way in the 16th century. The central stage of the instrument consists of a reversible sand-glass contained in a cylindrical housing. The front of the cylinder opens on hinges to reveal the glass, which is held in a frame to the front of which is attached a male term. The glass pivots around the central point of the frame, the end of the pivot being covered with the favourite Flemish device of a lion's mask with a ring pendant from its mouth. The interior surface of the cylinder behind the sand-glass is divided into three panels of arabesques. The shallow cylindrical member with a goat's-head bracket at each side contains the compass that was required to set the equatorial sundial, of which one half is held by each of the two cherubs. The compass is also shown separately at the side of the drawing. In order to consult it, it was apparently necessary to lift the whole cover which rested on the three goat's heads. A note in a contemporary hand on the right side, opposite the sketch of the compass, reads *compassu superior.* This seems to suggest that there may have been a second compass in the base. If this surmise is correct, it might explain the purpose of the crystal panel in the latter. There would, however, be no need for two compasses on the same instrument and the annotation may merely mean that the compass was set above the sand-glass. On the heads of the two cherubs rests a dial marked with divisions from one to twelve like a watch, and this in turn is surmounted by a royal

crown. This dial presumably belonged to a spring-driven watch, but two factors make this uncertain, firstly its small size for the period and secondly the absence of divisions for the half hours or quarters. It may, therefore, be no more than an indicator dial to show how many times the glass below has been turned. The pointer would in that case have to be moved forward by hand each time. About 1544.
British Museum.

Plate 48.
Pen, ink and wash drawing, an alternative design for Sir Anthony Denny's time measuring instrument, after the lost original by Hans Holbein. The base of this instrument has a bold profile, typical of Italian bronze vessels of the mid-16th century. Above the base is, in conformity with the other design, a drum-shaped stage which was intended to be embossed or engraved with the arms of Henry VIII within the Garter; the elements that compose the ornament of the drum – the cartouches with rolled over ends, the lion's mask and the ribbons with pendants – are typical features of English drum salts. No drawing of this instrument survives that shows the drum open; it probably contained a spring-driven clock rather than a clepsydra (water-clock), though the vertical scale above the drum with the numeral one at the top and twelve at the bottom would seem to be more appropriate for a water-clock than a spring-driven one, since the indicator could be attached to a float and so descend as the water ran out of the container. In order, however, to function effectively for a twelve-hour period, a water-clock must be of reasonable size with a water depth of some ten to twelve inches. The design does not suggest that the clock was intended to be of such large dimensions, nor is there any indication of a receptacle below large enough to contain the water as it ran out of the container. If the clock was not a clepsydra, then the vertical indicator must have been attached to a straight rack that engaged with a toothed wheel driven by the clockwork inside the drum. The clock would only function for twelve hours, after which the pointer would have to be raised by hand back to the top of the scale. In other respects the design of this second instrument corresponds to that of the sand-glass (pl. 47). The scale is again supported by two putti, each of whom holds one half of an equatorial sundial. The compass for regulating the position of the sundial cannot have been placed above the drum in this case as it would have interrupted the passage of the pointer. It would, perhaps, have been accommodated in the base and consulted through the rock-crystal panel set therein. It is also possible that Holbein was not fully conversant with the functioning of a clepsydra and produced his design without having made a sufficiently profound study of the problems involved. This is unlikely as Holbein was well acquainted with Henry VIII's astronomer, Nicholas Kratzer, whose portrait he had painted as early as 1528, and whose advice he would surely have sought before drawing up his designs. About 1544.
Private collection.

Plate 49.

Design for a covered salt-cellar attributed to Michelangelo Buonarotti. This drawing shows the salt as though it were flat, but it was presumably intended to stand on three feet, from each of which springs an S-shaped bracket terminating above in a volute to which is attached one end of a festoon, which extends to meet a skull or grotesque mask beneath the rim, halfway between the brackets. In this drawing the artist has shown little concern for rational construction and Mannerist features can be detected. The salt receptacle is slung between the brackets in such a way that it is not clear whether it is supported from below or suspended from above. The furry treatment of the feet continues beyond the angle between bracket and foot up the lower part of the S-scroll. The placing of the monster's head between the two furry legs is anomalous and the goldsmith would have had considerable difficulty in arriving at a satisfactory junction between them. Finally the bird's-head termination of the two (or three?) mouldings, which run from the centre of the cover to the rim, is a curious and unexpected detail. The proportions of the piece are, however, impeccable and the figure of a cupid on the cover is far superior to the usual finial design. This salt is believed to be that designed for Francesco Maria della Rovere, Duke of Urbino, and referred to in a letter to the Duke from Girolamo Staccoli, his agent in Rome, dated 4 July, 1537. The text (in translation) is as follows 'In reply to your letter of the twenty-second of the last month, I inform you that the model of the salt-cellar with relief decoration was finished some months ago and some of the animals' legs on which the vase of the salt is to be placed are begun in silver; and around this vase run festoons with masks and on top of the cover is a figure in the round with other foliage, just as Michelangelo prescribed, and as it appears in the finished model referred to above. Considering that he has spent over eighteen ducats in its manufacture, and as it is going to cost more than this, I did not wish to proceed further without the knowledge and approval of your Majesty. However I can assure you that there is enough silver here to produce the desired effect, and should some four or six ounces be lacking I will supply them. As to the cost of the said salt cellar the goldsmiths who served your father in the past demand thirty scudi for making it and twelve ducats of Portuguese gold for gilding it'. It is not known if the salt was ever completed. The description in Staccoli's letter corresponds exactly to the salt shown in the drawing, of which there are two versions, one in the Victoria and Albert and the other in the British Museum.
British Museum.

Plate 50.

Pen and wash drawing of a ewer attributed to Polidoro Caldara da Caravaggio; perhaps intended to decorate a house facade and to be seen from below. Designs after or in the manner of Polidoro often show a coarseness of detail that must have made them inappropriate for execution in precious metal. Such bold effects could best be achieved by modellers working in a more plastic material such as majolica (see pl. 718). The complex profiles and the twisted-snake handle favoured by Polidoro are frequently found on 17th century Italian majolica ewers and vases. Polidoro's designs were engraved and three editions were issued between 1582 and 1638, indicating that they had a greater appeal to Baroque than to Renaissance taste.
Christchurch, Oxford.

Plate 51.

Engraved design by Enea Vico of a candlestick, one of a set of four published in 1552. The Classical Renaissance ornament is here combined with soft and fleshy forms that seem to anticipate the Dutch style introduced by the Utrecht family of van Vianen towards the end of the century. Vico's inventions include the sinking, flaccid drip-pan and the elongated ovoid stem; the elements of the design melt into each other instead of being clearly demarcated in the Renaissance manner.
Victoria and Albert Museum.

Plate 52.

Pen and wash drawing of a ewer attributed to Antonio Gentile of Faenza, or to an immediate follower. It belongs to a series, apparently executed for his patron, Cardinal Alessandro Farnese, that includes an alternative design for the ewer and preliminary versions of the pair of altar candlesticks he made for presentation by the Cardinal to the Basilica of St. Peter, Rome. The initials on the cartouche on the foot can be expanded as: *Alessandro Farnese Sacrae Romanae Ecclesiae Vice Cancellarius*, and the shield immediately above is charged with the Farnese arms. The design, with its curious frieze of aediculae running round the middle of the body, shows the influence of Michelangelo, but the artist is a more committed Mannerist than was his master. The drawing repeats many of the elements introduced by Gentile in his altar candlesticks but in less coherent manner. The treatment of the spout of the ewer as a monster's head is an ingenious feature which hardly accords with the architectural design of the body.
Victoria and Albert Museum.

Plate 53.

Pen and wash drawing of a covered tazza by Perino del Vaga; the circular or, perhaps, oval bowl with snake handles is supported on a knopped stem terminating, above, in six winged cherubs holding hands and, below, in four twin-tailed mermen; to the left of the bowl three small-scale sketches of similar but simpler tazzas. In the design of the bowl and cover the artist has kept close to a classical prototype.
Victoria and Albert Museum.

Plate 54.

Pen and wash drawing of a boat-shaped ewer attributed to Perino del Vaga, the body decorated with a bas-relief of nymphs and tritons, probably derived from a classical sarcophagus. The baluster foot with two applied female nudes. Such boat- or galley-shaped vessels, usually carved from rock-crystal or some other

semi-precious hardstone with gold mounts, were particularly favoured at the European courts and examples are still to be seen in the former dynastic collections.
Cooper-Hewitt Museum, New York.

Plate 55.

Two pen and wash drawings for a ewer and one for a hanging bowl by or from the studio of Perino del Vaga. The problem of adapting the human frame to the form of a ewer was one that appealed to the Mannerist designers and in particular to the school of Perino del Vaga, see also pl. 57. The two ewers show how, in one case, a demi-female figure and, in the other, a three-quarter one, could be transformed into the neck or neck and body of a vessel. The large ewer was probably intended to be made of hardstone, as would have been the body of the exceptionally elegant bowl with swinging handle to the left of the sheet.
Cooper-Hewitt Museum, New York.

Plate 56.

Two pen and wash drawings of candlesticks from the studio of Perino del Vaga. A characteristic device of Perino, seen in both these drawings and the ewer (pl. 54) was to perch female figures on projecting ledges or in some other commanding position; in each case they take up the same posture. The candlestick on the right of the sheet is a particularly inspired design with the knop formed as a Renaissance *tempietto* and with the three Graces grouped around the upper part of the stem. The influence of Michelangelo is apparent in the design of the bases. The elongated figures and their unconventional placing are Mannerist features of what otherwise is a typical Renaissance composition. A similar drawing in the Royal Library, Windsor (Vol. 196, fol. 65) is attributed to Luzio Romano.
Victoria and Albert Museum.

Plate 57.

Two pen and wash drawings of a ewer after Perino del Vaga. This peculiar ewer in the form of a crouching nude man with his arms folded above a glass or rock-crystal window through which the contents could be viewed, must rank as one of Perino's more ingenious but less successful inventions.
Victoria and Albert Museum.

Plate 58.

Pen and wash drawing of a basin by Perino del Vaga. In this design there seems to be a confusion of motifs, but this is because the artist has combined a number of alternative versions on the one drawing. Four different designs are provided for the frames of the oval cartouches, which were intended to contain rock-crystal or coloured hardstone panels. With the exception of the outermost border, nearly all the ornaments are shown in alternative versions. The legend in the central semi-circular area is a panegyric of Perino's qualities. Another version of this drawing is in the Hamburg Kunsthalle.
British Museum.

Plate 59.

Pen and wash drawing of a casket by Perino del Vaga, the base is supported on swans with outstretched wings, the front panelled. The side panels with oval cartouches within strapwork borders with curled over ends, the central one a drawer front with lion's-mask handle. The upper stage with two panels, one with classical figure subject, the other with a ribbon holding branches of laurel, the top surmounted by winged victories. The drawing provides alternative versions of panels and of other details, presumably for submission to the client. The stepped construction is a later development that replaced the more rectangular form derived from the Italian Renaissance *cassone*.
Galleria degli Uffizi, Florence.

Plate 60.

Pen and wash drawing attributed to Perino del Vaga, the basic form of bowl and cover corresponds to Renaissance convention, but is enriched by the addition of swags of drapery and by the ambitious group of a river god, a female nude emblematic of Abundance and a sleeping Cupid. Following the usual practice of the time, only the essential part of the design has been completed.
Victoria and Albert Museum.

Plate 61.

Pen and wash drawing of a tureen or salt-cellar by Giulio Romano, inscribed in his own hand *questo feci alo Sr do ferante Gonzaga* (I made this for Don Ferrante Gonzaga). The design is copied almost exactly from a Roman sarcophagus but with the addition of the demi-putto holding up a wine-jug.
Duke of Devonshire, Chatsworth.

Plate 62.

Pen and wash drawing of a candlestick by Giulio Romano, inscribed *Illmo sr. Feran(te) (Gonz)aga*. The hexagonal base supports four or, perhaps, six lions emerging from foliage, the socket supported by two cherubs also emerging from foliage.
Christchurch, Oxford.

Plate 63.

Pen and wash drawing of a ewer by Giulio Romano in the form of a dolphin supported on a foot composed of waves, a scallop-shell filling the curl of its body.
Christchurch, Oxford.

Plate 64.

Pen and wash drawing of a two-spouted ewer or flask by Giulio Romano, the body composed of two addorsed ducks whose beaks form the spouts and whose feet form the base. The flask is filled from a screw stopper in the form of a fruit.
British Museum.

Plate 65.
Pen and wash drawing of a ewer by Giulio Romano; this design is composed of various elements associated with marine life and the surface is given a soft effect into which the dolphins and molluscs seem to dissolve. *Christchurch, Oxford.*

Plate 66.
Pen and wash drawing of a tureen by or after Giulio Romano; three goats stand on a rocky base with vine trails and support on their backs the circular bowl with a frieze of linked dolphins. The cover surmounted by a demi-putto holding an oval medallion against his back. This design illustrates the tendency of the Italian masters to turn domestic vessels into elaborate works of sculpture. *Victoria and Albert Museum.*

Plate 67.
Pen and wash drawing by Giulio Romano of a fruit-dish composed of vine-leaves and bunches of grapes, a revival of the extreme naturalism also found in German late Gothic goldsmiths' work. *Duke of Devonshire, Chatsworth.*

Plate 68
Pen and wash drawing by Giulio Romano of a basin in the form of a whirlpool alive with fish, crabs, lobsters and turtles which are swept in a diminishing spiral into the mouth of a grimacing mask of Oceanus, the border composed of shells from which rivulets run into the basin. *Duke of Devonshire, Chatsworth.*

Plate 69.
Pen and wash drawing of a lamp by or after Giulio Romano, in the form of three baby tritons with intertwined tails supporting a vessel with four dolphin-head burners. *Christchurch, Oxford.*

Plate 70.
Pen and wash drawing of a candlestick after Giulio Romano, the foot is composed of addorsed winged harpies with a lion mask between, the stem wrought with foliage and seed-pods. Though shown as a flat composition, the foot would presumably have been completed with a third harpy. *Fitzwilliam Museum, Cambridge.*

Plate 71, 72.
Two pen and wash drawings of ewers after Giulio Romano, the first with handle and spout composed of basket work, the ovoid body with applied fruit and, around the bottom, a wave motif; the second with intertwined eel-handle, dolphin-spout, the body in three stages each decorated with marine subjects, swans and bullrushes. Both ewers intended to be of white silver, the ornament gilt. *Fitzwilliam Museum, Cambridge.*

Plate 73.
Pen and wash drawing of a salt-cellar after Giulio Romano, described as being of large size intended for the sideboard. The rim is wrought with basketwork, while the cover is formed as infants emerging from egg-shells, one of them embracing a swan, doubtless with reference to their mother Leda's alliance with Jupiter in the guise of a swan. A design in such high relief as this would present serious technical problems to the goldsmith, unless it were cast in several parts. *Fitzwilliam Museum, Cambridge.*

Plate 74.
Pen and wash drawing by Giulio Romano of a parcel gilt tazza; of familiar Renaissance type, many northern examples survive, whereas no single one has been definitely identified as Italian. The drawing is inscribed *Princ(ipe) federico Capriano*, presumably the name of the client. Giulio Romano is one of the few masters of goldsmith's design who noted the name of the customer on his drawings. *Oesterreichisches Museum für angewandte Kunst, Vienna.*

Plate 75.
Pen and wash drawing after Giulio Romano of a parcel-gilt goblet; this is of a specifically Italian form but no extant examples are known. The Fitzwilliam Codex, from which pls. 70-73 and 75 are taken, includes a large number of drawings of vessel types that must have been familiar in the 16th century but of which no examples are known to survive. *Fitzwilliam Museum, Cambridge.*

Plate 76.
Pen and wash drawing of a ewer by Francesco Salviati. One of the Graces forms the handle while the other two are seated by her side. The figure of a female satyr is so alive and powerful that she seems about to spring from her perch. A feature of this design and of many others of the school of Salviati is the ingenious combination of so large a variety of motifs in so confined a space. *Ashmolean Museum, Oxford.*

Plate 77.
Pen and wash drawing of a covered tazza attributed to Francesco Salviati, the decoration concentrated on foot and cover, the undecorated bowl probably intended to be made of hardstone. The terms with linked hands have smaller seated figures placed in the space between their arms and bodies, but with a curious difference of scale that was nevertheless acceptable in the climate of taste of the time. *Oesterreichisches Museum für angewandte Kunst, Vienna.*

Plate 78.
Pen and wash drawing of a combined table-centre

and salt-cellar from the studio of Francesco Salviati. The design suggests that the vessel was to be seen from the front only, whereas its function was such that it must be seen from all sides. Presumably the two figures, shown recumbent by the side of the central vase which supports a putto riding on a female tiger, must be joined by a third on the other side. The arrangement of the sides of the base with figures of winged putti holding garlands and separated by grotesque masks, alternating with oval panels containing figure subjects in low relief, can be paralleled in many other drawings by Salviati or his school.
Victoria and Albert Museum.

Plate 79.
Pen and wash drawing of a dish by Francesco Salviati; in the centre a river god, surrounded by a frieze with the Fall of Phaethon. The Phaethon subject is derived, but with considerable variation, from Michelanglo's famous presentation drawing of the same subject at Windsor Castle (Popham and Wilde, cat. no. 434). The outer border decorated with swans and sea-creatures. A similar drawing with a figure of Neptune in the centre is at Windsor Castle (Schilling and Blunt no. 6002).
Victoria and Albert Museum.

Plate 80.
Pen and wash drawing of a dish or tazza, school of Salviati, the centre with a figure of Amphitrite drawn on a shell by dolphins, the border with a frieze of nymphs sporting with tritons, the rim decorated with shells.
Victoria and Albert Museum.

Plate 81.
Pen and wash drawing of a large basin, school of Salviati; this design shows alternative treatments of the inner and outer borders: on the left are sea-centaurs in combat, on the right a Bacchic scene. Formerly attributed to Peruzzi, it is closer to Salviati's manner.
Pierpont Morgan Library, New York.

Plate 82.
Engraving by Cherubino Alberti of two table knives after the design of Francesco Salviati. The handles are composed of intermingled human and animal forms; in one of them the theme of the entrapped satyr is taken over, perhaps from some Flemish source. The satyr is not only bound by his hands to a tree but is undergoing the unwelcome attentions of an elderly man. The pommel of this same knife terminates in a Janus-like head with mixed animal and human features; Salviati has shown ingenuity in adapting the various elements that compose his handles to the shape required. The griffin that surmounts the second handle is a particularly happy solution.
Victoria and Albert Museum.

Plate 83.
Pen and wash drawing of a salt-cellar in the manner of Salviati; the contemporary annotation states that the salt-cellar has the form of a ship. All the figures that compose the design, mermaids, dolphins, swans, baby tritons, the river-god in the reserved panel and the Neptune on the top are associated with the sea. Another version of this drawing is in the Victoria and Albert Museum.
Formerly Perman Collection, Stockholm.

Plate 84.
Pen and wash drawing of a ewer attributed to Marco Marchetti of Faenza. Like Polidoro Caldara, this master was a fresco painter and his designs for vases are distinctly *malerisch* in approach. This lively drawing corresponds closely to the mid-16th-century Mannerist type with satyrs surrounding the body and a goat and dolphin handle.
Christchurch, Oxford.

Plate 85.
Pen and wash drawing of a ewer attributed to Francesco Salviati. This appears to be the earliest of numerous extant versions; there is a second version at Christchurch, others are in the Uffizi and the Oesterreichisches Museum für angewandte Kunst, Vienna. All show a massive body supported on a diminutive foot, and a frieze of nymphs and tritons derived from an antique sarcophagus, but there are variations in the form of the handle and spout. A similar frieze of nymphs and tritons appears on the basin design in pl. 81.
Christchurch, Oxford.

Plate 86.
Pen and wash drawing of a casket in the manner of Salviati; this design illustrates the typical Mannerist composition that was also used for the Farnese casket (pls. 322 to 327) and for some of the more ambitious German caskets (pl. 428). The recumbent figure of Vanity on the cover was a particular favourite of the Augsburg goldsmiths. In this drawing, as in the other Salviati school designs, the female nudes still display the rotund forms of the Renaissance rather than the long elegant figures of the Mannerist ideal that are seen in the designs of Perino del Vaga (pls. 53-60) or the contemporary goldsmiths' work of Benvenuto Cellini (pls. 313 to 314).
Formerly Perman Collection, Stockholm.

Plate 87.
Pen and wash drawing of a basin; in the centre a reclining river-god, surrounded by four panels separated by winged tritons with spirally twisted tails, representing the Rape of Europa, Diana and Actaeon and other subjects from Ovid's Metamorphoses. This is one of a number in the manner of Salviati bound up with a larger number of German drawings in a codex formerly in the library of the Emperor Rudolph II. Such

designs were equally suitable for the goldsmith or the painter of majolica.
Victoria and Albert Museum.

Plate 88.

Pen and wash drawing of a vessel, probably a salt-cellar but perhaps a nef, in the manner of Salviati, but by a different hand from pls. 86-87. This is another variation on the ship theme that was so favoured for table vessels in the 16th century. Although it has a spout which suggests use as a sauce-boat, the handle is hardly strong enough for it to be picked up. The banner with the Roman eagle, the paddle and the extraordinary masks at the stern, from which floats a sail-like length of drapery, combine to make this one of the most fantastic creations of the Italian goldsmith-designer. The design is based on a Roman lamp.
Victoria and Albert Museum.

Plate 89.

Pen and wash drawing of an altar candlestick in the manner of Salviati, but based on or, at any rate, strongly influenced by a lost Michelangelo design that was also used by Antonio Gentile in the set of altar plate he made for Cardinal Alessandro Farnese (pl. 307). The profile of this, as of other designs of the Salviati school, is dominated by salient, fleshy breasts of sphinxes, harpies or mermaids; Faith is strangely symbolised by a voluptuous recumbent female nude holding a Chalice and Cross.
Formerly Perman Collection, Stockholm. (Another version is in the Victoria and Albert Museum).

Plate 90.

Pen and wash drawing of a covered tazza in the manner of Salviati but with reminiscences (panther stem and putto frieze) of Giulio Romano. The artist seems to have known the original drawing by Salviati illustrated in pl. 77. The amendments he made include a taller stem composed of two addorsed female tigers holding bunches of grapes, the decoration of the bowl with Bacchic putti and the standing instead of the seated figure of Bacchus on the cover.
Formerly Perman Collection, Stockholm.

Plate 91.

Pen and wash drawing of a bowl by Bernardo Buontalenti, probably intended to be carved in coloured hardstone. It resembles lapis lazuli vases from the Medici workshop still preserved in Florence. A preliminary sketch, it has been pricked for a copy to be made, which would have served as the working drawing.
Galleria degli Uffizi, Florence.

Plate 92.

Pen and wash drawing of a salt-cellar, probably of triangular plan, the base with a mermaid at each corner, a heraldic cartouche supported by a coronet, above two

dolphins with a shell and a tortoise between. At the top a figure of Neptune seated on a rock with a trident under his arm, a vase in his arms. Probably Florentine.
Oesterreichisches Museum für angewandte Kunst, Vienna.

Plate 93.

Pen and wash design by Bernardo Buontalenti for the baptismal font of Prince Filippo, son of Grand Duke Francesco I of Tuscany; on the front the Medici arms impaling another surmounted by the Grand-ducal crown. The oval panel in the base is inscribed FLLPI. In working out this design Buontalenti seems to have remembered the Michelangelo salt-cellar in pl. 49. The main difference is the addition of a base and of the coat-of-arms. In view of the great importance accorded to Michelangelo in Florence during the second half of the 16th century, a conscious imitation on the part of Buontalenti is not unlikely. Dated 1577.
Galleria degli Uffizi, Florence.

Plate 94.

Pen and wash drawing of a basin, the central panel showing a seated female figure emblematic of Venice with Turkish prisoners bound at her feet; at her side the lion of St. Mark and in the background Venetian galleys with a Turkish prisoner being led by soldiers in Roman costume. The frieze represents the Triumph of Neptune accompanied by Amphitrite, tritons, nymphs, river-gods, etc., while numerous winged putti fly above, many of them bearing captured Turkish turbans, broken oars and other trophies. The composition of the frieze is masterly, particularly the rhythmic progression of the group of figures and sea-horses. The drawing is thought to be a German copy, perhaps by Rottenhammer, after a lost Venetian original. On the back is the date 1595 accompanied by a reference to the new Calendar. Other weaker versions are known and also details of individual groups from the frieze. The design probably goes back to the immediate circle of Paolo Veronese; it may well date from the years between the Battle of Lepanto in 1571 and the death in 1577 of Doge Alvise Mocenigo, whose arms are shown on the plinth of the column at the side of the figure of Venice and for whom the basin was presumably intended.
Kunstmuseum der Stadt Düsseldorf.

Plate 95.

Panel of ornament from the wall of the Gallery of François I, the stucco figures by Primaticcio, the painted oval panel of Danae by Rosso Fiorentino. In their decoration of this gallery, Rosso and Primaticcio divided the wall space into a series of rectangular or oval panels, each enclosing a painted or modelled scene, the stucco frame of which was supported by and in turn formed the support for numerous putti and nude male and female figures. These were surrounded by cartouches of interlacing strapwork executed in high relief and terminating in scrolled ends turning outwards from the plane of the wall.
Palais de Fontainebleau.

Plate 96.

One of a set of tapestry designs illustrating the story of Jason and the Golden Fleece, engraved by René Boyvin after Léonard Thiry. These designs introduced to a wider market the massive strapwork frames developed by Primaticcio for the stucco decorations of the Galerie François I at Fontainebleau. Published in Paris in 1563.
Victoria and Albert Museum.

Plate 97.

Original drawing in red chalk by Benvenuto Cellini for the figure of Juno, one of the twelve gods and goddesses commissioned in silver by François I for the Gallery at Fontainebleau. Cellini's autograph note states that 'Juno was full-length and made of silver, over life-size for Francis in Paris; there were to be twelve only the Jupiter was finished'. The bronze model (pL. 713) shows a slightly slimmer figure than that in the drawing.
Cabinet des Dessins, Musée du Louvre, Paris.

Plate 98.

Etching by Antonio Fantuzzi of a covered tazza perhaps after an original design of Rosso. This splendid design is the left hand half of a print with two tazzas which is dated 1543. The group of three figures with interlaced arms that forms the stem appears constantly in French Mannerist design.
Victoria and Albert Museum.

Plate 99.

Pen and wash drawing of a ewer attributed to René Boyvin, the body with a scene of Amphitrite in a shell chariot drawn by dolphins within interlacing strapwork surrounded by acquatic subjects. Perhaps based on an original drawing by Rosso.
Victoria and Albert Museum.

Plate 100.

Engraving of a ewer by René Boyvin or Pierre Milan, perhaps after an original drawing by Rosso; with its impracticable handle and mis-shapen spout this design shows some influence from Polidoro Caldara.
Victoria and Albert Museum.

Plate 101.

Engraving of a ewer from the same set as pl. 100 and showing the same Mannerist device of distorting a familiar conventional form in order to achieve surprise. In this case the handle is barely detached from the body and the spout could hardly function. These designs rival those of Polidoro in their grotesque ugliness.
Victoria and Albert Museum.

Plate 102.

Engraving of a nef by René Boyvin or Pierre Milan, probably after an original design by Rosso for François I. The nef was set beside the sovereign's place at table and contained napkin, knife and fork. In this case the folded napkin can be seen inside the lifted cover. The form is very similar to an incense-boat but the ornament with embracing nymphs and tritons is distinctly secular. The design illustrates Rosso's ingenuity in using strapwork. Here it is arranged to suggest the wooden frame of the vessel, while the scenes of sea-creatures engraved or embossed in the sides recall the element in which the vessel should float.
Bibliothèque Nationale, Paris.

Plate 103.

Engraving of a table-fountain from the same set of designs as pl. 102. While the actual form suggests that the object was intended to be a tureen, the micturating boys on the cover and the basin below show that this was a table-fountain. The small panels on the cover show two scenes from the story of Diana and Actaeon. The base is surrounded by snails alternating with tortoises and supported by dolphins.
Bibliothèque Nationale, Paris.

Plate 104.

The Triumph of Neptune, one of a set of engraved designs for the interiors of tazzas by Androuet du Cerceau. These were intended originally for the Limoges enamellers, but also proved useful to the goldsmiths.
Victoria and Albert Museum.

Plate 105.

The Triumph of Diana, engraving by Androuet du Cerceau from the same set as no. 104.
Bibliothèque Nationale, Paris.

Plate 106.

Engraved design for a salt attributed to Jacques Androuet du Cerceau; the stem is formed as a figure of Diana seated, rather unexpectedly, on a dolphin which has apparently strayed from its salt-water habitat, and supporting on her head a large scallop shell and cover, the handle of which is formed by the twisted body of a serpent. The figure follows the Fontainebleau type with small head, elongated limbs and slender body. The use of a figure modelled in the round as the stem, usual in late Gothic silver, was revived about the middle of the century and became a standard Mannerist device.
Bibliothèque Nationale, Paris.

Plate 107.

Engraving of a standing cup and cover by the monogrammist C.C. The long elegant figures composing the stem conform to the Mannerist ideal, but the combination of vegetable and human forms resembles the *Art Nouveau* of the twentieth century. It is probable that this vessel was intended to be executed in enamelled gold. The naturalistic detail suggests the casts from nature that were exploited by Palissy in France and by the northern goldsmiths of the second half of the century.
Bibliothèque Nationale, Paris.

Plate 108.
Engraved design by Etienne Delaune, one of a set of eight hand mirrors. In the centre is the subject of Medea. The border composed of emblematic figures seated on the convolutions of strapwork interspersed with jewels in cusped collets. This and the companion designs were probably intended to be executed in enamelled gold. Dated 1561.
Victoria and Albert Museum.

Plate 109.
Pen and wash drawing of a ewer by Etienne Delaune, the body decorated with oval panels containing scenes from the story of Apollo and Daphne, and, above, tritons and sea-centaurs. In this and the preceding design the scenes are carefully isolated from the surrounding ornament by broad straps and the whole arrangement is symmetrical. Such exact symmetry is not typical of contemporary fashion and it is not surprising that in the upper part of the ewer, above the girdle of ovals, the figures of tritons, masks and waves flow into each other. The handle is composed of the figure of Daphne partly metamorphosed into a tree in accordance with the legend. In this case the Mannerist obsession with metamorphosis coincides neatly with the theme of the ornament.
H.M. The Queen, Windsor Castle.

Plate 110.
Pen and wash drawing attributed to Etienne Delaune of a covered cup surmounted by a figure of Jupiter hurling a thunderbolt, the cover decorated with the fall of the Titans, the bowl with the Triumph of Neptune. The stem is composed of three men whose bodies are encircled by snakes, derived from the Laocoön theme. The actual medium to be used in this and in the preceding design is uncertain, the subjects shown could be embossed in silver, engraved in rock-crystal or painted in Limoges enamel.
Victoria and Albert Museum.

Plate 111.
Pen and wash drawing of a standing cup by Etienne Delaune. This design may have been intended for execution in Saint Porchaire pottery, but the complex profile and the hanging pearls indicate precious metal. The strongly projecting strapwork, which dominates the foot and lower part of the bowl, contrasts with the flat interlacing straps of the bowl and cover. As in other designs by Etienne Delaune the purpose of the vessel is suggested by its ornament; dolphins on the foot, mermaids on the stem and Neptune on the finial of the cover. The basket of fruit supported on the heads of the mermaids is a typical Fontainebleau motif.
H.M. The Queen, Windsor Castle.

Plate 112.
Engraving by Olivier Codoré of the silver-gilt centrepiece offered by the city of Paris to King Charles IX on his entry to the city after his coronation in 1571. This object, which was presumably a salt, was even more ambitious in design than the Cellini Salt (pl. 313). It consisted of a base supported by four dolphins with a frieze showing reliefs of victories, on this was a triumphal chariot drawn by lions in which were seated four gods, one of whom looked upwards in homage towards the mounted figure of Charles IX standing on a plinth composed of two Corinthian columns, around which wound a label with the device of the French king. An eagle held a large crown over the head of the king. At each corner of the chariot was one of the four French kings, Charlemagne, Charles V, Charles VII and Charles VIII. The design of the chariot and accompanying figures was evidently derived from one of the sheets of Hans Burgkmair's *Triumph of Maximilian*. Judging by the print, the salt must have been one of the most important works of sculpture in precious metal of its time.
Kunstbibliothek, Berlin.

Plate 113.
Pen and wash drawing of a tazza bowl by Etienne Delaune, one of three, originally part of a larger series; the design composed of a central circular medallion and four oval ones within strapwork borders enclosing scenes from the life of Samson. The areas between the panels filled with strapwork within the convolutions of which are satyrs, putti, and baskets of fruit.
Cabinet des Dessins, Musée du Louvre, Paris.

Plate 114.
Pen and wash drawing of the underside of a tazza in the manner of Etienne Delaune. The four cartouches contain figures of the Virtues, the intervening spaces, compositions of figures, masks, etc. The space left in the centre is for the junction of the top of the stem with the underside of the bowl. The restrained use of strapwork suggests the later Fontainebleau manner.
Victoria and Albert Museum.

Plate 115.
Pen and wash drawing of a standing cup, described in a contemporary inventory as having come from France, presented to the Emperor Matthias in 1612 when he entered the city after his coronation at Frankfurt am Main. The cup was gilt and set with twenty-five precious stones. Though of more advanced design than the St. Michael Cup (pl. 289), which was given to the Archduke Ferdinand of Tirol, it seems old-fashioned in comparison with the complex forms then being made by fashionable German goldsmiths such as Christoph Jamnitzer (pl. 516). The cup was probably nearly half a century old when it was presented. When such gifts were made the weight of silver was considered of equal or even greater importance than the design.
Staatsarchiv, Nürnberg.

Plate 116.
Engraved design by Etienne Delaune representing a female figure symbolic of *Phisique* from a set of the Sciences. These small prints were much exploited by

goldsmiths and jewellers who executed them in various techniques; engraving, embossing or in translucent or painted enamel.
Victoria and Albert Museum.

Plate 117.
Pen and wash design for a ewer, the masterpiece of Philip Ros of Barcelona, completed in 1597. This design shows striking evidence of the uniformity of style throughout western Europe during the second half of the sixteenth century. The beaded border around the lip of the jug is a feature that became popular towards the end of the century. A similar but less richly decorated ewer is illustrated in pl. 408.
Instituto Municipal de Historia de la Cuidad, Barcelona.

Plates 118, 119, 120, 121.
Four panels of engraved ornament for the borders of tazzas or the feet of cups by Virgil Solis of Nürnberg, probably after designs by Wenzel Jamnitzer, who in turn had derived his inspiration from Cornelis Bos. In these engravings the whole vocabulary of Mannerist decorative art, figure subjects, strapwork, monsters, grotesques and even architectural ornament are combined without regard to any rational association of themes. Nürnberg, mid-16th century.
Victoria and Albert Museum.

Plate 122.
Engraved design for a ewer signed by Virgil Solis but probably derived from an Italian source; the grotesque mask spout recalls the designs of Enea Vico or Agostino dei Musi, with which Solis was probably familiar. Nürnberg, mid-16th century.
Victoria and Albert Museum.

Plate 123.
Page of sketches for the decoration of a tazza or large dish from the sketch-book of Wenzel Jamnitzer. The large number of alternative designs for the frieze running round the central print illustrates the fertility of Jamnitzer's invention. The two drawings of watch-dials in the lower corner point to another of Jamnitzer's many skills. This drawing would have served as a guide to a member of his workshop who would produce a finished design.
Kunstbibliothek, Berlin.

Plate 124.
Page from Wenzel Jamnitzer's sketch-book, showing panels of interlaced strapwork and figures and a *Rollwerk* cartouche similar to the Virgil Solis engravings of pl. 118-121. Dated 1546.
Kunstbibliothek, Berlin.

Plate 125.
Pen and wash drawing of a standing cup, probably half a double cup, bearing the initials of and perhaps by Wenzel Jamnitzer. A fairly conventional design for the period; many cups of this type survive, both as double cups or as covered cups. Nürnberg, third quarter of the 16th century.
Germanisches Nationalmuseum, Nürnberg.

Plate 126.
Page from Wenzel Jamnitzer's sketch-book, with pen and ink drawing of a ewer decorated with strapwork enclosing arabesques, centering on a lion's mask; the half design on the right edge perhaps intended for a pendant jewel. See also pls. 123, 124.
Kunstbibliothek, Berlin.

Plate 127.
Pen and wash drawing of a table-fountain executed by Wenzel Jamnitzer for an unknown princely client. It is drawn on thirteen pieces of paper laid down on parchment, and shows the actual size of the object: another version of the drawing with minor variations is in the Basel Kupferstichkabinett. The large size of both of these drawings (151 cm high) implies that they were intended for workshop use, and it seems likely, therefore, that the table-fountain was actually made. The design displays the usual symbolism, beginning with a ring of various ores around the base from which spring grasses and moss over which crawl lizards, beetles and other insects. Presumably these were meant to establish a connection with the Earth, while the rest of the vessel was given over to the element of Water. Above the base, and supported on six large brackets in the form of cornucopiae, is a large basin and above this two more basins of decreasing size supported on stems of more slender proportion, while out of the top basin projects a plinth surmounted by a female figure holding a vase. Into each of the basins pour jets of water from the full breasts of female terms and, on the upper level, of mermaids. While the section of the fountain constantly changes between one stage and the next, there is no alteration of theme as the eye passes upwards. The fountain was intended to be enriched with enamel, probably true fired enamel as *Kaltemail* would deteriorate in the dampness of a fountain. Nürnberg, third quarter of the 16th century.
Kunstsammlungen, Veste Coburg.

Plate 128.
Pen and wash drawing of a standing cup and cover from the workshop of Wenzel Jamnitzer. This design shows the typical German cup of the middle years and third quarter of the 16th century, with mauresques playing an equal role with strapwork ornament. The lion's masks holding the Medici ring derive from an Italian source. Nürnberg, third quarter of the 16th century.
Victoria and Albert Museum.

Plate 129.
Pen and wash drawing of a parcel-gilt ewer in the manner of, and perhaps by, Wenzel Jamnitzer. The

girdle is shown with Jamnitzer's usual ornament, while above and below are panels of mauresques. Nürnberg, third quarter of the 16th century.
Victoria and Albert Museum.

Plate 130.
Pen and ink drawing heightened with watercolour of a basin en suite with the ewer in pl. XIV by or after Wenzel Jamnitzer. The outer border is in typical Jamnitzer manner; the inner borders include two of mauresques of differing design, one of nymphs and sea-creatures and one of basketwork. Nürnberg, third quarter of the 16th century.
Victoria and Albert Museum.

Plate 131.
Pen and wash drawing of an enamelled and gilt basin. This is a working drawing; its original purpose is shown, first by the fact that no more of the design is drawn out than was needed to guide the craftsman and, secondly, by the outlining in black ink of the intended profile of the basin in the lower part of the sheet. The drawing is coloured to show the goldsmith which areas should be white, which gilded and which enamelled. Workshop of Wenzel Jamnitzer, Nürnberg, third quarter of the 16th century.
Victoria and Albert Museum.

Plate 132.
Pen and wash drawing of the Merckelsche table-centre by Wenzel Jamnitzer. This is a preliminary design and differs in some respects, particularly the stem, from the piece executed (pls. 416 to 420). Nürnberg, about 1546.
Germanisches Nationalmuseum, Nürnberg.

Plate 133.
Pen and wash drawing of a standing dish or tazza, attributed to Matthias Zündt. This design combines the full vocabulary of Mannerist ornament with a frieze of putti borrowed from one of the Nürnberg *Kleinmeister* and with figures of Roman warriors after Virgil Solis, from whom the arabesque frieze around the lip is also derived. In spite of the Mannerist detail the vertical-horizontal scheme of the vessel shows the strength of Renaissance convention. Nürnberg, mid-16th century.
Victoria and Albert Museum.

Plates 134, 135.
Two engraved designs from the *Kraterographie* of 1551, attributed to Matthias Zündt of Nürnberg, showing a ewer and a flask. In the former design the artist has drawn upon all the creatures of the ocean; in spite of the proliferation of ornament the vessel is still balanced and graceful. It could, however, hardly have been executed in this form. The back of the handle is decorated with a row of beads of diminishing size, thus anticipating a fashion that was not generally adopted until the end of the century. The flask is a less original design,

but unlike the ewer would offer no insurmountable problem to the goldsmith. The closely packed ornament is typical of the Jamnitzer workshop. Nürnberg. 1551.
Victoria and Albert Museum.

Plate 136.
Engraved design from Zundt's *Kraterographie* of 1551; in spite of the profuse ornament, the strict horizontal piling up of elements shows that the artist still accepted Renaissance principles of structure. Nürnberg, 1551.
Victoria and Albert Museum.

Plate 137.
Engraved design for a standing cup and cover by Virgil Solis, probably after Wenzel Jamnitzer. In this combination-vessel the parts could be unscrewed, providing a salt-cellar and a separate cup on low foot. In other designs from the same set the figure on the cover could be unscrewed and the cover then reversed to form a dish or stand. For an Augsburg cup of this type, see pls. 442 and 444. Nürnberg, mid-16th century.
Victoria and Albert Museum.

Plate 138.
Title-page from a set of eighteen prints of designs for goldsmiths' work by Erasmus Hornick (c.1520-1583). The author's name, monogram and the date are inscribed in the middle of the flayed skin of an ass. Published in Nürnberg in 1565.
Kunstbibliothek, Berlin.

Plate 139.
Pen and wash drawing of a title-page for a projected but unpublished pattern book of goldsmiths' designs by Erasmus Hornick, dated 1560. In the middle is suspended by nails and ribbons a lion's skin very similar to the title-page of the 1565 publication (pl. 138). In the centre of the skin is a passage from Seneca, below which has been written at a later date its translation into German. The Latin inscription above, stating that the page is followed by 175 drawings of the Treasury of the Emperor Rudolph II, is a later and incorrect addition. Pl. Nos. 150, 151, 152, 153, 157, 158 and 159 all belong to this collection of drawings and may have been intended to follow this title-page. Nürnberg, 1560.
Victoria and Albert Museum.

Plate 140.
Pen and wash design by Erasmus Hornick for the title-page of a projected but unpublished pattern book of hunting equipment. The design shows a strapwork cartouche, with rolled over edges containing a Latin quotation from Plautus, and terminates above in a pair of antlers, flanked on each side by the head of a hound. Hunting-horns and a crossed bow and quiver are suspended from ribbons at the bottom.
Victoria and Albert Museum.

Plate 141.

Pen and wash drawing by Erasmus Hornick, title page of a projected but unpublished set of fifty-three drawings of goldsmiths' work. It consists of an elaborate *Rollwerk* cartouche from which hang swags of drapery, enclosing a panel inscribed with a quotation from Juvenal, which can be translated 'No-one asks how you got it, the important thing is to have it'. This epigram is particularly well suited to introduce the designs of a master who borrowed so liberally from his predecessors and his contemporaries in the field of engraved ornament. Dated 1569, when Hornick was resident in the city of Augsburg.
Formerly the Earl of Warwick Collection.

Plate 142.

Engraved design of a ewer by Erasmus Hornick probably from a set of designs for vases etc. The treatment of the human form with small head and long elegant body and the all-over decoration conform to Mannerist taste. For a ewer in this manner compare pl. 520. In the oval niche in front are figures of Venus and Mars.
Kunstbibliothek, Berlin.

Plate 143.

Pen and wash drawing by Erasmus Hornick of a vase of flowers; these were not intended to be natural blossoms but were made of silver wire and of cut and bent silver sheet.
From the Liechtenstein Codex.

Plate 144.

Pen and wash drawing of a tazza by Erasmus Hornick, the bowl decorated with the Fall of Phaethon, derived either from Michelangelo's presentation drawing of the subject (Popham and Wilde 430), or from Giovanni Bernardi's plaquette which is also based on Michelangelo. For Christoph Jamnitzer's set of tazzas embossed with subjects from the same legend, see pls. 509-10.
Staatsbibliothek, Munich.

Plate 145.

Pen and wash drawing by Erasmus Hornick, probably a design for the title-page of a projected pattern-book of silver vases containing flowers of cut silver sheet. Some twenty drawings of vases with bunches of flowers are preserved in one or other of the surviving collections of Hornick drawings, amongst them that illustrated in pl. 143.
Victoria and Albert Museum.

Plates 146 and 147.

Two pen and wash drawings of a covered salt-cellar and of a ewer in the manner of Erasmus Hornick, but perhaps executed by an assistant or follower. The salt-cellar is supported on three double-scroll brackets and its body and cover are ornamented with rather heavy scrollwork as is the ewer. The style is rather more florid

than that of Hornick's autograph works, but is closely related. About 1580.
Kunstbibliothek, Berlin.

Plate 148.

Etched design for a ewer from the 1565 pattern-book of Erasmus Hornick. In this design Hornick looks back to his Flemish origin; the surface is divided by a symmetrical arrangement of straps into small panels; masks or medallions mark the crossing points of the straps and the panels are either left blank or filled with delicate arabesques.
Albertina, Vienna.

Plate 149.

Etched design for a sauce-boat from the Hornick pattern book of 1565: human, animal, fish forms and a nautilus-shell are held in illogical and uncomfortable association.
Albertina, Vienna.

Plate 150.

Pen and wash drawing of a sauce-boat by Erasmus Hornick. Here the strapwork frame is omitted and the body of the vessel is composed of a writhing mass of human and animal forms, the mutual relationship of which is hardly comprehensible. From the Nürnberg collection, 1560.
Victoria and Albert Museum.

Plate 151.

Pen and wash drawing of a ewer by Erasmus Hornick. One of his favourite and most original devices was to compose a vessel from the confronted bodies of two or more animals or monsters apparently locked together in mortal combat. From the Nürnberg collection, 1560.
Victoria and Albert Museum.

Plate 152.

Pen and wash drawing of a ewer by Erasmus Hornick; in this, as in so many of Hornick's designs, there is an element of erotic suggestion. It may not always be explicit but there is no mistaking the meaning of the tumescent forms he so often employs. From the Nürnberg collection, 1560.
Victoria and Albert Museum.

Plate 153.

Pen and wash drawing by Erasmus Hornick of a ewer modelled in the form of a horse attacked by a lion, who digs his claws into the horse's neck and flank; the base formed as a tortoise. This subject, derived from an antique marble on the Capitoline Hill in Rome, was also exploited by the Florentine sculptor, Giovanni Bologna. Vessels of such bold sculptural form were much admired in the late 16th century when Baroque taste was developing. From the Nürnberg collection, 1560.
Victoria and Albert Museum.

Plate 154.
Etched sheet of jewellery designs by Erasmus Hornick from his first Nürnberg pattern-book. The two cartouche-shaped jewels are base mounts from aigrettes (hat ornaments), that on the left with a group of Mars, Venus and Cupid, that on the right mounted with a watch. In the centre a roundel composed of closely-set faceted stones. The cartouche in the bottom centre bears the legend (in translation) 'Beware for thou knowest neither the day nor the hour'. Nürnberg, 1562.
British Museum.

Plate 155.
Pen and wash drawing of a sauce-boat or ewer by Erasmus Hornick of fantastic form, the two groups of Amphitrite, drawn by dolphins in a chariot accompanied by a centaur, and Neptune in his sea-horse chariot probably derived from Italian bronze plaquettes.
Oesterreichisches Museum für angewandte Kunst, Vienna.

Plate 156.
Pen and wash drawing of a ewer by Erasmus Hornick, the body intended to be cut from rock-crystal, engraved and mounted in gold set with pyramid-cut diamonds and with numerous pearl pendants. From the Liechtenstein Codex.
Private collection, London.

Plate 157.
Pen and wash drawing of a flask by Erasmus Hornick; the central panel shows Bacchus seated in a pergola on which grow vines and attended by Bacchic infants. This design is presumably derived from an Italian majolica flask; Hornick appears, however, to have intended his version for the goldsmith or bronze founder, for, whereas the ornament on the majolica vessels was painted, in his design it is intended to be worked in low relief. From the Nürnberg collection of 1560.
Victoria and Albert Museum.

Plate 158.
Pen and wash drawing of a salt-cellar by Erasmus Hornick in the form of Neptune drawn on a shell chariot by three sea-horses. The composition is derived but with much adaptation from an engraving by Marcantonio Raimondi. From the Nürnberg collection of 1560.
Victoria and Albert Museum.

Plate 159.
Pen and wash drawing of a table centre or, perhaps, an inkstand by Erasmus Hornick. This design is derived from an Italian source such as the Salviati school drawing of a casket illustrated in pl. 86. In contrast to the Italian source, here the winged harpies at the angles are of insignifcant size and are weighed down by the volume they have to support. The horse is presu-

mably taken from a Paduan bronze. The base is somewhat crowded with panels of mauresque ornament, lion masks, swags and ribbons. From the Nürnberg collection of 1560.
Victoria and Albert Museum.

Plate 160.
Pen and wash drawing of a front saddle-plate from the workshop of Wenzel Jamnitzer; this piece was intended to be embossed in relief with strapwork enclosing a Roman warrior, prisoners, etc. A similar saddle-plate of silver was made by Wenzel Jamnitzer for the Emperor Maximilian II. The piece no longer survives, but a plaster cast from the front is in the Historisches Museum, Basel. This drawing is one of a group of six designs for front and rear saddle-plates. About 1560.
Universitätsbibliothek, Erlangen.

Plate 161.
Watercolour drawing by Hans Mühlich of a clock-salt from the pictorial inventory of the Treasury of Duke Albrecht V of Bavaria. The clock is, as in pl. 251, placed within a rock-crystal cylinder, but the salt receptacle is set below instead of above. It could easily be separated from the upper stage by lifting the latter clear of the supporting arms of the three miniature human figures. The detail of the ornament with its amorous couples and the interlacing strapwork of the cover recalls some of Erasmus Hornick's jewellery design. This clock-salt appears to be of Netherlandish or South German origin and to date from the third quarter of the 16th century.
Staatliche Graphische Sammlung, Munich.

Plate 162.
Sheet of drawings showing three designs for tazza feet and stems. The elongated vase form of the stems without separately indicated knop points to the end of the 16th or beginning of the 17th century. At this time Georg Wechter, Paul Flindt and other masters were using this type of strapwork (*Beschlagornament*). Probably Nürnberg, about 1600.
Private collection, Amsterdam.

Plate 163.
Pen and wash drawing of a chalice attributed to Hans Schebel of Augsburg; the contemporary note states that the chalice would weigh three marks if it were enamelled. The colour scheme was to be blue and gold. This sketch was one of three submitted to Duke Johann Wilhelm of Sachsen-Weimar in 1571.
Staatliche Kunstsammlungen, Weimar.

Plate 164.
Pen and wash drawing of a cup and cover by an anonymous master, submitted to Duke Johann Wilhelm of Sachsen-Weimar in 1571. The many annotations are in the hand of the Duke's agent, Matthis

Haug; that on the right above states that the cup would have to be wrought and would cost much more per mark weight than a cast one. The note on the right below gives the estimated weight of the cup (22 marks of silver) while that on the left is illegible. The ornament is no longer divided in Renaissance manner into horizontal zones but merges into a single highly ornate surface. This is especially marked in the bowl in which the various elements of ornament flow together in a loosely organized whole. The lion and the female masks which alternate with caryatids on the bowl are enclosed within strapwork cartouches of a familiar type. The reason for this apparent lack of originality on the part of a master, whose work was in other respects enterprising, is that these masks would have been cast from lead patterns supplied complete with their frame. The castings were soldered into holes cut in the bowl to receive them.
Staatliche Kunstsammlungen, Weimar.

Plate 165.
Pen and wash drawing of a standing cup and cover attributed to Hans Schebel of Augsburg: the drum of the bowl decorated with scenes of Adam and Eve in the Garden of Eden. The annotations explain that all the parts of the cup could be cast, while the lower part of the body was enamelled. It would weigh 18 marks or less, if made somewhat smaller.
Staatliche Kunstsammlungen, Weimar.

Plate 166.
Pen and ink drawing of the Deluge, intended to be embossed on a tazza bowl, the group of a nude woman with a child seated on a bull, perhaps derived from the subject of Europa and the Bull. In the distance is the ark towards which various animals swim. The design is less crowded than the usual Mannerist drawing of the late 16th century. By or from the immediate circle of Christoph Lencker of Augsburg. South German, about 1600.
Private collection, New York.

Plate 167.
Pen and wash drawing of the centre of an oval basin, attributed to Christoph Lencker of Augsburg. The subject, scenes from the legend of the Rape of Europa, is closely related to that on the dish in pl. 498. This may be a preliminary sketch which was rejected in favour of that executed, alternatively it may be the original design for one of the missing basins that originally accompanied the Europa and Bull ewers by Johannes Lencker. The drawing was formerly attributed to Friedrich Sustris, but masters so skilled as the Lenckers might well have been capable of producing this drawing, which is one of the finest goldsmiths' designs existing. While the central position for the ewer is indicated, the border is omitted. Early 17th century.
Germanisches Nationalmuseum, Nürnberg.

Plates 168, 169, 170, 171, 172.
Etched designs for ornament by Christoph Jamnitzer from the series of sixty etchings published in 1610. In these Jamnitzer departs from the then established practice of designing complete vessels and instead offers only details or ornament suitable for application in one form or other not only for silver, but for the whole field of decorative art. His reason for doing so may have been that his own style was too personal to appeal greatly to other goldsmiths of the time. Nürnberg, 1610.
Victoria and Albert Museum.

Plate 173.
Pen and wash drawing showing the race between Hippomenes and Atalanta, one of four original sketches for the *pointillé* decoration on the oval border of the Triumph basin by Christoph Jamnitzer (pl. 511). It is unlikely that the stippled decoration was carried out by Jamnitzer himself and it follows that these sketches are by another artist who was employed for this particular purpose. Nürnberg, about 1600.
Victoria and Albert Museum.

Plate 174.
Pen and wash drawing of a candlestick from the workshop of Christoph Jamnitzer. The scrolling foot is very much in Christoph's manner but one hesitates to attribute the confused perspective of the drawing to the great goldsmith. Nürnberg, early 17th century.
Kunstbibliothek, Berlin.

Plate 175.
Pen and wash drawing of a combined dish and centrepiece from the workshop of Christoph Jamnitzer. An effect of lightness is achieved in this design by reducing the stem to a slender baluster to which strength and profile without mass is given by the attached openwork brackets. Nürnberg. Early 17th century.
Kunstbibliothek, Berlin.

Plate 176.
Pen and wash drawing of a standing cup attributed to Jost Amman of Nürnberg. The design is unusual as the artist has rejected the all-over decoration of the Mannerist fashion and has left extensive undecorated areas, which contrast with the richly ornamented base of the bowl and the knop. The cup dates from the last years of the 16th century; its great height recalls the tall cups that were made in Hamburg for presentation to the Russian court. The attribution to Jost Amman rests on the final figure, but this could have been copied from him. Nürnberg, late 16th century.
Private collection, Paris.

Plate 177.
Etched design by Georg Wechter of a ewer from the set of thirty sheets published in Nürnberg, 1579. The all-over decoration shown on this piece was very popular during the last quarter of the 16th century. The mauresques have developed into interlacing strapwork and are now combined with naturalistic carnations.
Victoria and Albert Museum.

Plate 178.
Engraved design (*Punzenstich*) for a columbine-cup signed P.V.N., corresponding to the form followed by Nürnberg goldsmiths (see pls. 413-415). Paul Flindt of Nürnberg, about 1600.
Victoria and Albert Museum.

Plate 179.
Design for a standing cup with pear-shaped bowl from a set of dotted prints by Bernard Zan; the stem is formed as a tree-trunk which, instead of being felled by the usual wood-cutter, is supported by a cherub holding a lantern. The bowl of the cup in pl. 521 is based on this print. Published in Ansbach, 1581.
Victoria and Albert Museum.

Plate 180.
Engraved design for a nautilus-cup, the stem takes the form of a figure of Neptune holding his trident and accompanied by a dolphin. The violence of movement announces the beginning of Baroque. The scrollwork shown on the bowl would have been engraved on the nautilus-shell. Nürnberg, Paul Flindt, late 16th century.
Victoria and Albert Museum.

Plate 181.
Design for a tankard, the body embossed with scrolling strapwork enclosing bunches of fruit and masks, from a set of forty designs for drinking vessels by Bernard Zan. This dotted print shows a popular type of south German tankard of which many examples survive; only the boldly scrolled thumbpiece differs from the standard form of the period. Compare the Augsburg tankard in pl. 503. Published in Ansbach, 1581.
Victoria and Albert Museum.

Plate 182.
Engraved design for a drinking cup; in use the cup was reversed and could not be set down until it had been drained. It takes the form of a lady in fashionable dress of the time. Paul Flindt, Nürnberg, about 1600.
Victoria and Albert Museum.

Plates 183, 184.
Two pen and wash drawings from a set, some of which are signed with the monogram BV, attributed to Boas Ulrich of Augsburg. Pl. 183 represents the bowl of a columbine-cup of Nürnberg type. Pl. 184 shows the bowl of a double cup. The designs follow the style fashionable in late 16th century Germany.
Kunstsammlungen, Veste Coburg.

Plate 185.
Pen, ink and wash drawing of a silver, parcel gilt, travelling service consisting of a ewer and basin, a *Hansekanne,* a pair of candlesticks, two beakers, half a dozen dishes, plates and spoons, all contained in a travelling-case fitted below with one long and three shorter drawers. Workshop of Jakob Mores, Hamburg, early 17th century.
Kunstbibliothek, Berlin.

Plate 186.
Pen and wash drawing of a ewer and basin from the workshop of Jakob Mores of Hamburg, the ewer formed as a rampant lion bearing a halberd engraved with the arms of Charles Vasa, Duke of Södermanland, and, from 1604, King Charles of Sweden. Presumably made in 1592 on the occasion of his marriage to Christina of Holstein Gottorp, sister of Johann Adolf, Duke of Holstein Gottorp, who bore the charge of a rampant lion holding a halberd in the first quarter of his arms. The basin is of conventional form, the border embossed with recumbent figures symbolic of the Virtues.
Kunstbibliothek, Berlin.

Plate 187.
Pen and wash drawing of a ewer from the workshop of Jakob Mores of Hamburg, the body embossed with a scene of the Judgement of Paris while the spout is modelled as an eagle. Mores has not annotated this drawing and, as the shield surmounted by a helmet under the spout is left blank, we do not know for whom it was made. Late 16th century.
Kunstbibliothek, Berlin.

Plate 188.
Pen, ink and wash drawing of an ostrich-egg standing cup with gilt mounts from the workshop of Jakob Mores of Hamburg. The design of this vessel conforms to the type then fashionable in South Germany. Compare the Nürnberg cup in pl. 481. Late 16th century.
Kunstbibliothek, Berlin.

Plate 189.
Pen, ink and wash drawing of a table centre in the form of an elephant from the workshop of Jakob Mores of Hamburg. Probably intended to be made of silver with silver-gilt mounts set with precious stones. On the saddle-cloth the crowned cypher of the letters F and S for King Frederick II of Denmark (1559-1588) and Princess Sophia of Mecklenburg, married in 1572. The annotation in the corner states that 'this silver and gilt elephant was made by order of his Majesty King Frederick as a Welcome'. Presumably the top of the tower with the crew of soldiers could be removed when the vessel was to be used for drinking a toast. Compare the Christoph Jamnitzer elephant in pl. 517. About 1580.
Kunstbibliothek, Berlin.

Plate 190.
Pen and wash drawing of a basin decorated in three concentric rings with scenes from Ovid and other subjects; the hunting and battle subjects on the outermost rings are separated by four putti within elaborate *Rollwerk* cartouches. This drawing is a copy of an original, now lost, which has been attributed to Christoph

Murer. Another version is in the British Museum. The design is so complex that it would require considerable simplification by the goldsmith who endeavoured to execute it. Late 16th century.
Staatliche Kunsthalle, Karlsruhe.

Plate 191.
Pen and wash drawing of a two-handled vase and cover by an anonymous Italian or Flemish draughtsman, perhaps associated with the Prague Court Workshop. This vase is a pastiche composed of various elements taken from drawings by Giulio Romano. The careful finish suggests that it may have been a preliminary drawing for eventual inclusion in a pattern-book. Early 17th century.
Victoria and Albert Museum.

Plate 192.
Pen and wash drawing of a standing cup and cover by the same anonymous hand as 191 and showing the same combination of Italian and Flemish influence. While the design of the bowl and cover is conventional, the intertwined human and monstrous forms of the foot and stem create a disquieting but doubtless intentional effect. In the curious interpenetration of the figures composing foot and stem the artist has taken the Flemish theme of the entrapped satyr a step further. Other noteworthy features are the peculiar headgear composed of interlacing straps worn by the female half-figures on the bowl and the crustaceans on the cover and underneath the bowl. Early 17th century.
Victoria and Albert Museum.

Plate 193.
Pen and wash drawing of a double cup by the same hand as 191 and 192. Whereas the earlier double cup designs distinguish between the upper and lower parts, the former being smaller, here there is no difference in size or composition. In the placing of the armless satyr, that forms the lower part of the stem, the artist departs from the symmetrical arrangement which was usually mandatory at the time. The curled over straps on the knops recall·Flemish forms of the mid-16th century. Early 17th century.
Victoria and Albert Museum.

Plate 194.
Engraved panel of ornament by Cornelis Bos of Antwerp in which the Fontainebleau strapwork is developed and given more fantastic forms. This scene parodies one of the Triumphs popular with Renaissance artists and shows a nude female figure drawn in a chariot by villainous satyrs with dish-shaped mouths, who are imprisoned within its framework. Typical of contemporary taste is the filling of the whole surface of the panel with ornament or figures. From a set of designs dated 1550.
Victoria and Albert Museum.

Plate 195.
One of a set of four engraved designs for the interiors of tazza bowls by Adriaen Collaert of Antwerp, first published towards the end of the 16th century. The marine theme persisted as the most favoured form of decoration for basins and tazza bowls until well into the 17th century.
Victoria and Albert Museum.

Plates 196, 197, 198, 199.
Four engraved designs from a set of twenty vases and ewers by Cornelis Floris of Antwerp. Pl. 196 is copied from a similar design by Enea Vico published in 1543, while the remainder owe much to Vico's example. He follows Vico's practice of introducing numerous human figures, especially nymphs and fauns, whose contorted bodies form handle, spout or stem. Two of the designs (pls. 196 and 197) are constructed around nautilus shells, a natural object whose complex form had a special appeal to the Mannerist goldsmiths. Eight of the set include one of these shells. The satyrs, instead of being held securely bound within straps as in the Cornelis Bos designs, perform useful tasks such as supporting the body of a ewer (pls. 198, 199) or arching their backs to provide a handle. Published in Antwerp in 1548.
Victoria and Albert Museum.

Plates 200, 201.
Two pen and wash drawings by Erasmus Hornick for basins; these correspond to the standard types of the second half of the century. In pl. 200, one of his more ambitious designs, he divides the depression into two zones in which the inner circle is arranged to be seen from the outside looking inwards, while the outer circle is meant to be seen from the inside looking outwards. The two circles are not clearly separated and the effect is confused. In these designs Hornick uses stock figures of reclining river-gods and groups of nereids and tritons directly copied from Italian or from Flemish or French graphic sources. Antwerp (?), mid-16th century.
Victoria and Albert Museum.

Plate 202.
Pen and wash drawing of a ewer by Erasmus Hornick, the egg-shaped body with a frieze of nymphs and tritons in combat with sea-centaurs, crabs and other forms of marine life above and below. Antwerp (?), mid-16th century.
Victoria and Albert Museum.

Plate 203.
Pen and wash drawing of a large vase by Erasmus Hornick, the surface embossed with marine creatures and grotesque masks. Antwerp, mid-16th century.
Victoria and Albert Museum.

Plate 204.
Pen and wash drawing of a nef, perhaps intended to serve as a salt or ewer. The body decorated with strapwork enclosing oval cartouches of figures and in the centre classical shipping. The vessel is supported on a dolphin and is poled by two men standing in the stern. This design recalls the Boyvin engraving in pl. 102, upon which it is probably based. Antwerp, mid-16th century.
Kunstbibliothek, Berlin.

Plates 205, 206.
Two pen and wash drawings by Erasmus Hornick for standing cups, decorated with strapwork enclosing panels of arabesques or human and lion masks, the latter a detail frequently encountered on Netherlandish goldsmiths' work of the second half of the century. In place of the baluster stems of the typical Renaissance cup, Hornick used a form that was greatly favoured in Antwerp: an openwork basket decorated with lions' masks and filled with fruit. The same motif provided the knop on the cover. The lions' masks were sometimes linked by festoons of drapery which stood out free from the surface of the vessel. Antwerp, mid-16th century.
Victoria and Albert Museum.

Plate 207.
Pen and wash drawing of a tazza and cover by Erasmus Hornick, decorated with lions' masks and festoons of drapery, the cover intended to be embossed with oval cartouches enclosing reclining figures of rivergods, etc. surmounted by a figure of Judith with the head of Holophernes. The stem with applied volutes conforms to the contemporary Antwerp style. Antwerp, mid-16th century.
Victoria and Albert Museum.

Plates 208, 209, 210.
Three designs from a pattern book of goldsmiths' work published by Hans Vredeman de Vries in Antwerp in 1563. The design for a tazza follows the contemporary Antwerp manner with the inner surface of the bowl embossed with marine creatures and the upper part of the stem composed of straps ending below in volutes and above in terms. The salt-cellar is a typical Fontainebleau design, a combination of French and Florentine features, while the ewer derives from the mollusc-like style of Cornelius Floris, which was to be developed so brilliantly by the van Vianen family of Utrecht in the last decades of the century.
Victoria and Albert Museum.

Plates 211, 212, 213, 214.
Four engravings from the *Livre de grosserie et flaçons et bôites de poivre et du sel*, published by Balthasar Sylvius in Antwerp in 1568. The curious device of enclosing the vessels in architectural niches gives the impression that they were all intended to be of large size like the *acquareccie* described by Benvenuto Cellini, but the two flasks were quite small. The design of pl. 211 with the body centering on an oval relief of figures within a strapwork cartouche from which swags of drapery hang and also the rather coarse detail of the second flask (pl. 212) recalls the Fontainebleau style and, in particular, the border ornament of Leonard Thiry (pl. 96). Only the harpy-like figures of the handles suggest a Northern source. The designs for a covered cup (pl. 213) and a tazza (pl. 214) respectively are strikingly close to the work of contemporary Antwerp masters, far more so than is usually the case. Not only are the proportions similar — compare the Antwerp cup or the s'Hertogenbosch one of 1561 (pls. 606 and 613) — but the detail of the ornament corresponds closely. The stem with knop in the form of a wicker basket (pl. 214) is a familiar Antwerp form, but also the group of the Archangel Michael overcoming the Devil on top of the Sylvius cup is similar to that which surmounts the gold St. Michael Cup at Vienna, the Antwerp origin of which is still a matter of conjecture. Finally, the stem of the standing cup with three satyrs (pl. 213) is repeated in almost identical form on the Antwerp cup at Emden (pl. 605). Only the completely plain bowl seems out of accord with contemporary practice.
Victoria and Albert Museum.

Plate 215.
Pull from a silver tazza bowl engraved by Johann Theodor de Bry with Man receiving gifts from the Five Senses, probably after a drawing by Martin de Vos. This reproduction is printed in reverse so that the wording is legible. This is one of a set of four prints from engraved tazza bowls in the Victoria and Albert Museum. The tazzas were presumably melted down long ago. The pulls were taken by the engraver as a record of his work, but before he had completed engraving the text in the panel below.
Victoria and Albert Museum.

Plate 216.
Pen and wash drawing of a ewer based on a design by Cornelis Floris (pl. 197) which was in turn after Enea Vico. The grotesque mask at the base of the handle suggest familiarity with Leonardo da Vinci's drawings of grotesque faces. The intermingling of human and animal forms in the body of the ewer recalls some of Hornick's more fantastic designs. Attributed to an anonymous Flemish master. Late 16th century.
Museum of Fine Art, Budapest.

Plate 217.
Two designs in pen and wash for a salt-cellar by Adam van Vianen in his auricular manner. The upper of the two drawings was engraved by van Kessel as plate 20 in the *Modelles Artifciels du renommé Sr. Adam de Viane, Deuxième Partie*, published by Adam's son, Christian, in 1650. The familiar elements of mermaids and dolphins are used to compose these pleasing designs. Utrecht, first quarter of 17th century.
Nationalmuseum, Stockholm.

Plate 218.
Detail from pl. 220 of hilt and locket showing portrait of Charles V and devices of the Order of the Golden Fleece.

Plate 219.
Detail from pl. 220 of back of scabbard showing Wenzel Jamnitzer's signature and date.

Plate 220.
Pen, wash and body-colour drawing of the Sword of State of the Emperor Charles V by Wenzel Jamnitzer, dated 1544. The drawing, which is on three parchment sheets, shows each side of the sword. The pommel is cast and chased with four crowned female heads, the grip enamelled with mauresques in black and gold, the quillons formed as cornucopiae from which emerge female busts supporting baskets terminating in grotesque masks. The central point of the cross is adorned on each side with two lizards, those on the outside flanking a helmeted head. The front of the locket of the scabbard is decorated with a shield charged with the devices of the Order of the Golden Fleece surmounted by two rampant griffins; below the shield is a roundel enclosing a profile bust of the Emperor and below this the Imperial double eagle surmounted by the imperial crown and, further below, the Emperor's motto and device, *Plus Ultra* with the pillars of Hercules. Below this is a roundel with the head of Janus. The lower half of the scabbard is decorated with mauresques against a black ground and set with eight coats-of-arms, apparently intended to be executed in paintings under glass, though the Spanish inventory of 1602 describes the material as rock-crystal. The back of the scabbard is decorated with mauresques, those on the locket in black against a gilt ground, those on the lower part in gold against a black ground. The chape is decorated on each side with a blank shield supported by two winged female figures. Signed and dated W.I. 1544 by Wenzel Jamnitzer, Nürnberg.
Staatliche Kunstsammlungen, Schlossmuseum, Weimar.

Plate 221.
Drawing by Hans Holbein of a dagger and sheath probably intended for King Henry VIII. This dagger, which could only have been executed in gold or silver, is perhaps the most richly ornamented of its time. The pommel and quillons both terminate in demi-human figures whose bodies are twisted in spiral movement. Judging by the shape of the openings left between the figures and foliage, the dagger and scabbard were to be set with pearls or, perhaps, cabochon stones. The brilliant invention and superb execution of this drawing give it first place amongst all surviving 16th-century sword and dagger designs.
British Museum.

Plate 222.
Etched design by Wenceslas Hollar, after an original

drawing by Hans Holbein formerly in the Arundel collection, of a sword-hilt and scabbard mounts for Prince Edward (later King Edward VI). The ornament of the hilt introduces numerous infant boys, some armed and in combat, others more peacefully engaged. The design of the belt hook terminates above in a putto climbing up a helmet crest. This must have been one of Holbein's last drawings for the English court, executed shortly before his death in 1543.
Victoria and Albert Museum.

Plate 223.
Engraved design for a dagger scabbard signed VS for Virgil Solis of Nürnberg. In this and the other designs from the same series Solis makes use of the strapwork, masks and mauresques associated with Wenzel Jamnitzer and may indeed have been working from drawings provided by the Nürnberg goldsmith. His daggerhilts from the same series with their quillons terminating in volutes inhabited by human figures owe something also to the earlier designs of Hans Holbein. Mid 16th century.
Victoria and Albert Museum.

Plates 224 and 225.
Two pen and wash drawings of scimitars and scabbard mounts *en suite* with the title page (pl. 140). Pl. 225 is the best of all the Hornick hilt designs, in which he skilfully combines such disparate elements as classical figures within niches, strapwork and mauresques. The volute pommel is particularly original. The other design is more conventional. *Victoria and Albert Museum (pl. 224), Metropolitan Museum, New York, (pl. 225).*

Plate 226.
Pen and wash drawing of a garniture of rapier, dagger with sheath and purse-mount by Erasmus Hornick. In this design Hornick follows Jamnitzer's manner and it can therefore probably be dated to his period in Nürnberg. The protruberant grip form seems to have been fashionable about the middle of the 16th century. The elongated figures in niches are typical of the third quarter of the century.
Victoria and Albert Museum.

Plate 227.
Pen and wash drawing of a sword-hilt in the Spanish manner of enamelled gold, composed of a complex arrangement of scrolls and volutes, intermingled with human masks, cherubs and bunches of fruit with a standing classical figure in an oval medallion in the centre of the grip. The quillon terminals are pierced volutes from which putti emerge. Nürnberg, third quarter of 16th century.
Victoria and Albert Museum.

Plates 228, 229.
Pen and wash drawing of rapier and companion dag-

ger from the pictorial inventory of Duke Albrecht of Bavaria, completed by Hans Mühlich in 1570. The hilts of rapier and dagger are enamelled black and white and encrusted with rubies. The form of the grip corresponds to that in the Hornick drawing (pl. 226). The detail of the ornament is far more restrained than the turbulent *Rollwerk* of the Spanish gold hilts (pls. 700 and 701).
Bayerisches Nationalmuseum, Munich.

Plate 230.
Pen and wash drawing of a rapier hilt of enamelled gold decorated with polychrome translucent enamel. The ornament consists of scrolling foliage inhabited by animals including mice. Probably South German, third quarter of 16th century.
Victoria and Albert Museum.

Plate 231.
Pen and wash drawing of a *Landsknecht* dagger, the hilt and scabbard of silver engraved or embossed with strapwork, figures and masks. Probably part of a garniture with the rapier and hunting knife in pl. 232. Attributed to Jakob Mores of Hamburg.
Kunstbibliothek, Berlin.

Plate 232.
Pen and wash drawing of two rapiers and a hunting knife; the rapier hilts of silver sheet bent round a steel substructure, one hilt engraved with strapwork, the engraving probably intended to be filled with black enamel, the other embossed and chased with figures. The design of the two rapiers corresponds to Saxon fashion of the third quarter of the 16th century. Attributed to Jakob Mores of Hamburg.
Kunstbibliothek, Berlin.

Plate 233.
Pen and wash drawing of a dagger with golden hilt and scabbard mounts profusely set with jewels, probably intended, like pls. 231 and 232 for the Danish royal court. Attributed to Jakob Mores of Hamburg. Late 16th century.
Kunstbibliothek, Berlin.

Plates 234, 235.
Two designs submitted by Barcelona goldsmiths as masterpieces, showing a sword hilt and a dagger with sheath by Rafel Ximenis and Antonio de Valdes respectively. The ornament on both is similar, but the extreme crowding points to the breakdown of Renaissance proportion. While the form of the sword-hilt conforms to contemporary fashion, the curious snake quillons and unduly short blade of the dagger can only be described as mannered. The nature of the design makes it clear that both were intended to be constructed of enamelled gold. Dated 1537.
Llibros de Passantes, Instituto Municipal de Historia de la Cuidad, Barcelona.

Plate 236.
Design for an eared dagger from the Barcelona masterpiece book. The delicate arabesques could most effectively have been executed in black enamel on a gold ground. The design is dated 1538, and signed Cristofal Joan. It is probable that this hilt type, which is of Near-Eastern origin, came to Spain from Venice rather than that it persisted from the time of the Moorish occupation. It is referred to in 16th century inventories as *Façon d'Espagne*.
Llibros de Passantes, Instituto Municipal de Historia de la Cuidad, Barcelona.

Plate 237.
Pen and wash drawing of a sword-hilt, the vase shaped pommel surmounted by addorsed monsters, the knuckle-bow interrupted by a vase of classical form supporting two masks modelled in full relief. The cross is decorated with a grotesque mask from which festoons of drapery hang, the upper end of the knuckle bow terminates in a swan's head. Florentine, formerly attributed to Benvenuto Cellini. Third quarter of the 16th century.
Galleria degli Uffizi, Florence.

Plate 238.
Pen and colour wash drawing (Fol. D. VII) of a sword-hilt by Filippo Orso of Mantua; the artist's notes at the bottom state 'one may make this, as shown in the drawing, of white silver, or it may be browned or made of gold, or a mixture of silver or as you like, but one sees the fine chiselling best if it is left plain'. Mid-16th century.
Victoria and Albert Museum.

Plate 239.
Pen and colour wash drawing (Fol. D.III) of a sword hilt by Filippo Orso of Mantua, the notes at the bottom state 'this hilt of cornucopia design can be made of iron and decorated according to one's taste with gold or silver or plain or a mixture of the two, or as it is shown here'. Mid 16th century.
Victoria and Albert Museum.

Plate 240.
Pen and wash drawing (Fol. C.XII) of a sword-hilt by Filippo Orso of Mantua, the note at the bottom states 'this hilt is very light and beautiful as well; the guards are useful, it can be decorated by gilding and silvering or it can be done as you see here'. Mid 16th century.
Victoria and Albert Museum.

Plate 241.
Pen and wash drawing of a rapier-hilt of gold, enamelled and set with rubies, the quillons wound round with leafy trails terminating in volutes. Italian. Late 16th century.
Bodleian Library, Oxford.

Plate 242.

Sheet numbered five from a set of six designs for sword-hilts, ingeniously composed of figures and scrolls in Mannerist style, the grip with a vignette of Mars and Venus. Signed P.W.IN.F. for Pierre Woeriot, an artist from Lorraine who worked in Lyon. The set was published in 1555.
Victoria and Albert Museum.

Plate 243.

Gilt salt-cellar supported on paw feet, the sides decorated with a continuous frieze cast with dancing figures after the antique interrupted on two sides by a coat-of-arms on a separate plaque. In spite of the strictly classical form, the detail of the ornament does not derive exclusively from antique models; the upper face is engraved with a double border, the inner one with mauresques, the outer with a repeating pattern of birds. Italian, unmarked, about 1530-40. W. 8cm.
Victoria and Albert Museum.

Plate 244.

Gilt casket enriched with enamel and set on the sides and cover with rock-crystal panels engraved by Valerio Belli with scenes of the Passion of Christ in a manner that recalls classical reliefs. The mounts constitute little more than a frame for the rock-crystal panels and comprise a series of fluted Doric columns and mouldings embellished with delicate but simple filigree floral scrolls on an enamelled ground. It is not known whether Belli made the mounts as well as cutting the panels. He was paid the large sum of 2000 scudi fot the casket, but the high price may be explained by the excellence of the rock-crystals. Belli had previously asked Pope Clement VII for a commission to make a piece worthy of the Papacy, but according to a letter he wrote to his friend, the humanist Bembo, it was not till he retired to Vicenza in 1530 that he was able to concentrate on the casket. It was completed two years later and is signed and dated 1532. It bears both the arms and the *impresa* of the Medici Pope, Clement VII, but was presented to François I in 1535 on the marriage of his son, later King Henri II, to Catherine de'Medici. It was returned to Florence as part of the dowry of Christina of Lorraine in 1589. Italian, Valerio Belli, dated 1532. H. 15cm, L. 26.7 cm.
Museo degli Argenti, Florence.

Plate 245.

Silver-gilt basin enriched with polychrome translucent enamels and set with rock-crystal plaques, centring on the arms of Pope Leo X in relief, who presumably presented it to Duke Wilhelm IV of Bavaria, (1508-1550). The border is set with rubies and sapphires in tall collets. The enamelled decoration is of pure Renaissance design. Venice or Padua, unmarked, attributed to Valerio Belli, about 1520. Diam. 30cm.
Schatzkammer of the Residenz, Munich.

Plate 246.

Gold casket of sarcophagus form supported on four lion's paw feet, the sides and cover embossed and chased with acanthus scrolls inhabited by birds and masks. Italian, unmarked, first half of 16th century. H. 45 cm. L. 10.2 cm.
Metropolitan Museum, New York.

Plate 247.

Gilt casket, the sides filled with glass (*verre fixé*) panels painted inside with profile heads and mauresques against a gilt ground. The feet are formed as winged sphinxes and the frame holding the panels is enriched with inlaid borders of lapislazuli and open-work cartouches centering on jewels. This casket was an heirloom in the Florentine family of Strozzi and its interior is lined with silk embroidered with the arms of other families, presumably family alliances of the Strozzi. Probably Florentine, unmarked, mid 16th century. H. 20.4 cm.
Walters Art Gallery, Baltimore.

Plate 248.

Rear view of the mother of pearl and silver-gilt casket illustrated in pl. I. Paris, 1533-4. H. 29 cm. L. 40 cm.

Plate 249.

Pair of agate salt cellars mounted in silver-gilt; the bowls and stems of pink agate, the former spirally fluted, the latter facet-cut, the feet supported on four male heads, the concave foot mounts with applied scrolls terminating in figures of dragons, the knops with four applied rams' heads and terminating above and below in acanthus leaves; the rim mount with applied ornament. Unmarked, probably French, second quarter of 16th century. The French attribution is based on the silver mounts, similar agate salts with plainer mounts of German origin are represented in the Kunstkammer of the former Dukes of Württemberg, Stuttgart, and in the Kunsthistorisches Museum, Vienna. H. 12cm.
Private collection, London.

Plate 250.

Ciborium or Reliquary, mounts of silver-gilt set with cameos, gemstones and pearls, the bowl of rock-crystal. This is the finest of the group of six objects surviving, which were made by a goldsmith working for François I. It is accompanied in the Galerie d'Apollon by a pair of altar candlesticks of similar design; all three formed part of the French royal plate until they were given to the Order of *Saint Esprit*. The numerous cameos look back to classical precedent; its most attractive feature is the uncomplicated colour scheme of gold, red and white, achieved by the alternate use of rubies and pearls against a silver-gilt ground. Unmarked. About 1530-40. H. 33 cm.
Musée du Louvre, Paris.

Plate 251.

Clock-salt of rock-crystal and silver-gilt, formerly in the Treasury of King Henry VIII and perhaps presented to him by François I. Like the preceding cup, it is decorated with rubies and pearls, while the octagonal base is mounted with cameos. The clock movement (now replaced by another of early 18th century date) was originally enclosed within the rock-crystal cylinder while the chiming mechanism was in the base. In contrast to the other pieces in this group the sides of the base are enamelled blue. This piece has undergone much alteration in the course of time and the original salt receptacle had been removed, as well as the cover for the latter. The illustrations show it in its present restored state, which is thought to correspond to its original form, with the exception of the finial, which, according to the Tudor inventory description, was a figure of Jupiter seated upon an eagle. It still shows some Gothic features, such as the elaborate cresting around the upper stage; these are absent from the two other pieces from the same workshop, pls. 248 and 250. About 1530-40. H.39 cm.
Worshipful Company of Goldsmiths, London.

Plate 252.

Gilt salt in the form of a ship, the hull of nautilus-shell, supported on a mermaid and an octagonal base with open scrollwork frieze. The salt receptacle is placed in the stern of the vessel. The ball and claw feet and the arcading around the gunwale are Renaissance in character. In view of its delicate construction and the inaccessibility of the salt-receptacle, it seems likely that this was a ceremonial salt. Paris, 1528-9, maker's mark, a crowned fleur-de-lys over two crossed banners, a star below. H. 34.5 cm.
Victoria and Albert Museum.

Plate 253.

Silver-gilt nef supported on tall stem with applied leaf-ornament and circular foot; the shell bottom of the ship is missing and only the silver cage-work remains. The two friezes running around the body are, rather surprisingly, chased with hunting instead of with the more appropriate marine subjects. The ship is fully equipped with cannon, shields and naval gear and gives a convincing picture of a 16th-century vessel. There is no mark, but the presence of a French motto *Plus Penseer que Dier* on the knop suggests a French origin. About 1530-40. H. 42 cm.
British Museum.

Plate 254.

Carved agate standing cup mounted in enamelled gold and set with cameos of the twelve Roman Emperors, the two cameos of Caligula and Augustus set back to back on the cover surmounted by the French royal crown. This cup was formerly one of the French crown jewels and, like many other pieces from this source, it has not survived in pristine condition. It appears to have lost the bottom element of its foot and is now somewhat top-heavy. This is confirmed by the fact that the bottom of the screw securing the bowl to the foot can now be seen through the pierced foot, whereas originally it would have been hidden by an agate base that is now wanting. The design is closely related to the manner of Androuet du Cerceau; the gadrooning of bowl and knop, simple profile of the baluster stem and the openwork foot composed of dolphins, alternating with panels pierced with straps and scrolls, can all be recognised in his designs. The use of a large number of cameos, of which there were originally many more, follows du Cerceau's practice (see pls. 18 and 24). Paris, unmarked, mid 16th century. H. 28.3 cm.
Musée du Louvre, Paris.

Plate 255.

Gilt standing cup set with carved shell cameos of saints, angels, etc. The engraved ornament on the mounts is of international character but the cameos appear to be French and the cup corresponds to the designs of du Cerceau or the monogrammist CAP. The thistle foliage set between the cameos on the foot is a survival from the late Gothic, while the baluster stem with acanthus-leaf clasps is of early Renaissance type. The finial figure is a 19th-century restoration. French (?), unmarked. About 1530-40. H. 29 cm.
British Museum.

Plate 256.

Serpentine cup, the gilt mounts set with casts from Roman coins. The French attribution is based on the French motto, *Nulle Plus Aultre Ne Moy*, enamelled on foot and cover and on the dolphins above the knop and applied to the ring supporting the serpentine bowl. In other respects the cup is international in style. French (?), about 1530-40. Maker's mark, a cup or a well in a shield. (R3 no. 9486). H. 36.5 cm.
Imparmuveszeti Museum, Budapest.

Plate 257.

Spanish gilt brazier, the body embossed with scrolling foliage in the Renaissance style, perhaps after a German pattern book; four dragon handles, the circular foot rim pierced with Gothic quatrefoils. Described in the Ambras Inventory of 1596 as 'a Spanish brazier, gilt both inside and out with four handles ..... all wrought work'. Unmarked. Second quarter of the 16th century. H. 10.5 cm. W. 22.5 cm.
Kunsthistorisches Museum, Vienna.

Plate 258.

Spanish gilt casket traditionally presented to the Capilla Real of the Cathedral of Granada by King Ferdinand and Queen Isabella. The form is still medieval and the embossed ornament is late Gothic in feeling, but the bands of filigree that divide the surface into vertical panels are of Renaissance character. Unmarked. About 1520-30, but with later base and feet.
Granada Cathedral Treasury.

Plate 259.
Gilt triangular spice-plate, the angles with applied female terms, the sides embossed and chased with cherubs fighting dragons within scrolling foliage. Unmarked, probably Cordoba, second quarter of the 16th century. W.20 cm.
Victoria and Albert Museum.

Plates 260, 261.
Two views of the custodia of Saragossa Cathedral begun in 1537 by Pedro Lamaison. This custodia illustrates the culminating form of the plateresque style in which the architectural elements are almost lost in the profusion of ornament. The numerous pendant winged busts recall similar features in du Cerceau's designs and can, perhaps, be attributed to the goldsmith's French origin. The complex profile and rolled-over edges of the shields in the medallions point to a date in the last decade of the first half of the century. The sculptural enrichment was designed by Damian Forment, an alabaster carver from Valencia.
Saragossa Cathedral Treasury.

Plate 262.
Detail of cresting of the custodia made by Enrique de Arfe between 1515 and 1524 for Toledo Cathedral. While the general form and construction is still Gothic, the detail of the finials introduces Renaissance balusters and monsters' heads; the finely modelled cherub holding a staff and shield is of Italian Renaissance derivation. The sculpture as a whole recalls the tense and twisted manner of Alonso Berruguete (1486-1561) who was trained in Florence and Rome.
Toledo Cathedral Treasury.

Plate 263.
Detail of base of the custodia constructed between 1539 and 1544 by Antonio de Arfe for the Cathedral of Santiago da Compostella. This custodia still conforms to the Gothic spire type, but the detail shows Spanish plateresque ornament combined with a profusion of Italian Renaissance elements, including classical armour and monsters that seem out of place on an ecclesiastical vessel. This detail illustrates the mastery of low relief sculpture achieved by the d'Arfe family and other contemporary Spanish goldsmiths.
Santiago Cathedral Treasury.

Plate 264.
Gilt tazza with fluted baluster stem, the bowl with border of floral trails, the centre set with a relief medallion of Lucretia. The simplicity of this secular piece contrasts with the extreme elaboration of contemporary religious plate. Seville, maker's mark of Juan de Herrera. Mid-16th century. H. 13 cm.
Victoria and Albert Museum.

Plate 265.
Gilt dish, the outer border embossed with trophies of arms alternating with thistles and pomegranates; the central boss set with a profile bust plaque, in place of the original coat-of-arms, within a border of laurel leaves and another of winged cherubs' heads. Lisbon, unidentified maker's mark. About 1540. Diam. 32.5 cm.
Victoria and Albert Museum.

Plate 266.
Gilt dish, the outer border embossed with six scenes from mythology and the Old Testament, each scene separated by a Renaissance baluster column, the inner border with a hunting frieze; the central medallion of a female bust probably replacing the original coat-of-arms. The embossing is somewhat naive in comparison with Italian work of the same period. Lisbon, unidentified maker's mark, dated 1537. Diam. 34 cm.
Metropolitan Museum, New York, Pierpont Morgan Gift.

Plate 267.
Portuguese gilt dish, the centre embossed with a thistle, the border with soldiers in mid-16th century costume fighting lions and monsters within thistle foliage. The dress of the figures dates the piece towards the middle of the century, though the thistle foliage is in pure late Gothic taste. Unmarked. Diam. 25 cm.
Victoria and Albert Museum.

Plate 268.
Portuguese gilt ewer of Gothic form but with Renaissance features, such as the egg-and-tongue moulding round the top of the cover and the frieze of figures round the centre of the body. It represents the Manueline style which drew upon exotic as well as European sources. In spite of its originality this style gradually gave way to the conformist taste of the Renaissance. Unmarked. Early 16th century.
Seville Cathedral Treasury.

Plate 269.
Gilt cup and cover with chrysoprase bowl in the manner of Ludwig Krug of Nürnberg. The tree-trunk stem rises from Gothic foliage composed of cut and bent sheet, half way up the stem are a huge snail and a putto; the bowl held by four bands pierced with putti and candelabrum ornament. The finial is again formed as a tree-trunk up which a putto climbs to escape from another giant snail. At the top within the berried finial a knight defends himself against a now missing attacker. His shield bears the arms of a Hungarian nobleman, Johann Sigmund Zapolya (1540-1571). No town mark, about 1520, maker's mark (?), OP in monogram. H.56 cm.
Imparmuveszeti Museum, Budapest.

Plate 270.
Gilt cup and cover set with carved mother of pearl plaques, attributed to Ludwig Krug, Nürnberg. The body of the cup and the foot with applied cut and bent Gothic foliage. The six mother-of-pearl plaques are

carved with religious and mythological subjects after Italian plaquettes and Dürer prints. The figure of a Turkish warrior on the top of the cover is probably a later addition. This and the preceding cup illustrate how slowly Gothic gave way to the Renaissance in the north; only in the detail of the ornament can the new influence be recognised. Nürnberg (R³3756), about 1520, no maker's mark, H. 39.5 cm.
Imparmuveszeti Museum, Budapest.

Plate 271.
Coconut-cup with gilt mounts, the nut carved by Peter Flötner, the mounts attributed to Melchior Baier. This cup was made for the Nürnberg patrician family of Holzschuher, and the naked putto standing on the base holds a shield with their arms. Not only is Peter Flötner credited with making the original models for the figures on the base, stem and cover, but he is believed to have carved the three panels on the nut as well. The figures round the stem illustrate the effects of alcohol; they include a pair of rutting goats, watched by a maiden, who raises a cloth to her eyes to conceal in part their antics, and a girl who makes an explicitly erotic gesture towards a recumbent man. The panels on the nut carry on the same theme of the voluptuous effects of drinking. The stem is formed as a twisted tree-trunk, a form found in Dürer designs, which was reintroduced towards the end of the century. Nürnberg (R³3756), about 1530-40, no maker's mark but probably Melchior Baier. H. 43.5 cm.
Germanisches Nationalmuseum, Nürnberg.

Plates 272, 273.
Two details of figure sculpture on the foot of the coconut-cup, pl. 271.

Plate 274.
Gilt flask bearing the arms of Saxony. The two large circular panels are embossed on one side with knights in front of a besieged city and on the other with peasants, apparently copied from a graphic source close to the Danube school. The handle is treated with great ingenuity; it springs on each side from a tortoise modelled in the round and continues upwards in a series of scrolls, each in the form of a dolphin. German or perhaps Hungarian. Unmarked, about 1540. H. 82 cm.
Grünes Gewölbe, Dresden.

Plates 275, 276.
Agate standing cup with mounts of enamelled gold enriched with jewels, made for the Markgraf Georg von Brandenburg-Kulmbach, attributed to Melchior Baier of Nürnberg. While the foot, with its six portrait medallions of members of the family and their wives, and the stem are of conservative design and correspond to the Brosamer pattern book (pl. 33), the curiously shaped bowl is highly original. Not only is the cup unfunctional, but the treatment of the bowl is sophisticated: though carved in the form of a shell, it is made of agate; this device of one material being wrought in the

semblance of another is typically Mannerist. The perverseness of the style could hardly be better illustrated than by the bowl of this cup, although it was wrought when Mannerist conceits were making their first impact on the goldsmith. The cover (pl. 276) is embossed in low relief with four scenes illustrating Justice: the corpse of the father used as target by the sons disputing his testament, the skin of the unjust judge draped over his chair as a warning, the blinding of King Zaleukos and the Judgement of Solomon. Unmarked, Nürnberg, dated 1536. H. 30.5 cm.
Schatzkammer of the Residenz, Munich.

Plate 277.
Gilt tankard, the drum set with three plaques embossed and chased with scenes from the parable of the Prodigal Son, the figures shown in fashionable costume of the mid-16th century. The points of junction between the plaques masked by figures of putti seated on half columns. The handle cast and chased in the form of a nude woman, whose feet rest on the head of a bearded man, probably symbolising the weakness of man in the presence of sexual temptation. The cover is surmounted by a finial in the heraldic form of an eagle perched on an arm holding a sceptre. Unmarked but probably Nürnberg, about 1540-50. H.18 cm.
Hungarian National Museum, Budapest.

Plate 278.
Gilt standing cup and cover, the bowl set with thirty-three Renaissance casts from Roman coins, the cover with ten more, the finial a nude female holding two casts from Greek tetradrachmae. The pentagonal stem embossed and chased with hop-leaf trails, the rim chased with candelabrum ornament between the inset coins, the interior of the cover set with a finely wrought five-petalled rose. This cup is almost identical with another attributed to Melchior Baier of Nürnberg in the Museo Civico, Padua, which is dated 1534 on a medallion inside the cover. The latter cup is further enriched with enamelling. Unmarked, attributed to Melchior Baier, Nürnberg about 1535-40. H.33cm.
Private collection, Switzerland.

Plate 279.
Gilt standing cup the foot, base of bowl and cover chased with panels of foliage enclosing relief medallion heads, the body lobed, around the top a frieze engraved with figures of the earliest German kings after plaquettes by Peter Flötner. The finial a nude female figure supporting a beacon (now much bent). This cup well represents the style developed by Hans Brosamer in Germany and Androuet du Cerceau in France. The craftsmanship is of outstanding quality; during the first half of the century, the Ulm masters rivalled those of Nürnberg and Augsburg. Ulm, Augustin Ehinger (R³4754). About 1540. H. 44.8 cm.
Württembergisches Landesmuseum, Stuttgart.

Plate 280.

Gilt beaker standing on three pomegranate feet, the exterior engraved, the lip with cherub's masks and scrolling foliage, below this arches terminating in escutcheons engraved with initials and the date 1552; underneath each arch head a figure of a cherub, playing with an animal or holding an object or fruit, in the manner of Bartel Beham. The engraving probably by one of the Nürnberg *Kleinmeister*. In spite of the mid-century date the pomegranate feet are of Gothic inspiration. Probably Nürnberg, mid 16th century. H. 10.7 cm.
Messrs. Christies, London.

Plates 281, 282

Gilt double-cup, the two parts decorated with embossed and cast work. The stem of one embossed with the adoration of the Kings and the underside of the foot with the Last Judgement (pl. 282) the other with the birth of Christ and underneath with the Crucifixion. The bowls are set with eight apostles on one and eight Kings and Old Testament characters on the other. The lips engraved with Renaissance ornament. Attributed to the same master as pl. 288. Unmarked, Nürnberg, about 1530-40. H. 33 cm.
Kunsthistorisches Museum, Vienna.

Plate 283

Gilt cup, one of two almost identical cups made for Bishop Wilhelm von Honstein, the bowl, foot and cover set with rows of casts from classical Roman coins within frames of twisted wire and separated by minute balusters from which spring bundles of foliage. Within this cagework is a gilt cylinder which forms the bowl. The stem and baluster finial enclosed within applied acanthus foliage. The outer rim of foot and cover embossed with a border of gadroons. The rim of the bowl is finely engraved after designs by Dürer with pairs of tritons supporting a shield and sea-horses whose tails develop into volutes. Inside the lid is set a portrait medal of Wilhelm, Count of Honstein and Bishop of Strassburg, dated 1526. The cover surmounted by a figure of a warrior in fantastic classical costume, his head surmounted by leaves, holding in his left hand a blank shield, formerly that of the Bishop. Unmarked, Strassburg, attributed to Erasmus Krug, about 1530-40. H. 37 cm.
Private collection, London.

Plate 284.

Gilt standing cup, the body and cover set with forty-four casts from classical Roman coins. The cover surmounted by three shields, two enamelled with the arms of Bavaria and the Palatinate, the third now blank, probably made for the Pfalzgraf Ottheinrich. Two other covered cups of almost identical design were made for Count Wilhelm von Honstein, Bishop of Strassburg (see pls. 283 and 286). Its stylistic resemblance to contemporary Nürnberg fashion has led to the suggestion that it might have been made in Strassburg by Erasmus Krug, a member of the famous Nürnberg goldsmith family. Strassburg, maker's mark, a fleur-de-lys

(R36965) about 1530-40. H. 29.2 cm.
Schatzkammer of the Munich Residenz.

Plate 285.

Gilt standing cup, the foot, stem, body and cover embossed with rings of bosses or lobes with engraved foliate friezes between. This cup was presented in 1560 by Queen Elizabeth I of England to the Zürich pastor Heinrich Bullinger, in recognition of his help in looking after English Protestant clerics who had fled to Switzerland to escape persecution under Mary Tudor. Like other Strassburg pieces it shows strong Nürnberg influence. Strassburg, maker's mark, a house mark (R36973) mid-16th century.
Schweizerisches Landesmuseum, Zürich.

Plate 286.

Detail of the finial and top of the cover of pl. 283, made for Count Wilhelm von Honstein, Bishop of Strassburg. The figure of a bearded man in fantastic costume is of outstanding quality. Strassburg, attributed to Erasmus Krug, about 1530-40.
Private collection, London.

Plate 287.

Gilt standing cup, commissioned by fourteen clerics and presented to the Cathedral Chapter of the city of Constance. The bowl is decorated with casts from Flötner's series of figures emblematic of the Seven Liberal Arts. An unusual and pleasing feature is the circle running around the upper member of the base; this is enamelled with the coats-of-arms of the fourteen donors, each in proper colours against a green ground. The finial of the cover probably altered at a later date. Zürich, maker's mark of Jacob Stampfer, (R39035) dated 1545. H. 37 cm.
Musée de la Ville de Strasbourg.

Plates 288, 288a.

Gilt standing cup and cover, the bowl of cylindrical form, domical cover rising in the centre to a hemispherical handle. The whole surface embossed and chased in low relief with scenes illustrating the Tunis campaign of the Emperor Charles V. The top of the handle set with a plaquette of Salome holding the head of St. John the Baptist on a platter, inside the cover a plaque embossed with the figure of Charles V in armour riding on an armoured horse over his enemies, among them the Pope, others represented by their shields as follows, France, a cock; the Medici Dukes of Tuscany, the six balls; Venice, the Lion of St. Mark; England (?), the cross of St. George; the Turks, a crescent (pl. 288a). A feature of this cup and of the small group of related cups from the same workshop is the ambitious use of perspective and the skilled embossing of figures, especially horses, seen from the rear with their rumps projecting outwards from the surface of the cup. A rim is missing from the upper border of the bowl of the cup. A similar cup and cover in the Treasury of the Deutsches Ritter Orden, Vienna, is also embossed with scenes illustrating the victories of Charles V, and is dated 1536. A third cup, also embossed with battle scenes, in the British Museum is struck with the Nürnberg town mark but without a maker's mark. Unmarked, Nürnberg, about 1535-40. H. 28.5 cm. *Württembergisches Landesmuseum, Stuttgart.*

Plate 289.
Gold standing cup and cover enamelled and enriched with 88 diamonds, 27 rubies, two emeralds and 123 pearls, presented by King Charles IX of France to Archduke Ferdinand of Tirol. This cup has usually been accepted as French on account of its history and its similarity to the du Cerceau drawings of goldsmiths' work (pl. 24). Apart from the jewelled enrichment its design corresponds so closely with pl. 290 that there can hardly be any doubt as to their common origin. The main difference is that where the gold cup is set with pearls and jewels, the other is set with Roman coins. The Renaissance insistence on contrasting vertical and horizontal structure is apparent in both; in each case the drum is embossed with a figure frieze. Gadrooned borders, curious pendants with masks interspersed with rams' heads and strongly projecting S-shaped scrolls attached to the stem are features of each cup. The scrolls attached to the stem became a constant feature of Antwerp cups of the second half of the 16th century. The cup is known as the St. Michael Cup on account of the figure of the Archangel Michael overcoming the devil on the top. This is somewhat out of keeping with the frieze embossed on the bowl which refers to the pleasure of drinking wine and may have replaced another, probably smaller, figure. Unmarked, probably Antwerp, about 1540. H. 51.7 cm. *Kunsthistorisches Museum, Vienna.*

Plate 290.
Gilt cup and cover, the base gadrooned and decorated with applied masks, circular knop set with four medallions of Roman Emperors alternating with masks; the upper part of the stem with four openwork S-scrolls, the lower and upper parts of the bowl gadrooned, between them a frieze embossed and chased with a triumphal procession of horsemen. From the cornice, which surrounds the bowl, garlands of flowers hang from rings. The cover repeats the form of the foot and stem with a spherical knop similar to that on the stem. The original figure that surmounted the cover replaced by a cross. Antwerp mark, date letter for 1530-31. H. 44 cm. *The Vatican, Rome.*

Plate 291.
Gilt coconut-cup, the nut carved with acanthus foliage enclosing on one side a cartouche with the date 1540, on the other two armorial shields, *parti per pale*, of a man and wife, each surmounted by a crest in the form of a stork; presumably commemorating a marriage. The foot embossed and chased with acanthus foliage, vase stem of Renaissance pattern, three straps holding the nut terminating in winged cherubs' heads,

the lip finely engraved with arabesques. Very little Brussels silver survives, but this cup is of outstanding quality of design and finish. Brussels, maker's mark a mask ? dated 1540. H. 17.6 cm. *Private collection, London.*

Plate 292.
Gilt standing salt; the foot, bowl and cover each of hemispherical form developing from an octagonal moulding. Octagonal knop connected to the top of the base and underside of the bowl by an S-shaped scroll terminating in a monster's head. The cover surmounted by a vase finial on which stands a putto holding a serpent and shield. The foot and cover lobed, each alternate lobe embossed with floral ornament. The design seems to derive from a late Gothic chalice. Maker's mark, a sceptre. London, 1542-3. H. 25 cm. *The Goldsmiths' Company, London.*

Plate 293.
Rock-crystal ewer mounted in silver-gilt, the gadrooned foot, cover and the handle are of early Renaissance fashion, but the long spout with dragon's head terminal carries more than a suggestion of Gothic. Its resemblance to a drawing by Holbein has led to the tentative identification of the mounts as English; this receives some support from the English provenance, the collection of the Marchioness of Conyngham. It shows the stylish manner that one might expect from a goldsmith working for the court of Henry VIII. About 1530-35, the rock-crystal perhaps earlier. H. 18 cm. *Rijksmuseum, Amsterdam.*

Plate 294.
Ivory cup, the silver-gilt mounts enriched with semi-precious stones; the earliest surviving example of the use of Renaissance motifs by an English goldsmith. The design combines late Gothic and Renaissance details: the figure of St. George on the cover and the cresting of the foot mount are Gothic, while the openwork ornament round the base and the cover introduces Renaissance vases, masks and classical foliage. The mounts are engraved in the manner of the contemporary Grace cups (pl. 299) with inscriptions, but these relate to sobriety instead of a Latin Grace. The curious shape suggests that the ivory bowl is earlier than the rest and that it was re-mounted on a more grandiose scale in 1525. London, 1525-6, maker's mark, three implements crossed (Jackson p. 94). H. 30.5 cm. *Victoria and Albert Museum.*

Plate 295.
Gilt standing cup, probably originally completed with a cover. The lip and base gadrooned, the remaining areas chased with Renaissance foliage, the two borders of recessed foliage originally filled with black enamel. The design is sophisticated in comparison with most surviving English drinking vessels of so early a date. London 1529-30, maker's mark, a merchant's mark. H. 21.3 cm. *Victoria and Albert Museum.*

Plate 296.

Gilt standing cup and cover set with onyx cameos according to a design that closely follows the Holbein drawing illustrated in pl. 41. This cup has both a vase stem and a vase finial, the crowning figure of which is missing. The lower part of the bowl is gadrooned, the lip engraved with mauresques, the bowl, in the intervals between the cameos, embossed with winged putti and foliage. The main differences between this cup and the Holbein design, apart from its greater simplicity, is that cameos replace the jewels on the foot and cover of the latter. Perhaps English, about 1535-40, maker's mark: a stork with wings raised within a shaped shield. H. 15.9 cm.
Victoria and Albert Museum.

Plates 297, 298.

Pair of gilt tazzas and one cover, probably from a set of six or more; the foot of each embossed with bands of gadrooning and over-lapping scalework, the cover decorated *en suite* and surmounted by a ring and frame for a heraldic medallion, now replaced by a floral one. The interior of the bowl is wrought with a honeycomb pattern and engraved around the edge with the words of a Latin Grace. This is a larger version of the Grace cup in pl. 299 and, like it, belongs to a transitional stage between Gothic and Renaissance. Both have a frilly collar around the stem. Only two other examples of this size are known. The Deane Cup (pl. 299), these tazzas and other extant examples all owe their preservation to having been presented to churches at or after the Reformation for use as Communion cups. The cover, which fits both cups, must have belonged to a third cup of the set. All are by different makers, suggesting that the set must originally have been a large one, calling for the combined efforts of several goldsmiths.
Pl. 297 cup, London, 1528-9, maker's mark; a crescent enclosing a mullet.
cover, London, 1532-3, maker's mark; a covered cup. H. (with lid) 22.5 cm, (without lid) 13 cm.
Pl. 298 cup, London, 1530-31, maker's mark: a crown (Jackson p. 95). Diam. 21.5 cm.
British Museum.

Plate 299.

Parcel-gilt font-shaped cup (Grace cup), the edge of the bowl engraved with the words of a Grace in English, the cylindrical stem with stamped moulding at the top surmounting a frilly collar, the two tiered foot decorated with embossed and cast gadrooning, in the centre of the bowl a helmeted head, implying that this was a secular cup. London 1551-2, maker's mark; KD in monogram. Diam. 15.2 cm. H. 12.8 cm.
Formerly Parish Church of Deane, Hampshire.

Plate 300.

Gilt standing bowl of the Barber-Surgeons' Company of London, presented by Henry VIII to the Company in 1543, probably made after a design by Hans Holbein. The cover and foot embossed with Tudor roses, portcullises and fleurs-de-lys, the same devices engraved upon the rim; the cover surmounted by the Tudor royal arms. This was originally a standing mazer, but the wood bowl has been replaced later by a silver one. Holbein's English sketch-book contains several similar designs; the placing of the English royal arms on top of the cover, the intertwining foliage on the foot and cover and the knop can all be paralleled in Holbein's designs, as can the engraving on the rim, now obscured by later gilding. The pendant bells are later replacements for more elegant ornaments; the foot has also been given a wider base. Said to have been made by Morett, goldsmith to Henry VIII, London, 1543-4, maker's mark indecipherable. H. 26.75 cm.
The Barber-Surgeons' Company, London.

Plates 301 and 302.

Sand-glass with gilt mounts and wall-fitting, the glass enclosed within four baluster columns, the wall-fitting with cast and pierced cresting centering on a winged cherub. The suspension of the sand-glass is ingeniously arranged so that it can be swung over and hung from either the left or the right hand vertical member, thus enabling the sand to run in a reverse direction. The end mounts of the glass with candelabrum ornament. Possibly designed by Holbein himself; some of the designs in his English sketch-book are similar, amongst them a drawing for a mirror frame which introduces double columns, nearly identical to those framing the hourglass, and the same dolphin-foliate decoration. Probably English, unmarked, about 1530-40. H. 17.8 cm.
Museum of Fine Arts, Boston.

Plate 303.

Gilt beaker, the trumpet-shaped body follows a design by Albrecht Altdorfer, but with the addition of embossed lobes on the body closer in style to Hans Brosamer. The foot also follows Brosamer. Around the lip is an engraved foliate frieze interspersed with medallion heads. London, 1545-6, maker's mark, a head erased. (Jackson p. 96). H. 20.3 cm.
Church of St. Margaret Pattens, London.

Plate 304.

Two-handled cup and cover, gilt, gadrooned foot in two stages, the flattened spherical body fluted, the alternate flutes flat-chased with foliage, pierced dragon handles, the lip flat-chased with a wide bend of foliage. Paten type cover, the finial also serving as a foot. The cover is fourteen years older than the vase but seems to have been intended for a cup of similar type. London, 1555-6, maker's mark, the initials TL linked. (Jackson p. 97). H. 15.3 cm.
Corpus Christi College, Cambridge.

Plates 305, 307.

Altar cross and pair of gilt altar candlesticks by Antonio Gentile of Faenza: completed in 1581 and signed on the cross: *Antonio Gentile da Faenza.* Incorporated in both cross and candlesticks are a number of rock-crystal intaglios which were cut by Giovanni dei Ber-

nardi as early as 1539. The design of the Gentile altar set owes so much to Michelangelo that it has been thought to be based on an original drawing of his. This may be so, for Gentile did claim that in his studio he had 'many casts and models by many worthy men, by Michelangelo and others'. In every stage of their highly architectural composition are quotations from the Medici tombs; the figures round the knop have a dramatic force more powerful than one would expect to find on a late 16th-century production. Moreover, the candlesticks have the logical construction that had long been rejected by the Mannerists. In the absence of other comparable works by Gentile, it is impossible to determine whether the influence of Michelangelo was confined to the Farnese altar set or was a usual feature of his style. Their strongly conservative character may have been dictated by their ultimate destination, the High Altar of St. Peter's, or by the personal taste of Cardinal Farnese. Such designs were equally suitable for execution in bronze or silver and, while nearly all the silver examples have been melted subsequently, a number of bronzes survive. Silver examples such as these were given a finer finish than those made of bronze. Both cross and candlesticks have undergone later additions or alterations. H. of cross 112 cm, of candlesticks 100 cm.
Vatican Sacristy, Rome.

Plate 306.
Silver fork from a set including a knife and spoon after an original drawing attributed to Antonio Gentili. The modelling of the figures is of comparable quality to those of the Vatican cross foot. The grotesque masks developing out of scrolls point to a date towards the end of the 16th century. Unmarked, Rome.
Metropolitan Museum, New York, where the drawing is also preserved. L. of knife 21.5 cm.

Plates 308, 309, 310.
Silver hammer made for the Jubileum of Pope Julius III in 1550 and presented to Duke Ernst von Bayern in 1595 by Pope Gregory XIII. The precision of the cutting of the Papal arms and the relief of Moses striking the rock on the reverse, as also of the strapwork interlace on the side of the hammer and the beak, point to the hand of a goldsmith who was also trained as a diecutter. The two male terms that decorate the uppermost sides are modelled on a minute scale with a mastery that gives them a monumental quality. For its date the hammer is of advanced design; so imaginative and free is the use of the rolled over straps that it might have been designed by Primaticcio himself. Unmarked, Rome, 1550. L. with handle 37.5 cm., without 25.2 cm.
Bayerisches Nationalmuseum, Munich.

Plates 311-320.
The enamelled gold salt of François I. Originally commissioned from Benvenuto Cellini in Rome by Cardinal Ippolito d'Este in 1539; Cellini made a model for the Cardinal but got no further and took it with him to Paris to show to François I who instructed him to make it and gave him the gold that was necessary. It was completed and handed over in 1543. Cellini gives two lengthy accounts of its manufacture in the *Vita* and in his *Trattato dell'Oreficeria,* of which the more informative is the following:-

'. . . It was oval in form, standing about two thirds of a cubit, wrought of solid gold and worked entirely with the chisel. While speaking of the model, I said before how I had represented Sea and Earth seated, with their legs interlaced, as we observe in the case of bays and promontories; this attitude was therefore metaphorically correct. The Sea carried a trident in his right hand and in his left I put a ship of delicate workmanship to hold the salt. Below him were his four sea-horses, fashioned like our horses from the head to the front hoofs; all the rest of their body from the middle backwards, resembled a fish, and the tails of these creatures were agreeably interwoven. Above this group the Sea sat throned in an attitude of pride and dignity; around him were many kinds of fishes and other creatures of the ocean. The water was represented with its waves, and enamelled in the appropriate colour. I had portrayed Earth under the form of a very handsome woman holding her horn of plenty, entirely nude like the male figure; in her left hand I placed a little temple of Ionic architecture, most delicately wrought, which was meant to contain the pepper. Beneath her were the handsomest living creatures which the earth produces; and the rocks were partly enamelled, partly left in gold. The whole piece reposed upon a base of ebony, properly proportioned but with a projecting cornice, upon which I introduced four golden figures in rather more than half-relief. They represented Night, Day, Twilight and Dawn. I put moreover into the same frieze four other figures, similar in size and intended for the four chief winds; these were executed and in part enamelled with the most exquisite refinement'.

The elaborate symbolism that governs the design of this salt is typical of Mannerist art. The artist was not satisfied with the aesthetic merit of the object he had created but sought to subject it to a complex philosophical programme. The salt is of majestic form and worthy of the royal table, but the position of the two figures, especially the Neptune, who lean so far backwards as almost to lose their balance is disturbing. This restlessness of pose recalls the Mannerist tendency to sacrifice serenity and harmony in order to achieve a more striking and dramatic effect. Even more contorted are the figures emblematic of the times of the day, who recline most uncomfortably in the deep groove of the base. The spirit of tension is repeated in the winds, represented as half-figures struggling to escape from their ebony prison. In his modelling of the main figures on top of the salt, Cellini follows the contemporary ideal of long elegant limbs and small heads. The face of the woman is cold and expressionless. a feature that can also be seen on the figures of goddesses on the base of the Perseus and Medusa group in Florence. Completed in Paris, 1543. Unmarked. H. 26 cm. W. 33.5 cm.
Kunsthistorisches Museum, Vienna.

Plates 321-327.

Gilt casket, commissioned from the Florentine goldsmith, Manno di Sebastiano Sbarri (Manno Fiorentino) by Cardinal Alessandro Farnese, and mounted with rock-crystal plaques carved intaglio by Giovanni dei Bernardi. The crystals were ordered from Giovanni dei Bernardi in 1543 and completed by the end of 1544. Manno Fiorentino started work on the casket three years later, but it was not until 1561, eighteen years after the plaques were first commissioned, that the casket was finished. The long delay seems to have been as much due to lack of interest on the part of the Cardinal as to indolence on the part of the goldsmith. This casket, which rivals the Cellini Salt as the finest surviving example of Renaissance goldsmiths' work, represents the mature stage of Italian Mannerism. It shows the whole vocabulary of the style in a complex system of decoration that leaves no space unornamented, introducing broken pediments, elaborate frames, heavy volutes and numerous figures, often in contorted poses, and, finally, repeated changes of scale in figures set next to each other. The only element missing is the strapwork cartouche. Great care is taken in the design of the oval cartouches that surround the rock-crystal panels. There are six of these cartouches, two each of three different patterns (pls. 323-4-5). Each is surmounted by a pair of human figures, either nude or partly draped. Instead of the strapwork that one might expect on a piece that was not finished until after 1560, the cartouches are composed of fruit, birds and masks; on one side only is the cartouche supported on a console bracket flanked on each side by a massive C-scroll (pl. 326). The laurel swags that Michelangelo uses so sparingly in the upper corners of the Medici tombs are introduced more freely to link the volutes of the two halves of the pediment and as pendants running all round below the cornice. Both the interior of the cover (pl. 322) and the lower side of the base (pl. 327) are set with embossed plaques: that under the cover with the Rape of Proserpine, that under the base with the arms of Cardinal Farnese flanked by two medallions with his devices. Roman, circa 1547-1561. H. 49 cm, L. 42 cm, W. 26cm.
Museo di Capodimonte, Naples.

Plate 328.

Enamelled gold and jewelled cup (the Rospigliosi Cup). The design is not entirely successful; in particular the juxtaposition of the dragon and the tortoise is too close; similar designs can be seen in the series of engravings published in Antwerp by Hieronymus Cock after Cornelis Floris in 1548. The northern character of the design is not surprising, the Florentine workshops were staffed in part by Germans.

The form of the cup suggests that it was intended to serve as a salt, but it is too large for this purpose. Though 16th-century salts were often of monumental size, the actual salt container was usually quite small, as is that of the Cellini Salt. The fact that the bowl is formed as a scallop-shell might also be held to imply use as a salt, but at the time shells and sea-creatures were associated with any kind of drinking vessel. The bowl which is supported on the back of a dragon who in turn rests on a tortoise, is decorated with translucent enamels, as are both the dragon and the tortoise. The most richly decorated part is the winged sphinx that is perched on one side of the shell. Her body is enamelled and jewelled like the mounts of Florentine hardstone vessels of the period. An unusual feature is the tiny crab which hangs down from the sphinx into the bowl. Florentine (?). Last quarter of the 16th century. H. 19.7 cm.
Metropolitan Museum, New York.

Plate 329.

Lapis lazuli tazza with silver-gilt stem and mounts; the profile of this graceful vessel suggests French or Italian origin. The decoration of the stem recalls the German designs for tazza stems (pl. 162) but lacks the all-over decoration characteristic of northern Mannerism. The underside of the foot has a pierced gilt mount engraved with bunches of fruit and strapwork cartouches of international character. Probably Italian, last quarter of the 16th century.
Private collection, Dublin.

Plate 330.

Heliotrope ewer, the body of oval section fluted at the base and carved below the lip with a mask of the Medusa, silver-gilt mounts. The quality of the material and the carving of this ewer are so fine that one would expect it to be mounted in gold. The handle corresponds to contemporary Florentine fashion, but the foot seems too large and clumsy and may be later. This ewer is accompanied by a lapis lazuli basin of small size, which, though long associated with it, lacks its subtle form. Florentine, last quarter of 16th century. H. 20.3 cm.
Württembergisches Landesmuseum, Stuttgart.

Plate 331.

Lapis lazuli ewer with enamelled gold mounts, the spout formed as a swan's head and beak. Probably designed by Buontalenti and mounted by Giacomo Biliverti. Florentine, last quarter of the 16th century. H. 27 cm.
Museo degli Argenti, Florence.

Plate 332.

Lapis lazuli tazza in the manner of Bernardo Buontalenti, the bowl carved as an oval shell terminating in a grotesque mask, the trumpet shaped foot and stem carved with a dolphin whose tail twines around the stem. In this and other similar hardstone vessels from the Medici court workshop mollusc-like forms were developed that foretell the grotesques of Dutch Mannerism. Such vases were sometimes left unmounted in order to give maximum effect to the splendour of the stone and the ingenuity of its shaping. The best examples are now in the Florence Museo di Mineralogia, see Heikamp, 'Unbekannte Halbedelsteingefässe aus Medici Besitz', *Pantheon*, XXIX, 1971, p. 188. Florentine, late 16th century. Length of bowl 12.8 cm.
Formerly Gutman Collection, New York.

Plate 333.
Lapis lazuli tazza probably after a design by Buontalenti; the bowl carved as a shell supported on a small gold cockle-shell while the handle is an eel of gold with green enamelled scales. The mount probably made in the workshop of Giacomo Biliverti towards the end of the 16th century. Florentine. H. 8 cm.
Museo degli Argenti, Florence.

Plate 334.
Lapis lazuli ewer made from a design by Buontalenti: the small grotesque mask below the lip is typical of the Medici workshop. The enamelled gilt mounts by Giacomo Biliverti are of exceptional richness and were intended to contrast with the restrained form of the hardstone vessel. Although of vase form, the vessel is recognisable as a ewer by the lip for pouring and the small gold dolphin handle on the opposite side. The base is carved with the Medici arms and the vessel was delivered to the Tribuna in January, 1581, having taken five years to make. It was presented to the Emperor Ferdinand II in 1628. H. 36 cm.
Kunsthistorisches Museum, Vienna.

Plate 335.
Jasper flask constructed of two shell-shaped plaques set vertically and held by a silver-gilt band decorated with four small shells, each with a pin-set pearl. In the centre is an oval onyx cameo of a negro bust set in an enamelled gold strapwork frame enriched with four rubies. Formerly thought to have been made by Jacopo da Trezzo in Spain and sent by him to Francesco I of Tuscany, it is more likely to have been made in the Saracchi workshop in Milan. About 1560-70. H. 27.5 cm.
Museo degli Argenti, Florence.

Plate 336.
Rock-crystal ewer with enamelled and jewelled gold mounts, the lower and upper stages of the body intaglio-cut with hunting scenes, the central area with four recumbent figures within rectangular cartouches from which spring strapwork scrolls; the handle carved in the form of a serpent. The original foot replaced later in gilt metal. This vessel is carved from four separate pieces of crystal which are held together by the gold mounts. The intaglio cutting of superlative quality is attributed to the Saracchi workshop. About 1580. H. 40 cm.
Museo degli Argenti, Florence.

Plate 337.
Rock-crystal bowl of quatrefoil shape with winged harpy handles, the lower part of the body gadrooned and carved with acanthus foliage, in the centre of the base a wheel-cut intaglio of Neptune drawn by dolphins; Milanese, third quarter of 16th century; the gold foot mount, enamelled with mauresques in white enamel against a black and gold ground, probably of French workmanship. H. 7 cm. L. 24 cm.
Rijksmuseum, Amsterdam.

Plate 338.
Milanese rock-crystal tazza with mounts of enamelled gold enriched with rubies, emeralds and crystals, the flattened polylobate bowl engraved with scrollwork, birds and insects, the gold rim with blue enamelled edge enclosing a border of finely drawn black enamel scrolls, in the centre of the bowl two *verre fixé* coats of arms, apparently commemorating a marriage between members of the Augsburg family of Krafter and the Ulm family of Ott. Polylobate foot *en suite* with the bowl, the gold mount enamelled and set with eight crystals. Late 16th century. Diam. 25.. cm.
Private collection.

Plate 339.
Rock-crystal ewer, the body carved with three horizontal bands, the uppermost with anthemion ornament, the central one with scrolling foliage and flowers, the bottom one gadrooned; an old man's mask carved under the spout; the mounts of gold enamelled with mauresques in the French fashion. The crystal probably Milanese, the mounts French. Second half of 16th century. H. 24.5 cm.
Rijksmuseum, Amsterdam.

Plate 340.
Rock-crystal vase, probably after a design by Buontalenti, the enamelled gold mounts designed and executed in 1618 by Edouard Vallet, the French goldsmith of Grand Duke Cosimo II. This master was then aged 76, which presumably accounts for the Mannerist design of the mount at a date when the Baroque style was already established. H. 38 cm.
Museo degli Argenti, Florence.

Plates 341, 343 and 344.
Gilt ewer and basin, perhaps the most richly decorated and superbly wrought of the period in existence. They bear no maker's mark, but the arrangement of the scenes depicted on the basin, the crowded groups of figures in high relief and the bull-fighting scene on the innermost border of the basin, justify attribution to a Spanish or Portuguese master. The plaques on the outer border can be compared with those on the Spanish tazza in pl. 411. Both ewer and basin are struck with a later Rome mark, apparently dating from the 18th century. Like the ewer and basin in pls. 348-9 they may have been made by an Iberian master who had emigrated to Italy; alternatively they may have been imported as finished pieces. The ewer is constructed of four separate elements, foot, stem, body and spout with handle. The body is decorated in high relief with a frieze of a Roman Triumph in which various African animals are represented including an elephant, rhinoceros, giraffe, lion, tiger, etc. The outer border of the basin is set with twelve plaques of scenes from Ancient History and the Apochrypha, the subject being in each case identified on a label above (pl. 344). The circular band around the central boss is decorated with hunting scenes while the depression between this band and the

rim is embossed with two rings, the inner embossed with ovolos, the outer with shells, each alternating with grotesque masks. Much of the ornament on these vessels is cast and chased; the plaques around the rim are attached by screws. In order to conceal the unfinished appearance when the basin is seen from below, the back is covered by three concentric rings engraved with monsters along a river-bank and with scrolls in a lively and original manner. Such elaborate treatment is not unique, but is only found on pieces of great importance. The central boss, which originally bore the enamelled or engraved arms of the owner has been removed, doubtless when the vessels passed out of the family for which they were originally made. A *verre fixé* plaque of later date attached to the top of the handle and inscribed *Materiam superabat opus* now replaces another which probably bore the same arms as those once in the centre of the boss. The representation of the rhinoceros was probably based on an illustration in Juan d'Arfe's *Varia Commensuracion*, published 1585-7. About 1590. H. of ewer 47.3 cm.
Metropolitan Museum of Art, New York.

Plates 342 and 345.
Gilt ewer and basin, the basin signed by Antonio de Castro, a goldsmith of Portuguese origin working in Genoa in the second half of the 16th century. De Castro was commissioned by a Genoese nobleman, Francesco Lercaro, in 1565 to produce a ewer and companion basin which in fifteen scenes would commemorate the story of his 14th-century ancestor, Megollo Lercaro, who had conducted a private war against the Emperor of Trebizond. Four of these scenes are represented on four large panels on the ewer, while the remaining eleven are embossed in smaller panels on the basin. To the many figures contained in the scenes the goldsmith has added others separating the panels and seated on the cartouches which enclose them. Further figures are shown in a frieze running around the lower part of the body and in a panel under the lip. Both handle and spout, the latter of the drooping form found in Polidoro vases (pl. 50), are composed of animal, vegetable and architectural forms in a highly imaginative association. It has been conjectured that the figure scenes were wrought after designs by the Genoese painter, Luca Cambiaso. The design with its seemingly infinte number of figures recalls contemporary Felmish work, particularly in the profuse and convoluted strapwork which frames the scenes. H. of ewer 42 cm. Diam. of basin 53 cm.
Conte Cini Collection, Palazzo Loredano, Venice.

Plates 346 and 347.
Gilt ewer of exceptional construction in that the whole vessel is cast; the foot is screwed on to a threaded rim instead of being attached in the usual way be means of a nut under the base. Around the body runs a series of oval cartouches after the designs of Etienne Delaune; this does not, however, determine the nationality of the ewer as Delaune's engravings had a wide circulation outside France. Whereas embossed work tends to be executed in low relief with rather soft edges,

the detail of the ornament on this ewer is in high relief and very crisply finished, giving a different effect from other vessels of similar type and date. The ornament on both neck and body is divided by horizontal mouldings into four zones, each of which receives different treatment. The ewer shows a wide range of Mannerist ornament and follows Mannerist fashion in the small size of its foot in relation to the mass of the body. Unmarked, Italian or French. Late 16th century. H. 38.6 cm.
Bayerisches Nationalmuseum, Munich.

Plates 348 and 349.
Gilt ewer and basin from a service of plate bearing the arms of the Medici Pope Pius IV (1559-1566). The arms, which appear on a cast medallion in the centre of the basin and also on the lid of the ewer, are not contemporary but seem to date from the early 19th century. As the Pope's reign corresponds to the period of the pieces, the arms may have been added to preserve a well-founded tradition. Though similar in style the ewer and basin are not en suite, nor can the ewer be placed in its proper position in the centre of the basin. The two vessels may even be the work of different masters. The body of the ewer is embossed with a series of cartouches enclosing sea-monsters surrounded by male and female nudes, strapwork and bunches of fruit, while the handle is formed as a sea-serpent with twin heads and tails. The outer border of the basin is embossed with the Planets drawn in chariots, the depression with figures emblematic of the Elements, the innermost ring with the Seasons. Both basin and ewer are probably the work of an Iberian master working in Italy, perhaps Antonio de Castro: their design seems too unsophisticated for a goldsmith trained in the Italian Renaissance tradition. Unmarked, third quarter of 16th century. H. of ewer 47 cm. Diam. of salver 52.1 cm.
Wallace Collection, London.

Plate 350.
Silver parcel-gilt ewer, unmarked but in a style that combines both Italian and northern features, perhaps the work of one of the immigrant goldsmiths employed in the Medici court workshop. The body is divided into four panels, surmounted by grotesque masks and linked by swags of drapery, embossed with swans in white silver against a gilt ground. Florentine (?). Late 16th century. H. 32.8 cm.
Museo degli Argenti, Florence.

Plate 351.
Gilt salt-cellar from the same service as pls. 348,9, the drum embossed and chased with masks within strapwork cartouches separated by recumbent figures. Italo-Portuguese, unmarked, third quarter of the 16th century. Diam. 8.2 cm.
Wallace Collection, London.

Plates 352 and 353.
Gilt ewer and basin, the body of the ewer embossed

with three scenes from the history of Pompey within strapwork cartouches, flanked above by seated figures bearing palm branches, grotesque masks and bunches of fruit between, the handle cast in the form of a male term, the basin embossed with five scenes from the life of Julius Caesar. Both pieces bear the monogram of Anna Catherina Constanza, daughter of King Sigismund of Poland, who married the Elector Wilhelm of the Palatinate in 1642. The ewer and basin appear to have been made some thirty years prior to this date. Unmarked, but probably Italian. H. of ewer 45.3 cm, Diam. of basin 69.5 cm.
Schatzkammer of the Residenz, Munich.

Plates 354 and 355.
Gilt ewer and basin, the form of the ewer apparently based on a design resembling the larger vessel in pl. 55, though the body, instead of being left plain, is here divided into three oval panels separated by half figures of winged satyrs; the basin embossed with six panels enclosing figures within cartouches composed of foliate scrolls. In the centre a blank oval shield supported by two partly draped females. Venice, early 17th century. H. of ewer 43.5 cm. Diam. of basin 68 cm.
Victoria and Albert Museum.

Plate 356.
One of a pair of smaller identical ewers made *en suite* with pl. 358 for a member of the Lomellini family of Genoa. The frieze running around the body is cast and chased with nymphs and tritons above which are cartouches enclosing recumbent figures alternating with bunches of fruit and flowers; the shell spout is supported by young tritons and dolphins. On the foot of the ewer is a cartouche with the arms of Lomellini. The square base is apparently later. Unmarked but certainly Genoa, dated 1619. H. 46 cm.
Ashmolean Museum, Oxford.

Plate 357.
One of a pair of identical basins *en suite* with the ewer in pl. 356. In the centre a medallion cast with a figure emblematic of Genoa holding a shield charged with the Lomellini arms and placing a wreath on the head of Neptune. In the well of the basin a frieze of nymphs and tritons. The outer border embossed with recumbent figures within cartouches alternating with bunches of fruit. Unmarked but certainly Genoa. Diam. 51 cm.
Ashmolean Museum, Oxford.

Plate 358.
Large ewer from the set of three ewers and three basins made for a member of the Lomellini family of Genoa, dated 1621, the frieze running around the ewer cast and chased with scenes from the battle of the Po which took place in 1431, after M. Gaspari Bugati's *Historia Universale* published in Venice in 1571. On the foot opposite the handle an escutcheon charged with the Lomellini arms. The short foot cast with four

dolphins, the handle superbly modelled in the form of two tritons struggling with a satyr. The square base probably a later addition. This and the companion ewers and basins show Flemish influence and may be the work of one of the numerous Flemish goldsmiths working in Genoa in the early decades of the 17th century. Maker's mark the initials GBA within a trefoil and town mark of Genoa. H. 53.5 cm.
Victoria and Albert Museum.

Plate 359.
Detail of spout and handle of ewer in pl. 358.

Plate 360.
Detail of handle and spout of ewer in pl. 356. The handle composed of a putto seated on a dragon, whose body issues from a foliate sheath, is entirely in the Mannerist tradition.

Plate 361.
Detail of frieze of ewer in pl. 358.

Plate 362.
Detail of outer border of basin *en suite* with pl. 358. The embossed subjects represent scenes illustrating the maritime rivalry of the cities of Genoa and Venice. Unmarked but by the same maker as pl. 358. Diam. 64 cm.
Victoria and Albert Museum.

Plates 363 and 365.
Silver gilt tazza, the bowl embossed with scenes from the life of Galba surmounted by a figure of the Emperor Caligula: one from a set of twelve, once belonging to Cardinal Ippolito Aldobrandini, later Pope Clement VII (1592-1605). Lightly pricked on the back of each bowl (on one bowl only on the front) is the Aldobrandini arms surmounted by a cardinal's hat. This must have been done between 1585 and 1592 when Ippolito Aldobrandini was a cardinal, but the method of applying the arms is so inconspicuous that they must be a later addition. Presumably they were originally made for some other person and acquired by the cardinal by inheritance, gift or purchase. All twelve tazzas are unmarked, apart from later control marks, and are known as the Emperor tazzas because each is surmounted by a figure of a Roman Emperor modelled in the round, while the upper side of the circular bowl is divided into four segments, each embossed and chased in great detail with a scene from the life of the Emperor concerned (pl. 364). The four panels of triangular shape, embossed and chased with many hundreds of minute figures, are perhaps the most striking feature of these vessels. Their design and workmanship is northern in character; similar scenes are found on dishes of diverse provenance of about the same date, including those illustrated in pls. 602 (Antwerp) and 495 (Augsburg). More obviously Italian are the superbly modelled figures of Roman Emperors that surmount

them. As the tazzas are known to have been in Italian possession (Cardinal Aldobrandini) within a few years of their manufacture, there seems no reason to look outside Italy for their source though the chasing may be the work of a German or Flemish immigrant. They constitute the most important surviving set of Italian Renaissance silver vessels. Decorated as they are with forty-eight scenes illustrative of Roman imperial history, they provide the most convincing evidence of the co-operation between goldsmith and humanist in the production of a major commission. Last quarter of the 16th century. H. 42 cm.
Private collection, London.

Plate 364.
Detail of embossed scene from the life of the Emperor Otho on one of the Aldobrandini tazzas.
Victoria and Albert Museum.

Plate 366.
Rock-crystal incense-boat with silver-gilt mounts and silver-gilt incense spoon. The bowl carved with gadroons, the stem carved with spiral flutes. Typical of 16th century invasion of ecclesiastical design by pagan symbols is the grotesque mask at each end of the bowl, and the terms adorning the brackets of the stem. Unmarked, probably Italian. Second half of the 16th century. H. 12.7 cm. L. 17.8 cm.
Victoria and Albert Museum.

Plates 367. 368.
Glass ewer with enamelled gold mounts enriched with jewels. This vessel cannot definitely be identified as French, but the many masks developing out of strapwork cartouches,the scaly treatment of the spout and the human figure clasping the latter can all be paralleled in the Rosso-Boyvin designs for plate (see pls. 99-103). While the body is of 16th century Venetian glass, the foot and cover have been replaced later in the century with rock-crystal, presumably after damage, an indication of the importance then attached to the piece. Unmarked, Paris (?). Mid-16th century. H. 21.8 cm.
Kunsthistorisches Museum, Vienna.

Plate 369.
Shell powder-flask carved with tritons, nymphs and sea-horses and mounted in silver-gilt. This comparatively modest vessel bears the interlaced C's associated with Catherine de'Medici, but the reference is probably only patriotic. The quality of the goldsmiths' work is not what one would expect of a piece made for a Queen of France, the device of C's being roughly chased and the straps joining the upper and lower mounts cast with roughly finished female terms. The flask is certainly French and dates from a period that is otherwise very inadequately represented. A similar shell flask in the Kunsthistorisches Museum, Vienna, has silver mounts with a Vienna town mark. Unmarked, Paris (?). Mid-16th century. H. 20.7 cm.
Bayerisches Nationalmuseum, Munich.

Plates 370, 371.
Rock-crystal bowl mounted as a ewer in silver-gilt with enamelled blue ground. The rock-crystal bowl and cover appear to date from the late 15th or early 16th century, but the mounts are fifty years or more later and presumably replace others that seemed old-fashioned. The swirling cutting of the rock-crystal is similar to that of the Holbein cup (pl. 647). which has also been remounted subsequently. The design of the spout as a monster with twin snake tails supported by a satyr shows the influence of the Fontainebleau engravings. The rock-crystal ewer (pl. III), here catalogued as more probably Italian, has both bowl and spout of similar form. Unmarked, French. Third quarter of the 16th century. H. 24.5cm.
Musée du Louvre, Paris.

Plate 372.
Ewer of onyx mounted in enamelled gold and enriched with jewels presented by King Charles IX of France to the Archduke Ferdinand of Tirol in 1570. Its form is restrained and the onyx body is carved with bands of Renaissance stopped flutes and gadroons. The enamelled gold handle surmounted by a sea-monster seems to be derived from Enea Vico, perhaps through the medium of one of du Cerceau's copies. The modelling of the spout in the form of a dog is original, though somewhat out of accord with the dignified vase form of the body; here the Mannerist delight in the unexpected is evident. The ring handle is frequently encountered on hardstone vessels of the second half of the century. There is a comparable design amongst du Cerceau's earlier drawings (pl. 23); in this drawing the awkward insertion of cherub's heads between the gadroons points to the cavalier treatment of classical elements of ornament which one expects to find in Mannerist pieces, but the baluster stem and gadrooned foot are still firmly anchored in the Renaissance tradition. A striking feature is the double band of enamelled mauresques surrounding the body; an almost universal element of later Renaissance decorative vocabulary, the mauresque was especially favoured by the French goldsmiths. Unmarked, Paris (?). This vessel is not listed in the 1560 *Inventaire des Joyaux de la Couroune de France*, and must, therefore, have been made in the decade between 1560 and 1570. H. 27.1 cm.
Kunsthistorisches Museum, Vienna.

Plate 373.
Italian rock-crystal tazza with enamelled gold mounts, the cover of silver-gilt pierced and enamelled with the interlaced monogram HC of Henri II and his queen, Catherine de'Medici, and, on an inner zone, with three interlaced C's for Catherine, against a background of foliated tracery. Arrows project outwards from the central boss and the handle is formed as a crescent. In the centre a medallion of mauresques. A peculiar feature of this tazza is the lack of accord between the enamelled ornament of the cover and that of the mounts. The explanation is presumably that the rock-crystal tazza and its mounts are Milanese, while the cover was made in France subsequently. This type of

shallow tazza did not usually have a cover at all. It will be noticed that the cover is quite restrained in comparison with that made for Henry VIII of England from Holbein's design (pl. 645), though both share the mid-century fashion of combining Renaissance detail with mauresques of near-Eastern origin. This tazza formed part of the dowry of Christine of Lorraine, niece of Catherine de'Medici and was brought to Florence on her marriage in 1589. Unmarked, Milan and Paris (?). Mid-16th century (before 1559, death of Henri II). H. 23 cm.
Museo degli Argenti, Florence.

Plate 374.
Nautilus-shell cup with silver-gilt mounts, the stem, formed of three dolphins, resembles that of the agate cup from the French royal treasury in the Louvre (pl. 254); but this is a far less sumptuous vessel. The circular foot, embossed and chased with waves, bears a French mark. It is tempting to regard this construction as specifically French, but the dolphin has always been a popular decorative motif in western European art. The shell has been engraved in the Chinese manner, presumably in the Far East, and seems to be the earliest extant example of a shell cup with oriental decoration; the English example illustrated in pl. 661 is some ten or twenty years later. Paris, third quarter of the 16th century, maker's mark, a heart surmounted by fleur-de-lys and crown (R³6624). H. 17.5 cm.
Museo degli Argenti, Florence.

Plate 375.
Gilt tazza with jasper bowl, the foot and stem engraved with mauresques. French provincial, maker's mark, the initials IP in a shield, third quarter of the 16th century. H. 18.8 cm. Diam. of bowl 19.9 cm.
Musée du Louvre, Paris.

Plate 376.
Gilt basin embossed with designs after engravings by Androuet du Cerceau. Most of the figures of nereids and tritons in the inner frieze are copied from the tazza bowl design illustrated in pl. 104; the groups of a woman seated on the back of a marine centaur and of a woman between two marine centaurs are from du Cerceau's *Combat de centaures marines;* the strapwork around the central boss is derived with variations from another print in the same set of tazza bowls. The lively gesticulating groups of river-gods, tritons and nereids are rendered with great virtuosity. The foreshortenings, groups of interlaced bodies and rippling waves demonstrate the sculptural sense of the goldsmith. The same groups appear on the Antwerp basin illustrated in pl. 588. The English coat-of-arms of Featherstonhaugh on the central print is an early 19th century addition. Maker's mark illegible, Paris, 1560. Diam. 45.7 cm.
Fitzwilliam Museum, Cambridge.

Plate 377.
Gilt basin, the central print set with a Limoges enamel medallion of the centaur Nessus, the frieze around it embossed with dolphins and winged cherubs, the outer border with dolphins and marine subjects within oval cartouches. Unmarked, the attribution to a French goldsmith based on the border designs and the Limoges print. Third quarter of the 16th century. Diam. 53.6 cm.
Wernher Collection, Luton Hoo.

Plate 378.
Gilt basin, the centre embossed with a reclining river-god, his head surmounted by a crown of fleurs-de-lys, in the background a city dominated by a twin-towered cathedral, probably representing Paris. Around this is a frieze of combat scenes between mounted warriors in classical armour, armed with maces, some in extreme foreshortening. The outer border embossed with trophies of arms against which winged figures bearing palm branches recline, alternating with pairs of cupids bearing shields and crossed maces. The frequent repetition of the maces suggests a heraldic reference, perhaps to the family of Gondi, whose arms are a pair of crossed maces. The treatment of the battle scenes with the emphatic foreshortening recalls similar scenes on the armours made in the French royal workshops, but the most likely source is the *Victoires et Triomphes des Medicis,* engraved by Philippe Galle after Stradanus in 1583. The details of the towns in the background suggest Flemish influence. Maker's mark, the letters ILC in monogram surmounted by fleur-de-lys and crown (R³6628). Paris, 1586. Diam. 66 cm.
Musée du Louvre, Paris.

Plate 379.
Detail of border of basin in pl. 378.

Plates 380, 381, 382.
Gilt ewer and companion basin, the ewer standing on trumpet foot, apparently reduced in height; flattened globular body, cast and chased with a central frieze composed of plaques of the seasons within strapwork borders alternating with classical masks in the Fontainebleau manner, the upper frieze cast and chased with sea-monsters. The neck with a grotesque mask under the spout flanked by dolphins. The handle a triple-headed dragon. The basin embossed with three concentric rings of ornament surrounding a roundel now replacing the coat-of-arms of the original owner. The outer ring embossed with Old Testament subjects mostly after prints by Etienne Delaune alternating with classical masks and bunches of fruit. The subjects are the Creation of Eve, Adam and Eve eating the forbidden fruit, Cain killing Abel, the Ark in the Deluge, the Drunkenness of Noah, building the Tower of Babel, Abilech giving Sara to Abraham, Abraham receiving the three angels. The inner ring is also embossed with Old Testament subjects, including the Sacrifice of Abraham, Eliezar meeting Rebecca at the well, Jacob receiving the blessing of Isaac, Jacob's dream, Jacob being rescued from the well, Job in sickness, Lot and his daughters. The innermost ring is embossed with sat-

yrs' masks alternating with compositions of fruit and strapwork with snakes. The basin conforms to the international Mannerist style, but the ewer is of unusual form, though this is exaggerated by the apparent shortening of the foot which probably had a knop. Though wrought in heavy plate, the embossing and chasing of the basin is of the highest quality. The wave-scroll moulding between the inner and outer rings is particularly finely executed. Unmarked, French or, perhaps, Flemish, second half of the 16th century. H. of ewer 29.2 cm. Diam. of basin 52 cm.
Private collection, England.

Plates 383. 384.

Gilt basin; following contemporary fashion the whole upper surface is embossed and chased with figure ornament in three concentric circles. The anonymous master of this basin took the engravings of Etienne Delaune as his source: the scenes of the Labours of the Months on the outer border, the Seven Planets and Hercules taking the place of Atlas in supporting the world in the second ring and the four Elements in the inner ring all derive with minor variations from Delaune. The figures are shown in such minute detail that in comparison almost every other piece of 16th-century goldsmiths' work seems coarsely finished; one has to turn to vessels by one of the Utrecht masters of the van Vianen family to find comparable quality of execution. The goldsmith has wrought this dish in such high relief that he has had to work his metal very thin. He has, therefore, made it of double thickness with a shell covering the back and concealing the ugly underside. This shell was formerly attached to the front by the screw that held the (now missing) central boss and by a number of rivets at short intervals around the circumference, though these may be replacements for solder that may originally have held the two parts together. The back-plate is flat-chased with a composition of floral scrolls inhabited by insects and birds, etc. The closest parallel in design is the Temperantia dish, the model for which was cut by the model-carver and medal die-cutter, François Briot of Montbéliard, who in 1585 was appointed *Graveur de son Excellence,* Duke Frederick of Württemberg-Mömpelgard. It is tempting to think that he may have had some hand in this vessel. Alternatively it may be the work of a Flemish or Strassburg goldsmith who possessed a set of Delaune's prints. Unmarked, after 1568 (date of the Delaune Labours of the Months) Diam. 52 cm.
Private collection, Paris.

Plate 385.

Tazza, parcel-gilt, the baluster, knop and foot engraved with mauresque ornament, enclosing on the foot a cartouche with the arms of Bernard. Orléans, no maker's mark, third quarter of the 16th century. H. 13.3 cm.
Victoria and Albert Museum.

Plate 386.

Underside of a French tazza bowl, decorated with applied male and female terms within scrolling foliage inhabited by birds, the design derived from Etienne Delaune. The upper side of the bowl plain. Paris, 1560-1. Maker's mark, the letters MB with a chalice surmounted by a crowned fleur-de-lys. Diam. 19 cm.
Private collection, London.

Plate 387.

Gilt ewer, in the manner of Etienne Delaune. The body is embossed within oval frames with four figures emblematic of Charity, Hope, Fortitude and Faith. The arrangement of interlacing strapwork enclosing oval cartouches corresponds to that of the Etienne Delaune drawing in pl. 109. Unmarked, but probably French. Third quarter of the 16th century. H. 26.7 cm.
Fitzwilliam Museum, Cambridge.

Plates 388, 389.

Gilt tazza, the stem composed of the addorsed figures of two melusines, the bowl (pl. 388) embossed and chased with a scene of warships being attacked in a harbour while a figure of Fame passes in a sea-chariot drawn by marine elephants. Perhaps an allegory of Charles V's expedition to Tunis. French or Flemish, maker's mark, the initials AP and a sailing-ship. Third quarter of the 16th century. H. 13.4 cm.
Art Institute of Chicago.

Plates 390, 391.

Gilt tazza, one of two surviving from a set of the Four Continents. The central area is embossed with a scene of an elephant hunt, symbolic of the Continent of Asia. The other (not illustrated) is decorated with an European hunting scene. The two tazzas, though they belonged to the same set, bear the marks of different makers, but the same Paris date letter. The embossing was doubtless the work of the same artist. The central print is now engraved with the arms of an English family, of somewhat later date. The underside of the bowl is decorated with gadroons radiating outwards from the centre. The feet and stems are of plain design. Paris, 1583-4, maker's mark, a lion rampant holding a sword (?) surmounted by a crowned fleur-de-lys ($R^3$6636). Diam. of bowl 29 cm. H. 11 cm.
Private collection.

Plates 392, 393.

Covered bowl or tazza from a service of six originally made for the table but converted at a later date for use as reliquaries, when the crosses on top and the engraved names of the relics were added. The exterior of the bowl and the top of the cover embossed with a continuous frieze of hunting subjects in the manner of Stradanus. The wide blank band between the embossed frieze and the lip does not contribute to the beauty of the whole. The openwork stem composed of four brackets is typical of the early 17th century. From a service bequeathed by a Cardinal Sfondrati to the Convent of Santa Cecilia in Trastevere. Paris, 1606-7, maker's mark, the letters IC, a bird between, sur-

mounted by a crown and fleur-de-lys. H. 18 cm. with cover 35 cm.
The Vatican, Rome.

Plates 394, 395.
Gilt tazza from the service of Cardinal Sfondrati, view of the interior of the bowl and the top of the cover, the former showing a partly draped reclining man leaning against a vase and holding up a bowl to a fountain within a grape-vine arbour, in the foreground Bacchic infants collecting grapes; the cover with a continuous frieze of infants at the grape harves. A plaquette cut from another tazza bowl of the same set is in the collection of Lord Rosebery at Mentmore. Paris, 1595-6, maker's mark the same as pl. 392. H. 18 cm. Diam. (approx) 20.3 cm.
The Vatican, Rome.

Plate 396.
One half of a French gilt double-cup in the German manner; the bowl is decorated with the arms and names of several Swiss families, while around the lip are medallions engraved with portrait busts of French kings. This cup was presented to a Swiss officer, Colonel Pfyffer, by the officers who served under him in French service; he presumably specified the form he wished it to take, for double cups (*Doppelbecher*) of this type were specifically German and not otherwise known in France. Paris, 1567-8 maker's mark, a crowned fleur-de-lys over the letter D and another. H. 26.8 cm.
Schweizerisches Landesmuseum, Zürich.

Plates 397, 399.
Silver-gilt vase clock, the movement, of three trains each with its own fuzee, is contained in the vase. The neck of the vase is open and, between the Doric pilasters that support the rim, can be seen seven figures emblematic of the Planets; these figures are attached to a rotating steel base plate, the edge of which is damascened with foliage and the title of each planet in old French. A finely modelled silver figure of a youth seated on a small globe holds a pointer which indicates the hours. The vase is pierced both above and below to allow the sound of the chiming and musical bells to pass. The frieze around the body embossed with combat scenes between Roman warriors in the manner of Etienne Delaune. Though unmarked, the use of French names for the Planets and the similar treatment of the combat scenes to those on the Paris basin (pl. 378) justifies the attribution to a French goldsmith. According to tradition the clock was given by Queen Elizabeth to one of her ladies in waiting; its date would seem to support the tradition. French, third quarter of the 16th century. H. 33.1 cm.
Victoria and Albert Museum (Loan).

Plate 398.
Tureen from a service originally made for Cardinal Francesco Gioiosa (appointed cardinal in 1583, died

1615), whose arms it bears: it later passed into the possession of Cardinal Sfondrati, whose arms are engraved on the reverse. This vessel was subsequently converted for use as a reliquary; its large size precludes the possibility that it served as an incense boat, a purpose suggested by its shape. The heavy design illustrates the great contrast between fashionable and table plate at this date. Paris, 1586-7, maker's mark A B with a horse's head between, attributed to a member of the La Boissière family. H. 45 cm. L. 50 cm.
The Vatican, Rome.

Plate 400.
One of a pair of gilt tazzas from the plate of the Order of *Saint Esprit*, of simple form with deep bowl, the foot with stamped anthemion border, the cover with egg and dart moulding, ring handle. The bowl and cover engraved with the royal arms of France addorsed with those of Poland. Paris, 1581-2, maker's mark, the letters ILC in monogram, surmounted by fleur-de-lys and crown (R3 6628). H. 24.5 cm.
Musée du Louvre, Paris.

Plate 401.
One of a pair of French rock-crystal and silver-gilt altar candlesticks the bases and drip-pans embossed with gadroons, the design probably derived from du Cerceau. Paris, 1560-61, maker's mark, an elephant, fleur-de-lys above, a crescent below. (R³6634). H. 54 cm.
Private collection, U.S.A.

Plate 402.
Spanish parcel-gilt ewer, the body and handle engraved with conventional Renaissance foliage, the lower part of the body with protruding oval bosses. The design corresponds almost exactly to a drawing by Antonio Maltes dated 27 May, 1564 in the masterpiece book of the Barcelona Goldsmiths' Guild. Barcelona, about 1565. H. 21 cm.
Victoria and Albert Museum.

Plate 403.
Spanish ewer of helmet shape, the girdle embossed with monsters enclosing roundels with projecting heads. The spout supported by a putto standing on the eyebrows of a grotesque mask, the handle composed of intermingled animal and human forms. Attributed to a Castilian goldsmith who was perhaps of Flemish origin; the fantastic design on the handle, which recalls the prints of Cornelis Bos, suggests some Flemish connection. Unmarked, third quarter of the 16th century. H. 26.5 cm.
Victoria and Albert Museum.

Plate 404.
Two-handled vase and cover attributed to Fernando Ballestaros the Younger of Seville; one of a pair. The body is boldly embossed with floral scrolls and vertical

flutes. Four lively grotesque masks cast and chased in high relief are attached to a girdle running around the middle of the body. This is possibly the type of vase used by Pope Clement VII for disposing of unwanted morsels of food (see p.82). Seville. Last quarter of the 16th century. H. 39 cm.
Seville Cathedral Treasury.

Plate 405.
Spanish gilt altar cruet, the body divided into panels by vertical and horizontal bands engraved with arabesques and with Roman heads at the inter-sections, the spout a winged dragon, the handle with an applied bound satyr. Unmarked, Barcelona (?), mid-16th century. H. 18.5 cm.
Victoria and Albert Museum.

Plate 406.
Spanish gilt basin embossed with large foliate scrolls and enriched with applied panels of cloisonné enamel on a gold ground. The combination of the translucent enamels, in which red is the dominant colour, and the gold surface of the dish creates an exceptionally rich effect. The enamel plaques are of such delicacy as to make this piece quite unsuited to any practical use. The central boss is enamelled with the arms of Castile, Leon and France, Marks illegible, early 17th century. Diam. 66 cm.
Metropolitan Museum, New York.

Plate 407.
Spanish or Portuguese gilt dish presented to the Cathedral of Seville in 1668 by Donna Anna de Pavia, the outer border embossed and chased with strapwork enclosing figures, the inner frieze with four scenes of triumphs, the central plaque with the sacrifice of Isaac by Abraham wrought by another hand. The treatment of the border with its profuse strapwork recalls the manner of the Portuguese goldsmith, Antonio de Castro, who was working in Genoa about the time this dish was wrought. The scalloped edge is an Iberian feature, more usual in Portugal than Spain. Unmarked. Third quarter of the 16th century. Diam. 60 cm. (approx.).
Seville Cathedral Treasury.

Plate 408.
Spanish parcel-gilt ewer and basin, the former with egg-shaped body and girdle engraved with scrollwork, the border of the basin flat-chased with strapwork. Unmarked, late 16th century. H. of ewer 34 cm. Diam. of basin 38.5 cm.
Victoria and Albert Museum.

Plate 409.
Gilt dish, the border embossed with eight Roman profile heads alternating with panels embossed with masks, the alternate ones set on strapwork cartouches. The medallions are copied from Roman coins. In the centre is a boss bearing the enamelled arms of Davalos

or Nuevalos, pierced at a later date for the attachment of a plaque with the arms of a subsequent owner. Toledo, maker's mark of Juan Franci, (mid-16th century). Diam. 29 cm.
Victoria and Albert Museum.

Plate 410.
Ewer with body of egg-shape from which emerge four masks, two of wild men and two of lions, each within a strapwork cartouche, while around the lower part are applied buttress-like straps also within engraved cartouches; a cherub's head is applied below the spout, while a greyhound is seated on the end of the hinged cover. An acanthus leaf descends from the point of junction of the handle and back of the spout. This ewer dates from the first quarter of the 17th century; its restrained profile illustrates the change of fashion in Spanish silver that took place towards the end of the 16th century. Unmarked. H. 36.5 cm.
Private collection, London.

Plate 411.
Gilt dish standing on a low foot, perhaps by the same hand as the ewer and basin in pls. 342 and 343. The centre of the dish is embossed with a combat scene between horsemen and foot soldiers in classical costume, the border with six scenes from the story of Samson, each scene separated from the next by a winged term, the embossing executed in unusually high relief. The arrangement of the scenes corresponds to that of the basin (pl. 343). The figure groups are well composed and not crowded as on some contemporary Iberian goldsmiths' work. An attractive feature is the decoration of the foot with marine subjects executed in very low relief. Of exquisite quality, this work can only be seen when the dish is lifted up. Another dish apparently *en suite*, but on a taller base, is in the Metropolitan Museum, New York. Unmarked, Spanish or Portuguese. Third quarter of the 16th century. Diam. 30.5 cm.
British Museum.

Plate 412.
Detail of base of the Avila Cathedral Custodia by Juan d'Arfe, showing part of the master's signature and the date 1571. The bases of the columns supporting the upper stage are cast and chased in high relief with strapwork and pendant bunches of fruit. The relief panel is struck with the Valladolid town mark and the assayer's mark of Alonso Gutierrez.
Avila Cathedral Treasury

Plate 413.
Masterpiece cup in the form of a columbine (*Akeleybecher*) of the Nürnberg goldsmiths' guild. The manufacture of these masterpiece cups placed the greatest demands on the skill of the aspirant to admission to the guild as master of his craft. Though the design derived from the Gothic lobate cup, the section of the columbine-cup was even more complex and, fur-

thermore, the body was decorated with minute panels embossed or engraved with figure subjects. This particular cup is believed to be the original made by Martin Rehlein in 1572-3 from a model by Wenzel Jamnitzer as a pattern to be copied by aspirants to admission to the guild. The bowl is finely embossed and chased with minute figures of Diana, Lucretia and Judith with the head of Holophernes. Like most of the masterpiece cups, it has no mark, nor is it gilt. H. 21 cm.
Victoria and Albert Museum.

Plate 414.
Columbine-cup and cover, gilt, of a different type from the standard masterpiece; the bowl of strongly waisted form, the lower part embossed with panels of strapwork alternating with bosses, the centre with applied masks, the upper part etched with mauresques; stem with knop formed as a vase and cover, trefoil foot. Multifoil cover with scalloped edge, surmounted by an enamelled drum supporting a finial of triangular section enclosing three caryatids within niches, originally supporting a figure which is now wanting. The cast details derive from the Jamnitzer workshop. In his endeavour to break loose from the form imposed by the guild, the goldsmith has created almost a parody of the columbine-cup, exaggerating the horizontal members instead of the verticals. Masterpiece cups do not seem as a rule to have been supplied with covers. This cup has been embellished with additional enamel, pearls and gemstones at a later date. Nürnberg, Christoph Ritter II (R 3881k), c.1600. H. 25.5 cm.
Hermitage Museum, Leningrad.

Plate 415.
Masterpiece cup of the Nürnberg Goldsmiths' Guild. The body with three orders of ornament, the rim engraved with religious subjects, the central area with floral ornament, masks and strapwork, the lower part embossed and chased with religious scenes again. The stem follows the usual practice and is cast with ram's heads. There is no mark, nor is the cup gilt. Last quarter of the 16th century. H. 20.5 cm.
Germanisches Nationalmuseum, Nürnberg.

Plates 416, 417, 418, 419, 420.
The Merckel table-centre of silver-gilt and polychrome enamel, in part fired, in part applied cold. Completed by Wenzel Jamnitzer in or before 1549 and purchased by the City Council of Nürnberg, it has been aptly described as the *non plus ultra* of artistic virtuosity. Amongst its many original features are the individual form and profile, quite at variance with classical convention; its rejection of function, to such an extent that there are few points at which the piece can be picked up without the risk of damaging its delicate ornament; the profuse use of boldly curled over straps and of cartouches with *Rollwerk* borders, the frequent introduction of mauresque ornament in close association with classical detail; the striking contrast between the clinging classical draperies of the female figure of the stem and the wild growth of naturalistic grasses that

spring from the foot and from numerous points (pl. 417) in the upper structure of the piece. A last but not less important feature is the philosophical programme of the kind so admired by Renaissance humanists that lies behind the design. The central figure of the stem represents Mother Earth and the centre-piece as a whole symbolises her fruitfulness. This theme is suggested by the lizards, newts and other small reptiles cast from nature that inhabit the grasses growing from the base. The fertility theme of the centre-piece could, of course, be extended if real fruits were placed in the bowl at the top. Besides the casting of delicate grasses, two other special skills of Wenzel Jamnitzer can be recognised in this piece: the enamelling of the vase finial (pl. 418) and of the roundels set in the dish and the etching of the mauresques on the vase and the outer border of the dish. One of the most striking features is the inner zone of the dish; apart from the enamelled roundels (pl. 420) Jamnitzer has here used pure Renaissance ornament and the design is reminiscent of the cover of the Holbein rock-crystal bowl (pl. 645). The candelabrum designs on the bowl recall the engraved ornament of Daniel Hopfer, but it is unlikely that so original a master as Wenzel Jamnitzer would have used pattern sheets by other artists. Around the foot of the centre-piece, on the vase supported by Mother Earth (pl. 416) and again on the underside of the bowl are cartouches enamelled with Latin verses. Under the base is a blank cartouche, presumably intended for the coat of arms of the recipient, if it should have been presented by the Nürnberg Council. Nürnberg, Wenzel Jamnitzer (R³3822d). Before 1549.
H. 100 cm.
Rijksmuseum, Amsterdam.

Plate 421
Silver, parcel-gilt basin, the companion ewer missing, the reptiles in the depression cast from nature and coloured, the area around the central print cast with grasses. Nürnberg, Wenzel Jamnitzer, (R³3832aa), third quarter of 16th century. From the French royal treasury. Diam. 45 cm.
Musée du Louvre, Paris.

Plate 422.
Red jasper cup with gilt mounts; this hardstone cup was already an ancient object when it was given to Wenzel Jamnitzer to mount and it was presumably for this reason that the mounts he designed were so conservative. The foot, cover and the masks set on the upper corners of the handles are in Renaissance style; only the band of mauresques on the lip mount is more in accord with fashionable trends. Nürnberg, Wenzel Jamnitzer (R³3832mm). About 1560. H. 22 cm.
Schatzkammer of the Residenz, Munich.

Plate 423.
Silver bell, the whole surface covered with casts from nature of lizards, insects and mosses. The castings are remarkably fine, though the design can be criticized on account of the introduction of conventional lion and

faun masks amongst the naturalistic detail. The circular gap in the handle was presumably intended for the insertion of the owner's armorial bearings. A similar silver bell in the Bayerisches Nationalmuseum, Munich, is of less crowded design and two figures of lizards, also cast from nature, form the main ornament. The arms of Bavaria are inserted in the handle. The most successful example of Jamnitzer's technique of casting from nature is the silver inkstand in the Kunsthistorisches Museum. Nürnberg, Wenzel Jamnitzer ? (R³3835 but attr. to Hans Jamnitzer) 1558. H. 13.3 cm.
British Museum (Waddesdon Bequest).

Plates 424, 426.

Gilt standing cup known as the *Kaiser Pokal*, believed to have been presented to the Emperor Maximilian II on the occasion of his first state entry into Nürnberg on 7 June 1570. The heraldic and other details of the cup may relate to the Landsberger Bund, formed in 1556 from both Catholic and Evangelical powers with the aim of preserving peace and good order within the Empire. The programme of decoration of the cup is consistent with homage towards the Emperor and is, therefore, in accord with its presumed purpose. The cover is surmounted by a figure of the Emperor himself wearing his crown and holding sword and sceptre. The plinth on which he stands is surrounded by three ecclesiastical and one secular prince, the Archbishop of Salzburg, the Bishop of Würzburg, the Bishop of Bamberg and Duke Albrecht V of Bavaria. The bowl of the cup is decorated with the coats-of-arms of the cities of Nürnberg, Augsburg, Weissenburg and Windelsheim each supported by two female figures. Three studies for these figures by Wenzel Jamnitzer are preserved in the Erlangen University library. (See Pechstein, 'Zeichnungen von Wenzel Jamnitzer', *Anzeiger des Germ. Nationalmuseums*, 1970, p. 87). The very richly ornamented stem is adorned with four female figures emblematic of Virtues. The design is drawn from a variety of sources. The frieze with triglyphs and *bukrania* beneath the lip is strictly classical, the embossed lobes on this lip and on the foot are late Gothic in origin, while the confused design of the stem and the combination of figures, bunches of fruit, straps and cartouches on the drum reflect the fashionable Mannerist style. The taste of the period can also be recognised in the elegant *contraposto* of the figures of the bishops and of the Duke of Bavaria. If Jamnitzer really did model the figure sculpture (pl. 424) that adorns this cup, he ranks as high as a sculptor as he does as a goldsmith. Combining the workmanship of the foremost German goldsmith of all time with the historical interest of being a gift of some political significance from the city of Nürnberg to the Holy Roman Emperor, this cup ranks as the finest of its kind. Nürnberg, Wenzel Jamnitzer (R³3832), about 1570. H. 69 cm.
Kunstgewerbemuseum, Berlin.

Plate 425.

Gilt double cup made for the Tucher family in 1564. Unlike most of the Gothic Revival cups of the second half of the 16th century, no Renaissance detail is introduced even in the engraved borders of the lips. This cup constitutes striking proof of the survival of Gothic tradition in Nürnberg due to the influence of the goldsmiths' guild, unless, of course, it was made as a replica of, or a pair to, another late 15th-century cup. Nürnberg, Wenzel Jamnitzer (R³3832s), 1564. H. 43.5 cm.
Germanisches Nationalmuseum, Nürnberg.

Plate 427.

Gilt jewel-casket (side view) made for the Bavarian court and bequeathed by Duke Maximilian I to remain in perpetuity in the ducal treasury. The corners mounted with male and female herms alternately; triglyph frieze, the base supported on four ball feet, surmounted by a frieze of putti climbing over garlands, the sides and top set with rectangular plaques of heliotrope, inlaid with golden mauresques, each of different design, alternating with overlaid reliefs in gold representing the Labours of Hercules. In the central niches of front and back are statuettes representing *Opulentia* (wealth) and *Custodia* (watchfulness). The casket is further enriched with numerous rubies, emeralds and diamonds in tall collets and the inside of the lid is set with a cartouche of enamelled gold set with precious stones and enclosing the Sacred Monogram in diamonds. The casket contains an inner fitting with two drawers and and embossed silver-gilt mounts. This is the most sumptuous of all the Jamnitzer caskets, its effect being enhanced by the gold inlays and overlays against the dark green semi-precious stone. A drawing in the Berlin Kunstgewerbemuseum appears to be a preliminary design for this casket, which was executed with variations. The numerous jewels seem to have been an afterthought, though certainly added in the Jamnitzer workshop. The casket was evidently planned as a worthy setting for the richest Renaissance jewels. Nürnberg, Wenzel Jamnitzer, about 1560. H. 24.5 cm. W. 36.5 cm.
Schatzkammer of the Residenz, Munich.

Plate 428.

Jewel-casket of silver-gilt with plaques of mother of pearl and with semi-precious stones in gilt collets, on a wooden core. The upper stage of the lid is decorated with beetles and small reptiles cast from nature. The design as a whole is due to Wenzel Jamnitzer, who was also the master of the figures in the niches along the sides. The change of scale between these is a disturbing feature, which was presumably more acceptable to an eye accustomed to Mannerist proportion. The mounts are cast or stamped from thin silver sheet by the machine invented by Jamnitzer. The cover is surmounted by a recumbent female figure who lies on a bed of hardstone. The staff in her hand was intended to point the time on a clock dial (probably a revolving globe) at her side. This is now missing, though the movement is retained in the top of the casket. The effect of the whole is highly colourful; the figures and pierced plaques being set against panels of black painted glass, coloured velvet or silk. It must once have been even more brilliant, for the figures and other

details were finished with polychrome cold enamel. The colours are still preserved on the inside and can also be seen in the original drawing attributed to Wenzel Jamnitzer, preserved in Leningrad. The casket was a Christmas present from the Elector Christian I to his spouse. It was constructed or, perhaps, only finished by Nikolaus Schmidt, whose mark it bears (R³3832n). Nürnberg, before 1589. H. 36 cm. L. 54 cm.
Grünes Gewölbe, Dresden.

Plates 429, 430, 431, 432, 433, 434, 435.
Seven lead or pewter patterns from the collection of Basilius Amerbach of Basel; these show typical Jamnitzer designs and were obtained by Amerbach either directly from the Jamnitzer workshop in Nürnberg or through a Basel goldsmith who had himself obtained them from Nürnberg. The availability of such patterns explains the ubiquity of Jamnitzer ornament on silver vessels made elsewhere. Pl. 429 shows the well-known Jamnitzer frieze with *bukrania* alternating with medallions between the triglyphs used on the caskets in pls. 427, 428 and 444. Pls. 434 and 435 show two of the terms from the side of a Jamnitzer casket dated 1562. Pl. 430 is a slight variant of the cast frieze on the Lindenberger cup illustrated in pl. 436. Nürnberg, third quarter of the 16th century.
Historisches Museum, Basel.

Plate 436.
Gilt standing cup and cover, the panels of strapwork ornament of the drum cast from Jamnitzer workshop patterns, the base and lip etched with mauresques. In the cover a medal of Leonhart Tucher, dated 1568, Nürnberg, Christoph Lindenberger (R³3878), about 1570. H. 25.4 cm.
British Museum.

Plate 437.
Silver mirror frame copied from the frontispiece of Wenzel Jamnitzer's *Perspectiva* published in Nürnberg in 1563. In this pleasing composition, which apparently dates from the 1560's, instead of the brutal satyrs of Cornelis Floris or the nymphomaniacs of René Boyvin trapped in the convolutions of burdensome straps, cherubs and female figures emblematic of the Sciences recline gracefully on or between huge straps that resemble the backs of giant chairs rather than bonds. The figures are labelled *Arithmetica, Geometria, Architectura* and *Perspectiva* respectively, while the cherubs at the sides are labelled *Inclinatio* and *Diligentia,* the latter a quality not usually attributed to their kind. The calm beauty of the composition is free from the shock effect of fashionable Mannerist art. The present arrangement of the frame is possibly not original; the embossed area is cut out and set against a flat gilt sheet bearing the Jamnitzer mark. The embossed panel may once have formed part of some larger object. Nürnberg, Wenzel Jamnitzer (?) (R³3832u) about 1570. H. 39.8 cm.
Metropolitan Museum, New York.

Plate 438.
Embossed plaque from a silver tazza by the master H.G. (probably Hans Jamnitzer), showing fishing, hunting and hawking subjects with Jupiter seated on clouds at the top. The landscape background stretches back into the far distance and is treated with great mastery of perspective. Dated 1572 on a stone in the left foreground and signed H.G. on another in the right foreground. Nürnberg, 1572. Diam. 16.5 cm.
Bayerisches Nationalmuseum, Munich.

Plate 439.
Embossed plaque from a silver tazza attributed to Hans Jamnitzer, chased with Diana discovering the pregnancy of her nymph, Callisto, after an engraving by Cornelius Cort from the painting by Titian. Nürnberg, about 1570. Diam. 19.2 cm.
Victoria and Albert Museum.

Plate 440.
Lead plaquette after a silver plaque embossed and chased by the Master H.G. (probably Hans Jamnitzer), showing a fishing scene in a wide landscape with an Italian city to the left and a German village to the right, numerous others in the background. Nürnberg, signed H.G. and dated 1570. Diam. 15.3 cm.
Bayerisches Nationalmuseum, Munich.

Plates 441, 443.
Top and side views of a silver-gilt tazza. The modelling of the nude figures in the scene of the Judgement of Paris which is embossed and chased in the bowl shows exceptional mastery of the technique and is probably the work of a specialist. As on most first quality tazzas the underside of the bowl is concealed by a lower shell which is also embossed. The stem composed of three addorsed female caryatids is one of the most pleasing and most frequently used treatments of this part. Augsburg, maker's mark of Jakob Schenauer (R³405e), about 1570-80. H. 16.5 cm. Diam. 17.35 cm.
Thyssen Collection, Lugano.

Plates 442, 444, 445, 446.
Gilt double cup from a travelling service, originally including a pair of tazzas on low feet and other pieces. The cast ornament on the bases is apparently from a Jamnitzer pattern. The cups can be unscrewed (pl. 445,6) and then provide a pair of candlesticks and a pair of cups on low feet. Nürnberg, maker's mark of Jost Heberle (R³3990), last quarter of the 16th century.
Private collection.

Plate 447.
Silver-gilt, mother-of-pearl and hardstone jewel casket enriched with precious stones, by Hans Jamnitzer. This casket follows closely the style established by his father, Wenzel, and almost rivals his Dresden casket (pl. 428) in its brilliant colour effect, though not in quality. It also introduces the typical Jamnitzer cast frieze

composed of triglyphs and medallion and rams' head metopes. Mother-of-pearl plaques play an important part in its construction; this material, though not particularly precious, was much appreciated on account of its subtle and variegated colouring. It was increasingly used to decorate drinking vessels during the latter decades of the century. From the *Kunstkammer* of the Dukes of Württemberg. Nürnberg, Hans Jamnitzer, (R³3835c) third quarter of the 16th century. H. 19 cm. *Württembergisches Landesmuseum, Stuttgart.*

Plates 448, 449, 450, 451.

Front, back, side and interior views of silver-gilt and enamelled reading desk made by Hans and Elias Lencker of Nürnberg. The legacy of Jamnitzer can be recognised not only in the design as a whole but also in the use on the desk of his well-known triglyph and *bukranion* frieze (pl. 449). The arrangement of the panels on each side of the mirror inside the lid (pl. 451) is less sophisticated than the rest of the design; the central figures with their strictly frontal treatment belong to an earlier style than those of the inner frame and are derived from plaquettes by Peter Flötner. The introduction of panels of mauresques alongside classical ornament is a solecism often encountered in northern Mannerist art. The front of the desk (pl. 449), which is divided horizontally into two long panels shows the usual Mannerist lack of concern for scale, giving a curiously confusing effect to the composition. The restraint noted in the Jamnitzer frame (pl. 437) is absent in the design of the back of the desk (pl. 448) on which large numbers of figures, again varying in scale, are imposed on a background of interlacing strapwork together with bunches of fruit and jewels in elaborate settings. The composition conforms to the usual scheme with a central panel supported on each side by a classical warrior and with winged putti above and below. A sense of movement is given by the varied poses of the latter, sitting on scrolls with their legs swinging in *contraposto* to their bodies. These putti might well have been designed by Erasmus Hornick, who was in Nürnberg at the time the desk was made. While the figure scenes on the Hornick pilgrim bottle (pl. 157) and the ewer (pl. 142) are enclosed within frames of simpler form than those on the back of the desk, both belong to the same stylistic moment. A striking similarity exists between the warrior figures on each side of the central panel of the desk and in the oval panel on the ewer design. In spite of their martial associations these bearded and helmeted figures are given elegant S-curved bodies that are no less voluptuous than those of the nude females that strike such provocative poses. The figures on the outside of the desk are painted in cold enamel while the roundels inside are decorated with translucent fired enamel. Enough of this colour remains to give a good idea of its original brilliance. Nürnberg, Hans and Elias Lencker (R³3951dd) about 1560. Max. H. 23.4 cm. W. 39 cm. *Kunsthistorisches Museum, Vienna.*

Plates 452 and XVII

Triptych house-altar of ebony mounted with figures, ornaments and plaques of enamelled gold and further enriched with jewels, attributed to the Augsburg goldsmith, Abraham Lotter the Elder, and made between 1573 and 1574. While the facade conforms to Renaissance architecture, the web of polychrome ornament executed in encrusted and translucent champlevé enamel that covers the ebony surface follows Mannerist taste. An attractive feature is the frieze at the bottom which shows in three scenes Adam and Eve in Paradise, the eviction from there and Adam and Eve working. The central panel, which took the form of a Pieta, has been missing since the 17th century and is replaced by an openwork arabesque panel of enamelled gold transferred from the back. On the side wings are niches enclosing figures of the name-Saints of Herzog Albrecht von Bayern and his spouse: St. Albertus Magnus and St. Anna. The colour plate shows the resurection with Christ and the two watching soldiers executing dancelike movements. This house-altar would have required the co-operation of several masters, of whom Abraham Lotter was probably the most important. He is thought to have been assisted by Ulrich Eberl for some of the enamelling, while Hans Krieger carried out the cabinet work. It is one of a series of similar altars in the Munich Schatzkammer and the Reiche Kapelle; another, evidently from the same workshop, is illustrated in pl. 453. Augsburg, about 1573-4. H. 53 cm. *Schatzkammer of the Residenz, Munich.*

Plate 453.

Detail of central stage of house-altar of architectural form; ebony with figures and mounts of enamelled gold and silver-gilt. The central stage is set with an enamelled gold relief of the Last Supper within an arched niche, which is flanked by standing figures of saints, also in niches. The central panel pulls out as a drawer and the side panels can be slid across to reveal two further tiers of drawers. The upper stage is set with a scene of the Adoration of the Kings, the Holy Family being placed in a temple-like recess under a pediment, while in front the three Kings stand on an enamelled gold carpet. Above is a screen with enamelled gold busts and above this a scene of the Annunciation. At the top is a group of St. Martin and the beggar. This house altar is closely related to, and by the same masters as, two others in the Munich Schatzkammer (one in pl. 452) and a third formerly at Stift Andechs, near Munich, but now also in the Munich Schatzkammer. Augsburg, about 1570-80, un-marked. H. 38.1 cm. *Private collection, U.S.A.*

Plates 454, 455.

Enamelled gold cup and cover, the drum decorated with mauresques enamelled white and blue to which are applied three heraldic cartouches of the arms of Bavaria, Austria and the two impaled, the arms of Austria referring to the Duchess Anna, spouse of Albrecht V and daughter of the Emperor Ferdinand I. The foot, knop, base of the bowl and cover with cast and chiselled strapwork and bunches of fruit enamelled in colours. The cover surmounted by a rampant lion bearing a shield of the arms of Bavaria. The work of Hans Reimer, court goldsmith to the Duke of Bavaria, is cha-

racterised by his bold and effective colour-scheme. In this cup he has not departed far from the conventional profile of the period. Hans Reimer (R³3477) Munich, dated 1562. H. 9.9 cm.
Schatzkammer of Residenz, Munich.

Plate 456.
Standing cup of rock-crystal mounted in enamelled gold and set with rubies and emeralds. This cup differs from the contemporary Milanese type and was, perhaps mounted by the Augsburg goldsmith, Ulrich Eberl, who is known to have worked for the Bavarian court. The vase knop of the stem corresponds to that of the usual south German silver-gilt cup. The richness of the gold mounts and the numerous precious stones make this a piece of great splendour, though the rock-crystal bowl is without any cutting. The pearl hanging free in the finial is a noteworthy feature. The enamelled ornament relates this cup to a reliquary in the Reiche Kapelle, the case of which is struck with the Augsburg town mark. Probably Augsburg, late 16th century. H. 22.3 cm.
Schatzkammer of the Residenz, Munich.

Plate 457.
Standing cup of rock-crystal, heliotrope and agate mounted in enamelled gold and enriched with precious stones and pearls. This delicate cup combines nearly all the techniques of the Mannerist goldsmith and jeweller. The agate foot with its mounts of enamelled gold set with gemstones supports a stem composed of a Baroque pearl wrought in the form of a sea-centaur with a nymph. The plain rock-crystal cylindrical body has upper and lower mounts wrought with enamelled gold scrolls in relief surrounding gold collets set with rubies, diamonds and other stones. Around the upper border of the lower mount are six figures emblematic of the Virtues, the upper part of their bodies wrought in the round. The cover constructed of a plaque of heliotrope surmounted by a figure of the Venus Marina. According to an old inventory of the Stuttgart Schatzkammer the twelve stones set round the cover mount symbolise the twelve tribes of Israel. From the Kunstkammer of the Dukes of Württemberg. Probably Augsburg, last quarter of the 16th century. H. 22 cm.
Württembergisches Landesmuseum, Stuttgart.

Plate 458.
Gilt standing beaker of the Butchers' Guild (*Metzgerzunft*) of of the City of Augsburg, the body embossed and chased with figures emblematic of the Virtues. The chasing of the figures is of outstanding merit. These beakers on tall stems were either given all-over ornament, as in this case, or the bowl was left plain, apart from an engraved and gilt border around the lip. Augsburg, no maker's mark, late 16th century. H. 40.5 cm.
Bayerisches Nationalmuseum, Munich.

Plates 459, 460, 461.
Ewer and companion basin, gilt, enamelled and encrusted with large numbers of turquoises in the Turkish fashion. The border of the basin embossed with a continuous frieze of Neptune accompanied by Tritons and nymphs. The merit of these pieces lies more in their colour composition than in their design, which is conventional. The central boss of the basin and almost the whole surface of the ewer are enamelled with mauresques in blue and white against a black ground, each enamelled zone being framed by bands of silver-gilt. The contrast of black, white, blue and gold combined with the brilliant colour of the innumerable turquoises, gives to these pieces an effect of oriental splendour. Augsburg, maker's mark the letters HANS in monogram (R³426), about 1570-80. H. of ewer 30.3 cm. Diam. of basin 43.5 cm.
Schatzkammer of the Residenz, Munich.

Plate 462.
The *Landschadenbundbecher*, gilt and enamelled standing cup and cover commissioned by the Munich Court as a gift to the Archduke Karl of Steiermark on his marriage in 1571 and subsequently presented to the Styrian nobility by the Archduke Ferdinand II. Attributed to Hans Schebel of Augsburg, it closely resembles the Garden of Eden Cup design (pl. 165) believed to be by the same master. The subjects on the bowl differ; instead of the Garden of Eden scenes this cup is decorated with three cast plaquettes of favourite Old Testament scenes: Esther and Ahasuerus, Judith and Holophernes and the Queen of Sheba and King Solomon. The stem corresponds precisely with the drawing as does the lip decorated with etched mauresques. It also has the enamelled decoration referred to in the annotations on the drawing. The superlative quality of the chasing and enamelling and the vast proportions of this cup are unparalleled in surviving 16th-century goldsmiths' work. It weighs twelve and a half kilos. Augsburg, about 1570. Maker's mark, HS monogram (R³350). H. 105 cm.
Landesmuseum Joanneum, Graz.

Plate 463.
Rock-crystal cup and cover, the gilt mounts etched with mauresques and painted in green and blue lacquer colours (*Kaltemail*), the rock-crystal probably from Freiburg. Augsburg, maker's mark HANS in monogram, (R³426). Last quarter of the 16th century. H. 40 cm.
Grünes Gewölbe, Dresden.

Plate 464.
Gilt standing salt or cup with bowl of amethystine quartz, left in its natural state. As a rule the Mannerist goldsmiths liked to work these hardstones into sophisticated forms, thus demonstrating the triumph of art over nature, rather than leave them as rough crystals. The circular base is supported by three snails, creatures whose curious form particularly appealed to the goldsmith, not least because they could conveniently be cast from nature. The stem is a satyr-like marine monster seated on a tortoise, and the composition is com-

pleted by a lively figure of Neptune seated on a dolphin. It is derived with modifications from one of Cornelis Floris's designs for standing cups published in Antwerp in 1548 (see pl. 199). Augsburg, late 16th century, maker's mark AW in monogram (not in Rosenberg). H. 22.3 cm.
British Museum (Waddesdon Bequest).

Plate 465.

Gilt standing cup presented to the Zürich Painters' Guild (*Gesellschaft der Schildner zum Schneggen*) by Georg Albricht of Zürich in 1564. This cup, with bowl wrought in the form of a snail, is supported by a satyr astride a tortoise and bound by a ribbon around his waist to a post behind. The outer-most surface of the silver shell is divided by interlacing strapwork into small panels embossed with lion masks, cherubs' heads and bunches of fruit, while the inner spirals are embossed with crabs, dolphins and all the various monsters known to Renaissance fantasy. The lid in the form of a naturalistic snail emerging from its shell achieves the shock effect often found in Mannerist art. It was especially commissioned for presentation to the Guild that bore the curious device of a snail and can be dated to the years immediately preceding 1564. Augsburg, maker's mark of a member of the Hüter family. (R³363). H. 31 cm.
Schweizerisches Landesmuseum, Zürich.

Plates 466, 467.

Ewer and basin of shell mounted in silver-gilt, the ewer supported on the shoulders of a triton whose tail twists around the central stem, the basin composed of four large shells separated by mermaids whose twin tails hold a smaller scallop-shell and develop into volutes which frame the central boss on which the ewer stands. The basin is supported on four legs which are attached to the backs of the mermaids. Augsburg, maker's mark of Elias or Cornelius Grosz (*Meister der Hausmarke*). (R³476). Late 16th century. H. of ewer 32 cm. L. of basin 41.5 cm.
Kunsthistorisches Museum, Vienna.

Plates 468, 469, 470.

Gilt and enamelled standing cup and cover by Elias or Cornelius Grosz. Variety of effect is achieved by the use of both translucent and opaque enamel and by the numerous applied brackets and pendant swags that mask the otherwise conventional profile. The large brackets on the bowl are of exceptionally complex form (pl. 470): starting in a volute at the top of which is attached a baluster, like the thumb-piece on a tankard, they develop into a lion mask with pendant draperies resting on a cornucopia terminating below in a cherub's head, which grows out of a stem attached to the tail of a winged dragon. It would hardly be possible to find a more typical example of Mannerist delight in assembling into a connected sequence unrelated elements of ornament. Furthermore, the surface of the cup is embellished with precious stones and bosses decorated with mauresques in champlevé enamel. The body, foot and cover are embossed with satyrs entrapped within strapwork and set with cast medallions and masks. Practically every technique known to the goldsmith is represented: sculpture in the modelling of the figure that surmounts its cover (pl. 469) and in the putti, sphinxes, fauns, etc. applied to its surface; casting in the applied brackets and in the medallions set in the body (pl. 468); embossing and chasing in the classical masks and various figure subjects on foot, bowl and cover: etching in the band of mauresque ornament running round the bowl; champlevé enamel, in translucent colours in the band of birds and flowers below the lip, and in opaque colours on the bosses attached to foot and cover; and, finally, jewellers' work in the setting of the precious stones in their silver-gilt collets. Elias or Cornelius Grosz (*Meister der Hausmarke*) (R³476). Augsburg, about 1560-80. H. 62 cm.
Schatzkammer of the Residenz, Munich.

Plate 471.

Gilt standing cup and cover, the bowl embossed with gadroons alternating with winged cherubs' heads, the stem, bowl and cover decorated with four bands of bunches of fruit, animals, birds, drapery, etc. in translucent enamel in the manner of and probably from the workshop of David Altenstetter. Augsburg, maker's mark indecipherable. Late 16th century. H. 56 cm.
Museum of Art, Toledo, U.S.A.

Plate 472.

Standing cup and cover, silver, all parts except for the base moulding and lip decorated with champlevé translucent enamels in the manner of and probably by David Altenstetter. The delicate arabesques of Altenstetter's enamels had to be picked up in the hand and examined closely in order to be appreciated. Augsburg. Unmarked, late 16th century. H. 22.2 cm.
Wallace Collection, London.

Plate 473.

Nautilus-shell cup with silver-gilt mounts by Nikolaus Schmidt, one of the most elaborately composed cups of its type in existence. The sculptural detail is superbly modelled, especially the figure of Neptune riding on a hippocamp that forms the stem. The cup does, however, give the impression that Schmidt has assembled all the decorative elements he had and combined them without greatly concerning himself about their mutual relationship. A professional designer such as Erasmus Hornick, instead of applying sculptural ornament wherever it could be fitted in, would have modelled the cup as a coherent whole and so avoided the additive quality of Schmidt's design. It is in the base that the impression of one feature being added to another is strongest. The stem rests on an oval base with ovolo moulded border following the normal fashion of the period, but to this have been added a series of twin-tailed mermaids playing stringed instruments, interspersed with shells surmounted by winged terminal figures. Although thematically the mermaids can be related to the purpose of the cup, they form a

disturbing addition to its composition. In some later Mannerist vessels, such as those of Christoph Jamnitzer, the conventional oval base is replaced by a design of interlacing members (pl. 513) and the Schmidt cup looks forward to this development. Nürnberg, late 16th century. (R³⁴036). H. 50.8 cm.
H.M. Queen Elizabeth II.

Plates 474, 475.
Gilt covered tazza signed and dated by Jonas Silber of Nürnberg, 1589. The decoration of this vessel symbolises the history of the world. In order to achieve so ambitious a programme it was necessary to use every inch of its surface, and the subject manner begins already on the underside of the base, on which is shown a figure of Christ Triumphant over the powers of Hell. The foot is of trefoil shape, like the Nürnberg masterpiece cups, and each of the three lobes of the trefoil is embossed in hemispherical form and chased with a representation of one of the three Continents, Africa, Asia and America (described as Nova Hispania), which had not yet been converted to Christianity. From this base rises the stem, which takes the form of the Tree of Knowledge with Adam, Eve, and the Serpent; the knop, resting on the spreading branches of this tree, represents the Temple of Jerusalem with the High Priest, while on the pinnacle Christ is shown with the Devil tempting him. The bowl is composed of two shells, as was usual with good quality examples. That on the underside is embossed with the figures of the Emperor and the Electors with the coats-of-arms of the 97 Electoral bodies of the Empire, while the upper shell, which constitutes the inside of the bowl, is embossed with a curious map of Europe (pl. 475), copied from an engraving of 1587. Europe is represented as a woman wearing the Imperial crown; as Charles V was Emperor when the map was first devised, Spain occupies the position of the head, Italy the right arm with Sicily as the orb, the left arm is Denmark, while the city of Nürnberg is shown as the heart. The figure of Europe is surrounded by waves with ships and dolphins while the border is embossed with cloud scrolls interrupted at intervals by masks emblematic of the winds. On the far right of the bowl is a panel inscribed *Ionas Silber Nurmberga 1589.* The underside of the cover bears in the centre a figure of Germania enthroned over a Roman warrior and crowned by an eagle while a lion hands her her sceptre;.she is surrounded by figures of the twelve legendary ancient Kings of Germany, cast from the well-known plaquettes of Peter Flötner, under each of which is a cartouche with a verse relating their achievements. The top of the cover is embossed with a constellation and over this are two free-standing arches of silver wire, upon the intersection of which is a sphere supporting a figure of Christ in Judgement. Nürnberg, J. Silber, (R³³986) 1589. H. 34.3 cm.
Kunstgewerbemuseum, Berlin.

Plates 476, 477.
Ewer and companion basin of silver-gilt and mother-of-pearl by Nikolaus Schmidt. In its use of three trochus-shells to represent the wings and tail of a

dragon, the ewer is reminiscent of Wenzel Jamnitzer's design (pl. XIII), in which the body is composed of two trochus-shells set together. Since Schmidt was an assistant of the older Jamnitzer it is very likely that he knew the Munich ewer and borrowed his idea from it. His design can, however, be criticised inasmuch as the dragon is perched on a stem and foot of conventional form and no effort has been made to provide a fluent transition from one to the other. Corresponding to the three shells in the body are three round plaques of mother-of-pearl set in the trefoil foot, between each lobe of which sits a minute cast frog, suggesting the water-bearing function of the vessel. In the design of the chased ornament around the base of the foot, the master's imagination was less inspired and he has used a conventional floral design enclosing winged cherub's heads. The depression of the basin is covered with a mosaic of small mother-of-pearl plaques pinned to the silver foundation, while larger oval plaques are attached to the border between the figures of nymphs and river gods. The basin is further decorated with small figures of reptiles cast from nature. Nürnberg, late 16th century. Nikolaus Schmidt (R³⁴030fg). H. of ewer 45 cm. Diam. of basin 56 cm.
Staatliche Kunstsammlungen, Dresden.

Plate 478.
Gilt ewer set with mother-of-pearl roundels. The usual Renaissance ewer has a handle in the form of a female term and grotesque masks placed under both spout and handle; the sculptural detail on this ewer is more exuberant, consisting of a bold mask under the lower terminal of the handle, a female figure growing out of a winged mask on the handle and, most striking of all, a larger mask on the front out of which develops a female demi-figure modelled completely in the round, her head reaching up to the spout while her hands are supported on the upper surface of the body of the ewer. The figure is crisply modelled and recalls the manner of the contemporary Nürnberg sculptor, Benedikt Würzelbauer, the master of the Fountain of the Virtues in the Nürnberg market-place. Nürnberg, Nikolaus Schmidt (R³⁴030d, e,) late 16th century. H. 54. cm.
Kunsthistorisches Museum, Vienna.

Plate 479.
Trochus-shell cup with gilt mounts, the shell of unusually large size supported by a triton riding on a dolphin, the cover surmounted by a demi-figure of a nymph looking into a mirror. A pair of cups of exactly the same design by the same maker are in the Württembergisches Landesmuseum, Stuttgart. These cups were supplied by Petzoldt to the Nürnberg City Council for presentation to important visitors to the city. Nürnberg, Hans Petzoldt (R³⁴033dd), late 16th century.
H. 54.5 cm.
Imparmuveszeti Museum, Budapest.

Plate 480.
Gilt standing cup and cover wrought in the form of a bunch of grapes (*Traubenpokal*), the stem formed as an

emperor wearing armour and holding a banner in his right hand, a shield in his left. The cover is surmounted by a figure of a lion holding a shield of arms. The silver thistle foliage under the finial is a Gothic Revival feature. Formerly part of the city plate of Elbing. Nürnberg, Hans Petzoldt (R³⁴033x), about 1610, possibly one of the twenty cups in the form of grapes purchased by the city of Nürnberg from Petzoldt between 1610 and 1612. H. 50 cm.
Kunstgewerbemuseum, Berlin.

Plate 481.
Ostrich-egg cup with gilt mounts, the straps finely cast and chased with female terms surmounting lion heads. The egg painted and gilt with foliage and ribbons. Nürnberg. Hans Petzoldt (R³⁴033a) dated 1594. H. 52 cm.
Institute of Arts, Minneapolis.

Plate 482.
Gilt double cup made for the Usler family of Goslar, the bowls of the cups of Gothic Revival form but with applied Renaissance ornament. A medal of 1596 inset. Hans Petzoldt (R³⁴003b). Nürnberg, end of the 16th century. H. 54 cm.
Rijksmuseum, Amsterdam.

Plate 483.
Gilt standing cup and cover, the bowl composed of two cast plaques representing the Shame of Noah and the Birth of Christ — a curious combination chosen at random by the goldsmith from his stock of models — the lip etched with mauresques and embossed with lobes, the lower part of the body and the base of the finial cast from patterns derived from the Jamnitzer workshop. The cover set with a medallion of Hope after Peter Flötner, repeated three times. The upper finial restored. Another cup by the same master in the Metropolitan Museum, New York, is of almost identical form and shows only minor differences in the detail ornament. Such repetition does not accord with the modern conception of 16th-century practice, but was not exceptional; Hans Petzoldt did the same. Nürnberg, Jakob Fröhlich, (R³³923) last quarter of 16th century. H. 41.2 cm.
The Worshipful Company of Broderers, London.

Plates 484, 485.
Gilt standing cup and cover made for the Holzschuher family, perhaps Petzoldt's finest work. The stem is wrought in the form of a sea-lion with tail arching over its back, the device of the Imhoff family, while on the bottom is a dedication inscription from Georg Holzschuher to Andreas Imhoff. The bowl is embossed with interlacing strapwork forming six cartouches which enclose six scenes embossed and chased with the processes of mining silver ore and working the silver. These are arranged in two rows, those above being larger; that illustrated (pl. 485) is the last in the series and shows the interior of a goldsmith's workshop

with an apprentice holding a piece of silver in the kiln. Nürnberg, Hans Petzoldt, dated 1626. H. 46.5 cm.
Private collection, Switzerland.

Plate 486.
Gilt covered beaker. The body set with panels of *Hinterglasmalerei* (painting behind glass) and decorated with polychrome floral scrolls inhabited by birds, etc. in cold enamel. The cast decoration on the cover and also the frieze on the low stem taken from often-used Nürnberg models, Nürnberg, Jakob Fröhlich (R³³923) last quarter of the 16th century. H. 15.5 cm.
Kunstgewerbemuseum, Cologne.

Plate 487.
Gilt cup and cover, the form derived from the late Gothic columbine-cup. The bowl develops like a living flower from the tall delicate stem, while the bent and cut silver garlands that mask the junction of bowl and stem and separate the pronounced lobes on foot, bowl and cover give the effect of foliage. The skill of the goldsmith is demonstrated in the working of a vertical ridge on each of the lobes. The finial takes the form of a figure of Justice. This pattern of standing cup remained the standard formula well into the first half of the 17th century. Nürnberg, Hans Beutmüller, (R³⁴054) about 1600. H. 55 cm.
Museum of Art, Toledo, U.S.A.

Pl. 488.
Gilt standing cup and cover with exceptionally complex profile, the foot, bottom of the body and cover each with a frieze of niches enclosing allegorical figures, the central region of the body with a frieze of markedly smaller diameter than the mouth, embossed with Old Testament subjects, and set with oval panels of enamel. The rim of the bowl embossed with a frieze of New Testament subjects and also set with enamelled plaques. The cover surmounted by a bracketed finial terminating in a crowned double eagle of the Empire. This piece illustrates two trends in the architecture of standing cups of the early 17th century: the increasing contrast between the diameter of the centre and the lip of the bowl and the exaggerated height, even more marked than in pl. 487. This cup is believed to have been presented to the Emperor Charles VII in 1742 by the Jewish community of Frankfurt, hence the double eagle finial. Augsburg, about 1600, maker's mark LS in monogram (R³424) H. 78 cm. (The weight is no less than 5 kg.)
Schatzkammer of the Residenz, Munich.

Plate 489.
Gilt *Doppelpokal* (double cup) made for the Nürnberg patrician family of Holzschuher. The stems are wrought in the form of the crest and coat of arms of the family, each with a different model of helmet. The lower part of the bowl embossed with lobes, the upper with relief figures. Nürnberg, Elias Lencker (R³³951), dated 1575. H. 50.5 cm.
Museum für Kunst und Gewerbe, Hamburg.

Plate 490.

Gilt vase with two handles containing a spray of silver flowers by a member of the Epfenhauser family of Augsburg. The body of the vase is of gilt silver contained in a cagework of white silver. It is described in an inventory of the property left by the Archduke Ferdinand of Tirol, which was prepared in 1596, as 'A fine and artistic vase with a gilt body encased within a pierced cover, with two handles; in the vase stand ingeniously wrought flowers and grasses; it could not be weighed but is reckoned at 700 Gulden.' Apart from the flowers the vase is not remarkable; it conforms to the type that can be found in the designs of the *Punzenstecher*. Augsburg, Christoph Epfenhauser (R³336-7) about 1590. H. 74.8 cm.
Kunsthistorisches Museum, Vienna.

Plate 491.

Gilt and enamelled writing-cabinet, the surface decorated in polychrome translucent enamel with hunting scenes after prints by Stradanus and with panels of grotesques inhabited by birds and animals. The strictly rectangular structure is relieved by the snail feet, the dolphin brackets below the angles of the projecting upper stage and by the putti at the corners of the lower stage. Its main appeal lies in the brilliantly coloured panels of translucent enamel and the exquisitely modelled figures of cherubs seated on scrolls at the corners bearing attributes symbolic of *Grammatica, Mathematica, Astronomica* and *Musica* respectively. Enamelling has almost always been a specialist branch of the goldsmiths' craft and the enamelled ornament of this desk and the pieces that accompany it is not likely to have been the work of either of the Lenckers. They probably called upon the services of a specialist such as Hans Karl or David Altenstetter. While the panels of grotesques derive from much the same source as the translucent ornament by David Altenstetter and his school, the hunting scenes are more ambitious. The charming group on the top of the casket, consisting of a seated woman teaching a putto to read, symbolic of *Rhetorica,* is another proof of the sculptural powers of the goldsmith. The stool composed of open scrolls of curious construction than those supporting the cherubs is a delightful Mannerist conceit. Nürnberg, Hans Lencker the Elder and Elias Lencker, his younger brother (R³3905), about 1585. Dim. 30 x 39 x 28.6 cm.
Schatzkammer of the Residenz, Munich.

Plate 492.

Agate standing cup, the bowl carved as a shell, the gilt mounts bearing a Nürnberg mark. The rear terminal is modelled as a twin-tailed mermaid, the device of the city of Nürnberg. The presence of a town and maker's mark, unusual on a mounted hardstone, permits the precise attribution of this piece. Hardstone vessels were usually gold-mounted and hence escaped marking. Nürnberg, Jörg Ruel, (R³4086). Early 17th century. H. 21.7 cm.
Institute of Arts, Minneapolis.

Plate 493.

Nautilus-shell cup with silver-gilt foot, stem and mounts. This cup belongs to the transitional period between Mannerism and Baroque; this is indicated by the bold modelling of the figure sculpture and by the auricular ornament on the foot and the rim of the cover. The delicate festoons of fruit supported by winged mermaids look back to Mannerist taste, as does the figure of a mermaid on the cover with small head and long body. The placing of a second shell between the legs of the bearded Triton is an original feature. Augsburg, Jeremias Michael (R³469). First quarter of 17th century.
H. 42 cm.
Private collection, Switzerland.

Plate 494.

Gilt tankard, the body of rock-crystal within a silver filigree cage, bordered by a frieze of human masks within strapwork in cast relief; the foot and rim with etched mauresque borders. The device of concealing the rock-crystal drum within silver cagework presents the type of enigma beloved of Mannerism. Augsburg, Ulrich Schönmacher (R³349), third quarter of 16th century. H. 24.6 cm.
Royal Ontario Museum, Toronto.

Plate 495.

Gilt basin, the rim set with 45 *verre fixé* panels of the ruling families in the province of Bern; in the centre, the arms of the city of Bern and the Empire. The depression of the basin is divided into three panels each chased with scenes illustrating incidents from the history of the city of Bern. The battle scenes on the dish are shown in great detail, in particular the massed bodies of pikemen. The intervening spaces are chased with two handled vases of flowers set within strapwork cartouches. Together with a cup and a ewer in the form of a bear, this basin was presented to the city of Bern in 1583 by a merchant of Augsburg, Martin Zobel, in recognition of the grant to him of a lease of the Aelen salt mines for a further ten years. Augsburg, maker's mark, the initials GP (R³394), about 1583. Diam. 54.3 cm.
Historisches Museum, Bern.

Plates 496, 497.

Gilt tazza, the bowl embossed and chased with Minerva introducing the Art of Painting to the Muses, a temple to the left of the scene, a Roman City in the background, from an engraving by Goltzius after Hans von Aachen. Lead plaquettes were made from moulds taken from this tazza bowl; two are in the Bayerisches Nationalmuseum, Munich. The painting was originally executed for Duke Wilhelm V of Bavaria by the artist between 1588 and 1596, when he was for a while in Munich. The baluster stem is decorated with three oval cartouches, the intervening spaces above filled with projecting ram's heads. The lower side of the bowl covered with a separate plaque embossed with three recumbent female figures set within quadrilobate cartouches surmounted by masks and putti, between the cartouches compositions of masks, bunches of fruit

and birds (pl. 497). The foot embossed with recumbent figures of the Virtues and grotesque masks embossed in high and low relief. The form of the foot and stem and the lay-out of the underside of the bowl show strong Dutch influence. Augsburg, no maker's mark, about 1620-30. H. 15 cm. Diam. 18 cm.
Museé du Louvre, Paris.

Plates 498, 499.
Gilt basin by Christoph Lencker, the central area embossed with scenes from the story of Europa and the Bull, probably derived from a painting or drawing by one of the fashionable Mannerist artists such as Rottenhammer or Hans von Aachen. The border decorated with applied and pierced panels of enamelled scrollwork alternating with cherub's heads and swans. The basin is so designed that it had to be set up vertically like a painting for its embossed subjects to be appreciated. Instead of being divided up into panels, the central area is occupied by a single subject, though the oval seating for the base of the ewer is still reserved in the centre. The pictorial treatment reached its complete expression in basins such as that in pl. 500, in which there is no longer any central reserved place for the ewer. Augsburg, Christoph Lencker (R³412) early 17th century. L. 69 cm.
Kunsthistorisches Museum, Vienna.

Plate 500.
Large gilt basin embossed with Jupiter hurling his thunderbolt at the Titans. This is one of two basins made *en suite*, once accompanied by ewers which have since been lost or melted down. The absence of a mark on either suggests that they were made by one of the court goldsmiths of the Dukes of Bavaria. The basin is worked in heavy metal but the relief is high and much chasing has been done from the front. This and the companion basin have been attributed variously to Paul Hübner of Augsburg, to Paul van Vianen of Utrecht, Nikolaus Schmidt of Nürnberg and, more convincingly, to the Munich court goldsmith, Andreas Attemstett. The bold relief and violent gesticulation of the muscular figures resemble neither the rather flat manner of Hübner nor the more delicate and subtle style of the Utrecht master. The two basins are listed in the 1598 inventory of the Munich *Kunstkammer*. Unmarked, Augsburg or Munich, about 1590. Diam. 57 cm.
Schatzkammer of the Residenz, Munich.

Plate 501.
Gilt ewer by Christoph Lencker of Augsburg, given together with an oval basin by the same master to the Aegidien church in Nürnberg for use as a christening service, but originally intended for secular purposes. The boss of the basin (not illustrated because damaged in the Second World War) and a plaque attached to the handle of the ewer bear the Habsburg arms surmounted by the Imperial crown, indicating that this must have been an imperial commission. This ewer and basin probably date from the beginning of the 17th century; the oval shape of the basin corresponds to 17th-century fashion and the ewer no longer has the conventional Renaissance egg-form but rather resembles a sauceboat, recalling some of Hornick's more adventurous designs. The bold sculptural form of the handle contrasts effectively with the delicate low relief of the panel embossed with sea-monsters amongst waves, and the theme of water and water-creatures is suggested in every feature of the design. The figures of mermaids that form the stem are strikingly similar to those of the series of designs attributed to an anonymous Italo-Flemish master (see pls. 192 and 193). Augsburg, Christoph Lencker (R³412), marked on the basin only. Early 17th century. H. 16.5 cm.
Germanisches Nationalmuseum, Nürnberg. (Loan).

Plate 502.
Cup carved from petrified palmwood (agate) mounted in silver-gilt by Johannes Lencker and constructed in the form of a ship resting on the body of a triton and a dolphin. The bowl was already in the Bavarian *Kunstkammer* before 1598 but the mounts were ordered from Lencker at a later date, though before 1635, when the complete vessel was inventoried. The handle is surmounted by a young triton who holds up the arms of the Elector of Bavaria. The costliness of the piece is emphasized by the row of diamonds alternating with rubies around the foot. The strength and boldness of the modelling point to the incipient development of the Baroque style. Augsburg, Johannes Lencker (R³456) about 1625-30. H. 33.7 cm.
Schatzkammer of the Residenz, Munich.

Plate 503.
Gilt tankard, the tapering body embossed and chased with landscape panels within oval strapwork cartouches, the intervening spaces chased with nude demi-figures and scrollwork. The lid surmounted by a flat-topped finial engraved with a house mark; the thumbpiece cast from a Jamnitzer pattern with a bound satyr. The handle cast with a female demi-figure, the whole in the manner of Bernard Zan. Augsburg, maker's mark. the letter S in a shield (not in Rosenberg), late 16th century. H. 15.2 cm.
Private collection, London.

Plate 504.
Gilt cup, the body and cover wrought in the form of a performing bear held by a chain, the head serving as the cover. This piece would have been more serviceable than most of the vessels in the form of animals made at this time. Augsburg, probably Leonhard Umbach (R³399), end of 16th century. H. 18.6 cm.
Württembergisches Landesmuseum, Stuttgart.

Plate 505.
Standing cup in the form of a musketeer, his musket supported on his right shoulder, a powder flask at his right side, a sword at his left, the musket rests in his left hand; the figure wears a buttoned jacket of sharply tap-

ering cut and gorget round his neck, on his head a tall hat with wide brim. The oval base chased with scrolls. The head is removable and may be used as a cup. The figure is wrought from several plates of silver, the head being cast. The modeller showed great sculptural skill; whether he was identical with the goldsmith who struck his mark on the base is uncertain. Nürnberg, David Lauer (R³4040) first quarter of the 17th century. H. 26.5 cm. *Private collection, London.*

Plate 506.
Parcel-gilt cup wrought in the form of a huntsman dressed in the costume of the late 16th century, holding a boar spear in the ready position and leading a small dog. The oval base is covered with cast fern-like branches and lizards in full relief. A clockwork movement housed within the base enables the figure to move along the table. Nürnberg, Christoff Ritter (R³3880), late 16th century. H. 31.2 cm.
British Museum.

Plate 507.
Silver-gilt ewer by Johannes Lencker of Augsburg in the form of a nymph seated on the back of a sea-centaur. The goldsmith has here used the centaur's body as the water container, while the conch through which he blows serves as a spout. The vessel is supported on a dolphin, to which the upper part is attached by a large screw — the only unsatisfactory feature of the whole composition. The lithe figure of the nymph is the epitome of Mannerist sophistication. Augsburg, Johannes Lencker (R³456), early 17th century. H. 34.5 cm.
Rijksmuseum, Amsterdam.

Plate 508.
Gilt group of Diana seated upon a stag, the octagonal base containing clockwork: two hounds and a stag-hunting group, modelled in the round, are attached to the upper side of the base. These groups combined artistic appeal with the function of a toy. When used on the dining-table, the head was removed and the body filled with wine. The clockwork was wound up and the piece set in motion. It had to be emptied at a draught by the person in front of whom it came to rest. In comparison with the vessels modelled in the form of leaping animals, these stags with their goddess rider seem rather static, but motion was provided by the clockwork. The Diana group was one of the most popular conceits of the end of the 16th century; between twenty and thirty are recorded. Another version of this model by the same goldsmith appears on the jacket of this book (*Schatzkammer of the Residenz, Munich*). Augsburg, Matthäus Wallbaum, (R³428), about 1600. H. 16.4 cm.
Royal Ontario Museum, Toronto.

Plates 509, 510.
Two of a set of four gilt tazzas by Christoph Jamnitzer, embossed and chased with scenes from the story of Phaethon, showing him requesting permission from his father, the sun-god, Helios, to drive the chariot of the sun (pl. 509) and driving the chariot across the heavens (pl. 510). The third tazza shows the chariot falling from the heavens, the subject of Michelangelo's well-known presentation drawing for Tomaso dei Cavalieri at Windsor Castle, the fourth the lament of his sisters for his death. Jamnitzer's skill in representing a landscape receding into the far distance is well shown in the second tazza. He may have learnt this particular skill from his father, Hans Jamnitzer. The border ornament of dotted festoons is a typical Jamnitzer feature. Nürnberg, Christoph Jamnitzer (R³3839 m) about 1600. Diam. 23.8 cm.
Hermitage Museum, Leningrad.

Plates 511, 512, 513, 514.
Gilt and enamelled ewer and basin by Christoph Jamnitzer, made in the style of the Prague Imperial Court Workshop for the Emperor Rudolph II. The two vessels were probably made shortly before 1603, in which year Jamnitzer received the large sum of 4,024 florins through the Nürnberg City Council on the Emperor's instructions. The vertical movement of the ewer begins at the base in inter-penetrating scrolls that develop at intervals into grotesque masks. Above this a short stem, from which project four boldly modelled satyr-heads, leads to a lobed ovoid body. This is of exceptionally complex form and is divided into two zones; the lower, of circular section, is embossed with scenes of the Gods on Mount Olympus, while the upper and main part, which is of quatrefoil section, is divided vertically into four panels separated by beaded straps terminating above and below in bunches of fruit. The panels are embossed with scenes symbolic of the Triumph of Time (pl. 512), Truth, Death (pl. 514) and Fame (pl. 513) respectively. Particularly dramatic is the Triumph of Death with the human figures falling before a skeleton wielding a scythe. Above these panels the body is drawn up into a narrow neck surrounded by seated winged cherubs modelled in the round, while the spout is supported by a satyr who is held in position by a festoon of fruit and flowers (pl. 513). The satyr beneath the spout is one of the few conventional features in the composition of this extraordinary vessel. The cover, which cannot be moved, is surmounted by a swan with outstretched wings and gaping beak upon which rides a superbly modelled figure of Leda. The handle of the ewer is of S-form and is embellished with feather-like scrolls that develop at intervals into human or grotesque forms. The basin (pl. 511) is embossed in high relief with the Triumph of Cupid; it bears both signature and mark of Christoph Jamnitzer (R³3839, basin only). Nürnberg, about 1600. H. of ewer 43.5 cm. L. of dish 65 cm.
Kunsthistorisches Museum, Vienna.

Plate 515.
Silver columbine-cup in the manner of and probably made in the workshop of Christoph Jamnitzer. Its slim form, the applied brackets surmounted by female winged terms and the grotesque male masks with long

pendant dewlaps embossed between the lobes of the bowl are all characteristic of his documented pieces. The base of the bowl and the cover are both signed with the stamped initials B.C., while the bottom member of the stem is stamped BEN.CER., presumably by an Italian goldsmith in Christoph's employ. The finely engraved scenes from the Old Testament are copied from prints by Etienne Delaune, and one depicting Jacob's Dream is signed Jacobus F. and Jakob Scheib (?). The presence of two other signatures must exclude the old theory that this was Christoph Jamnitzer's masterpiece. As it bears no mark and is not gilt and is said to have come from the Nürnberg goldsmiths' chest (*Zunftlade*) the most likely explanation is that it is another of the sample vessels made to show aspirants for admission as masters to the guild. Signed but unmarked. Nürnberg, end of 16th century, the finial of the cover restored. H. 35.5 cm.
Victoria and Albert Museum.

Plate 516.
Gilt ewer, the companion basin was melted in the 18th century. This ewer derives its basic form from the columbine-cup, so long favoured by the goldsmiths of Nürnberg, but the profile is masked by the ornament applied around the lower region of the body, consisting of snail-shells between which spring large openwork brackets and figures of dragons. The body is composed of four large heart-shaped lobes, each decorated with a figure emblematic of one of the seasons, executed in *pointillé* technique and surmounted by a winged cherub's head, the massive features of which already anticipate the Baroque. No Mannerist goldsmith carried the process of breaking up the profile of a vessel into a confused and complex outline further than Christoph Jamnitzer. This treatment is particularly evident in the decoration of the cover with four lion masks rising from auricular scrolls between which project four large pierced brackets, each embellished with beaded rat-tail ornament. On a platform at the top of the cover stands a winged figure of Fame, precisely modelled and exquisitely finished, which might well have come from the workshop of the Nürnberg sculptor, Benedikt Würzelbauer. The quatrefoil foot is decorated with four rams' heads and develops into a stem from which spring applied brackets. Nürnberg, Christoph Jamnitzer (R³3839y) early 17th century. H. 46 cm.
Grünes Gewölbe, Dresden.

Plate 517.
Gilt ewer constructed in the form of the elephant of Hannibal at the Battle of Zama. It bears on its back a tower with warriors; its trunk is pierced with two holes for the water to run out, while the tail forms the handle. The modelling both of the elephant itself and of the lively little figures in classical armour in the tower illustrate Jamnitzer's skill as a sculptor. The ewer was originally accompanied by a large basin which was also embossed with a representation of the Battle of Zama and signed by Christoph Jamnitzer. The basin was last recorded in the late 18th century and is now lost. Unmarked, Nürnberg, about 1600. H. 43 cm.
Kunstgewerbemuseum, Berlin.

Plate 518.
Gilt wine-bottle wrought in the form of a double-headed eagle. This vessel was presumably presented to the Tsar of Russia by some German or Scandinavian diplomatic or trade delegation. In common with other vessels in the form of birds or beasts this was a show piece intended to excite wonder at the craftsman's skill. It is nevertheless rather coarsely worked, like many of the gifts sent to Russia, which were judged by size and weight rather than quality. Among them were pieces that had failed to find a buyer in the home market and, probably, secondhand ones as well. Nürnberg, Jörg Ruel (R³4086), early 17th century. H. 63 cm.
Hermitage Museum, Leningrad.

Plate 519.
Parcel-gilt ewer and detail of companion basin, the oviform ewer engraved with four panels depicting scenes from Genesis within scalework borders; around the lip, top and bottom of the body and the foot are etched bands of mauresques. The scroll handle is formed as a serpent with head attached by a hinge, while five simulated straps attach it to the scroll handle. The basin is engraved with biblical subjects and etched with mauresques. The scenes on the ewer after woodcuts by Virgil Solis. Most surviving ewers and basins of German origin are embossed and chased and these engraved and etched pieces are quite exceptional. The central boss of the basin is engraved with the arms of Pallandt (Lower Rhine) addorsed with Van Dorth. Nürnberg, makers' mark, the initials BI (not in Rosenberg), dated 1575. H. 40.5 cm.
Private collection, Germany.

Plate 520.
Gilt ewer, the oviform body embossed and chased with strapwork enclosing oval cartouches with figures of the Planets, the neck cast with a woman's head and bust above which is a shell. The all-over low relief decoration is typical of the late 16th century. Within the base is a plaquette with the arms of Geuder impaling Haller von Hallerstein, both Nürnberg patrician families. Nürnberg, maker's mark IB monogram, probably Joachim Bintzege, (R³3967), dated 1581. H. 36.5 cm.
Rijksmuseum, Amsterdam.

Plate 521.
Gilt standing cup, the bowl and cover of pear or gourd shape, embossed and chased with strapwork enclosing flowers and masks, the stem formed as a tree-trunk to which a figure of a man clings, the finial an infant looking through a telescope, perhaps a later alteration. The use of a form copied from nature for the bowl constitutes a return to the naturalistic element in late Gothic that is well represented in some of Albrecht Dürer's silver designs. The gourd cup is one of the few types of 16th-century German silver that was copied by English goldsmiths. Nürnberg, Heinrich Jonas (R³4004), late 16th century. H. 32.8 cm.
Hermitage Museum, Leningrad.

Plate 522.

Silver gilt mounted nautilus-shell cup, the stem in the form of a slim Mannerist Venus Marina, the lip mount with pieced panels alternating with oval ones embossed with reliefs of the Flood, Jonah and the Whale and Susannah and the Elders, each of which introduces the theme of water. The volute of the shell is surmounted by Neptune in his chariot drawn by sea-horses. Nürnberg, Thomas Stoer the Elder (R³4081), dated 1611. H. 43.3 cm.
Museum für Kunst und Gewerbe, Hamburg.

Plate 523.

Guild Welcome cup (*Willkommenbecher*) of a ceramic stove-makers' guild (*Hafnerzunft*), gilt and constructed in the form of a stove of of the type in fashion in the late 16th century. Such cups were used in the course of the ceremony of admittance of a new master to the guild. A touch of humour is given to the piece by the cat, dog and monkey perched upon it. No maker's mark, Augsburg, about 1600. H. 24 cm.
Württembergisches Landesmuseum, Stuttgart.

Plate 524.

Welcome cup of a shoemakers' guild, wrought in the form of a fashionable 16th century shoe, the mounts gilt, the lip mount engraved with a monster and with a huntsman about to attack a lion with a boar spear. The toe of the shoe mounted with a silver bell. Unmarked, German, third quarter of 16th century. H. 10.5 cm.
Fowler Museum, Los Angeles.

Plate 525.

Gilt beaker mounted with mother-of-pearl plaques modelled in the form of a woman bearing a basket of fruit on her head, her wide spreading skirt forming the bowl, which is covered with mother-of-pearl, each plaque being attached by a nail with decorative head. The goldsmith was probably influenced by the Paul Flindt design illustrated in pl. 182. This type of cup, if ever actually used, had to be drunk at one gulp; the form of the cup was doubtless the source of much bawdy humour. Nürnberg, Meinrad Bauch the Elder (R³3993), early 17th century. H. 22 cm.
Hermitage Museum, Leningrad.

Plates 526, 530.

Giant gilt standing cup; this piece illustrates the tendency to exaggerate the height of silver vessels in the early 17th century, sometimes at the expense of their proportions. Its maker had access to a large number of casting patterns which he has used without much regard to their relationship to each other. The lobate bosses under the lip are typical of the Gothic Revival fashion that persisted into the early 17th century. Unusual features for cups of this period are the bust portraits of contemporary German rulers, each with his name inscribed, embossed around the bowl, and the figures surmounting the cover, which are modelled in the round. Both these and the medallion heads retain most

of the cold enamel which once decorated much of the ornament of the cup. This vessel was made by Utermarke in Hamburg, after he had left Lüneburg where he made the mirror frame (pl. 527). It was once part of the Lüneburg Ratsschatz, to which it was presented in 1602 by the Tobing family. In 1706 it was presented by the city of Lüneburg to the Elector of Hanover. Hamburg, maker's mark of Dirich Utermarke, (Scheffler no. 835), about 1600. H. 76.5 cm.
Private collection, England.

Plates 527, 528, 529.

Gilt mirror frame made by Luleff Meyer of Lüneburg and his journeyman, Dirich Utermarke, before 1592, when it was delivered to the widowed Electress Sophia of Saxony. This mirror was a special commission from the Saxon court and is not, therefore, struck with the usual town and maker's marks. Instead, it bears two shields engraved with the initials of its joint makers. One, a crowned shield charged with three blossoms and a sickle flanked by the initials LM, is thought to be that of Luleff Meyer, while the other, a crowned shield charged with a lion rampant flanked by the initials DV, must be that of Dirich Utermarke. The mirror bears two dates, 1587 and 1592, perhaps recording its beginning and completion. As these dates are not on the silver frame but on the painted glass enrichment, they may not, however, relate to the goldsmiths' work. Even taking into consideration the extreme elaboration of its design, five years seems a very long time for such a piece to be in the making. The composition of the frame, in itself extremely elaborate, has been rendered more confused by the later addition of numerous jewels set in large silver-gilt collets, some of which interrupt the view of the figures. The large number of small shields, painted with coats-of-arms and applied to the two wide mouldings that divide the frame horizontally into three parts, seem also to be an afterthought, since they overload an area already highly charged with decoration and obscure the ornament of the moulding behind (pls. 528, 529). The production of painted glass panels of this type was a speciality of the Dresden goldsmith, Valentin Geitner (see p.265) and these embellishments were probably added by him after the frame arrived in Dresden. Like so many of the major works of the Mannerist goldsmiths, the design is based on a learned iconographical programme, taken from the Old Testament, with the exception of the small group in the triangular member at the base, which represents the Judgement of Paris. The remainder symbolizes the dream of Nebuchadnezzar as expounded by the prophet Daniel about the perpetual dominion of the Son of Man that will follow. Above the mirror is a roundel of glass painted on the back with a double eagle on whose breast is a crucifix, while on its wings are displayed 56 shields of arms of the constituent bodies of the Holy Roman Empire. On each side is a mounted warrior (pl. 528) while in niches below are two other warriors standing in niches; these represent the four Empires that had already passed, namely those of Nimrod, Cyrus, Alexander and Julius Caesar respectively. Finally, at the top is a fifth figure in Roman armour representing Nebuchadnezzar himself. The correct interpretation of all

the scenes and subjects represented is by no means certain, but as an achievement of the German goldsmith this mirror is unrivalled. Lüneburg, Luleff Meyer and Dirich Utermarke, about 1590 (Scheffler, no. 106). H. 115 cm.
Grünes Gewölbe, Dresden.

Plates 531, 532, 533.
Gilt flagon (*Hansekanne*), the drum finely embossed and chased with foliate strapwork enclosing three oval cartouches wrought with Andromeda chained to the rock and Perseus overcoming the dragon in the background (pl. 531), the death of Adonis (pl. 532) and the death of Thisbe with the corpse of Pyramus in the foreground (pl. 533). Around the bottom of the body, a hunting scene; on the lid, the arms of Riga. Hamburg, Dirich Utermarke (Scheffler no. 835), dated 1622. H. 42 cm.
Statens Historiska Museet, Stockholm.

Plate 534.
Gilt flagon, (*Hansekanne*) the body embossed and chased with strapwork, around the centre a pierced silver girdle, the base chased with winged cherubs and scrollwork. This flagon well illustrates the stately character of the north German *Hansekanne;* nowhere else was a vessel of such magnificence devised. The complex pierced thumbpiece and the terminal of the handle, from which spring wires ending in buds should be noticed. Their great weight made such vessels, once they were filled with liquid impracticable, but they made splendid sideboard ornaments for the city or guild council chamber. Lübeck, maker's mark, a rose (R³3193) early 17th century. H. 39 cm.
British Museum, (Waddesdon Bequest).

Plates 535, 536.
Gilt flagon (*Hansekanne*) of the Hamburg Cooper's Guild the cylindrical body engraved with interlaced strapwork and, in the front, with a circular cartouche engraved with the Last Judgement. Around the lower part of the body a hunting scene, and on foot and cover applied cast heads of Roman warriors and angels. Hamburg, no maker's mark, dated 1588. H. 38.7 cm.
Museum für Kunst und Gewerbe, Hamburg.

Plates 537, 538, 539.
Three details of the cross foot made by Anton Eisenhoit of Warburg for the church of St. Patroclus at Soest. Italian influence is much stronger in Eisenhoit's embossed work than in that of his German contemporaries, as can be seen in the beautiful female nudes set within the volutes of the triangular foot of the Soest cross. The biblical scenes within an architectural framework on the upper stage of the foot are also of Italian inspiration, each being apparently based on a design for a Pax. In the ornamental scheme of this cross foot the strapwork, which was almost *de rigeur* in contemporary German work, is absent. Unmarked. About 1600.
Treasury of the Cathedral of St. Patroklus, Soest.

Plate 540.
Parcel-gilt drinking-cup in the form of an owl, the detachable head serving as a cover. The owl was the most favoured bird-form, partly on account of its reputation for wisdom, and partly for the practical reason that its size made it convenient as a drinking vessel. A larger number of German cups in the form of owls exist than of any other bird or beast. The bells attached to its claws probably had no function other than adding to the merriment of the occasion when it was in use. The arms of Count Kolowrat of Bohemia added later. Ulm, Mathäus Hofherr, (R³4763), third quarter of 16th century. H. 16.3 cm.
Württembergisches Landesmuseum, Stuttgart.

Plate 541.
One of a pair of coconut flasks, the gilt mounts embossed with *Rollwerk*, masks and bunches of fruit; gilt chains. The nuts are carved with biblical subjects after woodcuts by Virgil Solis from a bible published in Frankfurt am Main in 1561. A coconut-cup carved with subjects after the same graphic source is in the Treasury of the Deutsches Ritter Orden, Vienna. Pilgrim flasks mounted with coconuts are distinctly unusual, no others are recorded. The surviving examples are mounted as standing cups or, more rarely, as tankards. Köln, Thomas von Hattingen (R³2696). about 1580. H. 32 cm.
Kunstgewerbemuseum, Cologne.

Plate 542.
Gilt standing cup, the bowl set with three cast medallions of figures symbolic of Faith, Christian Love and Charity; on the cover a figure of Abundance. The profusion of etched decoration is unusual; this appears on the cover, around the bowl as a background to the inset medallions and on the foot. Most of the casting patterns seem to be of Nürnberg origin. Strassburg, Linhardt Bauer, (R³6970) about 1560. H. 50 cm.
Museum of Art, Toledo, U.S.A.

Plate 543.
Gilt goblet, probably one of a set of four, the foot chased with three panels enclosing a lion, ram and bear respectively, alternating with bunches of fruit; baluster stem; the bowl chased with three strapwork cartouches chased with three of the Foolish Virgins from the New Testament parable, each holding a cup-shaped lamp from which the oil is spilling, one weeping at the same time, the intervals between the cartouches chased with vases of flowers; the rim engraved with three panels enclosing a fish and two water-fowl respectively, and with arabesques. The other goblets would have been chased with the remaining three Foolish Virgins and the six Wise Virgins. The figures are dressed in fashionable costume of about the year 1600. German, unmarked, town of origin uncertain. The absence of a mark makes it unlikely that this cup was made in one of the South German towns, such as Nürnberg or Augsburg, where the guilds enforced hall-marking with some severity. The quality of the chasing equals the best

South German work. Dated 1590. H. 16 cm.
Private collection, London.

Plates 544, 545, 546, 547.
Gilt standing cup set with *verre fixé* plaques and enriched with enamel. This cup was made to commemorate the association of the Rappolstein family with silver-mining and is said to have been made from a rich vein of silver discovered in 1530 in a mine on their property. The base is decorated with a series of finely embossed scenes of silver-mining. The plaquettes around the body, which are also embossed, relate to Roman history and above each, in typical Mannerist fashion, is a cast cartouche within a strapwork border enamelled with Latin hexameters explaining the subject of the scene below. In the next zone of the body above the cartouches is a row of coats-of-arms of the Rappolstein family and their alliances painted under glass. Surmounting the cover, is a finial in the form of a horse bearing a nude female figure whose long limbs reflect the Mannerist ideal. The three cast figures of Hope, Faith and Charity on the stem derive from models from the Jamnitzer workshop. Strassburg, Georg Kobenhaupt (R36967) about 1550-60. H. 75 cm.
Schatzkammer of the Residenz, Munich.

Plate 548.
Gilt ewer in the form of a galley, standing on a baluster stem with wrought foot, the body of the vessel engraved to represent waves. Not only is the ship fully rigged but the oars, crew, arquebusiers, halberdiers and a group of noblemen sitting down to a meal under an awning on the poop are all carefully rendered and painted with cold enamel. Only the conventional stem and foot detract from the illusion. The spike at the front of the galley can be unscrewed revealing an opening from which liquid can be poured. The ewer could be filled through an aperture in the rear of the deck. According to tradition this vessel belonged to the Knights of Malta and was captured from a French ship returning from that island during the Napoleonic Wars. The flag at the top is, however, engraved with the arms of the family of Aspremont. Strassburg, maker's mark, the letter D in a shaped shield, early 17th century. H. 52 cm.
Private collection, London.

Plate 549.
Rock-crystal tankard with gilt mounts supported on lion feet. The décor of this vessel does not follow south German practice. The vertical straps which secure the crystal drum are of unusual form with a figure of a putto supporting a vase of fruit on his head below and a Corinthian pilaster and capital above. Around the lip is a border of mauresques. Strassburg, Dibolt Krug (R36968) about 1560. H. 25.5 cm.
Private collection, Paris.

Plate 550.
Gilt cup of the Goldsmiths' Guild of Frankfurt am Main, of late Gothic form with spirally wrought lobate bowl and polylobate foot. The upper border engraved with classical figures within foliage alternating with female masks from which scrolling foliage emerges. Winged dragons are attached around the top of the bowl between the lobes and the pendant ring below the bowl is composed of monsters and dragon-headed brackets. The finial a pomegranate. This is one of the most faithful reproductions of a Gothic cup dating from the end of the 16th century. It illustrates the conservatism of taste that persisted amongst the German guilds. Frankfurt am Main, dated 1592, G. Haas (R32029). H. 41.8 cm.
Bayerisches Nationalmuseum, Munich.

Plate 551.
Rock-crystal cup with gilt mounts, the rock-crystal with the faceted cut typical of Freiburg im Breisgau. The stem and foot do not differ from the contemporary form of altar candlesticks and illustrate the industrial nature of Freiburg rock-crystal working. The lip-mount engraved with mauresques. Freiburg im Breisgau, maker's mark, the initials HGK in monogram, early 17th century. H. 31 cm.
Private collection, London.

Plates 552, 554.
Parcel-gilt ewer and companion basin bearing the arms of Abbot Jodocus Singeisen of Muri in Switzerland. The cast details are mostly derived from Jamnitzer workshop models. The medallions with cherubs' heads set in the basin have enamelled backgrounds. The beaded edge of the spout points to a date in the first quarter of the 17th century. These vessels were bought by the Abbot from a Jewish dealer in 1635 and his arms added at that time. Freiburg im Breisgau, maker's mark indecipherable. H. 30.8 cm. Diam. of basin 40 cm.
Schweizerisches Landesmuseum, Zürich.

Plate 553.
Gilt standing cup and cover, the body cast with a frieze of the Massacre of the Innocents, the lower part of the bowl embossed and chased with cherubs and garlands between masks. the upper part of the bowl and the foot etched with mauresques. The cover surmounted by a cherub holding a shield bearing the arms of the Swiss families of Graffenried and Michel. The chasing and finish as a whole of the very highest order. Swiss (?). Town mark of Sitten on the (added) foot ring, maker's mark (R38959). Dated 1562. H. 11.5 cm.
Historisches Museum, Bern.

Plate 555.
Bowl of parcel-gilt tazza embossed in low relief with the subject of a topsy-turvy world with a bull preparing to cut up a man, a wife beating her husband and hares chasing the hounds, against a landscape background with a castle. Around the edge are verses describing the scenes. Zürich, Abraham Gessner (R39037), about 1580. H. 15.5 cm. Diam. 15.5 cm.
Schweizerisches Landesmuseum, Zürich.

Plate 556.
Parcel-gilt globe cup by Abraham Gessner of Zürich, constructed as a double cup, the upper part being detachable around the Equator. It is completed with an armillary sphere which rests in the cage formed by the inverted base of the upper cup. When the latter was used for drinking, it was necessary first to remove the sphere. Zürich, Abraham Gessner, (R³9037), end of the 16th century. H. 50 cm.
Plymouth Corporation, England.

Plate 557.
Gilt standing cup and cover of Renaissance form but dating from the middle of the 16th century. The foot, base of bowl and cover embossed with lobes (*Buckeln*), etched arabesque borders, the cover surmounted by a figure emblematic of Astronomy. Inside the cover, a plaquette enamelled with the addorsed arms of von Willading and von Wyngarten and the date 1558. Although dating from the middle of the century, this cup is of extremely conservative design; this can probably be explained in part by the relative remoteness of Bern from the main centres of fashion and in part by the natural conservative taste of Swiss Burger families. Bern, Peter Rohr, dated 1558. H. 40 cm.
Private collection, London.

Plates 558, 560.
Gilt basin and companion ewer, the central panel embossed and chased with the contest between Apollo and Marsyas in the presence of King Midas. No graphic source for this subject has been identified but it derives from the Rudolphine court style at Prague. The borders are embossed in low relief with friezes of Putti and with four mythological scenes in very low relief. At each end and above and below is a large scallop-shell in which sits a cast figure of a putto, while two further putti recline on each side of the shells in the longer axis. The shells in the shorter axis are flanked by reclining figures of nymphs and river-gods. Along the border of the basin are applied cast scrolls developing into smaller scallop-shells. The ewer is unrelated in form to the basin but is connected thematically through the figure of King Midas, now shown with ass's ears seated on a shell on the cover. The vessel is composed entirely of cast work, the body modelled with the bodies of various wild animals, the spout a dolphin, the stem with vase knop in the form of two baby tritons set back to back, the base composed of four openwork brackets. Dresden, the basin signed and dated with the monogram of Daniel Kellerthaler (R³1748) and the year 1629. H. of ewer 42 cm. L. of basin 84.5 cm.
Grünes Gewölbe, Dresden.

Plate 559.
Gilt table-centre in the form of a triumphal car, supported on four wheels driven by clockwork. The front and rear panels of the car support baluster stems, apparently cast from the covers of standing cups, terminating in female figures, one bearing a shield of arms. The figure of a coachman in front is a later restoration.

On each side are enamelled medallions of the arms of the Mercers' Company of London and of the City of London, presumably added in England. This piece, together with a miniature wine barrel which can be carried upon the car, was presented to the Company in 1573: it was probably purchased second-hand, but cannot have been very old at the time of purchase. Breslau, Hieronymus Orth (R³1396), about 1560-70. L. 39.5 cm. H. 26 cm.
The Mercers' Company, London.

Plate 561.
Gilt ewer, the ovoid body set with two rows of convex mother-of-pearl plaques, the handle with applied winged half-figure of a harpy and a triton riding on a dolphin. The body and neck chased in low relief with bunches of fruit and foliage within strapwork borders, applied female masks. This ewer was made to accompany a basin of near-Eastern origin. Leipzig, Elias Geyer (R³3032) about 1600. H.35 cm.
Grünes Gewölbe, Dresden.

Plate 562.
Nautilus-shell drinking vessel in the form of a sea-horse ridden by a triton; the silver-gilt mounts by Elias Geyer, who specialised in mounting shells. The head of the horse can be removed at the neck to enable the vessel to be used but its real purpose was that of a table or sideboard ornament. Leipzig, Elias Geyer (R³3032), 1635. H. 22.5 cm.
Iparmuveszeti Museum, Budapest.

Plate 563.
Gilt ewer attributed conjecturally to a Salzburg goldsmith but showing marked Italian influence. The goldsmith who made this ewer seems to have had some knowledge of Giulio Romano's designs, for the similarity of this vessel to Giulio's drawing (pl. 63) can hardly be fortuitous. By the last decade of the 16th century and perhaps before, copies of Giulio's drawings were re-issued by Ottavio Strada and this may have been the source through which the goldsmith obtained the idea of so original a form. Since 1612 at the latest the ewer has been associated with an oval basin bearing the arms and devices of the Archbishop of Salzburg, but the workmanship of the ewer is so much coarser than that of the basin that they can hardly have been made by the same goldsmith. The basin was lost during the Second World War; it showed stylistic affinity with the Paul Hübner pieces from the Treasury of the Archbishops of Salzburg, and may have been by that master. Salzburg (?), late 16th century. H. 25 cm.
Museo degli Argenti, Florence.

Plates 564, 565, 566, 567.
Enamelled gold ewer and basin presented to Archduke Carl of Innenoesterreich and wife, Maria von Bayern on their wedding in 1571, by the nobility of Carinthia. The coat-of-arms in the centre of the basin is that of Carinthia. These vessels have been attributed

both to North Italian and to South German goldsmiths, but their origin remains uncertain. They may have been made in Vienna by a goldsmith working there or by one of the Spanish goldsmiths employed by the Emperor. There are various reasons for suggesting Spanish influence. Firstly the rather coarse finish; this is usual on Spanish goldsmiths' work; so important a commission would have been more precisely finished if it had been executed by an Italian or a German goldsmith. The decoration in the form of applied medallions of interlacing strapwork in translucent enamel is typical of Spanish goldsmiths' work of this period. The form of the ewer corresponds to a known Spanish type but this was, of course, used elsewhere. A striking feature is the treatment of the handle, the upper part of which is constructed of a central member enclosed by pierced strapwork and numerous volutes (pl. 567). Similar work can be seen on the handles of the gold swords presented by the Emperor Maximilian II to the Elector August of Saxony in 1575; these are known to have been made by his Spanish goldsmith, Juan Pery Pockh. Perhaps Vienna, before 1571. H. of ewer 34.5 cm. Diam. of basin 61.5 cm.
Weltliche Schatzkammer, Vienna.

Plate 568.
Gilt standing cup in the form of a leaping stag, its fore-feet resting on a heraldic shield charged with a coat-of-arms and the inscription *Hans Ernst Stadtrichter zu Closterneuburg 1580*. The head is removable to enable the figure to be used as a cup and there is a strapwork engraved collar round the animal's neck. The domed base is chased with grasses and animals in low relief. The gilding has worn sufficiently to show the joints marking the points where the sheets, from which the body is wrought, are joined. The neck is carefully chased with long hair, the body with short hair. Vienna, before 1580, maker's mark a hunting horn from which hang leaves (R³7922). H. 28 cm.
British Museum.

Plate 569.
Heliotrope standing cup with enamelled gold mounts from the *Kaiserliche Hofwerkstatt*. Baluster stem, the bowl carved with spiral gadroons; the champlevé polychrome enamel decoration of the mounts is composed of cartouches enclosing bunches of fruit linked by festoons with birds and flowers. Unmarked, Prague, late 16th century. H. 12 cm.
Museo degli Argenti, Florence.

Plate 570.
Fatimid rock-crystal perfume-pot mounted as a vase in the *Kaiserliche Hofwerkstatt*. This rare rock-crystal vessel was provided with enamelled gold mounts in the typical Prague style. The curious method of mounting it so that it could be stood either way up derives from the popular double cup. No effort was made to relate the design of the enamelled decoration to the antiquity of the piece itself. Devoid of purpose, it is a typical *Kunstkammer* piece. Unmarked, Prague. The mounts late 16th century. H. 15.4 cm.
Freer Gallery, Washington, D.C.

Plate 571.
Enamelled gold two-handled bowl from the travelling service of the Archbishops of Salzburg, the bowl enamelled with the arms of Marcus Sitticus von Hohenembs (1612-1619), the reverse with a mining scene; the handles terminate in the heads of mountain goats, the charge of the Archbishop's arms. This bowl is attributed to Hans Karl, who, after working in Salzburg for Marcus Sitticus' predecessor, Wolf Dietrich von Raitenau, went to Prague where he is believed to have worked on the crown of Rudolph II. The detail of the champlevé enamel work, especially the figure subjects around the foot, is typical of the Prague *Hofwerkstatt*. Prague, Hans Karl, about 1612. H. 12.5 cm.
Museo degli Argenti, Florence.

Plate 572.
Enamelled gold two-handled bowl attributed to Hans Karl of Nürnberg, but probably made when he was in Prague. The low bowl of lobate form enamelled in translucent colours, the handles in the form of female terms. The Mannerist taste is here expressed in sculptural terms; whereas the enamel decoration of this bowl derives from the Renaissance grotesque, the handles show the mixed animal, vegetable and human forms of Mannerism. In the centre of the base the enamelled arms of Prince Janusz Radizwill. Prague (?). Hans Karl, early 17th century. H. 12 cm.
Schatzkammer of the Munich Residenz.

Plate 573.
Salt-cellar with silver gilt mounts, the receptacle a scallop shell supported on the tail fin of a dolphin and the body of a snake twisting round the dolphin, surmounted by a demi-figure of a woman in fashionable dress, her breast formed from a smaller shell. The circular base chased with sea-creatures. This salt illustrates the persistence of Mannerist conceits into the 17th century at a time when Baroque taste was dominating the arts. Unmarked, South German or Saxon (manner of Elias Geyer), first quarter of 17th century. H. 31.5 cm.
British Museum.

Plate 574.
Enamelled gold small ewer profusely set with rubies in square collets, around the ovoid body are applied winged cherubs heads alternating with larger rubies and connected by festoons of leaves and fruit; on the handle the arms of Habsburg impaling Burgundy. This ewer has a classical elegance and sophistication of form that is less apparent in the larger ewer (pl. 565) which it replaced at Imperial Christening ceremonies. Probably made in the *Kaiserliche Hofwerkstatt*, Prague, about 1600. H. 15.5 cm.
Weltliche Schatzkammer, Vienna.

Plate 575.

Rock-crystal covered beaker with enamelled gold mounts, the beaker cut with a scrolling grapevine pattern enclosing a gardener, a rabbit, the sun, moon and stars. The gold mounts enamelled with formalised flowers in white, green and red, the ball feet enamelled and each set with a table-cut ruby in a gold collet, the knop of the cover also set with rubies. The enamelled decoration is German in style as is the engraving of the rock-crystal. The vessel is somewhat unsophisticated in comparison with the major productions of the court workshops. Unmarked, probably Nürnberg. Early 17th century. H. 11.5 cm.
Private collection, U.S.A.

Plates 576, 577.

Ewer and basin of rock-crystal mounted in silver-gilt with applied enamelled gold pierced scrollwork, set with 168 rubies. The ewer composed of four separate pieces of rock-crystal, the handle formed as a harpy, the body engraved with harpies bearing baskets of fruit and flowers on their heads; the basin composed of seventeen plates of crystal, those on the exterior engraved with scrollwork and winged creatures, the inner ones with flutes, in the centre the arms of Johann Friedrich, Duke of Württemberg and Teck, etc. Unmarked, the rock-crystal Prague or perhaps Freiburg im Breisgau, the mounts probably Prague, early 17th century. H. of ewer, 28 cm. Diam. of basin, 50 cm.
Schatzkammer of the Residenz, Munich.

Plate 578.

Smoky topaz cup and cover with enamelled gold handles and mounts, the bowl carved with a monster's head at one end and a spout at the other; the mounts decorated with delicate gold strapwork against a white enamel ground. In this vessel the Baroque taste for massive and unified forms is evident; only the minute detail of the enamelled mounts still derives from Mannerism. Probably by Dionysio Miseroni, *Kaiserliche Hofwerkstatt*, Prague, first quarter of the 17th century. H. 18 cm.
Walters Art Gallery, Baltimore, U.S.A.

Plate 579.

Carved Seychelles nut with silver-gilt mounts, the nut is supposed to have been presented by the Sultan of Bantam in Western Java to the Dutch Admiral Wolfer Hermanszen, who subsequently sold it to Rudolf II for the huge sum of 4000 gulden. The nut was given by the Emperor to one of his favourite goldsmiths, Anton Schweinberger, to mount and he produced a vessel that was of advanced design for its date. The mounts have something of the liquid fleshy quality of the Van Vianen workshop, but display a bolder treatment that anticipates Baroque fashion of succeeding decades. The bold and massive scrolls foreshadow the type that took over in early Baroque art the rôle of strapwork and *Rollwerk* in Mannerist art. The diffuse effect of some Mannerist goldsmiths' work is not apparent in this ewer, which has a unified organic form that well accords with the Baroque ideal. The treatment of the foot with its twin-tailed mermen set back to back recalls the work of an anonymous designer who was probably associated with Erasmus Hornick — compare the drawings illustrated in pls. 192 and 193. The group of a triton riding a sea-horse on the cover is of masterly quality. The nut is said to have been given to the Admiral in 1602. Schweinberger worked for the Emperor from about 1587 to about 1603, so the mounting of this shell was probably one of his last works. Unmarked, Prague, signed *Anthoni Schweinberger F.* About 1603.
H. 38.5 cm.
Kunsthistorisches Museum, Vienna.

Plate 580.

Ewer carved from jasper with gold mounts, the hardstone attributed to Dionysio Miseroni, the mounts by Paul van Vianen. The vessel is of conventional form with the exception of the thumb-piece. The mounts rank as works of sculpture rather than of goldsmithing. The cover is wrought with an exquisite figure of a nereid, while the foot is adorned with reclining figures of Jupiter, Juno, Neptune and Amphitrite with a goat's head set between each figure. They are embossed in high relief and arranged with a just sense of proportion without a trace of the conscious striving for effect (*Concetto*) typical of Mannerist art. Unmarked, Prague, signed by Paul van Vianen and dated 1608. H. 36 cm.
Kunsthistorisches Museum, Vienna.

Plate 581.

Gilt standing cup, originally surmounted by a cover, the stem of unusual length cast with three addorsed mermaids and, above and below, with drum-shaped members cast and chased with male and female recumbent figures; the shallow bulbous bowl embossed with four large masks set against drapery cartouches interspersed with seated female figures holding up swags of drapery; the lip etched with figures, bunches of fruit and strapwork. This form of cup was known in Augsburg and Nürnberg, but the Hungarian master has exaggerated its effect by increasing the height, crowding the ornament and depressing the bowl. Leutschau (Lőcse), Sebastian Aurifaber, late 16th century. H. 27.3 cm.
Private collection, London.

Plate 582.

Gilt tankard, the ornament of the drum cast from Jamnitzer workshop plaquettes. Such plaquettes were probably obtainable already bent for casting tankard bodies. Otherwise a wax mould could be taken from a flat plaquette, bent to shape and a lead model made from it. Kassa (Kosice), Johann Lippai (R^{39273}) dated 1578. H. 18.5 cm.
Hungarian National Museum, Budapest.

Plate 583.

Ostrich-egg cup with silver-gilt mounts, the bands enclosing the egg composed of pierced strapwork, the

cover surmounted by an ostrich holding a horseshoe in its beak, the stem cast in the form of a spirally twisted trunk entwined by a vine upon which are a lizard, a tortoise and a squirrel. The base embossed and chased with bunches of fruit. The design corresponds to contemporary south German work but does not make use of the otherwise almost ubiquitous Jamnitzer models. Prague, maker's mark AK in monogram (R³9331), last quarter of the 16th century. H. 38.4 cm.
British Museum (Waddesdon Bequest).

Plate 584.
Gilt cup modelled in the form of an ostrich, its head detachable at the neck, the body an ostrich egg, the legs and feet rendered naturalistically, oval base with small applied reptiles. A horseshoe is held in the ostrich's mouth, presumably in reference to its legendary digestive powers. Eger (Cheb), Sudetenland, Martin Burckhardt, early 17th century. H. 47 cm.
Staatliche Kunstsammlungen, Kassel.

Plates 585, 586.
Gilt basin and ewer, the whole surface of both pieces embossed and chased; the body of the ewer embossed with allegories of the four Elements, each figure being separated by a tree, and identified by a Latin inscription within a strapwork cartouche; beneath the spout a classical mask with draperies flanked by garlands supporting birds. The handle formed as a monster with applied beaded ornament. The main area of the basin is decorated with couples of men and women in fashionable dress against landscape backgrounds, each pair separated by a caryatid whose arms develop into a fruit tree; four panels of inscriptions on the border refer to Spain, France, Germany and Italy, separated by figures emblematic of Geometry, Arithmetic, Dialectic and Rhetoric. In the centre the the arms of Christoph Chodkiewicz, Voivode of Vilna, who died in 1560. On the reverse of the basin is an allegory of Vanity, represented by a putto seated on a skull and blowing soap bubbles. Unmarked but probably Polish, early 17th century, the arms of Chodkiewicz added later. H. of ewer 46 cm. Diam. of basin 59 cm.
Wawel Cathedral Treasury, Cracow.

Plate 587.
Gilt ewer, the body is divided horizontally into two zones, the upper with a frieze of the Rape of Helen after Raphael, the lower with strapwork enclosing satyrs and pendant bunches of fruit in the manner of Cornélis Floris. The handle is composed of a superbly modelled satyr, the lower part of whose body develops into a lion's leg and paw. Beneath the lip on either side is a grotesque mask. The body is signed and dated by the chaser with the monogram HR and 1559. Antwerp, 1559. Maker's mark the letters PS in monogram (R³5088). H. 35.5 cm.
British Museum.

Plates 588, 589.
Gilt basin *en suite* with the ewer in pl. 587. The

Triumph of Neptune on the outer border (pl. 589) is derived from the same two du Cerceau tazza designs that were used by the maker of the Paris basin illustrated in pl. 376. Such designs had a wide circulation and this one speedily found its way from Paris to Antwerp. The inner border is embossed with the Judgement of Paris copied in part, but in reverse, from the same graphic source as that on the Antwerp standing cup in pl. XXIII. Chaser's signature and date HR 1559. Antwerp, 1559. Maker's mark the letters PS in monogram (R³5088). Max. Diam. 48.3 cm.
British Museum.

Plate 590.
Gilt ewer, the egg-shaped body embossed and chased with a framework of straps with lions' masks at the intersections; snakes are twined around some of the straps and the areas they enclose are embossed and chased with monsters and with scrolling foliage and flowers. In the centre of each side is a cartouche embossed with figures of Neptune and Amphitrite respectively. From the collection of the Counts of Aspremont-Lynden. Antwerp, 1544-5. Maker's mark a pair of compasses (R³5103). H. 34 cm.
British Museum.

Plates 591, 592.
Gilt basin accompanying, but not made *en suite* with, the ewer in pl. 590. The ornament consists of cartouches enclosing scenes of the Plagues of Egypt (pl. 592) and the destruction of Pharaoh's army in the Red Sea. The border design of satyrs trapped in strapwork supporting cartouches and with baskets of fruit between is a typical Antwerp deign. The central boss is engraved with the arms of the Counts of Aspremont-Lynden. Antwerp, 1546-7, Joris Weyer (R³5105). Diam. 47.5 cm.
British Museum.

Plate 593.
Glass beaker with gilt mounts, the foot embossed with a frieze of foliage and strapwork alternating with lion masks, the cover embossed with a frieze of figure subjects representing the Triumph of Love and surmounted by a boar rising from a basket of fruit. The glass is of Renaissance form while the detail of the ornament and the volutes around the top of the cover are Mannerist. Antwerp 1546-7. Reinier van Jaersvelt (R³5687). H. 26. cm.
Rijksmuseum, Amsterdam.

Plates 594, 595.
Gilt tazza and cover; the decoration is based upon the usual symbolism of the element of water; within the bowl (pl. 594) is a circular panel representing Arion and the dolphin; around this is a frieze of marine creatures and nymphs. The cover is divided into two circular zones, the outer being embossed with scallop- and mussel-shells with bunches of fruit between. The inner zone is embossed with tritons, sea-serpents and other

aquatic creatures. The marine symbolism is continued on the finial, formed of three demi sea-horses surrounding a central stem from which rise the shields with the Mildmay arms. On the base, products of the earth replace those of the sea. The bowl is supported by four harpies whose feet rest on the knop formed as a basket of fruit to the sides of which are applied lion's masks. Below the knop is a trumpet shaped member embellished with four animal's claws and, finally, the base is embossed with four masks with serpents and floral scrolls between. Although the profile of this tazza is somewhat masked by its vociferous ornament, it is still composed of coherent and logically arranged elements. It dates from about 1550 and does, therefore, precede the more extravagant development of Mannerist design. Another indication of its early date can be found in the absence of elaborate strapwork, the only significant use of which is the application of four free-standing straps to the knop. Antwerp, date letter uncertain, mid 16th century. Maker's mark, a lion's mask, (R³5101 ?). H. 38.7 cm.
Emmanuel College, Cambridge.

Plates 596, 597, 602.

Gilt and enamelled ewer and basin made to commemorate the Emperor Charles V's expedition against Tunis in the year 1535. The body is encircled by a continuous frieze embossed with scenes of Charles V's campaign. Such friezes are usual features of Antwerp ewers of the period, but this one has additional features that mark it out from even the finest work of the time. Applied to both the upper and lower zones of the body on each side of the frieze are trophies of arms linked by swags, which are further enriched with polychrome enamels. The embossing of these trophies is carried out with a precision that shows supreme mastery of the goldsmith's art but the enamelling is opaque and lifeless. The neck is formed as a female head with plaited hair reaching down to the shoulders where it encircles a large snail on each side. The shell spout develops into straps of unusually massive dimensions, while the handle is composed of the intertwined bodies of snakes, probably copied from one of du Cerceau's prints. Below the handle and masking its junction with the body is a seated faun. This combination of snake-handle with a seated figure can also be seen on the Italian rock-crystal ewer illustrated in pl. III. The basin is apparently the earliest example of the recording of a contemporary event on a silver vessel. The surface is embossed and chased with scenes from the battles fought by the Emperor's army. These are depicted in considerable detail, the basin being treated like a canvas for their pictorial representation. It has to be set vertically, like a picture, in order for its subjects to be understood, and in view of its vast size it could hardly have been intended to serve any practical purpose. A series of small strapwork cartouches are attached to the border; these are enriched with enamel like the trophies of arms on the ewer. The detail illustration of the border of the dish (pl. 602) shows companies of mounted knights and galleys bearing the Imperial double eagle flag. Antwerp 1558-9. Maker's mark on both ewer and basin, the initials PR in monogram (R³5093). H. of ewer 43.5 cm.

Diam. of basin 64.5 cm.
Musée du Louvre, Paris.

Plate 598.

Coconut-cup with gilt mounts, the foot embossed with bunches of fruit, vase stem with the applied straps typical of Antwerp, the nut carved with biblical subjects, on the front, the drunkenness of Noah, the cover surmounted by a male figure rising from a tall stem. Antwerp, maker's mark, the pipes of Pan, 1560-61. H. 30 cm.
Private collection, London.

Plate 599.

Gilt cup wrought in the form of a falcon perched with folded wings on a mound worked in imitation of earth, on top of an oblong box with egg-and-tongue moulded edges; the front delicately engraved with a bust of a Roman Emperor within a laurel wreath, the sides engraved with bunches of fruit and with ring handles springing from monster's heads. The head of the falcon is removable, but this piece can hardly have been intended for other than decorative purposes. Antwerp, maker's mark, the pipes of Pan, 1561-62. H. 28.8 cm.
Clare College, Cambridge.

Plates 600, 603, 604.

Gilt standing cup, the finest surviving south Netherlandish cup of the third quarter of the 16th century. The composition corresponds to that of the cup in pl. XXIII and it also has four scenes emblematic of the Elements on the cover. Its precious quality is stressed by the insertion of an agate urn held within cagework as the knop of the stem and of a cylinder of rock-crystal as the body of the cup. Two pieces of rock-crystal are set in the centre of the foot and the cover. Below the lip is a band of arabesques. The numerous brackets terminating in volutes applied to the stem soften the contrast between horizontal and vertical of its composition and illustrate the originality of the Antwerp masters. The cup was probably further enriched with pearls or precious stones. unmarked, attributed to Antwerp, about 1560. H. 40 cm.
Private collection, England.

Plate 601.

Detail of embossed figure of a reclining man, emblematic of Autumn, from the cover of the Antwerp cup (pl. XXIII).

Plate 602.

Detail of embossed ornament of border of the Antwerp basin (pl. 597) showing the galleys of Charles V with the double eagle flags of the Holy Roman Empire.

Plate 605.

Gilt standing cup presented in 1598 by the Company of Merchant Adventurers of London to the City of

Emden, the cover surmounted by a figure bearing a shield enamelled with the arms of the Company. The cylindrical bowl embossed with plaques of the Virtues with lion masks between, the stem surrounded by satyrs. The volute brackets, typical of Antwerp silver, play an important role in its composition. Though the detail of the ornament is drawn from Mannerist sources, the cup is far from elegant. Unmarked, attributed to Antwerp, about 1560. H. 47 cm.
Ostfriesisches Landesmuseum, Emden.

Plates 606. 607.

Gilt standing cup presented in 1564 by King Frederick II of Denmark to the Malmö Guild of St. Knud. The stem with vase shaped knop and applied brackets. The upper part of the bowl is embossed with figures of Diana and her nymphs and hunting scenes; the lower part of the bowl embossed with grotesque masks alternating with applied figures of twin-tailed tritons terminating in volutes. The lip, of unusually large proportions, is engraved with mauresques. Antwerp, maker's mark, a swan (R³5098a) attributed to Hans de Hanns or Johan van Sicken, about 1560. H. 73 cm.
Malmö Museum, Sweden.

Plate 608.

Gilt trochus-shell cup, the stem cast from the same mould as the standing cup in pl. XXIII. The knop follows the standard Antwerp form of a basket of fruit, the shell is secured by pierced straps with applied lion masks. The mauresque border is exceptional on Antwerp pieces of this date. The shape of the stem distinguishes this vessel from German trochus-cups of the third quarter of the century. Unmarked, attributed to Antwerp, about 1560. H. 21.4 cm.
Musees Royaux d'Art et d'Histoire, Brussels.

Plate 609.

Gilt nautilus-shell cup, the shell painted with festoons of flowers, the stem in the form of a satyr whose waist is secured by a fetter-like strap, derived from a print by Cornelis Floris. The volute of the nautilus is concealed within the jaws of a monster on whose back a satyr rides. The front and rear straps are formed as terms, those at the sides are composed of the familiar Mannerist combination of putti, rolled-over straps, snakes and masks. The oval foot is embossed with a frieze of sea-creatures. Antwerp, maker's mark, a pair of compasses (R³ 5103) about 1560-70. H. 25 cm.
Staatliche Kunstsammlungen, Kassel.

Plate 610.

One of a pair of large twin-spouted ewers, the frieze embossed with biblical and mythological subjects, the lower part of the ovoid body embossed with groups of three male and female demi-figures supporting baskets of fruit on their heads. The loop handle and the spouts spring from grotesque masks. They seem to be an afterthought as they obscure the detail of the frieze. Antwerp, third quarter of the 16th century. H. 60 cm.
Seville Cathedral Treasury.

Plate 611.

Gilt cup, the cover wanting, the bowl embossed with the Triumph of Neptune and Amphitrite. In this cup the influence of Cornelis Floris is unmistakable, both in the three satyrs placed back to back who form the stem and in the female fauns bound by straps on the lower part of the bowl. Antwerp, maker's mark, a pair of compasses (R³ 5103), 1557-8. H.33.8 cm.
Schatzkammer of the Residenz, Munich.

Plates 612, 616.

Parcel-gilt tazza, the interior of the bowl embossed with David killing Goliath, the border engraved with mauresques. The sturdy practical form of the base departs from Mannerist fashion. Though made after the Sack of Antwerp in 1574 this tazza shows no decline in quality. It follows contemporary Dutch fashion without individual local features. Antwerp, 1582-3, maker's mark, a heart pierced by two arrows. H. 15 cm. Diam. 17.5 cm.
Victoria and Albert Museum.

Plate 613.

Gilt standing cup and cover, the tall thistle-shaped body with an engraved frieze of mauresques, interrupted by applied profile heads. Vase knop with applied brackets, the foot and cover embossed with bunches of fruit, drapery and cartouches. The cover surmounted by a Roman warrior. The thistle-shaped body is typical of Dutch fashion of the second half of the 16th century. s'Hertogenbosch, 1561, maker's mark of A. de Groet. H. 27.8 cm.
Rijksmuseum, Amsterdam.

Plate 614.

Gilt standing cup and cover, a sleeve slipped over the bowl is embossed with the Parable of the Prodigal Son. Vase stem, the foot and cover with masks between strapwork and bunches of fruit. The cover surmounted by a seated boar. The form corresponds to the Antwerp type of the mid-16th century. The date letter is usually read as 1569 but may be a series earlier. Amsterdam, 1546 or 1569, maker's mark a fire steel. H. 28 cm.
Rijksmuseum, Amsterdam.

Plate 615.

Gilt standing cup and cover, the bowl embossed with female figures of Faith, Hope and Charity within strapwork cartouches separated by masks and bunches of fruit. The lip engraved with a border of mauresque ornament. The cover embossed with three strapwork cartouches enclosing lion masks interspersed with military trophies and lion masks. The finial a warrior riding a sea-horse. This cup was presented to Arent Fabricius, Burgomaster of Haarlem, after the siege of Ostend in 1603. The Hague, Bowvens van der Houven, 1603, H.32.5 cm.
Frans Hals Museum, Haarlem.

Plate 617.

Coconut-cup with cover, the nut carved in low relief with the story of Jonah and the whale, and held by straps in the form of male terms supporting vases of fruit on their heads. The baluster stem chased with wave ornament, the rim engraved with a band of strapwork enclosing floral scrolls. The foot embossed with cherubs' heads alternating with bunches of fruit. Following the Dutch custom, the cup is not gilt. The Dordrecht town mark closely resembles that of Norwich and their pieces are for this reason sometimes confused. Dordrecht, maker's mark, a flower, dated 1576. H. 33 cm.
Victoria and Albert Museum.

Plate 618.

Gilt nautilus-shell cup, the oval base chased with fish, crustacea and shells amongst waves, the stem formed as a satyr seated upon a dolphin with upstretched arms supporting the shell, the valve formed as a sea-monster with open jaws, upon whose head kneels a naked man holding a sword and a shield. The straps securing the bowl formed as mermen and a sea-god wrestling with dolphins, the rim engraved with fish, ships and figures in a stormy sea. Dated on the base *Anno 1596.* Utrecht, Jan Jacobz van Royesteyn, 1596. This cup is identical with one shown in a still life painting by Pieter Claesz dated 1630 in the Kunsthistorisch Institut, Utrecht. H. 29.3 cm.
Private collection.

Plate 619.

Nautilus-shell cup with silver-gilt mounts, the shell enriched with garlands and applied precious stones and secured on each side by a sea-monster surmounted by a triton blowing a conch, at the front by a female term, while at the top is a figure of Neptune riding on a dolphin. Baluster stem and domed foot embossed with strapwork and set with plaques of mother-of-pearl, enriched with stones. The Dutch goldsmiths were the foremost makers of nautilus-cups, their productions being both richer and more delicate than those of other countries. Rotterdam, maker's mark, a coat-of-arms, 1590. H. 29 cm.
Boymans-van Beuningen Museum, Rotterdam.

Plates 620, 621.

Gilt ewer and companion basin, the body of the ewer and the inner border of the basin finely embossed and chased with friezes of marine subjects, that on the ewer representing the Triumph of Neptune. The handle of unusually complex triple scroll form, introducing a dolphin, a winged female figure and a grotesque mask. The outer border of the basin is embossed with six cartouches enclosing marine subjects alternating with grotesque masks flanked by bunches of fruit. The central boss, set with a plaquette of the Magdalen washing the feet of Christ, is a later substitution, probably for the coat-of-arms of the original owner, who may have been the Earl of Arundel, the patron of Wenceslas Hollar and a famous collector of antiquities. These are the finest surviving ewer and basin bearing an English hall-mark but they are included amongst the Dutch silver as they bear no resemblance to English goldsmiths' work of the early 17th century. The design of the ewer is closest to another made by Balthasar Grill of Augsburg, which is in the Grünes Gewölbe, Dresden, but other features justify attribution to a Dutch goldsmith: in particular the form of the handle and the arrangement of the border of the ewer with cartouches alternating with panels of grotesques. Another Dutch feature is the domed shape of the foot. These pieces were either made in Holland and assayed and marked in London on their import into England or made in London by a Dutch immigrant master. It is no longer possible to determine which. The fact that they show no trace of the van Vianen influence that was so strong in the northern Netherlands by the early 17th century suggests that they may have been made by an immigrant. They were presented to the Corporation of Norwich by Henry Howard, 7th Duke of Norfolk. London, 1617, maker's mark IV over a mullet. Ht. of ewer 35.3 cm. Diam. of basin 45.5 cm.
City Corporation, Norwich.

Plates 622, 623.

Gilt tazza, the bowl embossed with the death of Meleager; he is supported by an old man and Atalanta while Venus and Cupid mourn behind him. The back of the bowl is covered by a circular plaque embossed with acanthus leaves. The stem of unusually large circumference is embossed with trails of husks, bunches of fruit and rams' heads. The embossing which is executed with great delicacy is attributed to Ernst Jansz van Vianen, though the tazza bears the mark of Aelbert Verhaer. Utrecht, 1602. H. 17 cm. Diam. 21.6 cm.
Victoria and Albert Museum.

Plates 624, 625.

Tazza, the bowl embossed with the Judgement of Solomon, the foot with grotesque masks; the ovoid stem chased with bunches of fruit and further enriched with applied cast masks. This tazza illustrates Adam van Vianen's early style just before he adopted the auricular manner of which he was the most skilful master. The embossed scene in the bowl shows the greatest mastery of the art of the chaser: the variation of relief from the minute figures of soldiers looking though the first-floor windows in the background to the superbly modelled executioner and the two mothers in the in the foreground. The subject is presented in a pictorial manner with little emphasis on plastic qualities; this manner soon gave way to Dutch Baroque in which form and relief were of prime importance. Utrecht, Signed AV in monogram for Adam van Vianen, 1612. H. 16 cm. Diam. 20 cm.
Victoria and Albert Museum.

Plates 626, 627.

Tazza, the bowl embossed with the Judgement of Paris, with Paris seated on one side and Mercury handing the apple to Venus on the other, Juno and Minerva

in the background. The baluster stem with plum-shaped knop decorated with three oval cartouches within auricular borders enclosing landscapes, the lower side of the bowl and the foot embossed with landscapes also within auricular cartouches. This appears to be the earliest of the van Vianen vessels to show fully developed auricular ornament and establishes Paul van Vianen's claim to be its creator. Its date shows that it was wrought by Paul van Vianen in Prague. Signed with the monogram PV and dated 1607. H. 17 cm.
Rijksmuseum, Amsterdam.

Plates 628, 629.
Gilt ewer, the foot formed as a squatting monkey on a base of auricular scrolls, the handle wrought as a crouching nude figure whose neck is prolonged until it ends in a fantastic mask which composes the front of the body. The cover of irregular shape rises up in a form resembling the head and neck of a swan. The rear of the body breaks out into a serrated ridge like huge vertebrae. This vessel, entirely wrought out of one piece of silver − except for the cover − was commissioned from Adam van Vianen by the Amsterdam Goldsmiths' Guild to commemorate the memory of his brother, Paul. Utrecht, maker's mark of Adam van Vianen, 1614. H. 25.4 cm.
Private collection, Scotland.

Plates 630, 631, 632.
Ewer and companion basin by Paul van Vianen, the ewer with vase-shaped body embossed with two reliefs, one of Jupiter disguised as Diana violating Callisto, the other of Juno punishing Callisto; the foot, neck and handle composed of supple scrolls, a grotesque mask embossed below the spout. The oval basin is unique in being decorated on both sides, the border being finished so that the ornament is effective both above and below, while a second plaque is attached to the inner panel of the underside. The inner surface of the upper side is embossed and chased with Diana accompanied by her nymphs being disturbed by Actaeon, while the plaque below shows Actaeon, changed into a stag, being attacked by huntsmen and hounds. The decoration of the rim is composed of fully evolved Dutch auricular ornament and is one of the finest examples of its use. The ewer and its companion basin were copied by another goldsmith as early as 1637 (see p.293). Signed and dated PV in monogram 1613. Wrought by Paul van Vianen when working for the Emperor Rudolph II in Prague. H. of ewer 34 cm. Diam. of basin 52 by 41 cm.
Rijksmuseum, Amsterdam.

Plates 633, 634.
One of a pair of wall-sconces by Adam van Vianen, each constructed of three elements, a wall plaque, a cresting and a candle-branch with drip-pan and socket. Each wall-plaque is signed at the bottom in a cartouche *A. D. Viane FE. ANNO 1622* and is composed of a central panel within a pierced border of auricular scrolls inhabited by human figures and monsters; the cresting which slots into the plaque also consists of a central embossed panel within a pierced border and is signed A.D.V.F. and is surmounted by a heraldic cartouche with a later coat-of-arms. The scenes embossed in the panels are (upper panel) Stag-hunting scene; (lower panel) Diana with her maidens watching Actaeon being turned into a stag (pl. 634). On the other wall-sconce the scenes are (above) Mercury holding the decapitated head of Argus, (below) Syrinx being pursued by Pan and turning into reeds. The subjects depicted in the panels were much favoured by the van Vianen family and were used by Paul as well as by an unknown Utrecht goldsmith associated with the Vianen workshop (see pls. 635-6). Utrecht, Adam van Vianen, dated 1622. H. 59.8 cm.
Private collection.

Plates 635, 636, 637.
Gilt ewer and companion basin, the body of the ewer embossed and chased with a continuous frieze illustrating the story of Mercury and Argus, on one side with Jupiter dispatching Mercury to the Earth where Io is being guarded by Argus, on the other, Mercury with the decapitated head of Argus (pl. 637). The handle with beaded rat-tail edging. The border of the basin embossed with a continuous frieze depicting the Forge of Vulcan, Mars and Venus trapped in Vulcan's net, Diana and Callisto, Juno chastising Callisto and Callisto being turned into a bear. These subjects are all recorded on vessels wrought by Paul van Vianen or on the plaquettes after his models, suggesting that these vessels were embossed by a master working either in Prague or Utrecht, who had access to his drawings or plaquettes. The basin is struck with the mark of the goldsmith, the monogram G.B., and also with the engraved monogram of the master who decorated them, the letters MAF. Utrecht (?) early 17th century. H. of ewer 32.7 cm. Diam. of basin 45.5 cm.
Rijksmuseum, Amsterdam.

Plate 638.
Ewer, the body of irregular vase-form, decorated with four medallions illustrating scenes from Roman history, Mucius Scaevola and Lars Porsena, the fight between the Horatii and the Curatii, the beheading of Brutus's sons, and Claelia, framed within writhing auricular scrolls which develop at intervals into masks and wings, the base modelled as a snail. In this vessel the goldsmith has endeavoured to arrive at a compromise between the Mannerist auricular style and traditional representational ornament. Signed with monogram and name of Adam van Vianen. Utrecht, about 1620. H. 30 cm.
Rijksmuseum, Amsterdam.

Plate 639.
Embossed and chased plaquette from a tazza bowl with the subject of Lot and his daughters, one daughter asleep, the other almost naked holding up a wine cup, while her father caresses her, the whole within a laurel-wreath border. Probably Munich, Paul van Vianen, signed *PAUL. D.V.F.*, about 1600. Diam. 17.2 cm.
Rijksmuseum, Amsterdam.

Plate 640.
One of a pair of gilt tazza bowls engraved by Johann Theodor de Bry with Adam and Eve in Paradise. The scene is accompanied by an extract from the 104th Psalm at the bottom and is surrounded by a narrow border engraved with a passage from Genesis. Two very similar tazzas, also engraved with religious subjects, were acquired from de Bry by the Archduke Maximilian of Tirol, Grand Master of the *Deutsches Ritter Orden* in or about 1604 and were subsequently presented by him to the Treasury of that Order. Yet another pair of tazzas of similar character and design belong to the parish church of Esher in the county of Surrey. All six may have formed part of a set of a dozen which were meant to go *en suite* but for which de Bry had not been able to find a customer. Signed by the artist in the left foreground. Frankfurt am Main, J. T. de Bry, early 17th century. Diam. 17.8 cm.
Musée d'Art et d'Histoire, Geneva.

Plate 641.
Silver plaquette embossed and chased by Arent van Bolten with the Crucifixion, signed with his monogram. This master's works represent a transitional style between late Mannerism and early Baroque. Zwolle, Arent van Bolten, first quarter of the 17th century. H. 28.9 cm.
Rijksmuseum, Amsterdam.

Plates 642, 643.
Ebony inkstand enclosed with silver cagework, the exterior engraved with four roundels each enclosing a figure of an Evangelist accompanied by his symbol, the interior set with two panels showing Moses and Isaiah respectively and with a text from the Gosel according to St. John. The remainder of the silver cagework, both inside and outside is pierced and engraved with foliage and scrollwork inhabited by figures. In this piece two different hands can be recognised; that of the master de Bry who engraved the main figures, and that of an assistant who engraved the border strips. Unmarked, attributed to Theodor de Bry, Frankfurt am Main, late 16th century. H. 10.7 cm. L. 24.1 cm.
Victoria and Albert Museum.

Plate 644.
Bowl of a silver tazza engraved by Hans Bol with a Dutch interior with a family seated at table saying grace before the meal; a view of a bedroom at the back and of a landscape through an open door on the right. Above and below the scene and in a border running round it are quotations from the Psalms in German and French. The arrangement of the texts and the figure subject corresponds to that adopted by Johann Theodor de Bry who produced a large number of similar engraved tazzas. The family is unpretentious and the array of dishes and plates on the left side would have been of pewter. Amsterdam, about 1590, Hans Bol. Diam. 15.3 cm.
Private collection.

Plate 645.
Details of enamelled gold cover of pl. 647, set with two rock-crystal roundels.

Plates 646, 647.
Enamelled gold and rock-crystal bowl, the design attributed to Hans Holbein. This bowl was originally in the Tudor Royal Treasury and is one of the three surviving pieces from it. It is described in detail in Tudor inventories (see p.299). The bowl of rock-crystal with spiral fluting, the foot of enamelled gold decorated with three embossed female half-figures alternating with three white enamel cartouches bearing inscriptions relating to the dangers of wine. The cover decorated with two concentric zones, the inner with five cartouches enamelled white and bearing Latin verses in praise of moderation alternating with mauresques in translucent enamel, the outer zone set with five rock-crystal medallions alternating with compositions of strapwork and grotesques in high relief (pl. 645). The original finial to the cover has been lost and is now replaced by a silver-gilt button. The spout-like projection under the rim (pl. 646) was apparently intended to serve as a handle; it is, however, too short and stubby to be used for this purpose. The confused compositions of masks, animals, drapery and bunches of fruit set against strapwork seem to derive from one of the pattern-sheets of Cornelis Bos or Cornelis Floris. Unmarked, probably by an English court goldsmith, about 1540. H. 16 cm.
Schatzkammer of the Residenz, Munich.

Plate 648.
Detail of the finial of the Holbein bowl from a still-life by Willem Kalf, showing original arrangement with tiers of pendant pearls. Dated 1678.
Statens Museum för Kunst, Copenhagen.

Plate 649.
Scent flask, the body embossed and chased with strapwork centering on a roundel, now engraved with a later crest; the stopper later. This little vessel is, after the Holbein bowl, one of the earliest recorded examples of the use of Flemish strapwork cartouches in English silver. London, struck only with date letter for 1546-7. H. 11.7 cm.
Victoria and Albert Museum.

Plate 650.
Gilt cup and cover, the bowl and cover wrought in the form of a pomegranate with one segment open to show the seeds; the stem is wrought as a twisted stalk from which numerous tendrils spring. The naturalistic style recalls the Dürer designs for cups in the form of an apple or a pear; the archaism may in this case have been due to the special wish of the client. London, maker's mark, HW with two pellets within a quatrefoil. (Jackson p.97). 1563-4. H. 26.2 cm.
The Inner Temple, London.

Plate 651.

Part of a gilt standing cup, this piece is defective, the present bowl of agate (not shown) is a later restoration for the original, which was probably of rock-crystal. What now serves as the foot was originally the cover and only the knop and stem are in their former position. This piece is of particular interest as it appears to be the work of a Flemish immigrant. The baskets of fruit on the knop and the base of the bowl, the straps with lion masks at the intersections, the snails, crabs and the dolphins applied to the bottom of the foot (cover) are familiar features of Antwerp silver of the same period. London, maker's mark, the letters ER in monogram. (Jackson p. 100). 1567-8. H. 19.9 cm.
Victoria and Albert Museum.

Plate 652.

Rock-crystal cup with gilt mounts presented to the Goldsmiths' Company of London in 1561 by Sir Martin Bowes, Lord Mayor of London in 1545 and Prime Warden of the Goldsmiths' Company in 1558. The body is a crystal cylinder supported by four Atlas figures and further decorated with brackets. The domed cover is surmounted by a rock-crystal faceted hemisphere supporting a vase with a female figure holding a shield enamelled with the arms of Bowes. The embossed decoration is, like much English work of the second half of the 16th century, coarse in comparison with western European standards. London, maker's mark a monogram crowned (Jackson p. 97), 1554-5. H. 49 cm.
The Goldsmiths' Company, London.

Plate 653.

Gilt standing cup and cover presented to the church of St. Peter Mancroft, Norwich in 1633. This cup shows both English and German features. Among the latter are the continuous frieze around the bowl, showing King David rising from his throne to receive Abigail who kneels before him, while a trail of camels bearing gifts approaches from behind, the vase-shaped knops on both stem and cover and the three cast medallions set in the calyx of the bowl. These represent Justice, Fortitude and another of the Virtues whose attribute cannot be identified. Medallions of this type were produced in Nürnberg and lead models taken from them were widely exported. The bunch of flowers worked from cut sheet is also of German fashion, though in this case the flowers are restored. English features are the flangelike members with turned down edges on both foot and cover and the wide engraved border on the lip. This is executed with great delicacy in a manner that can be paralleled on many other English silver vessels of the period. It is composed of arabesques developing at intervals into cartouches which frame Tudor roses. This combination of German and English styles of decoration can probably be explained by the fact that a German immigrant goldsmith employed an English engraver to execute the decoration of the lip. London, maker's mark indecipherable, the date letter is not clearly struck, but probably 1565-6. H. 46 cm.
St. Peter Mancroft, Norwich.

Plate 654.

Gilt standing cup in the form of a pelican in its piety; originally a nautilus-shell cup, the shell was broken long ago and replaced by a silver one realistically engraved with feathers. The subject of the pelican standing in her basketwork nest and drawing blood from her breast to feed her young, is medieval and recalls late Gothic vessels such as the Pelican and Phoenix reliquaries in the *Hallesche Heiltum* (Halm and Berliner, pls. 136, 179). While the pelican theme is archaic, the foot with its frieze of animals in a landscape, symbolic of the Earth on which we live is more contemporary. The knop displays typical Mannerist confusion: classical masks within strapwork are applied to a vase, around the neck of which is a garland of fruit and scrolls, while the top ends in a basket of fruit. A satyr is bound to each of the three openwork brackets. London, maker's mark, a bird in shaped shield (Jackson p. 104). 1579-80. H. 39 cm.
Victoria and Albert Museum (Loan).

Plate 655.

Gilt standing cup and cover, the lower part of the body gadrooned, the upper engraved with a frieze of strapwork and festoons of drapery enclosing three coats-of-arms, of Queen Elizabeth I, of the Drapers' Company and of Sir William Cordelle, Master of the Rolls, alternating with three profile heads. The strapwork cartouches enclosing the arms taken from one of the Flemish pattern-books. The finial a later restoration. London, maker's mark, a bird in a shaped shield (Jackson p. 104) 1578-9. H. 31.4 cm.
The Drapers' Company, London.

Plate 656.

Gilt standing cup and cover, the gourd-shaped bowl engraved with mauresques which spread over onto the cover, calyx of leaves of cut and shaped silver sheet, the stem a twisted branch, the foot, embossed with cartouches alternating with bunches of fruit, baluster finial, perhaps restored. This gourd shape was popular both in Germany and in England during the last quarter of the century. London, maker's mark, the letters SB between two mullets (Jackson p. 104), 1585-6. H. 29.2 cm.
Private collection.

Plate 657.

Gilt standing cup and cover, made from the Great Seal of Ireland, the bowl inscribed within a leafy frame 'This Cuppe was made of the greate sealle of Irelande in Ano 1593. Adam Loftus beinge then Lord Chancelor: He was also Lord Justice in Ano 1582 and in anno 1583 in which yeare he builded his howse at Rathfernan.' On the termination of office the Great Seal became a perquisite of the Lord Chancellor and it was the custom to convert it, sometimes with added metal, into a silver vessel. The representation and inscription on the Seal was usually engraved on the piece made from it. Baluster stem and trumpet shaped gadrooned foot. The stepped cover surmounted by a vase finial supporting

two angels holding a shield (probably a later alteration). The late date of this cup is indicated by the tall foot. London, maker's mark, the letters HL conjoined, a star below in a shaped shield (Jackson p. 106) 1592-3. H. 49.9 cm.
Ulster Museum, Belfast.

Plate 658.
Tazza, with baluster stem and vase knop, the inside of the bowl embossed with the scene of the meeting of Eliaser and Rebecca, within an embossed inner laurel wreath and an outer engraved border of strapwork and mauresques. The subject is derived from a plaquette attributed to Hans Jamnitzer, but the engraved border is typically English. This appears to be the only recorded example of a German plaquette copied by an English goldsmith. London, maker's mark, a bunch of grapes (Jackson p. 100), 1567-8. H. 14.6 cm.
City Museum, Southampton.

Plate 659.
Gilt tazza and cover, the exterior of the bowl plain, the inside engraved with strapwork and bunches of fruit and, in the centre, a cartouche enclosing a Roman profile head. Domed foot embossed, like the cover, with cartouches enclosing lion masks interspersed with bunches of fruit. The cover with vase finial supporting a figure of a Roman warrior holding a shield and spear. This tazza differs from the contemporary Dutch or German form in having a narrower but deeper bowl. The large flange below the vase on the finial is a typically English feature. London, maker's mark the letters IG in a shield (Jackson p. 105), 1584-5. H. 34.3 cm.
The Goldsmiths' Company, London.

Plate 660.
One of a set of six gilt spice plates, the centres engraved with scenes from the parable of the Prodigal Son, the inner borders with a frieze of sea-monsters after Androuet du Cerceau or Adriaen Collaert, the roundels on the outer border with birds after Virgil Solis. The surviving sets of Elizabethan spice plates are in perfect condition, indicating that such use as they received did not involve any surface wear. London, 1573-4, maker's mark FR conjoined (Jackson p. 103). Diam. 154. cm.
Victoria and Albert Museum.

Plate 661.
Gilt nautilus-shell cup, the shell decorated with engraved ornament in the Far East. The stem is formed as a triton seated on a dolphin while the straps securing the shell are composed of a giant crayfish, snails and caryatids, the oval foot is chased with marine subjects. The mounts correspond to contemporary Flemish fashion but the floral scrolls terminating in roses engraved on the lip are recognisably English in style. London, maker's mark, the letters TR in monogram, 1585-6. H. 23.8 cm.
Fitzwilliam Museum, Cambridge.

Plate 662.
Gilt ostrich-egg cup and cover, the stem formed as three ostrich legs standing on a high circular base, the foot embossed with a frieze showing ostriches in a landscape. The cover surmounted by an ostrich standing on three plumes on a circular plinth with three attached dolphin brackets. This cup exemplifies the tendency common to both English and German goldsmiths' work of the early 17th century to increase the height of vessels unduly. Probably London, unmarked, dated 1610. H. 50.6 cm.
Exeter College, Oxford.

Plate 663.
Gilt standing cup and cover, the body, cover and foot decorated with alternate bands of applied and engraved ornament. The master of this cup, who is represented by at least seven extant pieces, devised an original method of decoration, which he repeated on all the pieces referred to: delicate scrolling and interlacing foliage with berries applied against a matted ground. The intervening bands of this cup are finely engraved with hunting scenes. The stem and finial are of vase form, the latter surmounted by a small spray of flowers cut out of bent silver sheet in a manner usually associated with German goldsmiths' work. This goldsmith's works are of outstanding quality, though the general trend at the time was for a lowering of standards. London, maker's mark the letters TvZ in monogram. (Jackson p. 112). 1611-12. H. 42 cm.
Victoria and Albert Museum.

Plate 664.
Gilt standing cup and cover, of 'steeple' or 'pyramid' form; ovoid bowl embossed with conventional foliage, short baluster stem with three attached brackets; tall trumpet-shaped foot embossed with foliage; the domed cover chased en suite with the bowl and surmounted by an openwork three sided pyramid with a Roman warrior finial. This was the standard type of presentation cup in England during the first third of the 17th century and many hundreds must have been made. London, maker's mark of F. Terry (Jackson p. 110) 1611-12. H. 61.2 cm.
The Carpenters' Company, London.

Plates 665, 666, 667.
Gilt standing cup and cover, the bowl decorated with three almost circular cartouches embossed with figures of Jupiter, Diana (pl. 666) and Venus (pl. 667) respectively; the intervening spaces filled with putti, fruit and flowers. While the steeple cup of this period was usually coarsely decorated with marine subjects, this piece is finely embossed with ten cartouches enclosing figures of classical gods, goddesses and warriors. The style of the embossing recalls contemporary Dutch pieces (pl. 615) and the cup as a whole shows little resemblance to the English steeple cup. The peculiar formation of the lower part of the bowl as two members, each with rounded profile, the lower embossed with gadroons, the upper with lion masks alternating

with cartouches containing sea-monsters, while unfamiliar on English silver, can be paralleld on a number of Dutch ones. The cup might be an imported Dutch piece marked in England, but this seems unlikely as the engraving on the broad lip of the bowl is typically English, and Tudor roses appear in the stamped borders of both cup and cover. London, maker's mark a trefoil within an oval. (Jackson p. 114), 1616-17. H. 63.5 cm.
St. John's College, Cambridge.

Plate 668.
Rock-crystal and silver-gilt standing salt and cover, the body constructed of a rock-crystal cylinder enclosing a draped female figure standing on a pedestal. The receptacle for salt gadrooned, the foot embossed with running foliate scrolls and enriched with three scroll brackets terminating above in female terms. The cover embossed en suite and set with a hemispherical piece of rock-crystal. This material was greatly appreciated in England and many vessels of the second half of the century have rock-crystal bowls or feet. London, maker's mark, a swan's head erased (Jackson p. 97), 1549-50. H. 20.5 cm.
Trinity College, Oxford.

Plate 669.
Gilt standing salt and cover, the cylindrical body embossed with a crowded composition of strapwork and bunches of fruit enclosing three medallions containing satyr masks in high relief; the foot supported on three tortoises. The cover embossed with cherub's heads and surmounted by a vase pepper-box, supported by three sea-horses. Presented to Corpus Christi College by Matthew Parker, Archbishop of Canterbury, on 1 September, 1570. London, maker's mark, RD monogram (Jackson p.96), 1562-3. H. 29.2 cm.
Corpus Christi College, Cambridge.

Plate 670.
Standing salt of silver-gilt and rock-crystal enriched with semi-precious stones. The curious construction of this salt with elements of rock-crystal of various shapes secured by silver brackets columns and straps, surmounted by a circular receptacle with pendant faceted crystal beads and by a cover with baluster finial, is explained by its having been composed from fragments of medieval reliquaries which had been destroyed at the Reformation. The design shows Mannerist features but was to some extent determined by the need to accommodate as many ancient fragments as possibie. London, maker's mark IR, with a fleur-de-lys between, in a shaped shield, 1577-8. H. 26.8 cm.
British Museum.

Plate 671.
Standing salt of silver-gilt and rock-crystal; of architectural form, the salt is supported by a figure of Neptune enclosed within a rock-crystal cylinder of pentagonal section, around which is a peristyle of four free-standing Ionic columns. The salt stands on four baluster feet. Each of the columns is surmounted by two circular members and, above by a small dome on the cover. In the centre of the cover a larger dome supporting a large vase finial. This salt is the finest of the whole group of English rock-crystal and silver examples. The architectural theme is carried through from the base to the cover with great skill and the proportion of the columns is excellent. London, maker's mark, three trefoils within a trefoil (Jackson p. 103), 1576-7. H. 30.5 cm.
The Goldsmiths' Company, London.

Plate 672.
Gilt standing salt and cover of clock shape. The square body is embossed and chased on each side with a figure of one of the Cardinal Virtues after plaquettes by Peter Flötner, an indication of the availability of foreign goldsmiths' models in England. The shells applied at the centre point of the arched scrolls over each of the Virtues recall the German fashion of taking casts directly from natural objects. The angles between the panels are masked by male caryatids. The foot is supported on four sphinx feet, the domical cover surmounted by a vase on which stands a female figure holding a shield engraved with the arms of the Vintners' Company of London. London, maker's mark, a falcon (Jackson p. 101), 1569-70. H. 30.5 cm.
The Vintners' Company, London.

Plate 673.
Gilt standing salt and cover, set with panels of *verre fixé*. The rectangular body is supported on four lion feet and set with four panels painted with designs adapted from an emblem book published at Leyden in 1586. Domed cover set with four roundels painted with heads of Roman Emperors, it is surmounted by a free-standing figure emblematic of Justice. The combination of silver-gilt and *verre fixé* is extremely rare on English silver. This salt illustrates a new fashion in that the cover is raised from the receptacle on four openwork brackets, on which a dish could be placed. London, maker's mark, the letters WH with a flower (Jackson p. 107) 1592-3. H. 34 cm.
Victoria and Albert Museum.

Plate 674.
Gilt standing salt mounted with mother-of-pearl plaques, supported on three agate ball feet. The mouldings of base, rim and cover stamped with ovolo ornament. The cover is held clear of the salt receptacle by three double-scroll brackets with applied beaded rat-tail ornament and is surmounted by a bud finial. Mother-of-pearl, which was obtained from the Eastern Mediterranean, was favoured throughout Western Europe as a material for mounting articles of silver during the last quarter of the 16th and the early 17th centuries. English, unmarked, about 1600. H. 19.7 cm.
Royal Ontario Museum, Toronto.

Plate 675.
Gilt trencher salt, triangular, supported on three

shell-shaped feet, the upper surface engraved with floral scrolls incorporating the owner's arms in one corner. This type of salt was common in Germany and many examples survive. Only one other earlier English one is recorded and examples are extremely rare, but this may be due to later melting rather than to few having been made. London, maker's mark G in a shaped shield (Jackson p. 110) 1607-8. H. 3.5 cm. L. of side 9.2 cm.
Royal Ontario Museum, Toronto.

Plate 676.

Double tiered gilt salt, the cover and the upper tier originally detachable but now fixed, the whole surmounted by a four-sided pinnacle. This type of salt is the complement of the steeple cup so popular in England during the first quarter of the 17th century. London, maker's mark, RB (Jackson p. 112), 1614-15. H. 41.5 cm.
Victoria and Albert Museum.

Plate 677, 678.

Ewer and basin, the ewer in the form of a mermaid, holding a comb in her right hand and, formerly, a mirror in her left, her body wrought entirely from sheet, her tail engraved with scales, her hair hanging down her back; the stem fluted and of oval section, the base a scallop-shell, of the same pattern used for English spice-box covers of the period. The tip of the tail can be unscrewed to allow the body to be filled with water, which can then be poured out through the nipples. Below the breast an oval escutcheon engraved with the arms of Wilson, probably for Sir Thomas Wilson (1560-1629). The accompanying basin (pl. 678) is wrought in the form of a large scallop-shell and embossed with marine motifs. The quality of the modelling does not fall below contemporary continental work. London, maker's mark, the letters TB conjoined, (Jackson p. 112), 1610-11. H. of ewer 31.7 cm. Max. width of basin 45.5 cm.
Victoria and Albert Museum.

Plate 679.

Gilt covered beaker, the body engraved with canopies connected to strapwork cartouches by festoons and inhabited by dolphins, snails, birds and animals. The engraved detail copied from Flemish pattern sheets; a laurel wreath is engraved around the lip. The cover embossed with bunches of fruit. The relatively modern name of 'Magdalen cup' for this type of vessel derives from its similarity to the cup carried by St. Mary Magdalen in 16th-century religious painting. London, maker's mark, MH in monogram. (Jackson p.113), 1573-4. H. 19.7 cm.
City Art Gallery, Manchester.

Plate 680.

Gilt tankard, the upwards tapering cylindrical body flat-chased with bands of mauresques enclosing medallions, the S-scroll handle with volute thumb piece attached below to a large projecting semi-circular moulding. One of three similar tankards presented by Matthew Parker, the second Protestant Archbishop of Canterbury, to Cambridge colleges on New Year's Day 1571-2. The tankard was a piece of useful rather than show plate and its ornament was usually more restrained than that of cups, ewers or basins. London, maker's mark FR in monogram in a shaped shield (Jackson p. 100), 1570-1. H. 16 cm.
Trinity Hall, Cambridge.

Plates 681, 682.

Parcel-gilt ewer and companion basin, the basin with central circular panel embossed with fruit and masks enclosing a shield enamelled with the arms of the See of Norwich impaling those of Parkhurst. The vase-shaped ewer with wedge spout has a chased girdle interrupted by cartouches enclosing Roman heads, the body rises from a gadrooned bottom. The cover embossed *en suite* with the central medallion of the basin, in the centre the same arms as on the basin. Bold S-scroll handle with volute thumb-piece. This was the standard type of ewer of the second quarter and third quarter of the century. The ewer was made at a later date to match the earlier Flemish basin and illustrates how very little difference existed between English and Flemish silver at this period. The ewer, London, maker's mark a hand holding a hammer in a shaped shield (Jackson p. 100), 1567-8; the basin, Antwerp, maker's mark a pelican in her piety, 1543-4. H. of ewer 23 cm. Diam. of basin 42 cm.
Corporation of Guildford, Surrey.

Plates 683, 684.

Gilt ewer and companion basin, the former of agate, the latter set with agate plaques, probably the finest surviving English examples of this period. The ewer design departs entirely from the conventions of the period, though its originality was partly due to the need to deal with the problem of constructing a ewer out of four cylinders of agate of differing diameter. The four free-standing brackets, that are so curious a feature of its construction, have an important function in supporting the agate cylinders one above the other. It seems curious that four cylinders should have been used rather than a single piece of agate cut to the appropriate shape. Agate was not readily available in England and possibly the cylinders were originally intended for some other purpose. The ewer was once even more splendid, for the four holes drilled in front of each bracket must have secured collets set with precious stones. The parallel lines and sharp angles of the body give a restless disorganised appearance which is enhanced by the curved brackets and the merman handle with his twisted tail, on whose back is unsteadily perched a large snail with another smaller one on his back. Other small snails are at the base of each of the vertical brackets; all seem to have been cast from nature. The basin is set with a circular agate boss in the centre and with twelve oval bosses in two concentric circles. The intervening spaces between the bosses on the bowl are decorated with a dolphin, turtle, lobster and crayfish respectively.

Between the eight spaces on the rim are embossed lion masks and female heads, while the whole of the remaining surface is elaborateiy embossed with birds, monsters, snails and bunches of fruit surrounded by strapwork. London, maker's mark, three trefoils within a trefoil (Jackson p. 104), . 1579-80.
The Duke of Rutland Collection.

Plate 685, 686.
Gilt ewer and companion basin, both the body of the ewer and the inner and outer border of the basin embossed with crudely modelled animals within a landscape; the frieze on the ewer interrupted in front by an applied grotesque mask, while another mask is applied under the spout. The body, instead of conforming to the usual egg shape is wrought in two stages, the lower being decorated with gadroons. Among the animals depicted are an elephant, giraffe and camel, implying that the maker had access to a pattern-book of exotic animals. The ewer with its companion basin used up a lot of metal and was bound to be expensive; they are, therefore, usually of high quality but the embossing and chasing of these examples is naive. London, maker's mark, an escallop (Jackson p. 105), 1586-7. H. of ewer 36.5 cm. Diam. of basin 50 cm.
Rijksmuseum, Amsterdam.

Plate 687.
Gilt ewer, the oviform body chased with a frieze of dolphins and rushes against a background of waves, the front with an applied cast mask, the spout embossed with a similar mask, the handle of scroll form terminating above in the forepart of a lion after the engraved design by Agostino Veneziano, of 1531 (pl. 12). London, maker's mark, a fleur-de-lys (Jackson p. 105), 1583-4. H. 33.6 cm.
Victoria and Albert Museum.

Plate 688.
Oil painting showing the treasure of the East Anglian family of Paston. While the background and the Negro servant are probably imaginary additions by the artist, the survival of at least five of the pieces represented proves that the collection existed as shown. Thirteen pieces of goldsmiths' work are included; of these the flagon decorated with shells, held by the Negro boy in the bottom left hand corner of the painting, and the large strombus-shell mounted on a gilt and enamelled brass stem that lies on its side in front of him are certainly English. Both survive, the flagon being one of a pair bearing the London hall-mark for 1597-8 in the Metropolitan Museum, New York, while the mounted shell is in the Castle Museum, Norwich. The shell flask to the right of the painting beneath the sand-glass is illustrated in pl. 690. The Paston family seems to have been particularly attracted to mounted shells, for, of the thirteen pieces of goldsmiths' work shown in the picture, eleven are of this type, a twelfth, the flagon, is embossed with shells and only the large tankard in the centre background has no marine association. Two of the nautilus-cups in the painting have been identified in

Dutch museums; they are shown in the right background and are of Dutch make, one by a Delft master, the other unmarked. The strombus-shell bottle lying on its side, the nautilus-cup in the centre and the very elaborately worked cup to the left of the painting are also probably of Dutch origin, as is the small powder-flask to the far right with body formed of two tortoise-shells. One can only guess at the origin of the other pieces but they appear to be of Dutch, Flemish or German origin. It is significant that only two or, perhaps, three pieces from this collection of goldsmiths' work belonging to a wealthy East Anglian family should be of English origin. Dutch School, mid 17th century.
Castle Museum, Norwich.

Plate 689.
One of a pair of silver-gilt and rock-crystal candlesticks, of German, probably Freiburg im Breisgau origin, converted in England by the addition of the domed base and substitution of candle-socket and silver drip pan for the original pricket. The stick now has a double base, one beneath the other, the lower one of typically English form, embossed with gadroons alternating with overlapping scale ornament. Originally altar candlesticks, the conversion made them suitable for domestic use. As far as is known rock-crystal was not worked in England, hence the necessity to adapt a pair of Continental sticks. Probably London, maker's mark the letter P or monogram IP in a shield, about 1600. H. 24.4 cm.
Museum of Art, Philadelphia.

Plate 690.
Mother of pearl flask with silver-gilt mounts, the body composed of segments of mother of pearl attached to a silver carcase. The cover surmounted by a cast silver shell. This vessel is shown in the painting of the Paston treasure on the far right of pl. 687. English or Dutch, first half of 17th century. H. 29.5 cm.
Private collection, London.

Plate 691.
Lead model for a Swiss dagger-sheath in the manner of Hans Holbein, cast from the carved wood original. The subject is the Parable of the Prodigal son, shown in four scenes running from right to left: the departure, debauch, money lost to loose women and work as a swineherd. Swiss, mid 16th century.
Historisches Museum, Basel.

Plate 692.
Dagger and sheath, silver-gilt; the upper part of the sheath embossed and pierced with Job seated naked, his breast pierced by a sword held in the hand of God. Above on a ribbon is the legend: *Etiam si occideris me Domine in te sperabo* (Even if thou killest me, Lord, I shall place my hope in thee). Below this is a lion's mask and a female caryatid whose arms are bound by straps. The hilt has a fluted grip while the pommel and quillons

are cast and chased with acanthus foliage. German, mid 16th century.
Staatliche Kunstsammlungen, Kassel.

Plate 693.
Dagger-sheath in the manner of Hans Holbein, of cast and gilt bronze, pierced and chased with a scene from the legend of Virginia, showing Appius Claudius in the seat of Judgement. The ferrule composed of addorsed dolphins. Swiss or South German, mid 16th century.
Wallace Collection, London.

Plate 694.
Two lead patterns for the two sides of a sword- or dagger-hilt; though probably from a Nürnberg workshop, they derive from an Italian source and may have been cast from an Italian original. They were intended to serve as models for producing a mould for casting in silver or bronze, but similar designs were executed in chiselled iron. The drawing (pl. 225) shows similar elements of ornament but interpreted by a German-Flemish artist. Third quarter of 16th century.
Historisches Museum, Basel.

Plates 695, 697.
Sword of State with hilt and scabbard mounts of silver-gilt, the former cast and chased, the latter embossed with *Rollwerk* cartouches centering on masks; the quillons terminating in eagle heads, the chape of the scabbard embossed with a standing figure of Minerva. Swords of this type were carried before civic officers and symbolised the power of giving justice delegated to them by the sovereign. They were usually carried by a sword-bearer with the point held upwards and for this reason the decoration was sometimes planned, though not in this case, to be seen in this position. South German, second half of 16th century.'
Kunsthistoriches Museum, Vienna.

Plates 696, 698.
Sword with hilt of gilt iron, the scabbard mounts of silver-gilt embossed with panels of ornament in the Jamnitzer manner and with Old Testament subjects. The back of the scabbard locket etched with mauresques. This was a fully functional sword; apart from the band of silver round the upper part of the blade which fitted over the top of the scabbard, the hilt is left plain. South German, third quarter of 16th century.
Kunsthistorisches Museum, Vienna.

Plate 699.
Rapier-hilt of gold, the ground champlevé enamelled with black scrollwork, to which are applied blue-enamelled snakes winding over the surface and biting into bunches of green and white enamelled fruit. Presented before 1567 to the Elector August of Saxony by Duke Albrecht of Bavaria. Probably made by one of the Munich court goldsmiths. The ricasso of the blade damascened in gold and silver. About 1560.
Historisches Museum, Dresden.

Plate 700.
Rapier-hilt of gold wrought with white enamelled interlacing strapwork inhabited by tortoises and snails enamelled blue, the gold ground enamelled with translucent green and red flowers. This sword and a companion dagger were presented to the Elector August of Saxony by Maximilian (later the Emperor Maximilian II) on the occasion of his election as King of Rome in Frankfurt am Main in 1562. Probably the work of a Spanish goldsmith at the Habsburg court, perhaps Pery Juan Pockh. About 1560.
Historisches Museum, Dresden.

Plate 701.
Rapier-hilt of gold wrought with garlands of floral scrolls enamelled white, blue and black against a matt gold ground. The cross with a grotesque mask, the central point of the grip with an enamelled blue wing. Presented by the Emperor Maximilian II in 1575 to Prince Christian (later the Elector Christian I) on the occasion of his visit to Dresden. This hilt is very similar to that presented to the Elector August (pl. 703) and is probably the work of the same Spanish goldsmith.
Historisches Museum, Dresden.

Plate 702.
Rapier-hilt of gold, dated 1571, composed of wrought and cast elements enriched with polychrome enamel. The pommel set with six figures within niches, the quillons composed of scrollwork, masks and bunches of fruit inhabited by putti and animals, the grip divided into panels by trelliswork, the panels enclosing figures of classical Gods. Probably Spanish, dated 1571.
Schatzkammer of the Residenz, Munich.

Plate 703.
Rapier-hilt of enamelled gold composed of relief strapwork through which wind snakes with enamelled blue scales; the quillons, also decorated with strapwork, terminate in buds, numerous masks and shells interrupt the straps. This sword with its dagger was supplied by the Spanish goldsmith Pery Juan Pockh and presented by the Emperor Maximilian II to the Elector August in 1575.
Historisches Museum, Dresden.

Plate 704.
Sword-hilt of gilt-bronze, the pommel and guard cast and chased with masks and male and female figures modelled in the round, the grip with strapwork and a girdle of acanthus foliage. The design is based upon one of the prints of Pierre Woeriot, compare pl. 242. French, about 1560-70.
Musée de l'Armée, Paris.

Plate 705.
Rapier-hilt of gold wrought with white enamelled interlacing strapwork, inhabited by blue and black enamelled snakes against a matt ground. The quillons

terminate in grotesque monsters' heads. This sword with a companion dagger was presented to the Elector August of Saxony by the Archduke Ferdinand of Tirol, probably when the latter visited Dresden in 1574. Probably the work of a Spanish goldsmith at the Habsburg court (Pery Juan Pockh?). About 1570.
Historisches Museum, Dresden.

Plate 706.
Rapier, the hilt of gilt-bronze cast and chased with strapwork enclosing numerous grotesque masks, recumbent figures and griffins and set with pearls and forty cabochon-, table- and pyramid-cut stones (mostly foiled crystals) in cusped gilt bronze collets, the pommel of cartouche shape with a female figure in a niche on each side. The main ring of the guard set with two shell cameos of cupid heads, the whole of the interior surface of the hilt finely cast and chased with masks and scrollwork and figures from classical mythology. Signed *ISRAEL SCHUECH M.1606,* the only signed work of this master. He seems to have been influenced by the *Eisenschneider,* Othmar Wetter, who worked for the Munich court before coming to Dresden. In view of the lavish enrichment of this hilt, it must have been made for the Elector Christian II or for his brother, Duke Johann Georg. Dresden, dated 1606.
Metropolitan Museum, New York.

Plate 707.
Hilt of iron wrought with nereids and tritons in low relief on the grip and pommel, in the round on ringguard and quillons, the whole surface of the hilt heavily encrusted with gold and oxydised silver. The chiselling of the free-standing figures in iron is an outstanding example of this particular technique. Probably Italian, third quarter of the 16th century. From the Markgräfliche Sammlung, Erlangen.
Bayerisches Nationalmuseum, Munich.

Plate 708.
Sabre-hilt, the cross and pommel sheathed in gold, enamelled and enriched with rubies and emeralds, the ends of the guard and pommel terminating in volutes. Made by Gilles Coyet, a Flemish goldsmith, who emigrated to work for the Swedish court, for King John III of Sweden. About 1575-80.
Kunglige Livrustkammaren, Stockholm.

Plate 709.
Sword-hilt of gold wrought with foliage, angels' heads and volutes and enamelled in polychrome translucent colours. This sword with a companion dagger was presented before 1552 to the Emperor Maximilian II by Wratislaw II von Bernstein, a Bohemian nobleman. It was subsequently given by Maximilian to his younger brother, the Archduke Ferdinand II, Statthalter of Bohemia. This sword is generally recognised as the finest surviving piece of its kind. It is described in the old inventories as a Spanish sword, but this may refer to the enamelled decoration. The closest parallels

to its decoration can be found on the mounts of Florentine semi-precious hardstone vessels. Probably Italian. Mid-16th century.
Kunsthistoriches Museum, Vienna.

Plate 710.
Shield of wrought iron covered with gold and enamelled, made for Charles IX, king of France, whose monogram decorates the rim. It was wrought in the royal workshops, probably in the Louvre, and then plated with gold and enamelled by the Paris goldsmith, Pierre Redon, whose widow received 5000 *livres Tournois* for it in 1572. The decoration conforms to that of a series of parade shields, preserved in the former royal armouries; the design is attributed to Etienne Delaune. Two main types were made, of pointed oval form such as this, or with rolled over corners, such as examples in the Vienna Waffensammlung and in the castle of Skokloster. The morion helmet made by the same goldsmith to go en suite with this shield is illustrated in colour plate XXIV. The Royal Armoury, Paris, and Pierre Redon, about 1570. H. 68 cm.
Musée du Louvre, Paris.

Plate 711.
Burgonet helmet of gilt copper, the bowl, cheekpieces and crest embossed with combat scenes between mounted men in classical armour, the roped border on the comb and the rivet heads of silver. The silver border struck with the Augsburg mark and an unidentified house-mark. This helmet was presented to Elector Christian I of Saxony by his wife Sophie in 1589. It was accompanied by a saddle mounted with two plates embossed in a similar manner.
Historisches Museum, Dresden.

Plate 712.
Burgonet helmet of blued steel embossed with bunches of fruit and enriched with gilt copper borders and with pierced strapwork cartouches enclosing figures of Roman warriors and trophies of arms. Augsburg, last quarter of 16th century.
H. M. Armouries, Tower of London.

Plates 713, 714.
Front and rear view of the bronze figure cast from Benvenuto Cellini's wax model of Juno. The wax was a preparatory sketch for the life-size silver figure that with twelve others was to decorate the Galerie François I at Fontainebleau. The completed candlestick would have been seen from all sides, hence the *forma serpentinata* of the model. Cellini relates that the bronze base and the wax model for the Juno were completed but the full-size figure was never cast. For Cellini's drawing see pl. 97. H. 26 cm.
Private collection.

Plate 715.
Gilt copper foot of an altar cross; though dated 1541,

this foot is in early Renaissance style. Comparison with the designs in pls. 9 and 10 illustrates the degree of simplification that was required in order to translate an artist's drawing into a form that could be executed by the goldsmith. Italian, dated 1541. H. 35.5 cm.
Victoria and Albert Museum.

Plate 716.
Venetian bronze inkstand, the receptacle supported by three figures of putti seated on a scrolled base, the cover surmounted by masks and a figure of Hope holding an anchor. Though not directly associated with one of the Salviati school designs, this inkstand illustrates how they might be executed in bronze. Venetian, attributed to Tiziano Aspetti. Third quarter of the 16th century. H. 27.3 cm.
Victoria and Albert Museum.

Plate 717.
Bronze casket bearing the arms of Organtino Scarola, Bishop of San Marco from 1568 to 1572; this is a simplified version of a casket design in the manner of Salviati in the Victoria and Albert Museum, from which it differs by the omission of one stage of the cover and a reduced scheme of ornament. Venetian, third quarter of the 16th century. H. 22.9 cm. W. 29.2 cm.
Victoria and Albert Museum.

Plate 718.
Majolica salt-cellar with polychrome decoration based on a design in the manner of Francesco Salviati. Urbino, mid 16th century.
Walters Art Gallery, Baltimore.

Plate 719.
Gilt-copper and gilt-bronze salt-cellar constructed in three tiers; the embossed decoration represents sea-battles instead of the more usual denizens of the sea. The pyramid top is embossed with trophies of arms, the lowest receptacle with sea-fights while the whole is supported on the backs of four naked prisoners. The vertical towerlike construction is well adapted to serve as a centre-piece; similar tiered salts were produced in both Spain and England in the early 17th century. Italian. Early 17th century. H. 48.5 cm.
Victoria and Albert Museum.

Plates 720, 722.
Monstrance of gilt copper and gilt bronze in the form of a three-storyed temple, the container for the Host flanked by three pairs of columns, the inner ones having censing angels attached to them, the outer in the form of turbaned prophet terms holding scrolls. Between each pair of columns is a kneeling angel (pl. 722). The stem embossed with strapwork, the six-lobed foot embossed with Evangelists within strapwork cartouches alternating with angels holding crystal shields. Unmarked, Spanish, third quarter of the 16th century. H. 53 cm.
Victoria and Albert Museum.

Plate 721.
Gilt bronze salt-cellar, composed of three bearded tritons supporting three scallop shells. North Italian, second half of 16th century. H. 28 cm.
Victoria and Albert Museum.

Plate 723.
Gilt bronze salt-cellar, one of a pair, composed of a figure of Jupiter standing on a pedestal rising from a platform set between three scallop-shells supported on the backs of tritons resting on a base, the corners of which develop into sea-horses. Probably Venetian, last quarter of the 16th century, derived from a design in the manner of Salviati. H. 30.5 cm.
Victoria and Albert Museum.

Plates 724, 729.
Detail of dial plate of embossed, chased and gilded-copper from a table clock, the case cast and chased with scenes from the legend of Orpheus. The decoration is composed of interlacing vine foliage inhabited by birds, snakes and a lizard while the background is finely punched. The working of this dial has been attributed to Wenzel Jamnitzer but, while it is certainly worthy of him, the attribution is conjectural. Whoever was its master must have had a powerful personality or he would not have succeeded in imposing upon the clock-maker so impracticable a design. In the illustration of the dial (pl. 724) it is quite impossible to recognise the hand (pl. 729) at all and, though this is less difficult when one is confronted with the clock itself, there is no doubt that its functional efficiency has been sacrificed to the artist's wish to create a masterpiece. South German, third quarter of the 16th century. Diam. 23 cm.
Württembergisches Landesmuseum, Stuttgart.

Plate 725.
Gilt-copper shield, the central boss embossed and chased with a victor being carried in triumph by his prisoners, the inner frieze with combats between horsemen in classical armour, the outer with trophies of arms within strapwork cartouches alternating with hunting scenes. Attributed to Jakob Knoll of Augsburg, the assistant of Jörg Sigman. Dated 1556.
Hermitage Museum, Leningrad.

Plate 726.
Goblet of cast, chased and gilt bronze, the rim etched with mauresques. The ornament on the bowl cast from plaquettes from the Jamnitzer workshop. In order to produce the curved models required for casting the bowl, a soft material, such as wax or lead which could be bent to shape, was used. South German, last quarter of the 16th century. H. 14 cm.
Württembergisches Landesmuseum, Stuttgart.

Plate 727.
Gilt-bronze plaquette, the centre cast and chased with a standing figure of Minerva, flanked by lion heads

and surmounted by two cornucopiae upon which are perched reclining nude figures of Juno with her peacock and Venus with Cupid. Signed and dated *Paulus de Vianus fecit et invent.* Attributed to Vianen's Munich period. About 1600. H. 11.7 cm.
Rijksmuseum, Amsterdam.

Plate 728.
Two bronze casts after panels from the Briot Dish (pl. 736). The high quality of these casts suggests that they are contemporary models and not, as were many bronze casts from 16th century plaquettes, made at a later date for collectors. French, late 16th century. L. of part illustrated 15 cm.
Kunstgewerbemuseum, Berlin.

Plate 730.
Carved limewood model of the side of a clock-case, one of a set of four, intended to be cast in bronze. The low relief design is probably based on a drawing by Matthias Zündt of Nürnberg, but executed by an unidentified *Formenschneider* about 1560-70. H. 13.5 cm.
Germanisches Nationalmuseum, Nürnberg (Loan).

Plate 731.
Model carved in boxwood by Wenzel Jamnitzer or a Nürnberg *Formenschneider* for the Earth Mother figure that composes the stem of the Merckelsche table-centre. This was a preliminary model and the position of the arms differs from those of the figure as executed. Nürnberg. Before 1549. H. 29 cm.
Germanisches Nationalmuseum, Nürnberg.

Plates 732, 734.
Two carved wood figures of the Muses, Clio and Erato, from a larger set, intended as models for goldsmiths to cast reliefs for the decoration of caskets or clocks. The figures are based on originals by Hans Kels but the execution is noticeably inferior to the Jamnitzer model (pl. 731). South German, second half of 16th century.
Staatliche Museum, Berlin.

Plates 733, 735.
Carved fruitwood model for a tazza, the bowl, lower part of the stem and foot dating from the second quarter or middle of the 16th century, the group of three che-

rubs surrounding the upper part of the stem and the foliage above apparently of somewhat later date. The hop-leaf foliage around the rim of the bowl in the manner of Aldegrever is interrupted by projecting relief busts of Roman warriors. The centre carved with a relief of Roman Charity within a wreath. Such precise models were probably made only in the case of more important commissions where the patron required to see the exact effect intended. South German, about 1530-50.
Metropolitan Museum, New York.

Plate 736.
French pewter dish by François Briot with central print representing Temperantia. The design follows the convention of the period with the figure of Temperantia surrounded by four oval cartouches, each enclosing one of the four Elements and separated by terms within strapwork. The outer border is composed of eight cartouches enclosing reclining figures of Minerva and the Seven Liberal Arts separated by four panels of strapwork and four grotesque masks. The importance of the dish lies less in originality than in the harmonious arrangement of the composition and the sensitive treatment of the relief. The long elegant figures conform to the Fontainebleau canon. The dish was recognised as a *tour de force* at the time and was repeatedly copied, in Nürnberg by Caspar Enderlein and also in Strassburg. Versions in silver were also made. Diam. 44.5 cm.
Victoria and Albert Museum.

Plates 737, 738, 739.
Back and two details of a standing toilet mirror, constructed of iron plaques, damascened with gold and silver within dotted silver borders, nailed to a wood carcase, and further enriched with numerous gilt-bronze figures modelled in the round and set within niches. Some of the figures show the influence of Michelangelo (pl. 738) while the tall figures with bunches of fruit on their heads (pl. 739) and the bold straps ending in volutes at the base of the stem suggest the more evolved Fontainebleau Mannerism. With a surprising reversal of the usual order of priority the front is devoted to secular subjects while religious ones are relegated to the back (pl. 738). The mirror is of burnished steel and is concealed behind the central plaque incised with a Roman warrior suppliant before a victor (pl. 739). This mirror is a base metal version of the elaborate silver ones mentioned in contemporary inventories and shown in paintings of ladies at their toilet. Milan, last quarter of the 16th century. H. 116.4 cm. W. 63.5 cm.
Victoria and Albert Museum.

Part Three

MONOCHROME PLATES

1 Alessandro Fei, workshop of the Medici court goldsmiths, Florence, 1572

2

2, 3 Etienne Delaune, goldsmith's workshop, Augsburg, 1576

3

4

4 Titian, portrait of Jacopo da Strada, goldsmith and Court Antiquary of the Emperor Rudolph II, 1566

5

5 Nicolas de Neufchatel, portrait of Wenzel Jamnitzer of Nürnberg, c.1560-65

ÆTATIS SVÆ 34.
ANNO, 1597,

6

6 Lorenz Strauch, portrait of Christoph Jamnitzer of Nürnberg, 1597

7

7 Nicoletto Rosex of Modena, panel of grotesque ornament, c.1510
8 Giovanni Antonio of Brescia, after the antique, c.1510-20
9 Paduan (?), early 16th century

8

9

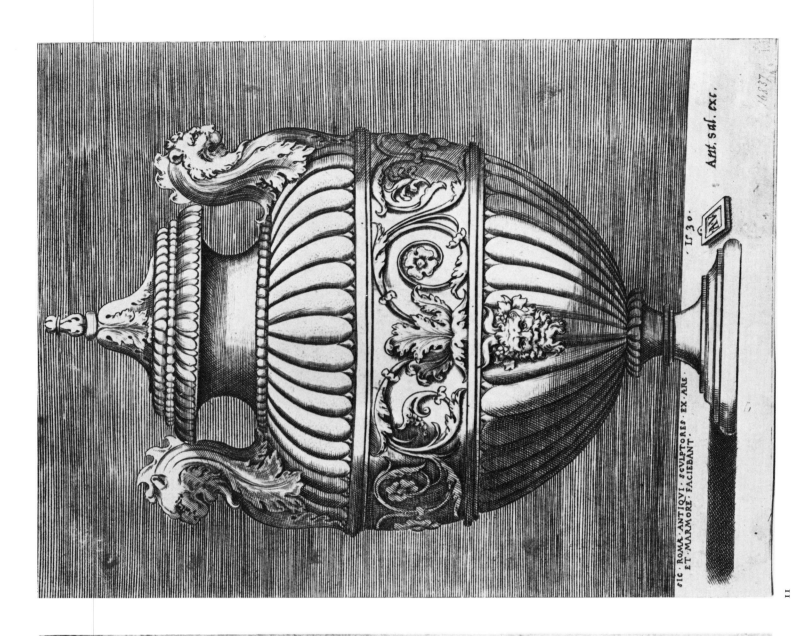

SIC · ROMÆ · ANTIQVI · SCVLPTORES · EX · ARE
ET · MARMORE · FACIEBANT.

1530.

Ant. sal. exc.

11

Baldassa   Peruzi

10

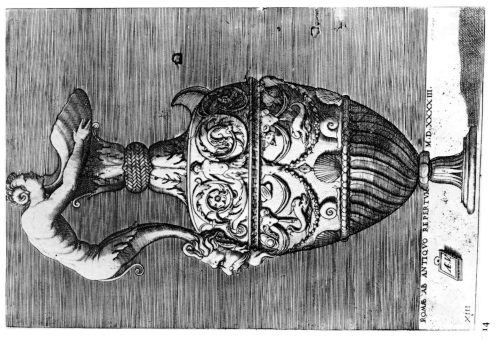

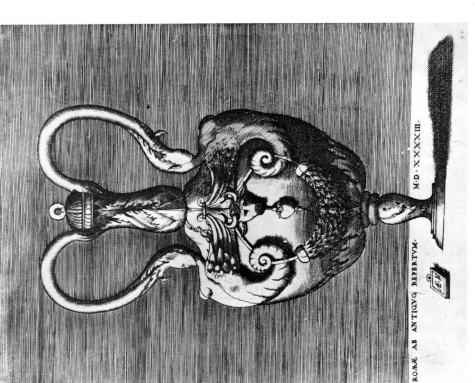

10 Venetian (?), c.1520-40

11 Agostino dei Musi, after the antique, Rome, 1530

12 Agostino dei Musi, after the antique, Rome, 1531

13, 14 Enea Vico, after the antique, Rome 1543

15

15, 16, 17 Androuet du Cerceau, Paris, c.1540-45

18 Androuet du Cerceau, Paris, c.1540-45

19, 20, 21 After Androuet du Cerceau, Paris, c.1530

16

17

18

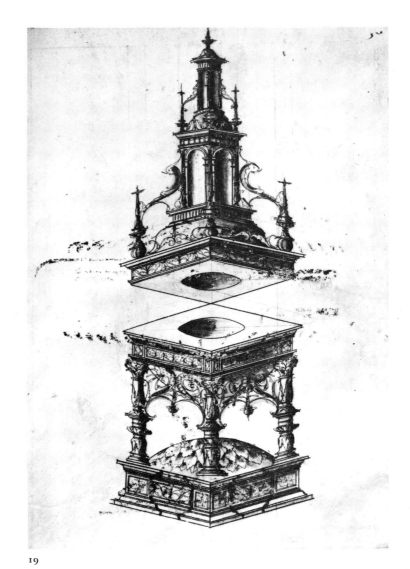

19

20

21

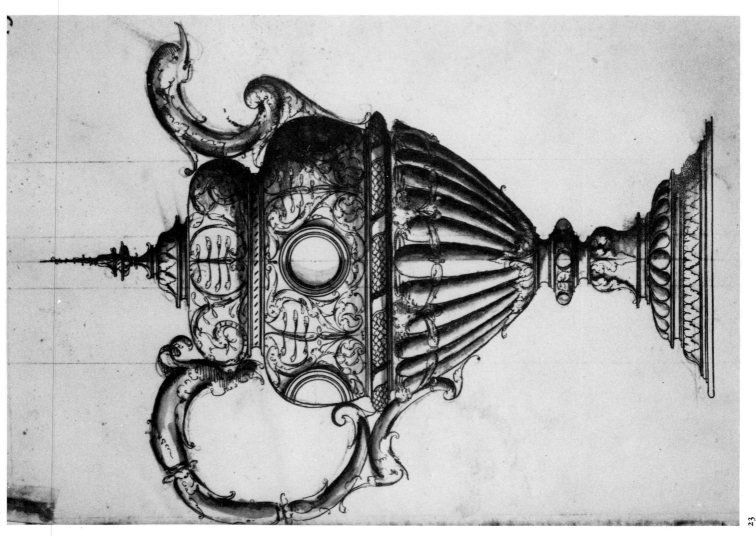

23

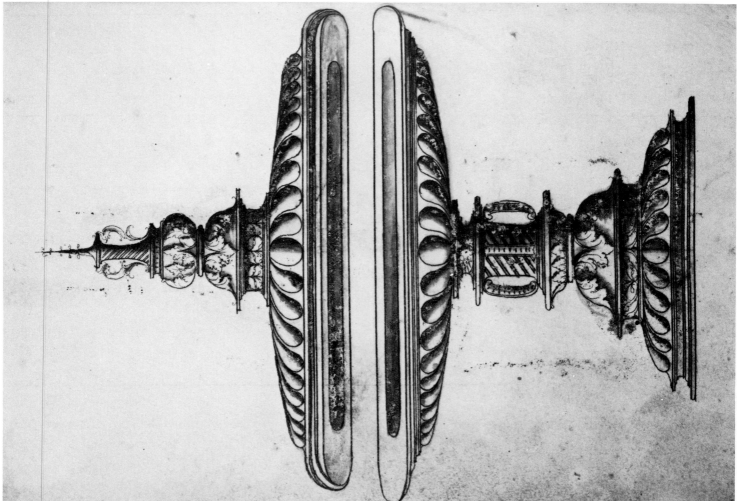

22

25

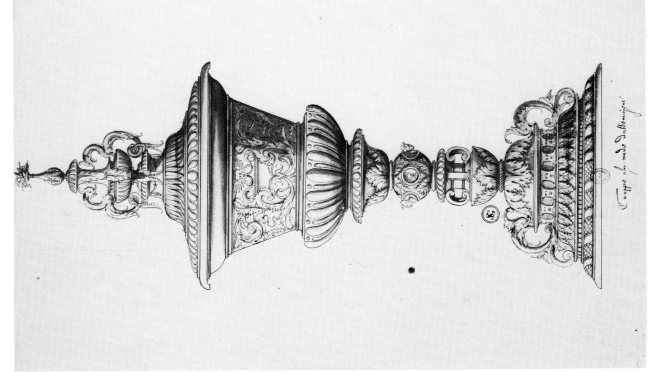

22, 23 After Androuet du Cerceau, c.1530

24 Androuet du Cerceau, Paris, c.1540

25 Androuet du Cerceau, Paris, mid 16th century

24

26

27

28

29

30

31

26, 27 Monogrammist CAP, French, mid 16th century

28, 29 Augustin Hirschvogel, Vienna, 1543

30 Albrecht Dürer, Nürnberg, 1526

31 Albrecht Altdorfer, Regensburg, c.1525

32

33

34

35

36

37

32, 33, 34, 35 Hans Brosamer, 1540

36 Kunz Welcz, Joachimstal, 1532

37 Hans Holbein, London, c.1532

38

39   40

38, 39, 40 Hans Holbein, London, c.1532-35

41 Hans Holbein, London, c.1535

42 Wenceslas Hollar, after Holbein's original drawing, c.1535-40

41

42

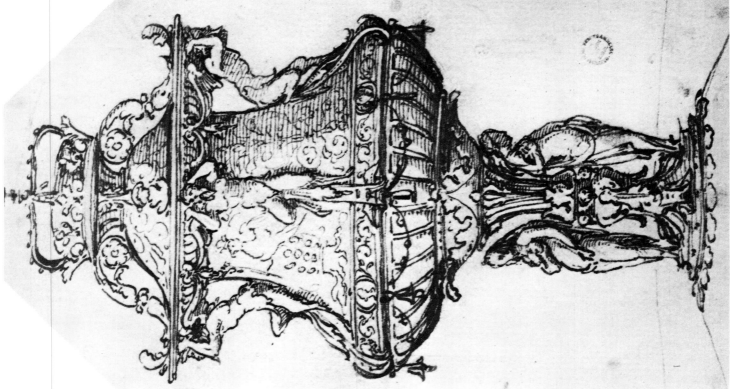

44

43

43, 44 Hans Holbein, London, c.1533-5

45 Hans Holbein, London, c.1536

46 Wenceslas Hollar, after Holbein's original
drawing, c.1535-40

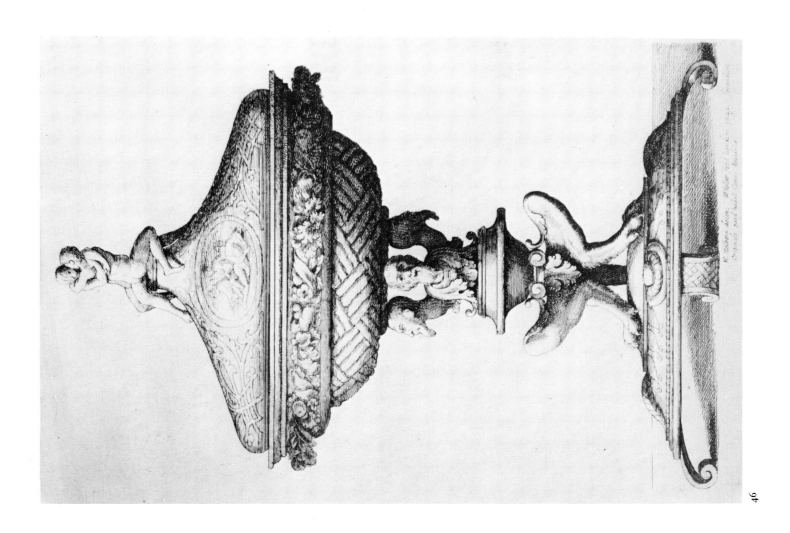

46

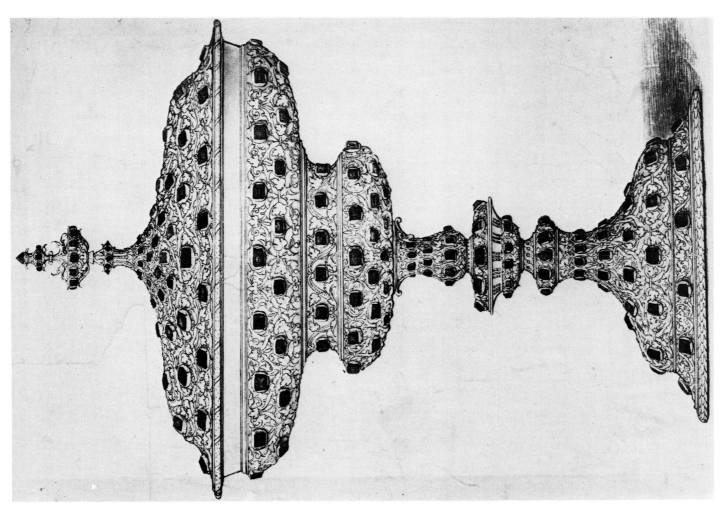

45

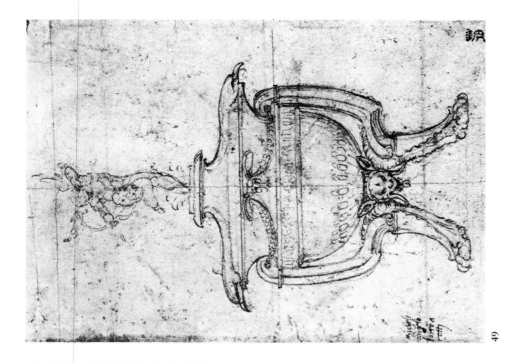

49

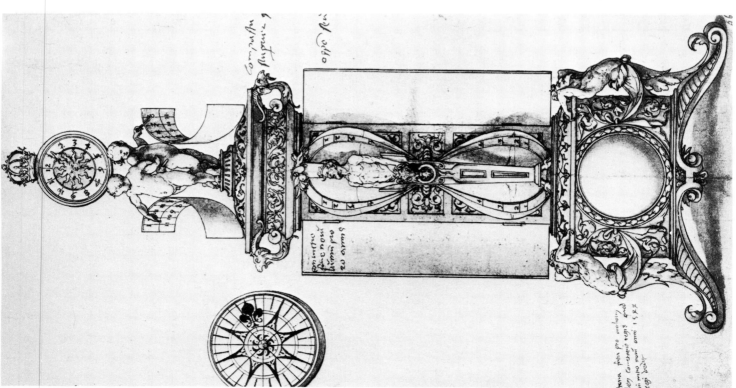

47, 48 Hans Holbein, London, 1544
49 Attributed to Michelangelo, 1537

48

47

92

92 Florentine, third quarter of the 16th century
93 Bernardo Buontalenti, Florence, 1577

93

94

94 Johann Rottenhammer, probably after a Venetian original, Augsburg, late 16th century

95 Primaticcio, Gallery of François I, Fontainebleau, c.1535-40

96 René Boyvin after Léonard Thiry, school of Fontainebleau, Paris, 1563

95

96

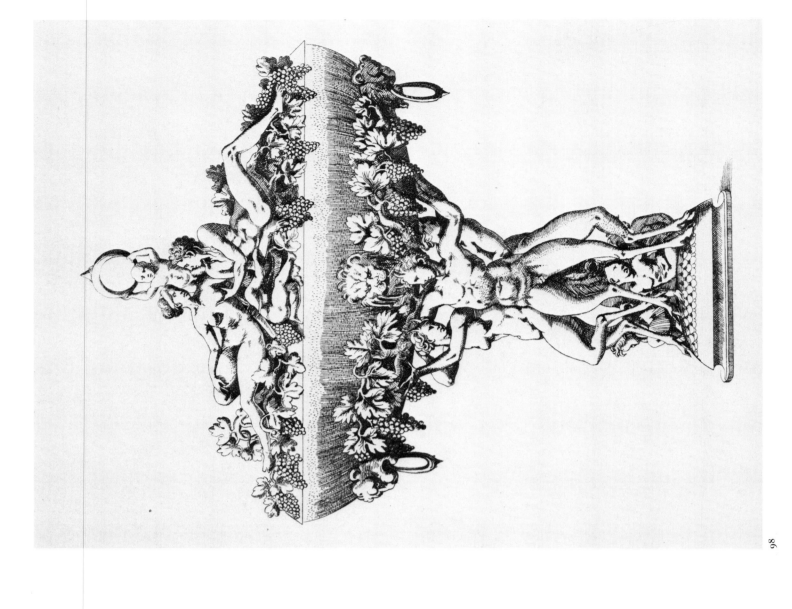

97 Benvenuto Cellini, c.1540

98 Antonio Fantuzzi, perhaps after Rosso Fiorentino, Fontainebleau, 1543

99 Attributed to René Boyvin, perhaps after Rosso Fiorentino, school of Fontainebleau, third quarter of the 16th century

100, 101 René Boyvin, or Pierre Milan, perhaps after Rosso Fiorentino, school of Fontainebleau, third quarter of the 16th century

101

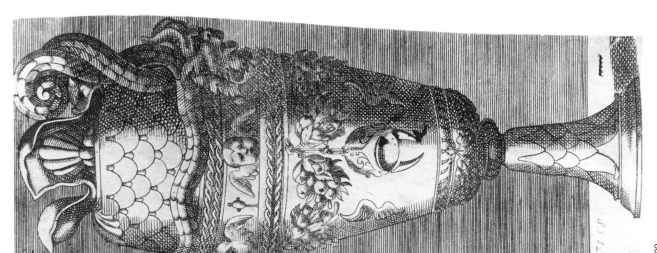

100

99

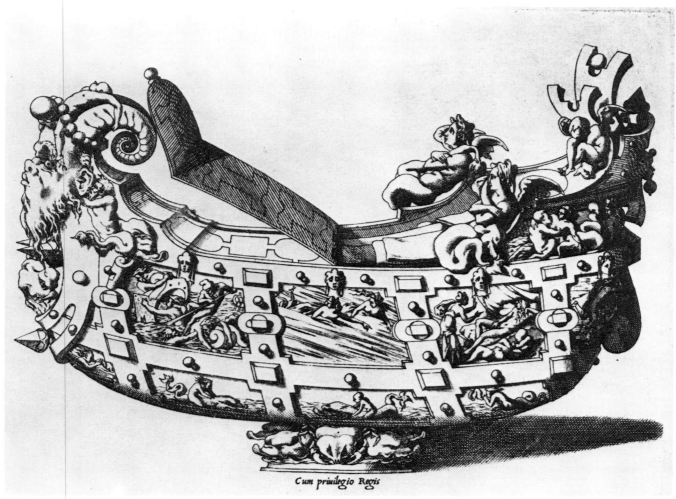

Cum priuilegio Regis

102

103

102, 103 René Boyvin, or Pierre Milan,
perhaps after Rosso Fiorentino, school
of Fontainebleau, third quarter of the
16th century

104, 105 Androuet du Cerceau, Paris,
mid 16th century

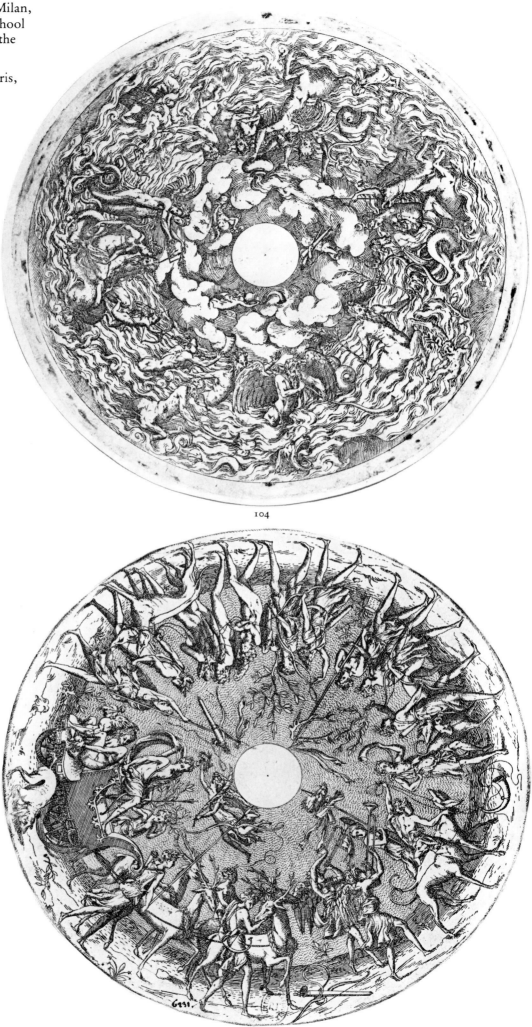

104

105

106

107

108

106 Attributed to Androuet du Cerceau, Paris, third quarter of the 16th century

107 Monogrammist C.C., school of Fontainebleau, third quarter of the 16th century

108 Etienne Delaune, Paris, 1561

109, 110, 111 Etienne Delaune, Paris, third quarter of the 16th century

112 Olivier Codoré, Paris, 1571

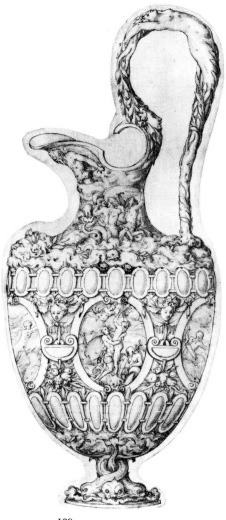

109

110

111

112

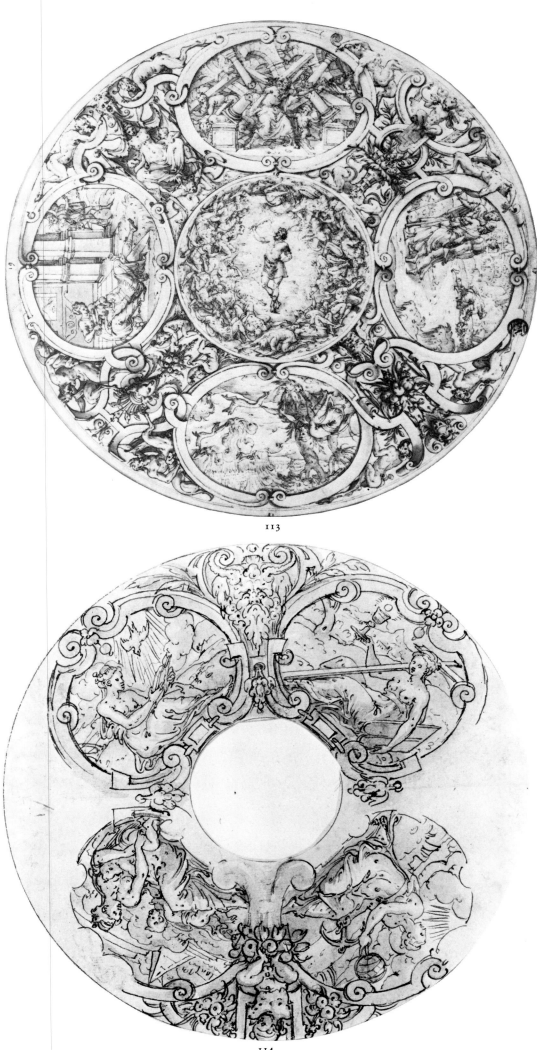

113

114

113 Etienne Delaune, Paris, third quarter of the 16th century

114 School of Etienne Delaune, second half of the 16th century

115 French (?), mid 16th century

116

116 Etienne Delaune, Paris, third quarter of the 16th century

117 Philip Ros, Barcelona, 1597

118, 119, 120, 121 Virgil Solis, probably after Wenzel Jamnitzer, Nürnberg, mid 16th century

122 Virgil Solis, Nürnberg, mid 16th century

117

150

151

150, 151, 152, 153 Erasmus Hornick, Nürnberg, 1560

152

153

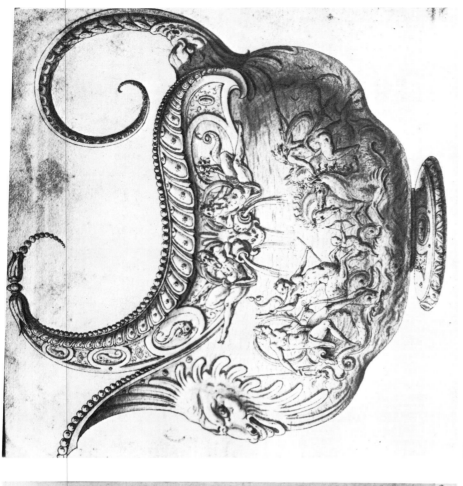

154 Erasmus Hornick, Nürnberg, 1562

155 Erasmus Hornick, third quarter of the 16th century

156, 157 Erasmus Hornick, Nürnberg, 1560

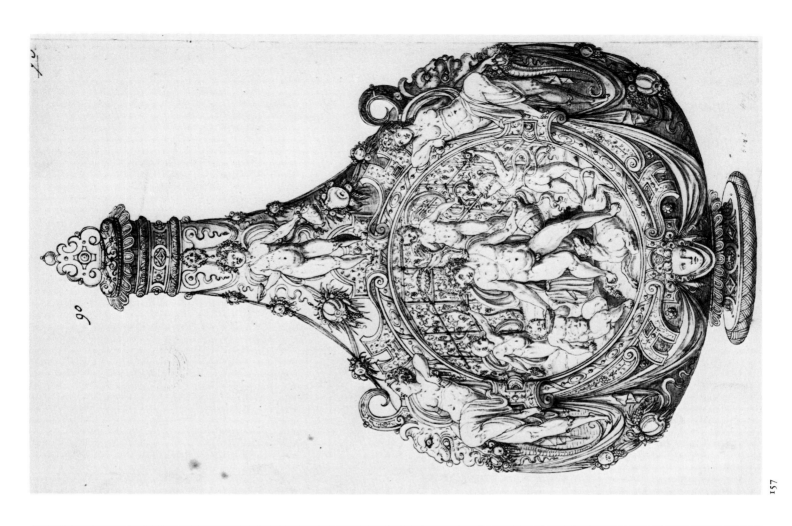

90

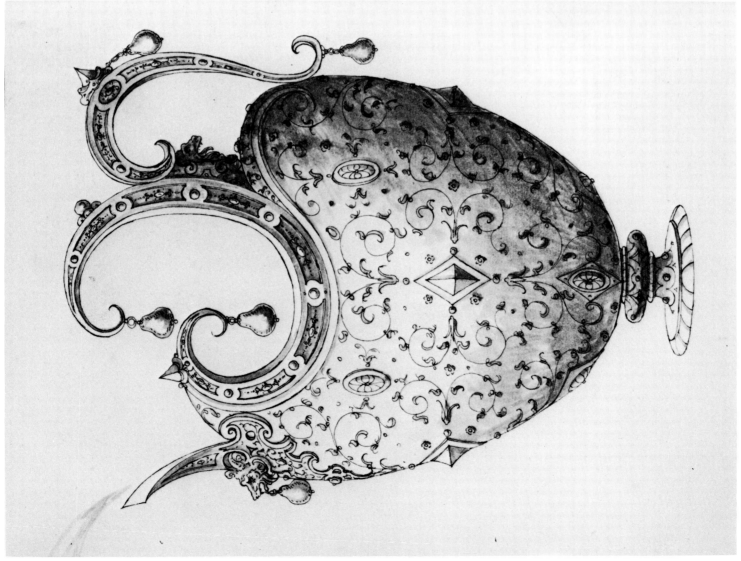

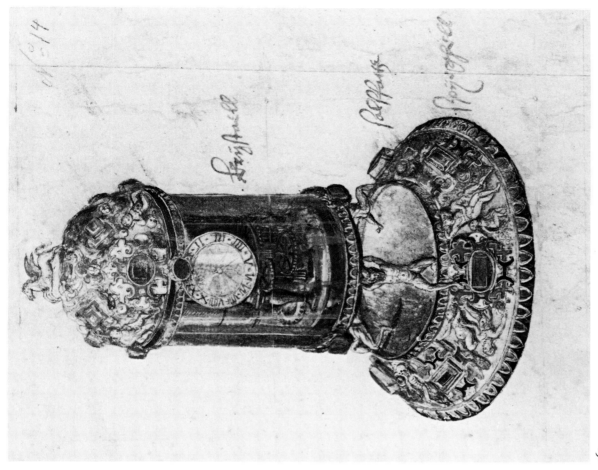

161

160

158, 159 Erasmus Hornick, Nürnberg, c.1560

160 Workshop of Wenzel Jamnitzer (?), Nürnberg, third quarter of the 16th century

161 Hans Mühlich, Munich, 1570

162

163

162 School of Paul Flindt, c.1600

163 Attributed to Hans Schebel,
Augsburg, 1571

164 Anonymous, South
German, 1571

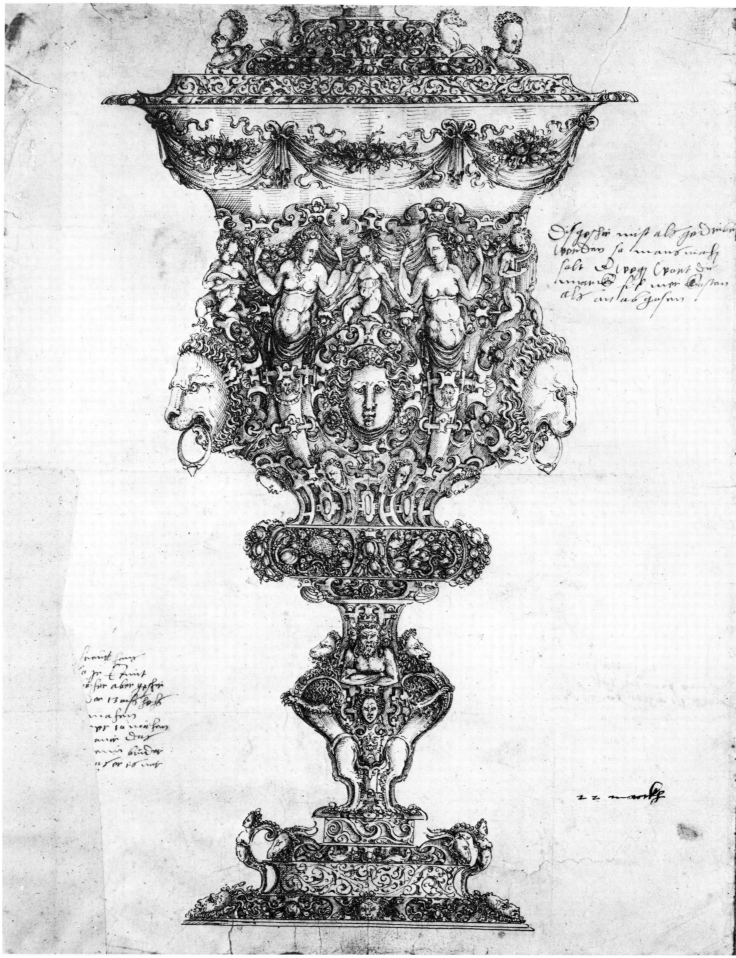

164

166

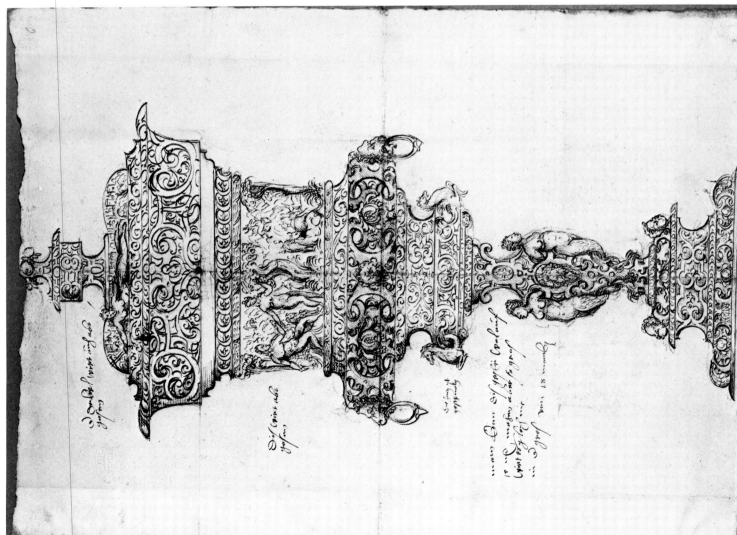

165

165 Attributed to Hans Schebel, Augsburg, 1571

166 Attributed to Christoph Lencker, Augsburg, c.1600

167 Attributed to Christoph Lencker, Augsburg, early 17th century

168

168, 169, 170, 171, 172 Christoph Jamnitzer, Nürnberg, 1610

173 Christoph Jamnitzer(?), Nürnberg, early 17th century

174, 175 Workshop of Christoph Jamnitzer, Nürnberg, early 17th century

169 172

173

174

175

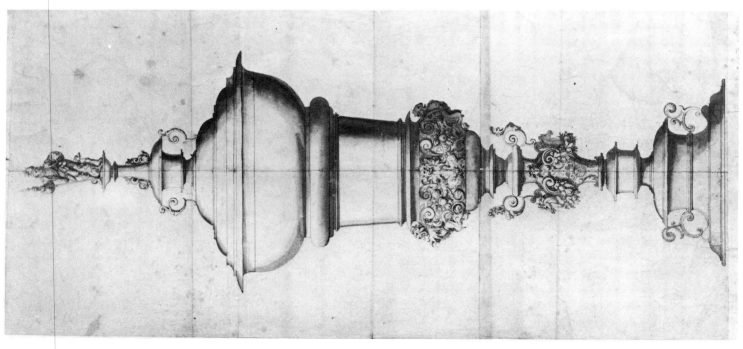

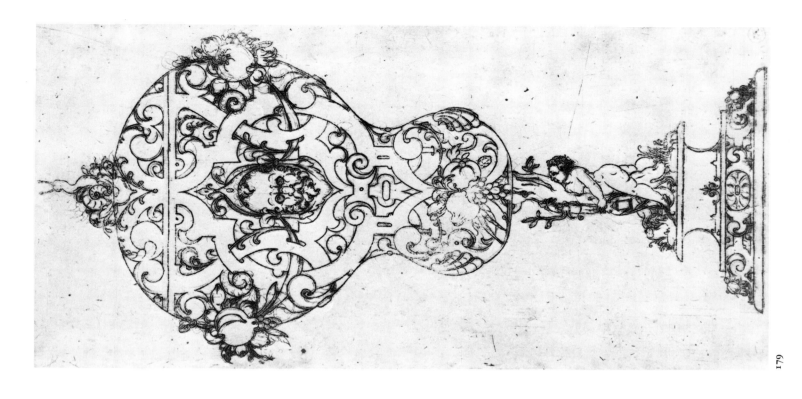

179

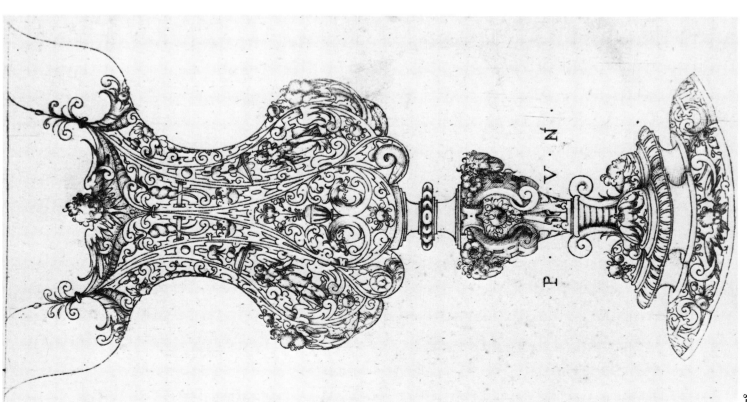

178

176 Attributed to Jost Amman,
Nürnberg, later 16th century

177 Georg Wechter, Nürnberg, 1579

178 Paul Flindt, Nürnberg, c.1600

179 Bernard Zan, Ansbach, 1581

180

181

182

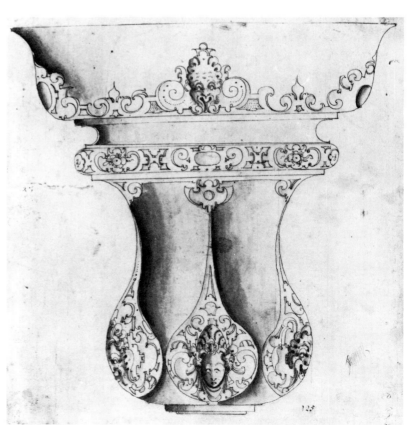

183

180 Paul Flindt, Nürnberg, c.1600

181 Bernard Zan, Ansbach, 1581

182 Paul Flindt, Nürnberg, c.1600

183 Attributed to Boas Ulrich, Augsburg, late 16th century

184 Attributed to Boas Ulrich, Augsburg, late 16th century

185 Workshop of Jakob Mores, Hamburg, early 17th century

184

185

186

187

188

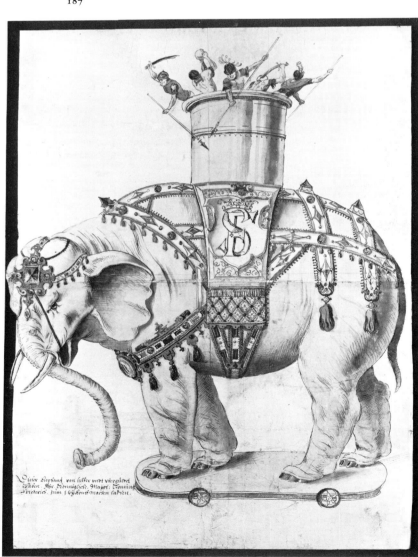

189

190

186, 187, 188, 189 Workshop of Jakob Mores, Hamburg, last quarter of the 16th century

190 After Jost Amman, Nürnberg, or Christoph Murer, Strassburg, late 16th century

191 Italo-Flemish master, perhaps Prague, early 17th century

192, 193 Italo-Flemish master, perhaps Prague, early 17th century

193

192

194

4   *Adrianus Collaert fecit.*   *Phis Galle excudit.*

195

194 Cornelis Bos, Antwerp, 1550

195 Adriaen Collaert, Antwerp,
late 16th century

196, 197, 198, 199 Cornelis Floris,
Antwerp, 1548

196

197

198

199

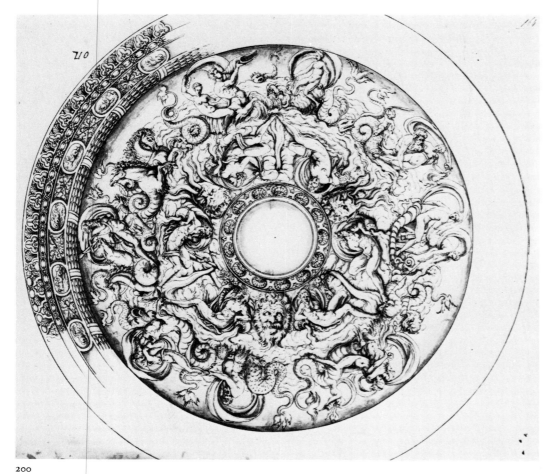

200

200, 201 Erasmus Hornick,
Antwerp (?), mid 16th century

202, 203 Erasmus Hornick,
Antwerp (?), mid 16th century

204 Anonymous, Flemish or
French, mid 16th century

201

202

203

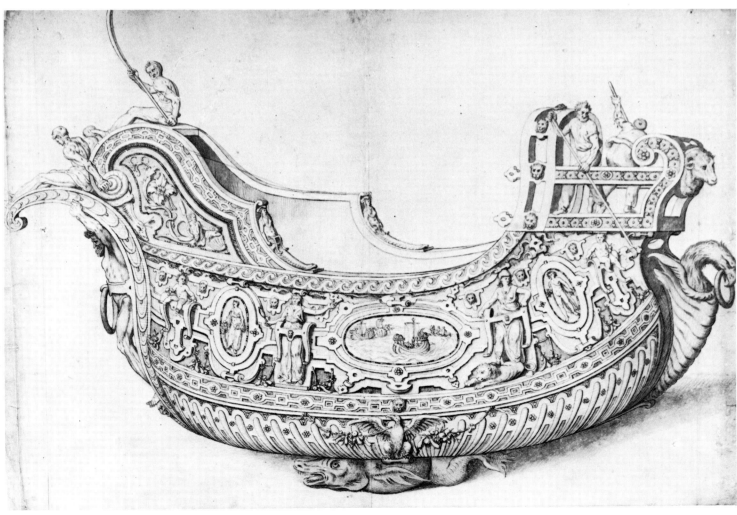

204

205

206

207

205, 206, 207 Erasmus Hornick, Antwerp (?), mid 16th century
208, 209, 210 Hans Vredeman de Vries, Antwerp, 1563

208

209

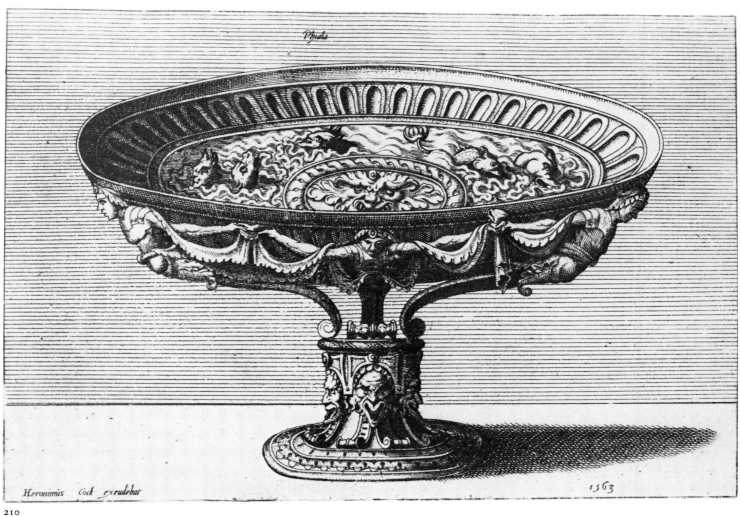

210

211

212

213

214

215

211, 212, 213, 214 Balthasar Sylvius, Antwerp, 1568

215 Johann Theodor de Bry, Frankfurt am Main, early 17th century

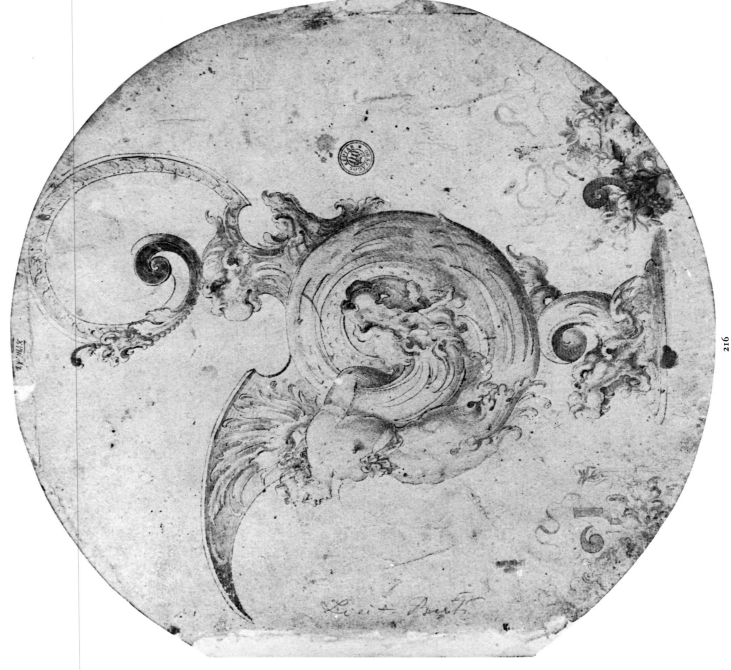

219

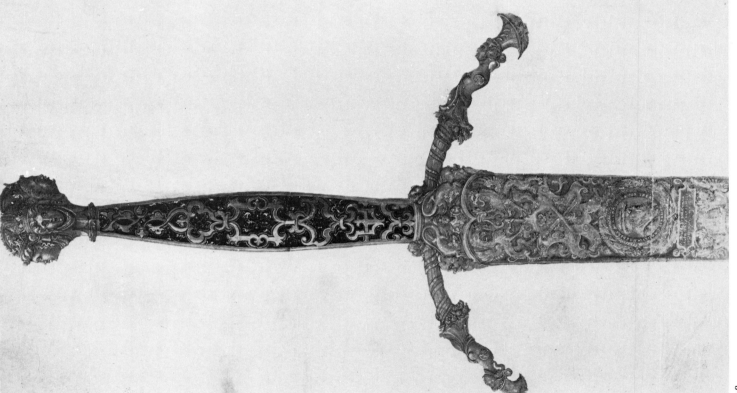

218

216 School of Cornelis Floris, Flemish, late 16th century

217 Adam van Vianen, Utrecht, first quarter of the 17th century

218, 219 Wenzel Jamnitzer, Nürnberg, 1544

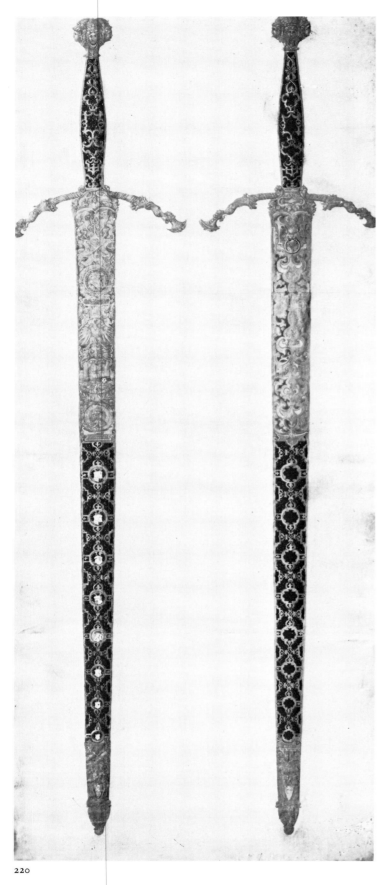

220

221

220 Wenzel Jamnitzer, Nürnberg, 1544

221 Hans Holbein, London, c.1540

222 Wenceslas Hollar, after an original by Hans Holbein, c.1540

223 Virgil Solis, Nürnberg, mid 16th century

224, 225 Erasmus Hornick, Nürnberg, third quarter of the 16th century

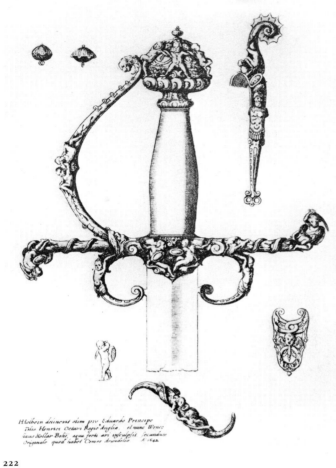

Holbein delineavit olim pro Eduardo Principe
filio Henrici Octavi Regis Angliæ, et nunc Wenceslaus Hollar Bohe: aqua forti æri insculpsit secundum
Originale quod habet Comes Arundeliæ A: 1644

222

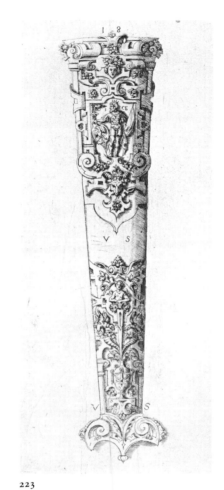

223

224

225

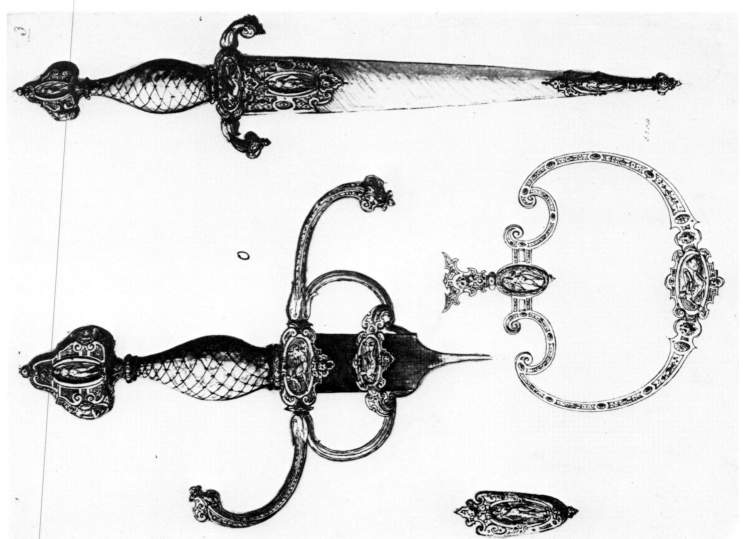

230

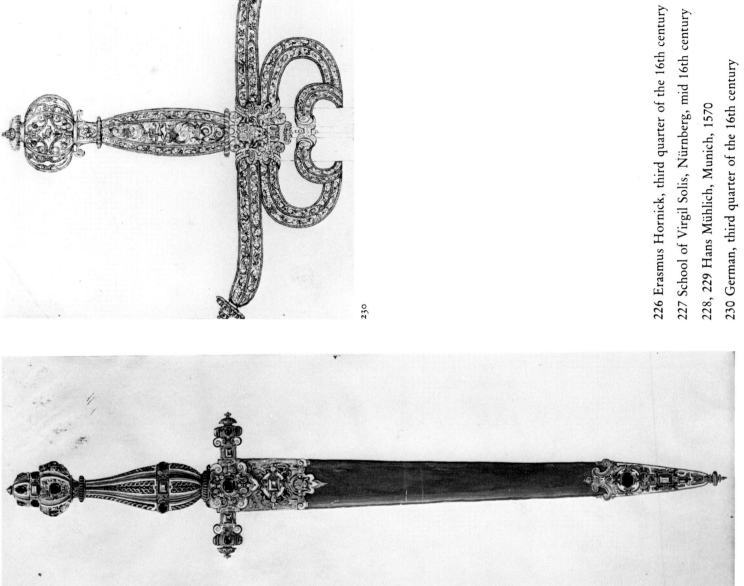

229

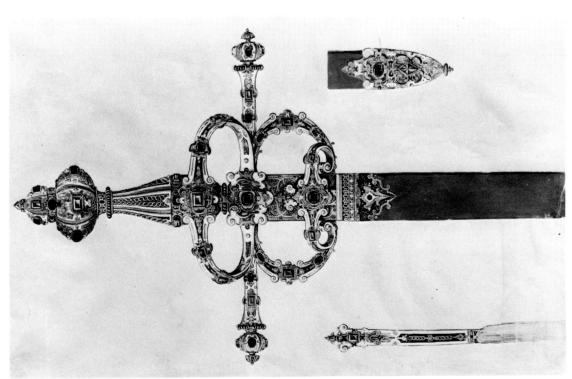

228

226 Erasmus Hornick, third quarter of the 16th century

227 School of Virgil Solis, Nürnberg, mid 16th century

228, 229 Hans Mühlich, Munich, 1570

230 German, third quarter of the 16th century

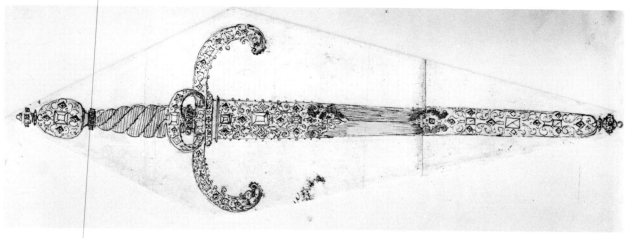

233

232

231, 232, 233 Workshop of Jakob Mores, Hamburg, second half of the 16th century

234 Rafel Ximenes, Barcelona, 1537

235 Antonio de Valdes, Barcelona, 1539

236 Cristofal Joan, Barcelona, 1538

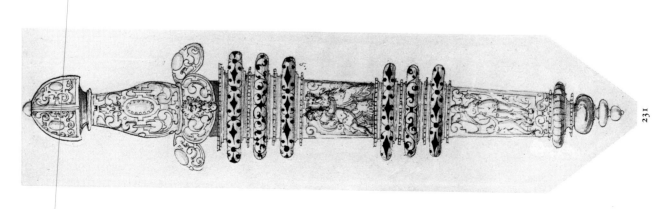

231

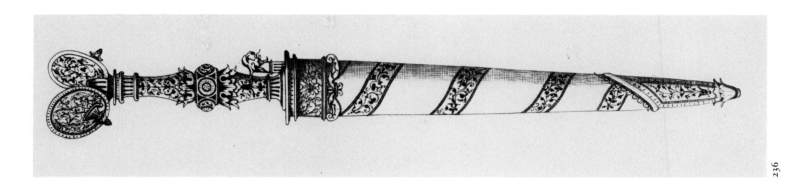

236

235

234

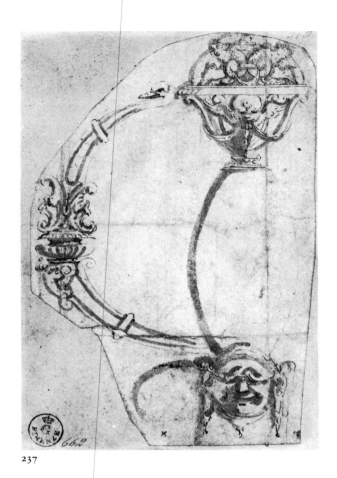

237

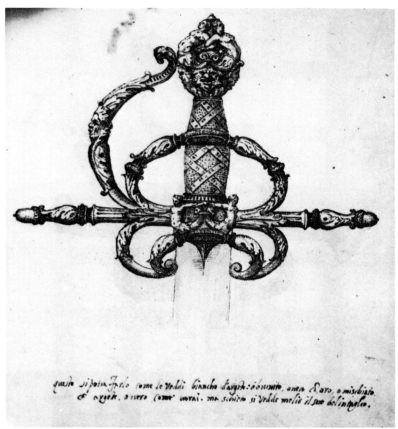

quanto si poin Ipilio come le veddi bianche d'argento conento, onca di oro, o misdiato
di argento, o uero come uorai, ma scricto si vedde molto il suo bel intaglio.

238

questo fatto a cerna Copia si poria parlo di macie ferro, er amado suo smalto
di oro, argento, o schieto o mischiato, capio come sta qui.

239

quasto similmente è molto intaglio sil fatto di aricio guido, maximamente
potrano smado suo a mario argento a bianco, come si vedde qui.

240

237 Florentine, third quarter of the 16th century

238, 239, 240 Filippo Orso, Mantua, mid 16th century

241 Italian, late 16th century

242 Pierre Woeriot, Lyon, 1555

241

242

243

244

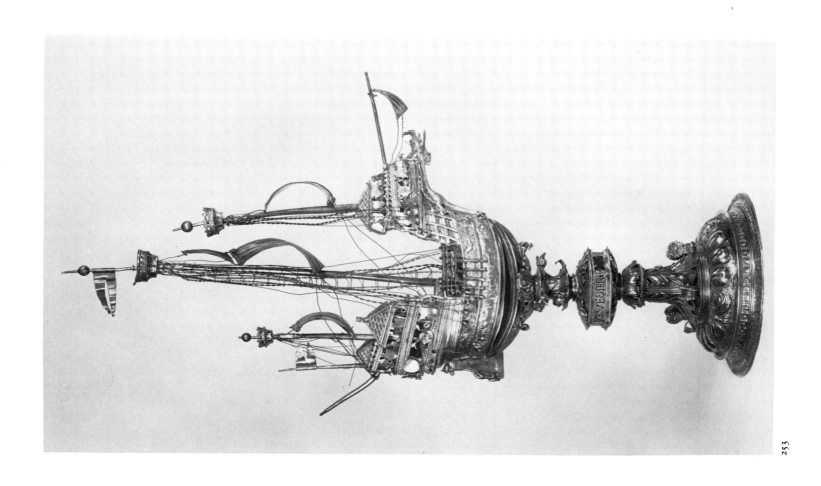

253

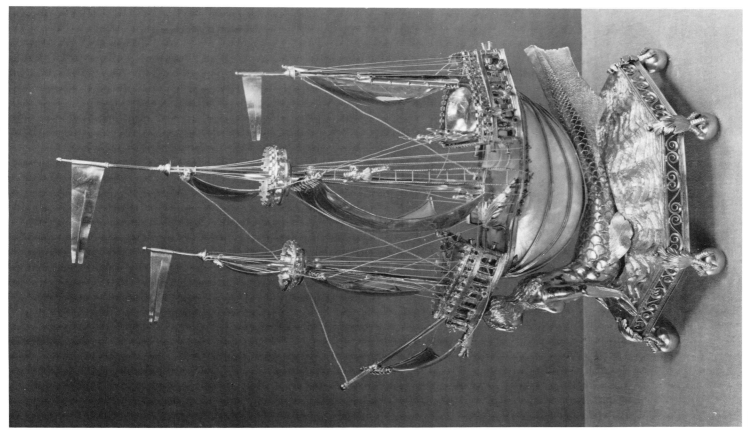

252

254

255

256

254 Paris Court goldsmith, mid 16th century

255 French (?), c.1530-40

256 French (?), c.1530-40

257 Spanish, second quarter of the 16th century

258 Spanish, c.1520-30

259 Cordoba (?), second quarter of the 16th century

257

258

259

260 Pedro Lamaison and Damian Forment, Saragossa, 1537-45

261 Detail of 260

262 Enrique de Arfe, Toledo, 1515-24. Detail of custodia

263 Antonio de Arfe, Santiago da Compostella, 1539-44. Detail of custodia

261

262

263

264

265

266

264 Juan de Herrera, Seville, mid 16th century

265 Lisbon, c.1540

266 Lisbon, 1537

267 Portuguese, mid 16th century

267

268

268 Portuguese, first quarter of the 16th century

269 Manner of Ludwig Krug, Nürnberg, c.1520-30

270 Attributed to Ludwig Krug, Nürnberg, c.1520

269   270

271

271 Attributed to Melchior Baier and Peter Flötner, Nürnberg, c.1530-40

272, 273 Details of 271

274 German or Hungarian, c.1540

272

273

274

276

275 Attributed to Melchior Baier,
Nürnberg, 1536

276 Detail of 275

277 Nürnberg (?), c.1540-50

277

278

279

280

278 Attributed to Melchior Baier, Nürnberg, c.1535-40

279 Augustin Ehinger, Ulm, c.1540

280 Nürnberg (?), 1552

281 Nürnberg, c.1530-40

282 Detail of 281

281

282

284

285

286

283 Strassburg, c.1530-40

284 Strassburg, c.1530-40

285 Strassburg, mid 16th century

286 Detail of 283

287

288

288 A

287 Jacob Stampfer, Zürich, 1545

288, 288a Nürnberg, c.1540

289 Antwerp (?), c.1540

290 Antwerp, 1530-31

289

290

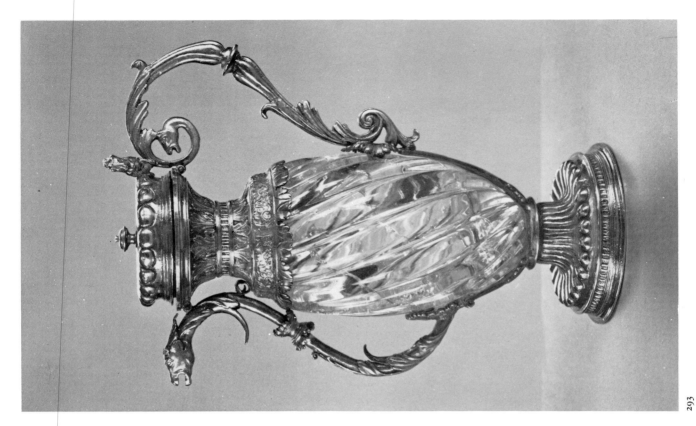

293

292

291

296

295

294

291 Brussels, 1540   294 London, 1525-6

292 London, 1542-3   295 London, 1529-30

293 English (?), c.1530-35   296 English (?), c.1535-40

298

297

297 Tazza: London, 1528-29, cover: London, 1532-33

298 London, 1530-31

299 London, 1551-52

300 London, 1543-44

300

299

301

302

303

304

305

306

301, 302 English (?), c.1530-40

303 London, 1545-46

304 Cup: London, 1555-56, cover: London, 1541-42

305 Antonio Gentile, Rome, 1581

306 Attributed to Antonio Gentile, Rome, end of the 16th century

307

308

310

309

307 Antonio Gentile, Rome, 1581

308, 309, 310 Rome, 1550

311

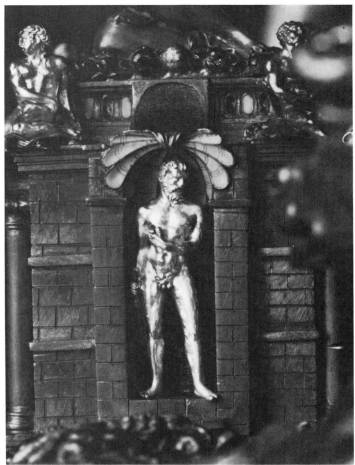

312

313

314

311, 312, 313 Benvenuto Cellini, Rome, Paris, 1540-43

314-320 Details of base of 313

315

316

317

318

319

320

321

321, 322 Giovanni dei Bernardi (rock-crystal plaques) 1543-44, Manno di Sebastiano Sbarri, Florence and Rome, 1547-61

322

323

323, 324 Details of 321

324

325

326

325 Manno di Sebastiano
Sbarri, Florence and Rome,
1547-61

326 Rock-crystal plaque,
Giovanni dei Bernardi, 1543-44

327 Manno di Sebastiano
Sbarri, Florence and Rome,
1547-61

327

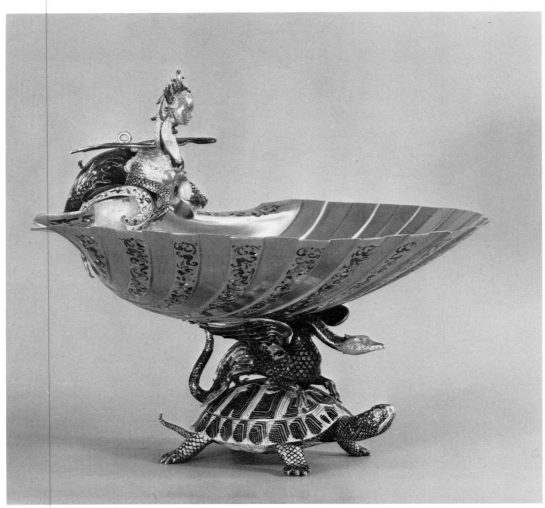

328

329

330

331

328 Florence (?), last quarter of the 16th century

329 Italian, last quarter of the 16th century

330 Florence, last quarter of the 16th century

331 Attributed to Giacomo Biliverti, Florence,
last quarter of the 16th century

332 Florence, late 16th century

333 Attributed to Giacomo Biliverti, late 16th century

332

333

335

334 Giacomo Biliverti, Florence, c.1580

335 Saracchi workshop (?), Milan, c.1650-70

337

338

336 Attributed to Annibale Fontana, Milan, about 1580

337 Milan (rock-crystal), Paris (mount), third quarter of the 16th century

338 Milan, late 16th century

339

340

339 Milan (rock-crystal), Paris (mount), second half of the 16th century

340 Edouard Vallet, Florence, 1618 (mounts)

341 Italo-Spanish, late 16th century

341

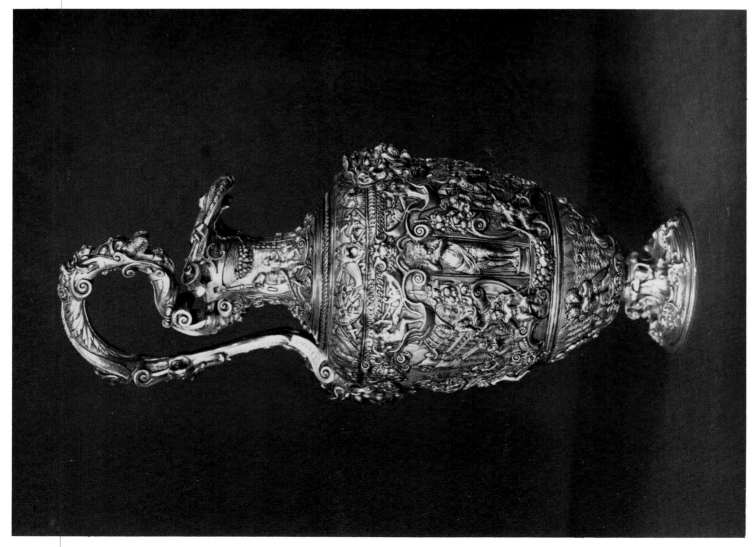

345

344

342 Antonio de Castro, Genoa, 1565

343 Details of 341 and 344

344 Italo-Spanish, late 16th century

345 Antonio de Castro, Genoa, 1565

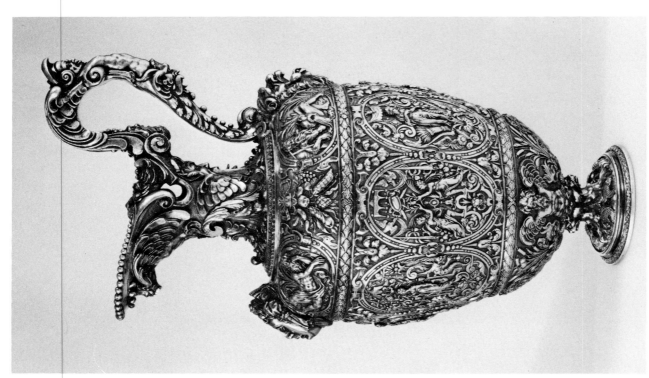

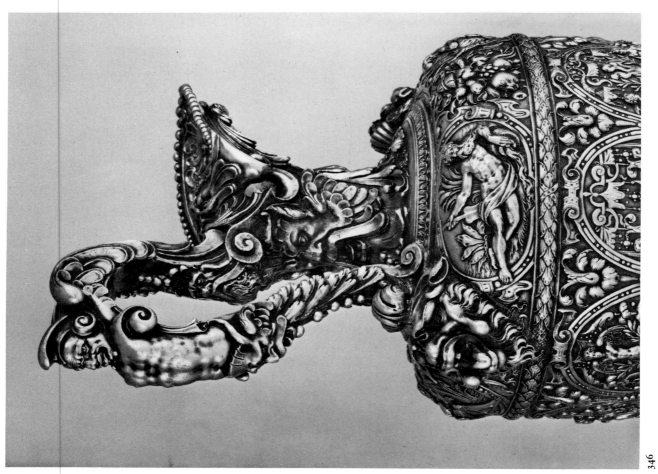

346

346, 347 Italian or French, late 16th century

348, 349 Italo-Iberian, third quarter of the 16th century

349

348

351

350

350 Florence (?), late 16th century

351 Italo-Iberian, third quarter of the 16th century

352, 353 Italian (?), early 17th century

353

352

355

354, 355 Venice, early 17th century
356, 357 Genoa, 1619

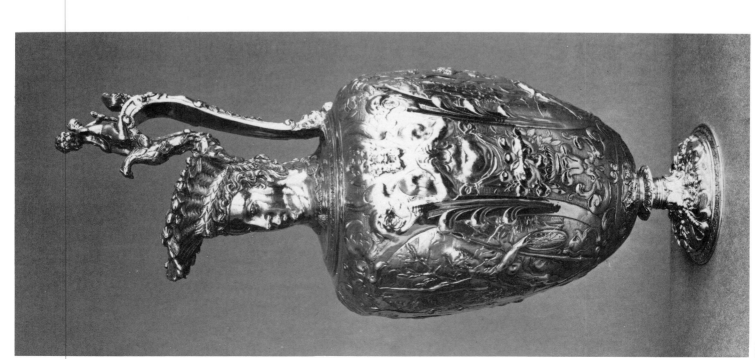

354

357

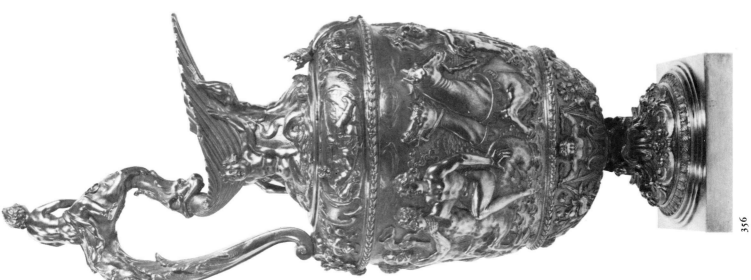

356

358

359

360

358 Genoa, 1621
359 Detail of 358
360 Detail of 356
361 Detail of 358
362 Genoa, 1619

361

362

363

363 Italian, c.1580

364 Detail of tazza bowl, Italian, c.1580

365 Italian, c.1580

366 Italian (?), second half of the 16th century

364

365

366

367

368

369

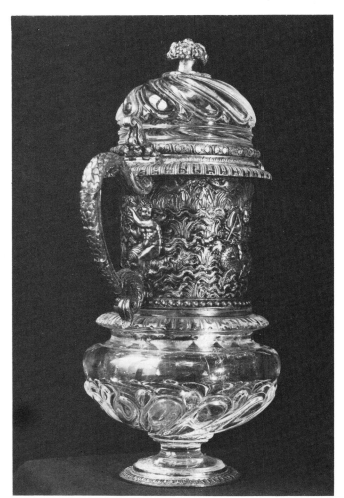

370

371

372

373

367, 368 Paris (?), mid 16th century

369 French, mid 16th century

370 French, third quarter of the 16th century

371 French, third quarter of the 16th century

372 Paris, 1560-70

373 Milan (rock-crystal). Paris (cover), mid 16th century

374 Paris, third quarter of the 16th century

375 French Provincial, third quarter of the 16th century

374

375

376

377

376 Paris, 1560-61

377 French, third quarter of the 16th century

378 Paris, 1586-87

379 Detail of 378

378

379

380

381

382

380, 381, 382 French or Flemish,
second half of the 16th century

383 Paris (?), c.1570-80

384 Detail of 383

383

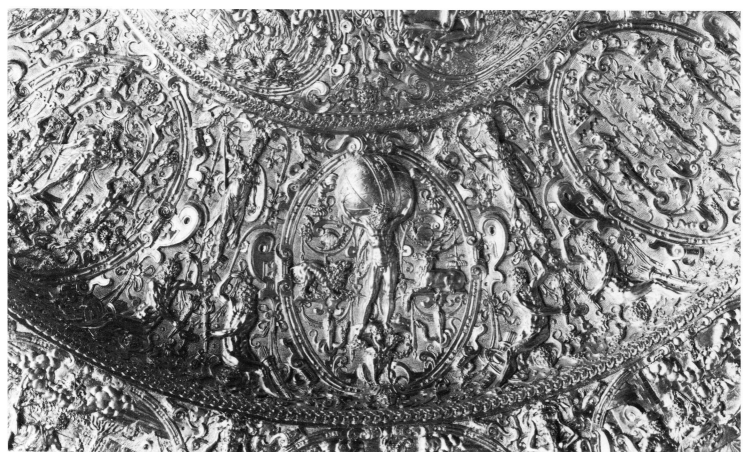

384

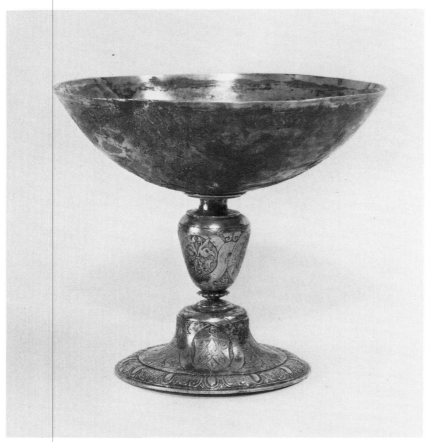

385

385 Orleans, third quarter of the 16th century

386 Paris, 1560-61

387 Paris (?), third quarter of the 16th century

388 French or Flemish, third quarter of the 16th century

389 Detail of 388

386

387

388

389

390

391

392

393

394

395

390, 391 Paris, 1583-84

392 Paris, 1606-7

393 Detail of 392

394, 395 Paris, late 16th century

396

397

398

399

400

401

403

402

402 Barcelona, c.1565

403 Spanish, third quarter of the 16th century

404 Seville, last quarter of the 16th century

405 Barcelona (?), mid 16th century

405

404

406

407

408

409

410

412

411

411 Spanish, third quarter of the 16th century

412 Juan de Arfe, Valladolid, 1571

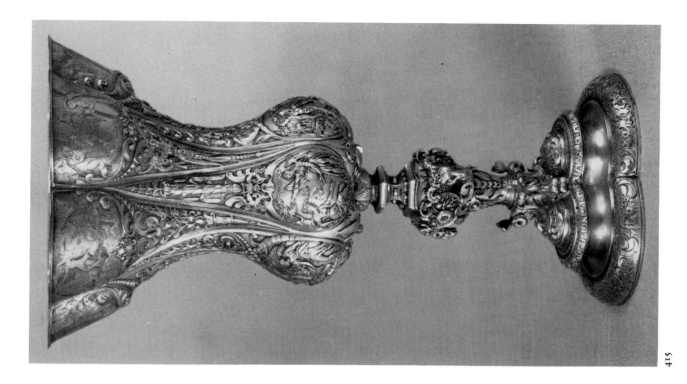

413 Attributed to Martin Rehlein, Nürnberg, 1572-3

414 Christoph Ritter II, Nürnberg, c.1600

415 Nürnberg, last quarter of the 16th century

415

414

413

416 Detail of 417

417 Wenzel Jamnitzer, Nürnberg, 1547-48

418 Detail of 417

417

418

419

420

421

422

419, 420 Details of 417

421 Wenzel Jamnitzer, Nürnberg, third quarter of the 16th century

422 Wenzel Jamnitzer, Nürnberg, c.1560

423 Wenzel Jamnitzer, Nürnberg, 1558

423

424 Detail of 426

425 Wenzel Jamnitzer, Nürnberg, 1564

426 Wenzel Jamnitzer, Nürnberg, c.1570

427 Wenzel Jamnitzer, Nürnberg, c.1560

425

424

427

426

428

429

430

431

432

433

434 435

428 Wenzel Jamnitzer and Nikolaus Schmidt, Nürnberg, c.1570-80

429, 430, 431, 432 Wenzel Jamnitzer, patterns of ornament, Nürnberg, third quarter of the 16th century

433, 434, 435 Wenzel Jamnitzer, patterns of ornament, Nürnberg, third quarter of the 16th century

436 Christoph Lindenberger, Nürnberg, c.1570

437 Wenzel Jamnitzer, Nürnberg, c.1570

436

437

438

439

438 Hans Jamnitzer, Nürnberg, 1572

439 Attributed to Hans Jamnitzer, Nürnberg, c.1570

440 Hans Jamnitzer, Nürnberg, 1570

441 Jakob Schenauer, Augsburg, c.1570

440

441

442

443

444

442, 444 Jost Heberle, Nürnberg, last quarter of the 16th century

443 Side view of 441

445, 446 Jost Heberle, Nürnberg, last quarter of the 16th century

447 Hans Jamnitzer, Nürnberg, third quarter of the 16th century

445

446

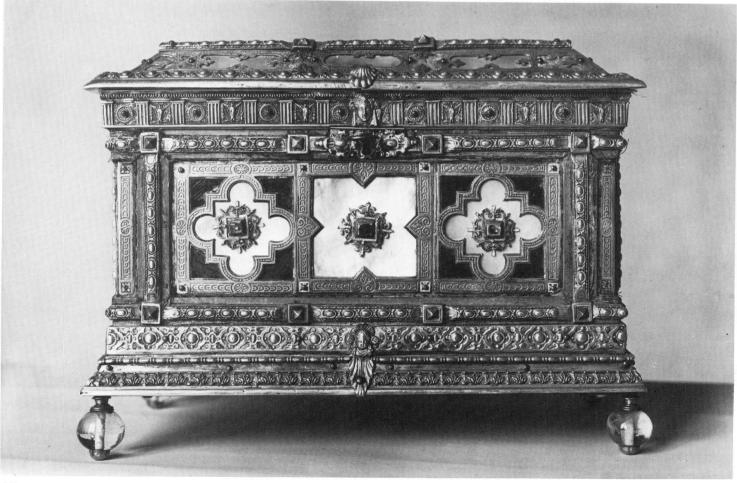

447

448

449

450

448, 449 Hans and Elias Lencker,
Nürnberg, c.1560

450, 451 Details of 449

451

452

452 Attributed to Abraham Lotter the Elder, Augsburg, c.1573-74

453 Attributed to Abraham Lotter, Augsburg, c.1570-80

454 Detail of 455

453

454

455

456

455 Hans Reimer, Munich, 1562

456 Attributed to Ulrich Eberl, Augsburg, late 16th century

457

458

457 Augsburg (?), last quarter of the 16th century

458 Augsburg, late 16th century

459

460

461

459, 460, 461 Augsburg, c.1570-80

462 Attributed to Hans Schekel,
Augsburg, c.1570

463 Augsburg, last quarter of the
16th century

464 Augsburg, late 16th century

462

463

464

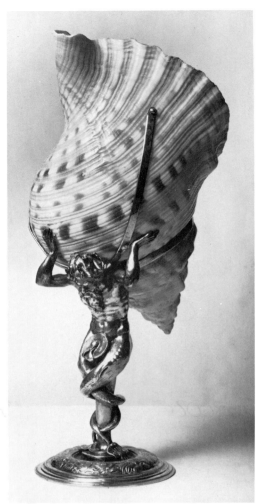

465 Augsburg, c.1560

466, 467 Elias or Cornelius Grosz, Augsburg, late 16th century

468, 469, 470 Elias or Cornelius Grosz, Augsburg, c.1560-80

465

466

467

468

469

470

471

472

471 Augsburg, late 16th century

472 David Altenstetter (?), Augsburg, late 16th century

473 Nikolaus Schmidt, Nürnberg, late 16th century

473

475

474, 475 Jonas Silber, Nürnberg, 1589

476, 477 Nikolaus Schmidt, Nürnberg, late 16th century

474

477

476

478

479

478 Nikolaus Schmidt, Nürnberg, late 16th century

479 Hans Petzoldt, Nürnberg, late 16th century

480

481

480 Hans Petzoldt, Nürnberg, c.1610
481 Hans Petzoldt, Nürnberg, dated 1594

482

483

482 Hans Petzoldt, Nürnberg, end of the 16th century

483 Jakob Fröhlich, Nürnberg, last quarter of the 16th century

484

485

486

484 Hans Petzoldt, Nürnberg, 1626

485 Detail of 484

486 Jakob Fröhlich, Nürnberg, last quarter of the 16th century

487

488

489

490

487 Hans Beutmüller, Nürnberg, early 16th century

488 Augsburg, c.1600

489 Elias Lencker, Nürnberg, 1575

490 Christoph Epfenhauser, Augsburg, c.1590

491 Hans and Elias Lencker,
Nürnberg, c.1585

492 Jörg Ruel, Nürnberg,
late 16th century

493 Jeremias Michael,
Augsburg, first quarter of the
17th century

493

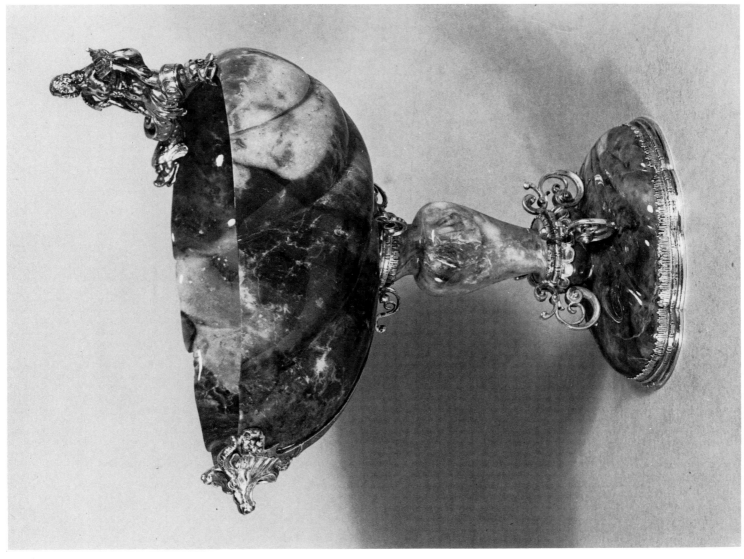

492

495

494

494 Ulrich Schönmacher, Augsburg, third quarter of the 16th century

495 Augsburg, before 1583

496 Circle of Paul van Vianen, Munich or Prague, c.1600

497 Reverse of 496

499

498

498 Christoph Lencker, Augsburg, early 17th century

499 Detail of 498

500 Augsburg or Munich, c.1590

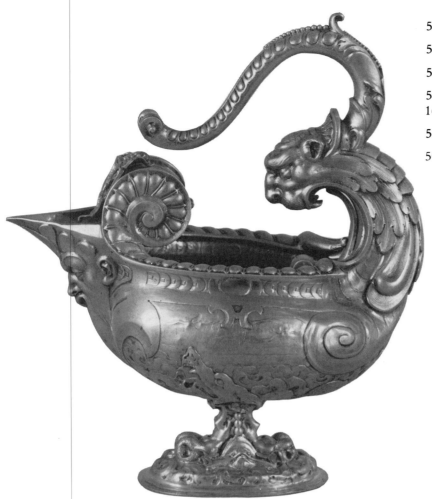

501 Christoph Lencker, Augsburg, early 17th century

502 Johannes Lencker, Augsburg, c.1625-30

503 Augsburg, late 16th century

504 Leonhard Umbach (?), Augsburg, end of the 16th century

505 David Lauer, Nürnberg, early 17th century

506 Christoph Ritter, Nürnberg, late 16th century

501

502

503

504

505

506

510

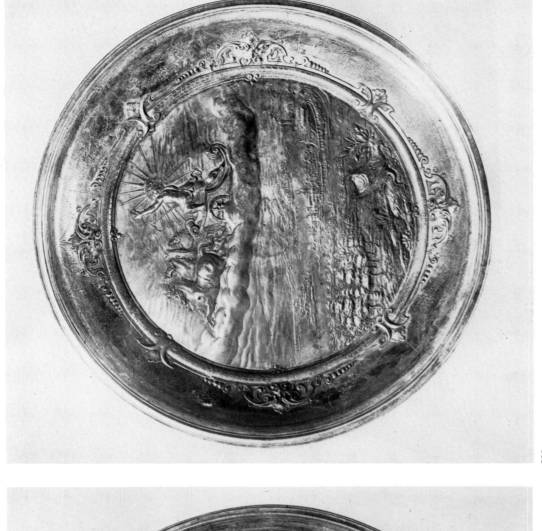

509

507 Johannes Lencker, Augsburg, early 17th century

508 Matthias Wallbaum, Augsburg, c.1600

509, 510 Christoph Jamnitzer, Nürnberg, c.1600

511 Christoph Jamnitzer, Nürnberg, c.1600

512, 513, 514 Christoph Jamnitzer,
Nürnberg, c.1600

514

513

512

516

515

518

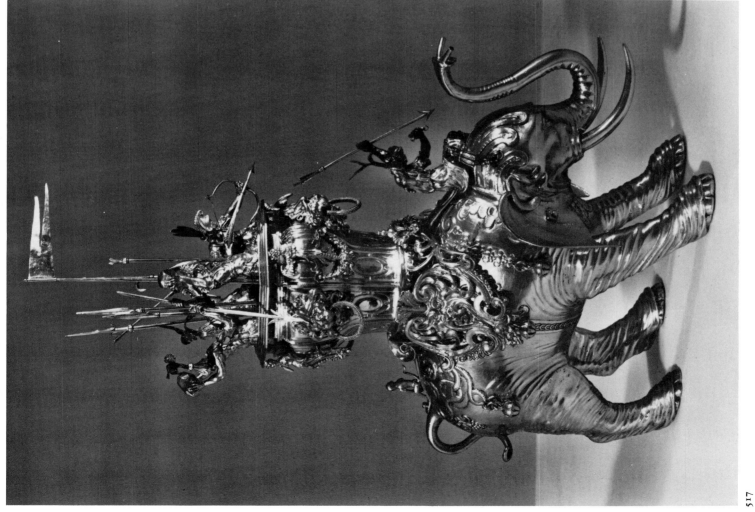

517

519

520

519

521

522

519 Nürnberg, 1575, ewer and detail of basin *en suite*

520 Joachim Bintzege (?), Nürnberg, 1581

521 Heinrich Jonas, Nürnberg, late 16th century

522 Thomas Stoer the Elder, Nürnberg, 1611

523

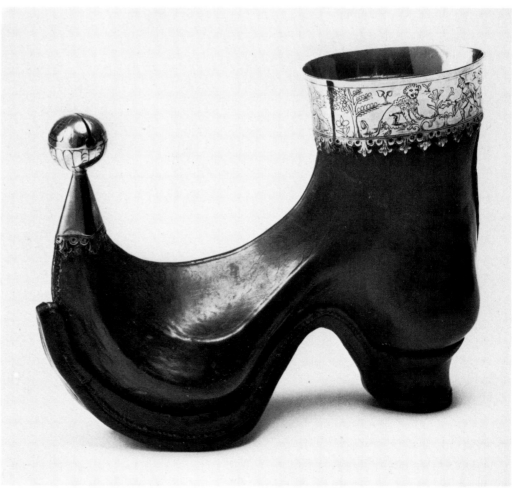

524

525 Meinrad Bauch the Elder, Nürnberg, early 17th century

526 Dirich Utermarke, Hamburg, c.1600

528

527 Luleff Meyer and Dirich Utermarke,
Lüneburg, c.1580-90

528, 529 Details of 527

530 Detail of 526

529

530

531, 532, 533 Dirich Utermarke, Hamburg, 1622

534 Lübeck, early 17th century

535, 536 Hamburg, 1588

534

535

536

537

538

539

540

541

542

537, 538, 539 Anton Eisenhoit, Warburg, c.1600

540 Mathäus Hofherr, Ulm, third quarter of the 16th century

541, Thomas von Hattingen, Cologne, c.1580

542 Linhardt Bauer, Strassburg, c.1560

545

544

543

547

546

543 German 1590

544 Detail of 545

545 George Kobenhaupt, Strassburg, c.1550-60

546, 547 Details of 545

548

549

550

551

548 Strassburg, early 17th century

549 Dibolt Krug, Strassburg, before 1567

550 G. Haas, Frankfurt am Main, 1592

551 Freiburg im Breisgau, early 17th century

552

553

552 Freiburg im Breisgau, first quarter of the 17th century

553 Sitten (?), 1562

554 Freiburg im Breisgau, first quarter of the 17th century

555 Abraham Gessner, Zürich, c.1580

554

555

556

557

556 Abraham Gessner, Zürich, end of the 16th century

557 Peter Rohr, Bern, 1558

558 Daniel Kellerthaler, Dresden, 1629

559 Hieronymus Orth, Breslau, c.1560-70

558

559

561

562

563

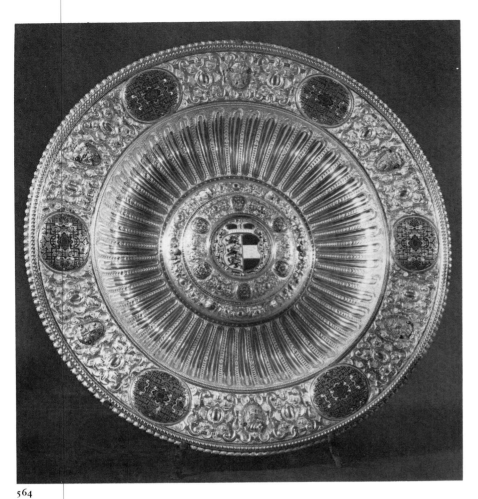

564

565

566

567

568

569

570

571 Hans Karl, Prague, c.1612

572 Hans Karl, Prague, early 17th century

573 South German or Saxon (manner of Elias Geyer), early 17th century

574 Prague Court Workshop, c.1600

571

572

573

574

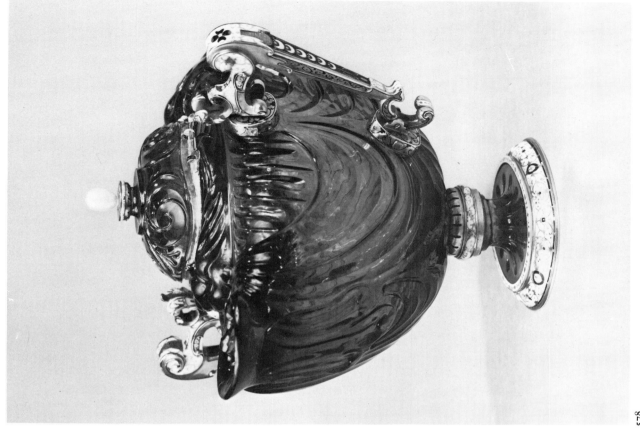

578

577

577 Prague Court Workshop (?), early 17th century
578 Dionysio Miseroni, Prague, first quarter of the 17th century

575 Nürnberg (?), early 17th century
576 Prague Court Workshops (?), early 17th century

579

580

581

582

579 Anton Schweinberger, Prague, c.1603

580 Dionysio Miseroni (jasper vase), and Paul van Vianen (mounts), Prague 1608

581 Sebastian Aurifaber, Leutschau, late 16th century

582 John Lippai, Kassa, 1578

583 Prague, last quarter of the 16th century

584 Martin Burckhardt, Eger, early 17th century

585, 586 Polish Court Goldsmith (?), early 17th century

583

584

585

586

587

588

587, 588 Antwerp, 1559

589 Detail of 588

590 Antwerp, 1544-45

591 Joris Weyer, Antwerp, 1546-47

592 Detail of 591

589

590

591

592

593

594

595

593 Reinier van Jaersvelt, Antwerp, 1546-47

594 Detail of 595

595 Antwerp, mid 16th century

596 Antwerp, 1558-59

597

598

599

601

602

603

604

601 Detail of pl. XXIII

602 Detail of 597

603, 604 Details of 600

605 Antwerp, c.1560

606 Hans de Hanns or Johan van Sicken, Antwerp, 1563-64

605

606

607

608

609

610

611

612

613

607 Detail of 606

608 Attributed to Antwerp, c.1560

609 Antwerp, c.1560-70

610 Antwerp, third quarter of the 16th century

611 Antwerp, 1557-58

612 Antwerp, 1582-83

613 A. de Groet, s'Hertogenbosch, 1561

614

615

614 Amsterdam, 1546 or 1569

615 Bouwvens van der Houven, The Hague, 1603

616 Detail of 612

617 Dordrecht, 1576

618 Jan Jacobz van Royesteyn, Utrecht, 1596

619 Rotterdam, 1590

616

617

618

619

620, 621 London, 1617, attributed to a Dutch immigrant goldsmith

622, 623 Aelbert Verhaer, the embossing attributed to Ernst Jansz van Vianen, Utrecht, 1602

620

621

622

623

624

624, 625 Adam van Vianen,
Utrecht, 1612

626, 627 Paul van Vianen, Prague,
1607

625

626

627

628

629

630

628 Adam van Vianen, Utrecht, 1614

629 Detail of 628

630 Paul van Vianen, Prague, 1613

631, 632 Paul van Vianen, Prague, 1613 (*en suite* with 630)

631

632

633

633 Adam van Vianen, Utrecht, 1622

634 Detail of 633

635 Detail of basin in 636

636 Utrecht, early 17th century

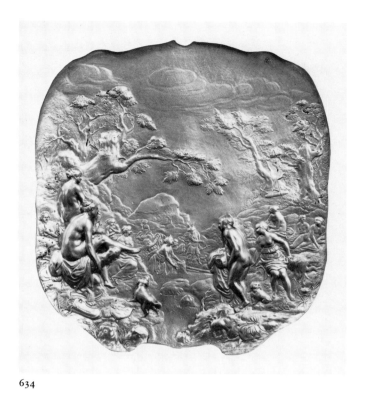

634

635

636

637

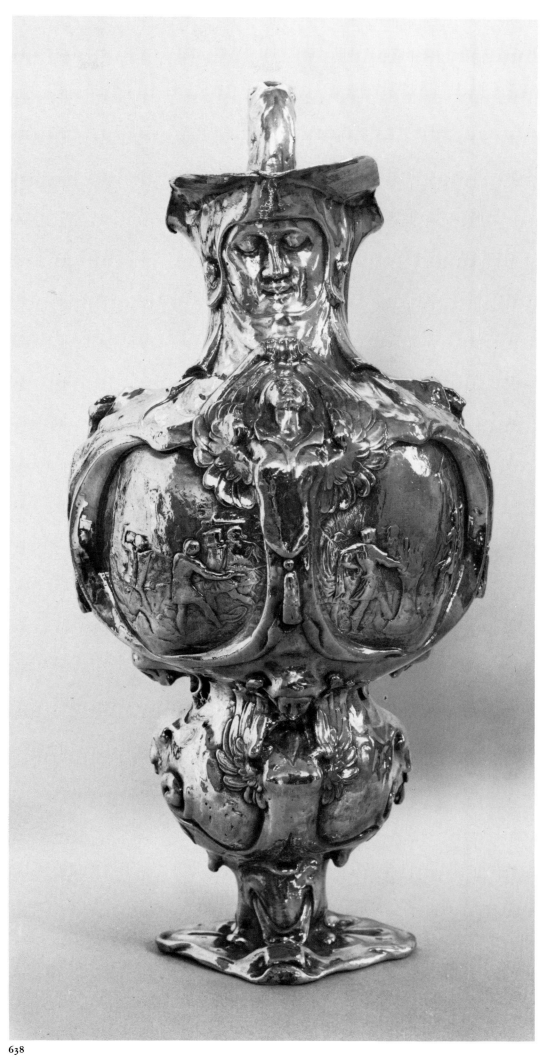

637 Detail of ewer in 636

638 Adam van Vianen, Utrecht,
c.1620

638

639

640

641

639 Paul van Vianen, Munich, c.1600

640 Johann Theodor de Bry, Frankfurt
am Main, early 17th century

641 Arent van Bolten, Zwolle, first
quarter of the 17th century

642, 643 Attributed to Theodor de Bry,
Frankfurt am Main, late 16th century

642

643

644

644 Hans Bol, Amsterdam, c.1590

645, 646, 647 English Court Goldsmith,
design attributed to Hans Holbein, c.1540

648 Detail from painting by Willem Kalf, 1678

649 London, 1546-47

650 London, 1563-64

651 London, 1567-68

645

646

647

648

649

650

651

652

653

652 London, 1554-55

653 London, 1565-66

654

655

654 London, 1579-80

655 London, 1578-79

656

657

656 London, 1585-86

657 London, 1592-93

658

659

658 London, 1567-68

659 London, 1584-85

660 London, 1573-74

660

661 London, 1585-86

662 London (?), 1610

663 London, 1611-12

664 F. Terry, London, 1611-12

665 London, 1616-17

666, 667 Details of 665

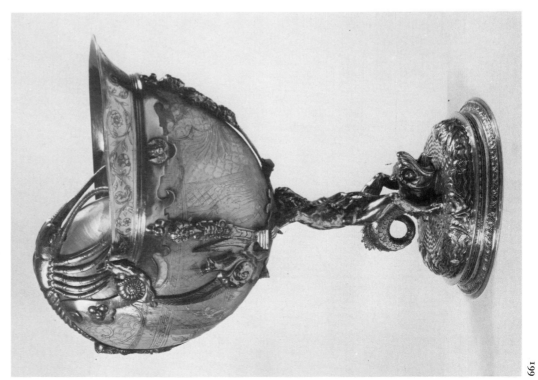

670

669

668

668 London, 1549-50

669 London, 1562-63

670 London, 1577-78

673

672

671 London, 1576-77

672 London, 1569-70

673 London, 1592-93

671

674

675

676

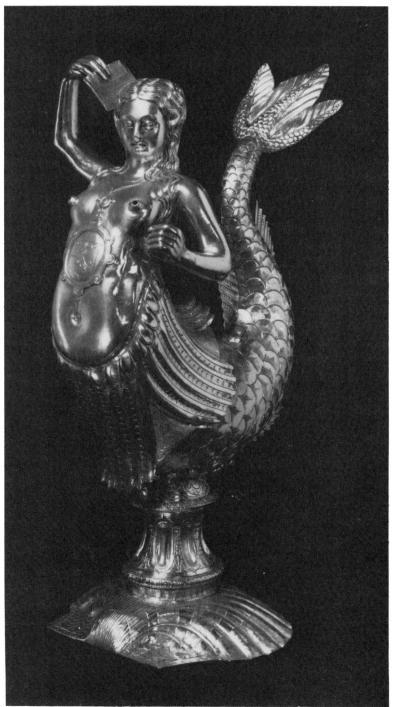

677

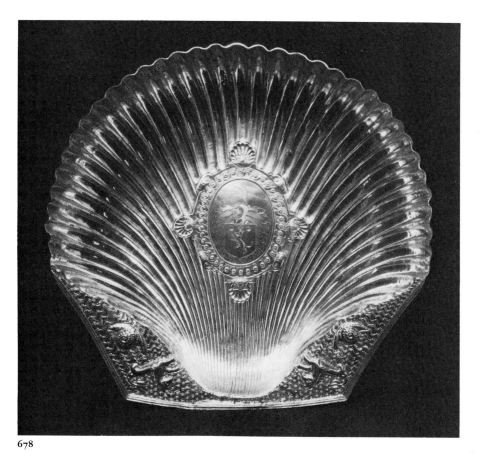

678

679

674 English, c.1600

675 London, 1607-08

676 London, 1614-15

677 London, 1610-11 (*en suite* with 678)

678 London, 1610-11

679 London, 1573-74

680 London, 1570-71

681 London, 1567-68 (*en suite* with 682)

680

681

682

683

682 Antwerp, 1543-44

683 London, 1579-80 (*en suite* with 684)

684 London, 1579-80 (*en suite* with 683)

685, 686 London, 1586-87

684

685

686

687 London, 1583-84

688 The Paston Treasure, Dutch School, mid 17th century

689 London, c.1600

690 English or Dutch, first half of the 17th century

687

688

689

690

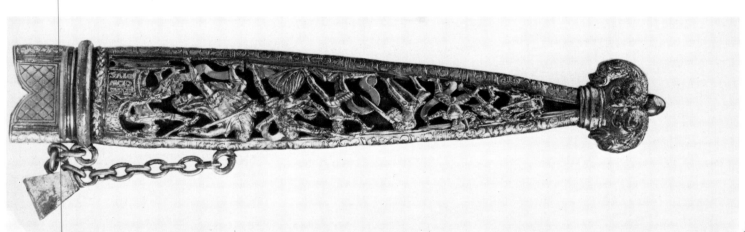

694

693

692

691

691 Lead model in the manner of Holbein, Swiss, mid 16th century

692 German, mid 16th century

693 Swiss or South German, mid 16th century

694 Lead models, Nürnberg (?), third quarter of the 16th century

695, 697 South German, second half of the 16th century

696, 698 South German, third quarter of the 16th century

698

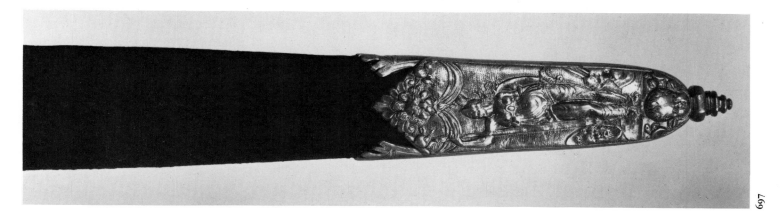

697

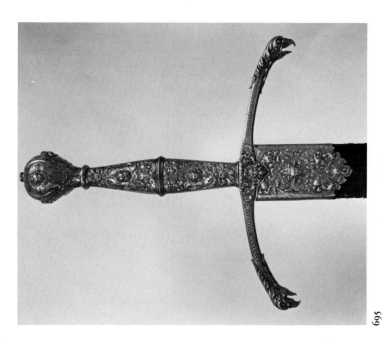

695

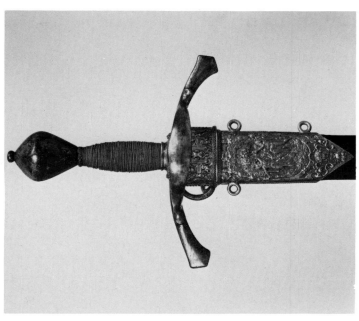

696

699

700

701

702

699 Munich Court Goldsmith, c.1560

700 Spanish goldsmith at the Habsburg Court, c.1560

701 Spanish goldsmith at the Habsburg Court, c.1570

702 Spanish (?), 1571

703

704

705

706

703 Pery Juan Pockh, Vienna, 1575

704 French, c.1560-70

705 Spanish goldsmith at the Habsburg Court, c.1570

706 Israel Schuech, Dresden, 1606

707

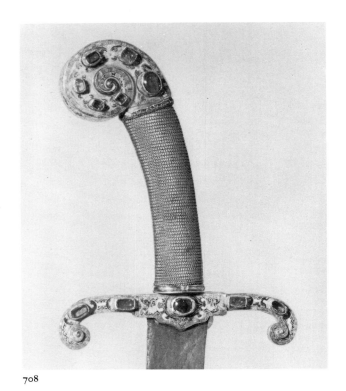

708

707 Italian (?), third quarter of the 16th century

708 Gilles Coyet, Stockholm, c.1575-80

709 Italian (?), mid 16th century

710 Pierre Redon, Paris Royal Armoury, c.1570

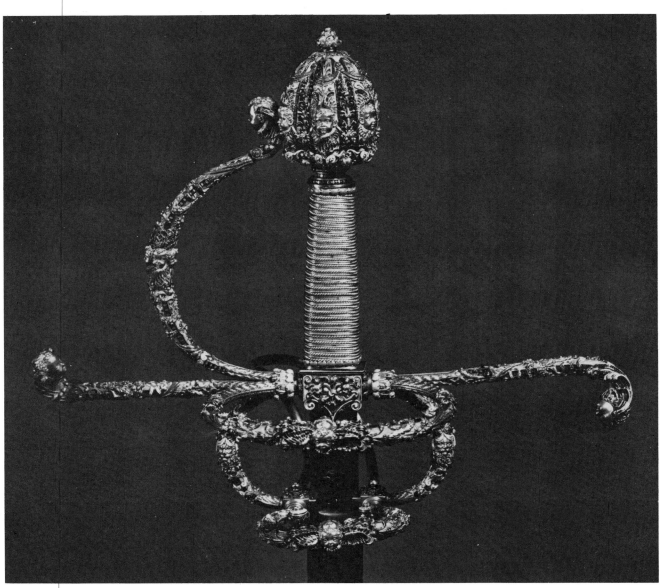

709

710

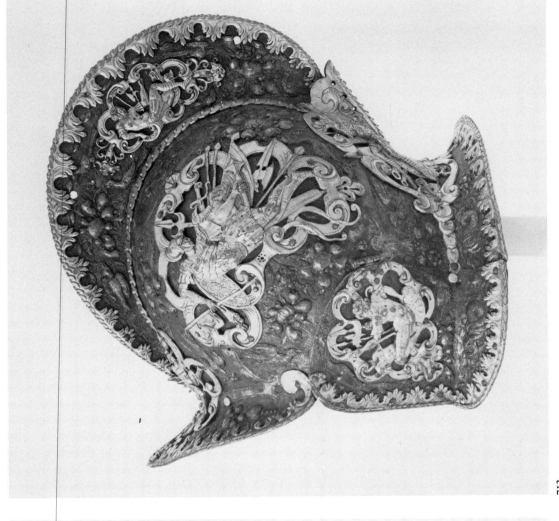

711 Augsburg, 1589

712 Augsburg, last quarter of the 16th century

713, 714 Benvenuto Cellini, Paris, 1540-45

711

712

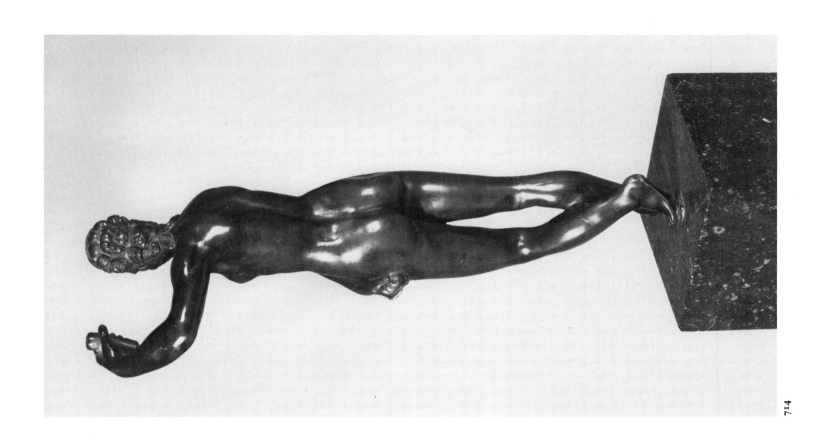

714

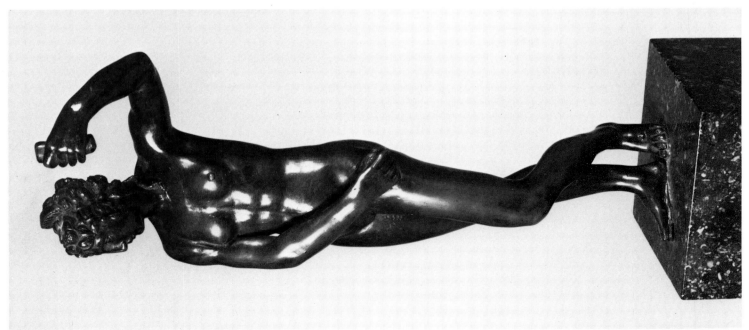

713

715

716

715 Italian, 1541

716 Bronze, attributed to Tiziano Aspetti, Venice, third quarter of the 16th century

717 Bronze, Venice, third quarter of the 16th century

718 Majolica, Urbino, mid 16th century

717

718

719

720

719 Italian, early 17th century

720 Spanish, third quarter of the 16th century

721

722

723

721 Bronze, North Italian, second half of the 16th century

722 Detail of 719

723 Bronze, Venetian (?), last quarter of the 16th century

724

725

726

727

724 South German, third quarter of the 16th century

725 Attributed to Jörg Sigman or Jakob Knoll, Augsburg, 1556

726 Jamnitzer Workshop (?), Nürnberg, last quarter of the 16th century

727 Paul van Vianen, Munich, c.1600

728 François Briot, French, late 16th century

729 Detail of 724

728

729

730

731

732

733

734

735

730 Wood model, attributed to
Matthias Zündt, Nürnberg,
c.1560-70

731 Wood model, Wenzel
Jamnitzer, Nürnberg, before 1549

732, 734 Wood models, after
Hans Kels, South German, second
half of the 16th century

733 Wood model, South German,
c.1530-50

735 Detail of 733

736, Pewter, François Briot,
Montbéliard, last quarter of the
16th century

736

737

737 Damascened iron, Milan, last quarter of the 16th century

738

738, 739 Details of 737

739

Select Bibliography

THIS bibliography is confined to basic works and to books and articles that are referred to more than once in the text. In order to avoid unnecessary repetition of titles, those listed in this bibliography are referred to in the notes by the author's name alone. Where more than one work by the same author is the subject of repeated reference, the works in question are numbered, I, II, III, etc.

D. Alcouffe, 'Le Collezioni di Gemme del XVI Secolo', *Arte Illustrata*, 59, 1975, p.266.

B. P. Baader, *Der Bayerische Renaissancehof Herzog Wilhelms V*, Leipzig, 1943.

J. Babelon, *Jacopo da Trezzo*, Paris, 1922.

L. Becherucci, *Manieristi Toscani*, Bergamo, 1944.

E. Berckenhagen, *Die Französischen Zeichnungen der Kunstbibliothek, Berlin*, Berlin, 1970.

Berlin Ornamentstich Katalog, *Katalog der Ornamentstichsammlung der Staatl. Kunstbibliothek*, Berlin, 1936-9.

R. Berliner, *Ornamentale Vorlage-Blaetter*, 3 Vols., Leipzig, 1926.

L. Berti, *Il Principe dello Studiolo*, Florence, 1967.

H. Bethe, *Die Kunst am Hofe der pommerschen Herzöge*, Berlin, 1937.

E. Bock. *Die Zeichnungen in der Universitätsbibliothek, Erlangen*, Frankfurt am Main, 1929.

E. Böhm, *Hans Petzoldt*, Munich, 1939.

C. Bosson, 'Les Dagues Suisses' Vol. XII, *Geneva*, Geneva, 1964.

J. Bousquet, *La Peinture Manieriste*, Neuchâtel, 1964.

E. W. Braun, *Die Silberkammer eines Reichsfürsten*, Leipzig, 1923.

G. Briganti, *Italian Mannerism*, London, 1962.

H. Brunner, *Schatzkammer der Residenz München, 3. Auflage, 1970.*

E. Camesasca, *Tutta l'opera del Cellini*, Milan, 1962.

B. Cellini,
Cellini I, *Vita*, ed. E. Camesasca, Milan, 1954.
Cellini II, *Trattato dell'Oreficeria*, ed. Rusconi e Valeri, Rome, 1901.
Cellini III, *Documenti*, Vol. II of *Vita* ed. Rusconi e Valeri, Rome, 1901.

A. J. Collins, *Jewels and Plate of Queen Elizabeth I*, London, 1955.

R. H. Cust, *Life of Benvenuto Cellini*, (revised edition), London, 1935.

C. Davilier, *Recherches sur l'Orfèvrerie en Espagne*, Paris, 1879.

H. Demiani, *François Briot, Caspar Enderlein*, Leipzig, 1897.

O. Doering, 'Des Augsburger Patriziers Philipp Hainhofer Beziehungen zum Herzog Philipp II von Pommern - Stettin', *Quellenschriften für Kunstgeschichte*, N.S. Band VI, Vienna, 1894.

K. Drexler, *Goldschmiedearbeiten in Klosterneuburg*, Vienna, 1897.

J. D. Farmer, *The Virtuoso Craftsman*, Exhibition Catalogue, Worcester, Mass., 1969.

H. Fillitz und E. Neumann, *Die Wiener Schatzkammern*, (5th ed. 1971, Vienna.

C. W. Fock, 'Der Goldschmied Jacques Bylivelt aus Delft', *Jahrbuch der Kunsthistorischen Sammlungen in Wien*, Vol. 70, 1974, pp. 89-178.

Fontainebleau I, 'Inventaire des Joyaux de la Couronne de France, Fontainebleau 1560, *Revue des Arts*, Brussels, Vols. III & IV, 1856.

Fontainebleau II, *L'Ecole de Fontainebleau*, Catalogue de l'Exposition, Paris, 1972-3.

M. Frankenburger, *Beiträge zur Geschichte Wenzel Jamnitzer und seiner Familie*, Strassburg, 1901.

J. W. Frederiks, *Dutch Silver*, 4 Vols., The Hague, 1952, 1958, 1960, 1961.

W. Friedlander, *Mannerism and anti-Mannerism in Italian Painting*, New York, 1965.

L. Fröhlich-Bum, *Parmagianino und der Manierismus*, Vienna, 1921.

H. de Geymuller, *Les du Cerceau*, Paris, 1887.

T. Hach, *Zur Geschichte der Lübeckischen Goldschmiedekunst*, Lübeck, 1893.

Y. Hackenbroch, *English and other Silver, the collection of Irving Untermyer*, London, 1963.

E. Haenel, *Kostbare Waffen*, Dresden, 1923.

Ph. Halm und R. Berliner, *Das Hallesche Heiltum*, Berlin, 1931.

T. Hampe, 'Nürnberger Ratsverlässe über Kunst und Künstler im Zeitalter der Spätgotik und Ranaissance 1474-1618' *Quellenschriften für Kunstgeschichte*, Vienna, 1904, Band XI, XII. 31.

F. Hartt, *Giulio Romano*, Yale, 1958.

A. Hauser, *Der Manierismus*, Munich, 1964.

H. Havard, *Histoire de l'orfèvrerie française*, Paris, 1896.

R. Hedicke, *Cornelis Floris und die Florisdekoration*, Berlin, 1913.

D. Heikamp, 'Zur Geschichte der Uffizien-Tribuna und der Kunstschränke in Florenz und Deutschland', *Zeitschrift für Kinstgeschichte*, Berlin, Band 26, 1963, p.193.

D. Heikamp and A. Grote, *Il Tesoro di Lorenzo il Magnifico*, Florence, Vol. I, 1972, Vol. II, 1974.

G. R. Hocke, *Die Welt als Labyrinth, Manier und Manie in der europäischen Kunst*, Hamburg, 1957.

F. W. Hollstein, *Dutch and Flemish Etchings, Engravings and Woodcuts*, Amsterdam, 1949.

W. Holzhausen, *Prachtgefässe, Geschmeide, Kabinettstücke*, Tübingen, 1966.

K. Hüseler, *Hamburger Silber*, Darmstadt, n.d.

Jahrbuch, *Jahrbuch der kunsthistorischen Sammlungen des allerhöchsten Kaiserhauses*, Vienna, 1883-1926 and thereafter *Jahrbuch der kunsthistorischen Sammlungen in Wien*.

P. Jessen, *Der Ornamentstich*, Berlin, 1920.

A. M. Kersting, *Anton Eisenhoit, Ein Westphälischer Kuperferstecher und Goldschmied*, Münster, 1964.

J. H. Kolba and A. T. Nemeth, *Treasures of the Hungarian National Museum, Goldsmiths Work*, Budapest, 1973.

H. Kohlhaussen, *Nürnberger Goldschmiedekunst des Mittelalters und der Dürerzeit*, 1240 bis 1540, Berlin 1968.

E. Koszeghy, *Merkzeichen der Goldschmiede Ungarns*, Budapest, 1936.

U. Krempel, 'Augsburger und Münchner Emailarbeiten des Manierismus,' *Münchner Jahrbuch der bildenden Kunst*, 1967.

E. Kris,
  Kris I, *Steinschneidekunst in der italienischen Renaissance*, 2 Vols. Vienna, 1929.

  Kris II, 'Der stil "Rustique"' *Jahrbuch der Kunsthist. Sammlungen in Wien*, N.F. I, Vienna, 1926.

  Kris III, *Goldschmiedearbeiten des Mittelalters, der Renaissance und des Barock Teil I*, Kunsthistorisches Museum, Vienna, 1932.

E. Kris und O. von Falke, 'Beitrage zu den Werken Christoph und Hans Jamnitzer', *Jahrbuch der Preussischen Kunstsammlungen*, Vol. 47, 1926, p. 196 ff.

M. Landenberger, *Kleinodien aus dem Württembergischen Landesmuseum, Stuttgart*, Pfullingen, 1973.

A. Lhotsky, *Die Geschichte der Sammlungen, Festschrift des Kunsthistorischen Museums zum Feier des 50 Jährigen Bestandes*, Zweiter Teil, Erste Hälfte, Vienna, 1941-5.

A. Lipinsky, *Oreficeria e argenteria in Europa*, Novara, 1965.

A. Legner, 'Freiburger Werke aus Bergkristall', *Schau ins Land*, 75 Jahresheft des Breisgauer Geschichtvereins, 1957.

G. Mariaux, *Armes et Armures Anciennes*, Musée de l'Armée, Vol. II, Paris, 1927.

J. J. Marquet de Vasselot, *Bibliographic de l'orfèvrerie et de l'émaillerie franĉaises*, Paris, 1925.

J. Menzhausen, *Das Grüne Gewölbe*, Leipzig, 1968.

S. Mihalik, 'Die Ungarischen Beziehungen des Glockenblumenpokals', *Acta Historiae Artium*, Budapest, 1959.

C. Monbeig-Goguel, *Il Manierismo Fiorentino (I Disegni dei Maestri)*, Milan, 1971.

A. Morassi, *Art Treasures of the Medici*, London, 1964.

G. Morazzoni, *Argenterie Genovesi*, Milan, 1951.

P. Morigia, *Della Nobilta di Milano*, Milan, 1595.

P. Muller, *Jewels in Spain*, New York, 1972.

J. Neudörfer, *Nachrichten von Künstlern und Werkleuten*, 1547, ed. G. W. Lochner, *Quellenschriften für Kunstgeschichte*, Band X, Vienna, 1875.

C. C. Oman,
  Oman I, *The Golden Age of Hispanic Silver*, London, 1968.
  Oman II, *English Silver in the Kremlin*, London, 1961.
  Oman III, *Medieval Silver Nefs*, London, 1963.
  Oman IV, *English Domestic Silver*, (4th ed.), 1959, London.

A. Omodeo, *Grafica per Orafi, Modelli del Cinque e Seicento*, Florence, 1975.

K. Pechstein
  Pechstein I, *Goldschmiedewerke der Renaissance*, Kataloge des Kunstgewerbemuseums, Band V, Berlin, 1971.
  Pechstein II, 'Zeichnungen von Wenzel Jamnitzer', *Anzeiger des Germanischen Nationalmuseums*, 1970.
  Pechstein III, 'Jamnitzer Studien', *Jahrbuch der Berliner Museen*, Band VIII, 1966.
  Pechstein IV, *Bronzen und Plaketten*, Kataloge des Kunstgewerbemuseums Berlin, Band IV, 1968.

C. Piacenti, *Il Museo degli Argenti a Firenze*, Milan, 1968.

E. Plon, *Benvenuto Cellini*, Paris, 1883.

A. E. Popham and J. Wilde, *The Italian Drawings of the XV and XVI Centuries at Windsor Castle,* London, 1949.

P. Pouncey and J. Gere, *Italian Drawings, Raphael and his Circle,* London, 1962.

W. Prideaux, *Memorials of the Goldsmiths' Company,* 2 Vols. London, 1896-7.

H. Read and A. Tonnochy,

Read and Tonnochy I, *The Waddesdon Bequest, Jewels, Plate and other Works of Art,* 2nd ed. London, 1927.

Read and Tonnochy II, *Catalogue of Silver Plate, Franks Bequest,* London, 1928.

A. P. Robert-Dumesnil, *Le Peintre-Graveur François,* Paris, 1850.

M. Rosenberg

Rosenberg I, *Der Goldschmiedemerkzeichen,* 3. Auflage, 4 Vols., Frankfurt am Main, 1922.

Rosenberg II, *Jamnitzer,* Frankfurt am Main, 1920.

K. Rossacher, *Der Schatz des Erzstiftes Salzburg,* Salzburg, 1966.

F. Rossi, *Capolavori di oreficeria italiana,* Milan, 1956.

J. von Sandrart, *Academie der Bau – Bilt und Mahlerey-Künste,* 1675, ed. A. R. Peltzer, Munich, 1925.

R. dos Santos, *Catálogo das Jóias e Pratas da Coroa,* Palacio Nacional da Ajuda, Lisbon, 1954.

W. Scheffler, *Die Goldschmiede Niedersachsens,* Berlin, 1965.

S. Schele, *Cornelis Bos, A study of the origins of the Netherlands Grotesque,* Uppsala, 1965.

E. Schilling and A. Blunt, *The German Drawings at Windsor Castle and Supplement to Italian and French Drawings,* London, 1971.

J. V. Schlosser, *Die Kunst und Wunderkammer der Spätrenaissance,* Leipzig, 1908.

H. A. Schmidt, *Hans Holbein der Jüngere,* Basle, 1945.

J. Shearman, *Mannerism,* London, 1967.

J. L. Sponsel, *Das Grüne Gewölbe,* Leipzig, 1925.

E. Steingräber, *Royal Treasures,* London, 1968.

J. Stockbauer, 'Kunstbestrebungen am Bayrischen Hofe unter Albrecht V und Wilhelm V' *Quellenschriften für Kunstgeschichte,* Vienna, 1874, Band VIII.

I. B. Supino, *L'Arte di Benvenuto Cellini,* Florence, 1901.

H. Thoma, *Kronen und Kleinodien,* Deutsche Kunst Verlag, 1955.

B. Thomas, O. Gamber und H. Schedelmann, *Die schönsten Waffen und Rüstungen,* Munich, 1963.

Valencia de Don Juan, *Catalogo Armeria Real,* Madrid, 1898.

G. Vasari, *Le Vite di piu eccellenti Pittori,* ed. Milanesi, Florence, 1868-1885.

I. Weber, 'Bildvorlagen für Silberreliefs in Palazzo Pitti' *Mitteilungen des Kunsthistorischen Instituts in Florenz,* 1970.

H. Weihrauch
Weihrauch I, *Europäische Bronze Statuetten,* Braunschweig, 1967.
Weihrauch II, 'Italienische Bronzen als Vorbilder Deutscher Goldschmiedekunst', *Studien zur Geschichte der Europäischen Plastik,* Festschrift Theodor Müller, Munich, 1965.

A. Weiss, *Das Handwerk der Goldschmiede in Augsburg,* Beiträge zur Kunstgeschichte, N.F. Vol. XXIV, 1897.

A. Werner, *Augsburger Goldschmiede,* Augsburg, 1913.

F. Würtenberger, *Mannerism,* New York, 1962.

H. Zerner, *Ecole de Fontainebleau,* Paris, 1969.

The following publications on sixteenth-century goldsmiths' work appeared after this book went to press and were not, therefore, consulted.

S. Alcolea, *Artes Decorativas en la Espana Cristiana* (Ars Hispaniae Vol. XX) Madrid, 1975.

R. Distelberger, 'Die Sarachi Werkstatt und Annibale Fontana' *Jahrbuch der Kunsthistorischen Sammlungen,* Vienna, Vol. 71, 1975.

R. Lowe, *Matthias Wallbaum,* Munich, 1975.

G. A. Markowa, *Deutsche Silberkunst des XVI-XVIII Jahrhunderts,* Moscow, 1975

I. Weber, *Deutsche, Niederländische und Französische Renaissance Plaketten,* Munich, 1975.

Index of Goldsmiths, Artists and Craftsmen

Index of Museums and Collections

General Index